The Free Grace movement has been accused by some within the Reformed tradition of being new or novel and diminishing the gospel. Is that a fair characterization? *A Defense of Free Grace Theology* is a scholarly yet irenic response to the overextended criticism of Grudem and others of Free Grace theology by five of its leading scholars. The nature of faith and its relationship to assurance is a crucial issue in theology and practice. Here is a work of clarity and charity that not only addresses the concerns of the critics but outlines a robust theology of Salvation solidly built on a biblical foundation. For all of us who are concerned about the gospel, this is a must read.

—David L. Allen, Ph.D.
Dean and Distinguished Professor of Preaching
Southwestern Baptist Theological Seminary

Those committed to a clear proclamation of the gospel of grace do not have to dot every "i" and cross every "t" the same way. We do have to agree though that we are saved by grace through faith and secure by grace through faith. Both our salvation and our assurance of it is not based on what we have done for Christ but gratefully on what He did for us on a cross. Regardless of where you stand on this issue, you will be helped by studying what these authors have to say and why they say it. One must applaud them for the fact that their conclusions are based on their personal study of Scripture and presented in a positive and caring way. It is incumbent upon ever believer to study the Scripture with the same thoroughness so we know what we believe and why we believe it.

—Dr. R. Larry Moyer
Founder and CEO
EvanTell

Five-point Calvinism offers a tight logical system—but not a biblical one. Given their understanding of total depravity, all the points of their TULIP fall into place. But what if their premise is mistaken?

This excellent book challenges the foundations of deterministic theology. The first chapter alone, by Dr. Fred Chay, should be enough to discredit Dr. Wayne Grudem's recent book attacking Free Grace theology in favor of Calvinistic determinism. But the reader will also see how Dr. Ken Wilson brilliantly exposes the pagan notions that influenced Saint Augustine who influenced John Calvin who influenced Grudem. Then Dr. David Anderson adroitly explains a biblical perspective on spiritual death and total depravity. Indeed, the reader will see that five-point Calvinism is balanced shakily on a pebble of reasoning. Furthermore, Dr. Jody Dillow exposes the weakness of Grudem's view of [no]assurance with powerful logic and exegesis of Scriptures. But all the authors resoundingly refute Grudem and TULIP Calvinism through their theological and biblical presentations. Irenic, but honest, this book is not just an answer to Grudem and others of his view; it is a powerful presentation of the centrality of unconditional grace in the gospel.

—Charles Bing, Ph.D.
President, GraceLife Ministries

What step of faith begins a relationship with God that lasts forever? What steps of faith can deepen your relationship with God and transform you forever? This book carefully examines the Biblical texts that answer these two questions.

—C. Craig Glickman, D.Theol. J.D.

A DEFENSE

— OF —

FREE GRACE
THEOLOGY

With Respect to Saving Faith,

Perseverance, and Assurance

Edited by Dr. Fred Chay

A Defense of Free Grace Theology: With Respect to Saving Faith, Perseverance, and Assurance

Published by Grace Theology Press

The website addresses recommended throughout this book are offered as a resource to you. These websites are not intended in any way to be or imply an endorsement on the part of the author or publisher, nor do we vouch for their content.

ISBN 10: 0998138541
ISBN 13: 9780998138541
eISBN 10: 099813855X
eISBN 13: 9780998138558

Printed in the United States of America

First Edition 2017

Contents

PART II: Biblical Texts

Preface

Today there are many theological issues and arguments concerning a variety of significant theological topics. However, the topic of and biblical evidence for Soteriology is perhaps the most important issue of the day or for any day. Although Evangelicals do agree Salvation is by Grace Alone through Faith Alone in Christ Alone, they do not always agree on some of the implications and consequences.

In a recent book, reformed theologian Dr. Wayne Grudem has voiced a concern and issued a challenge that *Free Grace Theology* is not only novel but dangerous to the church. His reasoning is founded upon the Reformed Theology of Puritan Calvinism and its underlying and assumed textual support.

This book is a rejoinder to his critique and a response to other Reformed theologians' articulations and conclusions. The contributors to this book seek to biblically describe and defend a true Grace Theology and answer the deficiencies and criticisms that have been expressed.

All sides of this theological discussion desire to know the truth. However, as theologian Helmut Thielicke asked, "Do we not have to accept the fact that under the shadow of forgiveness, different decisions are possible and different loyalties and liberties may exist?" To ask the question is to answer it. Different decisions and different loyalties have been the hallmark of the church with its diverse theological articulations and declarations. The question is, how do we handle those differences.

The Church has always engaged in discussion, dialogue and at times debate. This dialogue is a "family issue" and an "insiders debate." It is hoped that clarity of argument, charity of heart, communicated with an irenic spirit will be sensed by all.

Introduction

Fred Chay, Ph.D.

In "The Progress of Dogma," James Orr (Scottish divine, 1844-1913) realized there was a difference between the apostles' teaching (the static word of God) and the teaching of the church.[1] The history of the church has manifested a variety of theological discussions and disputes. But even the apostles found themselves entertaining theological differences and, at times, locked in theological dialogue and debate concerning doctrine.

The history of the church has created a variety of creeds and confessions that have sought to clarify the theological positions of the church. The theological topics have and still include both the nature of the authority of the Bible and the extent of the atonement. Ancient and recent debates continue concerning the nature of the Godhead, the Trinity, and the eternal subordination of the Son. The nature, duration and population of hell have always been topics of contention. The issue over spiritual gifts comes and goes, and of course, that is the actual point of contention. The perennial problems regarding eschatological events and end times figures as well as exit timelines have always held

---

1 See *Our Legacy: The History of Christian Doctrine*, John Hannah, Nav Press 2001, 26.

theological interest. But the foundational and fundamental topic of soteriology is essential for present and eternal life. To be more precise, our understanding and articulation of the nature of faith and the relationship to assurance need to be both precise and accurate. The misunderstanding concerning faith and assurance has produced a variety of theological errors as well as pastoral complications for both the ancient and modern church.

This theological question has always been at the center of contention. After all, it is the devil who desires to confuse as well as blind people concerning the goodness and the glorious grace of God. Many look to the Protestant Reformation led by Luther, Calvin and Zwingli and fueled by Augustine's theology as the determinative event that settled the issues. This was followed by concessions, creeds, and confessions to provide correction for the church and catechetical indoctrination for its members. But it is often forgotten or perhaps unknown that the relationship of faith and assurance and the resulting issues concerning the Christian life were not easily or uniformly connected. Both in the European Reformation and the American Puritan Movement, there was an unevenness and uneasiness as to how faith and assurance are related.[2]

All evangelicals would agree that we are "saved by faith alone." But is it biblically true that "the faith that saves is never alone"? The determination of both the origin of assurance (Augustine saw it as a gift) and the role of assurance (Puritans saw it as the primary evidence of genuine salvation) in the life of the Christian has tremendous consequences.

And so it is today that the church must continue the dialogue and debate when necessary to clarify if assurance is the essence of saving

---

2   See Michael Eaton (a charismatic Reformed theologian like Wayne Grudem), *No Condemnation: A New Theology of Assurance* (Downers Grove, Ill.: InterVarsity Press, 1997); M. Charles Bell, *Calvin and Scottish Theology: The Doctrine of Assurance* (Edinburgh: Handsel Press, 1985), his dissertation published by Cambridge University; Robert W.A. Letham, "Saving Faith and Assurance in Reformed Theology: Zwingli to the Synod of Dort" (Ph.D. dissertation, University of Aberdeen, 1979).

faith and if faith must always work. And what do we conclude if it does not?

There have been some recent attempts to deal with this issue,[3] but the most recent is by a tried and true and thoroughly trusted evangelical theologian and an astute student of the history of doctrine, Wayne Grudem, Ph.D., D.D. His recent book strikes an irenic tone as he shares his concerns with those who hold to what is called Free Grace theology. His concern has to do with definitions of terms and deficiencies in the theology and what he sees as errors of doctrine that diminish the gospel of Jesus Christ. His book, *"Free Grace" Theology: 5 Ways It Diminishes the Gospel,* is a simple and sharp expression of the seriousness of the issue.

Having been a colleague of Dr. Grudem's for 13 years and having enjoyed many a dialogue on a variety of theological topics, I know that he is sincere in his concerns and has an unwavering commitment of his convictions concerning Reformed theology. However, neither sincerity of heart nor theological tradition is the test for truth. Although traditions are often the *tramway of intellectual transportation, traditions are not to be assumed automatically, accepted unconsciously, or assimilated uncritically.*[4] Like all dogma or doctrine, a theological position is to be inspected and, if necessary, rejected.

The purpose of this book is to clarify certain theological definitions and doctrinal positions regarding soteriology. We will seek to interact

---

3 The most recent is Matthew W. Bates, *Salvation by Allegiance Alone: Rethinking Faith, Works and the Gospel of Jesus the King* (Grand Rapids, Michigan: Baker Academic publishing, 2017). Also see, Sujaya T. James, *Salvation and Discipleship Continuum in Johannine Literature: Toward an Evaluation of the Faith Alone Doctrine* (Lewiston, N.Y.: The Edward Mellen Press, 2014); Thomas R. Schreiner and Matthew Barrett, *Faith Alone -- The Doctrine of Justification: What the Reformers Taught . . . and Why It Still Matters* (Grand Rapids, Michigan: Zondervan Publishing House, 2015); Bradley G. Green, *Covenant and Commandment: Works, Obedience and Faithfulness in the Christian Life,* (Downers Grove, Illinois: IVP Academic, 2014); Alan P. Stanley, *Did Jesus Teach Salvation by Works?: The Role of Works in Salvation in the Synoptic Gospels,* ed. David Baker, Evangelical Theological Society Monograph Series 4 (Eugene, Oregon: Pickwick Publications, 2006).

4 See José Ortega y Gasset, *The Revolt of the Masses* (N.Y.: W.W. Norton, 1994).

with some of Dr. Grudem's concerns as we integrate exegetical detail, form theological decisions, and evaluate historical theological dogma. Since many of the authors of this book were evaluated in Dr. Grudem's book, we have both a personal and professional desire to understand and be understood. It is also our desire that we articulate our views with both clarity and charity.

"The past will not tell us what we should do, but it will often tell us what we should avoid."[5] It is neither to the recent past nor the reformational past but to the ancient past of the Scriptures that we must turn to find ultimate truth.

---

5 Ibid.

PART I

Theological Topics

Chapter 1

The Perennial Problem for Protestants

Fred Chay, Ph.D.

Introduction

"Grace: You don't deserve it. You can't buy it. You can't live without it."[1] On this, all evangelicals can agree. However, we enter into difficulty when we discuss exactly how God's grace operates in our lives.

Defining the gospel has been difficult from the beginning. This seems counterintuitive since it is simply the presentation of a free gift that needs only to be received and believed for one to be justified forever and possess the gift of eternal life. It is a gift you can never earn and a gift you can never lose. But the simplicity of the gift of the gospel from the glorious grace of God has always raised issues, issues brought on from the Judaizers of the first century, with whom Paul had contentious debates, or from the Roman Catholic Church locked against Luther and the Protestant Reformation. The conditions and circumstances regarding how the gift of God's love is received have

---

1   R.T. Kendall, *Grace: You Don't Deserve It. You Can't Buy It. You Can't Live Without It.* (Lake Mary, Florida: Charisma House, 2006).

always been argued. We should all agree that, by definition, grace is a gift and therefore free to the recipient, even if costly for the benefactor.[2]

Nevertheless, the modern evangelical church has engaged in a number of dialogues and debates regarding the presentation of the gospel and the proper response to the gospel. This is a "family issue," it is an "insider debate" among brothers and sisters in Christ who have a high sense of fidelity to Scripture and wish to be faithful in presenting the Savior and his life-giving gift to a lost and dying world.

As a young Christian, the words of the Apostle Paul always struck me as strange, but no longer. He told the Corinthians, "When you come together as a church, I hear that divisions exist among you; and in part, I believe it. For there must also be *factions* among you, in order that those who are approved may have become evident among you" (1 Corinthians 11:18-19; emphasis added).

To say it in a more modern way, "Our critics keep us on our toes." The term "factions" or "divisions" that Paul selected under the inspiration of the Holy Spirit is the Greek term αἵρεσις (*hairesis*), anglicized into the English term "heresies."

Divisions come from confusion, and we must confront confusion with clarity, courage, compassion, and, above all, charity. This book is a call for theological clarity delivered with genuine Christian charity.

Dr. Wayne Grudem, Research Professor of Theology and Biblical Studies at Phoenix Seminary, has written a book that expresses both a personal burden and a concern for the corporate church concerning both Systematic and Biblical Theology and their impact on Pastoral Theology. The title says it all, *"Free Grace" Theology: 5 Ways It Diminishes the Gospel.*[3]

---

2   The term "free grace" is even utilized in the Westminster Confession of Faith to describe the essence and nature of the gift of eternal life (see Westminster Confession of Faith, 3:5, 11:3, 15:3 and Westminster Longer Confession 70, 71, 74, 194 and the Shorter Confession 34, 35).

3   Wayne Grudem, *"Free Grace" Theology: 5 Ways It Diminishes the Gospel* (Wheaton, Ill.: Crossway 2016). Dr. J. I. Packer has written a similar four-point critique, "Understanding the Lordship Controversy" n.p. [cited 20 August 2016]. Online: http://www.mountainretreatorg.net/other_studies/understanding-the-lordship-controversy.shtml. His points include: "The

This is a provocative title and an essential topic of theology. I became aware of this theological battleground, having been introduced to Lordship Salvation under the teaching of Dr. Ray Steadman, my first pastor, and then under the teaching of Dr. John MacArthur in 1970. Both had a wonderful impact on my life and formed my early theological commitments. I was then challenged at Dallas Theological Seminary, in particular by Dr. Charles Ryrie and Zane Hodges. I began to embrace Free Grace theology and formalized my views with my master of theology thesis: "Lordship Salvation as Taught by John MacArthur." Dr. MacArthur was gracious enough to read and re-read the chapters to make sure that I understood him correctly and quoted him accurately. As we met for the last time at breakfast, he affirmed that I expressed his views faithfully and then said to me, "I think I need to write a book on this topic." He wrote what has become the classic text on the topic of Lordship Salvation—*The Gospel According to Jesus*.[4]

After a number of years serving as a pastor, I had the honor of being a Professor of Theology at Phoenix Seminary for 21 years. The school was founded by Dr. Earl Radmacher as a Free Grace seminary.[5] During my last 13 years at Phoenix Seminary, I had the privilege of having Dr. Wayne Grudem as a colleague. His commitment to the inerrancy and sufficiency of the Scriptures, as well as his courageous stance on complementarianism, was encouraging, and his personal commitment to a charismatic theology was enlightening. Concerning soteriology, both "Reformed" and "Free Grace," we dialogued on many occasions in my office or over a pizza dinner or before a friendly card game of Hearts. Anyone familiar with his award winning *Systematic*

Error about Christ," "The Error about Works," "The Error about Repentance," and "The Error about Regeneration."

4   John MacArthur, *The Gospel According to Jesus* (Grand Rapids, Mich.: Zondervan Publishing House, 1988).

5   Phoenix Seminary is no longer a Free Grace school. All of its full-time faculty in the Theological and Biblical Studies Department and the Missions and Intercultural studies department hold to a Reformed position on soteriology.

Theology: An Introduction to Biblical Doctrine[6] knows that he has addressed this topic in some detail.[7] But our discussions provided him a more up-to-date report on the status and defense of the views of Free Grace theology.

Dr. Grudem became convinced that Free Grace theology was a danger to the church and hence presented a lecture on "Conversion" to The Gospel Coalition, Arizona Chapter. It was a clear frontal attack against Free Grace theology and implored the audience, mainly pastors, to stay away from such dangerous teaching. Having attended the lecture, he and I had a "debriefing session" a few days later. He then provided a similar lecture to his adult Sunday school class, which happened to be at the same church I attended. We had another debriefing session later. Finally, he delivered a similar talk in a workshop presentation at the national Evangelical Theological Society meeting in San Diego, California. Again, we debriefed later as to its contents and his portrayal of Free Grace theology.

Each of these presentations remained fairly consistent, and as such, the final form of his research is presented in his book *"Free Grace" Theology: 5 ways It Diminishes the Gospel.*[8]

---

6   Wayne Grudem, *Systematic Theology: An Introduction to Biblical Doctrine* (Grand Rapids, Mich.: Zondervan Publishing House, 1994).

7   Ibib., 709-717.

8   Other recent critical analyses of Free Grace theology have been presented by Matthew W. Bates, *Salvation by Allegiance Alone: Rethinking Faith, Works and the Gospel of Jesus the King*, (Grand Rapids, Mich., Baker Academic, 2017); Sujaya T. James, *Salvation and Discipleship Continuum in Johannine Literature: Toward an Evaluation of the Faith Alone Doctrine*, (Lewiston, New York: The Edward Mellen Press, N.Y. 2014); Thomas R. Schreiner and Matthew Barrett, *Faith Alone -- The Doctrine of Justification: What the Reformers Taught . . . and Why It Still Matters* (Grand Rapids, Mich.: Zondervan Publishing House, 2015); Alan P. Stanley, *Salvation Is More Complicated Than You Think*, (London, UK: Paternoster, 2007) and *Did Jesus Teach Salvation by Works: The Role of Works in Salvation in the Synoptic Gospels*, (Eugene Ore., Pickwick Publications, 2006) originally from The Evangelical Theological Society Monograph Series Volume 4; Bradley G. Green, *Covenant and Commandment: Works, Obedience and Faithfulness in the Christian Life*, (Downers Grove, Ill.: IVP Academic, 2014). Also, much of Dr. Grudem's book has been anticipated

In response to his book we will seek not only to answer the questions and alleged dangers that Dr. Grudem presents, but also to explore some of the issues that are an integral part of the discussion. [9] Dr. Grudem has stated that he had a limited focus and did not wish to wander off in certain directions of theological articulation such as "Lordship Salvation," which he feels is not an accurate description of the issue[10] or the topic of "carnality."[11] However, it is precisely with such issues that one finds resolution to some of his difficulties with Free Grace theology. Hence, we will endeavor to show the correlation of theological concerns that cause confusion, along with answering directly his points of disagreement.

Finally, before examining the specifics of Dr. Grudem's arguments against Free Grace theology, there are three matters of prolegomena that need to be addressed. As a paradigm for doing theological studies, it is agreed that the best paradigm is one that handles the most data with the least assumptions. Hence, theology must be comprehensive, congruent, and complete as far as a proper theory of validation will allow us to go. Complete verification awaits the glory of a future day, in which we are unimpeded by dimensional limitations. For now, we see dimly, but we do see some things.

---

by Dr. J. I. Packer in his article, "Understanding the Lordship Controversy," n.p. [cited 20 August 2016]. Online: http://www.mountainretreatorg.net/other_studies/understanding-the-lordship-controversy.shtml. For similar lines of argument see Mike McKinley, *Am I Really a Christian?*, 9Marks Series (Wheaton: Crossway, 2011); Greg Gilbert, *What is the Gospel?*, 9, Marks Series (Wheaton: Crossway, 2010); and Thomas Schreiner, *New Testament Theology: Magnifying God in Christ* (Grand Rapids, Michigan: Baker Academic, 2008), 551-560 for similar categories of Dr. Grudem's presentation.

9   There are two others works that have sought to interact with Dr. Grudem's book. *Free Grace Theology: 5 Ways It Magnifies the Gospel*, ed. Grant Hawley, (Allen, Tx. Bold Grace Ministries, 2016) and *Free Grace Theology on Trial*, Anthony Badger, (Createspace Independent Publishing Platform, 2017).

10 Grudem, *"Free Grace" Theology*, 22, 143.

11 Ibid., 143.

Theological Logic

The first issue has to do with Theological Logic. Labels and catchwords can be clarifying or confusing depending on one's context. In his presentation, Dr. Grudem graciously refers to Free Grace teachers as "genuine brothers and sisters in Christ" working for the kingdom of God.[12] He also affirms that the Free Grace gospel is not a "false gospel," because people can be saved by believing it and coming to genuine faith.[13] Although in his *Systematic Theology* he refers to Free Grace theology as teaching "a half gospel,"[14] in his present work he describes the Free Grace gospel as being a "weakened" message,[15] a "watered down" message,[16] or a "diminished gospel," as the title of the book describes. But he would agree that the presentation of the gospel is sufficient to bring persons to saving faith in Christ Jesus and result in eternal life being granted to them.

On one occasion in my office, I asked Dr. Grudem, "Wayne, do you think I am a false teacher in my presentation of the gospel?" He answered, "No. I do not." I then asked him, "Do you think I am a heretic?" He answered, "No, and I have never used that term concerning you." I thanked him for that and asked him, "If I present the Free Grace gospel and someone believes it, are they saved?" He answered, "Yes, they are." I then responded, "That does not sound like a weak gospel to me. If they believe the gospel I preach, and they are justified and have gained eternal life allowing them to go to heaven, then what is the problem?" His response was, "I am afraid there are people who only think they believe, and you will give them false assurance." I reminded him that in his Reformed system of election and his version of double predestination, no one will get into heaven that was not elected before the foundation of the world and that everyone will go to hell whom

---

12 Ibid., 17, 144.

13 Ibid., 73, 74, 77.

14 Ibid., 717.

15 Ibid., 74, 77.

16 Ibid., 145.

God determined would go to hell. He reiterates his concern as he explains:

> The weakening of the gospel message that I discussed in the previous chapter should be a major concern for evangelical Christians today. In spite of the fact that some people come to genuine saving faith under Free Grace preaching, I am deeply concerned that such a weakened gospel message, which lacks any call for people to repent from their sins, will result—and has resulted—in many unsaved people who think they are saved. But they are not.
>
> If you ask them if they are sinners in need of salvation, they will agree. If you ask them if they believe that Jesus died to pay the penalty for their sins, they will agree. They heard that teaching in a church one time and decided that they thought it was true. They "changed their minds" about sin and about Christ and about their need for salvation. Intellectually they believed those things to be true facts about history and about themselves. And on this basis some Free Grace pastors and teachers have assured them that they are saved.
>
> *But they have never truly repented from their sins.* They are still lacking a necessary component of genuine saving faith, according to frequent and repeated New Testament presentations. They still lack genuine repentance, and so they have never had genuine New Testament faith. They are not born again. They are lost because of a weakened gospel message.[17]

The obvious question begging to be asked and answered remains: Is the "weakened Free Grace gospel message" able to save a person when believed or not? Dr. Grudem appears to say both "yes" and "no." This displays an inconsistent theological logic. In terms of soteriology (as in pregnancy), it is a binary option. You are either pregnant or you are not. So also, you either have eternal life or you do not have eternal life.

---

17 Ibid., 77-78.

If you believe the gospel, you have eternal life. If you do not, you do not![18]

This confusion or lack of consistent clarity is also seen in his recent book where in one place he affirms that a person can believe the Free Grace message and be saved, but then later asserts that many who believe the same Free Grace message are not saved.[19] Furthermore, he opines that the Free Grace message is harmful to evangelicalism around the world, but then he claims that many Free Grace ministers are engaged in many kingdom-advancing ministries.

> As is evident in the previous pages, I cannot say that I appreciate any of the doctrinal distinctives of the Free Grace movement that set it apart from historic Protestantism. And I think that those distinctives have had, for the most part, a harmful influence upon evangelicals around the world.

> However, as I mentioned at the beginning of the book, I am thankful for the friendships and the exemplary Christian lives and ministries of numerous Free Grace supporters whom I have known. Many of them have, in spite of this distinctive teaching, developed very significant, kingdom-advancing ministries around the world.[20]

This theological logic is less than clear. I appreciate that Dr. Grudem does not call us false teachers or heretics and that he affirms a person can be saved by believing the gospel we preach based on John 3:16, 5:24, and Ephesians 2:8-10. However, it seems incongruent then to say that the Free Grace gospel is weak, watered down, and diminished, and that it is not enough to save a person if believed, especially after he affirms that many are saved when they believe the Free Grace message. It also seems strange that the Lord would use such poor theology to develop "significant kingdom-advancing ministries."

---

18 The category of "false faith" or "non-saving faith" as Calvin and Reformed theology articulates will be taken up later in Chapter 3.

19 Ibid., 112.

20 Ibid., 144.

He explains that there is a true gospel that is affirmed in Scripture and a false gospel that Scripture warns us to avoid. But in between these two polarities is a "weak gospel," which is the Free Grace gospel. It is weak and incomplete. But it still can save. Dr Grudem says:

> My conclusion in this chapter is that the Free Grace movement preaches a weakened gospel because it avoids any call to people to repent of their sins. This is no minor matter, because repentance from sin is such an important part of the gospel in many New Testament summaries and presentations (see above) that it cannot be omitted without grave consequences in the lives of people who hear such a weakened message.

> However, I am not willing to say that the Free Grace Gospel is a false gospel. That is far too strong a category to apply here, and it calls to mind Paul's extremely strong condemnation in Galatians 1:6-10. I think it is certainly possible to distinguish between a *true gospel* that is presented in an incomplete or weakened form (such as with Free Grace teaching), and a *false gospel* that simply proclaims falsehood rather than truth about Jesus Christ and his work of redemption.

The covenant of the Free Grace Alliance says this:

> The sole means of receiving the free gift of eternal life is faith in the Lord Jesus Christ, the Son of God, whose substitutionary death on the cross fully satisfied the requirement for our justification.[21]

That statement is a wonderful summary of the New Testament gospel message, and it is inconceivable to me that anyone could read that statement and say that people who believe and advocate those truths are preaching a false gospel. That would just be a slanderous and wrongful accusation.

---

21 Free Grace Alliance, "Covenant" n.p. [cited 15 February 2016]. Online: http://www.freegracealliance.com/covenant.htm.

Another thing that demonstrates that this is not a false gospel is the fact that many people who have heard the gospel proclamation as explained by Free Grace advocates have come to genuine saving faith in Christ. Even though the message of the need for repentance from sins was omitted, every unbeliever who ever comes to Christ comes with a guilty conscience and comes to ask for forgiveness, and there is often an instinctive awareness of the need to somehow turn from sin, even though that is not made explicit in the gospel presentation. Therefore, many such people actually do repent of their sins in their hearts, at least to some extent, and God looks on that heartfelt repentance and sees it as part of genuine faith. Many others start attending a Free Grace church and then repent later, perhaps as they begin reading the Bible, and at that point they first come to genuine saving faith.

Nevertheless, it still seems to me that a deliberate omission of the need to call people to repent of their sins constitutes a significant departure from New Testament patterns, and such a departure cannot be taught and practiced without significant harmful consequences to the church and to many of the people who hear such a gospel.[22]

So it appears that the Free Grace gospel is a "weakened form" of the "true gospel" and an "incomplete form" of the "true gospel" but not a "false gospel." But the all-important question to ask remains: Is it a saving gospel? To that Dr. Grudem has answered yes, no, and sometimes.[23]

---

22 Grudem, *"Free Grace" Theology,* 74-76. See also 112.

23 This view of acceptance is clearly not endorsed by J. I. Packer whose endorsement on the back of the book declares: "The so-called Free Grace version of the gospel of Jesus Christ is un-biblical, anti-evangelical, and sub-Christian. . . ." This view was also expressed by Dr. Packer earlier as he said, "If I seem harsh in my critique of Hodges' redefinition of faith as barren intellectual formalism, you must remember that once I almost lost my soul through assuming what Hodges teaches, and a burned child always thereafter dreads the fire." J. I. Packer, "Understanding the Lordship Controversy," n.p.

On one hand, it is declared by Dr. Grudem that even though the Free Grace gospel is weak, it can save a person when believed. On the other hand, as Dr. Grudem states, "they are still lacking a necessary component of genuine saving faith according to frequent and repeated New Testament presentations. They still lack genuine repentance and so they have never had genuine New Testament faith. They are not born again. They are lost because of the weakened gospel message."[24] Dr. Grudem's lack of both clarity and consistency creates difficulty responding to his essential critique about the eternal consequences of the Free Grace gospel.[25]

Theological Methodology

Dr. Grudem earned his Doctorate of Philosophy in New Testament studies from Cambridge University. His research and writing emphasis over the past 40 years has been in theological and biblical studies. The approach and the evidence for his views comes from three sources: first, Historic Reformed Dogmatics in the forms of creeds and confessions; second, Systematic Theology; and third, the two preceding sources of evidence are said to be built off of exegetically sound and historically confirmed New Testament exegesis.

The claim to the accuracy of his view and the alleged error of the Free Grace view is strongly affirmed by what he states is the deviation of Free Grace theology from the theological views based on the Protestant Reformation exposited in its creeds and confessions. Dr. Grudem provides ample selections from both creeds and confessions of the Reformation to verify his particular Calvinistic viewpoint (one

---

[cited 20 August 2016.] Online: http://www.mountainretreatorg.net/other_studies/understanding-the-lordship-controversy.shtml.

24 Grudem, "Free Grace" Theology, 78.

25 See the recent theological rebuttal of Dr. Grudem's book entitled, *Free Grace Theology: 5 Ways It Magnifies The Gospel*, ed. by Grant Hawley, (Allen, TX. Bold Grace Ministries, 2016) and Anthony B. Badger, *Free Grace Theology on Trial*, (n.p. accessed on Create Space Amazon 2017).

of many viewpoints from the Reformation).[26] He implies that given the lack of coherence of Free Grace theology with his particular Reformed views, Free Grace theology is not in theological correspondence with the Reformation, and therefore it is in theological error.[27]

One aspect of his historical/theological defense is based upon the idea that Free Grace theology cannot be the correct view given that no one has ever held to these "eccentric views" of Scripture during the Reformation (1450-1500) or the past 500 years. He refers to Free Grace interpretations as idiosyncratic, eccentric, novel, and therefore unlikely to be accurate.[28]

---

26 Grudem, *"Free Grace" Theology*, 28-32. "Speaking candidly, some Reformed theologians acknowledge the danger for Reformed theology of reading creeds and confessions into Scripture. While the confessions have tended to control our understanding of Scripture, something even less frequently recognized has added to our difficulty. At least until the present century, our conservative systematic theologies have tended to be expositions of the confessions even when that was not immediately apparent. The reason for this is not far to seek: the systematic theologian doing the writing was usually already bound to a confession by being a member or theologian of a confessional church. He could keep neither his credentials as a minister nor his post as a theological professor if he varied appreciably from the confession of his church. . . . The central matter is that those who study the Scriptures must have liberty to follow them wherever they may lead. How can we obtain such liberty in a creedal world?" Tom Wells and Fred G. Zaspel, *New Covenant Theology* (Frederick, Md: New Covenant Media, 2002), 265.

27 Grudem, *"Free Grace" Theology*, 34.

28 "It is not my purpose to interact with all of those explanations in detail at this point, except to say that I think Free Grace 'insiders' have no idea how strained, how idiosyncratic, how artificial and contrived, how insensitive to context, and how completely unpersuasive and foreign to the New Testament these explanations sound. Again and again they bear the marks of special pleading. In some cases, they are not even mentioned as legitimate exegetical alternatives in the standard commentaries because no serious interpreter in history of the church has held these interpretations" Grudem. *"Free Grace" Theology*, 119-120. However, it is interesting that Dr. Grudem acknowledges that "the Free Grace movement gained a remarkable worldwide influence . . . " Grudem. *"Free Grace" Theology*, 22.

It may be true that a Free Grace interpretation of a select passage of Scriptures is wrong. But we are not Roman Catholics—validity in interpretation does not depend upon its antiquity. If Dr. Grudem's reason and the evidence used to validate the error of our interpretation is that no one since the Reformation has ever held to such views until Zane Hodges in the early 1970s, it must be pointed out that the Roman Catholic Church used this argument to condemn Luther as a heretic. Augustine's later views were never held in the early church until the fifth century. The Roman Catholic Church held views different from Augustine for 1,000 years before Luther's "idiosyncratic, eccentric, and novel" interpretations. The text is the determiner of truth.

It must also be remembered that many do not sense that the Reformers went far enough, nor were they accurate enough in their reforming of the church. T. F. Torrance declared, "It is my firm conviction that the misunderstanding of the Gospel which took place as early as in the second century, with the consequent relapse into non-Christian ideas, has resulted in a doctrine that is largely un-biblical, and that has been only partially corrected by the work of Augustine and the Reformers."[29]

There is one final methodological procedural problem to address. It has to do with the construction of hypothetical or theoretical theological scenarios. It is true that the New Testament uses the diatribe formula with its "imaginary objector" to frame an issue. However, biblical illustrations were created under the inspiration of the Spirit and are thus infallible Scripture. In challenging theological positions, we construct theoretical problems, which often are creative but may not comport to reality and therefore are not the best tools to arrive at truth.[30]

The following is my summary of a common Reformed theology example of a hypothetical theological conundrum. "We all know that when a person becomes a Christian they are a new person and have a

---

29 Thomas F. Torrance, *The Doctrine of Grace in the Apostolic Fathers*, (Eugene, OR.: Wipf and Stock Publishers, 1996), vi. (Previously published Edinburgh: Oliver and Boyd Publishers, 1948.)

30 Theologians of all stripes engage in this creative process. The essential problem is with the methodology, not the theology.

new heart by virtue of being regenerated (i.e., born again). As such, it is impossible that they will not demonstrate a new lifestyle. We know that 'works' do not save them, but works are a necessity, a necessary result to demonstrate and prove that they actually had 'genuine saving faith.' We are not talking about perfection but an ongoing change of lifestyle and behavior right up to when they die. We know that they will persevere in faithfulness because God will preserve them in godliness to the end. Imagine a person goes to a Christian outreach camp as a teenager and becomes a Christian but then comes home and shows no interest in Jesus or the church, living a life of total disobedience and moral rebellion, perhaps even saying that he or she hates Christ or never believed in Christ, and then that person becomes a Buddhist. We know that such a person never became a Christian, because God would not allow that type of behavior to occur in his children. We know he or she never truly believed."

I am sure you have heard some form of this hypothetical illustration. It is usually followed by the theological question, "You are not saying that a person who does that is actually a Christian are you?" This is presented as some sort of litmus test, as if one's orthodoxy is dependent upon, decided by, or proven by one's orthopraxy (practice).

I have decided that it is not very helpful to try to answer hypothetical scenarios like these, since they never reveal all the "facts." More importantly, these types of descriptions are not found in the New Testament. I prefer to use what the New Testament does in fact provide as actual realities with real people. I prefer to look at Ananias and Sapphira (Acts 5:1), or the sin unto death (1 John 5:16) written as a real danger for believers,[31] or the reality that sin can kill Christians

---

31 Dr. Grudem was the general editor of the ESV Study Bible. He did not personally write the notes for each book of the Bible, but he had oversight responsibility and did evaluate each note for theological accuracy and acceptability. The note on 1 John 5:16 refers to a sin that a non-believer commits and is evidenced by his lack of love, lack of obedience, and a lack of commitment to Christ, which is a sign of a "lack of saving faith which will not be forgiven" and leads to death [ESV Study Bible (Wheaton, Ill.: Crossway Bibles, 2008), 2437].

(James 1:15), or those at Corinth about whom Paul said some of these Christians are weak, sick, or asleep (a euphemism for death) because of their sinful lifestyles and actions (1 Corinthians 11:30-31).[32] I look at Demas (2 Timothy 4:10) or Simon the sorcerer (Acts 8) or Solomon of the Old Testament.[33] Scripture seems to indicate that they are believers (with which Dr. Grudem has agreed), even if some theological traditions and systems demand we view them as unbelievers.

As Calvin said, we must go as far as Scripture and no farther. Theology tends to extrapolate as it constructs theories. Hypothetical theological situations seem to take us into territory that is farther away from scripturally sanctioned truth.

Historical Abnormalities

Dr. Grudem makes the charge that Free Grace theology is built on idiosyncratic and eccentric views of passages in the Bible that no one has articulated until Zane Hodges. The charge is that they are not only eccentric and novel but also original with Hodges. However, it seems that Dr. Grudem has failed to read many writers and documents in his assessment.

First, there is a vast field of literature that advocates for and promotes a Free Grace theological perspective predating Hodges. Robert Govett (1860) was a fellow at the University of Oxford who wrote voluminous exegetical and theological works advocating Free

---

32 The ESV Study Bible study note at 1 Corinthians 11:31 indicates that the disciplines of 11:30 are for "Christians." *ESV Study Bible*, (Wheaton, Ill.: Crossway Bibles, 2008), 2208.

33 I also find it difficult to say that one million or more people who came out of Egypt covered by the Passover blood, under the leadership of Moses and the personal direction of the Lord himself, imHimselfwho also declared they believed the Lord as they came out of the Red Sea, were then lost to eternal hell (Exodus 14:31). This is especially difficult in light of the fact that the Lord was asked by Moses to forgive/pardon this people, which God did for the very sin of disbelief in the midst of their belief (see Numbers 14:3-33, especially verses 20-23). Also, Moses did not enter the land but died because of his sin of "breaking faith with the Lord" (Deuteronomy 32:50-51). But he was on the Mount of Transfiguration (Matthew 17:3).

Grace interpretations. The massive three-volume work of George N. H. Peters, *The Theocratic Kingdom* (New York: Funk and Wagnalls, 1884), republished by Kregel Publications in 1972, puts forward many views of Scripture that support a Free Grace view. The work of Alexander Patterson, *The Greater Life and Work of Christ: As Revealed in Scripture, Man and Nature* (Chicago: Fleming H. Revell Publishers, 1896) presents an eschatology and soteriology that affirms the Free Grace perspective. Others include D.M. Panton (1900), G.H Pember (1890), Watchman Nee (1925-35), G.H. Lang (1940-50), R.E. Neighbor (1920), Edwin Wilson (1950), and Kenneth Dodson (1950), who all held to views that incorporated Free Grace theological convictions.[34]

Second, there are those from Dallas Theological Seminary that predate Hodges and who held and taught much of a Free Grace perspective in general, if not in every nuance of the view, such as Drs. L. S. Chafer, founder of Dallas Theological Seminary in 1924, J. Dwight Pentecost (1940s), Howard Hendricks (1950s), Roy Zuck (1950s), and Charles C. Ryrie (1950s). Not all would hold to each specific exegetical nuance, but overall they articulate a Free Grace theology.[35]

---

34 It is true that not all of these authors would agree on every point of theology or every point of Free Grace theology. But the fundamentals are clearly in place. For an example of diversity see Robert Govett, who created the Partial Rapture Theory that was also held by Pember, Panton, and Lang. But I do not know of any Free Grace theologians who hold to this view and neither did Hodges.

35 It should not go unnoticed that when Dr. S. Lewis Johnson, (a five-point Calvinist whose credentials are impeccable for a spokesman of Reformed theology) was leaving as Department Chair and Professor of New Testament at Dallas Theological Seminary, he recommended Zane Hodges to replace him as chairman of the department. The president at that time, Dr. John Walvoord, (a four-point Calvinist of the Amyraldian type) accepted the recommendation, and Mr. Hodges accepted the post. Dr. Johnson was a five-point Calvinist. One would assume that Dr. Johnson, as well as Dr. Walvoord, did not perceive Free Grace theology to be heretical or dangerous, even though they both did not agree with all that it taught. Hodges taught at Dallas Seminary for 27 years, although he resigned from being chairman of the New Testament department to continue full-time teaching as opposed to holding an administrative role.

Third, there are authors who published contemporaneously with Hodges who affirm many of the Free Grace views, yet who had little if no contact with his teachings. From the previous generation, Erich Sauer has written many books that not only mention "free grace"[36] but also articulate a theology of free grace in many ways. He did his writing in Germany from 1940 to 1965. His works were also published by mainstream publishers, such as *The King of the Earth* (Grand Rapids, Mich.: Eerdmans, 1962), *From Eternity to Eternity* (Eerdmans 1954), and *The Arena of Faith: The Call to the Consecrated Life* (Grand Rapids, Mich.: Eerdmans, 1955). In these works, he articulates many of the teachings and distinctions that are found in Free Grace theology. In this generation, there is the Oxford dissertation by R.T. Kendall that was later published by Oxford Press (1977) and endorsed by J.I. Packer. He also wrote *Calvin and English Calvinism through 1649* that rocked the evangelical world in his assessment of Calvin and Beza's view of faith and assurance and their connection to American Colonial Calvinism along with a detailed analysis of the antinomian controversy. Dr. Kendall has written *Grace* (Lake Mary, Fla.: Charisma House, 2006), published by a leading charismatic publisher. He also wrote *Justification by Works* built upon an exposition of James 1-3.[37] In it he articulates two types of justification as most adherents of Free Grace theology hold.[38] Dr. Kendall held the post of pastor at Westminster Chapel for

---

36 See *The King of the Earth* (Grand Rapids, Mich.: Eerdmans, 1962), p.149, where he uses the term "free grace" twice.

37 R. T. Kendall, *Justification By Works*, The New Westminster Pulpit Series (Waynesboro, Ga.: Authentic Media, 2005). Many have read his Oxford dissertation regarding the teaching of Calvin and English Calvinism.

38 In fact, this view is even anticipated to some degree by John Calvin himself in his commentary on James where he identifies two types of justification—one for Paul and one for James, although Calvin seems unable to understand or appreciate the textual, literary, and logical issue in the passage. He simply is looking for a way to disagree with the "sophists," aka the Roman Catholic Church. But if one is looking for clarity of exegesis, this is not it. Dr. Grudem, on page 135, footnote 21, cites Tom Nettles' review of Hodges ["Review of Zane Clark Hodges' *Absolutely Free: A Biblical Reply to Lordship Salvation*," Trinity Journal 11 (Fall 1990): 245-246] on James 2 and states that Calvin in no way endorses Hodges' view and, in fact, that Calvin is clearly against it as

25 years following the ministry of Martin Lloyd Jones. Dr. Kendall is a well trained and credentialed theologian published by reputable publishers and is also charismatic, as is Dr. Grudem.

This view of James 2, to a large degree, is held by Martin Dibelius in his commentary on James in the Hermeneia Commentary Series.[39] This is not meant to endorse all of this redaction critic's conclusions, but simply to offer that the Free Grace view on James 2 is not an isolated, idiosyncratic interpretation. It is true that Zane Hodges, having done the textual critical work on the Greek textual variants in this theologically significant passage, as well as his structural analysis,[40] came out with a popular book, *The Hungry Inherit*

---

demonstrated in other parts of Calvin's work. However, if one reads the entire section of Calvin covering all of James 2:1-26, it is clear that Calvin is not able to follow the argument and as such is forced to equivocate on the passage. At the beginning of the chapter, on verse 1 he admits that these Christians' faith in the glorious Lord Jesus Christ has "lost all its vitality." But concerning the last verse, 26 (including James' illustration of a dead person having been alive but now only a corpse devoid of all vitality), Calvin does not even comment on the verse. He simply stops his commentary at verse 25. It is a bad sign in a commentary not even to acknowledge a problem text and the final verse that provides the punch line to the whole argument. He fails to see the symmetry of the whole passage and does not understand the issues of the "quotation" of the imaginary objector and the literary formula that is being utilized. It should be noted that perhaps Calvin was unaware due to the fact that he was writing before many exegetical methodology tools were discovered or refined over the past 500 years since his writing. For example, he defers to the Latin text as his evidence to decide the textual critical difficulty [John Calvin, *Calvin's New Testament Commentaries—A New Translation*, ed. David W, Torrance and Thomas F. Torrance, trans. A. W. Morrison (Grand Rapids, Mich.: Eerdmans Publishing Co., 1972), 3:276-287].

39 Martin Dibelius, *James*, ed, Helmut Koester, trans. Michael A. William, rev. Heinrich Greeven Hermenia Commentary Series (Philadelphia, Pa.: Fortress Press, 1976).

40 Zane Hodges, "Light on James Two from Textual Criticism" *Bibliotheca Sacra* 120 (October 1963): 343. It appears that for many decades the assumed position regarding the structure of the book of James was that of a series of wisdom and proverbial literature without much structure within the text. However, after Hodges' article, structural studies came from every quadrant

(Chicago: Moody Press, 1972), to articulate his findings and that many in the Free Grace movement have followed his view. The fact that many in the Reformed camp were unfamiliar with this line of interpretation does not mean that it did not exist prior to Hodges.

Reformed scholar Dr. Michael Eaton, a Charismatic Reformed theologian like Dr. Grudem, in his work, *No Condemnation: A New Theology of Assurance* (Downers Grove, Ill.: InterVarsity Press 1997), articulates a Free Grace theology. Dr. M. Charles Bell published his dissertation from Cambridge University, *Calvin and Scottish Theology: The Doctrine of Assurance* (Edinburgh: Handsel Press, 1985). He evaluates Calvin and Scottish theology much as Kendall did in his evaluation of Calvin and English theology down to the Westminster Confession of 1649. Both reach similar conclusions regarding Calvin's view of faith and assurance and the inaccurate pastoral theology of the secondary Reformers and their impact upon American religious life.[41]

Dr. David Allen, Dean and Distinguished Professor of Preaching at Southwestern Baptist Theological Seminary, provides a sterling defense of Free Grace theology and a devastating evisceration of Dr. Grudem's classic Reformed articulation of Hebrews 6 (in which Grudem attempts to validate his Reformed position) in *Hebrews: An Exegetical and Theological Exposition of Holy Scripture* (Nashville, Tenn.: B & H Publishing Group, 2010).[42]

---

of evangelicalism on the book of James. (See Peter Davids, *The Epistle of James: A Commentary on the Greek Text* [Grand Rapids, Michigan: Eerdmans, 1982]. Father Davids is now a Catholic priest and charismatic. One wonders how his work in James has impacted his overall theology.) Although this is not meant to prove a causal relationship between Hodges' article and the transition to structural studies in James, it is interesting to note in light of the history of New Testament interpretation.

41 See Robert L. Dabney, *Lectures in Systematic Theology* (Grand Rapids, Mich.: Baker, 1985) for his observation that Calvin and Luther were wrong in their view of "assurance being the essence of saving faith" and how the Westminster Assembly corrected their error. Dabney concludes that Calvin's view of Faith and Assurance was "extreme" (see Section 2, Chapter 27 "Assurance of Grace and Salvation").

42 Even Thomas Schreiner, in his commentary on Hebrews, admits that Grudem is wrong when he says that the warnings in Hebrews 6 are addressed to people

Dr. Grudem also chides the Free Grace position because it has had only two of its works published by "recognized, mainstream, evangelical, academic publishers (such as Zondervan, Baker, Crossway, InterVarsity Press, P&R, B&H or others). This means that (with two exceptions) their publications have not made it through the rigorous editorial vetting process that publishers undertake before they will publish a manuscript."[43] It is to be noticed that all of these aforementioned authors are trained scholars who have had their works published by reputable publishing companies who come from Reformed, Arminian, dispensational, and charismatic backgrounds. Perhaps the reason these resources have been overlooked is that these authors were not writing theology books of Free Grace theology per se. However, their views seem to fit with a Free Grace perspective. It appears that Dr. Grudem has only looked at a few of the dozens of Free Grace theologies, commentaries, or articles that touch the issue.[44]

There are others who are contemporary Free Grace teachers who also have had their books published and who are read widely. Some of these are in the academic world, and others are not.

Dr. Charles Ryrie, former President of Philadelphia College of the Bible and Dean of Doctoral Studies and Professor of Systematic

---

who are "almost Christians" (p. 181). Schreiner admits that these people are "Christian believers in the fullest sense of the word" (p.186). He must utilize a unique view of the warnings to ultimately end up in the reformed view of perseverance of the saints. See Tom Schreiner, *Biblical Theology for Christian Proclamation; Commentary on Hebrews* (Nashville, Tenn., Holman Reference, 2015), 185-188.

43 Grudem, *"Free Grace" Theology*, 138, note 30. Dr. Grudem was operating under false information saying that Dr. Charles C. Bing's book *Simply by Grace: An Introduction to God's Life-Changing Gift* (Grand Rapids, Mich.: Kregel Publications, 2009) was out of print. It is not out of print. In fact, the book was reviewed in 2010 by the late Dr. Roy Zuck, former Professor of Bible and Academic Dean at Dallas Theological Seminary and longtime editor of *Bibliotheca Sacra* in which he affirms Free Grace theology (see Roy Zuck, "Simply by Grace," *Bibliotheca Sacra* 167, no. 2 [April-June 2010]).

44 Numerous articles have appeared in *Bibliotheca Sacra*, Journal of the Evangelical Theological Society, and the Journal of the Southwestern Baptist Seminary discussing this issue from both sides of the theological perspective.

Theology at Dallas Theological Seminary for over 30 years, wrote on Free Grace theology. His book, *Balancing the Christian Life* (Chicago: Moody, 1969) is a classic as well as *So Great a Salvation: What It Means to Believe in Jesus,* (Chicago: Moody Publishers, 1997; republished by Victor Books 1989). Dr. Lewis Sperry Chafer, founder and President of Dallas Theological Seminary wrote *He That is Spiritual* (Chicago: Moody, 1918 and later republished by Zondervan publishers in 1967) and *True Evangelism* (originally published in 1919 and later by Zondervan 1967). Dr. Earl Radmacher, former President of Western Seminary and Phoenix Seminary, wrote a Free Grace perspective in his textbook, *Salvation* (Nashville: Thomas Nelson Publishers, 2000) in the series of theology texts by faculty and graduates of Dallas Theological Seminary. The foreword of the book is by Chuck Swindoll and provides an enthusiastic endorsement of Dr. Radmacher and his theology that has been taught in some form at Dallas Theological seminary since L. S. Chafer. Another form of Radmacher's book on *Salvation* was published in *Understanding Christian Theology,* (Nashville: Thomas Nelson Publishers, 2003) edited by Charles Swindoll and Roy Zuck. Dr. Swindoll himself, former President of Dallas Theological Seminary, wrote a book opening up the doors of Free Grace theology to millions of readers in *The Grace Awakening* (Nashville: Word Publishing, 1990). The book is similar to *One Way Love: Inexhaustible Grace for an Exhausted World* (Colorado Springs: David C. Cook, 2013) by Tullian Tchividjian, a Reformed pastor whose book articulates many of the Free Grace perspectives of the gospel and assurance without using the label or affirming his association.[45]

Going for the Gold by Dr. Joe Wall (Chicago: Moody, 1991), *The Believer's Pay Day* by Dr. Paul Benware (Chattanooga, Tenn.: AMG Publishers, 2002), *Grace Walk* by Steve McVey (Eugene, Ore. Harvest House, 1995), Charles Stanley's *Understanding Eternal Security*

---

45 Mr. Tchividjian was the Senior Pastor at Coral Ridge Presbyterian Church; he resigned his position due to marital infidelity. He has also been accused of holding to a form of what has been termed "Hyper Grace" or Free Grace. His books have a distinct grace perspective, but he does not give enough of a systematic approach to be able to label him Free Grace. It is curious that his fellow ministers and critics label him that way.

(Nashville, Tenn: Thomas Nelson, 1998), and Dr. Tony Evans' *Totally Saved: Understanding, Experiencing and Enjoying the Greatness of Your Salvation* (Chicago: Moody Publishing, 2002) all articulate a Free Grace viewpoint. Also Ray E. Baughman, former Dean of Southeastern Bible College, wrote *The Kingdom of God Visualized* (Chicago: Moody Press) in 1972, presenting a view of the kingdom and a rewards system similar to many in the Free Grace camp.

Finally, Dr. Larry Moyer, Professor of Evangelism at Dallas Theological Seminary for over 25 years and founder and President of EvanTell, a ministry that has taught in thousands of churches and para-church venues to hundreds of thousands of people how to share the gospel with his book, *Free and Clear: Understanding and Communicating Gods Offer of Eternal Life* (Grand Rapids, Mich.: Kregel 1997), teaches a free grace theology.[46]

There are many others at both the academic and popular levels, but this partial list shows that there are authors who are credentialed and published by "recognized, mainstream, evangelical publishing companies"—contrary to Dr. Grudem's charge—who hold to a Free Grace theological perspective. Dr. Grudem seems to believe and affirms Michael Horton who says, "As James Boice, J. I. Packer and others have argued in their works, no respected mainstream Christian thinker, writer or preacher has ever held such extreme and unusual views concerning the nature of the gospel and saving grace as Zane Hodges."[47] This erroneous statement may be why it came as a surprise to Dr. Grudem that so many in evangelicalism were adopting this view, as he states, "Many evangelicals today who have never heard of the Free

---

46 Dr. Moyer was also on the board of directors of the Free Grace Alliance and a regular plenary speaker at the national Free Grace Alliance conference.

47 Grudem, *"Free Grace" Theology*, 139-140, quoting Michael Horton, *Christ the Lord: The Reformation and Lordship Salvation* (Eugene, Ore.: Wipf and Stock, 1992), 11. Since Dr. Grudem has made Zane Hodges the ground zero of all that is wrong, claiming Hodges alone had originated this view, it must be pointed out that Hodges' views on the Hebrews warning passages, 1 John, John 15, 2 Peter 1:10 and some on Romans had all been articulated before he began publishing his works in 1972. Even his views on James 2 had been anticipated in some form by others.

Grace movement have unknowingly moved too far in the direction of Free Grace teaching anyway."[48]

Concluding Thoughts

Over the years, Christian voices have exhausted themselves in a cacophony arguing these complex issues. I have focused on Dr. Grudem as a prior colleague and friend who represents the recent criticisms of Reformed theology concerning Free Grace theology. It was disappointing that Dr. Grudem did not allow Free Grace theologians to evaluate the accuracy of his book prior to its publication. Nevertheless,

---

48 Grudem, *"Free Grace" Theology*, 9. This "movement" toward a free grace direction is also being experienced to a large degree in the Southern Baptist convention under the title of "Traditionalist Soteriology." Historically, Southern Baptists did not follow the Westminster catechism as a group, and even those who did follow it to some degree do not follow many points of its Presbyterian-Reformed theology. Most followed the New Hampshire Confession as opposed to the second London Confession. For a historical view of this movement and its theology see, "History or Revisionist History? How Calvinistic Were the Overwhelming Majority of Baptists and Their Confessions in the South until the Twentieth Century," by Steve Lemke, Journal of the Southwestern Theological Baptist Seminary, 57, no 2 (Spring 2015). Also see "Whosoever Will: A Biblical-Theological Critique of Five-Point Calvinism," edited by David Allen and Steve Lemke, (Nashville, Tenn., Broadman & Holman, 2010) and Leighton Flowers, *The Potters Promise: A Biblical Defense of Traditional Soteriology* (Evansville, Ind.: Trinity Academic Press, 2017). The division inside the Southern Baptist association is mainly felt in the academic institutions. But "Traditionalist Soteriology" that does not include total inability, limited atonement and irresistible grace is the norm on the mission field and the pastorate, although many inside the convention are fighting for the heart and soul of pastors to become and lead as Five Point Calvinists. See "Traditionalists" websites: "SBC Today" and "Connect 316" and its statement: A STATEMENT OF THE TRADITIONAL SOUTHERN BAPTIST UNDERSTANDING OF GOD'S PLAN OF SALVATION. From a theological perspective, the advance of a form of Molinism seems to have also enhanced a non Calvinistic-Hard deterministic form of theological expression. See the extensive argument from Kenneth Keathley, *Salvation and Sovereignty: A Molinist Approach*: (Nashville, Tenn.: B& H Academic, 2010).

we would like to respond with genuine grace and what we believe to be the truth.

As Quintilian said, "We should not speak so that it is possible for the audience to understand us, but so that it is impossible for them to misunderstand us."[49] We do not wish to be misunderstood or to be mistaken in our views. Hence, we accept the challenge to clarify our views and hope that iron will sharpen iron.

Harry Ironside, Pastor of Moody Memorial Church in Chicago, identified the tension in 1896:

> The Gospel is not a call to repentance, or to amendment of our ways, to make restitution for past sins, or to promise to do better in the future. These things are proper in their place, but they do not constitute the Gospel; for the Gospel is not good advice to be obeyed, it is good news to be believed. Do not make the mistake then of thinking that the Gospel is a call to duty or a call to reformation, a call to better your condition, to behave yourself in a more perfect way than you have been doing in the past.[50]

This is not the first time people have debated this seminal question, and it may not be the last. But both sides desire to honor the Lord and his word and feed, lead, and protect the flock.[51]

The authors of this book agree with Dr. Grudem that regarding this topic, as viewed from both sides, a "family intervention" is needed.[52]

---

49 Marcus Fabius Quintilianus, *Instiutio Orartoria*, VIII, 2.24.

50 Dr. Harry A. Ironside, "What Is the Gospel?," n.p. [cited 12 September 2016]. Online: http://www.jesus-is-savior.com/BTP/Dr_Harry_Ironside/what_is_the_gospel.htm.

51 See John Stott and Everett F. Harrison, "Must Christ be Lord?" *Eternity Magazine*, September 1959, and William Hogan, "The Relationship of the Lordship of Christ to Salvation" (PhD diss., Wheaton College, 1958). See also Michael P. Winship, *Making Heretics*, (Princeton N.J.: Princeton University Press, 2002) for a delineation of the Free Grace Controversy that issued forth from high Calvinism in Colonial Puritanism. Free Grace theology has been a part of the American church from its inception.

52 Grudem, *"Free Grace" Theology*, 145.

We would implore those who disagree with Free Grace theology to be open to engage or re-engage the evidence under the illuminating ministry of the Holy Spirit. It is our sincere desire to engage the issue with exegetical care, theological skill, academic rigor, evenhandedness of presentation, and an extension of grace to all.

Chapter 2

A Theological and Historical Investigation

Ken Wilson, M.D., D. Phil.

D r. Wayne Grudem, as we all do, writes from a particular theological persuasion that influences his exegesis of Scripture. He claims "Free Grace" theology not only diminishes the gospel, but also lacks a foundation as a recent and idiosyncratic, unbiblical theology popularized by a fringe group.[1] The Roman Catholic Church leveled the same accusations against Martin Luther—the "wild boar" who invaded the Lord's vineyard and instigated the Protestant Reformation.[2] But Reformed and Arminian theologies are not the only Protestant options.

---

1   Wayne Grudem, *"Free Grace" Theology: 5 Ways It Diminishes the Gospel* (Wheaton, Ill.: Crossway, 2016), 21, 27, 119-20.

2   See Pope Leo's AD 1520 papal bull *Exsurge Domine* against Luther in which he asks the Lord to arise against the wild boar who has invaded the Lord's vineyard. He mockingly doubted a single simple monk could be right.

An ideal systematic theology combines biblical theology with historical theology to develop a logically coherent set of doctrines. That is, a systematic theology is only as good as its foundation. Reformed and Arminian theologies are both built on Augustine's unstable foundation through Martin Luther (an Augustinian monk) and Calvin (an ardent disciple of Augustine). This chapter will demonstrate that Grace views are not novel, nor are they idiosyncratic. Rather, they are based on a foundation of ancient ideas taught by early church fathers prior to Augustine and a contextual exegesis of Scripture.[3]

Theological truth is not primarily measured by its antiquity, but by its conformity to Scripture and logic. The 500-year-old theology of John Calvin was directly derived from Augustine who strayed from the foundation of traditional Patristic theology over 1,000 years prior to Calvin. We need to explore the foundation on which Augustine laid his novel Christian theology. This will expose the fact that Augustinian Calvinism's impressively logical edifice has been built upon an unstable foundation of pagan syncretism (mixing pagan and Christian ideas). In contrast, the foundation of Grace theology was laid in general by AD 180 and was specifically taught since AD 400.

Augustine of Hippo's Traditional Theology AD 386-411

As a young man Augustine was trained as a rhetorician and adhered to three highly deterministic philosophies—Stoicism, Neoplatonism, and Manichaeism. He spent ten years as a hearer in the heretical Manichaean religion.[4] Manichaeism was the pinnacle of Gnosticism. It taught that the physical body was evil and the spirit was good, so that even the birth of a child was sin. Persons were unilaterally pre-determined before birth by the good god (who did not create physical matter) to be either elect

---

3 This chapter briefly summarizes my doctoral thesis at the University of Oxford, 2012. See Kenneth Wilson, *Augustine's Conversion from Traditional Free Choice to "Non-free Free Will: A Comprehensive Methodology"* (Tübingen: Mohr Siebeck, 2017).

4 Henry Chadwick, *Augustine: A Very Short Introduction* (Oxford: Oxford University Press, 1986), 14. A hearer was a disciple attempting to be one of the elect. Chadwick proved ten years, not the commonly accepted nine.

or damned independently of human choice—Divine Unilateral Pre-
determinism of Individuals' Eternal Destinies (DUPIED).[5] A second
deterministic influence was Stoicism, which taught the causal nexus was
controlled by fate. Seneca the Younger pronounced, "The fates lead the
willing and drag the unwilling."[6] Augustine's first work, *On Providence*,
reiterates this Stoic philosophy. The falling of a leaf to the exact location
is predetermined by a meticulous micromanaging God and the precise
neck muscle actions of two roosters fighting are predetermined by God.[7]
The third influence for determinism was Neoplatonism, instituted
by Plotinus (*c.*250) and popularized by Porphyry (*c.*350). Scholars
recognize Augustine was heavily influenced by the deterministic
writings of Plotinus and Porphyry, as well as Cicero.[8] In addition to
these three influences for determinism, Augustine struggled with strong
sexual desires. His son Adeodatus resulted from sex with a concubine
whom he loved, and then after sending her from Milan back to Africa
for professional advancement reasons, he acquired a second concubine
for a short time.[9]

---

5   In my Oxford doctoral thesis, I used this neutral term DUPIED to analyze
     the pre-Christian religious and philosophical views on determinism so
     that the biblical word "predestination" would not be prejudiced by modern
     understandings. Ancient pagan DUPIED was a non-relational, unilateral,
     unconditional election independent of foreknowledge of eternal (not
     temporal) destinies for individuals (not nations or groups).

6   Lucius Seneca, *Epistle to Lucilius*.

7   Augustine, *De providentia*, 1.12-25.

8   Gerard O'Daly, *Platonism Pagan and Christian: Studies in Plotinus and
     Augustine* (Variorum Collected Studies Series 719, Farnham, UK: Ashgate,
     2001) and Augustine Curley, O.S.B. "Cicero, Marcus Tullius," in Allan D.
     Fitzgerald, ed. *Augustine Through the Ages: An Encyclopedia*. Grand Rapids,
     Mich.: Wm. B. Eerdman's, 1999), 190-3.

9   François Decret, *Early Christianity in North Africa* (Le christianisme en Afrique
     du Nord Ancienne, 1978). Translated by Edward Smither (Cambridge: James
     Clarke & Co Ltd., 2011),163; Chadwick, *Augustine*, 16; *Stanford Encyclopedia
     of Philosophy* "Saint Augustine: 3. The Mysterious Woman from North Africa"
     (Mar 24, 2000; substantive revision Nov 12, 2010) accessed 9-1-2016 at http://
     plato.stanford.edu/entries/augustine/.

Augustine was baptized into Christianity in AD 386 by his spiritual father, Ambrose, bishop of Milan. He gradually moved from Neoplatonic and Manichaean ideas to embrace the Christian theology of his time. A decade later Augustine discovered God's grace apart from the merit of human works after reading the commentaries of Victorinus and then Jerome on Galatians.[10] When he became co-bishop of Hippo, Augustine was teaching traditional theology against the Manichaean heretics, as Christian leaders had taught for centuries against the Stoics and Gnostics. God's responses to humans and God's election to heavenly bliss were based upon God's "foreknowledge" of future human choices, not a unilateral and non-relational pre-determinism (as in Augustine's prior Gnostic Manichaeism, Stoicism, and Neoplatonism).[11] Augustine taught these traditional theologies defending human free choice and election based upon God's foreknowledge for over twenty-five years until AD 412.[12]

The early Augustine's traditional theology is pervasive that humans can respond to God without divine assistance. "But miserable friends could be masters of this world if they were willing to be the sons of God, for God has given them the power to become his sons" (V.rel.65).[13] Contra the Manichaean misinterpretation of Ephesians 2:3 ("were by nature children of wrath," meaning at birth), Augustine

---

10 Stephen Cooper, *Marius Victorinus' Commentary on Galatians: Introduction, Translation, and Notes* (Oxford: Oxford University Press, 2005), 136-9; Andrew Cain, *St. Jerome: Commentary on Galatians in the Fathers of the Church* (Washington, D.C.: The Catholic University of America Press, 2010), 16-33.

11 Because God is omnitemporal, the term "foreknowledge" is an anthropomorphism. God lives in the past, present, and future simultaneously. See Richard Swinburne, "God and Time," in Eleonore Stump, ed., *Reasoned Faith* (Ithaca: Cornell University Press, 1993), 204-222.

12 Virtually all scholars claim Augustine converted to his novel theology in AD 396/7 with *Ad Simplicianum* 1.2ff. I have demonstrated that Augustine revised this work just as he revised others many decades after they were written. See Ken Wilson, (2012) "Augustine's Conversion" and "Redating Augustine's *Ad Simplicianum* 1.2 to the Pelagian Controversy," *Studia Patristica* 96, 2017.

13 *vera.rel.*65: «Sed miseri amici hujus mundi, cujus domini erunt, si filii Dei esse voluerint, quoniam dedit eis potestatem filios Dei fieri».

denounced alienation by nature, proclaiming, "Remember what the apostle said, 'In our lifestyle [behavior] we are alienated from God,'" and, "Augustine said: 'I say it is not sin, if it be not sinned by one's own will; hence also there is [a] reward, because of our own will we do right.'" (*c.Fort.*21).[14] Augustine clarifies that his free will statements concern current persons, not merely Adam's original nature.

> For this reason, those souls, whatever they do, if by nature and not voluntarily, that is, if they lack the movement of the free soul/mind of doing and not doing, if, in short, no power is granted to them to abstain from their own deeds, we are not able to lay hands on their sin. But all admit, both bad souls are justly condemned and those who have not sinned are unjustly condemned. (*an.immor.*17; cf.,12; translation mine).[15]

"For by his free will man has a means to believe in the Liberator and to receive grace" (*exp.prop.Rm.*44.3).[16] God's foreknowledge allows him to predestine only those whom he knows will respond in faith: "Nor did God predestine anyone except him whom he knew would believe and would follow the call, whom he [Paul] calls 'the elect.' (5) For many do not come, though they have been called." (*exp.prop.Rm.*55).[17]

"By all means he has mercy on whom he wants, and he hardens whom he wants, but this will of God cannot be unjust. For it springs from deeply hidden merits, [*occultissimis meritis*] because, even though

---

14 *c.Fort.*21 : «AUG.dixit: Ego dico peccatum non esse, si non propria voluntate peccetur: hinc esse et praemium, quia propria voluntate recta facimus»

15 *An.immor.*17: «Quamobrem illae animae quidquid faciunt, si natura, non voluntate faciunt, id est, si libero et ad faciendum et ad non faciendum motu animi carent; si denique his abstinendi ab opere suo potestas nulla conceditur, peccatum earum tenere non possumus. At omnes fatentur, et malas animas juste, et eas quae non peccaverunt, injuste damnari».

16 «In libero autem arbitrio habet, ut credit liberatori et accipiat gratum» (*exp. prop.Rm.*44.3)

17 «Nec praedestinavit aliquem, nisi quem praescivit crediturum et secuturum vocationem suam, quos et electos dicit. Multi enim non veniunt, cum vocati fuerint» (*exp.prop.Rm.*55).

sinners themselves have constituted a single mass on account of the sin of all, still it is not the case that there is no difference among them" (*Div.Q.O.*68.4; *cf.*, 82.2). "Through foreknowledge God chooses believers and damns unbelievers" (*exp.prop.Rm.*62.15).[18] "Therefore God did not elect anyone's works [which God himself will grant] by foreknowledge, but rather by foreknowledge he chose faith, so that he chooses precisely him whom he foreknew would believe in him; and to him he gives the Holy Spirit. . . . Belief is our work, but good deeds are his who gives the Holy Spirit to believers" (*exp.prop.Rm.*60.11-12).[19] Consummate with all other extant early Christian writings, Augustine viewed free will as critical to defending the Christian God against the highly deterministic Gnostic and Manichaean heresies and from Stoic fate.

> Now, however, when God punishes a sinner, what else do you suppose he will say to him than "Why did you not use your free will for the purpose for which I gave it to you, that is, in order to do right?" . . . For neither is it sin nor done right, because it [choice] is not made voluntarily. For this reason, both punishment and reward would be unjust, if man did not have free will. (*lib.arb.*2.3, translation mine)[20]

"Scripture teaches that God himself placed this in our power when it says, 'He gave them the power to become sons of God' [John 1:12].

---

18 «deus praescius eligat credituros et damnet incredulos» (*exp.prop.Rm.*62.15; cf., 60.4–15).

19 «Non ergo elegit deus opera cuiusquam in praescientia, quae ipse daturus est, sed fidem elegit in praescientia, ut quem sibi crediturum esse praescivit ipsum elegerit, cui spiritum sanctum daret…Quod ergo credimus, nostrum est, quod autem bonum operamur, illius qui credentibus in se dat spiritum sanctum.» (*exp.prop.Rm.* 60.11-12). Translation by Paula Fredriksen Landes, *Augustine on Romans* (Chico, Cal.: Scholars Press, 1982).

20 «Nunc vero Deus cum peccantem punit, quid videtur tibi aliud dicere nisi, Cur non ad eam rem usus es libera voluntate, ad quam tibi eam dedi, hoc est ad recte faciendum? … Non enim aut peccatum esset, aut recte factum, quod non fieret voluntate. Ac per hoc et poena injusta esset et praemium, si homo voluntatem non haberet liberam» (*lib.arb.*2.3).

But people are called sons of the devil when they imitate his impious pride, fall away from the light and the height of wisdom, and do not believe the truth."(*c.Adim*.5).[21] For twenty-five years Augustine was solidly within traditional Christian doctrine of the first four centuries, fighting the Stoics, Gnostics, and Manichaeans by teaching God's foreknowledge of free choice determined his election of persons.[22]

Augustine's Conversion in Paedobaptism to Stoic "Non-free Free Will" AD 412

When Rome fell to the Vandals in AD 410, Pelagius and Caelestius came to Augustine's home of North Africa (present day Tunisia) instigating the infamous Pelagian controversy.[23] These Christians were teaching doctrines not accepted by other churches. For example, Adam's fall was merely a personal moral failure so each human born subsequently remained in the same state as Adam when he was created. There was no traditional Christian original sin (a sin propensity, moral weakness, and resultant physical death).[24] The Pelagians had

---

21 «Quod in potestate nostra ab ipso Deo esse positum docet Scriptura, cum dicit: Dedit eis potestatem filios Dei fieri. Filii autem diaboli dicuntur homines, cum imitantur ejus impiam superbiam, et a luce atque celsitudine sapientiae decidunt, et non credunt veritati.» (*c.Adim*.5).

22 James Swindal and Harry Gensler, *The Sheed and Ward Anthology of Catholic Philosophy* (Lewiston, NY: Sheed and Ward, 2005), 39-40. Swindal and Gensler admit that Patristic thinkers embraced human free will, but somehow they miss that the later Augustine refuted what the saints, bishops, and presbyters since Justin Martyr and Irenaeus had championed. This occurs despite their admission that Manichaeism's parent, Gnosticism, "combined biblical, Neoplatonic, and Persian elements."

23 N. Joseph Torchia, *Creatio Ex Nihilo and the Theology of St. Augustine: The Anti-Manichean Polemic and Beyond* (New York: Peter Lang, 1999), 239.

24 David Weaver, "From Paul to Augustine: Romans 5:12 in Early Christian Exegesis," *St. Vladimir's Theological Quarterly* 27.3 (1983), 187-206 and "The Exegesis of Romans 5:12 Among the Greek Fathers and Implications for the Doctrine of Original Sin: The 5th-12th Centuries," 29.2 (1985), 154-6; Johannes van Oort, "Augustine on Sexual Concupiscence and Original Sin," *Studia Patristica* 22 (Louvain: Peeters, 1989), 261.

no answer as to why infants were baptized.[25] Jerome, Augustine, and numerous other Christian leaders attacked these views so fiercely that excommunication of the Pelagians eventually ensued.[26]

One critical question remained throughout the Pelagian conflict. Why did the church practice the tradition of baptizing infants? Tertullian had spoken out against paedobaptism over two-hundred years earlier, pointing out that the child should wait until he or she was old enough to make his or her own decision.[27] About AD 405, Augustine admitted that he did not know why infant baptism was practiced.[28] The conflict with Pelagius caused him to rethink this tradition about AD 412 and convert to his later DUPIED.[29] His reasoning started with church tradition then logically progressed:

1. The church baptizes infants.

2. Water baptism is for forgiveness of sin and reception of the Holy Spirit.

---

25 These concepts are outlined by Augustine in *nat. et. gr.* 2, 6, 7, 10, 20, 21, 47, 58.

26 Innocent responded to Epistle176 from the Council of Milevis with excommunication of Caelestius and Pelagius.

27 Tertullian, (*De bapt.*18): "The Lord said, 'Do not prohibit them to come to me.' Therefore, let them come while adolescents, let them 'come' while they are learning, while learning where to come; let them become Christians when they have become able to know Christ! Why does the innocent age rush to the remission of sins?" «Ait quidem Dominus: Nolite illos prohibere ad me venire (Matth.XIX,14). Veniant ergo dum adolescunt, dum discunt, dum quo ueniant docentur; fiant christiani cum christum nosse potuerint! quid festinat innocens aetas ad remissionem peccatorum?»

28 Augustine, *an.quant.*80: "In this context, also, how much benefit is there in the consecration of infant children? It is a most difficult (obscure) question. However, that some benefit exists is to be believed. Reason will discover this when it should be asked." «amvero etiam puerorum infantium consecrationes quantum prosint, obscurissima quaestio est, nonnihil tamen prodesse credendum est. Inveniet hoc ratio, cum quaeri oportuerit».

29 Ken Wilson, "*Augustine's Conversion*" (2012). See also Henry Chadwick, *Early Christian Thought and the Classical Tradition* (Oxford: At the Clarendon Press, 1966), 110-11.

3. Some dying infants are rushed by their Christian parents to the bishop for baptism but die before this can occur, while other infants born of prostitutes are abandoned on the streets when a church virgin rushes them to the bishop who baptizes them.

4. These infants have no control over whether or not they are baptized and receive the Holy Spirit to become Christians.

5. Therefore, God must unilaterally and unconditionally predetermine which infants are damned and which are justified.

Augustine eventually taught even when "ministers prepared for giving baptism to the infants, it still is not given, because God does not choose" (*perseu.*31). God's election must be unconditional since infants have no personal sin, no merit, no good works, and no choice.

Because infants have no personal sin, he deduced their baptisms for forgiveness of sin must be based upon their inherited guilt (*reatus*) from Adam's sin. No prior author taught infants were guilty and damned from Adam's sin and required water baptism for salvation.[30] Contrary to God's rebuttal of this theology in the book of Job, Augustine's theodicy (a defense vindicating God for apparent evil) demanded that every punishment, pain, and loss in a person's life be justly deserved from God for that individual (due to his Stoic Providential micromanagement).[31] If infants die, they must be guilty and be damned.

---

30 This included Augustine's mentor Ambrose who held the traditional view of inherited sin propensity within the physical body but without *reatus* (guilt, crime, fault) whereas Ambrose and others had used the milder *culpa* (imperfection, wrongdoing, sin, error). Henry Chadwick, *Saint Ambrose: On the Sacraments, The Latin Text* (London: Mowbray and Co., 1960; reprint, Chicago: Loyola University Press, 1961), 74, fnt.3 and 136, fnt.6. See Ambrose's *De poenitentia*, 1, Ep. 41.7, and *De mysteriis* 6. Cf., Wilson, "Augustine's Conversion," (2012), 105-7; *Oxford Latin Dictionary*, s.v. "*reatus*" and "*culpa*"; *Dictionary of Ecclesiastical Latin*, s.v. "*reatus*" and "*culpa*."

31 Chadwick, *Augustine*, 109.

I am myself keenly aware of how problematic this question is, and I recognize that my powers are not sufficient to get to the bottom of it. Here too I like to exclaim with Paul, *Oh the depths of the riches!* (Romans 11:33). Unbaptized infants go to damnation; they are like the apostles words, after all: *From one to condemnation* (Romans 5:16). I cannot find a satisfactory and worthy explanation... [he cites all of Romans 11:33-36]. (*s*.294.7).[32]

Augustine brought into Christianity the Manichaean concepts of total inability (infants cannot make a choice), damnable sin at birth, and unconditional election (God chooses unilaterally). This logical deduction from infant baptism was then extrapolated to all humans. Note that the basis for this logical argument was the salvific power of water baptism for an infant combined with the Stoic philosophy of divine meticulous control of all events. No prior extant Christian writings had taught these three pagan ideas.

Augustine admitted he had abandoned the centuries-old Christian doctrine of human free choice.[33] "In the solution of this question I struggled in behalf of free choice of the will, but the grace of God won out." (*retr.* 2.1). "When I began my books on Free Choice [3.68]... I still doubted the condemnation of infants not born again [baptized]" (*pers.*30) and "before this heresy [Pelagianism] arose, they did not have the necessity to deal with this question, so difficult of solution. They would undoubtedly have done so if they had been compelled

---

32 Edmund Hill, O.P., *The Works of Saint Augustine: A New Translation for the 21st Century*, Sermons III/8, Sermon 294 (Hyde Park, NY: New City Press, 1994), 184. Augustine reverses the apostle Paul's exclamatory praise for God's undeserved mercy into praise for his [Manichaean] God's undeserved eternal damnation of innocent infants!

33 William Babcock, s.v. "Sin" in *The Encyclopedia of Early Christianity*, 2nd ed., Everett Ferguson, ed. (New York and London: Garland Publishing, 1998): "It could also be represented by speaking—as Augustine did, in what was a significant break with the previous tradition—of the impairment of the human will and the vitiation of human nature, after Adam's sin, with the result that human beings, on their own, are no longer capable of willing and doing the good (*Nat. et Grat.* and the anti-Pelagian writings...)."

to respond to such men." (*pers*.2.4; *pred*.44). The famous scholar Pelikan appropriately lamented Augustine's departure from traditional theology and his feeble excuse.[34]

Augustine attempted to use "divine persuasion" as his means to avoid summarily rejecting the free will defense of all prior Christian authors against Stoicism and Manichaeism. Of the extant authors who taught on the topic, all forty-seven from AD 95 through AD 412 supported and defended this view of free choice against the Stoics, Gnostics, and Manichaeans.[35] For them, election was according to God's foreknowledge (cf., 1 Peter 1:2),[36] as Augustine himself had taught for decades.[37] To avoid violating centuries of Christian teaching

---

34 Jaroslav Pelikan, *The Christian Tradition: A History of the Development of Doctrine*, vol. 1 (Chicago: University of Chicago Press, 1971-1989), 278-280, esp. 280.

35 Ibid. Aside from all of the primary sources listed in my thesis, see also Hall (1979), 42; Hinson (2005), "Irenaeus"; Orbe (1969), 296–7; Sesboüé (2004), 105; Floyd (1971), 28 (Cf., Strom.1.34, 6.4, 6.7); Osborn (1997), 100; O'Leary (2004), 115; cp., C.Cels.6.55; McIntire (2005), "Free Will and Predestination: Christian Concepts"; Williams (1927), 297; Kelly (1960), 149; Harrison (1992), 130–31; Streck (2005), 173,180–82; Moxon (1922), 40; Chadwick (1960), 136, fnt.6; Blowers (1999), "Original Sin."

36 Note the bias of *BDAG* (3rd ed.) in considering κατά in verse 3 as meaning "because of" without admitting this in the κατά of the immediately preceeding verse (2). A *Greek-English Lexicon of the New Testament and Other Early Christian Literature*, Third edition, rev. and ed. by Frederick Danker (Chicago: University of Chicago Press, 2000), κατά.B.a.5.δ. "Oft. the norm is at the same time the reason, so that *in accordance with* and *because of* are merged:...1 Pt 1.3."

37 J. Wetzel, "Simplicianum, Ad" in A. Fitzgerald, ed. *Augustine Through the Ages: An Encyclopedia* (Grand Rapids, Mich.: Wm. B. Eerdman's, 1999): "As late as the first part of *Ad Simplicianum*, Augustine rests secure in his belief that it remains to a person's free choice to seek the aid of the divine liberator, regardless of how debilitating addiction to sin has become (1.1.14)" Cf., Lenka Karfíková, *Grace and the Will according to Augustine* (Leiden: Brill, 2012), 7-61; Peter Brown, *Augustine of Hippo: A Biography* (London: Faber and Faber, 1967; revised edition, Berkeley: University of California Press, 2000), 141-2; Marianne Djuth, "Will," in Allan D. Fitzgerald, ed. *Augustine*

Augustine redefined free will. He concluded God must micromanage and manipulate the circumstances that would guarantee a person would "freely" respond to the invitation of God's calling to eternal life.[38] A millennium later, Calvinists would call this irresistible grace.

The Roman statesman Cicero (*c.*50 BC) and numerous philosophers had argued the incompatibility between divine omniscience and human free will. They cannot co-exist. But Augustine's refutation (*ciu.*5) claimed divine foreknowledge of the future occurs only through God's pre-determination of everything both good and bad (*ordo*), a concept absent in Cicero's Platonic philosophy (*De Divinatione*) and Christianity, but common in Stoicism. "God foreordains human wills."[39] But Origin (*c.*250) had differentiated the Christian God's foreknowledge from pagan divine foreknowledge—God's foreknowledge is not causative (*Com.Rom.*7.8.7) which allows human free choice.

Another novel doctrine emerged many years later—perseverance of the saints. Some baptized infants would become responsible adult Christians while other baptized infants would fall away from the faith and perhaps live immoral lives. What could explain the difference since both possessed the Holy Spirit? Augustine concluded (logically) that God must give a second gift of grace called perseverance. The gift of perseverance is only given to some baptized infants.[40] Without this second gift of grace, a baptized Christian with the Holy Spirit will not persevere and ultimately will not be saved.[41]

Through the Ages: An Encyclopedia (Grand Rapids, Mich.: Wm. B. Eerdman's, 1999), 883; Augustine, 83Div.Q 68.3 and *Gen.c.Man.*1.6.

38 Patout Burns, "From Persuasion to Predestination: Augustine on Freedom in Rational Creatures" in P. Blowers, et al., eds. In *Dominico Elquio, in Lordly Eloquence: Essays on Patristic Exegesis in Honour of Robert Louis Wilken* (Cambridge: Eerdmans, 2002), 307. But Burns would not assent to my use of micromanage and manipulate.

39 Christopher Kirwan, *Augustine (The Arguments of the Philosophers)*, (London and New York: Routledge, 1989), 98–103.

40 Augustine, (*persev.*1, 9–12, 21, 41); Peter Burnell, *The Augustinian Person* (Washington, D.C.: The Catholic University of America Press, 2005), 85–86.

41 Augustine, *corrept.*18.

And this led to another doctrinal change. Back in AD 411, Augustine held to the traditional Christian doctrine on the atonement—that God loved and Christ died for the whole world. "Who indeed can doubt that in the term *world* all persons are indicated who enter the world by being born?" (*Pecc.mer.*1.26; cf., *conf.*6.7-8). But after his syncretism with Gnostic Manichaeism, Augustine attempted at least five answers over a decade of time trying to explain 1 Timothy 2:4— "who desires all men to be saved and to come to the knowledge of the truth"—on the extent of Christ's redeeming sacrifice.[42] His major premise was the pagan idea that God receives everything he desires (a philosophical McEar error variant).[43] Omnipotence (Stoic and Neoplatonic) is doing whatever the One desires, ensuring everything that occurs is exactly the Almighty's will and so must come to pass (*s.*214.4).[44] He concluded that because God gets everything he wants, God does not desire all persons to be saved, otherwise every human

---

42 Alexander Hwang, "Augustine's Various Interpretations of 1 Tim. 2: 4," *Studia Patristica* 43 (2006), 137-42.

43 The McEar error may have been first explicated by Ockham against the inadequate or problematic definition of the word 'omnipotence.' Augustine's earlier variant of the error concludes that omnipotence necessarily results in God receiving everything he desires. See Leftow (2009), 168, where he exposes this McEar error from Augustine's "will" element; cf., John Rist, *Augustine: Ancient Thought Baptized* (Cambridge: Cambridge University Press, 1994), 272, 286; Richard La Croix. "The Impossibility of Defining 'Omnipotence.'" *Philosophical Studies* 32.2 (1977): 181-190; Alvin Plantinga. *God and Other Minds: A Study of the Rational Justification of Belief in God* (Ithaca, NY: Cornell University Press, 1967), 170; Edward Wierenga, "Omnipotence Defined," *Philosophy and Phenomenological Research* 43.3 (1983): 363-375 and *The Nature of God: An Inquiry into Divine Attributes* (Cornell Studies in the Philosophy of Religion, Cornell University Press, 2003), Chapter 1.

44 Augustine, (*symb.cat.*2): "He does whatever He wills: that itself is omnipotence [by definition]. He does whatever He wishes well, whatever He wishes justly, but, whatever is evil, He does not will. No one resists the Omnipotent and not do what God wills." «Facit quidquid vult: ipsa est omnipotentia. Facit quidquid bene vult, quidquid juste vult: quidquid autem male fit, non vult. Nemo resistit omnipotenti, ut non quod vult faciat.»

would be saved. The Oxford Patristics expert Chadwick concluded that because Augustine's God does not desire and so refuses to save all persons, Augustine elevated God's sovereignty as absolute and God's justice was trampled.[45] This also logically demanded that Christ could not have died for those who would not be saved. Therefore, Christ only died for the elect since God does not waste causation or energy.[46]

Finally, for the first time in his massive corpus, Augustine affirms perseverance itself is God's gift (*corrept.*10) by decontextualizing 1 Corinthians 4:7.[47] In *corrept.*16, he first posits that all the "true elect" inevitably persevere. Therefore, a person can be genuinely regenerated and receive the Holy Spirit but be damned to hell by not receiving the additional necessary gift of perseverance from God (*corrept.*18), which he astutely exclaims as stupefying. He reverts to the Gnostic/Manichaean interpretation of Romans 11:33. Augustine then conscripts Philippians 1:6 as a proof-text completely out of context of Paul's confidence that the Philippians will continue their partnership/fellowship in the gospel through their financial contributions to him.[48]

---

45 Henry Chadwick "Freedom and Necessity in Early Christian Thought About God" in David Tracy and Nicholas Lash, eds. *Cosmology and Theology.* (Edinburgh: T. & T. Clark Ltd, 1983), 8-13.

46 See Donato Ogliari, *Gratia et Certamen: The Relationship between Grace and Free Will in the Discussion of Augustine with the so-called Semipelagians* (Leuven: University Press, 2003). Not distinguishing between the early Augustine (386-411 CE) who taught traditional doctrines versus his later extreme writings (412 through 430 CE) leads to scholarly confusion regarding his teachings on faith, grace, the extent of the atonement, etc. This is compounded by many of his writings (e.g., *En.Ps., Io.eu.tr., Gn.litt., doc.chr.*) being written over a time period of fifteen to twenty-five years from c.400 through c.425, and therefore those works contain both sets of doctrine.

47 By asking, "And what do you have that you did not receive?" Paul rebukes prideful boasting in human abilities that created rivalries instead of crediting spiritual gifts to God who gave them. Cf., John Barclay, "I Corinthians" in *The Oxford Bible Commentary*, John Barton and John Muddiman, eds. (Oxford: Oxford University Press, 2001), 1115. Augustine reverts to Manichaean heresy—God regenerates giving initial faith.

48 David Black, *Linguistics for Students of New Testament Greek*, 2nd ed. (Grand Rapids, Mich.: Baker Books, 1995), 177-8. Compare 4.10-20 where the

Despite this contextual error, he proclaims, "by this gift they cannot fail to persevere" (*corrept*.34).

Augustine's five points of total inability, unconditional election, limited atonement, "irresistible" grace, and perseverance are now recognized as the TULIP of Calvinism. Thus, Augustine was the inventor of the five points of Calvinism. Calvin admitted, "Augustine is so wholly within me that I could write my entire theology out of his writings."[49] Calvin was not the only one influenced by Augustine. The originator of the Protestant Reformation, Martin Luther, was an Augustinian monk who revived Augustine's pagan deterministic theology in AD 1525 with *De servo arbitrio* (*On the Bondage of the Will*).[50] Both Luther and Calvin mistakenly believed that Augustine was merely teaching what all of the earlier church fathers had taught.[51] But in fact, Augustine himself admitted that he had tried but failed

---

concluding good work of financial support matches the beginning 1.5 of fellowship in the gospel that Paul is confident will continue. Nothing suggests eternal life or perseverance.

49 John Calvin, "A Treatise on the Eternal Predestination of God," in John Calvin, *Calvin's Calvinism*, trans. Henry Cole (London: Sovereign Grace Union; reprint, 1927), 38.

50 As an Augustinian monk, Luther could not allow Erasmus of Rotterdam to continue the traditional doctrine of free choice and responded to Erasmus' "Free Will" with "Bondage of the Will." Although orthodox regarding Christian doctrine, Erasmus believed righteousness was more important than nit-picking orthodoxy.

51 Martin Luther, "Letter to Spalatin" (October 19, 1516) and *Lecture on Romans*, Glosses and Scholia, Chapter 4 in *Luther's Works*, vol. 48, Letters I, J. Pelikan, H. Oswald, and H. Lehmann, eds. (Philadelphia: Fortress Press, 1999); John Calvin, *Institutes of the Christian Religion* I.xiii.29; Cf., Kenneth Wilson, "The Mortal Wound to the Anthropological *Regula Fide*" (Unpublished Master's Thesis, Golden Gate Baptist Theological Seminary, 2006), 101-2; Wolfson, *Religious Philosophy*, 158-76 in which he explains the centuries-old traditional Judeo-Christian understanding of free will (despite the sinful inclination) that persisted until the "later Augustine" introduced Stoic ideas into Judeo-Christian theology, and especially Augustine's misunderstanding of *concupiscentia* in his Latin translation of *Wisdom of Solomon 8:21*.

to continue in the Christian doctrine of free will of the first four centuries.[52] He consistently utilized the same Christian terms but inserted new meanings into those terms.[53]

Augustine Reverted to Manichaean Interpretations of Scripture

Of course, Augustine used Scripture to prove his new doctrines. Unfortunately, he used the Manichaean interpretations of passages he had previously refuted. The Gnostic Manichaeans cited John 6:65, 14:6, and Ephesians 2:8-9 as proof of unconditional election against Christian free choice. Fortunatus the Manichaean had quoted Ephesians 2.8–9 as evidence for initial faith being God's gift by grace (DUPIED).[54] Fortunatus also cited John 14:6, "No one comes

---

52 As cited earlier, "In the solution of this question I struggled in behalf of free choice of the will, but the grace of God won out." (*retr.* 2.1).

53 This includes the terms original sin, grace, predestination, free will, etc. See Andre Dubarle, *The Biblical Doctrine of Original Sin* (London: Geoffrey Chapman, 1964), 53: "For example, in the early patristic writers we find references to the *origin of sin*, to a *fall*, and to the *inheritance of sin*, but what is meant is often different from the meaning given to those terms in the later classical tradition influenced by Augustine"; Ralph Mathiesen, "For Specialists Only: The Reception of Augustine and His Teachings in the Fifth Century Gaul" in *Collectanea Augustina: Presbyter Factus Sum*, eds. Joseph Lienhard, Earl Muller, and Roland Teske (New York: Peter Lang, 1993), 30-31; Rebecca Weaver, s.v. "Predestination," in *Encyclopedia of Early Christianity*, 2nd ed., Everett Ferguson, ed. (New York and London: Garland Publishing, 1998): "The now centuries-old characterization of the human being as capable of free choice and thus accountable at the last judgment had been retained, but the meaning of its elements had been considerably altered"; Peter Leitheri, "*Review of Adam, Eve, and the Serpent* by Elaine Pagels," *Westminster Theological Seminary Journal* 51.1 (Spring, 1989), 186: "Augustine's concept of free will certainly differs from that of earlier theologians"; C.f., Wilson, "*Augustine's Conversion*," (2012), 159, 164, 171, etc.

54 The first extant "Christian" writing claiming faith itself was a gift of God instead of a human response was from the gnostic Basilides who was refuted by Clement of Alexandria c.190 (*Strom.*2.3–4; cp., *Strom.*4.11, *Quis Dives Salvetur*, 10).

to the Father, but by me," since "He has chosen souls worthy of Himself according to His own holy will" (*c.Fort*.3, 16). But Augustine had previously correctly attacked this error: "'I say it is not sin, if it be not committed by one's own will; hence also there is reward, because of our own will we do right.'" (*c.Fort*.21). Unbelievably, in AD 412, Augustine accepted Fortunatus's Manichaean DUPIED interpretation of John 14:6 (*gr.et.lib.arb*.3–4,10). Augustine reconverted back to a Manichaean proof-text interpretation of Ephesians 2:8 for God regenerating the dead will and infusing faith (*gr.et.lib. arb*.17).

Augustine had earlier taunted the Manichaeans for inventing a god who damned persons eternally when the persons had no ability to do good or choose good.

> And by this you stand to say that those horrible mass of souls are being collected to be eternally damned, not by their will, but by necessity enemies sent away from the holy light; and such a just god you establish for yourselves! . . . whose hostility against you and Himself, not willingly, but you will testify are sent away by necessity, without any power to obtain an indulgence. What a most shocking cruelty! (*Contra Faustas* 22.22, translation mine).[55]

Such pagan ideas had been refuted by Augustine until AD 412 when he readopted the Manichaean interpretations against all prior Christian authors. Psalm 51:5 had never been cited by a Christian author as proof of separation from God at physical birth (a Manichaean doctrine) until Augustine used it to turn traditional original sin (sin propensity, moral weakness, and physical death) into Augustinian

---

55 *c.Faust*.22.22: «Ac per hoc restat ut dicatis etiam illas animas in horribili globo aeterna colligatione damnandas, non voluntate, sed necessitate inimicas lumini sancto exstitisse; talemque deum vestrum judicem constituatis, [...] quorum inimicitias adversus vos et ipsum, non voluntate, sed necessitate exstitisse perhibetis, nec indulgentiam impetrare valeatis. O immanissimam crudelitatem!»

original sin (inherited sin and guilt from Adam producing damnation at birth and total spiritual inability).[56]

In AD 395, his traditional view of Romans 5:12 ("Therefore, just as through one man sin entered the world and death through sin, and thus death spread to all men, because all sinned") allowed him to omit this verse in his commentary on Romans:

> But we also use it in speaking of the nature with which we are born mortal, ignorant and subject to the flesh, which is really the penalty of sin. In this sense the apostle says: "We also were by nature children of wrath even as others" . . . But if any of Adam's race should be willing to turn to God, and so overcome the punishment which had been merited by the original turning away from God, it was fitting not only that he should not be hindered but that he should also receive divine aid. In this way also the Creator showed how easily man might have retained, if he had so willed, the nature with which he was created, because his offspring had power to transcend that in which he was born. (*De Libero Arbitrio* 3.54-55)

After AD 411, his Manichaean view of inherited birth guilt and his Stoic view of micromanaging Providence pervaded his theology with infants being damned at birth by divine unilateral choice (*Pecc. mer.*1.29-30).[57] But there was a problem: Christianity required personal

---

56 This represents hyperbole by comparing Ps.57.4 LXX since sinners from the womb cannot yet speak lies as newborns: "ἀπηλλοτριώθησαν οἱ ἁμαρτωλοὶ ἀπὸ μήτρας, ἐπλανήθησαν ἀπὸ γαστρός, ἐλάλησαν ψεύδη." Origen specifically cited but denied any guilt for sin at birth in Ps. 51 when combating pagans and Gnostics (C.Cels.7.50) although the sin nature (*genuinae sordes peccati*) enters through physical birth (*Hom.Lev.*8.3, 12.4; *Com.Rom.*5.9; *C.Cels.*7.50). Cf., Wilson, *Augustine's Conversion*, 311-16, where Horace, whose works Augustine had read (*c.mend.*28; *s.*2.6; *ep.*1.7), utilized hyperbole to express the pervasiveness of human vices, particularly as beginning from birth (*Serm.Q.Hoarti Flacci* 1.68: «nam vitiis nemo sine nascitur, "For nobody is born without vices/faults."

57 Johannes van Oort, "Augustine on Sexual Concupiscence and Original Sin," *Studia Patristica* 22 (1989): 382-86.

faith for baptismal regeneration. So Augustine utilized a syncretistic approach by combining Stoic determinism while changing Christian doctrine by inventing a proxy salvation whereby one person can believe for another, so that the one being baptized need not believe in Christ. "There is not indeed a man among the faithful, who would hesitate to call such infants believers merely from the circumstance that such a designation is derived from the act of believing; for although incapable of such an act themselves, yet others are sponsors for them in the sacraments" (*Pecc.mer.*1.38). Personal faith was no longer required.

> And so, even if that faith that is found in the will of believers does not make a little one a believer, the sacrament of the faith itself [baptism], nonetheless, now does so. For, just as the response is given that the little one believes, he is also in that sense called a believer, not because he assents to the reality with his mind, but because he receives the sacrament of that reality. (*ep.*98.10).[58]

Using John 3:5 as his first scriptural defense for salvific infant water baptism (*an.et or.*1.1), it became his essential foundation, yet the Catholic scholar Redmond doubts its validity.[59] Furthermore, the Catholic Augustinian scholar Hill exposes, ". . . babies who die unbaptized therefore go to hell. Augustine assumed that baptism was the only means of liberating grace available to them. And it is

---

58 Translation by Roland Teske, S.J., *The Works of Saint Augustine: A Translation of the 21st Century*, Letters 1-99, II.1 (Hyde Park, NY: New City Press, 2001), 432.

59 Richard Redmond, "Infant Baptism: History and Pastoral Problems," *Theological Studies* 30 (March 1969): 79–89, esp. 84: "For, as Raymond Brown says, John's concern here is one of contrasting flesh and spirit....The negative universal of this verse, then, does not prove the necessity of infant baptism. Nor do we find any '*quamprimum*' urgency about baptism, since for a long time in Rome Easter and Pentecost were the only dates for baptism." The context clarifies the physical birth versus spiritual birth with the mother's "water breaking" being the common terminology for a physical birth even in our modern time. The context is not water baptism.

precisely this assumption that renders his whole argument weak, and his conclusion highly questionable."[60]

The scholarly literature contains numerous discussions of the Latin mistranslation of Romans 5:12 (in whom, *in quo*) versus NT Greek (because, ἐφ' ᾧ).[61] Augustine did not know Greek until later in his life.[62] He upheld this mistranslation as his definitive proof for his syncretistic Manichaean-Christian doctrine of separation from God at birth with all humanity damned by guilt from Adam's sin.[63] Traditional original sin with physical death from personal sin (ἐφ' ᾧ, because) became Augustinian original sin with spiritual death from Adam's sin (*in quo*, in whom [all sinned]).[64] So the traditional interpretation that all die physically as a result of Adam transformed into the Manichaean-Augustinian view that all sinned in Adam, and all are therefore damned at birth.

---

60 Edmund Hill, O.P., *The Works of Saint Augustine* (Sermon 294), 196.

61 Bruce Harbert, "Romans 5:12: Old Latin and Vulgate in the Pelagian Controversy," *Studia Patristica* 22 (1989), 262; Philip Quinn, "Sin" in *Routledge Encyclopedia of Philosophy* (London: Routledge, 1998); G. Vandervelde, *Original Sin: Two Major Trends in Contemporary Roman Catholic Reinterpretation* (Amsterdam: Rodopi N.V., 1975), 22; David Weaver, "From Paul to Augustine: Romans 5:12 in Early Christian Exegesis," *St. Vladimir's Theological Quarterly* 27.3 (1983); J.N.D. Kelly, *Early Christian Doctrines*, 2nd ed. (New York: Harper and Row, 1960), 181-2; Bradley Nassif, "Toward a 'catholic' Understanding of St. Augustine's View of Original Sin," *Union Seminary Quarterly Review* 39.4 (1984), 287-299, esp. 296; N.a., s.v., "Original Sin" in *The Oxford Dictionary of the Christian Church*, 3rd ed. (Oxford: Oxford University Press, 2005).

62 Augustine admits his poor knowledge of Greek (*c. litt.* Pet. 2.91), interpreted disparately but which can be ascertained as he chronologically improves his knowledge from c.400 through the next decades: «et Ego quidem graecae linguae perparum assecutus sum, et prope nihil: non tamen impudenter dico, me nosse ὅλου non esse unum, sed totum.» (PL 43, 292).

63 William Mann, "Augustine on Evil and Original Sin," in *The Cambridge Companion to Augustine*, ed. Eleanore Stump and Norman Kretzmann (Cambridge, UK: Normal Publication, 2001), 47; Anthony Padovano, *Original Sin and Christian Anthropology* (Washington, DC: Corpus Books, 1967), 11.

64 G. Vandervelde, *Original Sin*, 5.

The Augustinian scholar Bonner wrote, "It has been remarked that the number of texts to which Augustine appealed to establish this doctrine of Original Sin is remarkably limited: Psalm 50:7 [51:5 EW]; Job 14:4-5: John 3:5; Ephesians 2:3; Romans 5:12."[65] Augustine's reversal to his prior Manichaean interpretations of these verses is unmistakable.

Augustine Taught Pagan Determinism (DUPIED) not Biblical Predestination

Prior to AD 250, Gnostics and heretics had used Scripture to justify their false doctrines. They quoted these Scripture verses as proof of their deterministic DUPIED (*P.Arch.*3.1.18-21): Philippians 2:13, "for it is God who works in you, both to will and to work for his good pleasure" and Romans 9:18-21:

> So then he has mercy on whomever he wills, and he hardens whomever he wills. You will say to me then, "Why does he still find fault? For who can resist his will?" But who are you, O man, to answer back to God? Will what is molded say to its molder, "Why have you made me like this?" Has the potter no right over the clay, to make out of the same lump one vessel for honorable use and another for dishonorable use? (ESV)

The Valentinian variety of Gnostics derived their deterministic DUPIED from a Stoic interpretation of Romans 11 (Clement, *Exc. ex.Theo.*56.3-27) as explained by Bingham.[66] Valentinus taught the message of salvation was offered to all, but only the elect (πνευματικοί possessing Light particles) were empowered by God to accept the

---

65 Gerald Bonner, "Augustine, the Bible and the Pelagians," in Pamela Bright, editor and translator. *Augustine and the Bible* (Notre Dame, Ind.: Univ. of Notre Dame Press, 1999) 231–2.

66 Jeffrey Bingham, "Irenaeus Reads Romans 8: Resurrection and Renovation" in Kathy L. Gaca and Laurence L. Welborn, eds. *Patristic Readings of Romans* in Romans Through History and Culture Series (London: T&T Clark, 2005).

invitation and receive salvation (*Ev. Ver.* 11, 30–31; *Corp. Herm.* 1.26).[67] The Manichaean teachings (the theological pinnacle of Gnosticism) utilized these Gnostic ideas.

Yet no known major religion or philosophy has ever advertised itself as believing absolute determinism. Such a repugnant concept demands some accommodation for a "free will," even if it is disingenuous. This was precisely the manner in which Stoics, Gnostics, and Manichaeans presented their pervasive determinism. Even Augustine himself had previously accused the Manichaeans of carrying about the carcass of "free will" gutted of its Christian meaning.[68]

Although some scholars categorize Stoics as compatibilists, genuine free choice and moral responsibility are inseparably linked, presupposing and demanding each other. The contradictory Stoic "fated free will" rejects this common sense approach. Fate controls every minute occurrence in the universe in a moral imperative (Cicero, *Div.* 1, 125–6). Although the person had no possibility of actuating an opportunity, "free will" remains solely by definition (Cicero, *Fat.* 12–15).[69] Reesor correctly clarifies that even the infamously deterministic

---

67 Albrecht Dihle, *The Theory of Will in Classical Antiquity* (Berkeley: University of California Press, 1982), 151-4.

68 Faculty members (and others) at both Oxford and Cambridge have sounded this warning: Tim Mawson, *Free Will: A Guide for the Perplexed* (London: The Continuum International Publishing Group, 2011); Linda Zagzebski, "Recent Work on Divine Foreknowledge and Free Will" in Robert Kane, ed., *The Oxford Handbook of Free Will* (Oxford: Oxford University Press, 2002), 45-64; Christopher Stead, *Philosophy in Christian Antiquity* (Cambridge: Cambridge University Press, 1994), 50-52; Eleonore Stump, "Augustine on free will" in Eleonore Stump and Norman Kretzman, eds. *The Cambridge Companion to Augustine* (Cambridge: Cambridge University Press, 2001), 142: "On the contrary, unless Augustine is willing to accept that God's giving of grace is responsive to something in human beings, even if that something is not good or worthy of merit, I don't see how he can be saved from the imputation of theological determinism with all its infelicitous consequences." These present an astute discussion of covert determinism masquerading as free will (what I call pseudo-compatibilism).

69 A. A. Long and D.N. Sedley, *The Hellenistic Philosophers* Vol. 2 (Cambridge: Cambridge University Press, 1987), 392-3; cf., Epictetus, *Disc.* 1.1.7–12.

Stoics "took elaborate precautions to protect their system from rigid determinism."[70] Philo's *On Providence* appropriates a Stoic view. Even Dillon states a reading of this treatise by itself would lead one to the conclusion that Philo was a determinist.[71] Winston identified Philo's view as a "relative free will theory taught by the Stoics, and often characterized as 'compatibilism'" but not a genuine free will [but what I term a "non-free free will" of Stoicism] of traditional Judaism's varieties.[72]

Rejecting an outward Necessity, Plotinus (Neoplatonism) posits the Stoic theory of freedom to do whatever we desire, yet simultaneously subjects us to determinism since "the will" has been bound by innate universal wickedness (*Enn*.III,2.10). Evil produced a totally incapacitating fall, imprisoning us against our wills (*Enn*.I,8.5). Souls have neither genuine free will nor act by compulsion (*Enn*.IV,3.13). We are free to choose only what our corrupt will determines (Stoicism). His view of voluntariness required only that the act was not forced, done with knowledge, and that we were *kurioi* (masters) of the act (*Enn*. VI,8.1-4). The later Augustine incorporated all of these Neoplatonic theories now taught by Calvinism.

Plotinus rejected the Judeo-Christian account that Adam retained God's image (*imago Dei*) after the fall by positing a total loss of the original divine image only to be regained at death (*Enn*.I,1.12; IV,3.12; cf., Augustine's later view). Mimicking Stoicism, a person only achieves true freedom of will when (by renouncing pleasures and actions) the *autexousion* (self-determination/power) becomes totally dependent upon the Intellect (*Enn*.III, 3.19-21). For Plotinus, Providence controls every miniscule cosmic detail; nevertheless, the One (God) provides limited freedom for some events and persons

---

70 Margaret E. Reesor, "Fate and Possibility in Early Stoic Philosophy," *Phoenix* 19.4 (1965): 285–297, especially 201.

71 John Dillon, *The Middle Platonists: A Study of Platonism, 80 B.C. to AD 220* (London: Duckworth, 1977), 166ff.

72 David Winston, "Chapter 13: Philo of Alexandria" in Lloyd P. Gerson, ed. *The Cambridge History of Philosophy in Late Antiquity* (Cambridge: Cambridge University Press, 2010), 248, footnote 13. The analogies in Philo's *On Providence* are very close to the analogies in Cicero, *De Natura Deorum* II.

due to τὸ ἐφ' ἡμῖν (what depends upon us) made possible *solely* by the indwelling Reason-Principle to produce good (*Enn.*III,3.4-5; III,2.9.1, II,3.1.1).

When accused of Stoic determinism, Neoplatonists dissented by cleverly limiting "determinism" and "Fate" to astrology while still teaching Stoic "non-free free will." A totally incapacitating fall from "the One" produces a spiritually dead "evil will" thus requiring the divinely infused gift of love for free choice. The All-Soul (Spirit) gives the gift of love to individuals' souls as the Spirit who implants the desired love (*Enn.*III.5.4). Yet, the One's essential goodness (by definition) exculpates from charges of "unfairness" in Neoplatonic DUPIED.[73] Augustine's later theology incorporated all of these pagan ideas.

Space limitations do not permit a summary of my doctoral work analysis of Augustine's Stoic view of the human "evil will" along with his proof-text Latin mistranslations of Proverbs 8:35 and Philippians 2:13.[74] But, as Byers notes, "Augustine's account of the 'divided self' is deeply indebted to Stoicism."[75] Djuth summarizes Augustine's later premise drawn from Stoicism and Neoplatonism but without acknowledging those sources, "Hence, the good will by which someone begins to will to believe is a divine gift which comes from outside the will."[76]

The covert determinism of current Augustinian Calvinism embraces the same defenses as Augustine's pagan sources. Augustine followed

---

73 Long and Sedley (1987), 342, 392.

74 For example, the five other texts (Ps.5.13, 68.14, 144.16; Sir.15.15; Lk. 2.14) containing εὐδοκίας refer to *favor, acceptance,* or *good pleasure,* not a "good will" to live righteously in the Stoic sense that Augustine attempted to reinterpret Phil. 2:13 (cf., *gr.et.pecc.or.*1.6; *ep.*217.8).

75 Sara Byers, "Augustine on the 'Divided Self': Platonist or Stoic?" *Aug.Stud.*38:1 (2007) 105–118.

76 Marianne Djuth, "Stoicism and Augustine's Doctrine of Human Freedom after 396" in Joseph C. Schnaubelt and Frederick Van Fleteren, eds., *Augustine: Second Founder of the Faith.* Collectanea Augustiniana (New York: Peter Lang, 1990).

Plotinus's defense that fate must involve astrology, so fate from God does not count as fate. The Augustinian scholar, TeSelle noted,

> Augustine always reacted vigorously to the suggestion that he taught what amounted to a doctrine of *fate*. Now it is undeniable that he did hold to something like what is usually meant by fate.... To him fate meant something precise: the doctrine that external occurrences, bodily actions, even thoughts and decisions are determined by the position of the heavenly bodies (*C. duat ep Pel.*, II,6,12) or more broadly, universal material determinism (*C. duat ep Pel.* II, 6,12; *De Civ. Dei.* IV.33, V.1,8).[77]

Augustine admitted if anyone, "calls the will of God or the power of God itself by the name of fate, let him keep his opinion but correct his language." (*c.dua.ep.Pel.*1.2.4). Professor Wolfson, historian and philosopher at Harvard University's Judaic Studies Center, concluded Augustine's "doctrine of grace is only a Christianization of the Stoic doctrine of fate."[78]

God Desires All To be Saved but It's Their Choice

The early church viewed God as relational and responsive to human choices, having incorporated human choices into His prophecies. Wallace accurately identified the earliest Christian leaders using foreknowledge as their key defense against the Gnostics: "They interpreted προορίζω [predestination] as depending upon προγινώσκω (foreknow)".[79] Unlike Stoicism's causal nexus,

---

77 Eugene TeSelle, *Augustine the Theologian* (New York: Herder and Herder, 1970; reprint Eugene, Ore.: Wipf and Stock Publishers, 2002), 313.

78 Harry Wolfson, *Religious Philosophy: A Group of Essays* (Cambridge, Massachusetts: Belknap Press of Harvard University Press, 1961), 176; Cf., Michael Frede and Halszka Osmolska, *A Free Will: Origins of the Notion in Ancient Thought* (University of California Press, 2011), especially, "Chapter Nine—Augustine: A Radically New Notion of a Free Will?"

79 Dewey Wallace, Jr., "Free Will and Predestination," in *The Encyclopedia of Religion*, 2nd ed. (London: MacMillan, 2004).

Neoplatonism's One, and Manichaeism's god, Christianity's God did not decree everything—despite being sovereign. The first Christian patristic systematizing theologian, Irenaeus (c.185), argued that the Christian God was superior in power to the Gnostic god since He allowed free human choices and could still accomplish his plans (without Stoic divine micromanaging manipulation).[80]

Augustine cites 1 Timothy 2:4—"who desires all men to be saved and to come to the knowledge of the truth"—only once prior to 412 (*exp.prop.Rm.*74) and uses the traditional understanding. Beginning with his AD 412 departure, he attempts numerous explanations.[81] But only in AD 421 (*c.Jul.*4.8.42) did Augustine alter the text to mean "all who are saved" meaning those who are saved are only saved by God's will, which he repeats the next year (*ench.*97, 103). People fail to be saved, "not because they do not will it, but because God does not" (*ep.*217.19). Despite their certain damnation, God makes other Christians desire their impossible salvation (*corrept.*15, 47), which Rist identifies as "the most pathetic passage."[82] By AD 429, Augustine quotes 1 Corinthians 1:18 adding "such" to 1 Timothy 2:4, redefines *all* to mean as "all those elected," and implies an irresistible calling. As Hwang noted,

> Then the radical shift occurred, brought about by the open and heated conflict with the Pelagians. 'Desires' took on absolute and

---

80 Gustaf Wingren, *Man and the Incarnation*. Translated by Ross Mackenzie (Lund: C.W.K. Gleerup, 1947; reprint London: Oliver and Boyd, 1959), 35-6. "The essential principle in the concept of freedom appears first in Christ's status as the sovereign Lord, because for Irenaeus man's freedom is, strangely enough, a direct expression of God's omnipotence, so direct in fact, that a diminution of man's freedom automatically involves a corresponding diminution of God's omnipotence." Cf., Irenaeus, *Adv.haer.*II.5.4

81 Alexander Hwang, "Augustine's Various Interpretations of 1 Tim. 2: 4," *Studia Patristica* 43 (2006), 137-42.

82 John Rist, "Augustine on Free Will and Predestination" in Robert Markus, ed. *Augustine: A Collection of Critical Essays.* (New York: Doubleday, 1972), 239. John Dillon, *The Middle Platonists: A Study of Platonism, 80 B.C. to AD 220* (London: Duckworth, 1977), 166ff.

efficacious qualities, and the meaning of 'all' was reduced to the predestined. 1 Tim. 2:4 should be understood, then, as meaning that God saves only the predestined. All others, apparently, do not even have a prayer.[83]

The early Christian bishops and authors rejected Stoic and Manichaean unilateral determinism (DUPIED) while teaching God's sovereignty and biblical predestination utilizing foreknowledge of genuine human free choice.[84] For twenty-five years Augustine defended traditional Christian doctrines against the Gnostic Manichaeans. Yet, he persisted in his meticulous Stoic Providence from his first writings until his death, including every leaf and seed being micromanaged (s.D29.11). But, being unable to legitimately transfer it to his novel revised Christianity after AD 412, he defaults to Plotinus's (Neoplatonism's) inscrutability defense (s.D.29.10) by appealing to the inscrutable secret counsels of God, who is fair by definition.[85] Chadwick opined that Augustine was influenced by Platonism far more than even Origen, particularly with sin as privation (e.g., conf.7.22).[86] The scholar O'Daly concluded, "Condemned through the solidarity of all humans with Adam, they are predestined because God foreknows that he will not give them the grace to be saved. . . . Contrary to the view sometimes expressed, Augustine does

83 Hwang, "Augustine's Various Interpretations of 1 Tim. 2:4," *Studia Patristica* 43 (2006), 137-42.

84 For example, Clement and Origen had adapted Stoic concepts and terminology (e.g., πρόνοια; cp., Acts 24.2) but without succumbing to Stoic determinism. Cf., Van Der Eijk, Ph. „Origines' „Verteidigung des freien Willens in *De Oratione* 6,1-2," *Vig.Chr.*9.1 (2001): 339–351, esp. 347; Jon Ewing, *Clement of Alexandria's Reinterpretation of Divine Providence* (Lewiston, New York: Edwin Mellen Press, 2008), 167–186.

85 Hombert dates this to c.April, 412. Cf., *loc.Ex.*20; *s.*294.7.

86 Henry Chadwick, "Christian Platonism in Origen and Augustine" in Henry Chadwick, ed., *Heresy and Orthodoxy in the Early Church* (Aldershot, UK: Variorum, 1991), 229-30.

speak of the predestination of the damned."[87] His Christian God with Manichaean syncretism unilaterally damned even innocent infants in a deterministic pagan DUPIED.

Augustine's Christianized Stoic Providence, which directly (primarily and actively) micromanages every speck of minutia, somehow, does not sovereignly control evil (direct meticulous micromanagement), but only allows/permits it. This view demands that the perfectly holy God who micromanages and decrees everything also decrees evil (in some mysterious and non-culpable manner). This concept comes straight from Stoicism stating that this was the best of all possible worlds (cf., Leibniz, c.1710). But if God *only allows/permits* evil then he does not control everything meticulously by decree and thus is not "sovereign" in the Stoic-Augustinian-Calvinist sense. If God *does* decree evil then he is not the Christian God but the evil creator of matter in Manichaeism (this is then defended by the Neoplatonic appeal to mystery). So why does God eternally damn newborn babies? Augustine confessed, "I cannot find a satisfactory and worthy explanation—because I can't find one, not because there isn't one." (s.294.7).[88] No theologian or philosopher in the 1600 years since Augustine has found a satisfactory or worthy answer to this antilogy of God damning innocent infants.

Conclusion

Scholars recognize the significant influences of Stoicism, Neoplatonism, and Manichaeism upon Augustine.[89] No Christian bishop or author

---

87 Gerard O'Daly, "Predestination and Freedom in Augustine's Ethics" in G. Vesey, ed. *The Philosophy in Christianity* (Cambridge, 1989), 90. «quos praedestinavit ad aeternam vitam misericordissimus gratiae largitor: qui est et illis quos praedestinavit ad aeternam mortem, justissimus supplicii retributor; non solum propter illa quae volentes adjiciunt, verum etiam si infantes nihil adjiciant, propter originale peccatum. Haec est in illa quaestione definitio mea, ut occulta opera Dei habeant suum secretum, salva fide mea.» (*an.et or.*4.16)

88 Translation by Edmund Hill, *Augustine's Works* (Sermon 294), 184.

89 John Rist, *Stoic Philosophy* (Cambridge: Cambridge University Press, 1969); Marianne Djuth, "Stoicism and Augustine's Doctrine of Human Freedom

before Augustine had so extensively imbibed the Stoic Providence of Chrysippus and Cicero.[90] None had been so influenced by Plotinus and Neoplatonism's deterministic system. None had been a Gnostic Manichaean for a decade prior to becoming a bishop. The early church had forbidden prior Manichaeans from becoming bishops, and therefore Augustine was almost prevented. Bishop Megalius, Catholic Primate of Numidia who eventually ordained Augustine, had originally presented written accusations of Manichaeism against Augustine after Augustine had been sentenced *in abstentia* by the African proconsul Messianus (385/6).[91] Augustine wrote eleven definitive anti-Manichaean works in seven years (388-395). These allowed him to be ordained in AD 396.

Augustine was the only major Christian figure in history who was a serious disciple of all three highly deterministic pagan systems— Manichaeism (Gnosticism), Stoicism, and Neoplatonism. All other prior Christian bishops and authors rejected pagan determinism as Fergusson explained.

---

after 396" in Joseph C. Schnaubelt and Frederick Van Fleteren, eds. *Augustine: Second Founder of the Faith*. Collectanea Augustiniana (New York: Peter Lang, 1990); Gerard O'Daly, *Platonism Pagan and Christian: Studies in Plotinus and Augustine* (Aldershot, UK: Ashgate, 2001); Johannes Van Oort (2006). "Augustine and Manichaeism: New Discoveries, New Perspectives," *Verbum et Ecclesia JRG* 27.2 (2006): 710–728; N. Joseph Torchia, "St. Augustine's treatment of superbia and its Plotinian Affinities," *Aug.Stud.*18 (1987): 66–79; M. Testard, *Saint Augustin et Cicerón*, Bd.1: Cicerón dans la formation et dans l'œuvre de saint Augustin; Bd. 2 : Répertoire des textes (Paris, 1958).

90 Augustine credited Cicero's *Hortensius* as the impetus for abandoning his sin and seeking answers in Christianity (*Conf.*3.5-9). Cf., Robert J. O'Connell, *Augustine's Early Theory of Man* (Ann Arbor, MI.: Belknap Press of Harvard University Press, University of Michigan, 1968), 189, regarding *c.Acad.*1.1 and *sol.*1. Although overstating Augustine's dependence upon Plotinus and Porphyry in some areas [cp., Bonner (1984), 495–514; Dodaro and Lawless (2000); Ayres (2010), 13–41], O'Connell rightly identifies this Stoic/ Neoplatonic influence for Providence.

91 Jason D. BeDuhn, "Augustine Accused: Megalius, Manichaeism, and the Inception of the *Confessions*," *JECS* 17.1 (2009): 85–124.

Throughout the early centuries of the church, theology was marked by an emphasis upon the compatibility of divine foreknowledge and human freedom largely to combat Stoic determinism and astrological fatalism.... God's control over the future is determined by a foreknowledge of human choices. Divine election is in part a function of this foreknowledge. The manner in which God will determine and govern a human life is fixed by an awareness of the ways in which freedom will be exercised.[92]

Tertullian (c.200) defended humanity's current free choice as the epitome of the image and likeness of God.[93] Augustine admitted that he abandoned this powerful Christian doctrine of free choice (used to fight against those deterministic systems) in favor of the "grace of God." However, it was the grace of the Manichaean god, not the Christian God.[94] Augustine reversed his Christian anti-Manichaean

---

92 David Fergusson, s.v. "Predestination," in *The Oxford Companion to Christian Thought*, Adrian Hastings, Alistair Mason, and Hugh Pyper, eds. (Oxford: Oxford University Press, 2000).

93 *Adv.Marc.2.5*: «nullam magis imaginem et similitudinem dei in illo...sed in ea substantia quam ab ipso deo traxit, id est animae ad formam dei respondentis, et arbitrii sui libertate et potestate signatus est.» "In no better way does humanity display the image and likeness of God...in that essence which he obtained from God himself, which corresponds to the form of God, and in the freedom and power of his will."

94 Manichaean salvation emphasizes Christ's grace, dominating many hymns. One Manichaean prayer requests that Jesus "Come with Grace," eleven times (M.28.II). See Geo Widengren, *Der Manichismus* (Darmstadt: Wissenschaftliche Buchgesellschaft, Abt. Verl.,1977). 90: "Dann folgt das Hauptstück, das in einem Gebet um die Epihanie besteht: Komm mit Heil!" Cf., Gediliahu Stroumsa, "Titus of Bostra and Alexander of Lycopolis: A Christian and a Platonic Refutation of Manichaean Dualism" in Richard T. Wallis, ed. *Neoplatonism and Gnosticism* (New York: State University of New York Press, 1992), 337–349. Stroumsa summarized the response of Alexander of Lycopolis to Manichaean 'grace': "Alexander [of Lycopolis] is shocked by Manichaean limitation of the path to salvation to the elect. For him, this directly contradicts the idea of a Providence, by definition equally caring for

interpretations of John 6:66, John 14:6, Ephesians 2:3-9, Philippians 2:13, etc. by using Manichaean heretical interpretations of those exact Scriptures after AD 412, interpretations that he had previously refuted. His favorite proof-texts were the mistranslated Romans 5:12 and Philippians 2:13. Augustine's entire systematic theology was based upon the church tradition of infant baptism combined with his Stoic micromanaging Providence either allowing or thwarting salvific infant baptism in AD 412.[95] His doctrines of total depravity, unconditional election, limited atonement, "irresistible" (Manichaean) grace, and inevitable perseverance (due to a second gift of grace for only a select few of all baptized Christians possessing the Holy Spirit) were all subsequently derived on the basis of this foundational error. The five points of Calvinism (TULIP) were all created by Augustine.

In contrast, Christians had championed human free choice for hundreds of years prior to Augustine's syncretistic conversion incorporating pagan ideas. Jerome succeeded in battling the Pelagians without going to the extremes of Augustinian-Calvinism (*Against the Pelagians*, III) and retained the traditional belief in Christian grace and free will.[96] The belief in faith alone for justification by God's free grace (*sola fide*) was not first discovered in the Protestant Reformation. There were Christians in good standing with the church *c.*AD 400 who held the doctrine that a person received salvation by faith alone without repentance or good works. Much to Augustine's ire, baptism was practiced immediately if one of them believed in Christ, without first entering prolonged education in Christian faith and morals as a catechumen. For those early Christians, God's future judgment consisted only of payment (reward) or punishment (temporary) for how those Christians lived their lives before God—heaven or

---

all." (344). C.f., McFayden, *Oxford Companion to Christian Thought* (Oxford: Oxford University Press, 2000), 667. He correctly argues that Augustine changed his view of grace but does not understand the Manichaean origin and the precipitating cause of paedobaptism.

95 C.f., Jaroslav Pelikan, *The Christian Tradition*, 278, for Augustine's reversal of traditional Patristic anthropology, free will, and the priority of infant baptism.

96 Cf., Hušek, Vít. "Human Freedom According to the Earliest Latin Commentaries on Paul's Letters," *Studia Patristica* 44 (2010): 385–390.

hell was not in question. Faith alone saved. Augustine attempted a refutation (poorly argued) of this earlier Christian grace theology after weaving his novel theological syncretism (*ench*.18.67-9; *f. et op*.1-2).[97] Therefore, an appeal to historical theology attempting to demonstrate Grace theology as a recent development while claiming Calvinist (Augustinian) theology stands as the ancient gold standard displays an ignorance of historical theology. This explains why works by Calvinists do not explore in detail the early (pre-AD 412) Augustine, the major influences of his pagan and heretical heritage, and the particular reasons for his new theology.[98] They, along with others, mistakenly attribute it to a new understanding of God's grace when Augustine read Romans, Galatians, and 1 Corinthians.

But Augustine's pagan syncretism does not make him a heretic. He remains a doctor of the Roman Catholic Church despite teaching errors.[99] Augustine adhered fervently to the fundamental doctrines such as the person of Jesus Christ as the God-man who died as Savior for sin and the Trinity. Likewise, our Augustinian-Calvinist brothers

---

97 These Christians were appealing to 1 Cor. 3.11-14 which Augustine tried to refute with James 2.14ff. These Christians understood inheriting the kingdom as different from entering the kingdom as Augustine's reply evidences. According to Augustine, they did not view repentance and giving of alms (works) as required for justification or as inevitable proof of it, since justification was by faith alone.

98 For one example, see Charles Warren, *Original Sin Explained* (New York: University Press of America, 2002), 10-11. In his "Contents," he lists "Patristic Period (A.D. 100-451)," but he begins his actual discussion in that chapter with Augustine and the Council of Carthage in A.D. 418, thus bypassing over three hundred years of the early Patristic period that taught the opposite of what the later Augustine taught!

99 The brilliant Thomas Aquinas in *Summa Theologica* revised Augustine's errors into a more biblical view. However, note well that the native Greek-speaking Eastern church never did admit Augustine as a father of the church due to his departure from traditional doctrines. Michael Azkoul, *The Influence of Augustine of Hippo on the Orthodox Church*, Text and Studies in Religion, vol. 56 (Lewiston, N.Y.: The Edwin Mellen Press, 1990), 33-42, and iii: "There is good reason that Orthodoxy [Greek/Russian] has never recognized him as a Father of the Church."

and sisters are not heretics. Believing a wrong doctrine does not qualify one as a heretic unless it concerns the most essential principles.[100]

I appeal to my Calvinist brethren to research their Augustinian heritage with an open mind. I would not want to be in their awkward position of defending a theology founded singlehandedly by a man with a prolonged indoctrination in three different intensely pagan deterministic systems, who departed from centuries of orthodox teachings on free choice by appealing to "salvific" infant water baptism viewed from Stoic micromanaging determinism (that eternally damns newborns), who admitted he had departed from Christianity's centuries-old free choice defense against pagans, rested his case on numerous Latin mistranslations (without knowing the Greek language), then followed Plotinus's defense appealing to the inscrutable secret counsel of the One (*don.pers.*1/27, 7; *grat.et lib. arb.* 41, 45, *an.et or.*4.16) to explain the incomprehensible unreasonableness of his novel pagan-Christian syncretistic theology—Stoic/ Neoplatonic/Manichaean/Christian. Current Calvinist interpretations of "deterministic" scripture passages are pagan interpretations brought into Christianity through Augustine. The impressively logical edifice of Augustinian Calvinism teeters like a massive upside down pyramid resting on the pebble of salvific infant baptism. For those persons rightly disturbed by the precariously dangerous historical and biblical lack of foundation in Augustinian-Calvinist systematic theology, I invite you to consider the pre-Augustinian and Augustine's earlier, more firmly founded and universal perspective of a salvific free choice response, graciously offered by *Christianity's* sovereign God of grace.

---

100 Alister McGrath, *Heresy: A History of Defending the Truth* (New York, HarperOne, 2009), 12, 17-39 and *Christianity's Dangerous Idea* (New York, HarperOne, 2007), 227-230. McGrath correctly warns of the subtle nature of heresy that often unintentionally distorts essential truths, particularly about the person of Christ and distinguishes rival doctrines that should not be classified as heresy. This follows the emphasis of Georg Calixtus (d.1656) on error versus heresy as he attempted to unify the Protestant factions.

Chapter 3

The Faith That Saves

David R. Anderson, Ph.D.

I n some respects, Grudem's understanding of faith is closer to Free Grace theology than historic Reformed theology. Grudem claims that genuine, saving faith will produce fruit; so do we. When asked how much fruit would be evidence of genuine faith, Dr. Grudem says, "Some."[1] So do we. Although criticized by Grudem,[2] Zane Hodges wrote:

> Of course, there is every reason to believe that there *will* be good works in the life of each believer in Christ. The idea that one may believe in Him and live for years totally unaffected by the amazing miracle of regeneration, or by the instruction and/or discipline of God, his heavenly Father, is a fantastic notion— even bizarre. *We reject it categorically. . . .*[3]

---

1   Grudem, *"Free Grace" Theology*, 28.

2   Ibid., 67-8, 132-40.

3   Zane Hodges, "We Believe In: Assurance of Salvation," *Journal of the Grace Evangelical Society* 3 (Autumn, 1990): 7, emphasis added.

I am hard pressed to see how this differs from Grudem's answer to how much fruit is to be expected of a genuine believer: "Some." Hodges was defending the eleventh point of the doctrinal statement of Dallas Theological Seminary (DTS), which says:

> We believe it is the privilege, not only of some, but of all who are born again by the Spirit through faith in Christ as revealed in the Scriptures, to be assured of their salvation from the very day they take Him to be their Savior and that this assurance is not founded upon any fancied discovery of their own worthiness or fitness, but wholly upon the testimony of God in His written Word, exciting within His children filial love, gratitude, and obedience (Luke 10:20; 22:32; 2 Corinthians 5:1, 6–8; 2 Timothy 1:12; Hebrews 10:22; 1 John 5:13).[4]

If that is true, then fruit is not a **necessary** requirement to give a person assurance. Of course, modern Reformed theologians are slow to give a professing believer assurance because they think the fruit of faith must be demonstrated for men to see before men can give someone assurance of eternal life.

Many professors at Dallas Seminary no longer agree with the eleventh point of their doctrinal statement. One of them even told me he doesn't think it is possible to have assurance in this life. But such was not the case in the earlier history of DTS. It wasn't until the seventies that the influence of Five-Point Calvinism began at DTS. Just witness the debates between John F. Walvoord, the former president of DTS, and John Gerstner to see how distanced DTS was from Reformed theology. So, to claim that only a small number of DTS professors represent Free Grace theology today may or may not be true (I've never seen a survey), but Free Grace theology did not invade DTS. It was the other way around: Reformed theology invaded DTS.

---

4   http://www.dts.edu/about/doctrinalstatement/, accessed September 30, 2016.

Faith is More Than Intellectual Assent

Appreciated also is Dr. Grudem's definition of faith, which goes beyond intellectual assent. That is exactly the position of almost all Free Grace theologians. He goes on page after page telling us that "some" Free Grace theologians view faith as some kind of intellectual agreement with some facts.[5] I only know of one man who holds that view.[6] Grudem claims Joseph Dillow believes it: he doesn't. Before Grudem's book came out, Dr. Dillow had email correspondence trying to clarify for Dr. Grudem that he does not hold to a "mental assent" understanding of faith.

Dr. Grudem could have saved his readers from reading many pages in his book by simply giving some of the people he misrepresents a call. This "in family discussion" (as he describes this disagreement) would be better facilitated by Grudem participating in some personal interaction and clarification. He also claims that I hold to the mental assent view. Although he gives evidence of reading at least part of an article I wrote on faith, either he did not read the whole article or simply chose to ignore this statement:

> Well, R. T. Kendall likes to speak of believing more as a "persuasion" than a "decision." But I am not convinced that the word "decision" is wrong. However, it is important that we understand just what this decision is all about. I would suggest that a decision for Christ means that someone decided (chose) to trust Christ as Savior. That is a lot different from saying someone decided to obey Christ as Master of his life. Though we hope and pray that everyone who makes a decision to trust Christ as Savior will go on to total surrender and commitment to obey Christ, the issue is whether the latter is a condition for salvation

---

5 Grudem, *"Free Grace" Theology*, 39, 80, 99, 100-102, 109.

6 Bob Wilkin of the Grace Evangelical Society, discussed later in this chapter. In fact, Dr. Grudem's book could have been half its length if he had eliminated the straw men he blasts from its pages for "mental assent" and "repentance as change of mind."

and an integral element of faith or is it a desirable consequence of salvation.[7]

And again, in the same article:

We conclude that the charge of "mental assent" and "intellectual faith" as a less than adequate faith is both unfair and an inaccurate assessment of the position free grace adherents have taken on the meaning of saving faith. It is a "straw" man. Over and over in their writings they have defined faith as "trust," "confidence," "reliance," and "appropriation." These are the same words used by the beginners of the Reformation and many leading Reformed theologians of the last couple of centuries. It was only the English Puritans and those who have followed in their stream who have added the "obedience" element to the meaning of faith.[8]

Though this chart was not in the article, I have used it subsequently to clarify my own position:

THE NATURE OF FAITH

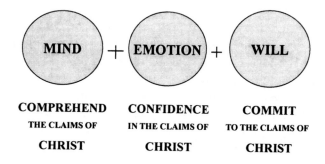

MIND	EMOTION	WILL
COMPREHEND	CONFIDENCE	COMMIT
THE CLAIMS OF	IN THE CLAIMS OF	TO THE CLAIMS OF
CHRIST	CHRIST	CHRIST

7   David R. Anderson, *Free Grace Soteriology* (The Woodlands, TX: Grace Theology Press, 2013), 172-73.

8   Ibid.

My chart is essentially following Berkhof's definition of faith, a Reformed scholar that many other Reformed scholars like to reference. Here is what he wrote:

> True saving faith is a faith that has its seat in the heart and is rooted in the regenerate life.... In speaking of the different elements of faith we should not lose sight of the fact that faith is an activity of man as a whole, and not any part of man.... In order to obtain a proper conception of faith, it is necessary to distinguish between the various elements which it comprises.
>
> A. *An intellectual element* (*notitia*). There is an element of knowledge in faith.... The knowledge of faith consists in a positive recognition of the truth, in which man accepts as true whatsoever God says in His word, and especially what He says respecting the deep depravity of man and the redemption which is in Christ Jesus. Over against Rome the position must be maintained that this sure knowledge belongs to the essence of faith; and in opposition to such theologians as Sandeman, Wardlaw, Alexander, Chalmers, and others, that a mere intellectual acceptance of the truth is not the whole of faith.
>
> B. *An emotional element* (*assensus*). When one embraces Christ by faith, he has a deep conviction of the truth and reality of the object of faith, feels that it meets an important need in his life, and is conscious of an absorbing interest in it – and this is assent.
>
> C. *A volitional element* (*fiducia*). This is the crowning element of faith. Faith is not merely a matter of the intellect, nor of the intellect and the emotions combined; it is also a matter of the will, determining the direction of the soul, an act of the soul going out towards its object and **appropriating** this. Without this activity the object of faith, which the sinner recognizes as true and real and entirely applicable to his present needs, remains outside of him. And in saving faith it is a matter of life and death that the object be **appropriated**. This third element

consists in a personal **trust** in Christ as Saviour and Lord, including the surrender of the soul as guilty and defiled to Christ, and a recognition and **appropriation** of Christ as the source of pardon and of spiritual life.[9]

Will you notice the number of times Berkhof uses the words "appropriating, appropriate, and appropriation"? Notice also the word "trust." But these are the very words Hodges uses to define faith in the very book Grudem uses as his source to say Hodges diminishes the gospel by defining faith as intellectual assent. Here is what Hodges wrote:

To describe faith that way [as mental assent] is to demean it as a trivial, academic exercise, when in fact it is no such thing. What faith really is . . . is the inward conviction that what God says to us in the gospel is true."[10]

Hodges further defines faith as "firm conviction,"[11] "childlike **trust**,"[12] an "act of **appropriation**" of the truth of the gospel,[13] an "act of **trust**."[14]

Do you see the words "trust" and "appropriation"? These are the same words used by Berkhof. So Grudem misrepresented Hodges (who agreed with Berkhof). But authors like John MacArthur[15] who have read Berkhof have changed his definition. In chart form it looks like this:

---

9   Louis Berkhof, *Systematic Theology* (Grand Rapids, Mich.: Wm. B. Eerdmans, 1939), 503-05.

10 Zane Hodges, *Absolutely Free* (Grand Rapids, MI: Zondervan, 1989), 31.

11 Ibid., 28.

12 Ibid., 38-39.

13 Ibid., 40-41.

14 Ibid., 32.

15 John MacArthur, *The Gospel According to Jesus* (Grand Rapids, MI: Academie, 1988), 173.

THE NATURE OF FAITH

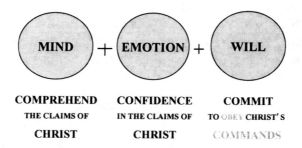

COMPREHEND	CONFIDENCE	COMMIT
THE CLAIMS OF	IN THE CLAIMS OF	TO OBEY CHRIST'S
CHRIST	CHRIST	COMMANDS

Notice in this second chart the will makes a commitment to **obey Christ's commands.** This is how MacArthur summarized Berkhof's explanation of *fiducia*, the volitional element of faith. Of course, Berkhof said nothing of the kind. He said, "This third element consists in a personal **trust** in Christ as Saviour and Lord, including the surrender of the soul as guilty and defiled to Christ, and a recognition and **appropriation** of Christ as the source of pardon and of spiritual life."[16] That's no different than what Hodges and Free Grace theologians are saying. MacArthur misrepresented what Berkhof wrote by adding obedience to Christ's commands.

Faith Alone[17]

Free Grace theologians disagree with Grudem that initial justifying faith is inevitably produced after God unilaterally regenerates us.[18] Augustine injected this Gnostic error into Christianity (based on salvific infant baptism devoid of human choice in Stoic "dead wills" which God "sovereignly" controls, discussed in chapter 2). For

---

16 Berkhof, *Systematic Theology*, 503-05.

17 Thanks to Dr. Ken Wilson for adding this section on Faith Alone.

18 Grudem, *Systematic Theology*, 699-706. Grudem stops short of directly teaching "faith is God's gift" but does so indirectly by making it the inevitable result of God's irresistible effectual calling.

Grudem, faith alone is nuanced to include inevitable works. He utilizes Calvin's cliché (paraphrased), "We are justified by faith alone, but the faith that justifies is never alone," which he attempts to explain with his "key" analogy.[19] But Grudem's key analogy fails.

Grudem must use the yellow key of works to enter the faculty corridor and then the blue key of faith to enter his office, both being on the same key ring and always together. However, his two keys are indeed separable and open different doors. Despite clever nuances, both keys are required to enter his office (heaven), although the first is "preparatory" for the corridor and not technically required to enter his office proper. But the blue key (faith) would still open his office door without the second yellow key (works) on his key ring. Likewise, the yellow key can open the corridor door without the blue key on the ring. But Grudem and other Calvinists demand both the key of faith and the key of works to enter heaven's one door. Faith alone will not open that door.

Calvin's cliché is written in a way that hides the equivocation fallacy. For the honest Calvinist, it reads: Faith alone saves but cannot save alone. We are justified by faith alone but faith alone cannot save (glorify). Calvin's faith alone saves (justifies) but cannot open the door to heaven (glorification) without works. The key of inevitable sanctification in good works must accompany faith alone because faith alone cannot save (glorify). The accompanying key of good works is required to open heaven, just as in Catholicism. The equivocation fallacy is exposed by separating the different meanings of saves in, "Faith alone saves (justifies) but the faith that saves (glorifies) is never alone." The first means justification and the second means glorification. So Calvinists can honestly say, "Faith alone justifies, but the faith that glorifies is not alone." Heaven requires works.

The reverse of Grudem's analogy fits with Free Grace theology. The first key (faith alone) accesses the faculty corridor (heaven) while the second key (works) opens Grudem's private office (special position/ reward in heaven). The Free Grace position states faith alone provides eternal life/heaven. Grudem's analogy and his use of Calvin's cliché hide the Calvinist disingenuous claim that faith alone "saves." It does

19 Grudem, *"Free Grace" Theology*, 28, 37-8.

not save in the sense of final salvation. It only justifies. No works—no heaven.

This error is the basis on which Grudem, MacArthur, Piper, and other lordship justificationists[20] teach the associated doctrine of a Christian's inevitable perseverance in good works.[21] "True faith" or "genuine faith" will persevere because it is God's perfect gift. In contrast, Augustine taught God must give a Christian a second grace of perseverance (which all Christians do not receive) to those having already received the Holy Spirit. So what about the popular concept of "true faith"?

"True Faith"

We should reexamine the teachings of John Calvin and Melanchthon, since Reformed scholars in general and Grudem in particular claim to have church history, especially Reformation history, on their side in this gospel discussion. Calvin claimed that his theology was completely Augustinian, and Augustine said, "Faith is nothing else than to think with assent."[22] No wonder, then, that Calvin wrote, "For, as regards justification, faith is something merely passive, bringing nothing of ours to the recovering of God's favor but receiving from Christ what we lack."[23]

---

20 Lordship justification (salvation) is the view that in order to be declared righteous, one must surrender his or her entire life to Christ. Free Grace teaches Lordship sanctification (salvation) in that surrender to Christ's lordship is required for progressive conformity to Christlikeness.

21 Grudem, *Systematic Theology*, 789: "All Who Are Truly Born Again Will Persevere to the End"; MacArthur, *Faith Works* (Dallas: Word, 1994), 49: "And faith endures. ... It perseveres."

22 A. Augustine, *On the Predestination of the Saints* 5, in *The Nicene and Post-Nicene Fathers of the Church*, 28 vols, trans. and ed. Phillip Schaff (Grand Rapids, Mich.: William B. Eerdmans Publishing Co., 1956), vol. 5: *St. Augustine: Anti-Pelagian Writings*, 499.

23 Calvin, *Institutes*, III. xiii. 5. Grudem follows Calvin (*Systematic Theology*, 699).

In contrast to "true" Augustinian-Calvinism, most who follow the Reformed tradition today affirm an active faith, one that produces good works and walks hand in hand with obedience. Anything less is false faith, they claim. But Calvin said, "We compare faith to a kind of vessel; for unless we come empty and with the mouth of our soul open to seek Christ's grace, we are not capable of receiving Christ."[24] R. T. Kendall evaluates Calvin this way: "What stands out in Calvin's descriptions is the given, intellectual, passive and assuring nature of faith."[25] M. C. Bell concurs with Kendall when he writes, "Calvin taught that faith is fundamentally passive in nature, is centered in the mind or understanding, is primarily to be viewed in terms of certain knowledge."[26]

Therefore, Calvin did not view faith as something that was akin to obedience or all-out commitment to follow Christ. Rather, as T. Lewellen observes, in Calvin's view obedience flows from faith and is part of the nature of the Christian life, and faith itself is reliance on the divine promises of salvation in Christ and nothing more.[27]

It seems the early Reformers were in complete agreement on this approach to faith, even if they had many other points of disagreement. P. Melanchthon, who wrote the Augsburg Confession, defined faith simply as "receptivity."[28] F. Pieper, the author of the modern standard theology of confessional Lutheranism wrote, "Saving faith is essentially the reliance of the heart on the promises of God set forth in the gospel. . . . In the preceding characterization of faith, we have

---

24 Ibid., III. xi. 7.

25 R. T. Kendall, *Calvin and English Calvinism to 1649* (Oxford: Oxford University Press, 1979), 19. See also Calvin, *Institutes*, III. 2. 36.

26 M. C. Bell, *Calvin and Scottish Theology: The Doctrine of Assurance* (Edinburgh: Handsel Press, 1985), 8.

27 T. G. Lewellen, "Has Lordship Salvation Been Taught throughout Church History?" *Bibliotheca Sacra* 147 (January 1990): 57.

28 *Apology of the Augsburg Confession*, IV. 56, 112, 257. Also see *The Formula of Concord, Solid Declaration*, III. 8-14. See also R. D. Preus, "Perennial Problems in the Doctrine of Justification," *Concordia Theological Quarterly* 45 (1981): 163-84, for a good summary of the approaches to faith taken by Melanchthon and Luther.

stated . . . that justifying faith must be viewed merely as the instrument or receptive organ for apprehending the forgiveness of sins offered in the gospel."[29]

While I was teaching a course at Jordan Evangelical Seminary in 2000, a group from the United States was visiting to see if they deemed the school worthy of their financial support. Leading the group was the brother of John Sailhamer, an Old Testament scholar and temporary Provost of DTS after Chuck Swindoll vacated the post of President. While we were visiting, Paul Sailhamer told me he had been MacArthur's right hand man for years. I asked him about MacArthur's statement on Berkhof and *fiducia*. He said, "Oh, my gosh. We got so much grief over that. I went to John and asked him about it, and he said, 'I didn't write that.'" Well, I don't know who wrote it, or how it got in *The Gospel According to MacArthur (Jesus)*, but it does not present Berkhof's explanation of faith correctly.[30]

Well, then, if the Reformers and even early American Reformed theologians like Berkhof understood faith to be passive and simply trust or confidence in the promises of God, where did this idea of an active faith that includes obedience and works originate? The answer is the English Puritans. R. T. Kendall's work (previously referenced) establishes this development beyond all reasonable doubt. And Lewellen emphasizes this when he says:

> In the Puritan era . . . there was a shift in the definition of saving faith. In the generations following the Reformation, some theologians subtly changed the Reformers' definition of faith

---

29 F. Pieper, *Christian Dogmatics*, 3 vols. (St. Louis: Concordia Publishing House, 1953), 2:426, 437.

30 The intrigue deepens when one reads MacArthur's explanations in *Faith Works*, 49-50: "trust is turning to Him in full self-surrender (cf. Deut. 30:12; 2 Kings 23:25; 1 Thess. 1:9). That was Berkhof's point. [...] Faith is an *internal* reality with *external* consequences. When we say that faith encompasses obedience, we are *speaking* of the God-given attitude of obedience, not trying to make *works* a part of the definition of faith." Calvin and Calvinists are not *trying* to make works part of the formal definition but they do so indirectly by following Augustine's error.

from a passive receptivity to an active response on the part of the sinner, centered in the will and containing both commitment and obedience.[31]

This shift in the understanding of faith from the Reformers' understanding is reflected in the Westminster Standards,[32] which Reformed theologians rely upon so heavily to prove their position. For example, in MacArthur's appendix whereby he tried to establish lordship salvation as the historic position of the church, ten of the seventeen pages of these "proofs" in his appendix are drawn from the Westminster Standards and the writings of post-Reformation English Calvinists.[33] It would certainly be fair to say that lordship salvation has its roots in one branch of traditional Christianity (to mix our metaphors), but to make a sweeping statement like, "The view of faith that Hodges decries as a modern heresy is exactly what the true church has always believed,"[34] is grossly misleading (to say it politely). To quote Lewellen once again:

> What is true . . . is that MacArthur's view *is* embodied in the Westminster Standards and *does* have a long and powerful history in the Christian church. The idea that faith is an active commitment, including obedience, is the view of one strand of church history—English Puritanism—which is of course a powerful strand. One should not confuse that strand, however,

---

31 Lewellen, "Lordship Salvation," 58.

32 *The Westminster Confession of Faith*, III. viii; XIV. ii (Philadelphia: Orthodox Presbyterian Church, n.d.). The Westminster Standards are the documents produced by the Westminster Assembly convened by the English Parliament from 1643 to 1649. These documents are the *Westminster Confession of Faith*, the *Shorter Catechism*, and the *Larger Catechism*. They form the doctrinal foundation of much of modern Presbyterianism. A slightly modified *Confession* called the *London Baptist Confession of Faith of 1689* also forms the doctrinal basis from which many of the modern Baptist churches have grown.

33 MacArthur, *The Gospel According to Jesus*, 221-37.

34 Ibid., 222.

with the "true church." Calvin disagreed with it; Lutheran theology has always opposed it; even today some Reformed theologians do not accept it.[35]

Wayne Grudem might be one of those Reformed scholars who does not accept it, for he says:

> On a related matter, I am also unwilling to say that initial saving faith requires absolute, total commitment of life, because then I do not think anyone in the world would be saved in this lifetime. Yes, I agree that Jesus demands total commitment of life from us (see Luke 9:23-24; 14:26), but because of our weakness in this lifetime we still fall short of that high standard, and we must trust him for forgiveness even of that failure.[36]

Grudem says Jesus requires total, absolute commitment of one's life for saving faith, but none of us can rise to that standard, so Jesus accepts our less than total commitment and forgives us of the sin of inadequate commitment? So, according to Grudem, when I make my conscious decision to trust Christ by committing to follow him almost everywhere he wants me to go, I am exercising saving faith but since this saving faith is sinful to the degree it is not a complete commitment, I should say a prayer of thanks for Jesus's forgiveness of my less than total commitment. That is very different than the stringent requirements of Piper and MacArthur.

John Piper tells us we evidence our commitment when we "believe . . . receive . . . repent . . . turn . . . obey . . . become childlike . . . deny self . . . love Jesus more than anything else . . . renounce all that you have . . . these are just some of the conditions that the New Testament says we must meet in order to be saved . . . This

---

35 Lewellen, 59. See G. H. Clark, *Faith and Saving Faith* (Jefferson, Md: Trinity Foundation, 1983), 110-18; R. T. Kendall, *Once Saved Always Saved* (Chicago: Moody Press, 1985); and M. C. Bell, *Calvin and Scottish Theology: The Doctrine of Assurance* (Edinburgh: Handsel Press, 1985).

36 Grudem, *"Free Grace" Theology*, 71, footnote 45.

alone is the way of everlasting life."[37] John MacArthur says essentially the same thing when he says there are "five essential elements of genuine conversion, all so inextricably linked that it is impossible to eliminate any one of them from the biblical concept of saving faith: humility . . . revelation . . . repentance [defined as 'a complete turnaround, a full change of direction' . . . faith . . . submission ['a willingness to have Him take control']."[38] And later in the same work MacArthur writes: "Fruit is the ultimate test of true salvation."[39] And, "Forsaking oneself . . . is the *sine qua non of saving faith.*"[40] "Absolute surrender . . . is the only response that will open the gates of the kingdom."[41] But Grudem disagrees, saying such all-out commitment is really impossible for an unbeliever. No wonder Reformed theologians cannot offer the new believer assurance of salvation immediately after a commitment to trust Christ. After all, we don't know just how committed they are, do we? How much commitment is enough for me to be saved?

A young woman asks, "Dr. Grudem, just how committed do I have to be to be accepted by God? What if the rich young ruler had given half his goods to the poor, would that be enough?" Grudem doesn't know, and neither does anyone else teaching lordship justification. We have returned to Roman Catholicism—we will find out if we have enough righteousness in our lives to be accepted only after we die. If one were to ask Grudem how committed the new believer has to be in order to be confident that she is one of God's children, what would he answer? Nobody knows. Assurance is impossible.

The straw-man "mental assent" criticism of Free Grace theologians is an old one but a very inaccurate one. Joseph Dillow is accused in Grudem's book, along with me, of espousing the "mental assent" view of faith. Before the book was printed, Dillow strongly denied holding

---

37 John Piper, *Desiring God* (Sisters, Ore.: Multnomah Publishers, 1986), 69-70.

38 MacArthur, *The Gospel According to Jesus* (Grand Rapids, Mich.: Academié Books, 1988), 108-13.

39 Ibid., 127.

40 Ibid., 135.

41 Ibid., 141.

to the "mental assent" view through email correspondence with Grudem. Yet Grudem made the accusation in spite of Dillow's protest. Here (by permission) is the follow-up email from Dillow to Grudem, after having read Grudem's book:

> I have clearly stated over and over that saving faith is not mere intellectual assent. For example (one of many), I say, "Mere mental agreement with facts about Christ is not genuine saving faith. Biblical faith is distinguished from mere assent in that it includes 'the assurance of things hoped for' (Hebrews 11:1-2) and reliance upon the person of Christ." (p. 687-88)
>
> It involves assent but it is much more than that—it is saving trust in the person and work of Christ. In fact, I include a separate section specifically distinguishing Biblical faith from intellectual assent (p. 685-86). It seems no matter what I say or how many times I say it, for some reason you refuse to believe it. . . . I agree with you that faith is assent plus trust in the person and work of Christ for salvation.[42]

So why can't we put this false charge of "mental assent" to rest? Hodges didn't believe it; Dillow doesn't believe it; I don't believe it. The only Free Grace theologian that has written much on the subject and does believe in the "mental assent" view, as far as I know, is Bob Wilkin. To project one man's views on others that are in print disagreeing with his views is highly unprofessional, and frankly, dishonest. The vast majority of Free Grace theologians and The Free Grace Alliance disassociated with Bob Wilkin due to his Grace Evangelical Society

---

42 Email correspondence between Joseph Dillow and Wayne Grudem, September, 2016. To his credit Grudem agreed to retract some of what he said about Dillow's views in future editions of his book and to also make corrections in any public settings. All this would have been unnecessary if Grudem had just called Dr. Dillow and gotten clarification on his views. The same would hold true of Grudem's inaccurate representations of my views. Grudem either did not give due diligence to scholarly research or deliberately misrepresented our views.

teaching new doctrines we consider unorthodox.[43] Lumping all Free Grace theologians in the same pot is not appropriate.

Trust in the Person of Christ

People of different theological persuasions have every right to express their own views and defend the same, but when you begin to tell the public what other people believe, you had better be accurate. Wayne Grudem has a whole chapter of his rather short book claiming that Free Grace theologians diminish the gospel by underemphasizing trust in the person of Christ. Again, he singles out Dillow and Anderson. Here is Dillow's response to Grudem on the assertion that he under-emphasizes personal trust in Christ as Savior:

> Faith is believing, acceptance of the facts of the gospel, and reliance upon Christ for the forgiveness of sins. . . . Faith involves believingly assenting to the facts of the Gospel and a personal reliance upon Christ as a Savior from sin. . . . Augustine defined faith as belief in propositions only and **failed to include the biblical requirement of reliance, or trust.** He says, "Faith is nothing else than to think with assent."[44] [Sounds like Grudem should be pointing out Augustine's errors instead of Dillow's.]

---

43 The most critical issue was a change in the statement of faith. GES now teaches that a person can be justified by believing that someone named Jesus guarantees eternal life without believing that Jesus is our Savior from sin and God incarnate. "Assurance is of the essence of believing in Jesus for everlasting life." And "To believe in Jesus ('he who believes in Me has everlasting life') is to be convinced that He guarantees everlasting life to all who simply believe in Him for it." That is, if you do not believe in eternal security at the moment of faith, you are not justified. See GES Affirmation of Belief accessed 11-24-2016, at https://faithalone.org/beliefs/ and Zane Hodges, "We Believe in: Assurance of Salvation," *JOTGES* 3.2 (1990): 3-17. For a refutation see David Anderson, "Is Belief in Eternal Security Necessary for Justification?" *CTS Journal* 13 (Spring 2008): 47-59 and Kenneth M. Wilson, "Is Belief in Christ's Deity Required for Eternal Life in John's Gospel?" *CTSJ* 12.2 (2006): 58-86.

44 Email correspondence between Joseph Dillow and Wayne Grudem, September, 2016.

In addition, Grudem also misrepresents my view from what I see as a clear rebuttal of mental assent. He quotes the following passage from my book on soteriology:

> Though saving faith *begins* as an assessment of revealed truth—most notably, God's promises—it is not *consummated* until one *trusts those promises*. One must appropriate those promises for himself and be fully persuaded and *confident in those promises* as his only hope for life eternal. Such faith is not a casual, detached, intellectual process and conclusion. It is an act of trust, whereby one puts the full weight and consequences of his sins on the cross of Christ to open the gates of heaven.[45]

From this paragraph Grudem deduces that I deemphasize trusting in the person of Christ, even though in small print at the bottom of the page he says, "On the other hand, on pp. 175-76 he [Anderson] does speak of 'the belief in Jesus which establishes a personal relationship with him.'"[46]

I find this reasoning either to be sloppy scholarship or disingenuous. First of all, is there something wrong with believing God's promises? Obviously not. And when it comes to the gospel promises, most of them center on the person and work of Jesus Christ. "Behold, the Lamb of God who takes away the sins of the world"—the person and work of Jesus. "One thing only do I make known among you, Jesus Christ and him crucified"—the person and work of Jesus Christ. How can you believe in the promises about Jesus without believing in Jesus? The Philippian jailer asks what he must do to be saved and gets the answer, "Believe on the Lord Jesus Christ and you will be saved." That was a promise. To believe the promise is to believe the content of the promise. This particular promise was a salvific one. It told the jailer to believe on the Lord Jesus Christ . . . and he would be saved. There are two objects of faith here: 1) The promise; 2) Jesus. The promise is that by believing on Jesus he would find salvation. How are you going

---

45 Anderson, *Free Grace Soteriology*, 174.

46 Grudem, *"Free Grace" Theology*, 103.

to separate believing this promise from believing in the person of Jesus as God and Savior? When Grudem claims believing in a promise about salvation through Jesus diminishes believing in Jesus he creates a logical impossibility, a *non sequitur*. Grudem appears to be grasping at straws in order to find something to criticize. In fact, he ultimately admits that this is not his real issue with Free Grace theology.[47]

Grudem makes the same criticism of Hodges. After acknowledging that Hodges says faith is more than "*mere* intellectual assent,"[48] he then makes this comment: "We look in vain in this entire chapter on faith [in Hodges' book *Absolutely Free!*] for any affirmation that includes trust in the person of Jesus that goes beyond mere agreement with statements about him in the Bible."[49] Yet in that chapter both Hodges's first sentence and his closing cite Bible verses emphasizing belief in the *person* of Christ—John 6:47 and 1 John 5:9-13.[50] I am at a loss to explain how a theologian like Grudem could repeatedly miss the obvious and attack as absent what is plainly present in so many Free Grace authors: Faith in the *person* of Christ. Grudem is either guilty of failure to exercise due diligence in scholarly research or guilty of deliberate misrepresentation.

Grudem's accusation that Free Grace theologians diminish the gospel because some put greater emphasis on the promises about Christ than on the person of Christ is both fatuous and gratuitous. He also accuses me of diminishing the gospel because I suggest that at

---

47 Grudem, *"Free Grace" Theology*, 102. "Some members of the Free Grace Alliance have also confirmed to me in personal correspondence and in private conversation that they do hold to faith in the *person* of Christ, not merely assent to facts about him. I have also found that to be true in personal interaction with number of Free Grace supporters. . . . But I still find that the emphasis is simply not there in how they write about the nature of saving faith." This exposes his Gnostic-Augustinian-Calvinist erroneous presupposition about faith as God's gift as the essential problem.

48 Then we have to wonder why Grudem accused Hodges of teaching faith in Christ is mere intellectual assent. Do you see how confusing and contradictory his writings are?

49 Grudem, *"Free Grace" Theology*, 102, footnote 6.

50 Hodges, *Absolutely Free*, 25 and 31-2.

the moment of salvation the sinner puts the entire weight of his sins "on the cross of Christ." Grudem claims that going to the cross "is still remembering a historical event in the past in distinction from placing trust in the person of Christ as a present, living Savior."[51] What was Paul's message? Jesus Christ and him crucified. Somehow he thought putting one's faith in the work of Christ on the cross was an important element of the gospel. In fact, in 1 Corinthians 1:18, Paul encapsulates his gospel as the message of the cross, "ο λογος γαρ ο του σταυρου." And in 1:23 he declares, "ημεις δε κηρυσσομεν χριστον εσταυρωμενον: but we preach Christ crucified" when he wants to summarize the content of his gospel. Should we criticize the great Apostle for focusing on this past historical event instead of emphasizing the risen Savior? Obviously, not.

It saddens me that Grudem wants to pick a fight over these things when we agree. We all believe in the personhood of the living Christ, and we also believe in his work on the cross to remove the barrier between us and God—our sins. As we keep reading Grudem, we begin to realize what he is trying to do. He believes this lack of emphasis on the person of the living Savior is the reason why we have so little emphasis on repentance. But again, he also misrepresents what we are saying about repentance, something we will address in the next chapter. We could have saved Grudem a lot of ink and embarrassment over retractions he has and will need to make by just sitting down with us in person to discuss exactly what we believe.

As we go through this chapter by Grudem on trusting in the person of Christ, we are getting a fuller picture of just what saving faith means to him: 1) Trust in the person of Jesus; 2) Repentance from sin (the flip side of faith/trust); 3) Obedience (though he denies this in one place, he affirms it in another[52]); 4) Coming into his presence and personal interaction with Christ[53]; 5) Believing in your heart instead of your head[54]; 6) Total commitment to the one who is trusted. So now we are

---

51 Grudem, 104.

52 Grudem, 106.

53 Ibid., 108.

54 Ibid, 109.

going to be putting our faith in our faith. In other words, Grudem tells us to go examine ourselves to see if we are in the faith.[55] To him this means we are to examine our faith to see if it is saving faith. Here is where we get into different levels of faith. Only faith that meets his seven qualifications above will open the doors of heaven. So, did I have enough trust, a sincere resolve to turn from sin, enough obedience, enough personal interaction with Christ, enough heart-felt trust, and enough commitment? No wonder so many Christians are full of doubt. No wonder so few believers have joy. In contrast, scholars recognize that the term "in the faith" (εν τη πιστει) of 2 Corinthians 13:5 does not refer to personal faith but to remaining within the accepted teaching of apostolic doctrine.[56] In the early church this came to be called Christianity's *rule of faith* (*kanon tes pisteos, regula fidei*).[57] We are not commanded to inspect the legitimacy of our personal faith but rather our obedience to God's commands as inspired by the Holy Spirit and written by the apostles as doctrine. The *New Living Translation* and the *Weymouth New Testament* both err by translating this as, "Examine yourselves to see if your faith is genuine" and "Test yourselves to discover whether you are true believers." The Bible never tells us to examine whether we "truly believe" or put our faith in our faith; we are to put our faith in the person of Christ as our God and Savior who died on the cross for our sins.

Conclusion

Grudem misrepresented the positions of Hodges, Dillow, Anderson, and others in his book through either sloppy scholarship or deliberate misrepresentation. He claims we, as Free Grace theologians, subscribe to the mental assent view of faith: we do not. He invents the accusation that we as Free Grace theologians minimize trust in the person of

---

55 Grudem, *"Free Grace" Theology*, 131.

56 Simon Kistemaker, *Acts* in NTC series (Grand Rapids, Mich.: Baker Academic, 1991), 225; and Daniel Schowalter, "Faith" in Bruce Metzger and Michael Coogan, eds., *The Oxford Companion to the Bible* (Oxford: Oxford University Press, 1993), 223.

57 *ABD*, II.757.

Christ: we do not. He only needed to read our writings explicitly stating such. The next chapter will correct his misrepresentation of our view of repentance. So Grudem claims *we* diminish the gospel, while *he* follows Augustinian-Calvinism in reciting faith alone saves (justifies) yet cannot save (glorify) since "true faith" perseveres in good works required to open heaven's door (Augustine's Gnostic-Manichaean error). In his "in family discussion," we had hoped to be represented by Grudem more fairly and accurately via personal communication. That did not happen. We look forward to his revised edition with fewer pages and numerous clarifying apologies.

Chapter 4

The Role of Repentance in Salvation

David R. Anderson, Ph.D.

How do we define repentance? We empathize with Grudem as he criticizes multiple definitions of repentance with the same criticism: there is not enough emphasis on turning from sin. Grudem seems lost in the different definitions used by Free Grace theologians for repentance:

1. Change of mind (Chafer, Ryrie)
2. Remorse for sin (Dillow)
3. Resolve to turn from sin (Anderson, Hodges)

Let's start with the "change of mind" view.

Repentance = Change of Mind

Again, we repeat that a misleading aspect of Grudem's book is the impression he leaves that the views expressed by Free Grace theologians are only about thirty years old and stemmed from the teachings of Zane

Hodges. This is inaccurate. The "change of mind" view on repentance was taught to all Dallas Seminary students while Charles Ryrie was head of the Systematic Theology department, who wrote:

> To repent is to change your mind. However, this only defines the word, not the concept, for you need to ask, Change your mind about what? Depending on how you answer that question, repentance might be a synonymous concept to believing in Christ or it might become an additional requirement for salvation. If repentance is understood to mean changing your mind about your sin—being sorry for your sin—this will not necessarily save. There are plenty of criminals in and out of jails who are repentant in this sense. . . .
>
> But if repentance means changing your mind about the particular sin of rejecting Christ, then that kind of repentance saves, and of course it is the same as faith in Christ. . . . everyone who is saved has repented in that sense.[1]

In fact, as we shall see, all of the Free Grace teaching Grudem deplores can be found in the teachings of Charles Ryrie. Ryrie wrote about surrendering to Christ as Lord:

> Must there be a commitment to Christ as Lord of one's life in order to be saved? Many today are answering yes. . . . [He then quotes J. I. Packer who says the sinner must trust Christ as a sin-bearer and also deny himself and enthrone Jesus as his Lord, as an example.] . . . In other words, one must believe *and* give Christ control of his life in order to be saved. Sometimes it is said only that there must be a willingness to surrender even if the surrender of life does not occur. At least this would allow for the existence of carnal Christians (of which there seem to be plenty). But, if willingness is required at the moment of believing in order to be saved, how much willingness is necessary? Can,

---

1   Charles Caldwell Ryrie, *A Survey of Bible Doctrine* (Chicago, Ill.: Moody Press, 1972), 139.

for instance, a man who is convinced in his mind that smoking is wrong (simply for medical reasons) not be saved until he is at least willing to give up his smoking? Or if surrender is necessary in order to be saved, why does the New Testament ask *believers* to surrender (Ro 12:1)?[2]

Let's go further back. Here are the words of the co-founder of Dallas Seminary in 1924, Lewis S. Chafer:

The word *metánoia* is in every instance translated *repentance*. The common practice of reading into this word the thought of sorrow and heart-anguish is responsible for much confusion in the field of Soteriology. There is no reason why sorrow should not accompany repentance or lead on to repentance, but the sorrow, whatever it may be, is not repentance. In 2 Corinthians 7:10, it is said that "godly sorrow worketh repentance," that is, it leads on to repentance; but the sorrow is not to be mistaken for the change of mind which it may serve to produce. The son cited by Christ as reported in Matthew 21:28-29 who first said "I will not go," and afterward repented and went, is a true example of the precise meaning of the word. The New Testament call to repentance is not an urge to self-condemnation, but is a call to a change of mind which promotes a change in the course being pursued. This definition of this word as it is used in the New Testament is fundamental. Little or no progress can be made in a right induction of the Word of God on this theme, unless the true and accurate meaning of the word is discovered and defended throughout.[3]

Now we know Grudem has read the paragraph above because in his writing on the warning passages in Hebrews he quotes Chafer's view of repentance as it relates to saving faith:

---

2   Ibid., 134-35.

3   Lewis Sperry Chafer, *Systematic Theology*, III (Dallas, Tex.: Dallas Seminary Press, 1948), 372-73.

Some evangelicals deny that repentance is necessary for experiencing justification and the other initial elements of the Christian life mentioned in this list (for example, Lewis Sperry Chafer says, "The New Testament does not impose repentance upon the unsaved as a condition of salvation" [*Systematic Theology*, 7 vols. (Dallas: Dallas Seminary Press, 1947-48), 3:376.][4]

So Grudem knew that Chafer (long before Hodges) was the one who pointed out the complete absence of repentance in this gospel designed to incite faith in Jesus Christ resulting in eternal life.[5] And again, quoting from Grudem's *Systematic Theology*:

The source of this view of the gospel [saving faith only requires an intellectual agreement with the facts of the gospel] is apparently Lewis Sperry Chafer, especially in his *Systematic Theology*, vol. 3, where he says, "The New Testament does not impose repentance upon the unsaved as a condition of salvation" (p. 376). Chafer recognizes that many verses call upon people to repent, but he simply defines repentance away as a "change of mind" that does not include sorrow for sin or a turning from sin (pp. 372-75). . . . Chafer provides a basis for the view that people must first accept Christ as Savior, and later as Lord, when he says that the preacher has the obligation "of preaching the Lordship of Christ to Christians exclusively, and the Saviorhood of Christ to those who are unsaved" (p. 387).[6]

Once again, we are trying to make sure the reader knows that Grudem's 2016 book about Free Grace reflects poor scholarship when

---

4   Grudem, *Still Sovereign*, ed. Thomas R. Schreiner & Bruce A. Ware, (Grand Rapids, Mich.: Baker Books,) 1995, 135.

5   Chafer, *Theology*, III, 376: "In like manner, the Gospel of John, which is written to present Christ as the object of faith unto eternal life, does not once employ the word *repentance*."

6   Wayne Grudem, *Systematic Theology* (Grand Rapids: Mich.: Zondervan Publishing House, 1994), 714.

it claims Free Grace teachings are relatively new and stem from Zane Hodges. Here are his words:

> Where did the modern Free Grace movement come from? *As far as I can tell* [italics mine], it stems primarily from a minority view among the faculty members at Dallas Theological Seminary. More particularly, it stems from an aggressive promotion of the Free Grace viewpoint by Zane Hodges (1932-2008), who taught New Testament at Dallas Theological Seminary for twenty-seven years, from 1959 to 1986.[7]

We have already shown that Chafer (1871-1952) predated Hodges by a generation. He was the primary teacher of systematic theology at DTS during his lifetime. It was his *Systematic Theology* published in 1948 that was the first fully developed dispensational, premillennial theology in print. Agreement with its major points was not optional for the faculty. It was mandatory. Hence, Grudem commits a serious error when he speaks of a "minority view among the faculty members at Dallas Theological Seminary." Even speaking of a majority would have been wrong. It was **all** the faculty members. Yet I would have to agree, sadly, with Grudem that today it may well be that only a minority of the faculty at DTS agree with Chafer's soteriology when it comes to the issues we are discussing (repentance, faith, lordship, and assurance). But it was not always so. So we have to ask ourselves why Grudem is so careful to avoid using the names of Chafer and Ryrie and Walvoord and Pentecost and Constable and Hendricks, all who openly taught Free Grace theology?

It's one thing to criticize people relatively unknown (Bing, Anderson, Dillow, Lybrand, Wilkin, and such). It's quite another to oppose the teachings of men who have been as influential in the Christian world as Charles Ryrie, who wrote a whole book in defense of Free Grace theology (*So Great a Salvation*). Even the current President of Dallas Seminary, Mark Bailey, claims to be a Free Grace theologian in the wake of Ryrie and recently spoke at a Free Grace Alliance banquet. Of course, just because Chafer and Ryrie taught it, doesn't make it right.

---

7   Grudem, *Free Grace Theology*, 21.

But these teachings did not begin with a little splinter group coming out of DTS as Grudem claims.

Chafer, Walvoord, Ryrie, and Pentecost all held to the "change of mind" view of repentance. And that would have to be acknowledged as an acceptable view based on one's understanding of what it meant to change the mind. However, the words "change the mind" may not go far enough and may be guilty of the "root fallacy." But even the first entry in third edition of BDAG states: μετάνοια, ας, ἡ (μετανοέω) prim[8]. 'a change of mind' and μετανοέω "1. *change one's mind*". So "change of mind" is not an inferior view. But Dillow does not think "change of mind" expresses the core of repentance, which he would equate with "regret" or "remorse" for one's sins. This is the second listing under μετανοέω, *"feel remorse, repent, be converted," and with μετάνοια*, " a change of mind (…), also w. the nuance of remorse."

Remorse for Sin

Since Grudem chose to quote Dillow so often, we thought it only fair to present Dillow's view of repentance, which he clarified for Grudem in their email correspondence:

> I do not believe that "repent," when related to saving faith, means "to turn." It means to admit guilt and regret it. It implies an openness to and desire to change, not as you say, "the resolute commitment to change." "Regret" is how the word is used in the LXX and that was Jesus's Bible. In the Septuagint there is no instance where *shub* ("to turn") is translated by *metanoeō* ("to repent")! The LXX translates *nicham* [Hebrew "*be sorry, repent, regret,*" "*change one's mind*" (Exodus 32:14; Jeremiah 26:19; Psalm 110:4)] by *metanoeō* . These facts indicate that the LXX does not understand things as Warfield and many do. *Metanoeō* does not mean "to turn"; it means what *nicham* means, "to regret, to admit guilt, feel sorry for." I absolutely believe repentance is a

---

8   Grudem's claim that only extra-biblical sources are used does not detract from the fact that this was the predominant understanding of the Greek word, so unless it can be proven otherwise, it should be the first meaning sought.

necessary precursor to saving faith, and one cannot be saved without repentance. You cannot trust in the person of Christ for forgiveness unless you believe you need to be forgiven, that is, unless you repent, admit your guilt and to some degree to regret it. But I don't think repentance means what you say it must **always** mean. Lexicons agree with me.[9]

Grudem is attacking a straw man. If we were to understand repentance as "the recognition of one's sin and his need for a Savior," then we know very few, if any, evangelical theologians who would not agree with that statement. As Dillow points out, ". . . you cannot trust in the person of Christ for forgiveness unless you believe you need to be forgiven." Even the "change of mind" view would include this meaning of repentance, for the person must change his mind about himself as a sinner and the solution to his sins, that is, Jesus. But Grudem thinks this is not enough, and I agree with him. Although Grudem and I have exactly the same definition of repentance, we have a major difference when it comes to the need for repentance. Here is our definition.

Resolve to Turn from Sin

As usual when it comes to understanding biblical terms and concepts, context is king. With very few exceptions the word "repent" or "repentance" is found in the New Testament connected to our sins. To just say that a person has "changed his mind" about his sins doesn't quite get it. For example, in Revelation 16:10-11 we read,

> Then the fifth angel poured out his bowl on the throne of the beast, and his kingdom became full of darkness; and they gnawed their tongues because of the pain. They blasphemed the God of heaven because of their pains and their sores, and did not repent of their deeds.[10]

---

9   Joseph Dillow in email correspondence with Wayne Grudem. Given by permission of both parties.

10 *The New King James Version*. (1982). (Revelation 16:10–11). Nashville: Thomas Nelson.

To say they "changed their minds" about their deeds doesn't have enough punch. Had they repented, they wouldn't be saying, "Oh, yes, now we see. We have been sinful. We did not realize that." No. These are people who are confirmed in their rebellion against God. They are blaspheming the God of heaven. This is war against God. The war wouldn't cease with a simple peace treaty in which these blasphemers agreed with God that they had been in rebellion. Repentance here would require some sort of resolve to turn from their wicked ways.

John the Baptist recognizes as much when he calls for the Pharisees that have come to be baptized by him to bring forth fruit that corresponds (áxios—BDAG) to repentance. By the way, when he does this he is also telling us that repentance does not mean "to turn" from our sins, a common misunderstanding. There is a different word in the New Testament for turning, which is epistrephō. But the New Testament word for repentance is metanoeō. By calling for fruit, John the Baptist is telling us that men cannot observe repentance; men can only observe the *fruit* of repentance. That tells us that repentance is **internal**, since the fruit of it is **external**. Repentance is internal; the turning from sin, which is the fruit of repentance, is external.

If repentance simply meant to change my mind about my sins, then John the Baptist could not legitimately call for fruit that goes along with repentance. He can only call for the fruit if indeed the fruit is the result of an internal resolve to turn from sin. Unfortunately, when Chafer was discussing metanoeō and using Matthew 21:29 (King James translation) as a definition of the word,[11] he apparently did not notice that the word for "repent" in Matthew 21:29 is not metanoeō at all; it is metamelomai, a word usually associated with being sorry because one is caught, not sorry for the deed itself. "Regret" is the first meaning listed by BDAG for metamelomai. It is the same word used for Judas when he was remorseful over his betrayal of Jesus. If that is "genuine

---

11 Chafer, *Theology*, III, 372: "The son cited by Christ as reported in Matthew 21:28-29 who first said 'I will not go,' and afterword repented and went, is a true example of the precise meaning of the word." See also 374: "As before stated, repentance, which is a change of mind, is included in believing." One could, as Chafer seems to have done, view repentance as a change of mind while seeing the fruit of repentance as a change of behavior.

repentance" in the sense that Grudem understands it (the flip side and concomitant with faith), then is Judas—the son of perdition—in heaven? We need a more accurate understanding.

We agree with Grudem that repentance involves more than the mind, just as we believe faith does. Just as faith (in our view) can well involve the mind, the emotions, and the will, so can repentance. We showed a chart of faith in which the mind comprehended the claims of Christ, the emotions had confidence in the claims of Christ, and the will made a commitment to the claims of Christ (per Berkhof, without MacArthur's added obedience). Repentance also can involve the mind, the emotions, and the will. With the mind we recognize our sinfulness, with the emotions we regret our sinfulness, and with our will we resolve to turn from our sinfulness.

So, we agree with Grudem's definition of repentance as given in his 2016 book. Although he does not use those precise words (a resolve to turn from sin) in his *Systematic Theology*, he does say it involves *"a sincere commitment to forsake it [sin] and walk in obedience to Christ . . . a personal decision to turn from it* (a renouncing of sin and a decision of the will to forsake it and lead a life of obedience to Christ instead)."[12]

REPENTANCE

MIND + EMOTION + WILL

RECOGNIZE   REMORSE   RESOLVE
MY SINS   FOR MY SINS   TO TURN FROM SIN

So, if Grudem and I have the exact same definition of repentance, why is he so critical of my view? It's because he claims Hodges and I

---

12 Grudem, *Systematic Theology*, 713.

make repentance "optional."[13] Grudem likes to talk about categorical errors, and he made a huge one here. Hodges and I are not saying repentance is optional at all. Whether repentance is necessary or not depends completely on the category of truth under discussion. For justification we would say that repentance is not optional; it is completely unnecessary.[14] However, for sanctification we would say repentance is *not* optional; it is absolutely *essential.*

My preferred way of discussing these categories of justification truth and sanctification truth is **relationship** truth and *fellowship* truth. We think understanding these categories resolves a lot of the misunderstandings on repentance. The difference between relationship and fellowship is easy to understand. It is as simple as the prodigal son and his father (Luke 15). Was the son in a family? Yes. Did he have a father? Yes. What was their relationship? Father-son. Were they enjoying their relationship when the son was off squandering his inheritance? No. In other words, the father and the son were not having much fellowship (intimacy), were they? No. So relationship truth deals with the eternal family; fellowship truth deals with intimacy with the family during time on earth. The concept of eternal security tells us that no sin on the part of a believer (or one of the elect, to satisfy some) can threaten the relationship with his or her heavenly father. Their relationship is intact—forever.

But fellowship (intimacy) is another issue. It's also another category of truth found within the Bible and in our daily lives. We might define fellowship as "enjoying the relationship." I have a son. I am his father. Nothing can ever change that relationship, even if one of the two of us spends eternity in hell. The relationship? Father-son. But if my son becomes a drug pusher and spends most of his life in prison, I think we could all agree we would not be *enjoying* our relationship. Another

---

13 Grudem, "Free Grace" Theology, 66ff.

14 Unless you use Ryrie's definition where "change of mind" becomes equivalent to faith. With that understanding we would agree with Ryrie that everyone who trusts in Christ as his Savior also repents. That kind of repentance would be absolutely necessary. But in Ryrie's discussion he makes it clear that the "surrender" view of repentance and commitment to turn from sin is not necessary at all.

way of putting that would be to say we are not having intimacy or fellowship with one another. Is it any different with our heavenly Father? Absolutely not.

The greatest example of this found in the Bible concerns God and Israel. An eternal relationship between Israel and God began with the Abrahamic covenant. That covenant was in effect regardless of Israel's behavior. One day a faithful remnant will enjoy the fulfillment of the covenant promises given to Abraham. That was relationship. But fellowship (enjoying the relationship) was another matter. Initially, one of the conditions for enjoying the relationship was for Abraham and his progeny to stay in the land. When Isaac tried to leave, God tells him to return to the land. When Jacob tries to leave, again God says, "Return to the land."

Finally, Israel leaves. Consequence? Four hundred years of slavery in Egypt. But God brings them out of Egypt and says, "OK, it looks like I'm going to have to spell it out for you. If you want to *enjoy* our relationship and be blessed, follow these commandments (the Mosaic covenant). If you do, things will go well for you (enjoying the relationship = fellowship). If you don't, I will put you out of the land (not enjoying the relationship = out of fellowship). But if you turn back to me, I will restore you to the land (enjoying the relationship = back in fellowship). The Abrahamic covenant established an eternal relationship with God; the Mosaic covenant was designed to maintain fellowship with God. When Israel broke fellowship by being disobedient to the Mosaic covenant, her eternal relationship was not threatened (the Abrahamic covenant). But she was subject to divine discipline. Her relationship was not in jeopardy, but her fellowship was. There was no intimacy with God while Israel was out of the land.

These same categories of truth are carried over from the Old Testament to the New Testament. Some truth is about our relationship with God; other truth is about our fellowship with God. Mixing these two has led to all sorts of confusion. Our proposal would be that repentance falls into the category of fellowship truth, not relationship truth. We would say that repentance is not a requirement for a relationship with God (unless you use Ryrie's definition), but it is an absolute requirement for fellowship with God.

Grudem might respond, "If repentance is for fellowship and not relationship, then why on earth does God tell us to preach repentance to all men?" Obvious. God wants to have fellowship with all people. It would be like walking around downtown New York with a placard on my front and back proclaiming, "GET RIGHT WITH GOD." To get right with God there are two steps: relationship + fellowship. As the "Four Spiritual Laws" proclaim in the first law, "God loves you and has a wonderful plan for your life." Does that statement, although true, have anything at all to do with justification? No, it speaks of God's ultimate purpose for creating that person. It's the end game. But to get to the end, you have to start at the beginning. So the second law deals with our sin; the third law deals with God's provision for our sin; the fourth law deals with our acceptance of his plan for our salvation. These last three laws all deal with relationship truth, or justification.

But the "Four Spiritual Laws" doesn't stop there. It goes on to help the new believer discover God's wonderful plan for his or her life. That's fellowship truth or sanctification. To GET RIGHT WITH GOD a person needs both justification and sanctification. Most Reformed people I know would agree that an elect person can slip into serious sin and spend some undefined period of time far from God (they will never agree the person could spend a long time away because that would go against their understanding of 1 John 3:4-10). Now, if we asked the question, "Is that elect person wallowing in sin RIGHT WITH GOD?" The answer would have to be no. Why not? The person is justified (if he is elect, an assumption we have made). He's not right with God because he is deep in sin. So how is this elect person going to GET RIGHT WITH GOD? Obvious answer. He must repent of his sins. So there you have a person with imputed righteousness (his position in the heavenlies) who was not righteous in his condition on earth. Hence, this Christian was not RIGHT WITH GOD. Repentance of his known sins is essential for him to be right with God. Intimacy demands repentance from sin.

The person on the street with the placard calling for a person to GET RIGHT WITH GOD is looking at the two steps necessary to be right with God: belief (for relationship) and repentance (for fellowship). It takes both to be right with God. Hence, when we preach repentance to unbelievers we are essentially asking them to GET RIGHT WITH GOD.

I sometimes ask parents what the highest desire they have for their children might be. Sometimes they reply, "I want them to know Jesus and go to heaven when they die." Really? That's your highest desire? Well, what if one of them trusted Christ and chose to live a life that was lukewarm toward God? They know Jesus and will go to heaven when they die. But is that your highest desire for your child? "Of course, not." Well, then, what is your highest desire? "It's that they know Christ and live a life that glorifies him." Exactly. Justification *and sanctification*. That's the goal. But you can't be sanctified until you are justified. And we are saying there is no way a person can be sanctified until he or she has repented of sins (made an internal decision to turn from them). Of course, it will take the Holy Spirit and his power to enable them to turn from their sins.

I once had a lengthy discussion with Robert Shank, a theologian with "the churches of Christ," as they like to be called. Being of the Arminian persuasion, Shank believes and teaches a child of God can lose his salvation. We studied 1 John 1 and began to speak of the difference between relationship and fellowship. He confessed he had never even considered the distinction. As far as he was concerned a person that had a relationship with God lost it when he or she sinned but could get it back when he or she confessed (1 John 1:9). This seems to be an absurd position. How many times would the same person get "saved" and get "lost" and get "saved" again in one lifetime or just one year, or one month or week? Wouldn't it be easier to say a child of God cannot be unborn, even if he wants to, that God's children have an eternal relationship with their heavenly Father? So what happens when they sin? They don't lose the relationship; they lose the fellowship. Confession and repentance restores the fellowship.

Neither Arminians nor Calvinists think in these terms. Grudem, like most Reformed theologians, understands 1 John to be a book about whether one is elect or not. But right in the beginning of the book (1:3-4) John tells us this is a book about "fellowship" with God, not our relationship with God. Grudem thinks 1 John 2:3-4 is a good test of whether one is elect or not:

Free Grace supporters reply that chapters 1-4 of 1 John give tests of who is in fellowship with God and who is not . . . , rather than tests of whether someone is born again or not. But the verses I have quoted here from 1 John will not bear that interpretation, because coming to "know him" and to be "in him" in 1 John 2:3-6 and 3:6 are descriptions of being born again . . . not descriptions of some additional level of relationship beyond initial salvation.[15]

Dr. Grudem may be unaware of K.L. McKay's article[16] demonstrating that stative verbs (verbs of state rather than action like to "know" versus to "hit") in the perfect *intensify* the meaning of the verb. Most of the translators of 1 John 2:3 translate the perfect of "to know" (*ginōskō*) as an extensive perfect ("have come to know," putting the emphasis on the initial saving experience with Jesus) or an intensive perfect ("know," putting the emphasis on the present results or the state of knowing Jesus). But if McKay is correct in his interpretation of stative verbs in the perfect tense, then this would be an intensive intensive perfect, a verb that intensifies the intensive perfect. It places the emphasis not only on the present state of being but also intensifies the meaning of the verb "to know." Thus it would be "to know well" or "to know intimately" or to "know deeply." It speaks of intimacy (fellowship) with Christ, not a test of whether one is a Christian.

Repentance in the Gospel of John

An Achilles heel for those who think repentance is a requirement for receiving eternal life is the conspicuous, total absence of the word (neither verb nor noun) in the Gospel of John. The point is made that John alone among the NT books explicitly sets forth evangelism as part of its purpose. Some would go further and say John 20:31 gives us **the** purpose statement for the book: "But these are written that you may believe that Jesus is the Christ, the Son of God, and that believing you may have life in his name." The "these" mentioned in the beginning

15 Grudem, *Free Grace Theology*, 81, footnote 3.

16 K. L. McKay, "On the Perfect and other Aspects in New testament Greek," *Novum testamentum XXIII*, 4 (1981), 297.

of the sentence refer to the signs he has written about in the book. He specifically selected these signs so his readers would believe and by believing find life through the name of Jesus. No other NT book states such a purpose.

The Gospel of John uses the word "believe" ninety-nine times but doesn't use the verb or the noun for repentance even once. Someone might say, "Perhaps John did not have that word in his vocabulary." Not if the same person wrote Revelation, because he calls for church after church to repent in Revelation 2-3. So because John purposefully avoids the word in his Gospel, someone should at least ask whether repentance was required to have eternal life. If so, and if John has written a twenty-one chapter book about how to have eternal life, you would expect him to mention the requirement of repentance numerous times, just as he mentioned "believe" many times.

This is an observation that theologians must answer if it is true that repentance is a requirement for receiving eternal life. John's omission of repentance is unthinkable and inexplicable if it is required for justification to eternal life along with belief. Grudem begins his answer to this question by quoting Hodges:

> The fourth gospel says nothing at all about repentance, much less does it connect repentance in any way with eternal life. This fact is the death knell for lordship theology. Only a resolute blindness can resist the obvious conclusion: *John did not regard repentance as a condition for eternal life.* If he had, he would have said so. After all, that's what his book is all about: obtaining eternal life (John 20:30-31).[17]

Grudem's answer to Hodges' claim is important to examine closely:[18]

1. Grudem says Hodges is wrong to base a doctrine on only one book in the Bible. "But here Hodges is basing his doctrine

---

17 Zane Hodges, *Absolutely Free! A Biblical Reply to Lordship Salvation* (Grand Rapids, Mich.: Zondervan, 1989), 148; emphasis original. Quoted in Grudem, 49.

18 Grudem, *Free Grace Theology*, 49-54.

of saving faith on only one book in the Bible, the Gospel of John, and implying that people are wrong to refer to the teachings of any other book of the Bible in defining saving faith." **But**, did Hodges make such a claim in the quote above? Hodges gleans much about saving faith from passages such as Ephesians 2:8-9.[19] Who doesn't? It's another of Grudem's multitudinous misleading and inaccurate statements. Hodges is merely observing what is obvious, except perhaps to those who are willfully blind: if repentance is a requirement to obtain eternal life, a book with the stated purpose of telling people how to get eternal life would mention it. Grudem knows he has a problem here, which is why he spends so much ink trying (unsuccessfully) to dismiss this argument. If John had not stated his purpose so plainly—to precipitate belief unto eternal life—then we would agree that a single book should not be used. John did.

2. Reformed and lordship proponents want to use the other Gospels and their use of repentance to argue that these authors (Matthew, Mark, and Luke) make it clear that repentance is necessary to obtain eternal life. But we have already agreed that repentance is perfectly right and legitimate to preach to unbelievers or believers as a call to GET RIGHT WITH GOD. Getting right with God involves not only believing and repenting; it also involves turning—*pisteuō* + *metanoeō* + *epistrephō*. Belief and repentance are on the inside; turning is the fruit of repentance and is observable on the outside. Grudem apparently sees Luke 15 as an evangelistic passage. What makes him think the sheep was not a sheep but a goat, and the son was not a son but a bastard? So many of the passages he uses both in the Synoptics and Acts are calls to fellowship, not relationship. But God's ultimate desire is both relationship and fellowship with his children. The requirement for a relationship is faith; the requirement for

---

19 Hodges, *Absolutely Free*, 72-73.

fellowship is faith plus repentance. But there is nothing wrong with starting off with a call to repentance.

3. According to Grudem, the Gospel of John assumes the truths concerning repentance taught in the Synoptics. His reasoning is that John was most likely written in the 90s, long after the Synoptics were completed. Hence, John would be supplementary to the Synoptics and would not repeat many of the stories about Jesus and the teachings contained in the Synoptics. **But** what if it could be shown that John was not written late? What if it could be shown that John was written before AD 70, something easy to establish. Again, we are surprised Grudem doesn't use his Greek training. John 5:2 says, "Now there is in Jerusalem by the Sheep *Gate* a pool, which is called in Hebrew, Bethesda, having five porches." The use of the present tense in 5:2 tells us the Pool of Bethesda was extant and in use when John was writing.[20] Anyone visiting Jerusalem today will most likely be taken to the remains of the Pool of Bethesda. The Romans destroyed it in AD 70. That means John must have been written before the destruction of the temple and the Old City. The assumption of a late John is just that, an improvable assumption that flies in the face of clear grammatical evidence that John was not written late. This is a weak argument for John's blatant omission of repentance.

4. Reformed and lordship justificationists argue that the changed behavior of those who follow Jesus in John presume they have all repented. As support Grudem quotes John MacArthur:

> Although John never uses *repent* as a verb, the verbs he *does* employ are even stronger. He teaches that all true believers love the light (3:19), come to the light

---

20 This cannot be a historical present because the historical present never uses the copulative (the verb "to be"). See Wallace, *Greek Grammar Beyond the Basics*, 531 and "John 5,2 and the Date of the Fourth Gospel," *Bib* 71 (1990): 177-205.

(3:20-21), obey the Son (3:36), practice the truth (3:21), worship in spirit and truth (4:23-24), honor God (5:22-24), do good deeds (5:29), eat Jesus' flesh and drink His blood (6:48-66), love God (8:42, cf. 1 John 2:15), follow Jesus (10:26-28), and keep Jesus' commandments (14:15) . . . All of them presuppose repentance, commitment, and a desire to obey.

As those terms suggest, the apostle was careful to describe conversion as a complete turnabout. To John, becoming a believer meant resurrection from death to life, a coming out of darkness and into light, abandoning lies for the truth, exchanging hatred for love, and forsaking the world for God. What are those but images of radical conversion?[21]

Here MacArthur falls into the same trap as Piper in his book *Desiring God*.[22] By the time they get through listing all the things Jesus asks his followers to do in the Synoptics, we get a list so long and difficult only the most dedicated of those who name the name of Christ can live up to them. When challenged on what appears to be a very works-laden orientation to salvation, they just retreat to Philippians 2:13 (meaning God does these works so it is not *synergism*), or say, "Many are called but few are chosen." So now Christian elitism is strutting about in all its finery: God only chose the very few (the elect) of his creation to spend eternity with him. He created all the rest (the vast, vast majority) to torture in the lake of fire forever for his glory and his good pleasure. That's exactly what Reformed theology teaches,

21 John MacArthur Jr., "Repentance in the Gospel of John," *Grace to You* website, accessed March 28, 2015, http://www. gty.org/resources/print/articles/A238, quoted in Grudem, 5.

22 John Piper, *Desiring God* (Sisters, Ore.: Multnomah Publishers, 1986), 65-66: believe, repent, turn, obey, become childlike, love Christ more than anyone, forsake our possessions, be willing to die for him.

but you don't see it on the front cover of their books. Not a very pretty picture of God, is it? No wonder Rob Bell went to the other extreme of universalism.[23] But the question still remains and has yet to be answered, "If John is going to give this long list of descriptions of a true follower of Jesus, things much harder to do than repentance, then why didn't he simply mention repentance?"

5. Grudem's comment about repentance—"This word is missing in this book"—is a misleading kind of argument and should be dismissed.[24] Why didn't he just say that at the beginning of his discussion on repentance in John? Grudem might have a point if it weren't for the fact that John openly states he is writing so his readers can obtain eternal life. He is as much as saying, "If you want eternal life, here is how to get it." His answer, over and over, is "believe." The only way you can get repentance in there is to use Ryrie's definition where changing the mind about one's sinfulness and the provision of Christ is roughly synonymous with faith. And that's fine. I think we have to say that is a fair and acceptable understanding of repentance. But, if you believe repentance is more than just a change of mind, as Grudem does and I do as well, then you have to deal with the absence of repentance in John. Because Grudem and most Reformed scholars see repentance as a requirement for obtaining eternal life, the Gospel of John presents an insurmountable and yet unanswered obstacle to an objective reader. I solve the problem by saying repentance is for fellowship, not relationship.

---

23 Rob Bell, *Love Wins: A Book About Heaven, Hell, and the Fate of Every Person Who Ever Lived* (New York: HarperCollins, 2011). For the opposing view, see Mark Galli, *God Wins: Heaven, Hell, and Why the Good News Is Better than Love Wins* (Carol Stream, Ill.: Tyndale, 2011).

24 Grudem, *Free Grace Theology*, 54.

Repentance, Saving Faith, and Obedience

We want to commend Grudem for not making obedience part of saving faith as so many of his Reformed friends do. He does claim that the "beginning of obedience" is part of saving faith,[25] but he also says, "*a resolve to turn from sin and begin obedience*" is not the same as obedience itself. And we must guard jealously the fact that *faith alone* is what saves us, not faith plus obedience."[26] He objects to the claim of some Free Grace proponents that many Reformed scholars include obedience in their definition of faith and says, "... to my knowledge ... no evangelical professor of theology" includes obedience in his understanding of faith. He goes on to say, "I am aware of no recognized Calvinist or Reformed theologian who says that faith is obedience or that faith is perseverance."[27]

Apparently, Grudem is not familiar with the works of D. A. Carson, who writes, "Hebrews virtually *defines* true believers as those who hold firmly to the end the confidence they had at first (3:6, 14). ... [P]art of the *definition* of saving faith includes the criterion of perseverance" (italics and emphasis mine). Perseverance is of the essence of saving faith, at least according to Carson. John MacArthur writes, "Scripture often equates faith with obedience."[28] Grudem responds to this clear reference to a Four/Five-Point Calvinist that includes obedience with faith by saying, "I think that MacArthur's sentence is unfortunate and claims too much."[29] We would agree, but it is yet another example of Grudem claiming too much, that is, that no Reformed scholar or theologian he knows includes obedience within faith. Then there is

---

25 Grudem, *Free Grace Theology*, 71.

26 Ibid., 71

27 Ibid., 74.

28 MacArthur, *Gospel According to Jesus*, 48. Cited by Grudem, *Free Grace Theology*, 71, footnote 46.

29 Grudem, *Free Grace Theology*, 71. But what about Daniel Fuller, *The Unity of the Bible*, (Grand Rapids, Mich., Zondervan Publishing, 1992) and one of Dr. Grudem's theology professors at Westminster Seminary, Norman Shepherd, who was forced to resign for his views on the relationship of obedience and justification. Both make obedience a requirement of the nature of saving faith.

the late John Stott, who claims, "Faith includes obedience."[30] Grudem counters, "Again I think that Stott's statement is too strong, and I clearly disagree with it."[31] We are glad he does, but Grudem seems to be waffling between two systems of theology. As long as Matthew 24:13 ("he who endures to the end will be saved") is misunderstood as justification and remains the *sine qua non* of Calvinism/Arminianism/Catholicism, works are undeniably a requirement for entrance to heaven.[32]

To say that a necessary result is not a requirement or a condition is simple mental gymnastics. As Zane Hodges so ably expressed it:

> Logan argues that faith is both cause and a condition for justification, while obedience (= works) is not a cause but it IS a condition (see pp. 42-48). Precisely this is the position logically necessitated by lordship salvation as well. If heaven really cannot be attained apart from obedience to God—and this is what lordship salvation teaches—then, logically, that obedience is a condition for getting there.[33]

MacArthur correctly replied that a condition and necessary result are not always synonymous in that glorification is a necessary result

---

30 John Stott, *Eternity* 10.9 (September 1959), 17.

31 Grudem, *Free Grace Theology*, 71.

32 Similarly, most Calvinists view repentance as a gift of God using 2 Timothy 2:25 interpreted from the Gnostic-Augustinian-Calvinist viewpoint. God does some things directly but many indirectly through nature and other people. To interpret this repentance as God's gift to regenerate an unbeliever does not fit the context of Christians (2:14-24). Nevertheless, the Gnostic-Augustinian-Calvinist paradigm demands these be unbelievers because they do not persevere to the end. See John Calvin, *1 & 2 Timothy & Titus: Calvin, The Crossway Classic Commentaries* (Wheaton, Ill.: Crossway, 1998), 145: "Since the conversion of a person is in God's hands, who can say whether those who today seem to be unteachable may be suddenly changed through God's power into different people?"; John MacArthur, Jr., *Faith Works* (Dallas: Word, 1993), 24. See chapter 2 for a refutation of this paradigm.

33 Hodges, *Absolutely Free!*, 214.

but not a condition for justification.[34] But Dillow has presented a more accurate analysis:[35]

> Here we can lay down a self-evident principle: a necessary result **for which we are responsible** which must be present for another result to occur is no different than an additional condition for the achievement of the second result. . . . There is no difference between a result **for which we are responsible** and a condition! Let the reader ponder this, and he will discover that it is impossible to come up with an illustration which contradicts this fact! (emphasis mine)

Free Grace theology teaches God grants us glorification independently of works (his or ours) based on faith alone, so it is therefore a necessary result without being a condition for justification.[36] Yet Calvinists (like Catholics and Arminians) demand good works to reach heaven. The maneuver Calvinists use to avoid this dilemma is to say the good works are of God and not human works (Philippians 2:13). That is, we are **not responsible** for them; God is. But again, this comes from Augustine's pagan influences and reverting to his Manichaean interpretations of Scripture. The system is logical, but the impressive upside-down pyramid still rests upon the pebble of salvific infant baptism.[37]

Repentance as a Summary of the Gospel

A final area of Grudem's argument against Free Grace theology is his statement that repentance from sin is mentioned in many of the gospel summaries in the NT. Here Grudem betrays not only the limitations from not thinking in categories but also a flawed application of the

---

34 MacArthur, *Faith Works*, 53.

35 Joseph Dillow, *Reign of the Servant Kings* (Hayesville, N.C.: Schoettle, 1992), 233.

36 See chapter 5.

37 See chapter 2.

historical-grammatical approach to exegesis. For example, he would view Acts 2:38 as a gospel summary: "Repent and let every one of you be baptized in the name of Jesus Christ for the remission of your sins, and you shall receive the gift of the Holy Spirit." Grudem seems to think these words were spoken to us today. He is not alone. From this verse more than any other the early church fathers, the Reformers, and most in Christianity today (including Catholics) believe water baptism is a requirement for receiving eternal life. And if this verse proves repentance is necessary to receive eternal life, then so is water baptism.

Despite citing this verse four times in his 2016 book (none in his *Systematic Theology*), Grudem fails to include water baptism along with his requirement of repentance.[38] But we would suggest neither repentance nor water baptism is required to receive eternal life. Why? Because, unlike Grudem,[39] we don't think this verse is a summary of the gospel. Rather, these words from the lips of Peter were directed toward the national leaders of Israel, just as they were in Acts 3:19.

As we have already seen, Israel as a nation already had an eternal relationship with God. Grudem avoids this discussion because he is a covenant theologian, who devotes all of eight pages in his lengthy (1,200 pages), one-volume work on systematic theology to the covenants. Then, as a covenant theologian, he speaks of three covenants (none of which is mentioned in the Bible): the covenant of works, the covenant of grace, and the covenant of redemption. The covenant of grace subsumes the Abrahamic covenant, the Mosaic covenant, and the new covenant all under its umbrella. He doesn't even mention the Davidic covenant. In light of this paradigm, I certainly don't fault Grudem for a lot of his interpretations of the Bible and thus his theology. But as dispensationalists we have a different understanding of the role of Israel and the Church than do covenant theologians. Covenant theologians not only discover covenants the Bible does not mention, they don't spend much time analyzing the covenants the Bible does mention, especially the Abrahamic, the Davidic, and the Mosaic. Grudem does

---

38 Grudem, *Free Grace Theology*, 43, 52, 53, 66.

39 Grudem, *Free Grace Theology*, 52.

not distinguish between the Suzerain-Vassal treaty (the Mosaic) and the Covenants of Grant (Abrahamic and Davidic). Among numerous differences, the latter are eternal from inception and the former is temporal. Grudem never discusses this and its implications for theology.[40]

When it comes to Israel, a dispensationalist believes God has an eternal relationship with the physical seed of Abraham established in his covenant with Abraham. But the rules for fellowship with God were established for Israel by the Mosaic covenant. When the cup of iniquity from Israel's disobedience was full, God judged or disciplined his wayward child: the Assyrians, the Babylonians, the Greeks, and the Romans were all God's response to the unfaithfulness of Israel. When the NT opens, John the Baptist is once again issuing a warning: repent or judgment will come. He claims the axe is already laid to the root of the trees. Judgment is on its way. But Jesus gives that particular Jewish generation (that would reject him) the length of one generation to repent and avoid the curse of having "all the blood from righteous Abel to the blood of Zecharias" exacted upon them (Matthew 23:35). To avoid the judgment of AD 70 at the hands of Titus, the nation itself would have to repent, which Jesus immediately announces next (see Matthew 23:37-24:2).

By "repent," John, Jesus, and Peter were not calling on the "nation" to believe for justification. As a nation they already had an eternal relationship with God. But to enjoy that relationship (or what we call fellowship) the nation needed to repent of its wickedness. Thus when those hearing Peter's sermon in Acts 2:36 are convicted by the Holy Spirit of the sin of crucifying Jesus, they are cut to the heart (i.e., they believed Peter's words about Jesus), and they ask Peter what they need to do. This was not a question for individual justification among the

---

40 For a more complete discussion see Anderson, *Soteriology*, 140-46. See Moshe Weinfeld: "Covenant Making in Anatolia and Mesopotamia," *Journal of Ancient Near Eastern Studies* 22 (1993): 135–39; *Deuteronomy and the Deuteronomic School* (Oxford: Oxford University, 1972); and the following for a Reformed theologian who admits this distinction: http://www.fivesolas. com/suzerain.htm and http://www.tyndalehouse.com/tynbul/library/tynbull _1963_13_01_thompson_anetreatypattern.pdf.

crowd. This was a question for their nation. If the nation were going to avoid the coming judgment (Acts 2:40), the nation needed to repent. But that's not all. These particular Jews under Jesus's curse also needed to be water baptized (a sign of their disassociation with the wickedness of Israel and a new association with the Messiah, Jesus) in order to receive the Holy Spirit.

In every instance in the book of Acts where the Holy Spirit was received some time after faith, it was a Jew or a half a Jew (Acts 2, 8, 9, 19). These are the only examples in the NT. But when Gentiles were in view—that were not under Jesus's curse and threat of the coming judgment of Titus—the Holy Spirit came upon them the moment they believed (Cornelius was the prototype of Gentile salvation, Acts 10). The Book of Acts is a book of transition. It begins in Jerusalem; it winds up in Rome. It begins with Peter; it winds up with Paul. It begins with the Jews; it winds up with the Gentiles. It begins with the Mosaic covenant; it winds up with the new covenant. Along the way it shifts from the requirements for the nation of Israel to avoid Jerusalem's destruction to the requirements for the individual justification of Jews and Gentiles.

Grudem will dismiss these kinds of distinctions between the Jews and the Gentiles simply because they do not fit into covenant theology. They fit his assumed theological covenant interpretations but not the actual biblical covenants. Nevertheless, I am a dispensationalist because it is a system of theology that answers more of my questions about God, man, and the Bible than any other system to which I have been introduced. For example, when did Jesus begin his ministry (AD 30)? When did Titus destroy Jerusalem (AD 70)? When we subtract: 70 – 30 = 40. Yes, exactly forty years, precisely according to Jesus's warning in Mathew 23:35-36. Covenant theology has no explanation for this.

When we look at Acts 3:19, we see it in its context, especially connected to 3:20-21:

Therefore repent and return, so that your sins may be wiped away, in order that times of refreshing may come from the presence of the Lord;

and that he may send Jesus, the Christ appointed for you,

whom heaven must receive until *the* period of restoration of all things about which God spoke by the mouth of his holy prophets from ancient time.

You will notice this does not say, "Believe and return." Grudem would explain this as the simple substitution of "repent" for "believe," for to him the words are interchangeable.[41] But consider for a moment the viewpoint of a dispensationalist. We believe Jesus is coming back some day to set up a millennium on earth, a thousand-year reign of Christ from Jerusalem. After that period of time, in which the Second Adam will fulfill what the first Adam was charged to do (take dominion over the earth), the eternal state in the New Jerusalem will begin.

Jesus made some promises to the Jews regarding the 1,000-year reign. One was to the disciples. "What are we going to get out of this because we have left everything to follow you?" Peter asks. "To you it will be granted to sit on the twelve thrones ruling over the twelve tribes of Israel," Jesus answers. There is no place for these verses in covenant theology. Israel is absorbed into the Church and there is no literal 1,000-year reign on the earth.

Acts 3:19-21 is spoken by Peter *after* Israel rejected Christ. And he is saying, "As a nation we Israelites have an eternal relationship with God. But to enjoy that relationship we need to repent and to turn (*metanoeō* and *epistrephō*)." The issue for Israel was fellowship, not relationship. And if the nation repents and turns to the Lord, what will happen? The Lord will return and set up his promised kingdom on earth for a thousand years. Now this makes a lot more sense to me than covenant theology. And thankfully Grudem did not condemn us for taking this approach. We appreciate that. Nor will we condemn him for his approach. However, we will not accept the charge that we have weakened the gospel in any way, shape, or form. We obviously believe our approach gives us a better explanation of the words in their biblical setting than does Grudem's approach.

---

41 Grudem, *Free Grace Theology*, 52, who misinterprets these as two aspects of the same action.

So, what we are saying is that many of these gospel summaries Grudem points to are calls for the nation to repent. Repent does not mean "believe." I completely agree with Grudem. Repent means "resolve to turn from one's sins." But the issue with repentance is fellowship, not relationship. Israel had a relationship with God (Abrahamic covenant), but she was sorely out of fellowship with God (Mosaic covenant). Judgment was coming (Titus). To avoid that judgment, she as a nation needed to repent.

By contrast the Gentiles were not required to be water baptized before receiving the Holy Spirit (Acts 11:15). And since the Gentiles comprised people from many nations, and since God had not singled them out as he had Israel, he deals with them as individuals. The requirement for the nation of Israel to avoid the judgment of AD 70 was to repent and be baptized. The requirement for a Gentile to GET RIGHT WITH GOD was to repent, believe, and turn (Acts 15:18-21). Remember, to get right with God they needed relationship (believe) + fellowship (repent and turn).

But what about individual Jews of that generation? Surely they weren't going to go to heaven just because the nation repented (if they had repented). No, of course not. But Peter, in his sermons found in Acts 2 and 3, is addressing *the nation* and asking them to turn. We know this because in Acts 2:14 Peter singles out the "men of Judea and those who live in Jerusalem." What about all the rest who were listening from all around the Mediterranean world? And in Peter's second sermon he addresses the people on Solomon's Porch (at the temple), but he references the rulers (v. 17) and at the end of the sermon he does not ask the people to believe; he asks them to turn (v. 26).

So although individuals in every age or dispensation had to believe in order to obtain eternal life, the nation of Israel as a whole had to turn in order to avoid the judgment of AD 70. Their covenant relationship with God was intact (see Acts 3:25), but to enjoy that relationship (fellowship) they had to repent, be water baptized, and turn. The water baptism did not justify them—it saved them from the perverse generation (Acts 2:40) subject to God's coming wrath in 70 AD by dispersing them out of Jerusalem through persecution (Acts 8:1). To get into Judaism, a Gentile had to be water baptized, just as in modern times with the *mitveh* ritual.[42] To get out of Judaism and avoid physical death, a Jew had to be water baptized in the name of Christ (to save his physical life and receive the Holy Spirit).

Conclusion

Grudem's main concern regarding repentance, as I understand it, is that Free Grace theologians have diminished the gospel with an understanding of repentance ("to change the mind") that does not make a strong call to sinners to change their ways. We would respond that this is an unfair assessment for these reasons:

1. "To change the mind" as taught by Chafer and Ryrie includes a recognition of a person's sinfulness and need for a Savior from their sins. The de-emphasis on sin we see in our American pulpits is primarily through the influence of Norman Vincent Peal, followed by Robert Schuller and then so many in the seeker sensitive church movement. Even some of these would say they draw people in with their positive, feel-good messages, and then lead people to Christ in a more private setting where people are confronted with their sin and their need for a Savior. We have several large churches of this brand here in Houston that are leading thousands to Christ. Grudem would probably say, "But how do you know they have exercised genuine faith?" I don't. Only God knows. But Grudem doesn't know they haven't.

---

42 Maimonides, Hilkh. Iss. Biah xiii. 5; Alfred Edersheim, *The Life and Times of Jesus the Messiah* (Oxford, 1883; updated edition, Peabody, Mass.: Hendrickson, 1993), 189 and 1014-16 (Appendix 12): "But we also have positive testimony (which the objections of *Winer*, *Keil*, and *Leyrer*, in my opinion do not invalidate) that the baptism of proselytes existed in the time of Hillel and Shammai. For, whereas the school of Shammai is said to have allowed a proselyte, who was circumcised on the even of the Passover, to partake after baptism of the Passover, the school of Hillel forbade it. This controversy must be regarded as proving that at the time (previous to Christ) the baptism of proselytes was customary (Pes. 8.8, Eduy. 5.2)."

2. Many teachers of Free Grace theology do not teach the "change of mind" view. Therefore, Grudem attacks a straw man when he lumps us all together. He undoubtedly would respond that he has not lumped us together. He has discussed both the "change of mind" view and the "resolve to turn from sin" view. But when he concludes his chapter on repentance, he lumps us all together by saying we do not have a strong call to deal with our sins. False accusation. Not only do we all deal with sin as a problem to be overcome if one is to obtain eternal life (via the cross), but some of us say repentance is absolutely essential (not optional) to have a relationship with God (Dillow) and/or fellowship with God (Hodges, Anderson). In either case, we do not minimize sin in the life of an unbeliever or a believer, and it is wrong to make such an accusation, especially without having a conversation with the accused.

3. Dispensationalists and covenant theologians will probably always talk past one another when it comes to the covenants. An understanding of the Abrahamic covenant to establish a relationship with Israel as a nation and the Mosaic covenant to provide fellowship for Israel as a nation helps many of us to understand many of the repentance passages in the Synoptics and Acts as a call to the nation of Israel back to fellowship, not a call to individuals within the nation to repent/believe.

4. Since some of us understand repentance as a fellowship issue, we also think it is perfectly right to preach repentance to unbelievers (Acts 17, Luke 24). It is perfectly right to preach to unbelievers God's highest desire for them, that is, to have both a relationship and fellowship with them. Christ did no different when the rich young ruler came to him. Depending on your understanding of the word "inherit," the ruler was asking either how to obtain eternal life or how to enjoy it to its fullest. In either case Jesus did not tell him how to obtain eternal life; he simply told him how to enjoy it to its fullest— by selling his goods, giving the money to poor, and following Jesus. Was that disingenuous on the part of Jesus? No. Jesus

went right to God's highest desire for the rich young ruler. But before the rich young ruler could get to point B (enjoy his life to the fullest), he had to go through point A (believe in Jesus as his Savior).

5. Repentance and faith are not inseparable. According to Grudem: "Repentance from sin and faith in Christ are two sides of the same coin, two aspects of the same decision of the heart."[43] And again, "This suggests that we should regard repentance and faith as two closely connected parts of one overall action, parts that cannot be separated."[44] I wonder what Grudem would say about all the rehab centers in America where alcoholics and drug addicts resolve to turn from their sins and do in fact turn by seeking professional help. To my knowledge, many, if not most, of these centers are not based on faith in Christ. So are there two types of resolving to turn from one's sins? And, according to Grudem's theology, a person must be born again (regenerated) before he can repent or believe. So are all these people going to rehab centers in America regenerated?

6. Grudem's underlying and unspoken (unwritten) concern seems to be a perception that Free Grace theology is slack concerning Christians who sin. Could a Christian die without repenting of a gross moral sin and yet still go to heaven? Grudem would respond, "No." That is the Roman Catholic view that a person must die "in a state of grace" in order to go to heaven. We respond, "Yes." Free Grace theologians believe that Christ's imputed righteousness is all that God requires since no attained holiness here on earth can add to it.[45] But those who choose to "wallow in sin" will suffer the consequences of sin in this life and the next. And those who simply waste their life chasing ignoble or even noble pursuits in this life will find themselves empty handed at the

---

43 Grudem, *Free Grace Theology*, 43.

44 Ibid., 45.

45 See chapter 5.

Judgment Seat of Christ if their pursuits were not connected
to the foundation of Christ (1 Corinthians 3:11-15).

So regarding the topic of repentance in his book, Grudem repeatedly
misrepresented Free Grace theology and apparently did so knowingly,
without responding to our offers to clarify. In addition, his scholarship
was deficient in this book in numerous inaccuracies. At least we can
credit him for his graciousness.

Chapter 5

The Role of Works in Justification

Joseph Dillow, Th.D.

In this chapter, we will demonstrate how Wayne Grudem's viewpoint on the warning passages in the New Testament logically leads to the conclusion that works are a condition for obtaining heaven. Advocates of this position say they are being misunderstood. The problem, they say, is that readers are not hearing their strong assertions that salvation comes by faith alone and are misrepresenting them. In order to clarify their position, Reformed theologians argue in two ways that what they teach is not a works-righteousness.

First, they say that, although works are indeed a condition for obtaining final salvation because they are non-meritorious works, there is no contradiction with *sola fide*. Secondly, since these works are produced by God's work in the believer, these works *can* save. Only human works or works produced by nonbelievers cannot save.

This chapter addresses these two responses to their problem of a works-salvation. However, before we begin, it will be necessary to correct a number of misunderstandings maintained by Dr. Grudem that affect some conclusions he arrives at throughout his book, *"Free Grace" Theology: 5 Ways It Diminishes the Gospel.*

Some Misunderstandings of Free Grace Theology

Grudem makes several inaccurate statements about the Free Grace view of salvation. For example, he asks, "Why do Free Grace advocates claim that we should not tell unbelievers that they need to repent of their sins when they come to trust in Christ?"[1] While some Free Grace advocates have said that, many would agree with Grudem that repentance is a necessary part of salvation.[2]

He asks, "Why do Free Grace advocates claim that we should not say that good works are a necessary result of saving faith?" Contra Grudem, Free Grace advocates do say that good works are a necessary result.[3] We do not believe that true believers will necessarily continue

---

1 Wayne A. Grudem, *"Free Grace" Theology: 5 Ways It Diminishes the Gospel* (Wheaton, Ill.: Crossway, 2016), 39.

2 See David R. Anderson's discussion in Chapter 4 of Free Grace thinking for a correct Free Grace view. See also my own book where I devote considerable coverage arguing, contra Grudem, that repentance is a necessary part of saving faith. Joseph C. Dillow, *Final Destiny: The Future Reign of the Servant Kings*, 3rd revised ed. (Monument, Col.: Paniym Group, Inc., 2016; reprint, 2016), Chapter 3. I define repentance as admission of guilt, sorrow for sin.

3 Hodges notes, "We must add that there is no need to quarrel with the Reformers' view that where there is justifying faith, works will undoubtedly exist too. This is a reasonable assumption for any Christian unless he has been converted on his death bed! But it is quite wrong to claim that a life of dedicated obedience is guaranteed by regeneration, or even that such works as there are must be visible to a human observer." *Zane C. Hodges, Absolutely Free! A Biblical Reply to Lordship Salvation* (Dallas: Redención Viva, 1989), 215. John Hart says, "It is not denied that genuine faith will result in some change in the believer. Those holding to the Free Grace teaching do not assert that faith can exist without any change whatsoever. Most, if not all, Free Grace proponents believe that good works will inevitably result from faith, but not necessarily as visibly as we desire them to appear and not necessarily as consistently as the Lord would desire them to appear." John F. Hart, "The Faith of Demons," *JOTGES* 8, no. 2 (1995): 40. See also my own statements in Dillow, *Final Destiny* 19.

in those good works to the end of life. We do not believe it because the Bible clearly gives numerous examples of true believers who did not continue (see chapter 10 in this book).

Grudem asks, "Why do some Free Grace advocates teach that saving faith is only intellectual assent?" No Free Grace writer that I know of believes this. We do believe that faith begins in the mind and then arises in the heart after reflecting on the Savior and the beauty of the gospel promise and results in personal trust in the person of Christ for forgiveness of sin.

He queries, "Why do Free Grace advocates adopt highly unusual and unprecedented interpretations of numerous New Testament texts that speak of the need for repentance?" He then cites some Protestant creeds and systematic theologies, which teach that "we are justified by faith alone but the faith that justifies is not alone."[4] His point is that these interpretations are new and therefore very unlikely.

However, as the Belgic Confession says:

Neither may we consider any writings of men, however holy these men may have been, of equal value with these divine Scriptures, nor ought we to consider custom, or the great multitude, or antiquity, or succession of times and persons, or councils, decrees or statutes, as of equal value with the truth of God, since the truth is above all.[5]

Schrotenboer illustrates the importance of this statement.

Throughout the centuries the church has repeatedly found new insights and sometimes rejected settled opinions of the "elders." For example, "It was held by some of the first-generation Reformers that the command of Jesus to proclaim the gospel to all nations was given exclusively to the apostles and did not

---

4   Grudem, *"Free Grace" Theology*, 28.

5   Belgic Confession, Art. VII.

place a responsibility upon the post apostolic church to engage in cross cultural evangelism" [6]

We admit that some of Free Grace interpretations are new. Job's counselors similarly admonished Job to accept only the traditions of the elders. *"Will they not teach you and tell you, and bring forth words from their minds?"* (Job 8:10). With an argument similar to Dr. Grudem's, they justified their approach to truth by saying, *"Can the papyrus grow up without a marsh? Can the rushes grow without water?"* (Job 8:11). All current knowledge, Bildad says, emerges from the "marsh," that is, the paradigm of those who went before. Job, of course, does not totally agree. The knowledge from former generations does not fit the facts of his experience. According to tradition, if someone suffers, it must be because of sin in his life. Job has not sinned. Similarly, we believe that the knowledge that comes from many of the creeds and former theologians does not fit the data of the New Testament.

In the final analysis, we all should heed the counsel of Jesus. "And he said to them, 'Therefore every scribe who has become a disciple of the kingdom of heaven is like a head of a household, who brings forth out of his treasure things **new** and old'" (Matthew 13:52). The church fathers and the creeds are to be respected, but they too must be submitted to the Scriptures; they are not infallible. If Luther and Calvin had avoided Christ's counsel, the Protestant Reformation would never have occurred. Most of the creeds and traditions of the church told them they were wrong. Even the majority of the church fathers had embraced a works salvation within 100 years of the close of the canon. [7]

---

6   Paul G. Schrotenboer, "An Evangelical View of Scripture and Tradition," *Evangelical Review of Theology* 19(1995): 193.

7   See Thomas F. Torrance, *The Doctrine of Grace in the Apostolic Fathers* (Edinburgh: Oliver and Boyd, 1948). William Cunningham, *Historical Theology: A Review of the Principal Doctrinal Discussions in the Christian Church Since the Apostolic Age*, 2 vols. (Bellingham, Wash.: Logos Research Systems, 2008). For one example among many, Tertullian says that Philippians 3:14 refers to "that judgment which we shall have to undergo as the recompense *of our deeds.* Tertullian, "On the Resurrection of the Flesh," in T*he Ante-Nicene Fathers Vol. III : Translations of the Writings of the Fathers*

The majority of Christians in the world reject Reformed theology. I know this first hand after almost 40 years of working with the church on four continents. Grudem admits this.[8] It is because of many unconvincing Reformed interpretations of numerous passages that the Free Grace movement was born. Thousands of Christians sitting under Reformed teaching simply dismissed it as too harsh, theoretical, and difficult to live. It has been very affirming to me to see believers from all over the world respond so positively to the Free Grace message. I cannot count the number of times I have received comments and letters saying that finally the Bible makes sense. Many say, "Free Grace interpretations put the Bible together for me and changed my life." Grudem's views hold up beautifully when he is preaching to the choir. Free Grace views appeal to believers of all theological backgrounds from all over the world.

Reformed Statements on Salvation by Works

Grudem says that Free Grace advocates misunderstand what Reformed theology teaches regarding soteriology. However, we do understand it, but simply disagree. In spite of their strong denials and claims that we do not understand, we hope to show in this chapter they do teach salvation by faith plus works. In fact, some of them openly say so.

For example, Reformed theologian Arthur Pink teaches that God requires that true Christians must "keep themselves" or risk eternal damnation.[9] Yet he unequivocally maintains the "absolute and eternal security of the saints."[10] He is attempting to show that God preserves his children through means, that is, by works. He quotes with approval John Owen, that prince of the Puritan expositors, who taught that

---

Down to A.D. 325; Latin Christianity: Its Founder, Tertullian, ed. Alexander Roberts, James Donaldson, and A. Cleveland Coxe (Oak Harbor, Wash.: Logos Research Systems, 1997), chapter 23, 155, 562.

8   Grudem, *"Free Grace" Theology*, 19.

9   Arthur Pink, *An Exposition of Hebrews* (Grand Rapids, Mich.: Baker, 1968), 601.

10 Ibid., 599.

works are a means of salvation: "We may say, with reference unto the **means** that He hath appointed, when storms and trials arise, **unless we use our diligent endeavors, we cannot be saved.**"[11]

Elsewhere, Pink asserts,

Holiness in this life is such a part of our "salvation" that it is a necessary means to make us meet to be partners of the inheritance of the saints in heavenly light and glory.[12]

They [good works] are requisite as part of the means which God has appointed: they are the means of spiritual preservation.[13]

R. C. Sproul agrees with this, "Endurance in the faith is a **condition** for future salvation. Only those who endure in the faith will be saved in eternity."[14]

Similarly, Thomas Schreiner writes,

Believers obtain eschatological salvation by continuing to believe until the end and by heeding the warnings given to them.[15]

The summons to persevere and the initial call to believe are conditions that must be fulfilled to be saved.[16]

---

11 John Owen, *Hebrews*, quoted in Pink, *Exposition of Hebrews*, 600.

12 Arthur Pink, *The Doctrine of Sanctification* (Swengel, Pa.: Reiner Publications, 1975), 28.

13 Arthur Pink, *An Exposition of the Sermon on the Mount* (Grand Rapids,Mich.: Baker Book House, 1974), 349.

14 R. C. Sproul, *Grace Unknown:The Heart of Reformed Theology* (Grand Rapids, Mich.: Baker Book House, 1997), 198.

15 Thomas R. Schreiner, *Run to Win the Prize: Perseverance in the New Testament* (Wheaton, Ill.: Crossway Books, 2010), 109.

16 Ibid., 104. Schreiner continues to confuse his readers by also saying, "Heeding warnings is not the basis of our salvation." Thus we obtain eschatological salvation "by heeding warnings," but heeding warnings is not the basis. So the warnings are not a "basis" of salvation but they are a "condition" and a means of salvation. I think I understand what Schreiner is getting at, but this

One might be tempted to explain this by saying, "Well, what Pink and others really mean is that because works are the necessary fruit of regeneration, we can understand them to mean that they are only a means in the sense of verifying that true faith has occurred." However, that is not what they mean. Pink clearly says, "That good works are neither the chief nor the procuring cause of salvation is readily admitted, **but that they are no cause whatever, that they are simply 'fruits' of salvation and not a means thereto, we definitely deny.**"[17] "Faith obtains the title [to salvation], good works secure the actual admission into the full and final benefits of redemption."[18] So according to Pink, works are "a" cause. "The doing of good works," he says, "is indispensable in order to the securing of full and final salvation, that is, in order to an actual entrance into heaven itself."[19]

In their book, *The Race Set Before Us*, Reformed writers Schreiner and Caneday boldly declare that works are a condition of salvation with much less hesitation than most within the Reformed community:

We must run the race with dogged determination to obtain the prize of eternal life, and it takes remarkable discipline and training to make it to the end.[20]

We are to use all the resources at our disposal in order to be saved on the last day. We must obey, pray, resist the flesh and

---

nuanced use of language explains why some believe he is in fact teaching a works righteousness even though he strongly denies it. I am also doubtful that a first-century fisherman or readers of Paul's epistles in the first century could comprehend this subtle defense of post-Reformation theology!

17 Pink, A*n Exposition of the Sermon on the Mount*: 343.

18 Ibid., 349.

19 Ibid.

20 Thomas R. Schreiner and Ardel B. Caneday, *The Race Set Before Us: A Biblical Theology of Perseverance and Assurance* (Downers Grove, Ill.: InterVarsity Press, 2001), 314.

yield to the Spirit to inherit salvation. No theology is acceptable that diminishes this call to work out our salvation.[21]

Roy Zuck responds,

A problem with this view is the authors' contradictory statements about works in relation to salvation. They "categorically deny that salvation can be earned by works" (p. 86). And yet in the very next sentence they write, "The prize to be won is eternal life . . . and we must strive to win that prize." When they say that "good works and following Jesus (Romans 2:6–7; Mark 10:29–30) are also necessary to obtain eternal life on the last day" (p. 67), is this not making salvation dependent on one's works? How can a gift be a gift if one must strive to attain it? Is this not illogical?[22]

"[H]ow," Zuck pointedly asks,

"can the authors say they are not adding a condition to salvation (p. 153), when they repeatedly say that "the promise of eternal life is conditional" (p. 166), that "God's promise of salvation is conditional" (p. 167), and that "if we fail to persevere we will perish" (p. 206)? Is it not adding a condition to salvation to say, "We must obey, pray, resist the flesh and yield to the Spirit to inherit salvation" (p. 315)?[23]

Schreiner and Caneday would reply something like, "Yes, but praying, resisting the flesh, and yielding to the Spirit are God-produced, non-meritorious conditions, and therefore no works-righteousness is involved in obtaining our final entrance into heaven."

---

21 Ibid., 315.

22 Roy B. Zuck, "Book Review of The Race Set Before Us: A Biblical Theology of Perseverance and Assurance by Thomas R. Schreiner and Ardel B. Caneday," *BibSac* 160, no. 638 (April-June 2003): 242.

23 Ibid.

Schreiner wants it both ways. He says those addressed in the warning passages are "true believers,"[24] but some may fall away proving they were not true believers.[25] He summarily dismisses the view that the warnings are related to loss of reward.[26] Of course, if they are not, well then, they are not. But that is the point in question.[27]

Maurice Roberts, a contributor to the Reformed journal, *The Banner of Truth*, writes, "There are conditions to be fulfilled if Heaven is to be ours."[28] His condition is perseverance. This condition, however, is to be fulfilled by God's effectual work in the regenerate. But we must cooperate with God in this work. So, salvation in this system is initial belief coupled with a lifelong synergism of human and divine work.[29]

Pink, Owen, Kling, Schreiner, Caneday, Sproul, and Roberts are simply being honest about the real meaning of the Reformed doctrine of salvation and perseverance. Their concern about antinomianism and Scriptures that contradict their system have boxed them into a distortion of their own doctrine. They clearly say that the warnings are the means of securing perseverance and that it is our obedience to those warnings that finally saves us. They make this claim because they are undoubtedly aware that merely warning a man will not guarantee he will obey. Thus, one needs to make his actual obedience the necessary ingredient for obtaining heaven. This indeed shuts out all possibility

---

24 Schreiner, *Run to Win the Prize*, 110.

25 Ibid., 105.

26 Ibid., 113.

27 It is interesting that an Arminian, Robert Shank, agrees with Pink and Schreiner and Caneday on this point, that salvation must be obtained by attention to the means of its attainment, namely, faithful perseverance. Robert Shank, *Life in the Son: A Study of the Doctrine of Perseverance* (Springfield, Mo.: Westcott Publishers, 1961), 299.

28 Maurice Roberts, "Final Perseverance," *Banner of Truth Trust*, no. 265 (October 1985): 11.

29 Sproul says, "As part of the process of our sanctification, perseverance is a synergistic work." The title of Sproul's book is revealing! Sproul, *Grace Unknown*, 212. See also John H. Gerstner, *Wrongly Dividing the Word of Truth: A Critique of Dispensationalism*, 1st ed. (Brentwood, Tenn.: Wolgemuth & Hyatt, 1991), 210.

of antinomianism, and for this they are to be commended. But is this really the gospel?

In response to the above citations, Reformed writers often complain they are being taken out of context and that those who disagree misunderstand. Their argument is that (1) God is the one who ultimately sanctified us, and therefore it is his work and not ours that finally secures our arrival in heaven. Furthermore, they assert (2) that these works are non-meritorious because God is the one who works them in us. They are, in effect, God-produced non-meritorious works. Finally, (3) they say that when they assert that perseverance is a condition to be fulfilled if heaven is to be ours, they are only stating the biblical truth that genuine faith will always result in perseverance. We believe that this core component of their system is contradicted by the testimony of Scripture (see Chapter 10). In the pages to follow, we will discuss the first two explanations above, which relate to Dr. Grudem's soteriology:

- Does Salvation Depend upon Works for Which We Are Responsible?
- Are Works a Non-Meritorious Condition of Salvation?

Does Salvation Depend on Results for Which We Are Responsible?

If it does, then, as we will now argue, salvation is in some sense "caused" by our own works and is not just a condition of final arrival in heaven. Who does these works? *If man has a part in their production, it would seem that man, in the final analysis, is partially responsible for his ultimate arrival in heaven.*

Dr. Grudem and other Reformed theologians maintain, and we certainly agree, that while salvation is a work of God, sanctification is a work of God in which believers cooperate.[30] For example, Grudem says, "The role that we play in sanctification is both a *passive* one in

---

30 Louis Berkhof, *Systematic Theology* (Grand Rapids,Mich.: Wm. B. Eerdmans Publishing Co., 1996), 534. He says, "Man is privileged to co-operate with the Spirit of God," and elsewhere that these kinds of works (i.e., those following

which we depend on God to sanctify us, and an *active* one in which we strive to obey God and take steps that will increase our sanctification."[31] Other Reformed writers agree,

There is no perseverance without man **working out his own salvation.**[32]

Authorities maintain that sanctification is not an autonomous human work **but a divine-human concursive operation** initiated by God.[33]

The vast majority of Reformed theologians would agree with Lewis and Demarest that while God's part in sanctification is to initiate, enable, motivate, and warn, there is still a sense in which "we sanctify ourselves."[34] We must take action; we must separate ourselves from immoral influences; we must initiate acts of love. Erickson puts it this way, "So while sanctification is God's work, the believer has a role as well, entailing both removal of sinfulness and development of holiness." It is not, he says, "a completely passive matter on the believer's part. . . . [T] he believer is constantly exhorted to work and to grow in the matters pertaining to salvation."[35]

But if man must cooperate, then he must choose to do this. If he does not choose to cooperate, then he will not be sanctified. The numerous biblical illustrations of failure prove (see Chapter 10) that a believer may not so choose. It is therefore incorrect to say, as Berkhof

---

regeneration), "are deserving of approval" and since a reward is attached to them are "sometimes called meritorious works." Ibid., 542.

31 Wayne A. Grudem, *Systematic Theology: An Introduction to Biblical Doctrine* (Grand Rapids, Mich.: Inter-Varsity Press, 2004), 754.

32 Leonard J. Coppes, *Are Five Points Enough? The Ten Points of Calvinism* (Denver: the author, 1980), 55.

33 Gordon Lewis and Bruce Demarest, *Integrative Theology* (Grand Rapids, MI: Zondervan Publishing House, 1987), 3:185.

34 Ibid., 3:207.

35 Millard J. Erickson, *Christian Theology* (Grand Rapids, Mich.: Baker Book House, 1985), 2:971.

does, that man deserves no credit. He certainly does deserve credit, and the Lord everywhere acknowledges that man will be rewarded for it in the future.[36]

Now, what shall we call this "cooperation" of man? What shall we call his decisions to pursue godliness? Could we not call them works for which he is responsible? Grudem says they are conditions of our ultimate arrival in heaven. And if so, could we not call the outcome of these works a wage earned based on meritorious effort? And if we can call them that, then are they not additional works necessary to obtain heaven? If they are not done, according to Dr. Grudem, the person will perish. If a person is responsible to do these works and if that person may choose not to (and both Scripture and experience confirm that he may), are not these works conditions for *and* causes of his salvation? If works are demanded as an essential part of the agreement that secures our final arrival in heaven, how does this differ from works being a condition or a cause? Indeed, the dictionary defines a condition as "something demanded as an essential part of an agreement"[37] and a cause as "something that brings about an effect or a result."[38]

Let us consider a human illustration and explore the parallels between spiritual and physical birth. We might say, "A condition for growing old is to be born." Now, on Reformed assumptions, certain kinds of results of birth are necessary for a person to grow old, such as eating. Hunger is a possible result of being born, and satisfying hunger is a necessary condition for, and cause of, growing old. Furthermore, unlike breathing, eating is a result for which we are responsible. Moreover, we can say that eating is a cause of growth and is not just a result of birth. We can choose to eat or not to eat. Here we can lay down a self-evident principle.

A necessary result **for which we are responsible** and which must be present for another result to occur is no different from an additional condition and cause for the achievement of that second result.

---

36 E.g., Mark 9:41; Matt. 6:1, 18; Luke 6:23, 35; Heb. 11:26; 2 John 8; Rev. 22:12.

37 Lexicon Webster Dictionary, s.v. "Condition," 1:211.

38 *Merriam-Webster's Collegiate Dictionary*, (Springfield, Mass.: Miriam-Webster, Inc., 2003), s.v. "cause".

In the analogy of physical birth, therefore, two conditions are necessary for growing old, birth and eating, the former making the latter possible and the latter making old age possible. In other words, there is no difference between a result for which we are responsible and a condition or cause!

Now, a person who has been born physically might do a lot of things, like brush his hair, shave his beard, and brush his teeth. None of these things, however, are conditions for or causes of growing old, and none of them are necessary results of birth. However, any result of birth that is a *necessary condition for growing old and for which we are responsible* is in fact a second cause and condition, added to birth, for growing old.

Imagine, after reflecting on this illustration regarding birth, you say to a friend, "Eating is a cause of growing old." Steeped in Reformed ways of thinking, your friend replies, "No, that is not true. Eating is not a cause of growing old but a necessary result of birth." Your reaction would understandably be one of amazement. Eating is both a condition and a cause.

Therefore, when Grudem quotes Calvin saying, "It is therefore faith alone which justifies, yet the faith which justifies is not alone,"[39] he is really saying that works are a cause of salvation. Reformed writers often cite this famous quote.[40] However, the cleverness of the prose serves to conceal the fact that what they are saying is, in effect, works are a cause of final entrance into heaven.

Proverbial sayings like this have been passed on in theology textbooks for centuries. They seem to have explanatory power, and they certainly left opponents of the Reformed system speechless, but they are also confusing. If the works are a necessary result of faith, and if a person cannot be saved without them, then the works are in fact a condition for and a cause of salvation. Since both God and the believer have parts to play in the production of these works, the believer is partially responsible to save himself. If they are not present, he will

---

39 Grudem, *"Free Grace" Theology*, 29.

40 John Calvin, Acts of the Council of Trent, 3:152.

perish. Necessary results for which we are responsible are the same as conditions.

Are Works a Non-meritorious Condition?

Faced with the troubling implications of their view, many Reformed writers respond, "Yes, works are a condition of salvation but they are a non-meritorious condition."[41] For example, Reformed writer Ed Neufeld asserts, "If God can graciously enable saving faith, he can also graciously enable saving obedience."[42] "Saving obedience"!? What is this "saving obedience"? For that writer, saving obedience is an obedience "rising from that same dynamic of God's grace and merit-less human response."[43] In other words, it is meritless because God does it in the believer.

---

41 This formulation has a long history, going back to Calvin himself. Calvin says, "There is nothing to prevent the Lord from embracing works as inferior causes. But how so? In this way: Those whom in mercy He has destined for the inheritance of eternal life, He, in his ordinary administration, introduces to the possession of it by means of good works. What precedes in the order of administration is called the cause of what follows. For this reason, He sometimes makes eternal life a consequent of works; not because it is to be ascribed to them, but because those whom He has elected He justifies, that He may at length glorify (Romans 8:30); He makes the prior grace to be a kind of cause, because it is a kind of step to that which follows. But whenever the true cause is to be assigned, He enjoins us not to take refuge in works, but to keep our thoughts entirely fixed on the mercy of God." *John Calvin, Institutes of the Christian Religion*, trans. Henry Beveridge, reprint ed. (Grand Rapids, Mich.: Wm. B. Eerdmans Publishing Co., 1964), 3.14.21. So instead of calling works a meritorious cause, they simply re-label them and call them an inferior one! But regardless of what they call these works, they are still saying that works cause final entrance into heaven, which is, if words mean anything, another gospel.

42 Edmund K. Neufeld, "The Gospel in the Gospels: Answering the Question 'What must I do to be saved?' From the Synoptics," *JETS* 51, no. 2 (June 2008): 268.

43 Ibid.

Thomas Schreiner agrees, and, because of this, he believes that he has been misunderstood when critics say he teaches "works-righteousness." In both of his books[44] he attempts to clarify. A works-righteousness, he says, is characterized by two things: (1) it is a righteousness produced by human effort, and (2) it is meritorious. Such righteousness Schreiner strongly asserts cannot save. In agreement with other Reformed writers, he believes that works are a condition for salvation but not a meritorious cause of final entrance into heaven. This distinction between a condition and a cause seems obvious to these writers.[45] Some Reformed writers, like Grudem, say that a believer's works are a *condition* for salvation, but not a *cause* of it. As far as I can tell, Dr. Grudem never uses the term "condition," but he would say works are requirements as evidence for genuine faith, which amounts to the same thing. Historically, as far as I can determine, we owe this distinction to Ulrich Zwingli.[46]

But why are these works non-meritorious?

Reformed writer Harold Hoehner explains, "Although salvation is based on grace (unmerited favor), it might appear that rewards imply merit. But on the contrary, rewards from God are not payment for services but a gracious gift from a generous God. They are independent

---

44 Schreiner and Caneday, *The Race Set Before Us*. Schreiner, *Run to Win the Prize*.

45 Chuck Lowe puts it this way, "Romans 6–8, no less than 8:1–2, indicate that good works are a precondition for—albeit not the meritorious cause of—eschatological salvation." Chuck Lowe, "There Is No Condemnation (Rom. 8:1): But Why Not?," *JETS* 42, no. 2 (June 1999): 246.

46 Summarizing Zwingli's teaching on this point, Gonzalez says, "Human works are the result of God's predestination. In those who are elected, God produces good works, and therefore good works are necessary to salvation, not in the sense they produce it, but in the sense that election is also an election to good works." Justo L. González, *From the Protestant Reformation to the Twentieth Century*, rev. ed., vol. 3, A History of Christian Thought (Nashville: Abingdon Press, 1975), 76. Similarly, Samuel Logan says, "Very simply, all causes are conditions but not all conditions are causes. Evangelical obedience is thus fully a condition of justification, but clearly is not a cause of justification." Samuel T. Logan, "The Doctrine of Justification in the Theology of Jonathan Edwards," *WTJ* 46, no. 1 (Spring 1984).

of human achievement." To support this thesis, Hoehner argues this from the parable of the laborers in the vineyard (Matthew 20:1-16)[47] where those who had worked one hour received the same pay as those who worked the entire day. However, contra Hoehner, merit certainly was involved. They were paid equally, some were paid over generously, but all were "paid." Furthermore, the parable is about rankings in the kingdom, not equality of reward (Matthew 20:16). There are two other major points being made by the parable: (1) there is no contractual and legal relationship between works and rewards as the early laborers required (Matthew 20:2). Instead, like those hired later, we should trust God to do "whatever is right" (v. 4). Secondly, (2) the parable teaches that whatever we received, it is overgenerous wages (vv. 12-15).

The problem with Dr. Hohner's view that these works are not meritorious is that all the Greek words used for reward imply merit of some kind. For example, Jesus says, *"For you will be repaid at the resurrection of the righteous"* (Luke 14:14). The word for "repay" is *antapodidōmi* and means, "to pay something back to someone as the result of an incurred obligation."[48] God, it seems, has graciously agreed to obligate himself to pay us "wages."

Jesus repeatedly refers to the works of the regenerate man as meriting compensation by using another common term for "wage" (Gr. *misthos*) and applying it to the believer's reward in heaven.[49] Seven Greek words are translated "reward," and twenty-nine passages having theological significance in the New Testament use *misthos* or cognate Greek words.[50] The basic idea of this word group means payment for work done. For example, *"He who receives a prophet in the name of a prophet shall receive a prophet's reward [Gr. misthos]; and he who receives a righteous man in the name of a righteous man shall receive*

47 Harold W. Hoehner, New Dictionary of Biblical Theology, ed. T.D. Alexander and B. S. Rosner (Downers Grove, Ill.: Intervarsity Press, 2001) 568. Also Dillow, *Final Destiny*, 997-99.

48 Louw-Nida, 1:574. See Col. 3:24.

49 Matt. 5:12, 46; 20:28; Luke 6:23; 1 Cor. 3:14; 2 John 8.

50 Harold W. Hoehner, "Rewards," in *New Dictionary of Biblical Theology*, ed. T. D. Alexander and B. S. Rosner (Downers Grove, Ill.: InterVarsity Press, 2001).

a righteous man's reward" (Matthew 10:41). The righteous man's "reward" is a *misthos*, "remuneration for work done, *pay, wages.*"[51] It is in addition to heaven!

In Romans 4:4, Paul explicitly says that a "wage" is an obligation that is owed to the worker, "*Now to the one who works, his wage* [Gr. *misthos*] *is not reckoned as a favor, but as what is due* [Gr. *opheilēma*]" (Romans 4:4). An *opheilēma* ("what is due") is a "debt" or "obligation." Clearly then, God has agreed to place himself in debt to the faithful Christian when in other passages he calls the reward granted a *misthos*. God has obligated himself to reward work! This is easily explained by the Free Grace view of rewards.

Part of the Reformed concern is that if these works are meritorious, that means that God is in some way under obligation to reward us or to save us by works. That would mean that their doctrine of non-meritorious works as a condition for salvation is false. They reject any idea of God being obligated to man. According to them, that is a Roman Catholic error.[52] Yet this is precisely why rewards are gracious. The point is that God freely chose to enter into a relationship with the believer in which he would reward him for work done. God was under no obligation to enter into this relationship. That he chose to do so is an act of grace. If it be argued that this means "God becomes indebted to man,"[53] we agree, but he willingly and freely chose to become indebted and was in no way obligated to obligate himself. Consider, in this regard, the many promises God gives to believers by which he obligates himself to fulfill.

There is no work that can place God in obligation to grant us entrance to heaven as Romans 4:4 says. However, God has obligated himself to pay what is due *in regard to rewards*. Faith alone is for salvation, but faith plus works are required for rewards.

Paul also says that the inheritance of the believer is a reward (Colossians 3:24), calling it an *antapodosis*, which means "that which

---

51 *BDAG*, 653.

52 G. C. Berkouwer, *Faith and Perseverance* (Grand Rapids, Mich.: Wm. B. Eerdmans Publishing Co., 1958), 126.

53 Ibid.

is given to someone in exchange for what has been done, *repaying, reward.*"[54] The writer of the epistle to the Hebrews tells us that God is a "rewarder" of those who believe him (Hebrews 11:6). The Greek word *misthapodotēs* means "one who pays wages."[55]

All the Greek words for reward (*misthos, antapodidōmi, misthapodosia, stephanos, brabeion, antapodosis, misthapodotēs*) express the idea of something obtained by means of effort, remuneration for work done, wages, or payment. They are singularly inappropriate terms to describe a "condition" for final entrance into heaven, which comes apart from payment, wages, work done, or remuneration and is obtained *"without cost"* (Revelation 21:6; 22:17). It is therefore lexically implausible to say, as some Reformed writers do, that while believers are judged according to their works, their works have no "merits, but in that they are the effects of faith."[56] Certainly, they are the effect of abiding in the Vine but they are also the effect of the believer choosing to abide and to do the work. If works have any meaning at all, they are meritorious.

Dr. Grudem believes that greater reward will be granted to some than others,[57] that is, there are degrees of glory. This requires that he see some kind of merit in rewards; there is something the believer can do to obtain more reward. However, in his books he seems unaware of the problem this causes for his view of salvation because he never discusses the issue. If they are meritorious, and if God AND man co-operate to produce the work necessary to obtain the reward (which Grudem believes[58]), then Grudem is teaching a salvation based in part upon good works, that is, on merit. Why? Because he teaches that these same works are necessary for entrance into heaven.

Free Grace writers have a plausible explanation for all these passages about merited works. Those passages refer to rewards, which are merited, and have nothing to do with entrance into heaven. Salvation

---

54 *BDAG*, 87.

55 *BDAG*, 653.

56 William G. T. Shedd and Alan W. Gomes, *Dogmatic Theology*, 3 vols. in 1 ed. (Phillipsburg, N.J.: Presbyterian and Reformed Publishing Co., 2003), 802.

57 Grudem, *Systematic Theology*, 757, 1141.

58 Ibid., 753.

is by faith alone apart from works of repentance on the front-end or a life of works on the back-end. Works, however, are for reward and relate to our accountability at the Judgment Seat of Christ. Paul says,

> For we must all appear before the Judgment Seat of Christ, that each one may be recompensed for his deeds in the body, according to what he has done, whether good or bad. Therefore, knowing the fear of the Lord, we persuade men, but we are made manifest to God; and I hope that we are made manifest also in your consciences." (2 Corinthians 5:10–11 NASB)

Summary

Alan Stanley has written a book entitled, *Did Jesus Teach Salvation by Works*.[59] He argues extensively that the answer is, "Yes." As a follow-up, he wrote a simplified version, *Salvation Is More Complicated Than You Think*.[60]

While Dr. Grudem would not go as far as Stanley, nevertheless he front-loads the gospel with repentance from sin and back-loads the gospel with many requirements of good works following.[61]

Imagine the following dialogue as an advocate of this viewpoint shares the gospel with an unbeliever, whom we will call Bill.

Counselor: Bill, I would like to share with you the wonderful good news of God's free offer of eternal life that comes "without cost."[62]

Bill: How can I obtain this free gift without cost? Please explain the gospel to me? How can I become a Christian?

---

59 Alan P. Stanley, *Did Jesus Teach Salvation by Works? The Role of Works in Salvation in the Synoptic Gospels* (Eugene, Ore.: Pickwick Publishers, 2006).

60 Alan P. Stanley, *Salvation Is More Complicated Than You Think* (Colorado Springs: Paternoster, 2007).

61 Grudem, *"Free Grace" Theology*, 34.

62 Revelation 21:6; 22:17

Counselor: You must believe on the Lord Jesus Christ, and if your believing is sincere you will be saved.

Bill: How will I know if I am sincere enough?

Counselor: You will progress to a point where you possess surpassing righteousness, and then you will be eligible to enter the kingdom.[63]

Bill: What does that involve?

Counselor: Well, you must never depart from fellowship with other Christians,[64] you must never wander from the faith,[65] you must grieve about your sins and turn from all of them,[66] you must persevere in good works to the end of life,[67] you must not stop going to church,[68] you must run the race with dogged determination to obtain the prize of eternal life (and it takes remarkable discipline and training to make it to the end[69]); you will need to obey all the commands,[70] sell your wealth and give it to the poor,[71] always forgive others,[72] be a peacemaker,[73] completely deny yourself to the point of possible martyrdom,[74] do the

---

63 Stanley, *Did Jesus Teach Salvation by Works*: 175.

64 1 John 2:19. Grudem, *"Free Grace" Theology*, 92, 135.

65 Hebrews 3:12. Ibid.

66 Quoting the Westminster Confession with approval. Ibid., 48.

67 Hebrews 3:14. Ibid., 89. Grudem, *Systematic Theology*, 788-89.

68 Grudem, *"Free Grace" Theology*, 78.

69 Schreiner and Caneday, *The Race Set Before Us*, 314.

70 Matthew 19:17; 1 John 2:4-6. Grudem, *Systematic Theology*, 804-05.

71 Matthew 19:21

72 Matthew 6:15

73 Matthew 5:9

74 Matthew 16:24-26

will of God and obey everything the Bible teaches,[75] develop a personal character that surpasses the highest known standards of character in Jesus's day;[76] you must continually examine your life to see if you have enough good works to verify that you are truly saved,[77] always struggle against lust,[78] never develop anger as a pattern of life;[79] you must keep adding good character traits to your life in order to verify that you are truly saved,[80] do acts of kindness toward others,[81] strive to be perfect,[82] abandon everything to follow Christ,[83] and a few other things.

Bill: Do I have to make a commitment to do all these things in order for my faith to be genuine?

Counselor: That seems to be what Jesus is teaching. You must commit to live out the principles of the Sermon on the Mount.

Bill: I thought you said salvation is by faith alone, is a gift, and is offered to me without cost.

Counselor: Well, Bill . . . salvation is more complicated than you think.

All of the requirements above would be the kinds of things that, according to Dr. Stanley ought to be characteristic of true believers.

---

75 Matthew 7:21; 1 John 2:3-6. See Grudem, *"Free Grace" Theology*, 81.

76 Matthew 5:20

77 2 Corinthians 13:5. Grudem, *"Free Grace" Theology*, 131.

78 Matthew 5:28-29

79 Matthew 5:21-22

80 2 Peter 1:10. Grudem, *Systematic Theology*, 806.

81 Matthew 25:31-46

82 Matthew 5:48; 19:21

83 Matthew 19:21

Dr. Grudem also agrees with many of these requirements, although he only requires that these things be evident to "some degree."[84]

In this chapter, we have demonstrated that, even though they deny it, Reformed writers are in fact teaching a salvation by works. Their argument that these works are produced by God in the believer and are therefore non-meritorious is not convincing. Furthermore, Scripture specifically says these works are meritorious.

"Perseverance," Schreiner and Caneday say, "is a necessary means that God has appointed for attaining final salvation."[85] With this, they fall into the cross hairs of the cannon fire that Calvin launched at the Council of Trent: "According to them [i.e., the Council], man is justified by faith as well as by work, provided these are not his own works, but gifts of Christ and fruits of regeneration."[86] We are partially responsible for these works, as Grudem maintains. Therefore we can conclude that,

> A necessary result **for which we are responsible** and which must be present for another result to occur is no different from an additional condition and cause for the achievement of that second result.

If, on the other hand, perseverance in works is not necessary for entrance into heaven and is not included within the compass of the word "faith," then the gospel of pure and free grace has been maintained.

---

84 Grudem, *Systematic Theology*, 843. Grudem, *"Free Grace" Theology*, 92.

85 Schreiner and Caneday, *The Race Set Before Us*, 152.

86 Calvin, *Institutes*, 3.11.14..

Chapter 6

Can That Faith Save Him?

Joseph Dillow, Th.D.

When James said, "*Faith without works is dead*" (James 2:20), and "*A man is justified by works, and not by faith alone*" (James 2:24), he no doubt was completely unaware of the volumes which would be written in the history of the church that would attempt to harmonize his words with those of the apostle Paul. This verse led Luther to conclude that James wrote "an epistle of straw."[1] James would also be surprised to learn that many would misconstrue his words to mean that those who have "true saving" faith will necessarily evidence this by a life of works and that, if they lack works, this proves their faith is not genuine, that is, not "saving" faith.

The apparent contradiction between James and Paul can be seen as follows:

---

1 Martin Luther, "Preface to the New Testament," in *Word and Sacrament*, ed. Theodor Bachman (Philadelphia: Fortress Press, 1960), 35:362.

Paul: "For we maintain that a man is justified by faith apart from works of the Law." (Romans 3:28)

James: "You see that a man is justified by works and not by faith alone." (James 2:24)

One can readily see the problem. By focusing on five key words: salvation, faith, justification, and "dead faith," different writers have suggested alternative solutions by proposing that Paul and James were defining or using these terms in different ways.

Calvin famously explained this contradiction by saying, "It is therefore faith alone which justifies, and the faith which justifies is not alone."[2] In the pages to follow, we will propose what we think is a better alternative.

Can *that* faith save him? Apparently, it cannot, because the question in Greek expects a negative answer. We must ask three questions. To whom is James writing, true believers or a mixture of saved and unsaved people? What is *that* faith? And, salvation from what?

Who is James's Intended Audience?

Wayne Grudem believes that James's epistle was addressed to a mixed group. To establish his thesis, he quotes James 2:14.

What use is it, my brethren, if **someone** says he has faith but he has no works? **Can that faith save him?** (ESV)

Grudem thinks that the use of "someone" (Gr. *su*) in the ESV, proves that a mixed group is the intended audience for James's epistle! He says that "James clearly signifies that he is not talking about all his readers or even most of his readers but rather 'someone' with whom they are in contact."[3] That is bare assertion with no evidence. Why doesn't he assume it means "someone" who is a born-again believer in the church?" Grudem assumes more than the indefinite pronoun can bear. The reader can just as equally assume that James's intended

---

2   John Calvin, *Acts of the Council of Trent: with the Antidote*, 6th Session, can. 11.

3   Grudem, *"Free Grace" Theology*, 133.

meaning is "someone *among you*." In fact, the context supports this view. In the following two verses, James gives an illustrative example of his question in v. 14.

If a brother or sister is poorly clothed and lacking in daily food, and one of you says to them 'Go in peace, be warmed and filled,' without giving them the things needed for the body, what good is that? (James 2:15-16 ESV)

It is not at all "clear" that a mixed group is James's intended audience, as the rest of the epistle makes plain. For example,

My brothers, show no partiality as you hold the faith in our Lord Jesus Christ, the Lord of glory. (James 2:1 ESV)

He is addressing "brothers" who "hold the faith in our Lord Jesus Christ." How can James make this clearer? He regularly addresses his readers as "brothers" (e.g. 2:5; 3:1; 4:11; 5:7, 10, 12, 19).

With it [the tongue] **we** bless our Lord and Father, and with it we curse people who are made in the likeness of God. From the same mouth come blessing and cursing. My **brothers**, these things ought not to be so. (James 3:9–10 ESV)

Notice how James includes himself as one of the brothers by using the first person plural pronoun "we". "We" refers to regenerate saints. James makes it plain that his readers are born again when he says:

Of his own will he brought us forth by the word of truth, that we should be a kind of first fruits of his creatures. (James 1:18 ESV)

He brought "us" forth, including James himself (v. 18). "Us" is not a vague term referring to believers and unbelievers because, by using that word, he is including himself and therefore likely refers to eternal life.

What Kind of Faith Is in View?

James says,

What good is it, my brothers, if someone says he has faith but does not have works? Can **that** faith save him? (James 2:14)

By inserting the word "that" in front of "faith," the translators are saying that there are different kinds of faith, true faith that would save him and "that" faith which does not. We agree that there *are* two kinds of faith in the Bible, but not as Reformed writers imagine. In their view, there is a faith that saves a person from final damnation and a false faith that does not. The way one identifies this false faith, in their view, is that it does not result in a life of works.

However, the text says nothing about faith that saves from eternal damnation versus a faith that does not. Rather, the focus in James is between a regenerate person who has a faith that works and produces blessings for himself and others in the church and a regenerate person who says he has a *walk of faith* but gives no evidence of it in his life. In other words, the contrast is between what Paul called a *living* faith (Galatians 2:20) and what James called a "useless" faith (James 2:20) or "dead" faith (2:17).

Faith in the book of James does not refer to the initial act of faith through which one is saved from damnation. It refers to *the ongoing walk of faith* that can save one from the pathway to "death" (James 1:15). "Death," however, is the progression to psychological, and spiritual ruin, or, possibly, the sin unto physical death resulting in a negative assessment of one's life at the Judgment Seat of Christ (2 Corinthians 5:20).

The Bible often speaks of faith as a walk of faith in distinction from faith as the initial event that procures salvation. Paul tells us to "walk by faith" (Galatians 5:25) and that our faith can grow (2 Corinthians 10:15). He speaks of faith "working through love" (Galatians 5:6) and says the righteous man "shall live by faith" (Galatians 3:11).

Scores of passages could be cited.[4] Indeed, the entire eleventh chapter of Hebrews is devoted to the life of faith, rather than faith that secures our initial justification.

We note that "[b]y faith" Enoch "pleased God" (Hebrews 11:5) and "walked with God . . . [for] 300 years" (Genesis 5:22). Likewise, "[b]y

---

4   See Romans 11:20; 14:1, 22, 23; 1 Corinthians 10:15; 2 Corinthians 5:7; Galatians 5:25; Ephesians 3:17; Philippians 1:25; 1 Thessalonians 5:2, 5, 7; 2 Thessalonians 1:3, 11; 1 Timothy 1:4-5, 19; 6:10, 12 (wandered away from true devotion to Christ); Philemon 6; Hebrews 6:12; 10:38.

faith Noah . . . built an ark," etc. (Hebrews 11:7) and others "through faith conquered kingdoms, performed acts of righteousness, obtained promises, shut the mouths of lions" (Hebrews 11:33).

All these achievements were obtained by the ongoing walk of faith (i.e., "*by faith*") and not the initial act whereby they were saved from damnation. Their faith was not "useless" or "dead," to use James's words, but was useful and alive and was "true piety, genuine devotion."[5]

But what does James refer to when he speaks of "faith"? Is the initial act in view, or is his subject the ongoing life of trust, the walk of faith? The question is important because if "that faith" in 2:14 is initial saving faith, then "save" must be deliverance from eternal damnation. If, on the other hand, faith means a walk of faith, salvation in 2:14 cannot mean initial justification, which occurs by a point-in-time faith and apart from works (Ephesians 2:8-9).

Usage in the epistle indicates that faith for James is the walk of faith. James uses the word "faith" fifteen times.[6] In the first instance (1:2-4) it is used of a faith related to testing and enduring trials; initial faith is not in view. Instead, the faith that endures testing is the subject.[7] Next, James writes of a faith that is to be exercised during a trial in which a believer asks for wisdom. One "must ask in faith without any doubting" (1:6). Once again, ongoing faith, that is, trusting God in one's daily walk, is the subject, not trusting Christ for deliverance from eternal damnation.

Next, in 2:1, James speaks of holding one's faith in Christ with an attitude of impartiality. Obviously, the continuing exercise of faith, "holding" it, is in view and not initial inception. James speaks of the poor who are "rich in faith and heirs of the kingdom" (2:5). To be "rich in faith" is not a reference to the initial act of faith that procures salvation from damnation; instead, as Dibelius says, it refers to being

---

5   *BDAG*, 819.

6   For example, see James 1:3, 6; 2:1, 5, 14 (2x), 17, 18 (3x), 20, 22, 24, 26; 5:15.

7   Craig Blomberg believes that faith in James is "full orbed trust in Christ" for salvation but seems to contradict himself when he says that the asking in faith in James 1:5 is a continuing thing. Craig L. Blomberg and Miriam J. Kimmel, *James*, Vol 16: Zondervan Exegetical Commentary of the New Testament (Grand Rapids, Mich.: Zondervan 2008), 129, 51.

"rich in the sphere of faith,"[8] the ongoing experience of their walk with God. The prayer "offered in faith" is not a prayer of the initial act of saving faith, but a prayer that emerges from a life of faith and genuine piety (James 5:15).[9]

If the above analysis of faith in James is correct, this will have significant impact on how statements like "faith without works is dead" or "can that faith save him?" are interpreted.

Grudem says, "These verses pose a significant challenge to the Free Grace position, because they seem to be saying that genuine faith will always result in good works."[10] However, this section poses no challenge at all to the Free Grace view. In agreement with Grudem, we do believe that the faith of which *James* speaks will always and inevitably result in some good works. Our disagreement is not with James, it is with Grudem. James is not speaking of initial saving faith, as Grudem believes, his epistle addresses the walk of faith, which will always produce fruit.[11] Thus, when Grudem says, "The paragraph

---

8 Martin Dibelius and Heinrich Greeven, *James: A Commentary on the Epistle of James*, 11th rev. ed., Hermeneia (Philadelphia: Fortress Press, 1975), 124.

9 In order to maintain his idea that faith means faith for initial salvation in James 2:14, Joseph Pak gratuitously argues, "In this passage faith means acceptance of revelation without corresponding behavior." He offers no proof beyond mere assertion, an assertion necessary to maintain his interpretation of James, which says that faith apart from works is not genuine. Joseph K. Pak, "A Study of Selected Passages on Distinguishing Marks of Genuine and False Believers" (PhD diss., Dallas Theological Seminary, 2001), 250.

10 Grudem, *"Free Grace" Theology*, 132.

11 Furthermore, Free Grace theology also teaches that *initial saving faith* will *always* produce works. John F. Hart, "The Faith of Demons," *JOTGES* 8, no. 2 (1995): 40. Zane Hodges agrees, "We must add that there is no need to quarrel with the Reformers' view that where there is justifying faith, works will undoubtedly exist too. This is a reasonable assumption for any Christian unless he has been converted on his deathbed! But it is quite wrong to claim that a life of dedicated obedience is guaranteed by regeneration, or even that such works as there are must be visible to a human observer." Zane C. Hodges, *Absolutely Free! A Biblical Reply to Lordship Salvation* (Dallas: Redención Viva, 1989), 215.

clearly implies that faith that 'does not have works, cannot save,'[12] we are in complete agreement! A *walk of faith* that does not have works cannot save a believer from the downward spiral of temptation, lust, sin, and death (1:14-5; 5:20), that is, spiritual ruin.

Now let us consider the third question regarding the context of James 2:14.

Salvation from What?

James asks, "*Can that faith save him?*" The question in Greek requires a negative answer, "No, it cannot." As argued above, a so-called "walk of faith" that does not manifest itself in deeds of charity and a life of obedience is not a walk of faith at all; it is an illusion. Such a Christian may claim he is living the Christian life, but he is not, and he is warned that his version of a walking faith cannot save. As James puts it, "*He deceives himself*" (James 1:26).

We ask, "Save from what?" There is extremely strong resistance to the idea that salvation can refer to anything other than deliverance from post-mortem condemnation to the lake of fire.[13] For example,

---

12 Grudem, "*Free Grace*" *Theology*, 133.

13 For example, Joseph Pak disagrees and asserts that "salvation" in the New Testament predominantly denotes deliverance from condemnation in hell. He makes this unfounded assertion with poor supporting evidence. Pak, "A Study of Selected Passages," 244. He cites only three other passages that do not necessarily refer to salvation from damnation (Matthew 10:28; John 12:25; 1 Peter 1:9). Pak sees the phrase about keeping one's soul for eternal life as something the believer does by means of hating the world (John 12:25). This is a novel way of guaranteeing one's arrival in heaven. It is better to understand keeping for eternal life as persevering and enhancing one's intimacy with God now and on into heaven when we die. Only by faithfulness can that intimacy be "kept" and thus experienced abundantly in heaven. As Billy Graham puts it, "Everyone's cup will be full, but the cups will be different sizes." Jesus referred to this "keeping" elsewhere as laying up treasures for ourselves in heaven. Pak understands 1 Peter 1:9, "obtaining the goal of your faith – the salvation of your souls," as a reference to final entrance into heaven. However, "obtaining" (Gr. *kōmizō*) refers to receiving something as a recompense (*BDAG*, 557, option 3) "to receive a recompense" and the salvation in view is

Thomas Schreiner writes, "The lengths to which advocates of this view [Free Grace] will go to preserve their theology are remarkable and. . . . [To take 'save' to refer to a deliverance from a temporal danger or physical death] is an astonishing move since salvation and justification are typically associated in the New Testament with entering heaven."[14]

However, this is not astonishing at all. It should be noted that the word *sōzō* rarely, if ever, means to save from damnation in the Old Testament. Also, in my own analysis of the 106 uses of the verb *sōzō* in the New Testament, I concluded that deliverance from damnation is the meaning only 27 times, that is 25% of the total.[15] I will grant that on 21 occasions (20%), the way I interpreted certain passages would be debated by Reformed writers.[16] I would see deliverance from some temporal trial or difficulty leading to reward at the Judgment Seat of Christ in many of those passages, whereas most Reformed writers would say that all 21 refer to salvation into eternal life.

That said, granting the Reformed the benefit of the doubt and assuming that their interpretations of all 21 of the debatable passages are correct and mine are wrong, that means there are 48 instances in the New Testament where *sōzō* refers to eternal salvation (45%). Therefore, at least 55% (58 times) of the usages of *sōzō* refer to deliverance from a temporal difficulty such as death, disease, or a meaningless life.[17]

On the other hand, assuming that Grudem is *incorrect* in his view of *some* of the 21 instances that debatably refer to eternal salvation, and the Free Grace view is correct, that means some of the passages

---

being experienced now resulting in reward at the Judgment Seat of Christ. It is a deliverance from the struggles his readers fight against in the present and has sanctification and reward as its focus.

14 Thomas R. Schreiner, "Perseverance and Assurance," *SBTJ* 2, no. 1 (1998): 45.

15 Luke 8:12; 19:10; John 5:34; 10:9; 12:47; Acts 4:12; 15:1, 11; 16:30, 31; Romans 5:9, 10; 8:24; 11:14; 1 Corinthians 1:21; 7:16; 10:33; Ephesians 2:5, 8; 1 Thessalonians 2:16; 2 Thessalonians 2:10; 1 Timothy 1:15; 2:4; 2 Timothy 1:9; Titus 3:5; 1 Pet. 4:18; Jude 23 = 27 times.

16 Matthew 1:21; 10:22; 16:25; Mark 10:26; Luke 13:23; 18:26; Acts 2:21; Romans 5:9; Romans 9:27; 10:9, 13; 11:26; 1 Corinthians 5:5; 15:2; Hebrews 7:25; James 1:21; 2:14; 4:12, 20; 1 Peter 1:9; Hebrews 10:39 = 21 times.

17 See Dillow, *Final Destiny*, 149 ff., esp. 51.

which he claims refer to rescue from eternal damnation do include a reference to temporal danger in the context. While I realize that there are limitations in how much one can cover in a book, shouldn't he first show why the Free Grace interpretations of some of these 21 passages are incorrect? Possibly, he is unaware of the numerous Free Grace books that address his misunderstandings of many of those 21 passages.[18]

However, statistics prove little (including mine); context determines word meanings. Therefore, the interpreter should consider the broader context of the pericope to see if that understanding coheres well with the details of the passage. Instead, Grudem assumes without any proof that all such examples lacking a specific reference to some local difficulty can *only* be explained by assuming that salvation to eternal life is the focus. Is it not possible that the biblical writer might have other legitimate reasons for omitting the specific mention of a temporal situation? "Free Grace" interpreters believe that in many of the examples that Grudem would cite, the broader context *does* imply a temporal crisis and in some cases, requires it. Perhaps the biblical writer *did not think it was necessary* to make a specific reference because he believed he had made it clear from the broader context that a rescue from a temporal, not eternal damnation, was his intended meaning.

Grudem's claim that "that whenever the word *sōzō* is used in the New Testament, it always refers to eternal salvation except where the context specifies that rescue is from some physical danger or sickness,"[19] is false.[20]

---

18 However, even though he apparently has not read them, he dismisses whatever they *will say* if he does read them as interpretations that would not occur to the "ordinary" Bible reader. Grudem says, "I am aware that for every New Testament passage I quote, Free Grace literature will have some alternative interpretation, usually an interpretation that would not occur to ordinary readers of the Bible." Grudem, *"Free Grace" Theology*, 80, fn. 1.

19 Ibid., 133-34.

20 As will be argued below, even the context of James 1:21 indicates salvation from temporal dangers (vv. 13-15; temptation, sin, lust, and death). If so, then on Grudem's premises, the salvation of the soul cannot refer to eternal life as he believes.

We disagree for four reasons.

First, even if that is true (and we believe it is not), the larger point is that "save" in the New Testament normally means salvation from some temporal, not eternal danger (78% of the time), such as rescue from a storm (Matthew 8:25), disease (9:21), or drowning (14:30). That at least opens the possibility that it may mean rescue from a temporal danger in James 2:14.[21]

Secondly, it is a gratuitous claim. One can equally say that unless the context indicates eternal salvation is in view, it normally means salvation from some temporal danger. There is no unambiguous indication of eternal salvation in the context of any of the 21 debatable passages. Therefore, in James, *sōzō may* normally mean salvation from some temporal danger and not an eternal one.

Thirdly, an exegete's normal approach should assume that there are two possibilities, not one: salvation from a temporal situation or salvation to eternal life. And in view of the fact that, as shown above, sōzō is predominantly used of deliverance from a temporal situation, Grudem should initially assume that the biblical writer may have salvation/rescue from a temporal situation in mind. He does not.

And finally, Grudem's claim is inaccurate. For example, according to 1 Timothy 2:15, "a woman will be saved [sōzō] through the bearing of children. Or, consider 4:16, where Timothy, a saved man, can "save himself." Yet there is no mention of physical danger or sickness in either of the texts. Does Grudem believe that eternal salvation is in view in these passages? Does he believe a woman must have children to escape damnation,[22] or that Timothy could save himself by being an example, using his gift, and maintaining correct doctrine? We doubt it.

---

21 For an extensive study of *sōzō* see Fred Lybrand, *Back to Faith: Reclaiming Gospel Clarity in an Age of Incongruence* (Lakewood, Fla.: Xulon Press, 2009).

22 Some Reformed writers actually believe this. For them "through childbirth" means through "the childbirth of Christ." See Ronald Y. K. Fung, "Ministry in the New Testament," in *The Church in the Bible and the World*, ed. D.A. Carson (World Evangelical Fellowship, 1987), 203; W. D. Mounce, *Pastorals*, Word Biblical Commentary (Grand Rapids, Mich.: Wm. B. Eerdmans Publishing Co., 2002), 145. Earle's interpretation is possible but seems a bit of a stretch.

In another example, Free Grace interpreters do not accept Grudem's interpretation of Matthew 10:22, "*the one who has endured to the end will be saved.*" Grudem understands this to mean that only those who persevere to the end of life will obtain *eternal* salvation. In other words, perseverance in good works and faith to the end of life is the required evidence to verify the presence of saving faith. However, since Grudem admits that Jesus is "warning people not to fall away in times of persecution,"[23] he should conclude that salvation to eternal life cannot be in view. In so doing, however, he would violate his own hermeneutical principle. Free Grace interpreters citing Solomon, Saul and many others,[24] argue that, biblically, there are saved people who have not persevered to the end and yet they will be saved to eternal life.

This phrase, "But the one who endures to the end, he will be saved," is also used in Matthew 24:13, and probably refers to a promise of physical salvation from the trials of the tribulation leading to entrance into and population of the Millennium. A few verses later Jesus says, "Unless those days had been cut short, no life would have been *saved*; but for the sake of the elect those days will be cut short" (24:22), which seems to define the salvation in 24:13 as the saving of one's physical life from the horrors of the tribulation era. Furthermore, the two preceding uses of the "end" in vv. 3 and 6 and the following v. 14, define "the end" as the end of the tribulation or end of the age

---

He says the salvation is from the evils of the time by means of motherhood. Also, see Ralph Earle, *1 Timothy*, ed. Frank E. Gabelein, The Expositer's Bible Commentary: Ephesians through Philemon (Grand Rapids, Mich.: Zondervan, 1981), 362. Better is the view of Litfin who says that to be saved is to be "preserved (from insignificance) by means of her role in the family." A. Duane Litfin, "1 Timothy," in *BKC New Testament*, ed. John F. Walvoord and Roy B. Zuck (Colorado Springs: Cook, 1985), 2:726. For a comprehensive study of this passage see Andraes Koestonberger, "Ascertaining Women's God-Ordained Roles: An Interpretation of 1 Timothy 2:15 " Bulliten for Biblicla Research 7 (1997).

23 Grudem, *Systematic Theology*, 793.

24 See chapter 10 in this book on The Possibility of Failure in the Christian Life.

and define salvation in a physical sense (vv. 9-13).[25] Therefore, it is likely that Jesus refers to the end of the age and not the end of life as Grudem believes.

Since all agree that *sōzō* has the basic meaning of "to rescue" from some danger we can then translate, "*the one who has endured to the end will be rescued*" from the trials of the tribulation at the end of the age. We agree with Walvoord that deliverance from persecution or possible martyrdom[26] is in view. Jesus says that "unless those days had been cut short, no life would be saved; but for the sake of the elect those days will be cut short" (Matthew 24:22). Perhaps, this cutting-short is one of the means by which those who have persevered will be saved.

In another passage that contradicts Grudem's hermeneutics, Peter says that baptism "saves" us.

"Corresponding to that, baptism now saves you—not the removal of dirt from the flesh, but an appeal to God for a good conscience—through the resurrection of Jesus Christ," (1 Peter 3:21, NASB95)

Since there is no mention of any temporal situation from which the believer needs to be rescued, based on Grudem's hermeneutical principle, he should believe that baptism saves us from eternal damnation. Which, of course, he does not.

In conclusion, we can say that Grudem's claim "that whenever the word *sōzō* is used in the New Testament, it always refers to eternal salvation except where the context specifies that rescue is from some physical danger or sickness,"[27] is false. Even the context of James 1:21 indicates salvation from temporal dangers: temptation, sin, lust, and

---

25 It seems that we owe the current spiritual understanding of these verses to Augustine. See David R. Anderson, "The Soteriological Impact of Augustine's Change from Premillennialism to Ammillenalism: Part One " *Journal of the Grace Evangelical Society* 15, no. 28 (Spring 2002): 25-36. Also see David R. Anderson, *Free Grace Soteriology* (Lakeland, Fla.: Xulon Press, 2010).

26 John F. Walvoord, "Christ's Olivet Discourse on the Time of the End," *Bibliotheca Sacra* 128, no. 511 (1971): 206-14.

27 Grudem, *"Free Grace" Theology*, 133-34.

death (vv.13-15). As demonstrated above, there are many uses of *sōzō* in contexts where eternal salvation is clearly not in view, even though there is no mention of physical danger or sickness.

Salvation of the Soul from "Death" (James 1:21)

James speaks of salvation five times in his epistle. A study of the four instances of sōzō outside of James 2:14 shows that none of them refer to salvation from damnation.

The first mention of "to save" (Gr. *sōzō*) in James is used of the *salvation of the soul.*

> Therefore, putting aside all filthiness and all that remains of wickedness, in humility receive the word implanted, which is able to **save your souls.** (James 1:21)

While the phrase "save your souls" is often understood as a reference to salvation from eternal damnation,[28] the author has been unable to find convincing biblical evidence that supports this. The immediate context suggests that this salvation is salvation from the downward spiral of temptation, lust, sin, and death.

> Let no one say when he is tempted, "I am being tempted by God," for God cannot be tempted with evil, and he himself tempts no one. But each person is tempted when he is lured and enticed by his own desire. Then desire when it has conceived gives birth to sin, and sin when it is fully grown **brings forth death.** (James 1:13–15 ESV)

---

28 For example, Robert Johnstone, *The Epistle of James*, reprint ed. (Minneapolis, Minn.: Klock and Klock Christian Publishers, 1871, 1978), 140. Dibelius and Greeven state that this is "an expression which here quite clearly must be understood eschatologically." Dibelius and Greeven, *James: A Commentary on the Epistle of James*, 113. Later, James uses the term in a way that does include an eschatological dimension. However, I believe that the reference is to the Judgment Seat of Christ, and not, as Dibelius suggests, to judgment in heaven or eternal damnation. This will be discussed below.

There are two interpretive issues here. What does "save your souls" mean—salvation from some temporal concern or salvation in the sense of eternal life? Secondly, what does "death" mean—final damnation or temporal spiritual and psychological ruin in a believer's walk with God?

Salvation of the Soul. Several factors indicate "salvation of the soul" refers to salvation from some catastrophe in the life of a believer and not salvation to eternal life.

First, it is important to note that, in every instance in the Old Testament, to "save a soul" and related expressions refer to being saved from some temporal danger (usually physical death) and not an eternal one.[29] That ought to be the starting point for understanding the phrase in the New Testament.

Secondly, this salvation appears to be salvation from the death spiral of temptation, lust, sin, and finally death (1:13-15), not damnation. Like 1 Timothy 4:16, this passage refers to the salvation of the saved. James says, God "brought us forth by the word of truth," a reference to regeneration, and one in whom the word has been implanted (James 1:18).

---

29 This phrase or similar ones are found 14 times in the LXX (Genesis 19:17, 20; 32:30; Judges 12:3; Psalm 3:3; 6:5; 34:3; 42:11; 68:2; 73:13; 85:2; Job 33:28; Amos 2:14, 16). In each case, the phrase suggests the notion of preserving one's physical life. In Genesis 19:17, the LXX translates "escape for your life" with *sōze tēn seautou psychēn* (lit. "save your soul"); and in Genesis 32:30, Jacob, after his struggle with the Angel of the Lord, exclaims, "My life (LXX Gr. *psyche*, "soul", Heb *nepeš*) has been *preserved* (i.e., "saved," Gr. *sōzō*, Heb *nāṣal*)." In one passage, it refers to delivering the needy from social injustice (Psalm 72:13) by preserving their lives. Even the warrior, declares Amos, will "not save his life" in the coming invasion (Amos 2:14, 16). In Psalm 42:11 (LXX 41:12), David's soul ("life," Gr. *psychē*), is in despair so he turns to God for "help of my countenance," which in the LXX is "salvation (Gr. *sōtēria*) of my countenance." In 1 Samuel 19:5 (LXX 1 Kings 19:5), David took his life (Gr. *psychē*) in his hand and killed Goliath, and this resulted in salvation (Gr. *sōtēria*) of all Israel, including, of course, David. Salvation from enemies is the meaning. Similarly, in Psalm 3:2, David once again finds many enemies, saying that God will not save (LXX Gr. *sōzō*) him. In Psalm 35:3, he asks the Lord to save his soul (LXX Gr. *psychē*), and God responds, "I am your salvation (Gr. *sōtēria*)." He wants deliverance from those who are his enemies and who fight against him (v. 2).

We know this is addressed to Christians,[30] because James includes himself (*he brought us forth*). This death is probably the experience of spiritual and psychological ruin, and possibly, like James 5:20, could refer to the sin unto death.[31]

The danger is likely directed to *the believer* who is approaching this death spiral sequence and whose "faith walk" is being tested by trials (James 1:3-4).

Since this salvation of the soul is ultimately salvation from death, and is the salvation of the Christian, we can rule out the interpretation that salvation of our souls refers to rescue from the lake of fire.

Third, James's half-brother (the Lord Jesus Christ), used the same phrase. In Matthew 16:24-27, Jesus says, "*For whoever wishes to save his life* ["*save his soul*"] *will lose it.*" To save one's soul in Matthew 16:24-27 and 10:38-39 refers to saving one's physical life from the possibility of martyrdom. This is the view accepted by most commentators.[32] According to Jesus, to save our soul means to find a rich life now instead of denying ourselves, taking up our cross and following Christ, even to

---

30 James refers to his readers as "brothers" (1:2) who have been "brought forth by the word of truth" (1:18) and who already have faith to hold on to (2:1) (see also 1:16, 19; 2:5, 14; 3:1, 10, 12; 5:12, 19). I have argued elsewhere that "death" is spiritual death but in the sense of the spiritual ineffectiveness of the Christian, and not a reference to eternal damnation. See Dillow, *Final Destiny*, 380, 418, 708, 13.

31 The sin unto death is mentioned in several passages (see Acts 5:1-5; 1 Corinthians 11:29-30; 1 John 5:16-17).

32 David L. Turner, *Matthew*, Baker Exegetical Commentary on the New Testament (Grand Rapids, Mich.: Baker Academic, 2008), 412. Donald A. Hagner, *Matthew 14-28*, Word Biblical Commentary (Dallas: Word Books, 2002), 484. R. T. France, "Matthew," in *The New Bible Commentary*, ed. D. A. Carson, *21st Century* (Downers Grove, Ill.: InterVarsity Press, 1994), 638. John Peter Lange, "The Gospel of Matthew," in *Commentary on the Holy Scriptures, Critial, Doctrinal, and Hommelitical*, ed. John Peter Lange (Grand Rapids, Mich.: Zondervan Publishing House, 1960), 303. William Hendriksen and Simon Kistemaker, *Exposition of the Gospel According to Matthew* (Grand Rapids, Mich.: Baker Book House, 2001), 657. Barclay Moon Newman and Eugene Albert Nida, *A translator's handbook on Paul's Letter to the Romans* (Stuttgart: United Bible Societies, 1973), 530.

the point of martyrdom, so that we will be favorably recompensed at the Judgment Seat of Christ.[33]

If James's Master understood the phrase "salvation of your souls" to refer to salvation of one's physical life, should we not assume that James understood it in the same way? Therefore, based on Grudem's own hermeneutics,[34] even though many agree with him,[35] salvation in 1:21 and 2:14 cannot refer to salvation from damnation, yet Grudem believes that it does.[36]

Salvation from death. James has told us that *"sin when it is fully grown brings forth death"* (James 1:15). But what kind of death does he have in mind—temporal ruin or eternal death?

First, if "death" refers to damnation, as Grudem believes, James is giving us a novel way of obtaining eternal life, by *"putting aside all filthiness and all the remains of wickedness"* (James 1:21). This would

---

33 For full discussion of Matthew 16:24-27, see Dillow, *Final Destiny*, Chapter 15.

34 That is, it always means eternal salvation except when the context specifies a rescue from some temporal difficulty (Grudem, *"Free Grace" Theology*, 133-34.

35 For example, Joseph Pak makes this unfounded assertion with poor supporting evidence (Pak, "A Study of Selected Passages," 244. He cites only three other passages that do not necessarily refer to salvation from damnation (Matthew 10:28; John 12:25; 1 Peter 1:9). All of these have been dealt with elsewhere (see footnotes above). Pak sees the phrase about keeping one's soul for eternal life as something the believer does by means of hating the world (John 12:25). This is a novel way of guaranteeing one's arrival in heaven. It is better to understand keeping for eternal life as persevering and enhancing one's intimacy with God now and on into heaven when we die. Only by faithfulness can that intimacy be "kept" and thus experienced abundantly in heaven. As Billy Graham puts it, "Everyone's cup will be full, but the cups will be different sizes." Jesus referred to this "keeping" elsewhere as laying up treasures for ourselves in heaven. Pak understands 1 Peter 1:9, "obtaining the goal of your faith – the salvation of your souls," as a reference to final entrance into heaven. However, "obtaining" (Gr. *kōmizō*) refers to receiving something as a recompense (*BDAG*, 557, option 3 "to receive a recompense"), and the salvation in view is being experienced now. It is a deliverance from the struggles his readers fight against in the present and has sanctification as one of its foci.

36 Grudem, *Systematic Theology*, 1202.

mean that James teaches that we must first change our lives before we can be saved. Then we must obey Scripture, that is, we must welcome the implanted word that can protect us from temptations. Yet Scripture says that the gift of eternal life comes to us "without cost" (Revelation 21:6).

Secondly, that "death" refers to spiritual and psychological ruin and not the lake of fire seems to be indicated in the way James appears to be echoing the book of Proverbs where Solomon speaks of salvation from the paths of sin. Wisdom, Solomon said, "*will save you from the ways of wicked men. . . . also from the adulteress woman, from the wayward woman*" (Prov. 2:12, 16). It is quite likely that James is thinking in Old Testament terms here. Solomon, for example, frequently contrasted the life-enriching benefits of righteousness with the death-producing effects of sin:

The truly righteous man attains life, but he who pursues evil goes to his death. (Proverbs 11:19)

The terms "life" and "death" are contextually defined in Proverbs 11 as "abundant life" and "carnality," to use contemporary terms. In a series of contrasts, Solomon defines death as "being trapped by evil desires" (Proverbs 11:6), physical death and loss of hope (11:7), being overwhelmed with trouble (11:8), destroying one's neighbor (11:9), destruction of a city by evil actions (11:11), a lack of judgment and a deriding of one's neighbor (11:12), and a lack of guidance resulting in the fall of a nation (11:14). Life, on the other hand, is defined as having a "straight way" (11:5), being delivered from evil snares (11:6), being rescued from trouble (11:8), giving blessing to a city (11:11), and sowing righteousness (11:18). Contrasts such as these define life and death not as entrance into heaven and final commitment to eternal damnation but as relative qualities of life now, qualities that depend on the faith-vitalizing property of good works.[37]

In Psalm 116, we find a remarkable parallel. The psalmist says the "*cords of death*" encompassed him. He equates "death" with distress and sorrow. He then calls on the Lord saying, "*Save my life*" (Heb.

---

37 See also Prov. 10:27; 12:28; 13:14; 19:16.

nephesh, "soul," Psalm 116:1-4). The salvation of a soul in the psalm is from spiritual distress and not final damnation.

The psalmist continues, "*For Thou hast rescued my soul from death, My eyes from tears, my feet from stumbling*" (Psalm 116:8). This rescue is from tears and stumbling, that is, from psychological/spiritual ruin. A key to the psalmist's deliverance was a determination to "*walk before the Lord*," that is, to do good works (v. 9) and to have a steadfast faith (v. 10), even during affliction. In other words, the salvation of which the psalmist speaks is like that of James. It is a temporal salvation from distress and trouble (death) and is obtained by faith plus works.

The parallelism between James 1:21-27 and 2:14-26 helps us to see how these passages explain each other. In 1:21-27, James tells us we will be "saved" by being doers and not just hearers of the word. In 2:14-26, we can now see that his meaning is the same. They will be saved in the sense of finding deliverance from the spiritually impoverishing consequences of sin if they energize their faith by works of obedience. Varner agrees with the Free Grace interpretation saying,

> *This expression "save your souls" does not refer to the initial experience of salvation, as in the exhortations that we should be evangelists who "save souls." The expression actually refers to the ongoing and continuous (imperfective aspect of δυνάμενον) work of restoring and rescuing the inner life of believers. This is obvious when one recognizes that James is addressing "brothers" (1:19) who have already been "birthed" through a supernatural word from God (1:18).*[38]

Salvation from loss at the Judgment Seat of Christ. The second instance where James speaks of salvation is in James 2:12-13. Just before asking, "*Can that faith save him?*" (2:14), James says,

> So speak and so act as those who are to be judged by the law of liberty. For judgment will be merciless to one who has shown no mercy; mercy triumphs over judgment. (James 2:12-13)

---

[38] William Varner, *James*, ed. H. Wayne House, Evangelical Exegetical Commentary (Bellingham, Wash.: Lexham Press, 2012), 190.

This judgment will fall on the justified saint who has "faith in our glorious Lord Jesus Christ" (James 2:1), who has received the "implanted word" (1:22-25), and who is one of the "brethren" (2:1). Some writers suggest that the judgment in verse 13 means the judgment of eternal damnation must be in view.[39] Assuming true believers are indicated, as Dibelius believes,[40] this would then teach that true believers can lose their salvation.

Douglas Moo explains the common Reformed viewpoint saying, "With these commands, James returns to the dominant theme in this section of the letter: the need for believers to *validate* the reality of their 'religion' by 'doing' the word (1:22; emphasis added)."[41] However, there is nothing in the context about *validating* one's initial "saving" faith. Also, since Moo believes that this judgment is a judgment on Christians,[42] why would they have to validate their faith at the end. Are they true believers or not?

The believer will never come into judgment regarding eternal life (John 5:24; Romans 8:32-33). Therefore, this judgment must be the Judgment Seat of Christ (2 Corinthians 5:9-11). In view of the many parallels between James and the Sermon on the Mount,[43] these criteria may include, as Craig Blomberg suggests, the precepts of the Sermon

---

39 Gale Z. Heide, "The Soteriology of James 2:14," *GTJ* 12, no. 1 (Spring 1991).

40 Dibelius and Greeven, *James: A Commentary on the Epistle of James*, 147. However, Dibelius is ambiguous regarding the outcome of this judgment.

41 He says that "the Greek text puts even more emphasis on the need for *Christians* to regulate their conduct with an eye on the judgment to come." Douglas J. Moo, *The Letter of James*, The Pillar New Testament Commentary (Grand Rapids, Mich.: Wm. B. Eerdmans Publishing Co., 2000), 116. McCartney seems to agree saying that "the quality of mercy exercised by the believer is the quality of genuine faith; it is the quintessential 'work' that manifests true belief in the God of mercy. In other words, showing mercy is a verification of true faith." See Dan G. McCartney, *James*, Baker Exegetical Commentary (Grand Rapids, Mich.: Baker Academic, 2009), 150. Also, Blomberg appears to take a similar view. Blomberg and Kimmel, *James*, 120.

42 Moo, *The Letter of James*.

43 Virgil V. Porter, "The Sermon on the Mount in the Book of James," *Bibliotheca Sacra* 162, no. 648 (October - December 2005).

on the Mount[44] and also the New Testament imperatives, summed up as "*the law of liberty*." When Christians ask, "What is the basis by which I will be judged at the Judgment Seat of Christ; how can I obtain reward there?" the answer is, "You will be judged by how you have applied the Sermon on the Mount to your life!"

Hart makes two points in favor of the idea that this judgment is a judgment on true believers. First, he notes that "James challenges his readership to act like those who have been forgiven and freed from guilt. But unbelievers or false believers cannot act like they have been freed from guilt."[45] This judgment is based on the "*law of liberty*," which is something believers intently look into (James 1:25). This law, which gives freedom, is a law that sets free those who know the truth (John 8:31-32).

Second, Hart notes that 2:12–13 corresponds to 3:1 as an *inclusio*. Therefore, the judgment mentioned in 3:1 corresponds with the judgment mentioned in 2:12–13. But in 3:1, James himself states that **he** will experience this judgment, and that it will involve greater strictness for **him** and for all teachers. "*Let not many of you become teachers, my brethren, knowing that as such we will incur a stricter judgment.*" Can anyone suppose that James thought of himself as appearing before God to determine his eternal destiny? Was heaven held in the balance for him?[46]

---

44 Blomberg and Kimmel, *James*, 119.

45 John F. Hart, "How to Energize Our Faith: Reconsidering the Meaning of James 2:14-26," *JOTGES* 12, no. 1 (Spring 1999): 52.

46 Ibid. Robert Wilkin agrees, "The verses immediately before and after James 2:14–26 are dealing with genuine believers. They are called 'my brethren' (2:1, 5; 3:1). These are not 'brethren' in the sense that all Jews refer to each other as brothers, but these are brothers in whom the Word has been implanted ('accept the word planted in you, which can save you,' James 1:21). These are brethren who have 'faith in our glorious Lord Jesus Christ' (James 2:1). Only believers will be at the Judgment Seat of Christ, to which James refers. James would never warn unbelievers to be cautious about becoming teachers in the church. Nor would he warn unbelievers of the need to be merciful to believers in the church." Robert Wilkin, "Another View of Faith and Works in James 2," *Journal of the Grace Evangelical Society* 15, no. 2 (Fall 2002): 20.

James also refers to the Judgment Seat of Christ at the end of the epistle. "Do not complain, brethren, against one another, so that you yourselves may not be judged; behold, the Judge is standing right at the door" (James 5:9). The salvation obtained by faith plus works is not soteriological entrance into heaven. Rather, it is a salvation of "brethren" (regenerate believers) from the temporal, psychological, spiritual, or possible physical consequences (sin unto death) of a non-working faith resulting in a negative assessment of one's life at the Judgment Seat of Christ.[47]

We are on familiar ground here. Elsewhere, Paul warns of judgment good and bad that can fall on the regenerate saint at the Judgment Seat of Christ (2 Corinthians 5:10) and John warns of the danger of losing what one has worked for (2 John 8; see also Matthew 4:25). James's point is that faith without works cannot save one from the negative consequences of a lifestyle of sin leading to death (1:21) and the resultant negative judgment at the Judgment Seat of Christ.

In fact, "save" is related by James not only to deliverance and perseverance in trial, i.e., sanctification, but also to obtaining an "advantage" (Gr. *ophelos*) at the Judgment Seat of Christ. He says,

> What use [Gr. ophelos] is it, my brethren, if someone says he has faith but he has no works? Can that faith save him? (James 2:14)

This raises two questions. First, what kind of good works? James answers,

> And one of you says to them, "Go in peace, be warmed and be filled," and yet you do not give them what is necessary for their body, what **use** is that? (James 2:16)

---

47 Heide disagrees, "The judgment that he has in mind does not look at the accomplishments of the person, rather it inspects the person's sinful transgression and judges upon that basis. This type of judgment is not with a view to reward, but with a view to convict and punish." Heide, "The Soteriology of James 2:14," 89. Apparently in Heide's theology, no negative could happen to the sinful believer at the Judgment Seat of Christ. All are to be happy there. The biblical idea that true believers can face "shame" (1 John 2:28) does not seem to dawn on him.

Faith without works is of no "use." The word "use" (Gr. *ophelos*) refers to an "advantage"[48] or an additional benefit or "increase."[49] The preceding context relates this to an advantage or increase of benefit at the Judgment Seat of Christ (2:12-13), where James warns his readers that one day they will be held accountable.

Second, saved from what?

Salvation from sin's penalties (James 4:12). The next instance of the word "save" in James (besides 2:14) is in 4:12, where we read of the divine Lawgiver, who is able to "save or destroy."[50]

> There is only one Lawgiver and Judge, the one who is able to save and to destroy (Gr. *apollumi*); but who are you who judge your neighbor? (James 4:12)

There is no need to assume, as Douglas Moo does, that "James . . . is thinking of 'judging' in terms of determining the ultimate spiritual destiny of individuals."[51] By "ultimate spiritual destiny" Moo means the lake of fire or entrance into heaven. But this is a bare assertion. There is nothing here about judging a man's state of redemptive salvation. Rather, James speaks of judging a fellow believer's behavior. These words, *sōzō* and *apollumi*, commonly refer to rescue from a temporal difficulty.

The phrase "save or destroy" (Gr. *apollumi*) may echo Jesus's statement to the Pharisees in Mark 3:4. "*And he said to them, 'is it lawful to do good or to do harm on the Sabbath, to save a life or to kill?'* [Gr. *apokteinō*]." The Greek words are different but the sentiment is the same, "to save a soul" or to destroy it.

---

48 Louw-Nida, 1:624. The word is used only three times in the New Testament (James 2:14, 16; 1 Corinthians 15:32).

49 *BDAG*, 743.

50 Alan P. Stanley assures his readers that "eschatological salvation is in view" because only God is able to save and destroy. However, this context is about temporal destruction and not damnation. Alan P. Stanley, *Did Jesus Teach Salvation by Works? The Role of Works in Salvation in the Synoptic Gospels* (Eugene, OR: Pickwick Publishers, 2006), 161.

51 Moo, *The Letter of James*, 199.

The opposite of "save a life/soul" is to kill. To "kill" and "*apollumi*," both being the opposite of "save a life," requires that "save a soul" refers to saving the soul from a temporal concern, not an eternal one. This is common in the New Testament.[52]

While *apollumi* does at times refer to damnation, the word often refers to the spiritual ruin of Christians,[53] or of physical death.[54] In some cases it apparently parallels a common Jewish expression which means "to trifle away one's life."[55] In 2 John 8, it means "to lose [Gr. *apollumi*] what you have worked for" (i.e., reward).

Since James's intended audience is saved people, and since believers will never come into the judgment of eternal damnation (John 3:18; 5:24), there is no need to introduce the doctrine of eternal salvation into this context.

When James says that the divine Lawgiver is able to "destroy," it is evident from the context that he does not have eternal destruction in

---

52 The verb *apollumi* is found ninety times in the New Testament. In a number of places it does mean "suffer damnation." There is only one clear instance of that meaning in the Gospels (John 10:28). What is of interest is that the verb is used nineteen times in seventeen verses in the Gospel of Matthew, and Matthew never uses it in the sense of damnation. It is used seven times of physical death (Matthew 2:13; 8:25; 12:14; 21:41 – he will "destroy those wretches" probably a reference to the judgment in time of AD 70 on the nation and not final damnation; Matthew 22:7; 26:52; 27:20). Peter was afraid of "perishing" by drowning (Matthew 8:25); Herod wanted to "destroy" Jesus (Matthew 2:13); the Pharisees likewise wanted to "destroy him" (Matthew 12:14). In one place it means "to ruin," where Jesus says that putting new wine into old wineskins "ruins" them (Matthew 9:17). See also Matthew 10:6; 18:13-14, "to go astray;" 12:14; 15:24; 22:7; 26:52; 27:20, etc. The verb is commonly used of a temporal perishing or psychological and spiritual ruin of believers: "*Do not destroy [Gr. apollumi] with your food him for whom Christ died*" (Romans 14:15); "*For through your knowledge he who is weak is ruined [Gr. apollumi], the brother for whose sake Christ died*" (1 Corinthians 8:11).

53 Matthew 10:42; 1 Corinthians 8:11.

54 Matthew 2:13; 8:25; 12:14; 22:7; 2 Corinthians 2:9.

55 For example, Matthew 10:39 (see Oepke, "ἀπόλλυμι, ἀπώλεια, ἀπολλύων," in TDNT, 1:394).

view.[56] The kind of destruction in this context is temporal, not eternal. This view is confirmed by his statement in verse 11, *"Do not slander one another,"* and the exhortation in verse 12, in which he asks, *"Who are you to judge your neighbor?"* James, who was a careful student of the Old Testament, likely has Psalm 101:5 in mind.

> Whoever secretly slanders his neighbor, him I will destroy (LXX Gr. *ekdiōk*); No one who has a haughty look and an arrogant heart will I endure. (Psalm 101:5)

Paul taught the same thing,

> Never take your own revenge, beloved, but leave room for the wrath of God, for it is written, "Vengeance is mine, I will repay," says the Lord." (Romans 12:19)

Only God has the right to revenge. Only God has the right to destroy someone. When the believers whom James addresses slander one another and judge one another, they assume a right they do not have. It is God's responsibility to deal with one's offender. To "save," in this context, means to deliver from the temporal consequences of sin, which can be spiritual and psychological ruin, physical illness (5:15), or possibly physical death (5:19-20).

Clearly, James has in mind his Lord's teaching given in his famous Sermon on the Mount where he said,

> Do not judge so that you will not be judged. For in the way you judge, you will be judged; and by your standard of measure, it will be measured to you. . . . You hypocrite, first take the log out of your own eye, and then you will see clearly to take the speck out of your brother's eye. (Matthew 7:1-5)

---

56 The phrase "save or destroy (Gr. *apollumi*), may echo Jesus's statement to the Pharisees in Mark 3:4. *"And he said to them, 'is it lawful to do good or to do harm on the Sabbath, to save a life or to kill?' [Gr. apokteinō]."* The Greek words are different but the sentiment is the same, "to save a soul" or to destroy it.

It is God's responsibility to "destroy" a sinning brother in this sense, and only God can ultimately save him from this kind of "destruction," that is, from spiritual and psychological ruin from a possible judgment unto physical death, or from a damaged reputation. Salvation, once again, has nothing to do in James with deliverance from damnation!

Salvation from disease (James 5:15). The next reference to salvation in James's epistle is found in the final chapter. James uses the word *sōzō* two more times.

> And the prayer offered in faith will restore [Gr. sōzō] the one who is sick, and the Lord will raise him up [Gr. sōzō, "save"], and if he has committed sins, they will be forgiven him. (James 5:15)

Clearly, salvation in this verse refers to salvation from disease, that is, physical healing. The one who is healed is a member of the congregation who believes in Christ and who calls on the elders of the congregation to pray for healing. He may need, as James suggests, forgiveness and restoration to fellowship with God. As Paul explained, sometimes a physical illness can be a divine discipline for a carnal life (1 Corinthians 11:30).

Salvation from physical death (James 5:19-20). Finally, we read in James 5:19-20,

> My brethren, if any among you strays from the truth and one turns him back, let him know that he who turns a sinner from the error of his way will save [Gr. sōzō] his soul from death and will cover a multitude of sins.

Once again, we see the phrase "save a soul," which, as demonstrated above, never in the Bible means salvation from eternal damnation. John Niemelä asks,

> Can an unbeliever wander away from that which he has never believed? The very absurdity of such a proposition is easily envisioned in geographic terms: Unless a person has been in China, how can he wander away from it? Likewise, can a person

be turned back to China, if he has never set foot in China? Indeed, James 5:19 speaks of anyone who left the truth that regenerated him, and is now turned back by a someone."[57]

Grudem doubts this interpretation, saying, "Because no physical danger is specified in the context . . . it is far better to understand salvation in this passage as a reference to eternal salvation."[58] However, one can also say, "Since there is no reference to eternal life in the context, it is far better to understand salvation in this passage as a reference to rescue from physical death." After all, James describes them as, "My **brethren**, if any **from among you** strays . . . " It is more natural to understand "save his soul" as it is used throughout the Bible and as it is used in 1:21, that is, the salvation of the saved, rescue from some temporal calamity leading to an advantage (Gr. *ophelos, 2:16*) at the Judgment Seat of Christ. Brothers do not need eternal salvation, they already have it!

All other references in Scripture relate the sin unto death to the physical death of a genuine believer (Genesis 38:7, Acts 5:5; 1 Corinthians 5:5; 11:30). Reformed theologians need this passage to refer to eternal death because of their false belief that all true believers will persevere in a life of good works and faith to the end of life.[59]

---

57 John Niemalä, "Faith Without Works: A Definition 1," *Chafer Theological Seminary Journal* 6, no. 2 (April 2000): 11.

58 Grudem, *"Free Grace" Theology*, 137.

59 See Reformed theologian, Hodge, in Archibald Hodge, *Outlines of Theology* (Simpsonville, S.C.: Christian Classics Foundation, 1998), 547. Dispensational writer Christopher Cone agrees. Concerning the meaning of "sin unto death," he says, "The final analysis usually depends upon which side of systematic theology—reformed or dispensational—one affirms. Typically, reformed theology proposes that the individual is a lost person: a false professor, a false believer. The outcome for such is rejection and the eternal flame of hellfire," Christopher Cone, "The Inevitability of Fruit Bearing: An Exegesis of John 15:6: Part 1," *Journal of Dispensational Theology* 15, no. 44 (2011): 61. Another Reformed writer, Henry Knapp, similarly excludes the possibility the sin unto death could be a sin unto physical death because that would contradict the Reformed doctrine of perseverance. He says, "Similarly, the elect cannot commit the sin unto death (1 John 5:16), because their election

Therefore, their system does not allow that a true believer could persevere in sin to the end of physical life because that would shatter his theological bias. This is theological exegesis in full flower!

Grudem calls this interpretation idiosyncratic and eccentric.[60] However, that conclusion is ridiculous. It is not idiosyncratic or eccentric at all. Grudem knows full well that this interpretation has been accepted by many scholars, except those who come from his Reformed tradition.[61]

---

and perseverance protects them from this sin." See Henry Knapp, "Augustine and Owen on Perseverance," *Westminster Journal of Theology* 62, no. 1 (2000): 75.

60 Grudem, *"Free Grace" Theology,* 119.

61 Charles Ryrie, *Basic Theology* (Chicago: Moody Press, 1999), 563. Robert Culver, *Systematic Theology: Systematic and Historical* (Ross-Shire, UK: Mentor, 2005), 366. Varner, *James*: 190. Varner says, "I doubt if anyone would interpret this verse as referring to anyone else than the converted sinner unless commentators had suggested differently," ibid., 560. Roger Ellsworth, *Opening up James* (Leominster: Day One Publications, 2009), 168. John F. Walvoord, "The Present Work of Christ in Heaven," *Bibliotheca Sacra* 121, no. 484 (1964): 274. Niemalä, "Faith Without Works: A Definition 1," 9-10. John A. Witmer, "A Review of Wrongly Dividing the Word of Truth: Part 1," *Bibliotheca Sacra* 149, no. 594 (1992): 142. Although he does not cite James 5:20, F. F. Bruce argues that the "sin unto death" refers to a sin unto physical death. He cites Acts 5:1-11; I Corinthians 5:5; 11:30. F.F. Bruce, *Answers to Questions* (Grand Rapids, IL: Zondervan Publishing House, 1974), 134. Rodney Decker, "Trampling the Son of God under Foot: The Warning of Hebrews 10:26-31," *Journal of Ministry and Theology* 6, no. 2 (2002): 34. Wiersbe says that the saving of the soul is the conversion of the converted, a brother, Warren W. Wiersbe, *The Bible Exposition Commentary* (Wheaton: Victor Books, 1996), 2:384. John Mitchell, "Does God Heal Today?," *Bibliotheca Sacra* 122, no. 485 (1965): 47. Tom Constable says, "Death represents the temporal destruction of the person, not his or her eternal damnation (cf. 1 Cor. 15:30; 1 John 5:16)," Tom Constable, *Tom Constable's Expository Notes on the Bible* (Garland, TX: Galaxie Software, 2003), s.v. "James 5:20". Zane C. Hodges, *The Epistle of James: Proven Character Through Testing: A Verse by Verse Commentary* (Irving, TX: Grace Evangelical Society, 1994), 120.

Conclusion

Because he believed, based on James 2:24, that James contradicted Paul's doctrine of faith alone, Luther wanted to eliminate James from the canon. In this chapter we considered James 2:14 where James says, "Can that faith save him?" referring to faith which does not result in a life of works. While Reformed interpreters consider that this phrase proves their doctrine of the perseverance of the saints, we have argued otherwise.

We have shown that true Christians are the intended addressees since James calls them brothers, includes himself as one of the brothers, and describes them as those who have been brought forth by the word of truth; and who hold their faith in the Lord Jesus Christ.

When James said, "Can that faith save him," we asked, To what kind of faith does James refer: the initial saving action or the ongoing walk of faith? We concluded that in all fifteen instances in the book of James, it is the walk of faith in view.

What then does James mean by "save"? Although Reformed interpreters understand this to refer to eternal salvation, we concluded that the salvation of a soul in 1:21 does not refer to eternal salvation but to the death-spiral of temptation, lust, and sin leading to physical or psychological ruin, that is, "death." James also refers to salvation from a negative assessment of one's life at the Judgment Seat of Christ, from disease, and from the sin unto physical death. However, he never refers to salvation as salvation from damnation. Because those he addresses are already saved to eternal life, they do not need to be saved from that.

James's question, "Can that faith save him?" is best understood this way: "Can a so- called walk of faith that does not result in a life of works deliver a believer from the death-spiral of lust, sin, and death or from the sin unto death, and give him any benefits at the Judgment Seat of Christ? It cannot. It is a delusion."

In the next chapter we will direct our attention to James's dialogue with an imaginary objector who disagrees with his theology that works are necessary for salvation and also consider the problem of the statement made in 2:24 that we are justified by faith plus works in apparent contraction to the teaching of Paul.

Chapter 7

What is Dead Faith All About?

Joseph Dillow, Th.D.

Few passages in the New Testament have been more controversial in the debate between believers of Reformed and Free Grace persuasions than James 2:18, "faith without works is useless." The reason for this is clear. The general moral decay of our culture has unfortunately impacted many in the church. This has correctly raised the question of whether or not all these people professing faith in Christ are really born again.

The Barna research group has regularly published the results of many surveys comparing the values and behavior of Christians as compared with non-Christians. The results are stunning.[1] I remember reading an article on marriage and divorce written by a prominent sociologist. The divorce rate in 1951 among sincerely professing believers in Christ was 1 in 1000. According to Barna, today the divorce rate among

---

1   Dan Barker, "National Surveys Question Christian Morality," *Freedom from Religion Foundation*, accessed Month ??, 2017, https://ffrf.org/component/k2/item/18390-national-surveys-question-christian-morality.

Christians is about the same as that for non-Christians (Christians: 27%; Non-Christians: 23%). Furthermore, the cohabitation rate among professing believers is now 25% and 13% believe it is permissible for married couples to have sex with someone else.

Barna concludes, "When we look at the values, lifestyles, the moral perspective and behaviors of Christians, we can see that there's virtually no difference between Christians and non-Christians."[2] In another, Barna reported, "of more than 70 other moral behaviors we study, when we compare Christians to non-Christians we rarely find substantial differences."[3]

These statistics make James's statement that "faith without works is dead," and "faith without works is useless," very relevant. How many of these professing Christians are truly born again?

What is Dead Faith?

James says, *"Even so faith, if it has no works, is dead, being by itself"* (James 2:17). There is no need to assume, as Grudem does, that this means a faith that does not manifest itself in a life of works is certainly not genuine saving faith.[4] Instead, James is teaching that just like the body is dead if its spirit has departed, so the believer's *walk of faith* becomes dead if works depart.

We ask, what does "dead" mean?

Normally, one would think that a dead faith signifies a faith that was once alive and then died. Not so, according to Grudem. Why? Because, he says, "This entire section begins with the question that has to do with eternal salvation."[5] Therefore, one must conclude that "death" is

---

2   "The Church and the Mosaic Generation" (an interview with George Barna), *Homiletics Online*, accessed Month ??, 2017, http://www.homileticsonline.com/subscriber/interviews/barna.asp.

3   Christine Wicker, "Survey Inspires Debate over Why Faith Isn't a Bigger Factor in Marriage," *Adeherents.com*, accessed Month ??, 2017, http://www.adherents.com/largecom/baptist_divorce.html.

4   Wayne A. Grudem, *"Free Grace" Theology 5 Ways It Diminishes the Gospel* (Wheaton, Ill.: Crossway, 2016), 134-35.

5   Ibid., 135.

the opposite, that is, eternal death. He then quotes 2:14 (*"can that faith save him?"*). For Grudem, the word "save" obviously means save from hell. However, as shown elsewhere in this book, that is not necessarily true. Furthermore, as shown in the preceding chapter, this section has nothing to do with eternal salvation. It deals with temporal salvation from the death-spiral, the salvation of one's soul, leading to favorable account at the Judgment Seat of Christ.

James refers to the kind of death experienced by the prodigal son. His father said, *"For this son of mine was dead, and has come to life again* [Gr. *anazaō*]; *he was lost, and has been found"* (Luke 15:24). He was once alive in the sense of intimacy with his father, but because of his carnality, he became dead. When he was with the pigs, he was "lost" (Gr. *apollumi*), not unsaved. He **was still a son,** but he was lost in the sense that his life was in ruins. His life had been destroyed, impoverished, psychologically and spiritually. In that sense, he was "dead." But he came alive "again" (Gr. *anazaō*, from *zaō*, "to live," and "*ana*" again, thus "be alive again"[6]). Of course, this means that he was alive before, but because of his lack of works he had become dead. For just as the body without the spirit is dead, so also faith without works is dead (James 2:26).

In James's analogy, the body is parallel to faith, and the spirit is parallel to works. Just as the spirit animates the body, so works animate faith. This obvious point is missed by Grudem and other Reformed writers because for centuries their thinking has been dominated by the idea that faith animates works. While that is true, the point in this text is that that *works animate faith.*

Hart is correct when he says,

> James is teaching that faith without works is simply a cold orthodoxy, lacking spiritual vibrancy. Practically speaking, we might think of a 'dead church.' This is not to say that those gathering as part of this assembly are not Christians. As noted earlier James' concerns are more practical than theological. The real issue for these believers is the absence of a freshness, vitality,

---

6 *BDAG*, 62.

and energy in their faith. When a Christian engages in practical deeds to benefit others, James says our faith comes alive."[7]

Also, the use of the term "death" to describe what can happen to Christians is not uncommon in the Bible:

But she who gives herself to wanton pleasure **is dead** even while she lives. (1 Timothy 5:6 NASB)

And to the angel of the church in Sardis write: He who has the seven Spirits of God, and the seven stars, says this: "I know your deeds, that you have a name that you are alive, but **you are dead.**" (Revelation 3:1)

Paul tells us that believers who were once alive can "die."

For if you live according to the flesh you will die, but if by the Spirit you put to death the deeds of the body, you will live. (Romans 8:13 ESV)

At one point in his Christian experience he felt he was dead. He asked,

Wretched man that I am! Who will deliver me from this body of death? (Romans 7:24 ESV)

Perhaps Grudem was led astray in his interpretation of the passage because he cannot give up the idea that "save" must mean deliver from hell. He says, "Because no physical danger or sickness is specified in the context, 'save' here must be understood to refer to eternal salvation."[8] However, as demonstrated in the previous chapter,[9] physical danger (lust, sin and spiritual and psychological ruin) is mentioned in the context.

---

7   John F. Hart, "How to Energize Our Faith: Reconsidering the Meaning of James 2:14-26," *JOTGES* 12, no. 1 (Spring 1999): 48.

8   Grudem, *"Free Grace" Theology*, 135.

9   See chapter 6, "Can That Faith Save Him?"

In each of these passages, the notion of death included a rather obvious point—they were once alive! Death is normally preceded by life, and in common biblical usage this is almost always true.[10] There is no reason to assume that James viewed it any differently. The dead faith to which James refers was unquestionably alive at one time, or it could not have died! This is not pressing the metaphor beyond its intent. It is an explicit implication of this same metaphor used elsewhere in the New Testament as the above passages reveal. As mentioned above, the experience of the prodigal son who was once alive and became dead is the kind of death to which James refers (Luke 15:24).[11]

---

10 Ephesians 2:1 can plausibly counter this statement. There we read that prior to being in Christ, we were dead in trespasses and sin. Obviously, this does not mean that men were once alive and then died. We entered this world dead, without spiritual life and unable to respond in faith or obedience to God. A possible response involves pointing out that we came into this world dead *in the sphere* [Gr. *tois,* dative] of sin, that is, in Adam. This may be as Wallace suggests a dative of sphere, "in the realm of sin." See Daniel Wallace, *Greek Grammar Beyond the Basics* (Grand Rapids, Mich.: Zondervan Publishing House, 1996), 145. Paul is speaking of our former sphere of life in Adam. In that sense were alive once before Adam sinned, and then we became dead. In other words, Paul may be speaking in terms of two federal headships. We were in the sphere of death, but God "raised us up with him, and seated us with him in the heavenly *places* in Christ Jesus" (Ephesians 2:6). We are now in the sphere of life. In Adam, Paul said, "through one man sin entered into the world, and death through sin, and so death spread to all men, because all sinned" (Romans 5:12). The federal headship view of this passage says we "sinned in Adam." We are viewed federally, that is, either in Adam or in Christ. Just as Adam was once alive, so were we. When Adam died, we died. It is also possible that an appeal to this verse is irrelevant. Ephesians 2:1 is probably not relevant anyway. The metaphor of "dead" in Ephesians 2:1 is almost certainly unrelated to the question of whether or not the person was once alive. Based on Ephesians 4:18, it appears that by "dead" Paul means "excluded from the life of God." If so, then the Reformed should not use this verse that proves that dead means "never alive." That would put a greater burden on the metaphor than it can bear.

11 The prodigal was a son of his father before and after he fell in with the pigs. For a full explanation of the parable see Joseph C. Dillow, *Final Destiny: The*

Furthermore, James seems to say this is the idea he intends to convey by the analogy he uses, "*For just as the body without the spirit is dead, so also faith without works is dead*" (James 2:26). The body dies, according to the Bible, when the spirit departs (John 19:30). Just as the body dies when our spirit departs, even so our faith dies when our works depart! Just as the spirit is the animating principle which gives the body life, so work is the animating principle which gives faith "life."

When believers do not animate their faith with works, James does not say their faith is nonexistent; he says it is useless (1:16), that is, it is of no value to others or themselves. This also helps define what he means by "dead," that is *useless* (v. 20 Gr. *argos*, "*unemployed*"[12]). This Greek word means that it does "not accomplish anything."[13] One lexicon translates it as "unemployed."[14] The whole point of James 2:14-26 is to exhort believers who already have faith to add works to it. In all of the uses of *argos*, it is talking about something that exists but is not functioning as intended.[15]

The passage is strikingly similar in this regard to 2 Peter 1:5-9.

Now for this very reason also, applying all diligence, in your faith supply moral excellence, and in your moral excellence, knowledge, and in your knowledge, self-control, and in your self-control, perseverance, and in your perseverance, godliness, and in your godliness, brotherly kindness, and in your brotherly

---

Future Reign of the Servant Kings, 3rd revised ed. (Monument, Col.: Paniym Group, Inc., 2016; reprint, 2016), Chapter 45.

12 *BDAG*, 128.

13 Louw-Nida, 1:452.

14 *BDAG*, 128.

15 One of the other uses is in Matthew 12:36-37. In v. 36, he speaks of "*careless*" words, and then, in v. 37, says "*by your words you will be justified* [or condemned]." The Greek words and construction are the same as James 2:20. Yet here, "justified" almost certainly does not have a forensic meaning but something like "vindicated." That would seem to give a foundation for the view that faith in James 2:14-26 talks about an actual faith that is useless if it doesn't work rather than a nonexistent faith.

kindness, love. For if these qualities are yours and are increasing, they render you neither useless (Gr. *argos*) nor unfruitful in the true knowledge of our Lord Jesus Christ. For he who lacks these qualities is blind or short-sighted, having forgotten his purification from his former sins. (2 Peter 1:5-9)

These believers are to add works (like self-control, kindness, love, and so forth) to their faith, and if they do, they will not be "unfruitful" (Gr. *akarpos*, "without fruit"), or, "useless" (*argos*). That is a good synonym for a dead faith, one which was once alive but is now "unemployed," having lost its vitality because it was not animated by a life of good works.

Apparently, some of the Christians to whom James was writing were deluding themselves (James 1:22). They imagined that their walk of faith was "living" and that they were walking in a life of faith even though it was not in accord with acts of charity. They had justifying faith, but some did not have the living faith with which the epistle is concerned. This is a typical situation faced by many pastors today. There may be some justified saints in his congregation who are lukewarm or even carnal, but they think all is well and that they are in fact living the Christian life when in fact they lack some of the essential attributes of a living faith. This was the problem John faced in 1 John. "*If we say that we have fellowship with him and yet walk in the darkness, we lie and do not practice the truth*" (1 John 1:6).[16] Also, like James' readers, John's readers faced a negative assessment of their lives at the Judgment Seat of Christ when some of them would draw back in shame (1 John 2:28).

A walk of faith by itself, if it is not vitalized by works, is a delusion. It is a dead faith and not a living and vital one.

---

16 As demonstrated elsewhere, the theme of 1 John is not tests of salvation, but tests of whether one is walking in fellowship. Like James, there were those among John's readers who had deluded themselves (James 1:22) and were walking in darkness (1 John 2:9) even though their sins had been forgiven (1 John 2:12). See discussion of the tests of 1 John elsewhere in Dillow, *Final Destiny*: Chapter 31; David R. Anderson, *Maximum Joy: First John - Relationship or Fellowship* (Woodlands, Tex.: Grace Theology Press, 2013).

Dialogue with the Objector

The words of an objector are now introduced in 2:18-19.

> *But someone will say, "You have faith and I have works."*

In our English translations, it is confusing where the words of the objector end and James begins to respond to the objection. In the Greek text that James wrote, there were neither punctuation marks nor lower/upper case letters. Any insertion of such distinguishing marks is an addition by much later editors or the various translators, and, as is often the case, is often informed by their prior theological beliefs.

In our discussion, we will assume the traditional punctuation reflected in the NIV, ESV, and NKJV. James has just said that "a walk of faith by itself, if it does not have works, is dead" (v. 17). He now turns his attention to an argument that apparently was voiced by some of those to whom the epistle was directed.[17] In the interpretation to follow, the present writer departs from a common Free Grace understanding as originally articulated by Zane Hodges.[18]

The objector's statement, "someone will say," indicates, according to Dibelius, "the form of fictitious discussion which is common in

---

17 Grudem's argument that this person is definitely a non-believer because he is called "someone" and elsewhere James contrasts "someone" with "my brothers" (James 2:14) is unlikely. There is no reason to believe that "someone" is not also one of "my brothers." To claim otherwise seems to be mere assertion and is contradicted by the clear evidence that James is not writing to a mixed audience, as Grudem believes, but is specifically writing to those who are born again (1:2, 9, 16, 18; 2:1; 4:2-3). Grudem, *"Free Grace" Theology*, 133.

18 Zane C. Hodges, *The Epistle of James: Proven Character Through Testing: A Verse by Verse Commentary* (Irving, Tex.: Grace Evangelical Society, 1994). See also Fred Chay and John P. Correia, *The Faith That Saves: The Nature of Faith in the New Testament* (Haysville, N.C.: Schoettle Publishing Co., 2008); Hart, "How to Energize Our Faith: Reconsidering the Meaning of James 2:14-26."

diatribe."[19] James himself introduces the interlocutor, and James himself answers him. The interlocutor objects to James's accusation of a "dead faith" saying, "You have faith, and I have works," and James's reply begins with "Show me," and continues through v. 20.[20]

---

19 Martin Dibelius and Heinrich Greeven, *James: A Commentary on the Epistle of James*, 11th rev. ed., Hermeneia (Philadelphia: Fortress Press, 1975), 149-50. In effect, the diatribe furnished him with a method of creating dialogues between himself and imaginary interlocutors (Romans 3:27–4:2)." Werner H. Kelber, "Oral Tradition, New Testament," in *Anchor Yale Bible Dictionary*, ed. David Noel Freedman, et al. (New York: Doubleday, 1992), 5:33. Stanley K. Stowers, "Diatribe,"ibid., ed. David Noel Freedman, et al., 2:191. According to Essel, "From a study of its literary forms J. H. Ropes concluded that the Epistle reveals many of the characteristics of the diatribe—the short moral or ethical address developed initially by the Stoics and Cynics. Certain stylistic features of the Epistle are similar to the peculiar style of the diatribe: dialogue (2:20); brief questions and answers (5:13f); rhetorical questions (2:14); harsh speech (2:20; 4:4); the introduction of an opposing speaker with 'but someone will say' (2:18); etc. The choice of illustrations, especially in 3:2–12, is significant." W. W. Essel, "James - Literary Character - Diatribe Theory," in *NISBE*, ed. G. W. Bromiley (Grand Rapids, Mich.: Wm. B. Eerdmans Publishing Co., 1988), 2:961.

20 Based on the fact that two other New Testament examples of diatribe connect "someone" with "you fool" directly following with no intervening verses (Romans 9:19-20; 1 Corinthians 15:35-36; also 4 Macc. 2:24), and James responds with "you fool" after some intervening verses, some believe therefore, that vv. 2:18b–19 must be on the lips of the objector, not James. See Hodges, *The Epistle of James: Proven Character Through Testing: A Verse by Verse Commentary*, 64-66. However, the phrase "you fool" or some negative comment about the objector is not a necessary part of a diatribe (see Epistle of Barnabas 9:6; Josephus, Wars of the Jews, 6, 8, 363; Xenophon 4.3.10). There is nothing in the diatribe style that requires that the phrase "you fool" follow immediately after the objection as it does in 1 Corinthians 15:35-36. It is perfectly acceptable and logical to end the objector's comment with v. 18b and James' response to include all of 18b-20. Dibelius agrees with our interpretation stating that James, not his opponent, is the speaker in 18b and v. 19-20. See Dibelius and Greeven, *James: A Commentary on the Epistle of James*, 154.

	Useless Faith
James:	But someone will say
Objector:	"You have faith; I have deeds" (2:18).
James:	Show me your faith without deeds, and I will show you my faith by what I do (2:18b).
	You believe that there is one God. Good! Even the demons believe that—and shudder (2:19)
	But are you willing to recognize, you foolish fellow, that faith without works is useless? (2:20).

James has just said that a faith-walk without works cannot save and is "dead." To this someone responded saying, *"You have faith, I have deeds"*? In other words, "James, some have faith and some have works."[21] A believer does not necessarily have a dead faith just because he does not have works. Some have a walk of faith without works and some have a walk of faith with works. There is no necessary connection between a walk of faith and works. The opponent's objection ends here (see table to the left).

Who is this "someone" (Gr. *tis,* "someone") and who is "you" (Gr. *su*) and "I" (Gr. *kagō*)? Do the terms refer to a specific objector or have a more general referent? Even though pages of ink have been written on the issue, in our view it is probably not critical for our interpretation.[22]

---

21 Dibelius says, "James treats the interlocutor as if he had said, 'The one has faith, the other has works.'" Dibelius and Greeven, *James: A Commentary on the Epistle of James*, 156.

22 Davids agrees, "the reference of σύ and κἀγώ is neither clear nor important" Peter H. Davids, *The Epistle of James: A Commentary on the Greek Text* (Grand Rapids, Mich.: Wm. B. Eerdmans Publishing Co., 1982), 123.

However, it does seem that "you" and "I" are most likely representative for general groups in James's audience.[23] Using synecdoche, a part of an idea or concept ("you" and "I") is put for the whole, or the whole is put for the part.[24] It is unlikely that a letter that is addressed to a broad number of churches (James 1:1) would address the argument of only one particular person.[25]

James replies to this travesty of grace saying,

Show me your walk of faith without deeds, and I will show you my walk of faith by what I do (2:18b).

Notice we have correctly defined faith as a "walk of faith." As pointed out in the previous chapter,[26] justifying faith is not in view in the book of James. Rather, the problem that James faced was that there were some who claimed to be walking by faith who had no evidence

---

23 Douglas J. Moo, *The Letter of James*, The Pillar New Testament Commentary (Grand Rapids, Mich.: Wm. B. Eerdmans Publishing Co., 2000), 129. While it is true the *su* and *kago* elsewhere do not refer to someone in general but instead point to specific persons, in this context they likely have a general referent because they have been defined by *tis* in the preceding phrase. Ralph P. Martin, *James*, Word Biblical Commentary (Dallas: Word, 2002), 59, 79, 90.

24 A synecdoche is "a figure of speech by which a part is put for the whole (as fifty sails for fifty ships), the whole for a part (as society for high society), the species for the genus (as cutthroat for assassin), the genus for the species (as a creature for a man), or the name of the material for the thing made (as boards for stage)" *Merriam-Webster's Collegiate Dictionary*: s.v. "synecdoche".

25 Apparently, according to Ropes, there are places in extra-biblical Greek where *su* is used as an equivalent to *tis* ("some" or "someone"), but in the New Testament *su* is found 174 times in 161 verses. It never means "someone." Also, the phrase 'and I' (Gr. *kai egō*) is found 80 times in 84 verses and never refers to "others." It always means "and I." J. H. Ropes, *A Critical and Exegetical Commentary on the Epistle of St. James* (New York: Scribner's Sons, 1916), 209. That said, it is clear that even if the terms refer to "you" and "I" they represent a common point of view held by a particular splinter group in James's audience. Thus, the intended sense is "someone" and "others."

26 See Chapter 6, "Can That Faith Save Him?" in this book.

of it in a life of works. They may or may not have been saved, but that is not James's issue.

While some have placed this comment on the lips of the objector, it makes no sense to do so. As Davies has noted, "The following clauses do not seem to oppose James's concepts."[27] Only James would say, "I will show you my faith by my works." Why would the objector state that he will show his faith by (Gr. *ek*) his works? The objector does not believe there is a necessary connection between a walk of faith and a life of works. In view of the fact that a reply to the objector is obviously being made and that reply squares exactly with James's point in the entire chapter, we understand this to be James' response to the view of his opponent. James is saying, "You will not be able to show faith without works."[28]

Therefore, we may paraphrase this way,

"A person cannot show he is walking by faith if he has no good works, but a believer can demonstrate by his works that he is walking by faith."

Or,

Show me your so-called walk of faith without (Gr. chōris) deeds (implying that this cannot be done) and I will show you by (Gr. ek) my works, my walk of faith.[29]

---

27 Davids, *The Epistle of James: A Commentary on the Greek Text*, 123. Similarly, Dibelius says, "This protest, in which the speaker ascribes works to himself and faith to another, does not seem to come at all from one who is an opponent of our author. Indeed, the speaker seems to appeal precisely to his works! Dibelius and Greeven, *James: A Commentary on the Epistle of James*, 155.

28 Dibelius and Greeven, *James, A Commentary on the Epistle of James*, 154.

29 There is a textual issue here. The Majority text substitutes *ek* (from) in place of *choris* (without). See William G. Pierpoint and Maurice A. Robinson, *The New Testament in the Original Greek: According to the Byzantine/Majority Textform* (Roswell, Ga.: Original Word Publishers, 1995). For a plausible defense of this textual variation see Chay and Correia, *The Faith That Saves: The Nature of Faith in the New Testament*, 141-48. See also George W. Peters,

Notice I added the word "cannot" even though that is not specifically in the Greek text. James is objecting, not agreeing!

James's point is that a "walk of faith" which does not manifest itself in a life of works is not really a walk of faith at all. He says that such a person is deceiving himself (1:20), and "deceives his heart, this person's religion is worthless" (1:22, 26). We might say today that his faith is mere intellectual assent and not daily trust in the person of Christ.

To demonstrate the foolishness of the belief that a true life of faith (in contrast to mere head knowledge) does not necessarily require a life of works, James drives his point home with this absurdity.

> You believe that there is one God. You do well. Even the demons believe—and tremble (v. 19).

Just believing the Shema (Deut. 6:4-9), while that is good, is insufficient. Even demons have an intellectual belief in the Shema.[30] But they have no good works. In other words, your so-called faith-walk is no better than the faith of demons. It is dead and useless. As Dibelius put it, "If Christianity is to be nothing more than what the demons also have, this faith is in bad shape. Thus, the author must already be speaking again in v. 19; he wants to show how unchristian 'faith without works' appears."[31]

> "Do you want to be shown, you foolish person, that faith apart from works (*chōris*) is useless? (Gr. *argos*)." (James 2:20, ESV)

"The Meaning of Conversion," *BibSac* 120, no. 479 (July - September 1963). Zane C. Hodges, "Light from James 2 from Textual Criticism," ibid., no. 480 (October-December 1963): 341-50. Fred Lybrand, *Back to Faith: Reclaiming Gospel Clarity in an Age of Incongruence* (Lakewood, Fla.: Xulon Press, 2009). John F. Hart, "The Faith of Demons," *JOTGES* 8, no. 2 (1995). These writers oppose the view of Joseph K. Pak, "A Study of Selected Passages on Distinguishing Marks of Genuine and False Believers" (PhD diss., Dallas Theological Seminary, 2001), 228-30.

30 Demons believe in God, Mark 1:24; 5:7; Acts 16:17; 19:15.

31 Dibelius and Greeven, *James: A Commentary on the Epistle of James*, 154.

When believers do not animate their faith with works, James does not say their faith is nonexistent; he says it is useless (2:20), that is, it is of no value to others or themselves. This helps define what James meant when he spoke of a dead faith; it is a useless faith. This Greek word, *argos*, denotes a faith-walk that is insufficient to save from the downward spiral of temptation, lust, sin, and spiritual and psychological ruin, that is, from "death" (1:14-15). Nor will it save anyone from a negative assessment of one's life at the Judgment Seat of Christ when all believers will be judged to see if their behavior is in accord with the Law of Liberty (2:12-16). In other words, it does "not accomplish anything."[32]

Our view of the argument of James 2:14-20 can be summarized this way:

James: A walk of faith without works is a delusion and, it cannot save a believer from "death" or from a negative assessment of his life at the Judgment Seat of Christ (v. 17).

Supposed objector: Some have a walk of faith without works, others have works, and both are legitimate in living the Christian life (v. 18a).

James's response: A life of faith and works cannot exist separately (vv. 18b-20), and it is foolish to say otherwise. Even the demons have that kind of faith.

Notice that both Free Grace and Reformed writers agree that faith without works is dead. They also agree that true faith should express itself and include a life of works. Furthermore, they agree that faith alone cannot save. The disagreement centers on the meaning of the words "faith," "dead," and "save." "True" faith, or "that" faith, in James never means the "initial act of faith whereby one is justified freely by his grace." It always refers to the walk of faith that follows initial salvation. Also, for James, "save" never means deliverance from eternal

---

32 Louw-Nida, 1:452.

damnation.[33] Rather, it speaks of the temporal salvation from a path leading to spiritual/psychological or physical death and the resultant negative judgment on one's life at the Judgment Seat of Christ. Finally, for James, for faith to be "dead" does not mean it never existed, it means it is not vital or living; or, to use James's words, it has no "benefit," it is *argos*.

When James rhetorically asks, "*Do you want to be shown, you foolish person, that faith apart from works is useless,*" he prepares his readers for the proof of this statement in the discussion to follow about Abraham and Rahab whose faith and good works operated together and they therefore obtained God's approval.

The Maturing of Abraham's Faith

As proof of the worthless nature of a delusional walk of faith apart from works, James now cites the illustration of Abraham:

> *Was not Abraham our father justified by works when he offered up Isaac his son on the altar? You see that faith was working with his works, and as a result of the works, faith was perfected; and the Scripture was fulfilled which says, "And Abraham believed God, and it was reckoned to him as righteousness," and he was called the friend of God. You see that a man is justified by works and not by faith alone.* (James 2:21–24)

What Paul asserts, however, is that Abraham was **not** forensically-justified by works (Romans 4:2), whereas James seems to say he was (James 2:21). But, surely James's readers knew that Abraham had been declared righteous before God long before he offered Isaac on the altar. The offering of Isaac occurred in Genesis 22:9, but he may have been declared righteous earlier (Hebrews 11:8; Acts 7:4) when he left Ur "by faith," as confirmed in Genesis 15:6. Abraham was already a saved man when he was "justified" in Genesis 22:9, about 25 years later.

---

33 See previous chapter, "Can That Faith Save Him?"

James makes two key statements.

- "A person is justified by what he does, and not by faith alone" (v. 24).
- "His faith and actions were working together" (v. 22).

In the former phrase, the word "alone" (Gr. *monon*) is crucial. While it is often translated as an adjective, there is no noun in the sentence that agrees with it in gender and number. So, it most likely should be understood as an adverb[34] modifying the verb "justified," rather than as an adjective modifying "faith."[35]

The resulting difference brings out more clearly what all translations imply. If *monon* is an adjective modifying "faith," we translate:

A person is justified by what he does and not by faith alone.

On the other hand, if *monon* is an adverb modifying "justified," we translate:

*A man **is justified** by works, and [is] **not** [justified] **only** [monon] by faith.*[36]

---

34 Martin, *James*, 95.

35 See John Niemelä, "James 2:24: Re-translation Required (Part 1 of 3)," *CTSJ* 7, no. 1 (January 2001): 2-15.

36 Ibid., 13. Jeff Phillips says, "The Greek is decisive here. The negative particle James uses is *ouk* (*ouk ek pisteōs monon*, "not by faith only"). But notice 1:22, where James uses the negative particle *mē* with *monon*. What is the difference between the two verses? In 1:22, James uses an imperative verb to tell his readers 'to prove yourselves doers of the word, *not only* hearers.' The reason James uses *mē* in 1:22 and *ou* in 2:24 becomes clear when one understands how verbs in different moods are negated in Greek. Verbs in the indicative mood are always negated by *ou* (Friedrich Blass, Albert Debrunner, and Robert Walter Funk, *A Greek Grammar of the New Testament and Other Early Christian Literature* [Chicago: University of Chicago Press, 1961], 220; *ou* and *ouk/ouch* are the same, the kappa and chi being added before words that begin with vowels). Verbs in non-indicative moods (such as imperatives) are always negated by *mē*. Therefore, because James uses *mē* in 1:22 and *ou* in

Or, more simply expressed in English,

A man is not only justified by faith, but is also justified by works.

This is the preferable translation and brings out more clearly that James has two different kinds of justification in view: one by works, and one by faith.[37] In other words, James is not suggesting that there are two conditions for justification, faith plus works, but there is a justification by faith and another one by works, and they are not the same kind of justification.[38]

This is his point in verse 24, when he refers to a justification by works that differs from the justification by faith alone mentioned by Paul. Abraham's justification in James 2:24 and Genesis 22:9 was a vindication-justification before God. His justification in Genesis

---

2:24, we can see that the negative particles are not modifying *monon* in either verse, but an understood verb that is not explicitly written out in the text. The reason the verb is not written is because it would be just a repetition of the same verb already written earlier in the sentence. Since, an unwritten verb is implied in the second half of each verse, it is grammatically preferable to understand *monon* as an adverb modifying the implied verb rather than an adjective modifying 'faith' or even an adverb somehow modifying the whole clause. Thus, we can understand 1:22 to say, "But prove yourselves doers of the word, and *do* not only *prove* to be hearers who delude themselves." And 2:24 can be rendered, "You see that a man is justified by works and not only *justified* by faith." This supports the idea that two distinct types of justification are in view—one forensic in nature before God and one having to do with one's reputation before men. I owe this observation to Jeff Phillips (personal communication, 5/22/2017).

37 Contra Stanley who sees the justification of Abraham as "an acquittal or declaration of righteousness." Alan P. Stanley, *Did Jesus Teach Salvation by Works? The Role of Works in Salvation in the Synoptic Gospels* (Eugene, Ore: Pickwick Publishers, 2006), 308. Joseph Pak similarly overlooks this point of grammar and thus his claim that "James cannot mean two different justifications" is not supported by the text. The text explicitly teaches two different kinds of justification! See Pak, "A Study of Selected Passages," 236.

38 R.T. Kendall, *Justification by Works: How Works Vindicate True Faith* (UK: Paternoster Press, 2001), 206.

15:6 was a soteriological-justification before God. In James 2:24, God
pronounced, "Well done!" But in the Genesis 15:6 he announced,
"Acquitted." The word "justify" is being used in James 2:24 in the sense
of declaring that someone is righteous in behavior (Matthew 11:19).[39]
That is, the declaration is based upon James 2:18 and 3:13, "*Who is
wise and understanding among you? Let him show it by his good life,
by deeds done in the humility that comes from wisdom.*"[40] What was the
outcome of this justification by works? It was not proof of genuine
faith as Grudem,[41] Blomberg, and other Reformed writers believe.
Instead it means that Abraham's faith was strengthened, matured,
and perfected by his obedience. To use James's words, it "was made
complete" (*eteleiōthē*, "matured," "perfected") by what he did. Recall
the opening words of the epistle where James sets out a major goal,
maturity (James 1:4): "*And let endurance have its perfect result, so
that you may be perfect [teleios] and complete [holoklēros], lacking in
nothing.*" "The point of verse 22 is not the substantiation of faith but the
maturation of it."[42] The "fulfillment" (v. 22) of justification is maturity.

How was this outcome achieved? According to James, Abraham's
"*actions were working together, and his faith was made complete by what

---

39 *BDAG*, 197.

40 It is possible that Abraham was already justified before God when he left Ur
(Hebrews 11:8; Acts 7:4) 30 or more years earlier, but was later vindicated
before God by his righteous life when he offered Isaac.

41 Grudem says, "At that point [sacrifice of Isaac] Abraham was 'shown to
be righteous' by his works, and in that sense James says that Abraham was
'justified by works, when he offered his son Isaac upon the altar' (James 2:21).
In other words, the declaration of righteousness in James 2:24 was verification
that Abraham was truly saved in Genesis 15:6." Wayne A. Grudem, *Systematic
Theology: An Introduction to Biblical Doctrine* (Grand Rapids, MI: Inter-Varsity
Press, 2004), 731. See also Craig L. Blomberg and Miriam J. Kimmel, *James,
Vol 16: Zondervan Exegetical Commentary of the New Testament* (Grand
Rapids: Zondervan 2008), 109. and William Varner, *James*, ed. H. Wayne
House, Evangelical Exegetical Commentary (Bellingham, WA: Lexham Press,
2012), 309.

42 Hart, "How to Energize Our Faith: Reconsidering the Meaning of James 2:14-
26," 44.

he did." It was not achieved by faith alone but by a life of faith working together (Gr. *synergeō*) with works (v. 22). *Synergeō* signifies "to engage in a cooperative endeavor,"[43] or "work together with, cooperate, assist."[44] For example, "*all things work together for good*" (Romans 8:28). James is saying that actions work together with faith; it says nothing about whether the good works inevitably result from a supposed genuine faith.[45] To be made complete is to become mature in one's faith. Lybrand

---

43 *BDAG*, 969.

44 Wolf-Henning Olbrog, "*suneros*" in *EDNT*, 3:303.

45 This passage also contradicts the Catholic assumption that claims that the result of this "working together" is final entrance into heaven. The text says nothing about heaven; rather it speaks of being made "complete." In this instance we agree, in part, with the Roman Catholic view of this passage. Catholics also see this as a synergy and not a sequence. See Robert A. Sungenis, *Not by Faith Alone: The Biblical Evidence for the Catholic Doctrine of Justification* (Goleta, CA: Queenship Publishing, 1997), 153. Sungenis protests that no one was around to "see" this vindication before men (ibid. 125)! However, James refers to the necessity of demonstration in 2:18-19. Sungenis also objects (ibid.) that James could have used a word that clearly does mean vindication "rather than a word commonly understood to refer to salvific justification." However, the verb *dikaioō* is used 39 times in the New Testament and commonly means "proved to be right" or "vindicated" (Matthew 11:19; 12:37; Luke 7:29, 35; 10:39; 16:15; 18:14, "proved to be right"; Romans 3:4; 6:7, "freed from sin," sanctified; 1 Corinthians 4:4; 1 Timothy 3:16). Thus, outside of James, the word is used 11 of 36 times in ways other than soteriological salvation or 33% of the time. If one adds the three usages in James 2, then it is used 14 of 39 times in a non-soteriological sense or 36%. So when Sungenis claims that "prove to be right" or "vindicate" is not a common sense, of the word, he is incorrect. Sungenis admits that the word often has a non-soteriological meaning (ibid. 126-27). Furthermore, Sungenis assumes that the context of James is soteriological. He bases this on one verse (2:14) "*Can that faith save him?*" He never answers the question "Save from what?" The context is about salvation from the spiritual/psychological death and a negative assessment of one's life at the Judgment Seat of Christ (1:14, 15, 21; 2:13). Sungenis makes a valid observation that in some of these instances, the nature of the context eliminates the possibility of it meaning soteriological justification (e.g., Matthew 11:19), and therefore, it is illegitimate to cite these passages against his Catholic view.

is correct when he says, "The combination of faith plus works is not to secure salvation from hell to heaven, but to propel the spiritual growth of the already-saved by giving fullness to a faithful walk with God, and a warning for avoiding 'death' through the failure to add works to one's faith."[46]

Abraham was already eternally saved, but the vitality and maturity of his faith could only be accomplished by works. Such an obedient response resulted in his being called God's friend (2 Chronicles 20:7),[47] a vindication-justification. Similarly, Jesus said, "*You are my friends, if you do what I command*" (John 15:14). There was no question about the disciples' regenerate state, but there was a question about whether they would continue to walk in fellowship with their King and be his "friend." When James says Abraham was justified by cooperative working of faith and works together he means that Abraham was declared to be morally righteous and mature, not that he was saved.

Thus James 2:24 is not in disagreement with Paul. James is simply saying that justification by faith is not the only kind of justification there is. Soteriological-justification by faith alone secures our eternal standing, but vindication-justification by works results from our obedient behavior and secures God's approval of our lives. Vindication-justification is our vindication before God at the Judgment Seat of Christ where we all hope to hear the Master say, "Well done!" James referred to vindication-justification when he spoke of being "saved" (2:14) from the death-spiral leading to spiritual ruin in this life, and at the Judgment Seat of Christ (James 2:12-13) because we have obeyed "the perfect law of liberty" (James 1:25; 2:12). That law is the law of the Spirit of life in Christ Jesus (Romans 8:3), which enables us to live out the Sermon on the Mount. Justification by faith alone secures our right standing before God; justification by works demonstrates our moral character as vindicated (justified) before God.

James's point then is not that perseverance to the end of life is the necessary and inevitable result of soteriological-justification, as

---

46 Fred Lybrand, "Does Faith Guarantee Works? Rethinking the Cliché" (DMin diss., Phoenix Theological Seminary, 2007), 85.

47 2 Chronicles 20:7; Isaiah 41:8.

Grudem believes.[48] Rather, he is saying that if works do not follow our soteriological-justification, our faith will shrivel up and die; we are in danger of spiritual impoverishment, "death." Nor does he say that the failure to work will result in the loss of our salvation. This is not a passage to prove the inevitable connection between forensic justification and progressive sanctification at all! Rather, it proves the desirable connection that we are all obliged to pursue.

But prove yourselves doers of the word, and not merely hearers who delude themselves. (James 2:22)

The Faith of Rahab

In the same way, was not Rahab the harlot also justified by works when she received the messengers and sent them out by another way? (James 2:25)

James does not say that Rahab was justified by faith plus works. But she was justified by works before God (and others). Like Abraham, Rahab was vindicated or shown to be ethically righteous by her works working together with her faith. There is nothing said here about her act being the result of faith. Rather, her act was combined with a faith she already had.

It may be significant that Rahab saved her life and that of the spies by works. She invited the spies in, she also sent them away by a different route. Until she sent them away and lied to the inhabitants of the city, she had not yet vitalized her faith by works. Just as saving a life in 1:21 and 2:14 referred, in part, to saving one's physical life, that is what Rahab did!

Summary

In this chapter and the previous one, we have shown that James is addressing believers and not mere professors of faith in Christ. His

---

48 Grudem, *"Free Grace" Theology*: 89.

burden is to show that in order for believers to be saved from the downward spiral of temptation, lust, sin, and "death," which would result in a negative assessment of their lives at the Judgment Seat of Christ (when they will be judged according to the perfect law of liberty), they must vitalize their walk of faith with good works. The subject is sanctification, not justification, living life, not gaining it. Some of his readers have argued that a walk of faith with no manifestation of works is acceptable. But James insists this is a "dead" faith.

We have argued in this chapter that a dead faith does not refer to non-existent faith. Instead it refers to a walk of faith that is not presently active and vital. Building on what we concluded in the preceding chapter, we have contended that the dead faith in view is a delusional and useless "walk of faith." It is only intellectual assent.

An imaginary objector replies, "some have faith and some have works." In other words, there is no necessary connection between a walk of faith with works and a walk of faith without works. Both are acceptable. To this James responds, "Show me your so-called walk of faith without deeds (implying that such a walk of faith is a myth), and I will show you by my works, my walk of faith." A faith-walk without works, James says, is mere head knowledge and not a real walk of faith. As proof of the ludicrousness of the interlocutor's viewpoint, James refers to the faith of demons. They also have an intellectual faith, but have no good works. In other words, the objector's so-called faith-walk is no better than the faith of demons. It is dead and useless.

James concludes his refutation of the interlocutor's foolish view of faith with proof from Scripture. Citing the illustrations of Abraham and Rahab, he shows that a true walk of faith always involves works and that those works not only bring faith to maturity, but they also result in vindication (approval) before God for a well-lived life, that is, justification by works. He concludes that there are two kinds of justification before God. The first is forensic and legal and results in our salvation. The second is a vindication-justification in which God says, "Well done!"

Chapter 8

Finding Assurance

Joseph Dillow, Th.D

John Duncan was born in 1796 in Aberdeen, Scotland, the son of a shoemaker.[1] Although not well known, his influence on Jewish missions was great. He was affectionately called "Rabbi" Duncan because of his immense knowledge of Hebrew literature and his espousal of the cause of the Jews. In fact, when he applied for the Chair of Oriental Languages in the University of Glasgow, there was no one who was qualified to examine him. He read fluently in Syriac, Arabic, Persian, Sanskrit, Bengali, Hindustani, and Marathi, as well as Latin, German, French, Hebrew, and Greek!

While studying in Budapest, he met a brilliant Jewish scholar, whom he led to Christ. This man was later to become the most learned writer on the life of Christ in the nineteenth century. His name? Alfred Edersheim.

---

1   This historical information is from John E. Marshall, "Rabbi Duncan and the Problem of Assurance (I)," *Banner of Truth*, no. 201 (June 1980): 16-27.

Becoming a Christian was not easy for Rabbi Duncan, and believing that he was saved was even harder. He struggled so desperately with doubt concerning his salvation that on one occasion, at a prayer meeting of professors and students, Duncan, who was presiding, broke down and wept, saying that God had forsaken him.[2]

In his quest to find subjective assurance that he was truly born again, Duncan turned repeatedly to Caesar Malan, through whom he was converted. Malan was ordained to the ministry in Geneva and apparently preached with great power and evangelical zeal. Malan's pastoral method of helping Duncan find assurance was through the use of a faith-based practical syllogism. He asked Duncan to consider the following logic:

Major Premise: He who believes that Jesus is the Christ is born of God.

Minor Premise: I believe that Jesus is the Christ.

Conclusion: Therefore, I am born of God.

As the implications of this reasoning dawned on his consciousness, Duncan said he sat still for hours, as many sermons he had preached came to his memory. The contemplation of the syllogism transformed his life—for a while. His new joy lasted for only two years and was followed by a time of terrible darkness. He was not sure he "really" believed. He says he prayed for the Holy Spirit and tried vainly to believe in Christ but could not. He then quarreled with God for not giving him his Holy Spirit and then rebuked himself for doing this. He thought that perhaps he was reprobate.

He pursued another version of the syllogism like the one advocated by Dr. Wayne A. Grudem.[3] He reasoned that those who are born of God will produce the fruits of regeneration.

---

2   John E. Marshall, "Rabbi Duncan and the Problem of Assurance (II)," *The Banner of Truth*, no. 202 (July 1980): 27.

3   Wayne A. Grudem, *Systematic Theology: An Introduction to Biblical Doctrine* (Grand Rapids, MI: Inter-Varsity Press, 2004), 803-06.

Major Premise:	Those who are born again will necessarily produce the fruits of regeneration in their lives.
Minor Premise:	I have the fruits of regeneration.
Conclusion:	Therefore, I am born again.

Duncan's problem was with the minor premise. He simply could not be convinced that there was sufficient evidence of the fruits of regeneration in his life for him to draw the necessary conclusion that he was indeed born of God.

He wrote one more time to his spiritual mentor, Caesar Malan. Malan told Duncan to reflect on his faith and scolded him for not believing the promises of the gospel.[4] Malan told him that the fruits of regeneration can come only after we have received assurance.

This did not help Duncan at all, and his struggles remained with him until his deathbed. In fact, his doubts were renewed with terrifying intensity: "I was in a terrible agony last night at the thought of a Christless state, and that I might be in it. The fear of it exhausted my faculties."[5]

He asked that the following words be published after his death:

I can't put a negative upon my regeneration. I don't say I can put a positive. Sometimes hope abounds, and at the worst I have never been able dogmatically to pronounce myself unregenerate. Sometimes I have strongly thought that what is formed between Christ and me shall last forever. At other times, I fear I may be in hell yet. But if I can't affirm my regeneration, I can't deny it; my self-examination can go no further.[6]

---

4 Malan asked Rabbi Duncan to reflect on his faith, which turned out to be a dead end. Instead, as the Free Grace view teaches, Duncan should have been encouraged to put his faith in the promises. Our trust is not in our faith but in Christ and his promises.

5 Marshall, "Rabbi Duncan and the Problem of Assurance (II)," 28.

6 John Duncan, quoted in Marshall, ibid., 27.

No doubt Duncan's healthy fear of taking the grace of God for granted contributed to his emotional state, but the methods employed by Caesar Malan and Dr. Grudem to secure confidence are only partially true to the New Testament. While Reformed interpreters like Dr. Grudem understand many passages in the New Testament exhort us to examine our works in order to discern our soteriological status, Free Grace interpreters understand all the passages Grudem cites in a different manner. According to the Free Grace understanding of the same passages, we look to our works to determine if we are in communion with God; to determine if we have a faith that is vital (that is, not dead); and to consider our lives in view of our final accountability at the Judgment Seat of Christ. For assurance of salvation we look to God's promises in Christ as declared in his Word. We agree with Calvin that our works cannot form a basis of assurance, but they can provide markers of our faithfulness and the vitality of our fellowship with him.

If, as Dr. Grudem believes, in eternity past God predestined some to hell (he prefers the term "passed over") and some to heaven,[7] how can a person be sure that he is among the elect? Dr. Grudem's question is, "How do I know that I have truly believed?"[8] In his recent book, he answers this question by listing five characteristics which must be present in order to verify the presence of saving faith. They are: (1) "a changed life," (2) "the internal testimony of the Holy Spirit," (3) "the leading of the Spirit," (4) "a deep inner sense of reliance on (also described as 'a personal, heart-felt trust in) Jesus Christ for

---

7 For example, he says, "When we understand election as God's sovereign choice of some persons to be saved, then there is necessarily another aspect of that choice, namely, God's sovereign decision to pass over others and not to save them. This decision of God in eternity past is called reprobation. *Reprobation is the sovereign decision of God before creation to pass over some persons, in sorrow deciding not to save them, and to punish them for their sins, and thereby to manifest his justice.*" Grudem, *Systematic Theology*: 685-85.

8 Wayne A. Grudem, *"Free Grace" Theology: 5 Ways It Diminishes the Gospel* (Wheaton: Crossway, 2016), 85.

salvation rather than reliance on oneself," and (5) "continuing in the faith."[9]

In this chapter, we will explore in more detail this approach suggested by Dr. Grudem. We begin with the viewpoint of John Calvin who would disagree strongly with Grudem's doctrine that we find our assurance by looking at the evidence of the Spirit's work in our lives.

John Calvin and Assurance (1509-1564)

The Basis of Assurance

Calvin would say that Christ is the source of our assurance. How? It is based on his atoning work. We look for peace "solely in the anguish of Christ our Redeemer."[10] We are to look to Christ who is the "pledge" of God's love for us.[11] When we look to him, he pledges eternal life to us. Unless we cling steadfastly to Christ, we will "waver continually."[12]

In other words, for Calvin the object of self-examination is not to see if we are saved but to be sure that we are trusting in Christ and not our works for our assurance.[13] He uses an excellent metaphor,

---

9 Ibid., 88-89, 105.

10 Ibid., 3.13.24.

11 John Calvin, *John*, Calvin's Commentaries (Albany, OR: Ages Software., 1998), s.v. "Jn. 15:9".

12 John Calvin, *Joshua*, electronic ed., Calvin's Commentaries (Albany, OR: Ages Software, 1998), s.v. 3:10.

13 Charles Bell explains that "while acknowledging that the Scriptures call on us to examine our lives, Calvin maintains that this is never to discern whether or not we are Christians: When we so examine ourselves, however, it is not to see whether our holiness, our works, or the fruit of the Spirit in our lives warrant assurance of salvation. Rather, it is to determine that such assurance rests on the proper foundation of God's mercy in Christ. Because of the phenomenon of temporary faith, we see that our feelings are an unreliable test of our standing with God. Therefore, if we are to be sure of our salvation, we must always direct our gaze to Christ, in whose face we see the love of God for us fully displayed." M. Charles Bell, *Calvin and the Scottish Theology: The Doctrine of Assurance* (Edinburgh: Handsel Press, 1985), 30.

saying that we must look to Christ who is the "mirror" in which we contemplate our election. He says,

> But if we are elected in him, we cannot find the certainty of our election in ourselves; and not even in God the Father, if we look at him apart from the Son. Christ, then, is the mirror in which we ought, and in which, without deception, we may contemplate our election.[14]

By this metaphor, Calvin means we must look externally to Christ and the beauty of the gospel promises. That is, we must look to the promise that whoever believes will be saved. If I believe in Christ, then I have the promise that I am saved. Christ, then, reflects back to us the image of the elect person. That is the basis for our assurance. This is also the Free Grace view.

Calvin feels strongly about this. He states that we cannot find assurance by examining our works.

> Doubtless, if we are to determine by our works in what way the Lord stands affected towards us, I admit that we cannot even get the length of a feeble conjecture: but since faith should accord with the free and simple promise, there is no room left for ambiguity. With what kind of confidence, pray, shall we be armed if we reason in this way—God is propitious to us, provided we deserve it by the purity of our lives?[15]

Although Dr. Grudem wishes to align himself with John Calvin's view of election, we find him at odds with Calvin in that Dr. Grudem believes one must work towards purity in order to assure oneself.[16] If we are not to trust in our works for justification, why should we trust in them for our assurance? While acknowledging that regeneration

---

14 John Calvin, *Institutes of the Christian Religion*, trans. Henry Beveridge, reprint ed. (Grand Rapids: Wm. B. Eerdmans Publishing Co., 1964), 3.24.5.

15 Ibid., 3.2.38.

16 Grudem, *"Free Grace" Theology*: 92.

has its fruits, such as love, Calvin avows that the presence in our hearts of love for our neighbor is an "accessory or inferior aid to our faith."[17] He insists, "if we are elected in him, we cannot find the certainty of our election in ourselves."[18] In his commentary on 1 Corinthians he says, "When the Christian looks at himself, he can only have ground for anxiety, indeed despair."[19] Furthermore, contrary to Grudem,[20] he says works cannot verify our saved status by their presence nor deny it by their absence:

> Should they begin to estimate it [assurance of their salvation] by their good works, nothing will be weaker or more uncertain; works, when estimated by themselves, no less proving the divine displeasure by their imperfection, than his good-will by their incipient purity.[21]

In his *Writings on Pastoral Piety*, he is even more emphatic saying, "*If you contemplate yourself, that is sure damnation.*[22] By this he means something like spiritual and psychological ruin, not loss of salvation.

---

17 John Calvin, *1 John*, electronic ed., Calvin's Commentaries (Albany, OR: Ages Software, 1998), s.v. "1 Jn. 3:19; 3:14".

18 Calvin, *Institutes*: 3.24.5.

19 Calvin, *1 Corinthians*: s.v. "1 Cor. 1:9".

20 Grudem, *"Free Grace" Theology*: 90.

21 Calvin clearly taught that works could be a proof of salvation. He says, "But as the fruits of regeneration furnish them with a proof of the Holy Spirit dwelling in them, experiencing God to be a Father in a matter of so much moment, they are strengthened in no slight degree to wait for his assistance in all their necessities." However, he clarifies that they are of no value unless the believer had already been assured by the promises. He says, "Even this [deriving assurance by works] they could not do, had they not previously perceived that the goodness of God is sealed to them by nothing but the certainty of the promise." Calvin, *Institutes*: 3.14.19.

22 John Calvin, *John Calvin: Writings on Pastoral Piety*, ed. Elsie Anne McKee and Bernard McGinn, trans. Elsie Anne McKee, The Classics of Western Spirituality (New York; Mahwah, NJ: Paulist Press, 2001), 76.

Good Works Are an Aid to Faith, Not a Basis of Assurance

Calvin says that if we seek assurance by works "they always give an occasion for trembling. Therefore no one can come with a tranquil mind to God's tribunal, except he believes that he is freely loved."[23] However, in agreement with most Free Grace interpreters,[24] Calvin states, that our good works give a "subsidiary aid to its [salvation's] confirmation."[25] In his *Institutes* he adds, "Then love is accessory or an inferior aid, a prop to our faith, not a foundation on which it rests."[26] But even with this concession, he insists that we must never "look to our works for our assurance to be firm."[27] If we want to know if we are elect, we must be "persuaded" that Christ died for us. We know this by a direct act of faith. We do not look for testimonies of good works in our lives to discern his love. Thus, Calvin affirms: "If Pighius asks how I know I am elect, I answer that Christ is more than a thousand testimonies to me."[28]

Calvin's view is eminently plausible. If works are necessary for assurance, as Dr. Grudem maintains (he says they are a "basis"),[29] then it is impossible for a person to have assurance until works have been manifested in his life. This leads to the curious conclusion that one can believe in Christ but not know that he has believed.

Calvin also taught that the reprobate could have similar feelings and evidences of regeneration as the elect.[30] This is also what Grudem believes as well.[31] How then does one know if he is one of the reprobate?

---

23 Calvin, *1 John*: s.v. "1 John 4:17".

24 Joseph C. Dillow, *Final Destiny: The Future Reign of the Servant Kings*, 3rd revised ed. (Monument, CO: Paniym Group, Inc., 2016; reprint, 2016), 19.

25 Calvin, *Joshua*: s.v. "Joshua 3:10".

26 Calvin, *1 John*: s.v. "1 John 3:19".

27 Ibid.

28 Jean Calvin and John Kelman Sutherland Reid, *Concerning the Eternal Predestination of God* (Louisville, KY: Westminster John Knox Press, 1997), 130.

29 Grudem, *"Free Grace" Theology*: 90, 92.

30 Calvin, *Institutes*: 3.2.11-12.

31 Grudem, *Systematic Theology*: 794.

Some means of discrimination are immediately thrust on the Christian mind: Is my faith only temporary? How can I know if my faith is saving faith? Wherein do they differ?

Theodore Beza (1519-1605)

Calvin grounded assurance in the death of Christ and reflection on the gospel promises. However, Calvin's successor at Geneva, Theodore Beza (1519-1605), departed from Calvin and grounded assurance in evidences of fruit in the life. Beza's starting point was his doctrine of limited atonement.[32] Calvin, according to R. T. Kendall, held to unlimited atonement.[33] If Christ died for all, Beza argued, then all would be saved. If Christ died only for the elect, as both Beza and Grudem maintain,[34] it would be illogical for a person to trust in

---

32 The definitive historical survey and theological critique based upon the New Testament against limited atonement to date is by David Allen, *The Extent of the Atonement* (Nashville: Broadman and Holman Academic, 2016). This monumental work of 800 pages is endorsed by many who hold to limited atonement such as Carl Truman of Westminster Theological Seminary. Craig A. Evans "finds its critique of the doctrine of limited atonement fully persuasive" (from the back cover of the book).

33 R. T. Kendall, *Calvin and English Calvinism to 1649* (Oxford: Oxford University Press, 1979), 13-18. He cites Calvin, *Institutes*: 3.1.1, *Commentary on Isaiah*, s.v. "Isaiah 53:12"; *Commentary on Hebrews*, s.v. "Hebrews 9:28." In both places, Romans 5:15 is referred to, and Calvin says "many" equals "all." In "Concerning the Eternal Predestination of God," p. 148, he says, it is "incontestable that Christ came for the expiation of the sins of the whole world." In his commentary on John 1:29, he observes, "And when he says *the sin of the world* he extends this kindness indiscriminately to the whole human race." "For God commends to us the salvation of all men without exception, even as Christ suffered for the sins of the whole world" (Sermons on Isaiah's Prophecy, 141). See also the extensive comment on this point in Bell, *Calvin and the Scottish Theology: The Doctrine of Assurance*: 13-19. Bell negatively critiques Paul Helm's response to Kendall in Paul Helm, "Article Review: Calvin and English Calvinism and the Logic of Doctrinal Development," *Scottish Journal of Theology* 34, no. 2 (1981). Allen also confirms Kendall's view. Allen, *The Extent of the Atonement*: 48-79.

34 Grudem, *Systematic Theology*: 594-96.

Christ's death unless he already knows he is elect. Why? It is because he cannot know if Christ died for him unless he already knows he is elect! Kendall, former pastor of Westminster Chapel explains the Reformed view in his doctoral dissertation, that it would, in fact, be dangerous for the non-elect to trust in Christ:

> We could be putting our trust in One who did not die for us and therefore be damned. Thus, we can no more trust Christ's death by a direct act of faith than we can infallibly project that we are among the number chosen from eternity: for the number of the elect and the number for whom Christ died are one and the same. The ground of assurance, then, must be sought elsewhere than in Christ.[35]

Beza, knowing this, suggests that we should look within ourselves for the evidence that Christ died for us. We cannot comprehend God's eternal decrees, but we can see if he is at work in our lives. "Beza directs us not to Christ but to ourselves; we do not begin with him but with the effects, which points us back, as it were, to the decree of election. Thus, while Calvin thinks looking to ourselves leads to anxiety, or sure ruin, Beza thinks otherwise. Sanctification, or good works is the infallible proof of saving faith."[36] Or, according to Grudem, they are a "basis" of assurance.[37] Free Grace interpreters would say that good works are a subsidiary encouragement, but are of little or no value apart from contemplation on the promises of eternal life. Because Grudem, like Beza, believes that Christ died only for the elect and not for all mankind (contrary to 1 John 2:2), he logically faces the same dilemma. He cannot logically direct a saved person to the promises because he does not know if the promises apply to that person. Christ may not have died for him! So, like all the heirs of Westminster Calvinism, Grudem needs to direct troubled souls to their works.

---

35 Kendall, *Calvin and English Calvinism to 1649*: 32.

36 Ibid., 33.

37 Grudem, *"Free Grace" Theology*: 87.

Free Grace theology, on the other hand, agrees with Calvin:[38] works are only a secondary confirmation, not a basis.[39] Furthermore, as I have stated elsewhere, those who have been born again will normally give some evidence of growth in grace and spiritual interest and commitment.[40] John Hart says it well, "It is not denied that genuine faith will result in some change in the believer. Those holding to the Free Grace teaching do not assert that faith can exist without any change whatsoever. Most, if not all Free Grace proponents believe that good works will inevitably result from faith, but not necessarily as visibly as we desire them to appear and not necessarily as consistently as the Lord would desire them to appear."[41] Zane Hodges agrees. "We must add that there is no need to quarrel with the Reformers' view that where there is justifying faith, works will undoubtedly exist too. This is a reasonable assumption for any Christian unless he has been converted on his deathbed! But it is quite wrong to claim that a life of dedicated obedience is guaranteed by regeneration, or even that such works as there are must be visible to a human observer."[42]

---

38 Calvin, *Joshua*: s.v. "Joshua 3:10"; 1 John 3:19.

39 Dillow, *Final Destiny*: 19.

40 See ibid.This is true because: (1) at conversion a person has believed and thus changed his perspective about sin and Christ. He knows who Christ is and what he has done for him and is therefore predisposed to allow Christ to change him. And (2) he has been flooded with new motivations toward godliness accompanied by the indwelling of the Holy Spirit. According to (3) the parable of the soils, the second man experienced some growth, a kind of fruit (see discussion of this parable in ibid., 522 ff.). But he may soon after conversion quench the Spirit, walk by means of the flesh, and thus fail to give visible evidence of these initial inner workings. A life of sanctification will not inevitably and necessarily follow justification.

41 John F. Hart, "The Faith of Demons," *JOTGES* 8, no. 2 (1995): 40.

42 Zane C. Hodges, *Absolutely Free! A Biblical Reply to Lordship Salvation* (Dallas: Redención Viva, 1989), 215.

Reformed Views for Obtaining Assurance

According to Westminster Calvinism, we can discern our soteriological status by three tests:

> Our assurance is based on three things: (1) the divine truth of the promises of salvation; (2) the inward evidence of those graces unto which these promises are made; and (3) the testimony of the Spirit of adoption that we are children of God.[43]

The problem, of course, is with number two. The Westminster divines required, as does Dr. Grudem, that this inward evidence must continue to the end of life. Thus, as a practical matter, most of the focus is upon the evidence of good works. This has resulted in various writers inventing lists of which works are necessary or must be avoided, which has understandably led to much legalism. For example, in one country in Eastern Europe the salvation of a woman was doubted because she came to church with lipstick and her dress came slightly above her knees. In some of the house church networks in China, if you disobeyed the network leader you could not be saved. And in another unless you could convince a group of observers that three days of crying and repentance was sincere, you could not possibly be a true believer.

Different Reformed scholars typically present different but overlapping lists of evidence that must be present to verify the presence of saving faith. John Murray, for example, says, there are five crucial evidences.[44] The beloved former pastor of Westminster Chapel, Martin Lloyd-Jones, however, says there are ten evidences which must be

---

43 *Westminster Confession of Faith*, ed. Phillip Schaff (Grand Rapids, MI: Baker Book House, 1985), 3:638; s.v. "18.2".

44 First, there must be intelligent understanding of the nature of salvation. Second, we must recognize the immutability of the gifts and calling of God. Our security rests in the faithfulness of God and not in the fluctuations of our experience. Third, we must obey the commandments of God. Fourth, there must be self-examination. He cites 2 Peter 1:10 and 2 Corinthians 13:5. Fifth, our assurance is based on the inward witness of the Holy Spirit. John Murray, *Collected Writings of John Murray*, 2 vols. (London: Banner of Truth Trust), 2:270.

present.[45] When we want to know the degree to which these evidences must be present, Lloyd-Jones says that a "glimmer" or a "mere trace" would be sufficient.[46] James Rosscup avows that "some vital degree" of evidence must be present.[47] Arthur Pink has a much higher bar.[48] Pink's list would surely call into question the salvation of every believer since the dawn of time, including even Pink himself![49]

---

45 (1) My outlook on life will be spiritual (1 Corinthians 2:12). (2) I will love the brethren. (3) I will seek God's glory: "A man who is led by the Spirit of God, is a man who desires to live to God's glory." (4) A man led by the Spirit always has a desire within him for greater knowledge of God, and a greater knowledge of our Lord and Savior Jesus Christ. (5) Anyone led by the Spirit is always concerned about his lack of love for God and for the Lord. (6) Anyone led by the Spirit has an increasing awareness of sin within. (7) A man led of the Spirit is increasingly sensitive to every approach of sin and evil and to temptation. (8) Are we putting to death the deeds of the body? (9) He is aware in himself of desires for righteousness and holiness. Do you long to be holy? (10) Are we manifesting the fruit of the Spirit? (Gal. 5). Martyn Lloyd-Jones, *Romans Chapter 8:17-39: The Final Perseverance of the Saints* (Grand Rapids: Zondervan Publishing House, 1976), 185-92.

46 Ibid., 193.

47 James E. Rosscup, "The Overcomers of the Apocalypse," *Grace Theological Journal* 3 (Fall 1982): 281-86.

48 He says, "One who regards sin lightly, who thinks nothing of breaking a promise, who is careless in performance of temporal duties, who gives no sign of a tender conscience which is exercised over what is commonly called 'trifles,' lacks the one thing needful. A person who is vain and self-important, who pushes to the fore seeking the notice of others, who parades his fancied knowledge and attainments, has not learned of him who is 'meek and lowly of heart.' One who is hypersensitive, who is deeply hurt if someone slights her, who resents a word of reproof no matter how kindly spoken, betrays the lack of a humble and teachable spirit. One who frets over disappointments, murmurs each time his will is crossed and rebels against the dispensations of Providence, exhibits a will which has not been Divinely subdued." Arthur Pink, *Eternal Security* (Grand Rapids: Baker Book House, 1974), 67.

49 Pink's list is completely arbitrary. How careless in our duties must one be? How lightly is sin regarded? How vain is too vain? If the professing Christian is too sensitive, he is not really saved. Yet if he is not sensitive enough, if his

Assurance According to Wayne Grudem

Tests of True Salvation

In his *Systematic Theology*, Dr. Wayne Grudem suggests three tests we can apply to see if in fact we are born again.[50] First, we should ask, "Do I today have trust in Christ to forgive my sins and take me without blame into heaven forever?"[51] With this encouraging statement, we can affirm that Dr. Grudem begins well. However, we are soon disappointed.

Secondly, the troubled believer should ask, "Is there evidence of a regenerating work of the Holy Spirit in my heart?" What are these evidences? In answer to this question, Dr. Grudem provides six pieces of evidence that should be present in a "true" believer's life.[52]

- Subjective testimony by the Holy Spirit in the heart.

- Holy Spirit produced character traits. Grudem differs from Calvin and argues that there is no possibility that a non-Christian can "convincingly fake" these traits.

- Am I having an influence on others in the church?

- Do I continue to believe and accept the teaching of the church?

- Do I have a continuing relationship with Jesus Christ?

- Do I live a life of obedience to God's commands? A perfect life is not necessary.

If Dr. Grudem had offered these tests as possible subsidiary evidence, we would heartily agree. However, when he requires that *they must be*

---

conscience is not tender enough, then this proves that "he lacks the root of the matter."

50 Grudem, *Systematic Theology*: 803-06.

51 Ibid., 803.

52 Ibid., 804.

present in "some" degree *to the end of life;*[53] are a "basis"[54] of assurance; and must be evident to be seen by others,[55] we are disappointed.

Thirdly, Dr. Grudem asks, "Do I see a long-term pattern of growth?"[56]

When we ask, "How much of these characteristics do we need to have to be sure we are saved," he says, "To be more specific, *some* change of life gives a basis for *some* measure of assurance" [emphasis original].[57] Since that is all that is required, is it not plausible to believe that there are many who are not saved and who have made an inaccurate profession of faith and would answer, "Yes," to all these questions? Dr. Grudem himself admits this.[58] They may reason that since they have not committed adultery; they go to church; they are moral and they read their Bible, and even say grace for dinner, they must be saved. They have believed (they think) and have Dr. Grudem's "some evidence" and Lloyd-Jones's "glimmer," and, perhaps they even think they have Rosscup's "some vital degree." However, they do not understand the gospel, nor are they personally trusting in the person of Christ for forgiveness, even though they can say the words. Also, there are many, like Rabbi Duncan, who are saved and who are introspective or discouraged, and they will conclude that they do not seem to have enough of the evidence Professor Grudem requires. The second test is therefore ineffective as a means of assurance.

This difficulty is illustrated by Dr. Grudem's fellow Five-Point Calvinist, John Piper.[59] Like Dr. Grudem, John Piper directs the

---

53 Ibid., 788.

54 Grudem, *"Free Grace" Theology*: 87. The only "basis" of assurance is reflection on Christ and his promises.

55 Ibid.

56 Grudem, *Systematic Theology*: 805.

57 Grudem, *"Free Grace" Theology*: 92.

58 Grudem, *Systematic Theology*: 794. See also his interpretation of Hebrews 6:4-7 where he argues that the unregenerate can manifest some of the same works that the regenerate do. See ibid., 796.

59 Piper might even be called a seven-point Calvinist. He says, "The 'sixth' point, double predestination, is simply the flip side of unconditional election." Then, "The 'seventh' point, the best-of-all-possible worlds, means that God governs

believer to examine his works to see if they are adequate to verify the presence of saving faith. This is an impossible standard that causes even a wonderful Christian like John Piper to wonder if he is saved. In response to a question about our imperfections in this life, Piper responded,

> I know people, and I would say this about myself, for whom the greatest threat to my perseverance and my ultimate salvation is the slowness of my sanctification. It's not theoretical questions like 'Did He rise from the dead?' or the problem of evil. I've got answers. But why I sin against my wife the same at age 62 that I did at age 42 causes me sometimes to doubt my salvation or the power of the Holy Spirit —This question is not theoretical.[60]

Thus, Piper admits that on Dr. Grudem's premises, one cannot really know for certain that he himself is a Christian—loved by God as his child—until he has finally persevered.

Another recent example of this approach to assurance is from Reformed theologian R.C Sproul. Sproul says that when he prayed for James Boice (who was then dying of cancer), his prayer was that he might die "in faith," because to do otherwise would indicate that he was never truly saved.[61] This is the logical ludicrousness of that position.

---

the course of history so that, in the long run, His glory will be more fully displayed and His people more fully satisfied than would have been the case in any other world." See Matt Perman, "What Does Piper Mean When He Says He's a Seven-Point Calvinist?" *Desiring God*, accessed Month ??, 2017, http://www.desiringgod.org/articles/what-does-piper-mean-when-he-says-hes-a-seven-point-calvinist

60 John Piper, "Why God is Not a Megalomaniac in Demanding to be Worshiped" 60th Annual Meeting of the Evangelical Theological Society. Recording available through ACTS Conference Products, # EV08487 (www.actsconferenceproducts.com/merchant/ev0108b.pdf).

61 R.C. Sproul, "Eternal Security," *Grace Bible Studies*, accessed July 6, 2017, http://gracebiblestudies.org/Resources/Web/www.duluthbible.org/g_f_j/EternalSecurity12.htm).

How does Dr. Grudem respond to this? He states that if a person is saved, his perseverance in good works is guaranteed by God. Therefore, the believer should reason, "I will certainly persevere to the end, because I am being guarded by God's power working through my faith (1 Peter 1:5)."[62] How does one know that he will be guarded by God? According to Grudem, he discerns it by his works, which will give him assurance of this on a progressive scale from some evidence to strong evidence and assurance.[63]

However, Free Grace interpreters believe that the quest for assurance based on self-examination is doomed for two seemingly conspicuous reasons. First, how can a man know that the good works he produces are in fact produced by the Holy Spirit flowing from a regenerate nature and not by his unregenerate flesh? Based upon Dr. Grudem's own interpretation of Hebrews 6:4-5, that is possible.[64] He doesn't provide a way to distinguish them outwardly (other than persevering to the end), and yet it is on the basis of these outward evidences that assurance is prematurely promised.[65] He admits that "[i]t is not always easy to tell" by looking at these evidences whether a person is saved. Furthermore, a person professing to be a Christian, but who is unsaved, can "give some external signs or indications that make them look or sound like true believers."[66]

However, Grudem's view is based upon an implausible understanding of Hebrews 6:4, namely that it refers to professing Christians who are not born again. We agree with Tom Schreiner who says that "Grudem's reading [of Heb. 6:4] fails to convince,"[67] and that "[t]he writer specifically addresses believers in the warning. The terms he uses don't

---

62 Grudem, *Systematic Theology*: 805.

63 Grudem, *"Free Grace" Theology*: 92.

64 Grudem, *Systematic Theology*: 796.

65 Grudem, *"Free Grace" Theology*: 87.

66 Grudem, *Systematic Theology*: 794.

67 Thomas Schreiner, *Biblical Theology for Christian Proclaimation: Commentary on Hebrews* (Nashville, TN: B & H Publishing Group, 2015), 185.

suggest inadequate or partial belief. Instead he uses expressions that designate Christian believers in the fullest sense of the word."[68]

Secondly, this view raises the question, "How much work and change are necessary to validate to one's conscience that he is born again?" Dr. Grudem dismisses this concern saying, "These questions give the impression that Free Grace supporters are looking for something like a mathematical formula by which one can be certain of salvation (How many? How long?)."[69]

Free Grace interpreters are *not* looking for a mathematical formula. But if assurance is to be found on Dr. Grudem's self-examination premises, such a formula might be helpful. He admits that "it would be impossible to put a numerical value on those qualities in our lives."[70] So rather than giving a number, his pastoral heart takes over, and he sets the bar very low; requiring only "some" evidence, like Lloyd-Jones's "glimmer."

Dr. Grudem proposes that there is a succession of various levels of assurance based on differing amounts of evidence ranging from mixed evidence, weak evidence, and strong evidence.[71] Only "strong" evidence can give strong assurance. Yet Dr. Grudem also says that "believers may obtain 'infallible' assurance of salvation and have 'certainty' that 'they are in a state of grace'" [emphasis added].[72] This raises the question, "Which is it – *strong* assurance or *infallible* and certain assurance?"

But even "strong" evidence would not be the certain evidence that Dr. Grudem says the verses he cites demand. Why? Because one of Dr. Grudem's requirements for certain evidence cannot be met until the person having this "strong" evidence has persevered in good works to the end of life.

The main difference between Dr. Grudem's scale and a numerical scale is the label he applied to it (mixed, weak, strong). On a scale of

---

68 Ibid., 186. See discussion by Paul Tanner in chapter 9 of this book.

69 Grudem, *"Free Grace" Theology*: 91.

70 Ibid.

71 Ibid., 92.

72 Ibid., 96.

one to ten, "mixed" might be a two or three, and "weak" might be a five? "Strong" may be an eight or nine, but it cannot be a ten because one cannot know that he has persevered until the end comes.[73] Thus, there is no certainty I am a child of God, only a high probability, and even that could possibly be false assurance.

I am unaware of any biblical discussion of such levels of assurance, and Dr. Grudem gives none. The Bible does speak of a full assurance and a certainty that a believer has eternal life. Faith comes by hearing, or reading, the Word of God (Romans 10:17), not by examining one's works.

Romans 8:16 and Assurance

Dr. Grudem curiously dismisses these legitimate concerns saying, "these questions fail to understand how the Bible talks about assurance."[74] He then appeals to the subjective testimony of the Holy Spirit (Romans 8:16), a view held by some evangelical scholars.[75] It is important to note that in his book he quotes this verse as saying the Holy Spirit "testifies **to** our spirit."[76] However, while some translations translate "testifies **to** our spirit,"[77] most of them render the Greek phrase "testifies **with** our spirit."[78]

---

73 Grudem, *Systematic Theology*: 788.

74 Grudem, *"Free Grace" Theology*: 61.

75 E.g. Daniel Wallace, "The Witness of the Holy Spirit in Romans 8:16: Interpretation and Implications," *Bible*.org, accessed July 6, 2017, https://bible.org/seriespage/2-witness-spirit-romans-816-interpretation-and-implications#P29_11697.

76 It is interesting to note that the ESV Study Bible, of which Dr. Grudem was the General Editor, renders Romans 8:16, "with our spirit."

77 NET, LB

78 NIV, NASB, ESV, NKJV, NRSV, KJV, HCSB, NLT, NAB, NCV, ISV, NIrv, RSV, 1901 ASV, YLT, TNIV, and the French, German, Spanish, Latin Vulgate, and Dutch translations. While it is true that the verb *summmartureō* (to testify with) could only be an intensification and not necessarily include the notion of "with," in the preceding context there are 8 *sun* verbs which all mean "with." Jewett, et al. say "This verb is in fact typically used to depict co-witnessing of

*"The Spirit himself testifies **with our spirit** that we are children of God,"* (Romans 8:16, NASB95)

If the Holy Spirit is testifying to our spirit with an internal confirmation that we are children of God, as Dr. Grudem maintains, this raises the question, "Would Paul think that the testimony of the Holy Spirit is insufficient, and therefore additional testimony by works are needed to be really sure? Would God leave the troubled believer with only vague hints derived from inner impressions produced by the Holy Spirit that he is saved?" If the Holy Spirit's inner testimony can only result in vague internal impressions and not absolute certainty, isn't this a demeaning view of the power and influence of the Holy Spirit?[79]

The Greek word for "testifies" means "to provide supporting evidence by testifying, confirm."[80] The idea seems to be that there are two persons addressing the Father, the believer's spirit crying "Abba, Father" (Romans 8:15) and the witness of the Holy Spirit praying with our spirit supplying supporting evidence. The Holy Spirit is not speaking "to" our spirit, rather he is speaking "with" our spirit to Abba, saying "this person is God's child."[81] A few verses later Paul explains

---

some sort. R. Jewett, R. D. Kotansky, and E. J. Epp, *Romans: A Commentary, Heremenia: A Critical and Historical Commentary on the Bible* (Minneapolis: Fortress Press, 2006).

79 As far as I can tell, there is no discussion in the Bible regarding how to discern whether an inner impression is from God or from the Holy Spirit. If the certainty of God's voice is tied to inner impressions, why is it that the New Testament never discusses how to discern this? Dr. Grudem, a champion of the ESV, was general editor of the ESV Study Bible, which translates it "with," so he is inconsistent. This exegetical decision may be based upon a "Charismatic" or "Vineyard" theological commitment to his overall theology. His work, *The Gift of Prophecy in the New Testament and Today*, (Westchester, IL: Crossway Books, 1988) brought a charismatic aspect into Reformed theology that has been frequently accepted among the young and new "Strong Calvinists".

80 *BDAG*, 957.

81 A similar construction is found in Romans 9:1, "my conscience testifies **with me** in (Gr. *en*, "with") the Holy Spirit" to you (implied). In 8:16, "the Spirit

that "in the same way" the Spirit "helps our weakness" and, in parallel to verse 16, "intercedes for us." The Holy Spirit within us prays to God for us (v. 23). In verse 16, he prays with us to God, and in verse 23 he intercedes for us to God.[82] The Holy Spirit addresses the Father in both passages, not the believer's spirit.[83]

Paul speaks of the Holy Spirit's ministry of prayer on our behalf in Galatians as well.

And because you are sons, God has sent forth the Spirit of his Son into our hearts, crying, "Abba! Father!" (Galatians 4:6, NASB)

---

testifies **with my spirit**" to God (implied). Both "me" in 9:1 and "our spirit" in 8:16 are dative. Paul is not saying that his spirit is testifying to himself. He is saying that both Paul and his conscience are testifying together to God. As further evidence for the dual-testimony view ("with"), Gunderson notes, "It is remarkable that there are eight *sun*-prefixed words bearing an associative sense from 8:17-9:1. There are four *sun*-prefixes in 8:16-17 alone, three with an obvious "together-with" meaning [*sugklaronomos*, "fellow heirs"; *sumpaschō*, "suffer with"; *sundoxazō*, "glorify with"]. See David A. Gunderson, "Adoption, Assurance, and the Internal Testimony of the Holy Spirit," *Jounal of Discipleship and Family Ministry* 2, no. 1 (Fall 2011): 26. Of course, this strong presence of other sun-prefixed words does not establish an associative, joint-witness meaning for *summarturei* in 8:16, but it certainly makes it much more likely."

82 Some object to this conclusion on the basis that God already knows that the saved person is his child. See ibid., 28. However the word "testifies" suggests a metaphor of a courtroom scene. Elsewhere John presents Jesus as our advocate in the heavenly courtroom testifying to the Father the believer's sins are forgiven (1 John 2:2). But the Father already knows that as well. In fact, the Father already knows everything that Jesus brings to him on our behalf in his high priestly ministry, so this is hardly a problem for the idea that Romans 8:16 could not express Jesus testifying to God because God already knows that the believer is his child. These are figures of speech.

83 This is the dual-testimony view (Holy Spirit plus human spirit both giving testimony to God.) The single testimony view, however, is also plausible. That is the Holy Spirit testifies to our spirit. Thomas Schreiner, along with many others, takes the dual-testimony view. See Thomas R. Schreiner, *Romans* (Grand Rapids: Baker Book House, 1998), 123. For an excellent discussion of the single testimony view see Gunderson, "Adoption, Assurance, and the Internal Testimony of the Holy Spirit," 18-32.

The word "hearts" is a plural noun, but the verb "crying" is a singular verb. It is clear therefore that this passage refers to the Spirit's prayer to God, and not the cry of our hearts to him. If so, why would the Holy Spirit address God as, "Abba, Father"? Is God the father of the Holy Spirit? While that form of address may be because his name within the Trinity is "Father," there is a more intimate reason. The Holy Spirt addresses God as the *believer's* Father. Since he is our Father, he will respond.

The New Testament tells us that Jesus also prays for us (Hebrews 4:13-16). What is the difference between the prayers of these two persons of the Godhead? It may be that because the Holy Spirit has a specific prayer ministry related to the fact that he dwells within our hearts, that he is, perhaps, assigned by the Father to intimately know our inner life. He knows our joy, our weeping, our dreams, and our burdens. Jesus told his disciples that he was going away but he would send the Holy Spirit and *"it is to your advantage that I go away; for if I do not go away, the Helper shall not come to you; but if I go, I will send him to you"* (John 16:7, NASB). He teaches that when he comes, he will be a "helper"[84] and he will be "in" us.[85]

This is a great encouragement to a troubled believer knowing that the Holy Spirit is affirming to the Father that the believer is God's child; that the Holy Spirit is praying for us in our weakness and that he intercedes for us with "groanings too deep for words" (v. 26). This should heighten our confidence that the Lord hears our prayers.[86]

---

84 John 14:26.

85 John 14:17.

86 Richard Lovelace notes that Puritan and Pietist legalism and their stress on self-examination led to "[a]n unbalanced stress on auxiliary methods of assurance—testing one's life by the inspection of works and searching for the internal witness of the Spirit." This stress "obscured Luther's teaching on assurance of salvation through naked reliance on the work of Christ." Richard F. Lovelace, *Dynamics of Spiritual Life: An Evangelical Theology of Renewal* (Downers Grove, IL: InterVarsity Press, 1979), 100.

Objections to Grudem's View of Finding Assurance

Grudem's View of Assurance Fails the Test of Human Consciousness

In 1643, the Westminster divines crafted a magnificent document, the Westminster Confession. There is no doubt that this confession and the Reformed movement that followed have contributed immensely to evangelical impact throughout the world. The doctrinal clarity and apologetic impact have served the church for 400 years as a bulwark against heresy and guide to holy Christian living. All evangelicals owe the Reformed faith an immense debt of gratitude.

Nevertheless, Calvinism has often enjoyed the sanctuary of the philosopher's hall. It revels in theoretical speculation and theological argument. However, with its doctrine of perseverance and assurance, in contrast to the doctrine of election, Calvinism must emerge from the halls of academia and submit itself to the test of the consciousness of men.[87]

In Reformed thought, the justified saint knows he cannot lose this salvation. But at the same time, when he fails for "a period of time,"[88] he must be warned that he might not have it because his initial faith may not have been genuine. Therefore, if that system is true, it would be difficult for believers to accept all of Scripture at face value at the same time. "He must oscillate between two contradictory

---

87 Many do not realize that Dr. Grudem's view of assurance is completely dependent upon his prior commitment to the Calvinist system and its views of sovereignty, unconditional election, irresistible grace, perseverance of the saints, and limited atonement. Free Grace writers along with the majority of Christians in the world throughout church history disagree with the Calvinist views on several of these doctrines.

88 Both Dr. Grudem and the Westminster Confession admit that believers can be carnal "for a period of time," but if they are truly believers they will always repent. See *Larger Catechism of the Westminster Standards*, ed. M. H. Smith (Greenville, SC: Presbyterian Theological Seminary Press, 1996), s.v. Answer: Question 195. Grudem, *"Free Grace" Theology*: 88.

persuasions, both of which are supposedly equally warranted by the Scriptures."[89]

Like other Reformed writers, Dr. Grudem must deal with the many warnings in the New Testament, which seem to be addressed to true believers.[90] These warnings are directly connected with all views of assurance. He believes that the purpose of the warnings is to produce sincere alarm to those *who have only professed faith, but may or may not be saved.*[91]

Elsewhere, Dr. Grudem says that the warnings are to be directed to *"those who are thinking of falling away or have fallen away."*[92] They should be cautioned that if they do this, it is a strong indication that they were never saved in the first place.[93] Furthermore, "the necessity of continuing in the faith should be used as a warning against falling away only after the person has already given evidence that his faith was never real."[94] That evidence, of course, would include a lack of the list of criteria above.

Yet he extends the warnings way beyond those who are thinking of falling away. He teaches that they also apply to those who think they are Christians but have not met his criteria, which must be present to verify the presence of saving faith. That is, professing Christians who are failing in their Christian lives.[95] He says the warnings also apply to "church goers (and those who claim to be a Christian but do not go to

---

89 Robert Shank, *Life in the Son: A Study of the Doctrine of Perseverance* (Springfield, MO: Westcott Publishers, 1961), 167.

90 E.g. Matthew 5:12; 21-22, 27-30; 18:1-6 John 15:6; Colossians 1:21-23; 2:18-19; 1 Corinthians 9:24-27; 10:12-13; 15:1-2; Galatians 5:1-4; James 5:19-20; 2 Peter 1:10-11; 3:16-18; Romans 8:12-13; 11:20-22; 1 Timothy 6:9-10; 2 Timothy 2:11-13; Hebrews 2:1-3; 3:1-6; 4:1; 6:4-6; 10:26-31;

91 Grudem, *Systematic Theology*: 793-94.

92 Ibid.

93 Ibid.

94 Ibid., 794.

95 Ibid., 792. Grudem, *"Free Grace" Theology*: 79-82.

church)."⁹⁶ So which is it, everyone (church goers), or only those who are thinking about apostasy?

How would Dr. Grudem counsel such a person? He explains, "I would tell him that I do not know if he is truly born again or not, but his present pattern of life gives me no reason to give him assurance of salvation."⁹⁷ In other words, Dr. Grudem would first raise the possibility to the unfaithful "Christian" that he may not be a Christian at all. On a case-by-case basis, Free Grace interpreters might do the same, but they would approach it differently (see below). As part of Grudem's counsel, he would direct him to three passages of Scripture, which in his interpretation, raise questions regarding a carnal person's final destiny (Hebrews 3:12; James 5:19-20; 1 John 2:19).⁹⁸ Since Dr. Grudem cannot know if the person whom he is counseling is saved or not, his counsel will also naturally fall upon the ears of a person who is saved, as well as the person who is unsaved. Dr. Grudem himself indirectly acknowledges this can be so when he argues extensively that no one can tell for sure if a professing non-Christian is saved, because he may exhibit many of the same characteristics of a saved person.⁹⁹ Dr. Grudem's approach would raise alarm in both the false "Christian" and the person who is justified. However, our concern here is the dynamics going on in the mind of the person who is saved.

In our journey to the heavenly city, all believers, including this author, often fail, even sin, and may lapse into doubt and disobedience for a period of time. When confronted with this common experience, Scripture counsels us to ask for forgiveness (1 John 1:9) and look to Christ who is the mirror in which we must contemplate our election.

In Grudem's system, however, the counselor should raise the specter that the person may not be saved. Based upon his misunderstanding of 2 Corinthians 13:5, Dr. Grudem teaches that when the believer sees inconsistencies in his life, he should regularly examine himself to see

---

96 Grudem, *"Free Grace" Theology*: 79.

97 Ibid., 93.

98 Free Grace interpreters deny that these verses raise questions about a person's saved status.

99 Grudem, *Systematic Theology*: 794-95.

if he is "in the faith" and may not have genuinely believed at first.[100] Free Grace interpreters understand "in the faith" to mean "in the faith way of life" and not "in a state of salvation."[101] How would Reformed interpreters relieve the justified saint's fear that he may not be saved?

On the one hand, he knows he is eternally secure, and on the other hand, because the evidences in his life may not rise to Dr. Grudem's standard of "some" to "strong" evidence, he is alarmed that he may end up in the lake of fire. A person cannot be motivated by the warnings until he has abandoned the promise that salvation cannot be lost. Until he concludes that his faith may not be "genuine," he will have no alarm. How is he supposed to determine if his faith is genuine? The answer is that he must heed the warnings. Would the Lord of grace motivate believers in this way? Does this ring true? Would the Bible demand that believers continually hold in their minds their assurance of salvation and at the same time hold that they must heed the warnings and persevere to the end for their assurance to be valid?

Free Grace interpreters also take the warnings seriously but find no contextual justification for Dr. Grudem's conclusion that the purpose of the warnings is to alert failing Christians that they may not be saved. Nor do we view the warnings as God's means of motivating believers to persevere in their quest for heaven. Instead, the purpose of the warnings is to warn justified believers of the possibility of negative assessment they might receive at the Judgment Seat of Christ and as a means of motivating true believers to persevere in good works (Ephesians 2:10). In the Free Grace view, they are not related to soteriology-justification, rather they are related to sanctification and rewards (Mark 4:25; Luke 6:23; 1 Corinthians 3:15; 9:27; 2 Corinthians 5:10-11; 1 John 2:28).[102]

In our view, Dr. Grudem's Westminster Calvinism and its view of assurance can only result in anxiety, as Calvin affirmed. Is it not confusing to say that men are to hold two contradictory sets of

---

100 Grudem, "Free Grace" Theology: 80-81.

101 See discussion elsewhere in this book, in chapter 19.

102 Also, we do not believe the Arminian conclusion that these warnings threaten loss of salvation. Rather, in each instance a millennial disinheritance or a judgment in time is forecast.

Scriptures in their minds at the same time and switch back and forth depending on whether their need is for assurance or admonition? They are unable, on Dr. Grudem's view of the warnings, to view the whole of Scripture with equal sincerity at the same time. Even Calvin fell into this trap: He says,

> As far then as Christians are illuminated by faith, they hear, for their assurance, that the calling of God is without repentance; but as far as they carry about them the flesh, which wantonly resists the grace of God, they are taught humility by this warning, "Take heed lest thou be cut off."[103]

In this view, when a person is "illuminated by faith," he knows that the calling of God is without repentance, that is, he cannot lose salvation. But in his struggle with the flesh, a person is supposed to fear going to the lake of fire. So, on the one hand, we are to have a consciousness that we are eternally secure (if we work hard enough to satisfy the claims of conscience that our faith is real), and, on the other hand, because of our flesh we are to be aware that we might be damned. But how can a person hold these two contradictory states in his mind at the same time? Being conscious of either one logically and subjectively excludes the other. It appears to Free Grace interpreters that Dr. Grudem's view of assurance fails the test of human consciousness.

Grudem's System for Obtaining Assurance Implies That Salvation Is Based on Faith Plus Works

Grudem's System Logically Requires that Salvation is By Faith Plus Works

When Dr. Grudem's system for obtaining salvation is carefully considered, although he would vigorously deny it, it implies that there are two causes of our arrival in heaven. The first, initial salvation, is God's part in causing our salvation and we have nothing to do with

---

103 John Calvin and John Owen, *Commentary on the Epistle of Paul to the Romans*, Calvin's Commentaries (Bellingham, WA: Logos Bible Software, 2010), s.v. Romans 11:22-24, p. 433.

it except believe. The second cause is our part in perseverance. While God strengthens, commands, warns and enables (his part), we, through definite effort, contribute to the final goal (our part). We are therefore partially responsible for our final salvation. Thomas Schreiner seems to agree, "We must run the race with dogged determination to obtain the prize of eternal life, and it takes remarkable discipline and training to make it to the end."[104] He continues, "We are to use all the resources at our disposal in order to be saved on the last day. We must obey, pray, resist the flesh and yield to the Spirit to inherit salvation. No theology is acceptable that diminishes this call to work out our salvation."[105]

Roy Zuck responds, "A problem with this view is the authors' contradictory statements about works in relation to salvation. They 'categorically deny that salvation can be earned by works' (p. 86). And yet in the very next sentence they write, 'The prize to be won is eternal life . . . and we must strive to win that prize . . . [I]s this not making salvation dependent on one's works? How can a gift be a gift if one must strive to attain it? Is this not illogical?"[106]

We have discussed this problem for Reformed theology elsewhere in this book.[107]

Grudem's System for Obtaining Assurance Is Logically Contradictory

His View of Perseverance to the End Can Lead to a False Assurance

Dr. Grudem's required tests to verify the presence of saving faith make assurance in this life an exercise balancing two contradictory ideas in

---

104 Thomas R. Schreiner and Ardel B. Caneday, *The Race Set Before Us: A Biblical Theology of Perseverance and Assurance* (Downers Grove, IL: InterVarsity Press, 2001), 314.

105 Ibid., 315.

106 Roy B. Zuck, "Book Review of The Race Set Before Us: A Biblical Theology of Perseverance and Assurance by Thomas R. Schreiner and Ardel B. Caneday," *BibSac* 160, no. 638 (April-June 2003): 242.

107 See chapter 5.

the mind at the same time. It results in doubts and hopelessness in the lives of many. Why? Dr. Grudem requires not only the presence of evident good works increasing assurance from weak to strong,[108] but critically, one must continue in belief and good works to the end of life. This leads to a logical contradiction. He states,

> It is clear that **continuing in the Christian life** is one of the evidences that a person is truly born again. It is important to keep this aspect of the doctrine in mind as well, lest false assurance be given to people who were never believers in the first place.[109]

In other words, the believer must be warned that he must continue in the faith to the end of life in order to verify that his initial belief was "genuine." How then, should the believer achieve assurance in the present—before the end of life?

Thomas Schreiner explains, a believer can "escape the threat of judgment by heeding the warning."[110] "Heeding warnings," he says, "is one of the means by which the promise of final salvation is obtained on the last day."[111] "By heeding the warnings, believers gain assurance in their lives."[112] Based on this approach, a true Christian, if he takes this seriously (and most do not), would be in tension regarding his saved status every time he fell into sin for "a period of time."

With these statements, Grudem and other Reformed writers are admitting that the *Reformed* approach also can give a false assurance. Why? Because no one can know that he is saved unless he "*continues in the Christian life*" and they "*persevere as Christians until the end of their lives*," and no one else could discern whether he has done that until

---

108 Grudem, *"Free Grace" Theology*: 92.

109 Grudem, *Systematic Theology*: 805.

110 Thomas R. Schreiner, *Run to Win the Prize: Perseverance in the New Testament* (Wheaton, IL: Crossway Books, 2010), 96.

111 Ibid., 101.

112 Ibid., 102.

the end of life arrives. Yet, Dr. Grudem requires that all these changes including perseverance to the end of life must be "evident."[113]

Furthermore, heeding the warnings would temporarily solve the problem until the next crisis of faith occurs. Then the troubled believer must doubt his salvation again. This is so because, as the believer progresses through life and falls into sin for a period of time, based on 2 Corinthians 13:5-6, Dr. Grudem would exhort the believer to examine himself once again to see if he has the evidence to verify the presence of saving faith. At the beginning of his journey he "thought" he believed. But what is to say that after self-examination later in life, he "believes" again, having concluded that his initial belief may not have been genuine? Will it be any different than when he "believed" the first time?

Thus, no matter how many times a person may conclude he or she had not really believed previously and then believes again in response to a self-examination, there is no certainty that this "new" belief is genuine. The cycle may only repeat itself. And how is this uncertainty to be corrected? According to Grudem, "One way in which we know that we have come to genuine faith in Christ is if we continue in faith until the end of our lives."[114]

David R. Anderson is certainly correct. According to the Reformed approach,

Present faithfulness is an unreliable basis for present assurance. Only future faithfulness can provide any grounds for assurance. But the future is always out there. Until one dies, one can always fall away. Present faithfulness is not firm footing for assurance of salvation.[115]

---

113 Grudem, *"Free Grace" Theology*: 87.

114 Wayne A. Grudem, *Systematic Theology: An Introduction to Biblical Doctrine* (Leicester, England; Grand Rapids, MI: Inter-Varsity Press; Zondervan Pub. House, 2004), 793.

115 David R. Anderson, *Free Grace Soteriology*, revised ed. (Woodlends, TX: Grace Theology Press, 2012), 212.

Grudem illogically responds to Anderson by quoting verses that say we can know we are saved.[116] Of course, all Free Grace interpreters agree we can know we are saved! However, we cannot know it by the manner Grudem suggests, because one can never know if he will fall away in the future. And we can only know that the Holy Spirit will guarantee our perseverance if we already know that we are Christians! Furthermore, for many, they would never find enough evidence of good works to satisfy the claims of conscience that they are born again. In agreement with Calvin, Free Grace interpreters believe we can only know if we are saved by looking to Christ who is the mirror in which we must contemplate our election. Changes in our lives are only helpful, secondary confirmations.

I wonder if Dr. Grudem knows of people who have met all his criteria of "strong evidence of belief," except perseverance to the end, and then, at some point many years later, rejected the faith altogether like Solomon did. I know such persons. My guess is that some reading this book have. The examples of Billy Graham's fellow evangelist, Charles Templeton and the New Testament scholar Bart Ehrman are well known. Both appeared to be solid evangelical Christians for many years and then denied the faith altogether[117] Based upon Dr. Grudem's

---

116 Grudem, *"Free Grace" Theology*: 95-96.

117 For example, Billy Graham and Charles Templeton were evangelists who rose to fame in the 1940s (Graham, of course, is still an evangelist). Early in their careers they were friends – close friends. Many have said Templeton was the one that everyone thought was going to overturn the world with the gospel. However, Templeton ended up leaving the Christian faith, eventually becoming an atheist." See Michael Patton, "Billy Graham and Charles Templeton: The Sad Tale of Two Evangelists," *Credo House Blog*, accessed July 7, 2017, http://credohouse.org/blog/billy-graham-and-charles-templeton-the-sad-tale-of-two-evangelists. More recently, Bart Ehrman, a well-known New Testament scholar wrote, "For most of my life I was a devout Christian, believing in God, trusting in Christ for salvation, knowing that God was actively involved in this world. During my young adulthood, I was an evangelical, with a firm belief in the Bible as the inspired and inerrant word of God. . . .This was my view for many years [the biblical explanation for the problem of pain and suffering in the world], and I still consider it a powerful theological view. It would be a view that I would still hold on to, *if*

criteria of "strong evidence," there is no question he should have concluded they were born again and should have given them assurance. However, in giving assurance to persons like this, Dr. Grudem would contradict himself. On the one hand, he says that everyone who gains assurance by reflecting on his criteria should conclude that he is saved and will persevere to the end.[118] There is little doubt that these two men had assurance, and Dr. Grudem would have gladly verified it. But on the other hand, Dr. Grudem says that continuing in the Christian life is one of the evidences that a person is truly born again.[119] Is this not circular reasoning?

Ken Mitchell illustrates the problem with this reasoning by citing his experience with a close friend named Jack. A few years after college Jack was saved. He and his wife were very dedicated to the Lord. Jack gave up high school coaching so he could travel and preach the gospel. He studied constantly. But something happened, and Jack left the faith. When his adult son died he prohibited the name of God or Jesus even to be spoken at his funeral. Like Templeton and Ehrman, Jack was an apostate. To say that Jack never truly trusted in the person of Christ for salvation means that all the time he was preaching and teaching and evangelizing and telling others how to be saved, he never really believed it himself. This is preposterous. To say that he never really believed it when he gave up his career in coaching to travel in a motorhome to preach the gospel simply defies all rationality. This would mean that every time that Jack shared the gospel, he would have to say, in the back of his mind, "But I really don't believe this." Because if he did ever believe it, if he ever trusted in the person of Christ, even just once, if he sincerely did, then he would be saved. Otherwise the promise of the gospel is not true, that whoever believes will have eternal life.[120]

I were still a Christian. But I'm not." See "Bart Ehrman: How the Problem of Pain Ruined My Faith," *Beliefnet*, accessed July 7, 2017 http://www.beliefnet.com/columnists/blogalogue/2008/04/why-suffering-is-gods-problem.html#5cUmAdGfsxmK3YjY.99.

118 Grudem, *"Free Grace" Theology*: 96.

119 Ibid., 88-89, 105.

120 Dr. Ken Mitchell, personal communication, 12/27/2016.

As quoted above, Dr. Grudem maintains that perseverance is one of the evidences that one is born again. However, we ask, "At what point in one's life is this true? Early life? Mid-life? Late in life?" Reformed writer Allan Stanley defines that point this way: "Somewhere along the way converted sinners become righteous and therefore eligible to enter the kingdom."[121] That point is probably what Dr. Grudem would call assurance based on "strong evidence" of salvation. What about Templeton, Ehrman, and Dr. Mitchell's friend, Jack, mentioned above? At one time, based on Dr. Grudem's criteria, he could have clearly pointed to evidence of their changed lives, which would be "strong evidence." But God did not cause them to persevere, despite very strong evidence.

Thus, in the final analysis, even though Dr. Grudem and the Westminster Divines may not intend this, in order to motivate believers toward perseverance Grudem's views logically seem to imply the need to hold the threat of eternal damnation over the sinning believer's head every time he fails "for a period of time"[122] or is thinking of falling away.[123] Can we seriously believe that our gracious heavenly Father terrorizes us into holy living? In a striking contrast, the writer to the Hebrews counseled that we should "take hold," or secure a "grip"[124] on grace and not threats of damnation (Hebrews 12:28).[125]

---

121 Stanley, *Did Jesus Teach Salvation by Works?*, 175.

122 See *Larger Catechism of the Westminster Standards*: s.v. Answer: Questdion 195. Grudem, *"Free Grace" Theology*: 88.

123 Grudem, *Systematic Theology*: 794.

124 Gr ἔχωμεν χάριν, "to take a hold on something, have, hold (to), grip, *BDAG*, 420, option #3.

125 Reformed writers are to be honored for their legitimate concern to build our faith. But it may be asked, "Are they unintentionally destroying faith through threats and intimidations which they actually believe will result in a highly moral lifestyle? Did not the author of the anonymous homily to the Hebrews teach the exact opposite view?" He said, "Therefore, since we receive a kingdom which cannot be shaken, let us hold fast to grace (ἔχωμεν χάριν), by which we may offer to God an acceptable service with reverence and awe" (Hebrews 12:28 – my translation).

One would assume that when Dr. Grudem gives assurance, he should then qualify it by warning the believer that he must persevere to the end of life in order for the assurance Grudem has just given to be proven genuine. The logic of his position requires this non-assurance. Why? Because *no one* can know for sure that he will continue in the Christian life until the end of his life, unless he already infallibly knows he is born again! Thus, in Dr. Grudem's view of assurance, *for any Reformed person to give assurance based upon Dr. Grudem's "strong evidence" is a logical impossibility*, because no one can know that the professed believer will persevere until he dies! Therefore, the potential danger of giving false assurance *occurs one hundred percent of the time* when Reformed teachers give assurance. It is *always* premature non-assurance because the Christian is not yet dead.

His Doctrine of Perseverance is Based upon a Circular Argument

Dr. Grudem attempts to circumvent the logical impossibility of assurance in his theology by saying that true believers can have assurance now because God will cause them to persevere as a Christian until the end of their lives.[126] However, it is assumed that this perseverance in belief and good works will occur only if that person is truly a Christian, and that is the point in question. Dr. Grudem is, in fact, guilty of arguing in a circle. On the one hand, he would give assurance to a professing Christian on the assumption that he is saved (because he meets Dr. Grudem's requirement of "some evidence" to "strong evidence"), and God's work of perseverance will keep him to the end.[127] But on the other hand, God will not do this work of perseverance unless the person is saved!

---

126 He says, "No one who has such assurance [based on Grudem's "some" or "strong" evidence] should wonder, 'Will I be able to persevere to the end of my life and therefore be saved?' Everyone who gains assurance through such a self-examination should rather think, 'I am truly born again; therefore, I will certainly persevere to the end, because I am being guarded "by God's power" working through my faith (1 Peter 1:5) and therefore I will never be lost. Jesus will raise me up at the last day and I will enter into his kingdom forever' (John 6:40)." Grudem, *Systematic Theology*: 805.

127 Ibid.

How does Dr. Grudem respond to this? In short, he doesn't. Instead, he says Free Grace interpreters misunderstand his position.[128] We don't misunderstand his position; we simply disagree. Supposedly, our lack of understanding is that we do not recognize the ministry of the Holy Spirit in giving us an internal subjective confirmation that we are children of God. He bases this on his misunderstanding of Romans 8:16, which, as explained above does not refer to the Holy Spirit testifying "to" our spirit but "with" our spirit to Abba that we are children of God.

His View of the Application and Purpose of the Warnings is Contradictory

Another area in which Dr. Grudem's theology of assurance appears to be internally at odds with itself relates to his misunderstanding of the purpose of the biblical warnings and to whom they apply. He says,

> The purpose is always to warn those who are thinking of falling away or have fallen away that if they do this it is a strong indication that they were never saved in the first place. Thus, the necessity for continuing in faith should just be used as a warning against falling away, a warning that those who fall away give evidence that their faith was never real.[129]

With this broad statement, he has removed the warnings from their intended purpose, which is to warn *all* believers of a danger, not just those who are "thinking of falling away." Yet he says elsewhere that the warnings are addressed to "church goers,"[130] many of whom are saved. Therefore, he is once again contradicting himself. In the quote above, he says the warnings are for those who are thinking of apostasy,

---

128 Grudem, *"Free Grace" Theology*: 95.

129 Grudem, *Systematic Theology*: 793-94.

130 Grudem, *"Free Grace" Theology*: 79.

and elsewhere he says they are a means God uses for all believers to increase their assurance (if they obey them).[131]

Furthermore, in Free Grace thinking, the danger taught in the verses Dr. Grudem cites is not that they might find out that they were never saved, but that they will forfeit their great future with Christ in the fulfillment of human destiny. In our view, one might "fall away" from the path leading to maturity (Hebrews 5:12-6:1) and face rebuke at the Judgment Seat of Christ and yet be saved "yet so as through fire" (1 Corinthians 3:15); lose their full reward (John 8); and "shrink back in shame at his coming" (1 John 2:28).

His View of the Warnings is Based on an Anachronism

Dr. Grudem is correct in saying that the warnings were addressed to entire congregations, that is, "church goers." However, he also limits the warnings only to those who were thinking of apostasy. If that is true, in view of the frequency and distribution of the warnings throughout the New Testament, one must believe that the New Testament writers considered this a major concern. They must have believed the early church to be packed with people who were only professing and not possessing believers. Normally one would think that most people in a Church under persecution would only join a Christian fellowship if they were serious. This was certainly my experience in working with the churches in Russia, Eastern Europe, China, and Vietnam during the communist era. I seriously doubt that people were different in the first century, especially since the persecution then was much more intense.

The picture we get in the book of Acts and the Epistles is of a vibrant growing church composed of intimate small church fellowships composed, in turn, of believers who knew each other and shared a common life. Those fellowships had some problems, but they were not churches full of many potential apostates. It is more credible to believe that there was a minority who were lazy or disobedient in their Christian lives and, perhaps, a few who were thinking of denying the faith and, fewer, who were never saved in the first place. It appears

---

131 Grudem, *Systematic Theology*: 805.

that Dr. Grudem is anachronistically viewing what he thinks he sees in a large church today and assuming it was like that in the first century.

Dr. Grudem correctly cites passages which prove that there were false brothers in the churches.[132] But that totally misses the crucial point, to *whom were the warnings addressed?* Paul never draws a distinction between wheat and tares, saved and unsaved, in the very epistles supposedly, according to Grudem, addressed to those kinds of groups. In nearly every case the distinction must be read into the text and read into the author's mind. Nowhere, for example, does the writer to the Hebrews say, "How can we *who claim to be Christians and may not really be,* escape if we neglect so great a salvation?" The writers never qualify the warnings and never introduce the distinction that Grudem's view specifically requires.[133] Since the writers themselves never explicitly say that their intended audience is a mixture and since they everywhere make statements to the effect that their intent is to address genuine Christians, we have no warrant for reading into their otherwise clear statements qualifications they themselves never make.[134]

The fact that a biblical writer **could be** speaking to wheat, tares, or both does not mean that he is. We can only discern his intended audience by studying the terms and themes he discusses in describing them. Everywhere, the writer of Hebrews uses terms like "brethren," "sanctified," "holy brethren," and "children" and describes them as having believed and manifested a life of works (Hebrews 10:35ff.). James describes his readers as those who "*hold the faith in our Lord Jesus Christ.*"[135] Paul addresses the carnal Corinthians as "*those who*

---

132 "Paul also speaks of '*false brethren* secretly brought in' (Galatians 2:4), and says that in his journeys he has been 'in danger from *false brethren*' (2 Corinthians 11:26). He also says that the servants of Satan '*disguise themselves* as servants of righteousness'" (2 Corinthians 11:15). Ibid., 794.

133 I am, of course, aware of the passages Dr. Grudem quotes to counter this statement. We will address them in later chapters.

134 Even Schreiner admits that the New Testament warnings "specifically address believers." Schreiner, *Run to Win the Prize*: 111.

135 James 2:1.

have been sanctified in Christ Jesus, saints by calling, with all who in every place call on the name of our Lord Jesus Christ, their Lord and ours.[136] The Apostle John explicitly calls his readers *"little children"* and says they have *"an advocate with the Father."*[137] While it is possible that mere professing Christians are in the audience, the existence of these kinds of people in the New Testament fellowships was not a major issue of concern reflected in the writings of the New Testament writers. The fact that they may exist does not logically require that the writer included them in his intended audience.

His View of the Warnings Places the Bible in Contradiction with Itself

What about the verses Dr. Grudem cites to prove that on his premises one can have full assurance now (2 Peter 1:10; 1 John 2:3, 5-6; 1 Peter 1:5)?[138] Grudem's interpretation of these passages leads to another logical fallacy. On the one hand, based on his interpretation of the four verses above he argues that the Bible says we can "know" we will go to heaven when we die, but on the other hand he says we can only have "strong," not certain assurance, that is, we cannot "know."[139] He admits that we should be careful giving assurance because it may turn out that the person receiving it will not persevere.[140] But on the other hand, he argues that a person who has assurance based on his criteria will persevere.

---

136 I Corinthians 1:2.

137 1 John 2:1.

138 Grudem, *"Free Grace" Theology*: 95-96. We will discuss those passages in a later chapter. However, a few comments are in order. Regarding 1 John 2:3, *"And by this we know that we have come to know him, if we keep his commandments,"* Free Grace interpreters do not understand the word "know" in this passage as a reference to knowing Christ in the sense of personal salvation. Instead, it refers to knowing him in the sense of fellowship. For example, Jesus said to Philip, *"Have I been so long with you, and yet you have not come to know me, Philip?"* (John 14:9). Philip already knew Jesus in a saving sense.

139 Ibid., 92.

140 Grudem, *Systematic Theology*: 788.

We are further confused when Dr. Grudem says that, on the one hand, continuing in the Christian life is "only one" of the evidences of regeneration, and we should keep this in mind lest we give false assurance.[141] He is therefore admitting that the person to whom he gives assurance may not continue (because continuing is "one" of the necessary evidences), and therefore he cannot be certain that he is saved unless he continues to the end. Then, on the other hand, he quotes four verses (1 Peter 1:5; 2 Peter 1:10; 1 John 2:3, 5-6), which (in his interpretation) say that even if he has only strong evidence of belief, he can be assured that he will persevere in good works to the end of life and be saved.[142] When he contends in one place in the Bible that perseverance in good works to the end is one requirement of "true" salvation, and in another, that these four verses say we can obtain full assurance of salvation *before the end has arrived*, his viewpoint is logically contradictory.

Several years ago, I had an interesting email exchange with a missionary who is strongly committed to Reformed theology. He has even written a book setting forth his views in a very compelling way. For several of our back-and-forth emails, the discussion proceeded along the lines above. I finally said to him, "Bill, [not his real name], you say you have a firm assurance that you are saved right now. But because you believe that perseverance in faith and good works is necessary to verify the presence of saving faith, how can you know for sure you are saved until the end has come? This seems like a contradiction."

He replied, "Jody, I see your point. All I can say is that I have peace."

That is one way of dealing with the contradiction. Bill's response is not uncommon. On occasions, I have met people who similarly maintain their assurance and also the doctrine that only the person who perseveres to the end is saved. In my experience, most people simply put the discussion out of their minds because the consequences are terrible or because theological conversation does not interest them. Only believers who care about the issue will be concerned about

---

141 Ibid.

142 Grudem, *"Free Grace" Theology*: 95.

assurance. For those believers, like Rabbi Duncan, the Reformed faith places a burden causing introspection and confusion. Most, however, simply choose not to think about it and leave it to the theologians and seminary students to discuss.

Free Grace interpreters can have infallible assurance because it is grounded outside of the vicissitudes of the believer's behavior and rests only in Christ and the wonderful promises he has made in the Word of God.

His View of Assurance May Unintentionally Involve God in a Falsehood

According to Dr. Grudem, the warnings are addressed to those who may or may not be saved.[143] For the person who has professed faith but is unsaved, or who is thinking of falling away or already has,[144] the warnings, according to Grudem, challenge him to examine his life to see if he has sufficient evidence to conclude that he is saved. If the evidence is weak, he is to reexamine his foundations, repent, and believe on Christ for salvation.

He also believes that the warnings are intended for many who may be saved, that is, "church goers." How, then are the warnings applied to those among the "church goers" who are saved, but whose lives do not meet Dr. Grudem's criteria to establish the presence of saving faith? Even though Dr. Grudem does not know if the professing Christian is a Christian or not, his counsel is, "You do not appear to be a Christian now—you must repent of your sins and trust in Christ for your salvation!"[145] In other words, (through Dr. Grudem) God would be warning one of his children with a destiny he knows will never befall them. He is telling the saved person that he might not be saved. Supposedly, God does this to motivate them by fear (a.k.a "healthy tension" or "wholesome fear") to persevere. According to Reformed

---

143 Grudem, *Systematic Theology*: 805-06.

144 Ibid., 793-94.

145 Ibid., 1201.

thought, this is one of the means God uses to guarantee that his elect will persevere.[146]

Consider how Calvin interprets Paul's famous warning to the Romans:

> *Behold the kindness and severity of God; to those who fell, severity, but to you, God's kindness, if you continue in his kindness; otherwise you also will be cut off.* (Romans 11:22)

In his commentary on Romans 11 he says:

> *We understand now in what sense Paul threatens those with excision whom he has already asserted to have been grafted into the hope of life through God's election. **For, first, though this cannot happen to the elect, they have yet need of such warnings**, in order to subdue the pride of the flesh; which being strongly opposed to their salvation, needs to be terrified with the dread of perdition.*[147]

Like Dr. Grudem's, Calvin's interpretation says that, even though God knows the sinning Christian is saved, God terrifies him with "the dread of perdition" to teach him humility! Lest this be considered simply an aberration of the sixteenth century, listen to Andrew Fuller as quoted approvingly by Arthur Pink:

> *It is necessary for those whom the Lord may know to be heirs of salvation, in certain circumstances, to be threatened with damnation, as a means of preserving them from it.*[148]

---

146 Schreiner and Caneday, *The Race Set Before Us.* Schreiner, *Run to Win the Prize*: 101.

147 Calvin, *Romans*: s.v. "Romans 11:22".

148 Arthur Pink, *An Exposition of the Sermon on the Mount* (Grand Rapids: Baker Book House, 1974), 88.

So, God, on the one hand, knows Christians will never go to the lake of fire, but, on the other hand, he tells them (through Reformed counselors and the New Testament warnings) that they might go to the lake of fire if they do not respond to the warnings! Don't Reformed thinkers see that they are *unintentionally* ascribing a falsehood to God?

How would Free Grace interpreters counsel a wayward professing Christian? Instead of warning him or her of final damnation, Free Grace interpreters might begin by attempting to clarify the person's understanding of the gospel. They would not begin where the Reformed begin by introducing the possibility that he is not saved. Instead, they would seek an opportunity to present the gospel of God's grace. In so doing, the person's saved status may become more evident. If in the course of the conversation it appears he is unsaved, the Free Grace counselor would clearly present the gospel and challenge him to believe in the person of Christ for salvation. If the person chooses to believe, revealing that he did not understand before, it might be appropriate to lead him in prayer.

On the other hand, if the Free Grace counselor discerns that he seems to be a genuine believer but is simply living a carnal life, he might say, "Unless you change your pattern of life, you face serious consequences at the Judgment Seat of Christ.[149] Also, you risk losing out on the fulfillment of human destiny: participation with Christ as one of his co-heirs in the future world."

Free Grace writers believe that the warning passages are directed mainly to truly saved persons, but the danger is not damnation, but rebuke, disinheritance, and loss of opportunities for service and honor in the final destiny of man. Therefore, God is not telling his elect they are headed for the lake of fire. Instead, he is truthfully warning them that they risk loss of the final meaning of their lives.

Free Grace interpreters do not claim to know if the person is saved, but instead direct him to the love and grace of God in Christ and attempt to lift his vision to the great future, becoming a partner of Christ in the fulfillment of human destiny, to rule and have dominion (Genesis 1:27-28; Hebrews 2:5-8). They ask, "Do you want to miss out on that?" and not, "If you don't change your ways this proves you are

---

149 Luke 19:24-26; Hebrews 5:12-6:1; 1 Corinthians 3:15; John 8; 1 John 2:28.

not really saved, and you are on the highway to hell." Why? Because only God can know with certainty the condition of a person's heart.

Grudem's Objections to Free Grace Views of Assurance

Dr. Grudem objects to the Free Grace view for many other reasons. Here we list three of them. First, he is troubled by the Free Grace view that says, "Just as the presence of fruit cannot prove whether a person is a Christian, neither can its absence deny it."[150] However, there is nothing idiosyncratic about this. Calvin said the same thing: "*Should they begin to estimate it* [that is, their saved status] *by their good works, nothing will be weaker or more uncertain; works, when estimated by themselves, no less proving the divine displeasure by their imperfection, than his good-will by their incipient purity.*"[151]

Secondly, regarding his understanding of Free Grace views of assurance, Dr. Grudem says that, "reading Bible verses about the atoning work of Christ tells me nothing about whether I have believed or not."[152] No Free Grace interpreter believes that this pejorative statement about merely "reading Bible verses" yields assurance. It is reading with an open, yielded, believing heart that yields assurance. It is a contemplation and meditation on these wonderful promises that Calvin encouraged, reflection on Christ who is the mirror in which we contemplate our election.

Finally, Dr. Grudem is concerned that Free Grace teachers will give people false assurance. If all a person must do is check a box on a revival card and can then live any kind of life he desires and still go to heaven, this would, according to Grudem, be giving a false assurance. However, Free Grace teachers agree with him! Grudem makes a false accusation when he says, "A Free Grace supporter would not hesitate to say this person is clearly saved based upon his earlier profession of faith."[153] Personally, after involvement in the so-called "Free Grace"

---

150 Dillow, *Final Destiny*: 684.

151 Calvin, *Institutes*: 3.14.19.

152 Grudem, *"Free Grace" Theology*: 85.

153 Ibid., 93.

movement for 26 years, I have never met anyone who believes this or would do this. Perhaps Dr. Grudem has, although he never gives any documentation from Free Grace writers or from personal conversations. However, he may be correct in the sense that the logic of the Free Grace position (i.e., a lack of works does not prove a person is unsaved) might mistakenly lead a person to believe that. Paul faced a similar challenge, "Are we to continue in sin that grace may increase" (Romans 6:1)? Since that would never be a possibility in Dr. Grudem's view of assurance and perseverance, we ask, "Does Dr. Grudem's system of assurance differ from that of the apostle Paul?"

The Free Grace View of How to Find Assurance

Richard Lovelace notes that Puritan and Pietist legalism and their stress on self-examination led to "[a]n unbalanced stress on auxiliary methods of assurance—testing one's life by the inspection of works and searching for the internal witness of the Spirit." He goes on to point out that this "obscured Luther's teaching on assurance of salvation through naked reliance on the work of Christ."[154] Many of Grudem's criteria would certainly be helpful as subsidiary aids and as encouragements to the believer, but not as a basis of assurance.

However, the only way to achieve the full assurance that the Scriptures promise is to ground it completely outside the believer's subjective experience and emotions and to ground it objectively in the person and work of Christ. There is perhaps no better way than to follow the method employed by the apostle Paul in Romans 8:31-39. Here the apostle asks four questions, each beginning with the word "who."

1. "Who can be against us?" (v. 31). His answer is no one, because Christ gave himself for all of us, and therefore God will graciously give us all things (v. 32).

2. "Who will bring any charge against those whom God has chosen?" (v. 33). His answer is no one, because God, the only One who could bring such a charge has already rendered his verdict, justified (v. 33).

---

154 Lovelace, *Dynamics of Spiritual Life: An Evangelical Theology of Renewal* 100.

3. *"Who is he that condemns?"* (v. 34). His answer is *no one*, because Christ has paid the penalty for sin and is at the right hand of God right now interceding for us.

4. *"Who shall separate us from the love of Christ?"* (v. 35). His answer is *no one*, because Christ's love for us is not conditioned on our loving him (Romans 5:8).

What is striking about all four of these answers is that Paul never asks the believer to look inwardly and test for evidences of regeneration, as Dr. Grudem requires. (We will discuss Dr. Grudem's view of 2 Corinthians 13:5-6 in a later chapter). Rather, in answer to all four questions, Paul directs him to Christ. Based on Romans 8:31-39, Sinclair Ferguson asks, "How does this bring assurance? It does so objectively because it provides the answers to my deepest doubts and fears. From such a premise, only one conclusion is possible. It is the conclusion of assurance."[155]

A believer may lack subjective assurance because of doubt, trials, or even an inconsistent Christian life. But for any Christian, he will only find his assurance if he looks to Christ. Attention must be focused on Christ and the answers Paul gives to the four questions above. This gives the objective foundation from which subjective feelings of assurance can flow. Assurance can be felt to greater or lesser degrees, but, as Calvin said, it is the product of looking at the "mirror in which we contemplate our election."

Conclusion

It would be a hateful father who entered into the following conversation with his son:

Son: "Dad, am I *really* your son?"

Father: "Well, young man, it depends on how you behave. If you really are my son, you will show this by doing the

---

155 Sinclair B. Ferguson, "The Assurance of Salvation," *The Banner of Truth*, no. 186 (March 1979): 5-6. Of course, Ferguson believes that the evidence of works is necessary as well.

things I tell you to do. If you have my nature inside you,
you can't help but be obedient."

Son: "But what if I disobey you a lot, Dad?"

Father: "Then you have every reason to doubt that you are truly
my son!"[156]

A child's greatest need when faced with doubt about his acceptance
is to have his father's unconditional love reaffirmed. No human father
would treat his child as Dr. Grudem and other Reformed theologians
imagine our divine Father treats his children!

Of course, it is very important that Christians regularly "examine
themselves." However, nowhere in the New Testament is such an
examination demanded in order to discern whether one is really
justified. Instead, we examine ourselves to see if we are in the faith
as a way of life, to see if Christ is expressing his life through us by
obedience to his commands.[157]

Paul counseled his readers to seek assurance by looking outward
to Christ and the beauty of the gospel promise (Romans 8:31-39).
After all, if Christ is for us, he pointed out, who can be against us? As
Calvin put it, one finds assurance not by examining one's works, but
by looking to Christ who is the mirror in which we contemplate our
election. This is the only path to infallible assurance.

---

156 This illustration is adapted from Hodges, *Absolutely Free! A Biblical Reply to
Lordship Salvation*: 17.

157 See Galatians 5:25 "If we live by the Spirit, let us [exhortatory subjunctive]
also [something in addition to being born again] walk by the Spirit [i.e. the
faith way of life]; Romans 8:5-13—It is the believer's choice to set his mind on
the flesh and walk according to the flesh or on the Spirit and walk according
to the Spirit (i.e., the faith way of life). We will consider 2 Corinthians 13:5
"examine yourselves" in another chapter in this book.

Chapter 9

Hebrews 6:4-6 and the Question of Christian Perseverance: A Case for Christian Rebellion Met by Temporal Judgment and Loss of Reward

J. Paul Tanner, Th.M., Ph.D.

Admittedly, the interpretation of Hebrews 6:4-6 is one of the most problematic passages in all the New Testament. Not surprisingly, this has generated numerous disparate interpretations, five of which have received particular attention.[1] These have been identified as

---

1 Helpful surveys can be found in H. Bateman, ed., *Four Views on the Warning Passages in Hebrews* (Grand Rapids: Kregel, 2007); T. Schreiner and A. B. Caneday, *The Race Set Before Us* (Downers Grove: InterVarsity, 2001), 19-45.

(1) the Loss of Salvation view (Arminian);[2] (2) the Hypothetical view;[3] (3) the Tests of Genuineness view (classical Reformed);[4] (4) the Means of Salvation view[5] (which is a variation of the Tests of Genuineness view); and (5) the Loss of Rewards view.[6] These five primary views are

---

2   Notable proponents include I. H. Marshall, *Kept by the Power of God* (London: Epworth, 1969), 137–57; Ibid., "The Problem of Apostasy in New Testament Theology," *Perspectives in Religious Studies* 14.4 (1987): 65–80; G. Osborne, "Soteriology in the Epistle to the Hebrews," in *Grace Unlimited*, ed. C. Pinnock (Minneapolis: Bethany Fellowship, 1975), 144–66; Scot McKnight, "The Warning Passages of Hebrews: A Formal Analysis and Theological Conclusions," *Trinity Journal* 13 (Spring 1992): 21-59; Gareth L. Cockerill, "A Wesleyan Arminian View," in *Four Views on the Warning Passages in Hebrews*, ed. H. W. Bateman IV (Kregel, 2007), 257-92; Ibid., *The Epistle to the Hebrews*, NICNT (Grand Rapids: Eerdmans, 2012).

3   See Thomas Hewitt, *The Epistle to the Hebrews*, Tyndale NT Commentaries (Grand Rapids: Eerdmans, 1960), 108; C. C. Ryrie, *The Ryrie Study Bible*, comments on Heb. 6:4-6.

4   This is the traditional Reformed position. Representative proponents include Roger Nicole, "Some Comments on Hebrews 6:4-6 and the Doctrine of Perseverance of God with the Saints," in *Current Issues in Biblical and Patristic Interpretation*, ed. G. F. Hawthorne (Grand Rapids, Eerdmans, 1975): 355-64; Robert A. Peterson, "Apostasy," *Presbyterion* 19 (Spring 1993): 17-31; Wayne Grudem, "Perseverance of the Saints: A Case Study from the Warning Passages in Hebrews," in *Still Sovereign*, ed. T. R. Schreiner and B. A. Ware (Baker, 2000), 133-82; and Buist M. Fanning, "A Classical Reformed View," in *Four Views on the Warning Passages in Hebrews*, ed. H. W. Bateman IV (Kregel, 2007), 172-219.

5   See G. C. Berkouwer, *Faith and Perseverance* (Grand Rapids: Eerdmans, 1958), 118–21; M. Erickson, *Christian Theology*, 2nd ed. (Grand Rapids: Baker, 1998), 1005; T. Schreiner and A. B. Caneday, *The Race Set Before Us*, esp. 38–45; 142–213; T. Schreiner, *Commentary on Hebrews*, Biblical Theology for Christian Proclamation (Nashville: B&H Publ., 2015); Christopher W. Cowan, "The Warning Passages of Hebrews and the New Covenant Community," in *Progressive Covenantalism*, ed. S. J. Wellum and B. E. Parker (Nashville: B&H, 2016), 189-213.

6   Thomas K. Oberholtzer, "The Thorn-Infested Ground in Hebrews 6:4-12; Part 3 of The Warning Passages in Hebrews," *Bibliotheca Sacra* 145:579 (July-September 1988): 319-328; J. Paul Tanner, "'But If It Yields Thorns and

carefully explained and evaluated by David Allen in his commentary, and, therefore, I will not attempt to repeat that information here.[7] But for the sake of clarification, the Means of Salvation view (popularized by Schreiner and Caneday) declares that the warnings of Hebrews 6:4–6 and other like passages are addressed to true Christians, but these are used by God, along with other divine promises, as the means by which he preserves his saints. That is, the warnings stimulate them not to *fall away* (and hence, genuine Christians do not). Although the forensic nature of justification is correctly affirmed in this view, they argue (incorrectly) that final justification awaits the completion of a life of perseverance. Such a view is certainly unbiblical, and Allen has correctly refuted the view in his commentary.[8] The position advocated in this presentation is a form of the Loss of Rewards view. Unfortunately, that label is insufficient, for it does not reflect the temporal judgment that properly accompanies it (more than loss of rewards are involved). Also, my particular expression of this view will differ on certain details from others holding the same general view. The purpose of this presentation, then, is to explain the meaning of Hebrews 6:4-6 in its biblical context. Furthermore, since all five major

---

Thistles': An Exposition of Hebrews 5:11–6:12," *Journal of the Grace Evangelical Society* 14:26 (Spring 2001): 19-42; Ibid., "The Epistle to the Hebrews," in *The Grace New Testament Commentary*, vol. 2 (Denton, TX: Grace Evangelical Society, 2010), 1031-98; Randall C. Gleason, "The Old Testament Background of the Warning in Hebrews 6:4-8," *Bibliotheca Sacra* 155:617 (January-March 1998): 62-91; Ibid., "A Moderate Reformed View," in *Four Views on the Warning Passages in Hebrews*, ed. H. W. Bateman IV (Kregel, 2007), 336-77. Although Gleason takes the view that the impending temporal judgment is the approaching destruction of Jerusalem in AD 70 (which differs from my view), he correctly understands the warnings to be aimed at rebellious Jewish Christians. His articles are extremely helpful in showing the Old Testament background to the warning passages, particularly the events at Kadesh-barnea in Numbers 13–14. For a thorough and more recent treatment of the Loss of Rewards view, see David L. Allen, *Hebrews*, The New American Commentary (Nashville: B&H, 2010); and Joseph C. Dillow, *Final Destiny; the Future Reign of the Servant Kings* (Grace Theology Press, 2013), 639-58.

7 Allen, *Hebrews*, 370-86.

8 Ibid., 373-76.

views consider the audience to be genuine Christians except for the Tests of Genuineness view (classical Reformed), I will give particular attention to interacting with advocates of that persuasion, especially Wayne Grudem's treatment.[9]

The Context of Hebrews 6:4-6 in Relation to the Author's Argument

Hebrews 1:1–7:28 forms the first major movement of the book of Hebrews. The author's thesis throughout this section is that the new covenant is superior to the old because of the superior person (God's Son) upon which it is based. He develops this thesis through three major units. In Hebrews 1:1–2:18, the Son is superior to the angels who mediated the old covenant. In Hebrews 3:1–5:10, the Son is superior to Moses through whom the old covenant came, and has a superior role compared to Joshua in leading God's people to the future greater "rest." This greater rest is not the mere land of Canaan, but the privilege that faithful believers will have to enjoy their eternal rest and inheritance in the future messianic kingdom.[10] Finally, in 5:11–7:28, the Son (as

---

9   For other critiques of Grudem from a slightly different perspective (Means of Salvation view), see Christopher W. Cowan, "'Confident of Better Things': Assurance of Salvation in the Letter to the Hebrews" (Ph.D. diss., The Southern Baptist Theological Seminary, 2012), 175-99; and T. Schreiner, *Commentary on Hebrews*, 182-86.

10 The *kingdom theme* was introduced as early as chapter one, especially vv. 8-9 where the Son's kingdom is explicitly mentioned. This suggests that the Son's appointment in 1:2 as "heir of all things" (an allusion to the messianic promise of Psalm 2:8 for God's king-designate) will find its fulfillment in this new world order. This, then, is "the world to come" that our author mentions in 2:5, and which he refers to directly in 12:28 as "a kingdom which cannot be shaken."

The concept of "rest" (κατάπαυσις) in Hebrews 4:1—where the author is concerned that some of his readers might come short of "entering his rest"— must not be interpreted as *being saved and going to heaven* (so F. F. Bruce, *The Epistle to the Hebrews*, rev. ed. [Grand Rapids: Eerdmans, 1990], 110; Philip E. Hughes, *A Commentary on the Epistle to the Hebrews* [Grand Rapids: Eerdmans, 1977], 161-62). The "rest" in chapter four depends on Psalm 95

High Priest) has a superior ministry to those of the Levitical priestly ministry. The predominant view throughout church history has been that the audience consists of Jewish Christians, which would explain the unusually heavy emphasis upon Old Testament quotations and allusions, reference to Old Testament persons and institutions, as well as the need to belabor the point that the old covenant has been replaced by the new.[11] That the audience are also Jews who had placed their faith in Jesus as Messiah is attested in the way he describes them as "holy brethren" (3:1), building on the argument in Hebrews 2:11 that Christ is not ashamed to call those who are sanctified "brethren."[12]

---

for its analogy, which in turn refers back to the Old Testament believers who rebelled at Kadesh-barnea and consequently forfeited their *inheritance rest* of the land (see Deut. 12:8-10). According to Hebrews 4:11, these Old Testament rebels failed on account of their "disobedience." The author also asserts in Hebrews 4:11 that believers today must be "diligent" (σπουδάζω) to enter God's future "rest," a term that implies "making every effort" (hardly a call to the gospel message for salvation from sins). In Hebrews 4:9, the author speaks uniquely of this future rest as a "Sabbath rest" (σαββατισμός, a NT hapax legomenon). "Here the repose typified by the Sabbath is seen as the spiritual rest to be realized fully in the life to come, 'for those who enter God's rest also cease from their labors as God did from his' (4:10 NRSV)" (Moisés Silva, ed., *New International Dictionary of New Testament Theology and Exegesis*, 2nd ed., [Grand Rapids, MI: Zondervan, 2014], 4:223).

11 Other arguments could easily be advanced to substantiate the audience as Jewish. The book begins with the note that God had spoken in days past to "the fathers" (Heb. 1:1). The superiority of the Melchizedekian priesthood and its replacement of the Levitical priesthood would have little significance to pagan converts (note Heb. 7:11). The author felt a need to insist on the superiority of Christ's blood to that of sacrificial animals (e.g., 9:13-14).

12 There is no need to make a distinction between the author's reference to his audience as "holy brethren" (ἀδελφοὶ ἅγιοι, which only occurs here in Heb. 3:1) and elsewhere as simply "brethren" (pl. of ἀδελφός; so Heb. 2:11, 12, 17; 3:12; 10:19; 13:1, 22). Hebrews 3:1 begins with the author drawing a conclusion (note Ὅθεν) based on his expositional comments in the previous chapter in which he had made the point in Hebrews 2:11 that "those who are sanctified" (οἱ ἁγιαζόμενοι, a cognate term to ἅγιοι) are now Jesus's "brethren" (ἀδελφούς). In light of the way the author has used the term "brethren" in Hebrews 2:11, the word is *theologically loaded* in the epistle to indicate

Yet they are also a particular community of believers, for they have a definite history (6:10; 10:32-34), some of their original leaders had died off (13:7), and the author had intentions of visiting them (13:23). Nevertheless, some of the community were in danger of drifting from the preaching of their original leaders (13:7-9), and apparently some of them had already come to the point of forsaking their assembling together with fellow believers (10:25). The primary cause appears to be the fact that they were facing severe persecution for their faith (10:32-34). Perhaps some were also becoming dismayed at the delay of Christ's parousia, since the author felt a need to remind them that "he who is coming will come, and will not delay" (10:37).

In the second major unit (3:1–5:10), the author felt pressed to remind this wavering community of Jewish believers that a previous generation of the nation (namely, those who came out of Egypt with Moses) had rebelled against God by refusing to enter the Promised Land and subsequently experienced temporal judgment by God (their "bodies fell in the wilderness," 3:17). Therefore, the author—calling them "brethren"—warned them there must not be in any one of them an evil heart of unbelief in *falling away* from the living God (3:12). What might lead to such falling away would be the hardening of their hearts by the deceitfulness of sin (3:13). For that reason, they must "hold fast the beginning of their assurance firm until the end" (3:14). [Notice that the solution is to *hold fast* (not repent and be saved), an exhortation which the author reiterates in Hebrews 10:19-24]. The point in reviewing the overall context and the author's concern for the audience is that there is a consistent concern for their perseverance in faith. He lays it on the line (so to speak) in Hebrews 10:35-36 with this exhortation:

Therefore, do not throw away your confidence (παρρησίαν),[13] which has a great reward. For you have need of endurance, so

---

genuine believers (he is not merely accommodating himself politely to a mixed audience).

13 This "confidence" is not a self-confidence, but as explained in a preceding verse (Hebrews 10:19) a confidence (παρρησίαν) that the brethren have of entering the (heavenly) holy place by the blood of Jesus.

that when you have done the will of God, you may receive what was promised.

Their need was not salvation from the penalty of their sins but to endure in faith and not retreat from their confession, so that they might ultimately inherit all that God had promised. While this does not prove the spiritual state of those being addressed in Hebrews 6:4-6, it certainly creates an expectation of their identity—barring any evidence to the contrary. A closer look at the preceding context of Hebrews 6:4-6 strengthens and affirms the fact that they are genuine believers.

Hebrews 5:11–7:28 (the general context for Hebrews 6:4-6), constitutes the third major unit of the book, in which the author argues for the superiority of Christ's priestly ministry to that of the Levitical priestly ministry. He senses, however, that this will be a much more difficult task, given the spiritual condition of his readers. They will need to be able to comprehend deeper spiritual truth, if they are to bear with him. They will need to be able to understand the Melchizedekian priesthood and its relationship to the old covenant priesthood based on Aaron and the tribe of Levi. Yet that is just the problem; the readers (at least a number of them) are not at a level of spiritual maturity to comprehend the significance of his argument. So, before diving into more detail about Christ in relationship to the Melchizedekian priesthood (which he will return to in 7:1), the author pauses to address the danger that their spiritual immaturity poses, and the risk they face of incurring God's judgment which ultimately will prevent them "inheriting God's promises" (Hebrews 6:12). Persistence in immaturity and resistance to moving forward can potentially lead—as it did with the wilderness generation at Kadesh-barnea—to hardness of heart and ultimately God intervening with temporal judgment. From the standpoint of the literary structure, the more immediate context for Hebrews 6:4-6 is the *pericope* defined as Hebrews 5:11–6:12, and for that reason the detailed discussion must begin at 5:11.

The Statement Of Their Spiritual Problem (5:11-14)

The author confronts the problem of his readers head-on when he says, "you have become dull (νωθροὶ) of hearing" (5:11). The word νωθρός means *slow* or *sluggish*.[14] They are sluggish hearers in that they do not hear well when it comes to comprehending spiritual truth. The adjective νωθρός is important to our evaluation of this whole unit, since it occurs only one other time in the New Testament, and that is in Hebrews 6:12. What we have, then, is an *inclusio* with νωθρός marking the beginning and ending points of the *pericope*.

> 5:11   "you are *dull/sluggish* (νωθροὶ) of hearing"
>
> 6:12   "that you might not be *sluggish* (νωθροὶ), but imitators of those who through faith and patience inherit the promises"

This observation of the *inclusio* is highly significant. There is no change of *addressee* in this unit of Hebrews 5:11–6:12. The ones he describes as *sluggish* in 5:11 are the same ones he continues to be concerned for all the way until 6:12. The point becomes quite clear at 6:12—he does not want to see them remain *sluggish*, but "imitators of those who through faith and patience inherit the promises."

Furthermore, their *sluggishness* is not simply a matter of their being "baby Christians" but rather a result of failure to make progress in the Christian life as they should have. This is rather obvious from a fair reading of Hebrews 5:12. "For though by this time you ought to be teachers, you have need again for someone to teach you the elementary principles of the oracles of God, and you have come to need milk and not solid food." He then closes the paragraph by stating that solid food is for those who are mature, for in their case, their *senses* (αἰσθητήρια) have been trained for distinguishing between good and evil.[15] One who would desire the "solid food" of God's Word must realize that

---

14 νωθρός does occur three times in the LXX (Prov. 22:29; Sir. 4:29; 11:12). The idea of "sluggish" is seen, for example, in Sirach 4:29 (=Ecclesiasticus) where it is contrasted with the idea of "hasty": "Be not hasty in thy tongue, and in thy deeds slack (νωθρός) and remiss."

15 "Senses" means the inner part of man where moral reasoning takes place (4 Macc. 2:22; see Jeremiah 4:19).

he cannot gain it apart from the process of maturing—a process that requires difficult training. The idea of stressful "training" is suggested by the word γυμνάζω (from which we get our English word gymnasium), meaning to exercise or train. But this maturing process is worth the price one pays, for in this way he comes to distinguish good and evil. This thought sets the stage for the author's exhortation in 6:1 in which he urges them to move on to maturity.

The Call To Maturity (6:1-3)

The Readers Must Choose the Goal of Maturing (6:1a)

The conjunction Διὸ ("Therefore") at the beginning of verse one underscores the connection to the preceding paragraph and suggests that pressing on to maturity is the only logical inference for the readers to make. They need to leave behind the elementary teaching about the promised Messiah and press on to maturity. The very fact that the author exhorts them to "press on" clarifies that there is still hope and opportunity for them to do so. But this is the decisive moment in which they must choose which way they are going to go [note that he is not suggesting a continued diet of "milk" for them]. Any appeals or inclinations they may have received to leave the faith and abandon their confession of Jesus as Messiah (note 3:6, 14; 4:14; 10:23) must be rejected in preference to the goal of maturing.

The Remedy is Not to Be Found in Laying Again the Foundational Truths (6:1b-2)

The author is not suggesting that the foundational truths they had learned about Messiah must now be discarded, as though they were unimportant. Rather, he is suggesting that these should not be re-laid. His readers must put their efforts into moving beyond these basic teachings that they had already come to know.

There is debate as to whether the teachings mentioned in these verses pertain to Jewish or Christian matters of faith. Lane points out that the latter option has been questioned

on the ground that in none of the six items mentioned in 6:1–2 is there any reference to anything specifically Christian (e.g., Adams, *NTS* 13 [1966-67] 379–84; Weeks, *WTJ* 39 [1976] 74-76). Each of the articles, however, is related to the high priestly Christology developed in the subsequent chapters, which makes explicit the christological structure of the foundation.[16]

The correct interpretation is probably not an either/or matter (i.e., that the teachings were either totally Jewish or totally Christian). Given the Jewish background of the readers, their faith in the Lord Jesus and participation in the new covenant called for a radical reassessment of their previous understanding of spiritual matters. In other words, their Jewish worldview needed to be recast and given new understanding in light of the new covenant Jesus Christ inaugurated.

The mention of "dead works" in v. 1 does not pertain to human works of the flesh in general, but more specifically to the external regulations of the Levitical cultus.[17] This is confirmed by the use of the phrase "dead works" in Hebrews 9:14 (the only other use of the phrase), in which the accomplishment of Christ's sacrifice is said to do so much more than Levitical sacrifices ever could. The "dead works," then, represent the efforts connected with the earthly sanctuary system to secure cleansing and acceptance before God. Now that the Messiah had come and made a perfect sacrifice (one that did not merely provide *external cleansing* but even made possible the cleansing of the conscience), those Jewish believers who turned to Christ repented of (changed their mind about) the Levitical approach to God and adjusted their theology to place their faith completely in the Lord Jesus as the sure and final atonement for their sins.

---

16 William L. Lane, *Hebrews 1–8*, Word Biblical Commentary, vol. 47A (Dallas, TX: Word Books, 1991), 1:140. See R. C. Sauer, "A Critical and Exegetical Reexamination of Hebrews 5:11–6:8" (Ph.D. diss., University of Manchester, 1981), 176–78.

17 Contra F. F. Bruce who holds that "they are works which issue in death because they are evil" (*The Epistle to the Hebrews*, rev. ed. [Grand Rapids: Eerdmans, 1990], 140).

Other teachings had to be adjusted in light of Messiah's coming as well. The four items remaining in v. 2 are all grammatically related to the word *instruction,* which in turn is related to *foundation* in v. 1:
  Not laying again a foundation

1. of repentance from dead works and faith toward God
2. of instruction about:

>   ritual washings
>
>   laying on of hands
>
>   resurrection of the dead
>
>   eternal judgment

The word *washings* (βαπτισμῶν) probably does not refer to Christian baptism but to Levitical washings connected with the cultus (note the use of βαπτισμοῖς in the plural in Hebrews 9:10). The "laying on" of hands was commonly practiced under the old covenant. This was associated with sacrifices (e.g., Leviticus 4:15 [by elders]; 8:14 [by priests]; and 16:21 [by the high priest on the Day of Atonement]). Also, hands were laid on the Levites when consecrating them to ministry (Numbers 8:10). Lane states,

> The discrimination between useless washings on the one hand and purification by the blood of Christ on the other (9:9–10, 19; 10:22), or between priests appointed by the imposition of hands according to the law, which in its weakness could not achieve the perfection of the people of God, and the high priest appointed by the oath of God and the power of an indestructible life (5:1–6; 7:5, 15–28) demonstrates the relationship between the foundational teaching and the advanced instruction provided in 7:1–10:18.[18]

Whatever understanding they previously had about resurrection and eternal judgment now had to be corrected in light of Messiah's coming. There was certainly a resurrection; since he had been resurrected, so

---

18 Lane, 1:140.

they would be also. Furthermore, the Father had entrusted all judgment into his hands (John 5:22). For believers, they must be prepared for giving an account of themselves at the Judgment Seat of Christ (2 Corinthians 5:10), while unbelievers will face condemnation to hell at the Great White Throne Judgment (Revelation 20:11).

Yet these foundational matters had already been dealt with in days past. There was no need to cover this ground again, but rather to "press on."

There is a Danger That the Readers May Not be Able to Press On (6:3)

Having mentioned the eschatological issue of "eternal judgment," the author suddenly stops his enumeration of what he considers "elementary teaching." The thought of judgment is a sober reminder of the potential danger his readers faced. If their present situation is not corrected, God himself may not permit them to "press on to maturity." This would surely result in a negative judgment experience for them, as the thought of "not permitting them" harks back to the experience of the wilderness generation coming out of Egypt that the author had previously commented on in Hebrews 3–4. They were not "permitted" to enter Canaan, and now this present generation of Jewish Christians faces a similar predicament, if they fail to make the right choice.

The phrase *if God permits* in 6:3, then, raises a note of alarm. While there is still the possibility of "pressing on," they must be confronted that they are dangerously close to grave spiritual disaster. Hence, in 6:4–6 the author will now confront them with the possible outcome that their spiritual lethargy and resistance to maturing could lead to.

The Danger Of "Falling Away" (6:4-8)

Though the readers desperately need to go on to maturity, the author issues a warning that *in some cases* this may not be possible. Hence, in 6:4–6 he describes a situation in which the readers might commit an offense so serious that God would not permit them to move on to maturity. This offense is described in 6:6 as "falling away" (παραπεσόντας). The seriousness of this sin of "falling away" has prompted great debate as to (1) whether genuine Christians are truly in view (can a Christian do such a thing?); and (2) what exactly is the judgment in store for anyone who might do this. In general, Reformed theologians have assumed that the ones described in 6:4-5 are not even genuine Christians. Yet some who take the Reformed view of these verses have admitted that they certainly *seem to* describe genuine Christian experience. Commenting on the descriptive participles in vv. 4-5 Fanning writes,

> On the face of it these seem to reflect different facets of a full experience of true Christian conversion. This is confirmed when parallel uses of the key words here are tracked down in other passages in Hebrews. . . . The sense of these phrases individually and their cumulative force when taken together have led many to the perfectly plausible conclusion that the people in view in 6:4b-5 are genuine Christians.[19]

Grudem concurs and states that "[t]he cumulative force of these terms can also be used as an argument to show that these people were genuine Christians before falling away."[20] For different reasons, however, both Fanning and Grudem go on to argue that despite the appearance that genuine Christians are in view, they conclude they are not. Their logic and arguments will be evaluated after first considering the exegetical details of Hebrews 6:4-5.

Theologians from the Arminian camp take the position that genuine Christians are in view but view the sin as apostasy resulting in their loss of salvation. Yet there is nothing in the passage that explicitly states—if they were to do this—that they would lose their salvation, any more than the sin of the wilderness generation meant loss of salvation for them, and certainly the author still has this old covenant failure in mind that he had brought to their attention in chapter three. Continuing the analogy, however, they may face temporal judgment

---

19 Fanning, "A Classical Reformed View," 177.

20 Grudem, "Perseverance of the Saints," 139.

and loss of their inheritance (as was true for the wilderness generation according to Psalm 95).[21]

As serious as the sin may be, however, the author is not actually charging his readers as having yet gone to that extent. Three observations confirm this: (1) he offers the possibility of "pressing on" in 6:1; (2) he makes a subtle shift from the first person in 6:1–3 to a less direct way by use of the third person in 6:4–6, and (3) he reaffirms his confidence in them in 6:9. Nevertheless, he recognizes that they are on a perilous path, and they need to quickly gain their senses and realize the seriousness of what is at stake. If they do not shake out of their spiritual lethargy, they may very well end up as one of those described in Hebrews 6:4–8.

The Spiritual State of the Offenders (6:4-5)

Verses 4-6 must be seen as one complete unit of thought. In the Greek text, the emphatic word *impossible* (Ἀδύνατον) is placed up front in v. 4, while the complement *to restore again to repentance* does not come until v. 6. In between, we have a series of five participles describing those who cannot be renewed to repentance. The first four are positive statements of their Christian experience, while the fifth and last ("have fallen away") in v. 6 is negative.

Significantly, all five participles are governed by the one definite article τοὺς in v. 4, which serves to unite them. As a result, these are not two different situations, but a single situation in which the one who "falls away" is the very one who had been enlightened, etc. The postpositive γὰρ at the beginning of v. 4, then, serves to connect v. 3 with the entire following paragraph and explains why, in some cases, God may not permit one to advance further to maturity if the situation described in vv. 4-6 proves true.

---

21 Although the wilderness generation rebelled at Kadesh-barnea, this did not mean that they lost their *eternal salvation*, but only that they forfeited their earthly inheritance as part of God's temporal judgment on them. According to Numbers 14:19-20, the LORD <u>pardoned</u> (סָלַחְתִּי) the people of their iniquity following Moses's intercessory prayer for them. If they had lost their eternal salvation, God's subsequent forgiving of their iniquity would have been superfluous.

Lane is undoubtedly correct when he states, "Together, the clauses describe vividly the reality of the experience of personal salvation enjoyed by the Christians addressed."[22] This is true for at least three basic reasons: (1) the author had expressed statements of concern about his readers in earlier portions of the epistle (e.g., Hebrews 3:12) while yet referring to them as "brethren;" (2) what he has to say about them in 6:4–6 cannot be divorced from what he has said about them at the beginning of this literary unit in 5:11-14, namely, that they are spiritual babes who have not matured; and (3) the terminology in 6:4–5 is most naturally descriptive of Christian experience, not of unbelievers.

To claim that they have merely professed to believe (in response to pre-salvation enlightenment), while yet remaining unregenerate, is to force one's theology on the text rather than allowing the text to speak for itself. Randall Gleason is precisely on target when he points out that this passage must be understood in light of its Old Testament background.[23] In particular, the author is still making allusions to the event that occurred at Kadesh-barnea:

> Most important to this study is the writer's use in chapters 3–4 of the Exodus generation at Kadesh-barnea (Ps 95:7b–11) as a type of the Christian community to which he was writing. In each case the Old Testament record of God's dealings in earlier redemptive history is used to bring understanding to the present situation of his readers.[24]

Gleason substantiates this claim by pointing out numerous instances of the author's use of the pilgrimage motif following chapter six.[25]

---

22 Lane, 1:141.

23 Gleason, "The Old Testament Background of the Warning in Hebrews 6:4–8." According to Gleason, the Old Testament is cited at least 38 times in Hebrews, and Longenecker has identified at least 55 additional allusions to the Old Testament (Richard Longenecker, "Hebrews and the Old Testament," in *Biblical Exegesis in the Apostolic Period* [Grand Rapids: Eerdmans, 1975], 166–70).

24 Gleason, 66.

25 See especially pp. 72–75 in Gleason.

The fateful decision of the wilderness generation at Kadesh-barnea is the Old Testament counterpart to a decision by those under the new covenant who would rebel and "fall away" from God.

The author's first statement about his readers in this verse is that they had been "enlightened" (φωτισθέντας). The author uses this term one other time in Hebrews 10:32 where he says, "after being enlightened, you endured a great conflict of sufferings." The context deals with their sufferings for the faith, a situation which would surely point to their regenerate state, for it is hardly imaginable that they (especially being first century Jews) would suffer persecution had they not truly come to know the Savior.

Secondly, he points out that they had "tasted" (γευσαμένους) the heavenly gift. Some have tried to argue that they had only "tasted" but had not fully partaken of, and hence were only *professing Christians*. The Greek verb γεύομαι, however, does not restrict itself to such a limited meaning. Furthermore, the author has already used the same verb in Hebrews 2:9 in reference to Christ having "tasted death for everyone." We would have quite a theological dilemma on our hands if Christ merely tasted death for us but did not fully undergo it. The Scripture is quite clear, however, that he fully experienced death for our sins.

As Ellingworth has noted, the author is using the word to mean "eat," not merely taste, and hence figuratively to "experience (to the full)."[26] Possibly, by the phrase *tasted the heavenly gift*, the author has in mind that they had partaken of God's free gift of eternal life in Christ (see John 4:10; Romans 6:23). As the wilderness generation ate of the heavenly provision of manna, so these new covenant believers had eaten the greater heavenly manna—the "bread of life" (John 6:33).

Thirdly, he states that his readers had been made "partakers of" or "partners with" the Holy Spirit. The word *partakers/partners* is the Greek word μετόχους, a word that was used earlier in 3:1 of the "holy brethren" who were <u>participants</u> in a heavenly calling and in 3:14 of those who had become <u>partners</u> with Christ by holding fast their

---

26 Paul Ellingworth, *The Epistle to the Hebrews; A Commentary on the Greek Text*. NIGTC (Grand Rapids: Eerdmans, 1993), 320.

confidence.[27] In Hebrews 6:4, the readers are "partakers of the Holy Spirit," because they had received the Holy Spirit when they believed. The Holy Spirit was God's "pledge" (or earnest payment) until the day of redemption when they would receive their resurrected bodies (Ephesians 1:13–14; Romans 8:23).

Fourthly, he says in 6:5 that they had "tasted (γευσαμένους) the good Word of God and the powers of the age to come." The word *tasted* is the same Greek word as used in v. 4, hence a true experiencing of. The Christian message had come to them accompanied by miraculous confirmations which they fully experienced (recall 2:3–4).

The Reformed Interpretation of Hebrews 6:4-5 Evaluated and Refuted

Despite these clear affirmations in vv. 4-5 that testify of their status as genuine Christians, theologians from the Reformed position generally deny that this is the case. Grudem, for example, though admitting that the participles in vv. 4-5 *could* be descriptive of genuine Christians, argues that they *could also be* descriptive of non-Christians, and therefore reasons from that premise that the ones in view were actually never saved.[28] The terms are "inconclusive," he argues, because had they truly become Christians, the text should have said *more* to this effect. For instance, the text does not say clearly that they had trusted in Christ for salvation, and whether their lives showed fruit that gives evidence of true salvation.[29]

---

27 The translation "shared in the Holy Spirit" given by the NIV (as though to suggest that the guilty ones had only participated in some of the Spirit's ministry rather than having received the Holy Spirit himself) is too weak in light of the use of the term in Hebrews 3:1 and would better be rendered "partakers of the Holy Spirit."

28 Grudem states that "this alternative view would argue that the terms in verses 4-6 by themselves are inconclusive, for they speak of events that are experienced both by genuine Christians and by some people who participate in the fellowship of a church but are never really saved" ("Perseverance of the Saints," 139).

29 Ibid., 140.

Grudem goes to great length to argue that the first participle, "have been enlightened" (φωτισθέντας) is inconclusive because most of the instances of the verb φωτίζω in the New Testament (used 11x) are not used in a soteriological sense but rather in a general sense of bringing something to light. While I readily agree that the word is not a technical term, Gundry too easily dismisses the obvious fact that it is used soteriologically in the only other instance in the book of Hebrews where it is used, namely, Hebrews 10:32: "But remember the former days, when, after being enlightened (φωτισθέντες), you endured a great conflict of sufferings." Gundry denies that this means they had heard and believed the gospel, but such a conclusion overlooks the fact that in view of first century AD Judaism, one would hardly have suffered for a faith he did not really possess.[30] So while the verb φωτίζω is not a technical term for soteriological enlightenment, it certainly can be, and Hebrews 10:32 (addressed to the same audience) shows that the author of Hebrews does indeed use it this way. This is further substantiated by the following context in Hebrew 10, especially vv. 35-36. Notice that the author does not tell the readers in this context that they need to be truly saved or justified. Rather he says, "Do not throw away your confidence, which has a great reward. For you have need of endurance, so that when you have done the will of God, you may receive what was promised." His remedy for these suffering saints is to have an enduring faith, not for initial saving faith in the gospel message.

In Hebrews 6:4-5, Gundry also asserts that the participle "have tasted" (γευσαμένους) in the phrases "have tasted of the heavenly gift" and "have tasted the good word of God" does not reflect that those addressed were truly saved. He states, "Inherent in the idea of *geuomai* when it means 'taste' are two factors: (1) the tasting is temporary, and (2) a more permanent experience of the thing might or might not follow."[31] From this, he goes on to assert that "mere tasting does not

---

30 Ibid., 141. Grudem (144) tries to dodge the weight of this evidence when he states, "We cannot establish a specialized sense for *phōtizō* in Hebrews in this way, for it is used only one other time in Hebrews, while it occurs nine other times in the rest of the New Testament." Yet the context of Hebrews 10 does indicate that the author is using *phōtizō* in this way.

31 Ibid., 145.

mean that they have made these things their own possession."[32] Gundry acknowledges that the only other use of γεύομαι in Hebrews 2:9 reflects genuine experiencing ("But we do see Him who was made for a little while lower than the angels, *namely*, Jesus, because of the suffering of death crowned with glory and honor, so that by the grace of God He might taste death for everyone").[33] Nevertheless Gundry insists, "The fact more important for our discussion is that the common factor in all instances of tasting is that the tasting is a temporary experience, not a continuing one, and it sometimes (or often) results in no permanent experience or permanent change in the person doing the tasting."[34] Gundry's comment, however, overlooks the main issue: the point is that, no matter the length of the experience involved in the tasting, it does often lead to a true resultant state. For example, in Matthew 16:28 we read: "Truly I say to you, there are some of those who are standing here who will not taste (γεύσωνται) death until they see the Son of Man coming in his kingdom." This is obviously not a false or insufficient experience of death; once dead, they would be *truly dead*, not a state short of being dead.

Gundry's claim that γεύομαι in Hebrews 6:4-5 does not mean that the readers had made these things their own possession (see above) is an invalid lexical assertion about the word. In 1 Peter 2:3, Peter speaks of growing in respect to salvation "if you have tasted (ἐγεύσασθε) the kindness of the Lord." Obviously, by this expression, Peter implies that his readers had entered into a true relationship with the Lord based on saving faith. It is at this point regarding "genuine experience" that Gundry's logic founders. He writes,

> Similarly, in Hebrews 6:4-6 the people had a genuine experience of the heavenly gift and the word of God and the powers of the age to come. But that is not the point. The question is whether they

---

32 Ibid.

33 Another helpful example is Matthew 27:34: "they gave him wine to drink mixed with gall; and after tasting (γευσάμενος) it, he was unwilling to drink." Yes, it was a mere taste, but Jesus truly had the wine, not a false experience of it.

34 Ibid., 145, fn. 27.

had a *saving* experience of these things, whether the experience was one that brought regeneration, saving faith, justification, etc.[35]

Yet Gundry fails to adequately explain how one can have a *genuine experience* of the heavenly gift without being saved. By analogy, how can one be said to experience justification without truly being justified? Gundry tries to dodge the meaning of "tasted the heavenly gift" when he claims that they have had some experience of the *power* of the Holy Spirit, yet that is not what the text says but only what Gundry wants to read into it. This leads him to conclude, "the tasting of the heavenly gift, and the word of God, and the coming powers, was temporary, and we cannot tell from the mere fact of such tasting if a more permanent experience of these things followed or not."[36] That, however, is a false conclusion. The context *strongly* argues that the readers had had a permanent experience of these things, for the author had just exhorted these readers who were "sluggish" to move on to maturity (Hebrews 5:11–6:2).

According to Hebrews 6:4 those being warned are also said to have been made μετόχους of the Holy Spirit, translated "partakers" by the NASB (the ESV says they have "shared in the Holy Spirit"). Gundry, however, argues that "they were partakers of some of the *benefits* that the Holy Spirit gives" (emphasis mine).[37] The word μέτοχος means either (1) adjectivally, to share or participate in; or (2) substantivally, a (business) partner or companion.[38] Yet to share in the Holy Spirit is not the same thing as sharing in *the benefits of* the Holy Spirit, and Gundry's interpretation does not hold up to close exegetical scrutiny. First, in other instances when μέτοχος is followed by a genitive of person(s), it does not mean to share in the benefits provided by that person but

---

35 Ibid., 146.

36 Ibid., 147.

37 Ibid., 148.

38 Arndt, William, Frederick W. Danker, and Walter Bauer, *A Greek-English Lexicon of the New Testament and Other Early Christian Literature.* 3rd ed. (Chicago: University of Chicago Press, 2000), 643. [Hereafter, *BDAG*].

rather in having an intimate relationship with that person (see Psalm 119:63; Hebrews 3:14). Second, a similar syntactical structure is found in Hebrews 3:14 involving μέτοχος, a form of the verb γίνομαι, and a genitive of person (μέτοχοι γὰρ τοῦ Χριστοῦ γεγόναμεν), and yet Gundry would not translate 3:14 "we have become partakers *of the benefits* of Christ."[39] This inconsistency of translation shows the weakness of his interpretation. Third, Hebrews 6:4 indicates that the addressees were "*made* sharers/partakers" (μετόχους γενηθέντας), the passive verb meaning they were *acted upon* by God, suggesting it was not an action on their part but what God had done to them (what he had made to happen). Logically this would suggest they were believers, since God can hardly be thought of as *making* them partake of the benefits of the Holy Spirit while stopping short of partaking of the person of the Holy Spirit.

Finally, Grudem's thesis that the participles of Hebrews 6:4-5 are "inconclusive" fails for several reasons. First, the author shows no change of subject in moving from 5:11 through 6:5; they were clearly believers who had not sufficiently matured in the faith. The author had already confronted them, telling them that they were "sluggish" and had had sufficient time in the faith to have progressed further by now ("by this time you ought to be teachers," 5:12). Second, the solution for their sluggishness according to Hebrews 6:1-3 was to press on to maturity, while there was a danger that some might not be able to do so on account of what 6:4-6 describes. Had they been non-Christians this would be irrelevant, for non-Christians rather obviously cannot move on to maturity. Third, drawing upon the wider context of the book, the warning passage in Hebrews 10:26-31 indicates that those in danger had been "sanctified" (Hebrews 10:29), a term used earlier in the same chapter for positional sanctification made possible by Christ's *once and for all* sacrifice (Hebrews 10:14; cf. 2:11).[40] Fourth,

---

39 See Grudem (167-168) where twice he translates Heb. 3:14 as "we share in Christ."

40 Grudem is aware of the reference to being sanctified in Hebrews 10:29, but he tries to build a case for what he calls a "nonsaving sense of *hagiazō*" (ἁγιάζω) in light of the general context of 9:1–10:39 and particularly the usage in Hebrews 9:13 (see Grudem, 177-79). He states, "In such a context, it is appropriate to

the author—in a brilliant articulation of biblical examples of faith in Hebrews 11—does not suggest that the readers needed "saving faith" but rather perseverance in their faith.

Other Reformed theologians holding to the Means of Salvation view of this passage also disagree with Grudem's interpretation. For example, Millard Erickson, a moderate Calvinist, confesses, "The vividness of the description, and particularly the statement 'who have shared in the Holy Spirit,' argues forcefully against denying that the people in view are (at least for a time) regenerate."[41]

The Impossibility of Renewal to a Repentant State (6:6)

The final participle of the series indicates that it is possible that one who had truly been enlightened and tasted of the heavenly gift (i.e., a truly

---

understand 'profaned the blood of the covenant by which he was *sanctified*' to mean 'by which he was given the privilege of coming before God with the congregation of God's people" (178). Yet this is clearly not the point, because in all other cases in Hebrews where Jesus (or Jesus' blood) is connected with *sanctification* (Heb. 2:11 twice; 10:10, 14, 29; and 13:12), it is always used in a soteriological sense. The usage in the immediate preceding context makes this clear: "For by one offering he has perfected for all time those who are sanctified" (10:14). This same observation would apply to those who might wish to translate Hebrews 10:29, "the blood of the covenant by which it (i.e., the covenant) was sanctified." The context of Hebrews 10 clearly has in view <u>people</u> who are sanctified, not the covenant.

41 Millard J. Erickson, *Christian Theology*, 2nd ed. (Grand Rapids: Baker, 1998), 1004. The majority of early church fathers who commented on Hebrews 6:4-6 understood the persons in view to be believers, as did Luther at the time of the Reformation. Calvin, however, laid the foundation for the non-Christian view that many in the Reformed tradition came to embrace. John T. McNeill, ed., *Calvin: Institutes of the Christian Religion 1*, (Philadelphia: The Westminster Press, 1960), 1:555. The non-Christian view was subsequently reinforced by John Owen, as David Allen explains: "Shortly afterward, John Owen made a distinction between inward, genuine repentance and outward, false repentance. He viewed the group described in Heb 6:4-6 in the latter category. Since Owen, the vast majority of Reformed commentators have argued the common theme that Heb 6:4-6 describes only apparent believers who are, in fact, not Christians" (Allen, *Hebrews*, 357).

regenerate person) can "fall away" (παραπεσόντας—from the verb παραπίπτω). Our understanding of this crucial term is handicapped by the fact that this is the only time this word is used in the New Testament.[42] Nevertheless, we are not completely empty-handed, for the verb is used eight times in the LXX.[43] It is used to translate several different Hebrew words (most often מעל, "to act unfaithfully, treacherously"). Frequently, παραπίπτω and its cognate forms have the meaning of "transgressing" against the Lord, though not in the sense of apostasy. In Ezekiel 20:27, for instance, the LXX (using the cognate noun παράπτωμα) reads "your fathers provoked me in their trespasses in which they transgressed (παραπτώμασιν) against me." In the preceding context, the main issues to their "transgressing" were the profaning of the Sabbath and turning to idolatry, acts of rebellion against the Lord. Josephus used παραπίπτω in the sense of "acting treacherously" or "transgressing against" (but not against the Lord).[44] From Moulton and Milligan, we find a few other examples shortly after the first century AD, including the following phrase: "if the terms of it

---

42 Although the verb παραπίπτω only occurs once in the New Testament, the nominal form παράπτωμα occurs 19x, but always in the general sense of "sin" or "transgressions" (e.g., Col. 2:13), never as "apostasy." The verb παραπίπτω does occur a number of times in ancient Greek literature. *LSJ* (Liddell, Scott and Jones, *A Greek English Lexicon*, 1321) indicates the primary meaning is "to fall beside," but their category IV would be the most appropriate for Hebrews 6:6, namely, "to go astray, err" or "fall aside or away from." So the verb and its cognate terms do not have a particular technical meaning. This has to be determined by context.

43 For παραπίπτω in the LXX, see Est. 6:10; Ezek. 14:13; 15:8; 18:24; 20:27; 22:4; Wisdom of Solomon 6:9; 12:2.

44 For Josephus, see *Ant.*, 13.362; 16.200; and 19.285. In the latter reference, the Roman Emperor Claudius wrote, "I will, therefore, that the nation of the Jews be not deprived of (παραπεπτωκέναι) their rights and privileges, on account of the madness of Caius." The idea would be that of acting treacherously against the Jews so as to deprive them of their rights. Similarly Philo, *On the Life of Moses*, I.142; and *Embassy* 120 and 201 (with the implication of "attacking").

(i.e., a contract) should be broken (παραπεσιν) or it in any other way be rendered invalid."[45]

A better clue of the author's intention, however, may be found in his use of the cognate form πίπτω (fall) earlier in the book. In Hebrews 4:11, he had warned the readers, "Let us therefore be diligent to enter that rest, lest anyone <u>fall</u> (πέσῃ—aorist subjunctive of πίπτω) through following the same example of disobedience" (see 3:17). In our author's thinking, one could "fall" rather than being diligent to enter God's rest. There is also a strong connection to his warning of "falling away from the living God" in Hebrews 3:12. In the case of Hebrews 3:12, the verb is ἀφίστημι rather than παραπίπτω, but the two verbs are still related.[46] As mentioned above, most of the instances of παραπίπτω in the LXX translate the Hebrew verb מעל, but the same Hebrew word is rendered by ἀφίστημι in another verse (namely, 2 Chron. 26:18). Though the expression "falling away" in Hebrews 3:12 is not lexically related to our verb παραπίπτω, conceptually it is. Lane concurs that it is "equivalent

---

45 B.P. Grenfell and A.S. Hunt, eds., *Oxyrhynchus Papyri I*, 9534 (AD 129), 1898; quoted in James H. Moulton and George Milligan, *The Vocabulary of the Greek Testament* (Grand Rapids: Eerdmans, 1930), 488–89. The point is that the terms of the contract were *transgressed*.

46 In commenting on ἀφίστημι in Hebrews 3:12, Fanning is a bit presumptive when he states, "The verb used in Hebrews 3:12 for 'turning away' and its cognate noun frequently denote a willful rejection of salvation and rebellion against God and his ways, and the warning passages in Hebrews lend support for this strong meaning (apostasy)" ("A Classical Reformed View," 181). Lexically, "rebellion" is at the heart of its meaning, but to claim it means a "willful rejection of salvation" exceeds the evidence. The word ἀφίστημι is used 14x in the New Testament, usually in the sense to "leave, depart from, draw away from," and typically in a physical sense (physical departure). For spiritual departure or falling away, see 1 Timothy 4:1. It is far more common in the LXX, where it is used 230x. There, it not only has the sense of physical departure but of *rebellion against another* (e.g., Gen. 14:4). In Joshua 22:18, it is used of the Israelites potentially rebelling against the Lord. Jeroboam *rebelled* against Solomon (2 Chron. 13:6; see also Ezek. 17:15; 20:8). Edom revolted against the rule of Judah (2 Chron. 21:8, 10). It has the sense of *going off into unfaithfulness* in regard to the Lord (2 Chron. 29:6). What we can safely conclude is that ἀφίστημι in Hebrews 3:12 ("to fall away from the living God") means to rebel against him, to turn away unfaithfully.

to the expression ἀποστῆναι ἀπὸ θεοῦ ζῶντος, 'to fall away from the living God,' in 3:12."[47]

We can thus conclude that "falling away" in Hebrews 6:6 is to transgress (or act treacherously) against the Lord in a way that parallels what happened at Kadesh-barnea when the Hebrews rebelled against the Lord with a heart of unbelief, the end result of becoming hardened in heart against the Lord.[48] More specifically, this would mean (in the context of what the author has stated thus far in the epistle) to not hold fast one's confession of faith in Christ—the very thing he had exhorted them to do in Hebrews 4:14 (see 3:6). This is a major concern of the author, for he reasserts this in Hebrews 10:23.

Of course, any drastic falling away from the faith was unlikely to happen without some prior development. They must be equally concerned about the root cause. Already, there was a passive drifting away from the word of Christ (2:1), they were sluggish hearers who had not moved on to maturity (5:11–14), and some were already avoiding Christian fellowship (10:25). Such a situation, if not soon corrected, would only bring on more hardening of heart until (like the Hebrews that fell in the wilderness) it would be too late. That is to say, God's judgment would fall . . . it would not be averted.

The author is telling them that there is a point beyond which it is impossible to restore them to a state of repentance. This would presume that their hearts would be gravely hardened. At this point (and only God knows when one has reached such a point), the guilty one does not recover to a repentant state, for this would be tantamount to crucifying the Savior and a severe public humiliation of him.[49]

---

47 Lane, 1:142.

48 There is no justification for arguing that the reference to "hardening of heart" in Hebrews 3:8—and alluded to in 3:12-13—is evidence that such a one is an "unsaved" individual. This is drawn from the warning in Psalm 95:8 ("do not harden your hearts"), but the preceding verse (Psalm 95:7) indicates that it is *God's people* that are being warned: "For he is our God, and we are the people of his pasture and the sheep of his hand." Hardening of heart can happen to a true child of God, as it did with Jesus' disciples (see Mark 6:51-52; 16:14).

49 Regarding the verb ἀνασταυροῦντας, there is no need to translate it "again crucify" (so NASB), as there is no practical difference between ἀνασταυρόω

Instead, the guilty one remains hardened against God and must face God's judgment. However, we must be careful what we conclude as to the form this judgment will take (and when it will take place).

By mentioning repentance (μετάνοιαν), the author is not suggesting they were never "saved." The author had just spoken a few verses prior to this of their repentance (μετανοίας) from dead works and of faith toward God (Hebrews 6:1). Obviously the author considered their repentance to have been "genuine," because—wishing to leave behind the foundational truths—he beckoned them on to maturity. At one point they had repented, but if they harden their hearts until at last "falling away"—an outright rebellion against the Lord—they would cut themselves off from being able to return to a state of repentance. The words "to again renew them to repentance" (πάλιν ἀνακαινίζειν εἰς μετάνοιαν) must carefully be noticed. The repentance the author has in mind is a repentance they had previously attained to. There is no need to assert (as Grudem does) that those being warned may have had some sort of deficient repentance (as though they had never *truly* repented). He states,

> it is possible to have a kind of repentance that falls short of saving repentance, a repentance that is not accompanied by saving faith. . . . We conclude that "repentance" means a sorrow for

---

and σταυρόω. For ἀνασταυρόω with the simple meaning "crucify" or "hang on a cross," see Josephus, Ant. 6.374; 11.17. Most translations put the causal conjunction "since" or "because" initiating the final clause ("since they crucify to themselves . . . "). In the Greek text there is no explicit conjunction, and this must be understood in light of the anarthrous participle. Technically, this could be translated "since" or "while," and some have opted for the latter temporal nuance, i.e., they cannot be restored to repentance *while* they continue in this state (which leaves open the possibility that this is not irreversible). However, the causal alternative is undoubtedly correct, because the whole point is that going on to maturity may be impossible in certain cases. Otherwise, there would be no need to make the statement about this, as F. F. Bruce has pointed out: "To say that they cannot be brought to repentance so long as they persist in their renunciation of Christ would be a truism hardly worth putting into words" (*The Epistle to the Hebrews*, rev. ed., 149).

actions that have been done or for sins that have been committed, and a resolve to forsake those sins.[50]

Though Grudem may be unsure if those warned have had "genuine saving repentance," the author of Hebrews does not suggest this at all.[51] God, in his judgment of their rebellion, may cut off the opportunity to be restored to a state of repentance, and hence they would never mature.[52]

An Illustration of the Two Main Alternatives (6:7-8)

The illustration that follows in Hebrews 6:7-8 has a great bearing on the interpretation of the warning itself, and hence this must be carefully taken into consideration.

1. Orientation. The author realizes that his audience could gravitate in one of two directions: they could either move on to maturity (6:1), or they could continue on the slippery slope that could ultimately lead

---

50 Grudem, *Perseverance* 149. In the context of Hebrews 6:1-6, however, the repentance mentioned in v. 6 most certainly refers back to the repentance in v. 1. Elsewhere Grudem argues that the repentance in Hebrews 6:1 was a genuine repentance that brought them salvation (*"Free Grace" Theology: 5 Ways It Diminishes the Gospel* [Wheaton, IL: Crossway Publishing, 2016], 41, 69).
The dispute with Grudem about repentance is not whether the Scriptures teach that non-Christians should repent (that is true in light of Luke 24:47; Acts 11:18; 17:30; 20:21; and 26:20). Rather the issue is what is meant by and what is entailed in the act of *saving repentance*. Grudem's definition exceeds the biblical evidence.

51 Grudem's uncertainty is evident when he states (150), "But none of this implies that the original repentance had necessarily led to saving faith and a forgiveness of sins. That is not specified, and we cannot therefore draw a conclusion on the basis of the term *repentance* itself."

52 Contrast Grudem's insistence that "salvation" is the issue rather than going on to maturity: "He wants to warn them that, although they have participated in the fellowship of the church and experienced a number of God's blessings in their lives, yet if they fall away after all that, they will not be saved" (154). This directly contradicts the author's point in Hebrews 6:3 that it is maturity that God might not permit.

them to an outright rebellion of "falling away" (6:6). Though, in reality, different ones among them were at different points of this spectrum, the author is primarily concerned with the direction they are headed. One leads to God's blessing, while the other may result in disaster. To help them see his concern, the author uses an illustration from agriculture involving the response of the ground to the care that it receives.

To understand the illustration, we should carefully note two important observations: (1) it is not "two grounds" being described but two possible outcomes of the same ground, and (2) regardless of the outcome, the ground has received the rain and what it needs for growth. Regarding the first point, we should notice that the NIV has obscured this matter:

> [7]**Land that drinks** in the rain often falling on it and that produces a crop useful to those for whom it is farmed receives the blessing of God. [8]**But land that produces** thorns and thistles is worthless and is in danger of being cursed. In the end it will be burned

In the Greek text, the word *ground* (γῆ) occurs only once (namely, in v. 7 . . . not twice as the NIV implies). So the point is that the *same ground* can have two possible outcomes, and by analogy there can be two possible outcomes for the "sluggish" readers to whom the author writes.

The falling of the rain upon the ground probably speaks of God's divine care and provision for the ground, i.e., God gives what is needed for growth. In this illustration, the ground should never be devoid of vegetation, because it is watered and sustained. This is what God does for the life of each believer. He waters and cares for him so that there will be fruitfulness. If fruitfulness does not result, it is not because God has not given his care and done his part.

2. Possible Interpretative Options. The illustration of vv. 7–8 could be interpreted in one of three ways:

1.   A contrast between a true believer and an unbeliever

2.   A contrast between a faithful enduring Christian and an "apostate Christian" who loses his salvation

3. A contrast between a faithful believer who is fruitful and an unfaithful believer [but not involving loss of salvation]

The decision about the correct interpretation should not be based upon one's preconceived theology *as primary resort* but first and foremost upon the exegetical details of 6:7–8 and the general context.

In regard to context, nothing explicitly has been said about loss of salvation, and the details of 6:4–6 do not seem directed at unbelievers (notwithstanding the fact that several commentators have opted for this suggestion). Context is more in favor of option three above, especially since mature and immature believers have been in view since 5:11.

3. Exegetical Details of Hebrews 6:7–8. Most of the concern is with v. 8, so attention will primarily be given to this.

a. An allusion to Genesis 3:17–18. The author of Hebrews is not simply making an illustration, but words his illustration in such a way as to allude to Genesis 3:17–18.

Hebrews 6:8 - ἐκφέρουσα δὲ ἀκάνθας καὶ τριβόλους, ἀδόκιμος καὶ κατάρας ἐγγύς

NASB	LXX
Cursed is the ground	ἐπικατάρατος ἡ γῆ
because of you;	ἐν τοῖς ἔργοις σου
In toil you shall eat of it	ἐν λύπαις φάγῃ αὐτὴν
All the days of your life.	πάσας τὰς ἡμέρας τῆς ζωῆς σου
Both thorns and thistles	ἀκάνθας καὶ τριβόλους
it shall grow for you,	ἀνατελεῖ σοι

Not only do we have the exact words for *thorns and thistles* (ἀκάνθας καὶ τριβόλους), but the noun *curse* (κατάρας) in Hebrews 6:8 has similarity to the adjective *cursed* (ἐπικατάρατος) in the LXX of Genesis 3:17.[53]

---

53 Note that Galatians 3:10 closely links the adjective ἐπικατάρατος with the noun κατάρα.

In the context of Genesis 3:17–18, the first man Adam received God's *curse* for disobedience. This is reflected in the words "By the sweat of your face you shall eat bread, till you return to the ground (γῆ)." Hence, the allusion to Genesis 3:17–18 (despite the fact that the order in Hebrews is inverted) brings to our mind the *temporal judgment* that fell on the first man's disobedience.[54]

b. Blessing-curse motif. Given the Jewish nature of the audience, the words *blessing* and *curse* would no doubt have particular significance to them in light of their Old Testament orientation. These words were juxtaposed in Deuteronomy 28–30, in which *blessing* was promised for obedience and *curse* (i.e., discipline) was promised for disobedience. Notice the use of the same word κατάρα in Deuteronomy 28:15, 45; 29:26; 30:1, 19. The word *curse* should not be taken as a technical term in Hebrews 6:8 for those who are unregenerate. From an Old Testament perspective, this designated God's discipline on his own children who were disobedient.

c. "If it produces thorns and thistles, it is worthless. . . ." The Greek adjective for *worthless* (ἀδόκιμος) is certainly not a technical term for unbelievers. The word means "'not standing the test' then *unqualified, worthless, base.*"[55] The particular nuance of the word, of course, depends on the context in which it is being used. In the LXX, δοκιμάζω and its cognate terms were often used in relation to testing or examining metals (especially by fire) to determine the acceptability of their quality (e.g., Proverbs 8:10; 17:3; 25:4; Isaiah 1:22). If they did not meet the standard, they were considered unfit and hence disapproved. The apostle Paul could use the term in relation to himself, as he does in 1 Corinthians 9:27, "lest . . . I myself should be disqualified." In this case, his eternal salvation was not the concern. Possibly, he thought about disqualification or disapproval. Lowery suggests that Paul was concerned that he might be disapproved by God and

---

54 There may also be similarity to the *song of the vineyard* in Isaiah 5. In that passage, ἄκανθα is used 3 times (5:2, 4, 6). God's discipline came upon it, because it did not produce good grapes.

55 *BDAG*, 3rd ed., 21.

thus face the disciplinary action of God that could even cut short his life.[56]

On the other hand, the preceding context (with its analogy of competition in the athletic games) might suggest that Paul was fearful of jeopardizing his eternal reward. Fee agrees that the athletic metaphor is still in view. He writes, "This has been the point of the metaphors from the beginning, that the Corinthians exercise self-control lest they fail to obtain the eschatological prize.[57]

The antonym to our term for *worthless* is δόκιμος, a word that emphasizes a *favorable evaluation*. In 2 Corinthians 10:18, for instance, it is used to indicate the approval of that Christian (but not every Christian!) that is commended by the Lord. Some Christians are "approved" and some are not (see 1 Corinthians 11:19). The Lord's approval may stem from the way one handles the Word of God (2 Timothy 2:15) or by the way one successfully endures divine trials in his life (James 1:12). Thus, the evaluation of the unfruitful ground of Hebrews 6:8 as being ἀδόκιμος probably implies no more than the fact that the offender is considered unfit and has not gained God's approval. He may be in store for God's discipline and eventual loss of reward, but there is nothing from a study of ἀδόκιμος or δόκιμος in the New Testament to establish that he loses his salvation, much less that he was never saved to begin with.

d. "Whose end (is) for burning" (ἧς τὸ τέλος εἰς καῦσιν). The "end" or outcome (τέλος) of the ground if it yields thorns and thistles is burning. Is the author trying to suggest (by analogy) that the individuals that "fall away" (6:6) are destined for hell? If so, then those who are in danger are either (1) Christians who lose their salvation, or (2) professing Christians who in actuality were never regenerate.[58]

---

56 David K. Lowery, "1 Corinthians," *Bible Knowledge Commentary, New Testament*, ed. John F. Walvoord and Roy B. Zuck (Wheaton: Victor Books, 1985), 525. Note that chapter 10 immediately launches into a discussion about God's discipline upon Israelites of old.

57 Gordon D. Fee, *The First Epistle to the Corinthians*, NICNT (Grand Rapids: Eerdmans, 1987), 440.

58 Grudem, failing to observe the allusion to Genesis 3:17-18 and the broader usage of fire as a metaphor in Scripture, *simply assumes* that "these

The Greek noun for *burning* (καῦσις) is used only once in the New Testament [see the mention of fire as a judgment in Hebrews 10:27], but it occurs seven times in the LXX. In Isaiah 4:4, it is used of God's judgment and purging of the land (including Jerusalem) for the millennium "by the spirit of judgment and the spirit of burning." In Daniel 7:11, it is used of the destruction of the little horn (the Antichrist) who is "given to the burning fire." The latter certainly has *hell* in mind (compare Revelation 19:20), though the word itself does not have to mean this.

Basically, *fire* is often used in Scripture to speak of God's judgment or sometimes of purifying something or someone. Though *fire* can be used to speak of the ultimate judgment of the unregenerate in hell, *fire* is also used to speak of God's judgment in connection with regenerate Christians. The latter is clearly the case in 1 Corinthians 3:12–15 where Paul is concerned about the "works" of believers in regard to God's church:

> [12]Now if any man builds upon the foundation with gold, silver, precious stones, wood, hay, straw, [13]each man's work will become evident; for the day will show it, because it is to be revealed with

---

consequences (being cursed and burned) are a picture of final judgment from God" (155). He goes on to say (156), "this bad fruit in a similar way revealed what their true status was all along: they had never truly been saved in the first place." The only rationale he offers for this conclusion is based on the present participles in vv. 7-8 (τίκτουσα and ἐκφέρουσα), which he thinks should be translated "*continuing to* bear" vegetation and "*continuing to* produce" thorns and thistles. Yet his insistence on the *continuous* nuance of these participles (as though the continuance of producing thorns and thistles is evidence of their being unsaved) is overstressing the force of the present participle, used here as a simple adjectival participle. [See D. B. Wallace, *Greek Grammar Beyond the Basics*, on "Aspect," 615-616]. The present participle is not emphasizing the durative nature of the verb but simply making a *statement of fact* (one bore useful vegetation and the other did not). That this is the case can be substantiated by comparison with the present participles in Hebrews 6:6 (ἀνασταυροῦντας and παραδειγματίζοντας). In that case, the author is not trying to point out that the sinner was "*continuing to* crucify" Christ and "*continuing to* humiliate" him, but simply that he was guilty of doing this by "falling away." Continual action was not the point.

fire; and the fire itself will test **the quality of each man's work.** [14]If any man's **work** which he has built upon it remains, he shall receive a reward. [15]If any man's **work** is burned up, he shall suffer loss; but he himself shall be saved, yet so as through fire.

In the case of this passage, fire is used for revealing the *quality* of the believer's works. The purpose is for assessing whether or not these are *rewardable good works*, but the person's eternal destiny is not the issue.

Hence, the motifs of *fire* and *burning* can speak of judgment in regard to the unregenerate (i.e., hades/hell) as well as evaluation of the regenerate (i.e., examination of one's works for the purpose of giving rewards). In the case of the latter, works that are unsuitable for reward are burned up.

So we must ask if in the case of Hebrews 6:8, the author is using *fire* to speak of the ultimate destiny of individuals in hell for their failure to put their faith in Christ, or if he is concerned about their *works* (i.e., a worthless life without rewardable good works). Two things in the following context argue for the latter: (1) he mentions their *work* in Hebrews 6:10; and (2) rewards are in view in Hebrews 6:12 when he speaks of those who *inherit the promises* because of their faith and patience.

Based on these two contextual observations as well as the other matters mentioned in points a-c above, the danger of *fire* is not related to hell. This probably looks at the discipline and judgment that can come upon an unfaithful Christian's life who has not brought forth fruit (as he should) but rather a life of worthless works (thorns and thistles). Such a person stands in jeopardy of receiving the Lord's discipline in this life ("near curse") and will certainly see his works burned up when examined at the Judgment Seat of Christ (Romans 14:10–12; 1 Corinthians 3:10ff.; see also 2 Corinthians 5:9–10). In contrast, the believer that is moving onward to "maturity" and walking in obedience to the Lord can expect to receive God's "blessing."

Encouragement And Hope For The Readers (6:9-12)

Despite the rebuke for being "dull of hearing" as spiritual babes and despite the ominous warning given in 6:4-6, the author has better hopes for his readers. It may be possible for these wayward believers to "fall away," but the author apparently does not think they have yet gone to that extreme. So, his warning of the fatal consequences is balanced by an encouraging note and exhortation to faithfulness in vv. 9–12.

An Affirmation of His Confidence in the Readers (6:9)

In the previous illustration, the unsuitable vegetation was burned off the unfruitful ground. That should not be seen as the normative outcome of the Christian life, and the author is concerned of "better things" for them, i.e., things that "accompany salvation." Most likely, *salvation* (σωτηρία) is being used in the same eschatological sense that it previously had in the book (see 1:14; 2:3, 10; 5:9) and in which it will be used in regard to the second coming in 9:28. Earlier in the epistle, the author anticipated Christ becoming heir of all things (1:2) and of those who would "inherit salvation" (1:14). In chapter two, the author connects this concept of *inheriting salvation* with the regaining of God's plan for man exercising dominion. This is the time when man shall be crowned with glory and honor... in the resurrected state ruling jointly with Christ. This is the glorious destiny of believers who are faithful to Christ in this life (see Revelation 2:26–27). These are the "better things" that the author has in mind for his readers. Faithfulness does bring a rich reward, both now and in the eschatological future.

Grudem, on the other hand, interprets the "better things" as meaning better characteristics of saving faith than were mentioned in Hebrews 6:4-5 (being enlightened, having tasted, made partakers of the Holy Spirit, etc.) rather than that which is depicted as burning up in v. 8. Since he regards the participles in Hebrews 6:4-5 as descriptives of non-Christians who stopped short of genuine salvation, the "better things" for him are the things mentioned in Hebrews 6:10, namely, their work, love, and service to fellow saints. He writes,

> Since things like love and service and faith in verses 10-12 are the kinds of good fruit that do give evidence of salvation, it is reasonable to think that the author would say that these are "better" than the enlightening, tasting, and partaking in verses 4-6, which in themselves do not give evidence of salvation. ... This

implies that the blessings in verses 4-6 were not things that belong to salvation.[59]

In defense of his interpretation, Grudem claims that "the adjective *kreisson*, 'better', in Hebrews is regularly used to contrast something better with something good (better covenant, better promises, better sacrifices, . . .), not something better with something bad."[60] While that statement by itself is correct, *BDAG* lexicon indicates that κρείσσων can be used in one of two ways, either (1) "pert. to being of high status, *more prominent, higher in rank, preferable, better;*" or (2) "pert. to having a relative advantage in value," adjectively "*more useful, more advantageous, better.*"[61] *BDAG*, however, put the verses mentioned by Grudem in category one but puts Hebrews 6:9 in category two. The word κρείσσων is used in the sense of "better" versus "bad" (*BDAG's* category two) in 1 Corinthians 7:9; 11:17; and 2 Peter 2:21. For example, "But in giving this instruction, I do not praise you, because you come together not for the better but for the worse" (1 Corinthians 11:17).

A second argument used by Grudem for "better things" is that (according to him) the author in Hebrews 6:9 would have used the singular κρεῖττόν τι (as in Hebrews 11:40) rather than the plural κρείσσονα, if he had meant "something better than *judgment.*"[62] This is an invalid point, as the author uses the plural κρείσσων in Hebrews 6:9 because he is contrasting the plural nouns "thorns and thistles" (ἀκάνθας καὶ τριβόλους) in Hebrews 6:8 with the promises of God they are destined to inherit (Hebrews 6:12) as a result of their "work" and "love" (Hebrews 6:10).

A third argument by Grudem that the "better things" are their *present* evidences of saving faith is that the present participle ἐχόμενα ("that accompany") in the phrase καὶ ἐχόμενα σωτηρίας ("that

---

59 Grudem, 159.

60 Ibid., 158.

61 *BDAG*, 3rd ed., 566.

62 Grudem, *Perseverance*, 158. The author of Hebrews does not use the word "judgment;" that is Grudem's choice of words (presumably for the "burning" mentioned in v. 8).

accompany salvation") "is most naturally understood as giving a sense of present duration over time, 'things *now presently* belonging to salvation, and continuing to belong to salvation.'" Yet this is based on a misunderstanding of the simple adjectival participle, which simply reports the fact of the action, not the duration of the action.[63] It is not the "present moment" that is in view, and this is confirmed by the use of salvation (σωτηρία) elsewhere in Hebrews as a future experience (see esp. Hebrews 1:14 and 9:28).[64]

The Reason for His Confidence in Them (6:10)

The conjunction *For* (γὰρ) in v. 10 signals the reason (illative use of γὰρ) for his confidence in his readers. Apparently, the author had firsthand knowledge of this group of believers, and he knew that they had been faithful to the Lord in days past. Notice that his commendation is not in regard to their personal justification, but in regard to their faithfulness *as Christians.* Their faithfulness is evidenced by their *work* (ἔργου) and their love. Later in the book (10:32ff.), he commends their past faithfulness again. Since they had begun their Christian pilgrimage well, they must not turn from the pathway of faithfulness.

The Exhortation to Remain Faithful (6:11–12)

They are to be diligent in having the "full assurance of hope" until the end. The word *diligence* translates the Greek σπουδή, a cognate term to the verb σπουδάζω in Hebrews 4:11 ("Let us be diligent to enter that rest"). The word means "eagerness, earnestness, diligence, willingness,

---

63 See comments under point 3d above where Grudem had made a similar mistake of Greek syntax. Note also that the article τὰ in the phrase τὰ κρείσσονα καὶ ἐχόμενα σωτηρίας does double duty (for both κρείσσονα and ἐχόμενα), and hence this is an adjectival participle.

64 Part of Grudem's misinterpretation is based on his misunderstanding of the "salvation" mentioned in Hebrews 6:9. It is not salvation from the penalty of sins that is in view, but the believer's future experience of salvation in conjunction with Christ's second coming (just as their "inheriting the promises" is contingent on persevering "until the end" [v 11]).

zeal."[65] They are to be diligent and eagerly make every effort to maintain a "full assurance of hope" until the end. The author has in mind the same concern as in 3:6—"if we hold fast our confidence and the boast of our hope firm until the end" (see 3:14; 10:23).[66] He is concerned that *each one of them* (ἕκαστον ὑμῶν) maintains his confession of Jesus as Messiah and is diligent to remain faithful to him.

---

65 BDAG, 3rd ed., 939.

66 The repetition of the verb "hold fast" (κατέχω) in the conditional statements found in Hebrews 3:6 and 3:14, suggests that the author has the same concern in both verses. The one who "holds fast" is the one who is said to be his "house" (οἶκός) in 3:12 and who has become one of "the μέτοχοι of Christ" in 3:14. How these expressions are translated and interpreted is crucial. In the first case (being his "house"), the metaphor must be understood in light of the preceding context. Based on the statement in Numbers 12:6-8, God said that Moses was faithful in all his "house" (LXX, ἐν ὅλῳ τῷ οἴκῳ μου πιστός ἐστιν). Note that "house" (οἴκῳ) in Numbers 12:7 is not being used in regard to the physical structure of the tabernacle, but of those who function within it (i.e., the *household* of worshipers). [Faithfulness has no meaning for the physical structure]. Moses was faithful as a member of the worshiping community (God's "house"). Of greater significance than the worshiping community in the wilderness, however, is the worshiping community (the "house/household") of Jesus. To equate Jesus' "house" with the body of Christ (which the Reformed view does) misses the point. The issue, in the case of Jesus' "house" is whether or not those who are *saved holy brethren* (Hebrews 3:1; see fn.12) are going to be faithful believer-priests in the worshiping community of which Jesus has the role of High Priest (see Hebrews 10:21; and compare 12:28 and 13:15-16).

In regard to the conditional statement in Hebrews 3:14, rather than translating μέτοχοι τοῦ Χριστοῦ as "partakers of Christ" (as though spiritual union with Christ was in view), I posit that we should translate the phrase "partners with Christ," in the sense that we are *partnering* with him in a common endeavor (see comments on μέτοχοι at discussion of Hebrews 6:4 above). The justification for this interpretation is simply the following verse and the danger for brethren of "hardening one's heart" (see fn. 48 for a defense of the notion that "hardening" is a danger for *genuine Christians*). We are to "partner with Christ" in the sense of drawing near to him for the sustaining grace needed to arrive victoriously at the destination of our eschatological salvation (Heb. 4:16; 7:25). In doing so, we will not fall short of God's *greater rest* (see fn. 10 above).

Not only must they be careful to hold fast their confession, but the author does not even want them to be *sluggish* (νωθροὶ). This is the same word he used to describe them in 5:11 when he charged them as being "dull of hearing" (νωθροὶ ταῖς ἀκοαῖς). Unfortunately, the NIV obscures the connection by its translation—"we do not want you to become lazy."[67] Indeed, they are *sluggish* at the present moment, but they must not remain so.

Alternatively, they can be "imitators of those who through faith and patience inherit the promises." *Inheriting the promises* is not automatic for any Christian, for this is based on the exercise of faith and patience. The verbal idea of "inheriting" is found four times in Hebrews, namely 1:4; 1:14; 6:12; and 12:17.[68] In the context of Hebrews, the *inheritance* in view is the "eschatological salvation" and full participation in the kingdom of Jesus Christ, entering God's rest and ruling jointly with Christ. Disobedience and unbelief may jeopardize these future promises (see Hebrews 3:12, 19; 4:1, 3, 11), but faith and patience help to bring them about.

Conclusion

From the preceding study, we have observed that the inclusio involving the word νωθρός in 5:11 and 6:12 marks the true parameters of the immediate context. This is an important observation, since it helps identify the readers addressed in 5:11–14 as being the same as those in 6:4–8. In both cases they are true Christians, and this is confirmed by the descriptive participles in 6:4–5. Their need is to press on to maturity, but a "falling away" (6:6) could eliminate that possibility for them. For committing such a sin, God would not permit them to move on in maturing.

The exact nature of the "falling away" (παραπίπτω, a New Testament hapax legomenon) in Hebrews 6:6 cannot be established by lexical

---

67 The verb γίνομαι can mean either "be" or "become." Note that the NASB chose the translation "be," which is better in light of the use of νωθρός in 5:11. The NIV's "become lazy" suggests they had not already entered into this state.

68 In addition, the noun κληρονομία ("inheritance") occurs in Hebrews 9:15 and 11:8.

definition alone, as LXX and extra-biblical usage simply identifies this as a general act of "transgressing, acting treacherously, or a breaking of agreement" (violating the understood expectations). Since "falling away" (παραπίπτω) in Hebrews 6:6 is not a technical term, the meaning of the term must be established on other considerations. First, there is the use in Hebrews 4:11of the cognate term πίπτω, translated "fall." One might "fall through following the same example of disobedience" as did the wilderness generation. For them, this came as a result of their refusal to enter the Promised Land. Second, there is the use of a *conceptually similar* term in Hebrews 3:12, namely ἀφίστημι ("fall away"), since both παραπίπτω and ἀφίστημι are in some cases translated by the same Hebrew verb מעל in the OT. This suggests that παραπίπτω is similar to "falling away from the living God" mentioned in Hebrews 3:12, i.e., an act of rebellion stemming from a progressive hardening of heart against God akin to what happened at Kadesh-barnea.

David Allen, though affirming the Loss of Rewards view, denies that this transgression is a willful rejection of Christ (apostasy) but rather a "falling into a permanent state of immaturity through a willful 'once for all' (*hapax*) refusal to trust God to deliver them from their present troubles."[69] His conclusion, however, fails to account for other significant statements in the book that would indicate that far more than a refusal to trust God must be involved. In particular these include the exhortations to "hold fast" (κατέχω) their confidence (Heb. 3:6), the beginning of their assurance (3:14), and the confession of their hope (10:23). Added to this are the exhortations to hold fast (κρατέω) their confession (4:14) and the hope set before them (6:18). Hence, they must not throw away their "confidence" in the blood of Christ that has been brought into the true holy place (10:19, 35). In light of (1) these exhortations, (2) the identity of the audience as Jewish Christians who were suffering for their faith (10:32-34), (3) the acknowledgment that some among them had already forsaken their assembling together (10:25), and (4) the closing warning against false teachings and the call to obey their leaders (13:9-11, 17), the transgression involved in "falling

---

69 Allen, 381. Elsewhere (390) he claims, "It is not apostasy that the author of Hebrews is warning against, but persistent rebelliousness comparable to the wilderness generation in the exodus."

away" appears to be that of turning away from active participation in the community of messianic believers and retreating into some form of Judaism. We cannot say for sure that this would have meant an explicit public renunciation of their faith in Christ, but such a withdrawal from the Christian assembly and reaffirmation of the blood of the Levitical sacrificial system would at least be *tantamount* to a rejection of their faith (and thus a "trampling under foot of the Son of God" and "regarding as unclean the blood of the covenant by which he was sanctified" (Heb. 10:29).

God, who sees the hearts of all mankind, would certainly know when one had gone too far, such that they can be said to have "fallen away." This would not mean a loss of eternal life, however, and we do well to observe that such an outcome is never clearly specified. In Hebrews 6:7–8, the author's deliberate allusion to Genesis 3:17–18 underscores that such rebels would forfeit God's blessing and divine discipline would be in store for them. So—just as with the rebels at Kadesh-barnea—they can expect to face *temporal judgment*, perhaps even loss of life. [In this regard, the designation "Loss of Reward view" is a misnomer; temporal judgment is also involved]. Also, by the fact that they could no longer progress in maturing, their rebellion would result in loss of usefulness for God and the absence of good works for which they would be rewarded at the Judgment Seat of Christ. Hence, there would be significant loss of reward and, in the context of Hebrews, even the opportunity to reign with Christ in the coming messianic kingdom—the greater rest to come (Hebrews 4:11; 6:11-12; 10:35-36). In the words of Hebrews 10:38-39, by shrinking back in unbelief, not only would God take no pleasure in them, but they would bring upon themselves a life of destruction (i.e., a ruined, wasted life).

A careful exegesis of Hebrews 5:11–6:12 reveals that Grudem's analysis of the passage and his defense of the Tests of Genuineness view (Reformed view) fails on multiple counts. The descriptive terms supplied in Hebrews 6:4-5 are indeed those of genuine Christians who are potentially in danger of "falling away." The Loss of Reward view— in contrast to Reformed theology—does not guarantee that a genuine believer will necessarily go on to persevere in a life of faithfulness and good works. Based on this study, rebellion and failure are certainly possible. For this very reason, Schreiner and Caneday charge that adherents of this view "radicalize eternal security by insisting that security in Jesus Christ guarantees that even those who fail to persevere in faithfulness to Christ and his gospel will never perish but are saved and will remain saved forever."[70] Pastorally speaking, it is difficult to imagine that any Christian would "fall away" as described in Hebrews 6:4-6—given the wonderful grace and love that Jesus has for his own. However, we should be willing to admit that *hardening of one's heart* is indeed possible for a Christian (Hebrews 3:12-13), and left unchecked this can certainly lead to serious spiritual deterioration and failure. This is what makes discipleship so imperative! Yet even in extreme cases of spiritual failure, the promise of eternal life is predominantly about the faithfulness of Jesus to his promises, not the faithfulness (or lack thereof) of those who believe him for it.

Fortunately, the author quickly turns in Hebrews 6:9 to encourage his readers that such negative warnings need not be their fate at all. Through faith and endurance, they can "inherit the promises." Hebrews 5:11–6:12 is a good reminder to each of us that we should be pressing on to spiritual maturity, but this is not an automatic or guaranteed outcome for any Christian. One attains to maturity as he responds in faith and obedience to God's Word, surrenders his life to the Savior, and endures in the pathway of discipleship. The price, of course, is high (death to self), but the rewards are great . . . and the rewards are for all eternity!

---

70 Schreiner and Caneday, *The Race Set Before Us*, 25.

Chapter 10

The Possibility of Failure in the Christian Life

Joseph Dillow, Th.D.

The Reformed theory of the saints' perseverance in holiness discussed in the previous chapter is, in principle, falsifiable. If the Bible offers illustrations of regenerate individuals who have persisted in sin for a lengthy period and finished life as failures before God, the theory of the saints' perseverance is simply wrong. No amount of special pleading that these are simply "descriptions of the failure of one man" rather than the "teaching" of Scripture will do. If one man who is born again fails to persevere in holiness, then the Scriptures cannot teach that *all* who are born again will "*continue in the Christian life*"[1] and "*persevere as Christians until the end of their lives*,"[2] as Dr. Grudem teaches.

---

1 Wayne A. Grudem, *Systematic Theology: An Introduction to Biblical Doctrine* (Grand Rapids, MI: Inter- Varsity Press, 2004), 805.

2 Wayne A. Grudem, *"Free Grace" Theology: 5 Ways It Diminishes the Gospel* (Wheaton: Crossway, 2016), 87.

In fact, we will demonstrate in this chapter that not just one or two passages describe such failing believers, but many passages are seen in both the Old and New Testaments that abundantly confirm this conclusion. Only one such illustration would be sufficient to falsify the Reformed doctrine of perseverance, but the existence of many of them leaves the theory in shreds.

Biblical Evidence for the Existence of the Permanently Carnal Believer

We begin with a few examples from the Old Testament.

Rehoboam

Rehoboam was the son of Solomon and Naamah and was the last king of the united kingdom and the first king of Judah (931-913 BC). Tired of the severe burdens imposed on them by Solomon, the elders counseled him to lighten the load so that the people would follow him (1 Kings 12:6-7). Foolishly, he took the counsel of some young men with whom he grew up and imposed greater burdens (1 Kings 12:8-11). As a result, united Israel split into the northern kingdom of Israel and the southern kingdom of Judah. The true Israel was now in Judah.

At the beginning of his reign, Rehoboam was obedient to Yahweh (1 Kings 12:24). He maintained the worship of Yahweh and the temple services in Jerusalem, and because of this the true followers of Yahweh left the north and migrated to Judah (2 Chronicles 11:13-17). Those who set their hearts on seeking the Lord, the God of Israel, followed the Levites to Jerusalem to offer sacrifices to the Lord (2 Chronicles 11:16). For three years, Rehoboam and followers "walked in the way of David and Solomon" (2 Chronicles 11:17).

Yet he abandoned the Lord, possibly because of the influence of his foreign wives, his associations with ungodly youth, and his youthful indecisiveness (2 Chronicles 13:7). He allowed pagan worship to prosper in Judah (1 Kings 14:22-24). In summarizing his life the Chronicler wrote, "He did evil because he did not set his heart to seek the Lord" (2 Chronicles 12:14).

Jehu

Jehu was the son of Jehoshaphat and reigned as the tenth king of the northern kingdom of Israel for 28 years (842-815 BC, 2 Kings 10:36). The Lord appointed him king (2 Kings 9:2-3) by the hand of Elisha the prophet (2 Kings 9:1-13). He stamped out the worship of Baal in Israel (2 Kings 10:10-28).

Yet he continued to worship the golden calves at Bethel and Dan (2 Kings 10:29-31). Jehu was a believer in Yahweh and was appointed to the throne by the Lord's prophet. Because he destroyed Baal worship, *"The Lord said to Jehu, 'Because you have done well in accomplishing what is right in my eyes and have done to the house of Ahab all I had in mind to do, your descendants will sit on the throne of Israel to the fourth generation'"* (2 Kings 10:30). He bears all the evidence of being born again, but he did not keep the law "with all his heart." *"Yet Jehu was not careful to keep the law of the Lord, the God of Israel, with all his heart. He did not turn away from the sins of Jeroboam, which he had caused Israel to commit"* (2 Kings 10:31). This man's life proves that the Reformed refusal to acknowledge the differing categories of believers presented in Scripture is incorrect. Here we have a believer who did not keep the Law of the Lord "with all his heart." He was a carnal believer. Some believers keep the Law of God with a whole heart. Some do not and end their lives in sin.[3]

Joash

That a king can be a follower of the Lord, genuinely saved, and yet compromise in aspects of his reign is a repeated refrain in the books of Kings and Chronicles. For example, "Joash did what was right in the eyes of the Lord all the years Jehoiada the priest instructed him" (2 Kings 12:2). For twenty-three years during this time, *"he did what was right in the eyes of the Lord"* (2 Chronicles 24:2), for he was under the influence of this devout priest. Yet after Jehoiada died, the princes of Judah came to Joash and asked for greater freedom in worship,

---

3 Grudem never mentions Rehoboam except to say that he made a "mistake" in listening to the younger men Grudem, *Systematic Theology: An Introduction to Biblical Doctrine*: 922.

and Joash granted their request (2 Chronicles 24:16-18). After idols and Asherim were set up all over the country, God sent a prophet, Zechariah, to warn the king. Because Joash had "forsaken the Lord," Zechariah said, "he has forsaken you" (2 Chronicles 24:20).

Joash responded by having Zechariah stoned. God passed judgment on him by bringing the army of Aram against him, leaving Joash severely wounded and his army defeated (2 Chronicles 24:24). His own officials conspired against him and killed him while he lay in his bed. He reigned from 878 to 838 BC. Here is an example of a regenerate man who did what was right in the eyes of the Lord for twenty-three years, but who then, like Solomon, abandoned the Lord and persisted in that state for the rest of his life. Reformed writers may say, "Well, the fact that he abandoned the Lord is proof that he never knew the Lord in a saving sense to begin with." That, however, is a theological premise read into the text and would not arise in the mind of a ninth-century BC Israelite unfamiliar with Calvin's or Beza's response to the Catholic Counter-Reformation, twenty-three centuries later.

Uzziah

King Uzziah did what was right in the eyes of the Lord in the early years of his reign (2 Chronicles 26:4). Around 767 BC, he became the tenth king of Judah. "*He sought God during the days of Zechariah, who instructed him in the fear of God. As long as he sought the Lord, God gave him success*" (2 Chronicles 26:5). So here is a king who did what was right in God's eyes, who sought the Lord, and who feared the Lord. But, in another falsification of Reformed doctrine, when he became powerful, he fell into sin because of pride (2 Chronicles 26:16) and became unfaithful to the Lord. As a result, while he was burning incense in the temple, which was a ministry reserved only for the Levites, he was struck with leprosy on his forehead (2 Chronicles 26:19-20). He had leprosy until he died, lived in a separate house, and was excluded from the temple of the Lord; and his kingdom was given to Jotham, his son.

Saul

Saul was clearly regenerate. He was anointed by the Lord as ruler over God's inheritance (1 Samuel 10:1, 24), the Spirit of the Lord came on him "*mightily*," and he prophesied and was "*changed into another man*" by means of the Spirit (1 Samuel 6-11). The Spirit of the Lord came on him on one occasion, provoking him to righteous anger (1 Sam. 11:6). He expelled all the mediums and spiritualists from the land (1 Samuel 28:3). Even in his carnality he remembered that God had answered his prayers in the past (1 Samuel 28:15), and he had some faith and inclination to goodness (1 Samuel 24:16-21). He still prayed (1 Samuel 28:6), and he could still repent. All these things should, of course, indicate to Reformed writers that Saul was regenerate (1 Samuel 26:21, 25). Yet his continued favor with God was conditioned on his obedience (1 Samuel 12:14 25). There was the possibility that he would fall away from the Lord. Becoming regenerate was not viewed as a guarantee of his perseverance in holiness.

The evidence above shows that he had believed and he had manifested his faith in a life of good works. Even Dr. Grudem seems to suggest that Saul was regenerate,[4] but then a page later he says "it is hard to tell."[5] Based on the Scriptures cited above, it is not hard to tell at all. It seems that the only reason for saying it is "hard to tell" is that if Saul was saved, the Reformed belief that regenerate Christians will always continue in the faith to the end of life would be falsified.

Saul was a saved man, but he became carnal. At first, he was repentant, a further evidence of his regenerate state (1 Samuel 15:24-25). But he became disobedient and forfeited his rulership over the kingdom (1 Samuel 13:13-14). This precisely parallels the experience of the carnal Christian who, like Saul, forfeits his inheritance and will not rule over the kingdom, that is, he will not inherit it. He became deceptive (1 Samuel 18:21). He continually persisted in his anger and sin (1 Samuel 18:29). There was no perseverance in holiness. The Lord disciplined him by sending an evil spirit on him (1 Sam. 19:9).

---

4   Ibid., 802.

5   Ibid.

Saul murdered the priests of the Lord (1 Samuel 22:17-18). When the writer of Chronicles summarized Saul's life, he said, "*Saul died because he was unfaithful to the LORD; he did not keep the word of the LORD and even consulted a medium for guidance, and did not inquire of the LORD. So the LORD put him to death and turned the kingdom over to David son of Jesse*" (1 Chronicles 10:13-14). Now here was a man who met all the conditions which Dr. Grudem would say are necessary for true salvation (except perseverance to the end).[6]

Saul was a regenerate man who became carnal. Furthermore, he persisted in his carnality to the point of physical death. Any doctrine that teaches that all who are regenerate will necessarily and inevitably persevere in a life of good works up to the point of physical death is falsified if only **one** regenerate person fails to do so. The life of Saul obviously falsifies Dr. Grudem's theory of perseverance.

Asa

A classic illustration of a regenerate man who falls into permanent carnality and dies in that condition is Asa, the third king of the southern kingdom of Judah (956–916 BC) and Rehoboam's grandson. The first ten years of his reign were prosperous and peaceful (2 Chronicles 14:1). Reformed theologians must admit that he was clearly regenerate. We are told that "*Asa did good and right in the sight of the Lord his God*" (2 Chronicles 14:2). As further evidence of his regenerate state, the Chronicler attests that he "*commanded Judah to seek the Lord*" (2 Chronicles 14:4). He removed the high places and introduced many reforms (2 Chronicles 14:5; 15:8). He rid the land of temple prostitutes which his father and grandfather had ignored (cf. 2 Chronicles 14:25–28; 15:3) and the "idols his father had made." When the country was in danger he

Called to the Lord his God, and said, "Lord, there is no one like you to help the powerless against the mighty. Help us, O Lord our God,

---

6   Grudem admits that Saul was "empowered for . . . special service," ibid., 636. He also notes that the Holy Spirit prophesied through Saul giving evidence of the Spirit's presence in his life, ibid., 637.

for we rely on you, and in your name we have come against this vast army. O Lord, you are our God; do not let man prevail against you." (2 Chronicles 14:11)

He sought the Lord with all his heart and soul and his heart, "But the high places were not removed from Israel; nevertheless, Asa's heart was blameless all his days" (2 Chronicles 15:17).

However, as his life wore on, he began to waver in his trust in the Lord (2 Chronicles 16:7). When God's prophet, Hanani, rebuked him for trusting in men rather than God and refusing to repent, as required by Reformed doctrine if he was "truly" saved, Asa became angry and put him in prison. Also, at this time Asa began to brutally oppress his people (2 Chronicles 16:10). In his later years, he became severely ill with gout, and yet *"even in his illness he did not seek help from the Lord, but only from the physicians"* (2 Chronicles 16:12). He died in his carnality. Once again, the Reformed assumption that those who are truly regenerate will persevere in a life of holiness to the final hour is shown to be false.[7]

In contrast to these kings (Rehoboam, Jehu, Joash, Amaziah, Uziah, and Asa), Hezekiah *"did what was right in the eyes of the Lord"* (2 Kings 18:3) and "removed the high places, and smashed the sacred stones and cut down the Asherah poles" (18:4). Here again, we have what Reformed theologians say do not exist, two classes of believers: carnal and spiritual. At the beginning, they believed and did what was right in the eyes of the Lord, but in the end they fell away from faith and obedience to Yahweh and persisted in that state to the end of life.

Solomon

First Kings 1-10 describes Solomon's glory and his dedication to God. The Lord granted his request for wisdom with discernment between good and evil (1 Kings 3:9). His childlike humility (1 Kings 3:7), his intimacy with the Lord (1 Kings 3:11-12), his prayer of dedication

---

7   Grudem mentions Asa's "mistake" of seeking doctors instead of the Lord for healing, but passes by the obvious contradiction to the Reformed doctrine which Asa's failed life illustrates. Ibid., 1064.

(1 Kings 8:23-53), and his God-given wisdom[8] and administration all confirm that he was regenerate. He declares his faith in God in 1 Kings 8:60, and Grudem admits that Solomon's prayer of dedication to the Lord is an example of prayer which students should study.[9] Solomon wrote three books of Scripture, which reveal divine wisdom available only to the regenerate mind.

But beginning in 1 Kings 11, he forsook the Lord. He began to love foreign wives (1 Kings 11:1), even though God had forbidden intermarriage. These wives turned his heart to "other gods," and his heart was no longer fully devoted to God (1 Kings 11:2). He became an idolater and worshiped the Ashtoreth, the moon-goddess of the Sidonians and female counterpart to Baal, and Molech, the detestable god of the Ammonites (1 Kings 11:5), to whom children were sacrificed in the Valley of Hinnom (*Gehenna*). He did evil in the eyes of the Lord and did not follow the Lord completely (1 Kings 11:6). He kept neither the Lord's covenant nor his decrees (1 Kings 11:11), and he became a worshiper of other gods. God began to bring divine discipline. He removed the kingdom from his house (1 Kings 11:11, 34). He raised up adversaries: Hadad the Edomite (1 Kings 11:14), Rezon, Hadadezer, king of Zobah, and others (1 Kings 11:23). Solomon tried to kill Jeroboam (1 Kings 11:40). Solomon was unrepentant. The kingdom was split because of his sin (1 Kings 12:1-33).

A popular Jewish legend indicates that he wrote the Song of Songs when he was young, Proverbs when he was middle-aged, and then fell away and returned and wrote Ecclesiates *when he was old.*[10] Yet the Scriptures specifically say, "*For it came about **when Solomon was old**, his wives turned his heart away after other gods; and his heart was not wholly devoted to the LORD his God, as the heart of David his father had been*" (1 Kings 11:4). The writer of 1 Kings summarizes his life saying, "*And Solomon did what was evil in the sight of the LORD, and did not*

---

8   Dr. Grudem equates Solomon's wisdom with the New Testament "word of knowledge". Ibid., 1080. Grudem admits that Solomon "turned away from the Lord" but never comments on how this refutes his theory of the saints' perseverance in holiness to the end of life. Ibid., 324).

9   Ibid., 36.

10 Some Old Testament scholars doubt that Solomon wrote Ecclesiastes.

follow the LORD fully, as David his father had done" (1 Kings 11:6), and *"Now the LORD was angry with Solomon because his heart was turned away from the LORD, the God of Israel, who had appeared to him twice,"* (1 Kings 11:9).[11] No evidence indicates that he repented. In fact, as Solomon grew older, he went farther away from God (1 Kings 11:33).

If we met a man today who had professed faith in Christ, been a well-known spiritual leader for years, manifested incredible divine wisdom, published numerous journal articles, and then rejected the Lord and began to worship idols, got involved in witchcraft and the New Age Movement, based on his criteria for verifying the presence of saving faith, Dr. Grudem would have to say he was never justified to begin with. However, even though he admits that Solomon "turned away from the Lord,"[12] he never discusses how this fact would falsify his entire system of assurance. Solomon was a born-again believer in Yahweh who finished life as a failure before God.[13] Once again, the Reformed theory of the saints' perseverance is falsified.

Saltless

The above illustrations are a few of many taken from the Old Testament. Now we must turn to the New Testament and see if similar failures are found.

Jesus tells his believing disciples,

> *You are the salt of the earth; but if the salt has become tasteless, how can it be made salty again? It is no longer good for anything, except to be thrown out and trampled underfoot by men.* (Matthew 5:13)

---

11 For a detailed discussion of Solomon's apostasy see Wayne A. Brindle, "The Causes of the Divisions of Israel's Kingdom " *BibSac* 141, no. 563 (July-September 1984): 230-33

12 Grudem, *Systematic Theology: An Introduction to Biblical Doctrine*: 324.

13 Fred Chay cites an interesting personal conversation with Dr. Grudem and one of his colleagues, Dr. Paul Wegner, a professor of Old Testament. When Dr. Chay asked Wegner where Solomon is today, Dr. Wegner replied he was in hell. Grudem then challenged him to rethink his position because Grudem clearly felt that Solomon was in heaven (Fred Chay, personal communication, 12/27/2016).

Salt had many uses in the ancient world. It was a seasoning for food (Job 6:6; Colossians 4:6), and it was associated with purity (Exodus 30:35; 2 Kings 2:19-22). Newborn babies were rubbed down with it for a cleansing (Ezekiel 16:4). It was also considered a preservative. It is difficult to know exactly how salt is used as an analogy in the life of the believer. However, Christianity has been a preservative for civilization.[14]

Because the chemical nature of salt is stable, the exact nature of this proverb has been problematic. Possibly, the salt in view here is what is derived from the Dead Sea by evaporation. The residue is impure and contains other minerals. Thus, salt becomes "saltless" when it "acquires easily a stale and alkaline taste,"[15] because of the presence of these foregoing elements. Apparently, believers can lose their saltiness and thus are "no longer good for anything." The word translated "tasteless" (Gr. *mōros*, "dull, sluggish, stupid, foolish") in its verbal form means to play the fool, to become foolish, or of salt to become tasteless, insipid (Mark 9:50).[16]

Furthermore, they can then be "thrown out" into the alleys and trampled on like garbage (Matthew 5:13). The foolish (tasteless) man is the failed Christian. The saltless metaphor is most likely a metaphor for uselessness. The negative consequence suggests the negative assessment of a useless and wasted life at the Judgment Seat of Christ when "saltless Christians" will lose their reward (2 John 8) and draw back in shame from Christ (1 John 2:28); be judged for the "bad" they have done (2 Corinthians 5:10), and lose what they have been given (Mark 4:25). These are Christians whose faith is not vital, living, and

---

14 See the extensive documentation of this fact in Alvin J. Schmidt, *Under the Influence: How Christianity Transformed Civilization* (Grand Rapids, Mich.: Zondervan Publishing House, 2001).

15 Friedrich Hauk, "ἅλας," in TDNT, 1:228. It is interesting to see how one Reformed commentator misquotes Hauk to imply that the gypsum which is mixed with the salt is then mistaken for the salt itself. Thus the reference is (supposedly) not to salt, but to gypsum which is said to have lost it saltiness (Donald A. Hagner, *Matthew 14-28*, Word Biblical Commentary (Dallas: Word Books, 2002), 99.

16 A.T. Robertson, *Word Pictures in the New Testament*, s.v. Matthew 5:13.

productive (i.e., it is dead), and lacks the energizing influence of good works (James 2:14). It is "useless" for sanctification (James 2:20).[17]

When the salt becomes mixed with impurities, it loses its savor. When Christians allow their lives to be mixed with "dirt," they become saltless. The supposed inevitable and necessary connection between genuine faith and a life of good works is refuted by this passage alone.[18]

How do Reformed teachers respond? Dr. Grudem cites this passage as teaching how Christians can positively affect the social order, seemingly affirming that those to whom Christ refers are regenerate.[19] However, like his discussion of Solomon, he does not comment on the obvious implication that this admission falsifies his system for obtaining assurance. A Christian who was once salt can become saltless (i.e., carnal).

---

17 Vincent suggests this historical background: "A merchant of Sidon, having farmed [sic?] of the government the revenue from the importation of salt, brought over a great quantity from the marshes of Cyprus—enough, in fact, to supply the whole province for many years. This he had transferred to the mountains, to cheat the government out of some small percentage of duty. Sixty-five houses were rented and filled with salt. Such houses have merely earthen floors, and the salt next to the ground was in a few years entirely spoiled. I saw large quantities of it literally thrown into the road to be trodden under foot of men and beasts. It was 'good for nothing'" (Marvin R. Vincent, *Word Studies in the New Testament* (Grand Rapids, Mich.: Wm. B. Eerdmans Publishing Co., 1946), 1:38-39.

18 Another biblical analogy is the "thorny soil" of the parable of the soils. Jesus described the thorns as "the worries of the world, the deceitfulness of wealth" (Matthew 13:22) and the "pleasures of this life" (Luke 8:14). The fruit in this parable is an indicator of usefulness and maturity in the kingdom of God, not an indicator of salvation. A plant that does not bring forth fruity to maturity is not a plant that never had life in it (regeneration). The seed obviously germinated and brought forth new life. Rather, such a plant is useless to the farmer. (Also, it should be noted that Luke only explicitly identifies the first soil by the road as those who are not saved.) The thorns correlate well with the other minerals that mix with salt and make it tasteless and thus worthless.

19 Grudem, *Systematic Theology: An Introduction to Biblical Doctrine*: 1203.

Some argue that the salt here refers to the Pharisees! Others say that when salt loses its flavor, this refers to "those who were trained in the knowledge of the truth but who then resolutely set themselves against the exhortations of the Holy Spirit and become hardened in their opposition [and] are not renewed unto repentance (Matthew 12:32; Hebrews 6:4–6)."[20] This, of course, is mere assertion, an assertion that flatly contradicts the text. The disciples, that is, "*you*," can "*become*" saltless. Some Reformed writers, like Dr. Grudem, while admitting that Jesus is referring to the failure of justified saints, do not comment on how this refutes their view of perseverance.[21]

Least in the Kingdom (Matthew 5:19)

In Matthew 5:19, Jesus says, "Whoever then annuls one of the least of these commandments, and so teaches others, shall be called least in the kingdom of heaven." The man in this verse is "in" the kingdom (i.e., he is saved), but he not only annuls (i.e., disobeys) even the least of the commandments (possibly the teaching of the sermon or of Torah),[22] but he actively teaches others to the do the same! In other words, he causes little ones to stumble (as in Matthew 18:6). According to Jesus, he is saved; he is "in" the kingdom! To teach others something that is contrary to what God has said is the ministry of a false prophet. Yet these false prophets are "in" the kingdom. Thus, while we agree that a carnal Christian without works is a monstrosity, Shepherd's statement that "faith alone justifies, but a justified person with faith alone would be a monstrosity which never exists in the kingdom of

---

20 William Hendriksen and Simon Kistemaker, *Exposition of the Gospel According to Matthew* (Grand Rapids, Mich.: Baker Book House, 2001), 283.

21 Craig Blomberg, for example, while avowing that the reference to being trampled on by men "neither affirms or denies anything about eternal security," nevertheless states that "believers who fail to arrest corruption become worthless agents of change and redemption" (Craig L. Blomberg, *Matthew*, New American Commentary (Nashville, Tenn.: Broadman and Holman Publishers, 2001), 102.

22 "Thus, the phrase 'the least of these commandments' refers to the final and full meaning of the law, but taken up and interpreted by Jesus." Hagner, *Matthew 14-28*: 108.

grace"[23] contradicts the teaching of Christ. Clearly, such monsters can exist "in" the kingdom of God.

The Carnal Christian (1 Corinthians 3:1-4)

In no uncertain terms, Paul makes it clear that it is possible for true believers to "*walk like mere men*" (1 Corinthians 3:3), something that Reformed teachers say cannot happen. Of course, they insert the qualifier, "for a limited period of time but not for the rest of their lives." If that is so, why, then, is it possible for one's life work to be burned up at the Judgment Seat of Christ (1 Corinthians 3:15; cf. 2 Corinthians 5:9-10)? How is it possible that a believer can persist in known sin up to the point of physical death (1 Corinthians 11:27-30)?

In dealing with this passage, it is common for Reformed writers to create a straw man regarding what the Free Grace position actually teaches. For example, Carson believes that those who disagree with him introduce "an ontological distinction in the congregation."[24] Ontological? With this he caricatures his opponents as believing there is a category of Christians whose *very essence* is carnal; that is, there is an "absolute, qualitative disjunction between those who are carnal and those who are spiritual." Having been involved in the Free Grace movement for many years, I am unaware of anyone who believes this. Then Carson goes on to give his understanding of 1 Corinthians 3. He says that the carnal man in this chapter is not ontologically different, but his behavior, not his essential being is carnal. Since this is precisely the Free Grace position, it is not clear where Carson derived his opinion of the Free Grace viewpoint. He gives no documentation.

But, by using the word "carnal" Carson adds an additional nuance. The carnal Christian in 1 Corinthians 3, he says, is not "someone who made a profession of faith at an evangelistic rally, followed the way of Christ for a few months, and then lived in a manner indistinguishable from that of any pagan for the next fifteen years, despite conscientious

---

23 Norman Shepherd, "Justification by Faith Alone," *Reformation and Revival* 11, no. 2 (2002): 88. Dr. Shepherd was a former teacher of Wayne Grudem's at Westminster Theological Seminary.

24 D. A. Carson, "Reflections on Christian Assurance," *WTJ* 54(Spring 1992): 8.

pastoral interest."[25] Carson admits that those addressed are "unspiritual believers." Also he curiously says that "the sins in view are not of the sort that make us think the Corinthians are distancing themselves from their baptismal vows.[26] In view of the fact that the Corinthians are fleshly and full of "jealousy and strife" (1 Corinthians 3:3), are practicing incest (1 Corinthians 5:1), are dragging one another into secular courts (1 Corinthians 6:1, 6), are participating in temple prostitution (1 Corinthians 6:15-16), are causing weaker brothers to stumble (1 Corinthians 8:9-10), are acting like the regenerate[27] but carnal Israel (1 Corinthians 10:4) in the wilderness (1 Corinthians 10:1-11), are participating in the Lord's table in an unworthy manner and as a result are judged by the sin unto death (1 Corinthians 11:27-32), are exercising spiritual gifts in sinful ways (1 Corinthians 14), and are denying the resurrection (1 Corinthians 15:12), it seems very appropriate, contra Carson, to describe them as those who "are distancing themselves from their baptismal vows."

Paul even insists that when these believers appear at the Judgment Seat of Christ, they face the possibility of all their works being burned up and entering eternity destitute of rewards. The danger in this passage is that they will persist in carnality to the end of life, which both Dr. Carson and Dr. Grudem say is impossible.

Apparently, Carson believes that Free Grace interpreters teach that anyone who makes a superficial commitment at an evangelistic rally and then lives like a pagan for fifteen years is a Christian. Supposedly, this is the Free Grace view of carnality. Dr. Grudem similarly misrepresents the Free Grace view.[28] What we do say, and what Carson does not believe, is that a carnal person *may* be a believer, but only God knows his heart. Carson thinks fifteen years of carnal behavior

---

25 Ibid.

26 Ibid., 9.

27 For proof that the biblical writers view the wilderness generation as a totality to be regenerate, see Joseph C. Dillow, *Final Destiny: The Future Reign of the Servant Kings*, 3rd revised ed. (Monument, CO: Paniym Group, Inc., 2016; reprint, 2016), 501-02.

28 Grudem, *"Free Grace" Theology: 5 Ways It Diminishes the Gospel*: 92-93.

would be sufficient to demonstrate that this man was not a genuine believer. Why not ten, or five, or how about one year? For how long would this man's carnality have to endure before Carson would feel free to announce that he was not a Christian?

In my view, 1 Corinthians 2:15–3:4 describes three categories of Christians: the spiritual (mature) Christian (1 Corinthians 2:15), the immature Christian, ("babes in Christ"; 1 Corinthians 3:1), and the carnal Christian (1 Corinthians 3:3). There is also an "ontological distinction" between the "natural man" who is an unbeliever, but not between the three types of Christians who are believers.[29]

Galatians

Can a Christian lose his joy (Galatians 4:15)? Yes! Can a Christian count an apostle as his enemy (Galatians 4:16)? Yes! Can Christians put themselves under the law (Galatians 4:21), fall from the grace way-of-life and become alienated from Christ (Galatians. 5:4)? Yes! Is it possible for a Christian to turn his freedom in Christ "into an opportunity for the flesh" (Galatians 5:13)? Yes! If it were not possible, there would be no point in warning them not to do something they could never do. Christians can "destroy" each other by their biting and devouring of each other (Galatians 5:15). Christians are capable of expressing the fruits of either the flesh or of the Spirit. The works of the flesh are warned against (Galatians 5:21). If they persist in them, they will not inherit the kingdom, that is, receive their reward-inheritance (Colossians 3:24).

Now if Christians can do all these things, how are they to be distinguished from the carnal Christian, which many Reformed writers say does not exist?

John 2:23

Many people saw the miraculous signs and *episteusan eis to onoma autou* ("believed on his name"). Yet Jesus would not *episteuen auton autois* ("entrust Himself to them") because he "knew all men." While

---

29 For more detail on this view see Stanley D. Toussaint, "The Spiritual Man," *BibSac* 125, no. 498 (April- June 1968): 139-46.

some have called this "spurious" faith,[30] this concept of believing on his name is used throughout John for saving faith. In fact, the first usage of the phrase in the book contradicts the view that it refers to a spurious faith.

> *Yet to all who received him, to those who believed in his name, he gave the right to become children of God—children born not of natural descent, nor of human decision or a husband's will, but born of God.* (John 1:12-13)

> *Whoever believes in him is not condemned, but whoever does not believe stands condemned already because he has not believed in the name of God's one and only Son.* (John 3:18)

The text does *not* say, "Many *said* they believed in his name." *John* says they *"believed in his name"* (Gr. ἐπίστευσαν εἰς τὸ ὄνομα αὐτοῦ). The word "believe" followed by "in the name" occurs only two other places in the Gospel of John. In John 1:12, it says the ones who believe in his name are children of God, and John 3:18 states that one who believes in his name is not condemned. Thus, the only other places in the New Testament where "believe" is followed by "in the name," teach that saving faith is indicated. In 1 John 3:23, God commands people to believe in the name of Jesus, and 1 John 5:13 states that believing in the name of Jesus gives assurance of having eternal life.[31]

The phrase *pisteuō eis*, "believe in," is John's standard expression for saving faith. One believes "on him" or "in his name."[32] To believe in a "name" in Semitic thought is to believe in a person. The faith in view here is faith in the person of Christ for salvation. When Calvin[33] says that they did not have true faith but were only borne along by

---

30 D. A. Carson, *The Gospel According to John* (Downers Grove, IL: InterVarsity, 1991), 184.

31 See Debbie Hunn, "The Believers Jesus Doubted: John 2:23-25," *TJ* 25, no. 1 (Spring 2004): 17.

32 See John 6:40; 7:39; 8:30; 10:42; 11:25, 26; 12:11.

33 John Calvin, *Institutes of the Christian Religion*, trans. Henry Beveridge, reprint ed. (Grand Rapids: Wm. B. Eerdmans Publishing Co., 1964), 3.2.12.

some impulse of zeal which prevented them from carefully examining their hearts, he is therefore flatly contradicting John's consistent usage in the rest of his writings.[34] Furthermore, in John 3:18, Jesus plainly states that the reason that a person is condemned is "because he has not *believed in the name* of the only begotten Son of God." Yet in John 2:23 they did *believe in the name*, therefore they are not condemned, that is, they are saved.

The fact that these Christians became believers in response to signs in no way requires that their faith was superficial. John makes it clear that he believes signs are *a* cause that may lead to faith, and he would be most perplexed to read in many modern commentaries that a faith that is generated in response to signs is not genuine.

Jesus did many other miraculous signs in the presence of his disciples, which are not recorded in this book. But these are written that you may believe that Jesus is the Christ, the Son of God, and that by believing you may have life in his name. (John 20:30-31)

In fact, John viewed a lack of response to signs as sinful rebellion! "Even after Jesus had done all these miraculous signs in their presence, they still would not believe in him" (John 12:37).

---

34 Martin Lloyd-Jones falls into the same error. He feels that those who "believed in His name" "did not truly believe in Him. They gave a kind of intellectual assent, they seemed to believe in Him; but He knew that they had not believed in Him in reality, and that is why He did not commit Himself to them." He cites John 6:60-66, where Jesus says there were some disciples "that believe not" and concludes that this explains the people in John 2:25. But isn't this directly contradicting the very words of John? John tells us that in John 2, contrary to the unbelieving disciples in John 6, these people specifically *did* believe. On what authority does Lloyd-Jones say they did not? How else could John say it if his intent was to indicate saving faith? Nowhere in the New Testament are adverbs, such as "truly" or "really" ever used to modify "believe" in a soteriological context. These adverbs are frequently inserted in front of the word "believe" in Reformed writings in order to sustain the fiction of the final perseverance of the saints in holiness to the final hour (Martyn Lloyd-Jones, *Romans Chapter 8:17-39: The Final Perseverance of the Saints* (Grand Rapids: Zondervan Publishing House, 1976), 282.

John does not reject a faith based on signs; he endorses it! Fred Chay and John Correia note, "In John 14:11, Jesus tells the disciples to 'believe because of the works themselves.'"[35] They add that it is true that a more mature faith, a more virtuous faith, does not rest only on visible signs (John 20:29).[36]

What then does it mean that "Jesus was not entrusting himself to them?" Debbie Hunn cites several examples from the first century which suggest that "entrusting oneself to another, in the examples known in the Greek of John's day, referred not to disclosure of truth, intimacy, or belief in the sayings of another, but to personal security."[37] This idea nicely fits the context of John 2:24. After driving out the traders from the temple, Jesus for the first time announced his coming death (John 2:18-22).

Chay and Correia add, "There is no reason to say that this lack of trust on Jesus's part was a permanent state of mind; all the text tells us is that Jesus was not yet ready to commit himself to their care. It seems apparent that Jesus was not entrusting himself to these people yet because their faith was infantile and weak. Jesus would not entrust his security in Judea to people whom he knew would eventually leave him. It was not the kind of faith that was mature enough to be trustworthy yet, but this does not mean it was not genuine faith.[38] To

---

35 Fred Chay and John P. Correia, *The Faith That Saves: The Nature of Faith in the New Testament* (Haysville, NC: Schoettle Publishing Co., 2008), 65.

36 Others see the expression as suggesting that he chose not to become "intimate" with them as in John 15:14-17. After the departure of Judas, the Lord turns to the disciples and says, "You are my friends if you do what I command" (John 15:14). Friendship with Christ is *not* a gift; it is conditional. When Jesus says he did not commit himself to them, there is no need to conclude they were unregenerate. Rather, it means he was not their friend and did not reveal to them additional truths learned from the Father (Zane C. Hodges, "Problem Passages in the Gospel of John: Untrustworthy Believers," *BibSac* 135, no. 538 (April 1978): 146-47.

37 Hunn, "The Believers Jesus Doubted: John 2:23-25," 19-21.

38 This is also seen in Paul commenting on the danger of shipwrecked faith or of a faith that can be overturned or made weak (1 Timothy 1:8-9).

ask the question, 'Do you have Christian friends that you do not fully trust' is to answer it."[39]

Christians Who Have No Part with Christ

Two kinds of Christians are referred to by the Lord in John 13:8:

Peter said to him, "Never shall you wash my feet!" Jesus answered him, "If I do not wash you, you have no part with me." (NASB)

He who has bathed need only to wash his feet, but is completely clean. (John 13:10)

Jesus refers to Christians who are "bathed" (Gr. *louō*), who are "completely clean," that is, regenerate (Titus 3:5). But a bathed, regenerate person sometimes needs washing (Gr. *niptō*). In fact, if he does not go through this washing (*niptō*) he has no part with Christ. To wash (*niptō*) means to wash in part, and to bathe (*louō*) means "to wash all over."[40] The former refers to cleansing from daily sin by confession (1 John 1:9), whereas the latter refers to regeneration. Christ teaches here that if a person who has been bathed refuses daily washing, he will have no part with him. This is what is meant by a carnal Christian.

Disgraceful Christians?

A concern of Reformed teachers is the fact that in the Free Grace view the character and works of a true believer can be very disparagingly described. The negative terminology that Jesus and the New Testament writers use to describe those whom the Free Grace writers believe are carnal Christians is quite severe. How could terms such as "evil servant" (Matthew 24:48) and "wicked" (Matt. 25:26) be applied to those who are truly born again?[41]

---

39 Chay and Correia, *The Faith That Saves: The Nature of Faith in the New Testament*: 69.

40 Richard Chenevix Trench, *Synonyms of the New Testament*, reprint ed. (Grand Rapids: Wm. B. Eerdmans Publishing Co., 1953), 161-62.

41 For full discussion of these passages from the point of view that those designated are born again see Dillow, *Final Destiny*: 787-95.

What other term besides "wicked," "evil," or "lazy" would be appropriate for the person who sins continually to the point of physical death? The wilderness generation trusted in the Passover lamb and worshiped the Lord (Exodus 12:27-28), believed in him (Exodus 4:31; 14:31), were "devoted to him," and "followed him" (Jeremiah 2:1-3). Yet though they believed on Christ (1 Corinthians 10:3); they were called "wicked" by God (Numbers 14:27) and were judged in the wilderness (1 Corinthians 10:5).[42] Carnal believers *can* be lazy and "neglect the so great salvation" (Hebrews 2:3). Born-again people are capable of murder and can live such a wretched life that they can be called "evildoers, thieves, and murderers" (1 Peter 4:15). Believers *do* sometimes mistreat their servants. Carnal believers harm other Christians when they gossip behind their backs (Titus 2:3), slander their character, ignore them in time of need (James 2:15), show partiality (James 2:3), drag them into court (1 Corinthians 6:6, 7), "ruin" them by their example (1 Corinthians 8:11-12), exhibit jealousy and strife toward them (1 Corinthians 3:3), steal from them (Ephesians 4:28), jealously and competitively cause them distress (Philippians 1:17), act with contempt toward them (Romans 14:3-4), judge them and cause them to stumble (Romans 14:13), quarrel with them (1 Corinthians 1:11), sleep with one's mother-in-law (1 Corinthians 5:1), treat fellow Christians as "enemies" (Galatians 4:16), "complain" about one another (Colossians 3:12), have sexual intercourse with another believer's wife (1 Thessalonians 4:6, 7), not provide for the needs of one's family (1 Timothy 5:8), betray and abandon a fellow believer because he is in

---

42 Jeff Phillips notes, "It is important to realize that God forgave the sins of the wilderness generation at Moses' request (see Numbers 14). But although he pardoned their iniquity (Numbers 14:20), he refused to let them enter into the Promised Land (i.e. receive their inheritance as children of Abraham; Numbers 14:23). This becomes an important hermeneutical key to understanding the book of Hebrews. The author of Hebrews uses the wilderness generation's example of failure and disinheritance to exhort his audience of Jewish believers not to go back to the old covenant. To do so would be to forfeit the Sabbath rest (sabbatismos), which corresponds to the wilderness generation not entering the land and should be understood as forfeiting the believer's inheritance in the kingdom (i.e. the millennial reign of Christ)." Personal Communication May 5, 2017.

trouble with anti-Christian authorities (2 Timothy 1:15), or upset the faith of fellow Christians (2 Timothy 2:17-18). Christians who do these things are carnal Christians, and one day this will be revealed for what it is, behavior that deserves rebuke! Reformed writers, of course, would agree that Christians can do these things but not continually or habitually. However, this is special pleading on their part.

Simon Magus

Under the preaching of Philip, a sorcerer named Simon Magus was converted. The text of Acts indicates he was a saved man. According to Luke, "Even *Simon himself believed*; and after being baptized, he continued on with Philip (Acts 8:13). Simon believed, was baptized and followed Philip as a disciple. This indicates he was regenerate. It is important to note that both the Samaritans and Simon "believed" (Acts 8:12-13). If the former were saved, on what basis can one argue that Simon was not?[43]

The gift of the Holy Spirit was delayed in Samaria until Peter and John arrived. When the Spirit was given, the external manifestations that Simon saw apparently motivated him to try to purchase the gift of being able to impart the Holy Spirit by the laying on of hands (Acts 8:18). Because of his sin, the apostle Peter responds:

May your silver perish with you, because you thought you could obtain the gift of God with money! You have no part or portion in this matter, for your heart is not right before God. Therefore, repent of this wickedness of yours, and pray the Lord that if possible, the intention of your heart may be forgiven you. For I see that you are in the gall of bitterness, and in the bondage of iniquity. But Simon answered and said, "Pray to the Lord for me yourselves, so that nothing of what you have said may come upon me." (Acts 8:20-24)

What was Simon's sin? It was selfish ambition. "Give this authority to me as well, so that everyone on whom I lay my hands may receive

---

43 Chay and Correia, *The Faith That Saves: The Nature of Faith in the New Testament:* 54-58.

the Holy Spirit" (Acts 8:19). Peter concluded that he wanted to buy the power to pass on the gift of the Holy Spirit with money and that his heart was not right with God. Surely the presence of prideful ambition is not a basis for concluding that a man is not saved! Who among us has not at one time or another been tempted in this way? Unholy rivalries and ambitions often plague relationships between true Christians. To say the presence of this sin invalidates the claim to regeneration is unrealistic.

The punishment for Simon's sin is that he will "perish." This refers to physical death. His money is to perish with him, and the perishing of his money is obviously temporal. This is another illustration of the sin unto physical death.[44]

While many Reformed writers say that Simon Magus could not have been saved because he did not persevere, and because Peter strongly rebuked him, surprisingly, others agree that he was justified.[45] This startling admission invalidates their theory of the saints' perseverance in holiness to the end.

Apostasy of Hymenaeus and Alexander

In some specific cases the possible became actual!

> Keeping faith and a good conscience, which some have rejected and suffered shipwreck in regard to their faith. Among these are Hymenaeus and Alexander, whom I have delivered over to Satan, so that they may be taught not to blaspheme. (1 Timothy 1:19-20)

These two men had "faith" and "a good conscience," but they rejected both and experienced shipwreck in their faith. The Reformed writers, of course, bring their theological system into the passage and

---

44 See also 1 Corinthians 8:11, where the perishing of the weaker brother has the same effect. See elsewhere in Dillow, *Final Destiny*: 534 ff.

45 See Ekhard J. Schnabel, *Acts*, ed. Arnold Clinton, Zondervan Exegetical Commentary on the New Testament (Grand Rapids: Zondervan, 2012), 409 and Craig Keener, *Acts: An Exegetical Commentary*, 2 vols., vol. 2 (Grand Rapids: Baker Book House, 2013), 1518.

say that the fact they rejected the faith proves they never had "true" faith to begin with.[46] Once again, however, this is the point in question. The spiritual state of these people must be determined from 1 Timothy 1 and not from a theological system. The Arminian writer, Howard Marshall, argues, "The language suggests a violent rejection of the claims of conscience, and the metaphor of shipwreck implies the *loss of a faith once held*."[47]

Three things are said about these two men: (1) they had believed; (2) they had given the internal evidence of regeneration in a good conscience; and (3) they needed to be taught not to blaspheme. If it were not for the third point, one would conclude on the premises of Reformed theology that they were saved people. They had believed, and they had given some initial evidence of it.[48] The only evidence against this conclusion is that they did not continue in the faith.

---

46 Sometimes this is done by translating the word "their" (Gr. *tēn*) as "the." This translation gives the sense that they became shipwrecked in regard to the objective faith and not in regard to their subjectively appropriated faith. However, the subjective sense agrees better with the previous verse as well as with the stress on faith in the whole book. Supporting "the faith" would also be the phrase *peri tēn pistin* (1 Timothy 6:21 and 2 Timothy 3:8 which seem clearly objective) and *peri tēn alētheian* (2 Timothy 2:18) which is clearly objective. The 2 Timothy passage seems conclusive enough that Hymenaeus was a believer who had gone astray.

47 I. Howard Marshall, *Kept by the Power of God: A Study of Perseverance and Falling Away*, 2nd ed.
(Minneapolis: Bethany Fellowship, 1974), 128.

48 Even this third argument paradoxically substantiates the thesis that they are regenerate. When Paul says they must be handed over to Satan, he calls to mind the only other illustration in the New Testament of a man being handed over to Satan, which is recorded in 1 Corinthians 5:5. In that passage a member of the congregation was involved in incest (1 Corinthians 5:1). However, even though he is obviously carnal, he will be saved in the day of Jesus Christ. Hymenaeus and Alexander needed to be "taught" (Gr. *paideuō*). In its other usages in the New Testament, this verb is commonly used of the divine chastening or discipline of the regenerate (1 Corinthians 11:32; Titus 2:12-13; Hebrews 12:5-6). See discussion in Dillow, *Final Destiny*: 511-14.

How does Dr. Grudem respond? He says that these men were unbelievers and "the Lord knows those who are His" (2 Timothy 2:17-18),[49] that is, "those who are saved and who are not." Grudem misunderstands the passage. He wants it to mean that the Lord knows (Gk. *ginōskō*) who are Christians and who are not.[50] However, the passage refers to a leadership quarrel between Moses and the sons of Korah who challenged whether or not Moses was sent by God as the appointed leader. Moses declared, "By this you shall *know* that the LORD has sent me" (Numbers 16:28). Faced with this challenge to his authority, Moses says, "Tomorrow morning the LORD will show (Heb. *yadah, hiphil, "cause to know, to reveal")* who is his" (Numbers 16:5). The context of the rebellion is not about who is regenerate and who is not, it is about who is the appointed leader and who is not. In other words, the Lord will show who is his appointed leader.[51] Like the sons of Korah, Hymenaeus and Alexander are not leaders of the people, even though they paraded themselves as teachers.

---

49 Grudem, *Systematic Theology: An Introduction to Biblical Doctrine*: 856. Grudem, *"Free Grace" Theology: 5 Ways It Diminishes the Gospel*: 92.

50 The Hebrew text has *yadah* in the *hiphil* which means "to make known, declare" (cf. Exodus 18:16, 20; Numbers 16:5; Deuteronomy 8:3; 1 Samuel 28:15; 2 Samuel 7:21; 1 Chronicles 17:19; 2 Chronicles 23:13; Job 32:7; 42:4; Psalms 16:11; 25:4, 14; 51:6; 77:14; 89:1; 98:2; 103:7; 105:1; 106:8). The idea is, "*In the morning the Lord will give consideration of (the situation) and declare who are his appointed leaders.*"

51 When Paul says, "The Lord knows those who are his," he is not saying that the Lord knows those who are truly regenerate in contrast to those who are not, implying that Hymenaeus was not regenerate. Paul quotes from the LXX (substituting *kurios* for *theos*). The translation of the Hebrew text of Numbers 16:5 reads: "*Tomorrow morning the LORD will **show who is his** and who is holy, and will cause him to come near to him*" (NKJV). The incident is instructive. Korah led a rebellion against Moses. The point at issue seems to be that Korah felt that since Israel was a community, all were in equal authority, and therefore it was only presumption, not God's appointment, that led Moses to assume the leadership of Israel. Furthermore, Moses had taken away the right of the firstborn of every household to be a member of the priesthood of Israel and had instead invested that right in a branch of his own family, the sons of Aaron.

The exegetical evidence seems to present these men as genuine Christians who have fallen away from their faith. Paradoxically, even Martyn Lloyd-Jones acknowledges that these men were saved, but, he says, "with respect to their belief, and their statement of their belief, they were in a state of chaos, shipwreck, utter muddle. The apostle does not say they were reprobate; all he says is that they have got in to this indescribable muddle, a shipwreck, a shamble, call it what you will."[52] We call it a carnal Christian who has denied the faith.

Two Categories of Christians

In 1 Timothy 1:20, we read that Hymenaeus and Alexander were turned over to Satan to be taught not to blaspheme. In 2 Timothy 2:17 Hymenaeus is mentioned again along with Philetus. They are both described as men who "have gone astray from the truth." Immediately following their apostasy and, perhaps further explaining it, Paul says,

> Now in a large house there are not only gold and silver vessels, but also vessels of wood and of earthenware, and some to honor and some to dishonor." (2 Timothy 2:20, NASB)

As a further explanation of the failure of Hymenaeus and Philetus, Paul explains that in a "large house," that is, the Church,[53] there are two kinds of Christians; some are "vessels of wood and of earthenware," and some are "gold and silver." The latter are "to honor" and the former are "to dishonor." The close association with 1 Corinthians 3:12-15 is obvious. There, Paul spoke of Christians whose works are "wood, hay, and stubble," and those whose works are "gold, silver, and precious stones." Even though the former will have all their works consumed by fire, they "will be saved, yet so as through fire" (1 Corinthians 3:16).

---

52 Lloyd-Jones, *Romans Chapter 8:17-39: The Final Perseverance of the Saints*: 284

53 In the Pastoral Epistles, Paul uses the overarching analogy of a household for the church of God (cf. 1 Timothy 3:14-16).

Clearly this parallels the classifications of 2 Timothy 2:20, "some to honor (εἰς τιμὴν) and some to dishonor (εἰς ἀτιμίαν)," and explains the final destiny of the two kinds of vessels. Hymenaeus and Philetus are "wood and earthenware" and their lives will lead to dishonor resulting in their works being burned up at the Judgement Seat of Christ. The preposition *eis* ("to") often takes the sense of an "end result."[54]

Apostasy in the Last Days

The apostle Paul specifically declares in 1 Timothy 4:1-3 that it is possible for believers to depart from the faith:

> But the Spirit explicitly says that in later times some will fall away from the faith, paying attention to deceitful spirits and doctrines of demons.

Now if the Spirit "explicitly says" that apostasy from the faith is possible, by what right do Reformed scholars deny this? These people who fall away are believers and are contrasted with the liars who have a seared conscience (1 Timothy 2). Non-Christians led these believers into apostasy. Marshall correctly observes that the use of *aphistēmi* ("fall away") "implies a departure from a position once held and therefore refers to apostasy from the faith by those who once held it."[55]

Apostasy of Demas and Others

Toward the end of his life, Paul found himself deserted by many of his fellow laborers. Among them were Demas (2 Timothy 4:10), Phygelus and Hermogenes (2 Timothy 1:15), and several unnamed people (2 Timothy 4:16).

Demas, according to Paul, was a "fellow worker" (Philemon 24). He is listed along with Luke as a traveling companion of the apostle

---

54 *BDAG*, option 4d, 290. Cf. "set apart for the gospel" (Romans 1:1).

55 Marshall, *Kept by the Power of God: A Study of Perseverance and Falling Away*: 129. Of course, Marshall believes that to fall away results in eternal damnation.

(Colossians 4:14). For most readers, this is strong presumptive evidence that he was saved. Yet he "deserted" the imprisoned Paul (possibly for a bribe)[56] and went to Thessalonica because he came to a point where "he loved this present world" (2 Timothy 4:10). To desert an apostle is to desert Christ, that is, to commit apostasy.

Dr. Grudem does not respond to the above. He simply asserts, without any evidence, that Demas was an unbeliever.[57]

Reformed Responses to These Examples

Reformed writers respond to all the examples of the permanently carnal Christian, and even apostasy, in two ways. The say,

1. "We do not have evidence to know 'for sure' that the men were born again."

2. "They could not have been born again because they did not continue to the end."

3. "New Testament fellowships included non-Christians."

These Professing Believers Could Not Have Been Justified

Why? Because if they were, they would have continued to the end. Often they will cite Calvin who famously said, "It is therefore faith alone which justifies, and the faith which justifies is not alone."[58] The argument is circular and needs no further response. They assume their conclusion is true before looking at the evidence that it is not. This is theological exegesis in full flower!

---

56 This is based on a questionable reference in the apocryphal Acts of Paul (Florence Morgan Gillman, "Demas," in *The Anchor Bible Dictionary*, ed. David Noel Freedman (New York: Doubleday Co., 1992), 2:134.

57 Grudem, *Systematic Theology: An Introduction to Biblical Doctrine*: 856.

58 John Calvin, *Acts of the Council of Trent: with the Antidote*, 6th Session, can. 11.

We Do Not Have Enough Evidence

Grudem requires the evidence that one is "really" saved to be "evident" to others.[59] Can we assume that when Luke said Simon Magus had believed, was baptized, and followed Philip (i.e., he became a disciple), there must have been something about his life that made it "evident" to Luke that Simon was saved? Also, when Paul refers to Demas as a "fellow worker" and took him on missionary trips, can we assume that Paul saw something in the life of this man that made it evident to Paul that Demas was saved? If Reformed thinkers claim that we do not have enough evidence to conclude that these two men were saved, they are saying that even Luke and Paul could not tell by outward appearance that a professing Christians was regenerate. If neither Luke nor Paul could be sure from the evidence that Demas and Simon were saved, Grudem's requirement that true faith will be "evident" to others is useless. There is good evidence to satisfy readers of these passages that these men were saved, unless certain interpreters have a prior agenda to maintain the theory of the saints' perseverance in holiness against the plain meaning of numerous passages.

While we believe the illustrations cited above provide sufficient evidence to falsify the Reformed doctrine of perseverance, we admit that for some no amount of evidence is satisfactory. I suggest that the reason for this intransigence is based on the concern that a denial of this fundamental aspect of Reformed theology will lead to antinomianism. Equally important is the emotional revulsion that a just and holy God might allow a failed believer into heaven. However, personally, I have always had a much bigger problem, "Why would he let *me* into heaven?"

Furthermore, all of us, including this writer, approach Scripture with certain biases that sometimes overly influence what the correct interpretation might be. While we always appeal to the Scriptures as our final authority, the reality is that our position, even when the evidence points toward a different view, often cannot be dislodged. As soon as a challenge emerges to what we have previously settled as something one no longer needs to think about, it is hard to give

---

59 Grudem, *"Free Grace" Theology: 5 Ways It Diminishes the Gospel*: 87.

an open-minded hearing to an alternative point of view. I know this happens, because it has happened to me. It took me over eight years to gradually give up my formerly Reformed approach to the New Testament and finally settle on the Free Grace paradigm.[60] When we have held certain viewpoints for a long time, they are not easily abandoned.

New Testament Fellowships Included Non-Christians

As pointed out in Chapter 8 above, Dr. Grudem correctly notes that there were "false brethren" in some of the New Testament churches.[61] However, as we explained in chapter 8 that is completely irrelevant. The issue is who is the intended audience, wheat or wheat and tares. We concluded that it is wheat only.

Conclusion

Other passages could be cited which establish the fact that true Christians can become carnal and even persist in their carnality up to the point of physical death.[62] Reference has already been made to the warnings in the New Testament. Each warning implies the possibility of failure, and almost all of them are specifically addressed to regenerate people.[63] If the interpretation of the above biblical references is correct, the Reformed doctrine of the perseverance of the saints in faith and holiness is left in shreds.

Dr. Grudem believes that one "evidence of genuine faith is continuing in his word, that is, continuing to believe what he says and living a life of obedience to his commands,"[64] and "those who do not

---

60 My own journey is described in some detail in Dillow, *Final Destiny*: 10-11.

61 Grudem, *"Free Grace" Theology*: 79-82.

62 1 Timothy 5:5-6, 11-15; 2 Timothy 2:22-26; James 1:12-16; Revelation 12:11

63 Dillow, *Final Destiny*: See Chapter 32, "The Carnal Christian"

64 Grudem, *Systematic Theology: An Introduction to Biblical Doctrine*: 792-93. He says that "continuing in the faith" is a requirement for genuine faith. Also, Grudem, *"Free Grace" Theology: 5 Ways It Diminishes the Gospel*: 83-84, 89.

continue in the faith show that there was no genuine faith in their hearts in the first place."[65]

The Free Grace contention is that the combined weight of the warning passages, the passages illustrating the fact of the carnal Christian, and the specific biblical illustrations of apostasy firmly establish the possible existence of the permanently carnal Christian. We maintain that it is extremely likely that this is true and that only prior adherence to a theological system could yield another result after careful examination of the biblical data.

---

65 Grudem, *Systematic Theology: An Introduction to Biblical Doctrine*: 793.

Chapter 11

The Doctrine of Rewards

Joseph Dillow, Th.D.

W hat is the Free Grace view of rewards? While it shares much with the view of Dr. Grudem and some other Reformed writers, there are some significant differences. In this chapter, we will address some of the objections to rewards advanced by a few Reformed theologians and also the interpretations of rewards that Dr. Grudem embraces in contradiction to the Free Grace approach. We will also note some of the omissions in his view that seriously diminish the motivational import of this central biblical doctrine and our final accountability. The Free Grace view of rewards could be grace plus accountability.

In addition, we will address the parable of the vineyard workers, which plays a key role in Reformed writer Craig Blomberg's view of rewards. Finally, we will define in more detail some biblical aspects of the doctrine of eternal reward as understood in Free Grace theology.

A critical omission in Dr. Grudem's recent book, *"Free Grace" Theology: 5 Ways It Diminishes the Gospel,* is the total lack of any discussion of a central emphasis in the Bible, rewards (good and bad;

cf. 2 Corinthians 5:10). As a result, Dr. Grudem often misunderstands Free Grace interpreters and makes astounding and unverified claims regarding the belief or implications of Free Grace theology in the practical lives of Christians.

Objections to Rewards as Motivation for Christian Living

A disconnect sometimes seems to exist between the many passages that urge us to action, service, and perseverance based on reward and what actually motivates some of us. This may explain why teaching about rewards is so rarely heard in our churches. For some, it is not perceived as highly relevant to daily life.

Why is this? We believe there are four reasons.

Striving for Rewards Can Result in a Performance-Based Relationship with God

Any kind of final accountability based on our performed work could possibly place many under a sense of legalism and a performance-based relationship with God. Did not the Reformation free us from the perspective that works are necessary as a means of securing God's ultimate approval?

Craig Blomberg and others have complained that the doctrine of differences in eternity future diminishes grace and "can have highly damaging consequences for the motivation and psychology of living the Christian life."[1] Furthermore, the way Free Grace writers present the doctrine, he says, smacks of legalism.

He recounts a conversation with one of his students, in which the student commented that "[i]n most of the conservative Christian circles of which he had been a part, the Christian life was like a free trial membership to an elite country club: The first year is wonderful, but after that you pay through the nose."[2]

---

1   Craig L. Blomberg, "Degrees of Reward in the Kingdom of Heaven?," *JETS* 35, no. 2 (1992): 160.

2   Ibid., 170.

Blomberg has a point. It is possible for sincere believers to be emotionally troubled in their relationship with God if they misunderstand the *fatherly context* of the call to rewards. Lacking that, there is a danger that the Free Grace of rewards might degenerate into a performance-based relationship with God, about which Blomberg is correctly concerned. We will discuss this issue later.[3]

He goes on to say, "Far too many Christians whom I have personally encountered think that God relates to them just like the taskmasters they have known in their families and at their work. If only they can be a little more obedient today, God will like them more and deal with them more favorably. Conversely, when they fail, especially when repeated failures plague them over a short period of time, they are convinced that God will be quick to punish them."[4]

We suspect, however, the sense of perceiving God as harsh has nothing to do with the Free Grace doctrine of rewards. Instead, it is more likely the result of a system of theology, embraced by Blomberg and Grudem, which dangles the threat of hell over the struggling Christian's head all his life[5] as a means of motivating him to persevere to the end of life.

Blomberg believes the notion of rewards results in a doctrine that implies believers in heaven "would live with some unending sense of regret and sadness if they realized that they had not attained to as high a level of enjoyment or privilege in heaven as they might have, had their lives on this earth proved more meritorious."[6] Hoehner responds clearly,

---

3   See Joseph C. Dillow, *Final Destiny: The Future Reign of the Servant Kings*, 3rd revised ed. (Monument, CO: Paniym Group, Inc., 2016; reprint, 2016), 1013 ff. and 985 ff.

4   Blomberg, "Degrees of Reward in the Kingdom of Heaven?," 169.

5   Of course, I realize that they do not state it so bluntly as I have, but there is no question that this is how their views are perceived by many in their churches.

6   Blomberg, "Degrees of Reward in the Kingdom of Heaven?," 162. While it is true that a few have held this idea (see Marty Cauley, *The Outer Darkness*, 2 vols. (Sylva, NC: Misthological Press, 1231 Monteith Branch Road, 2012), 519-64.), it is not held by the majority of those who hold the Free Grace view.

There will not be envy or jealousy, but rather praise. It will not be, "Why did you get more rewards than I?" but more likely "It is wonderful how you allowed the power of the Lord to work in you," or, "It is amazing what persecution you endured for the Lord." Finally, everyone in heaven will realize that rewards, like salvation, are of God's grace, and will give praise accordingly.[7]

Since All Will Know Joy in Heaven, Rewards Do Not Motivate

Since, according to the Free Grace view, everyone's cup will be full in eternity, although the cups will be of different sizes, what is the motivational benefit anyway? At the end of the day all are equally happy. With this observation Blomberg dismisses the subject of rewards because, he says, it fails at its core to motivate. No matter what one does, Blomberg incorrectly assumes, there will be no negative consequence.[8]

One reason Blomberg and others feel this way is that they have misinterpreted the vast amount of Scripture that speaks of the potential of a negative consequence at the Judgment Seat of Christ. They are incorrect when they say that everyone will be equally happy. That will not be true even in eternity future, and at the Judgment Seat of Christ

---

7   Harold W. Hoehner, "Reward," in *New Dictionary of Biblical Theology*, ed. T. Desmond Alexander and Brian S. Rosner (Downers Grove, IL: Inter-Varsity Press, 2000).

8   Nor does he discuss what being *rewarded* for "bad" work done means (Gr. *komizō* , "to cause someone to experience something on the basis of what that person has already done [Louw-Nida, 1:809, cf. Colossians 3:25]). The NIGTC describes being rewarded as being "duly requited for actions that we have carried out during our life on earth." Blomberg does mention being "saved through fire" in (1 Corinthians 3:15). He correctly says that all the believer's works are burned up. He then qualifies that the reference to suffering loss only applies to the Judgment Seat and that there is no loss once one arrives in heaven. That is merely an assumption he must add in defense of his central thesis. If this loss does not continue into heaven, then it does not. But that is the point in question. See Blomberg, "Degrees of Reward in the Kingdom of Heaven?," 165. Free Grace writers understand this loss in the sense of loss of special intimacy, loss of opportunities for service, and loss of honor, that is, hearing the Master say, "Well done."

there will be moments of terrible grief, weeping, rebuke, and possible millennial disinheritance for carnal Christians. Paul makes it clear.

*For we must all appear before the Judgment Seat of Christ, that each one may be recompensed for his deeds in the body, according to what he has done, whether **good or bad**. **Therefore knowing the fear of the Lord, we persuade men.*** (2 Corinthians 5:10-11)

Blomberg and those who share his viewpoint give little consideration to the teaching that something "**bad**" might be dispensed at the Judgment Seat of Christ. For some reason, they stop reading at the end of 2 Corinthians 5:10 and never consider (at least in their writings) verse 11, *"knowing the fear of the Lord."* John tells us that at the Judgment Seat of Christ, some will draw back in shame (1 John 2:28). He also exhorts his readers *"Watch yourselves, that you do not lose what we have accomplished, but that you may receive a full reward."* (2 John 8, NASB95).[9] Paul spoke of the Judgment Seat of Christ as a time when some would be saved as through fire (1 Corinthians 3:15) and our Lord said, *""I tell you that to everyone who has, more shall be given, but from the one who does not have, even what he does have shall be taken away"* (Luke 19:26, NASB95). These passages make clear that for some the Judgment Seat of Christ will not be all joy and rejoicing.

Rewards and Merit: A Protestant Dilemma in Regard to Rewards

Emma Disley in an excellent article, "Degrees of Glory," warns of the dangers of what she calls "spiritual commercialism." "The theology of future reward and punishment represents a constant latent propensity of the Christian faith to lapse into formalism, or spiritual commercialism, or legalism, which, in themselves, strike at the very heart of Christian disinterestedness and self-forgetfulness."[10]

---

9 Blomberg misunderstands this parable to teach that the reward here is "seeing the work of the ministry at Ephesus endure against false, gnostic teachers." Ibid., 169.

10 Emma Disley, "Degrees of Glory: The Protestant Doctrine and the Concept of Rewards Hereafter," *JTS* 42, no. 1 (April 1991): 77-105.

She introduces a difficult problem in the New Testament. On the one hand, the ethics of the New Testament are dominated throughout with the idea of reward as a recompense for work done. Yet, on the other hand, our Lord clearly teaches in numerous places that we should pursue disinterestedness. The New Testament ideal is selflessness and serving others, that is, freedom from selfish motive or interests (1 Corinthians 13:5; Philippians 2:1-11).

And he summoned the crowd with his disciples, and said to them, "If anyone wishes to come after me, he must deny himself, and take up his cross and follow me. For whoever wishes to save his life will lose it, but whoever loses his life for my sake and the gospel's will save it. For what does it profit a man to gain the whole world, and forfeit his soul? (Mark 8:34–36)

Are we not told, on the one hand, that we are to obey because of the mercies of God (Romans 12:1) and that "the love of Christ controls us" (2 Corinthians 5:14) rather than the love of rewards? Is not doing something for the purpose of obtaining a reward a far less worthy motive than doing it out of love and gratitude?

Yet, on the other hand, the reward motivation is clear. Each of the beatitudes comes with a promise. The poor in spirit are promised a reward, the kingdom of heaven. The pure in heart are promised that they will "see God." Those who endure persecution are promised that they will "receive" a kingship. Those persecuted are promised reward in heaven, and so forth.[11]

Jesus promises that those who are in the last position now may be first in the kingdom. He stresses rewards emphatically when he says to his astonished disciples,

Truly I say to you, that you who have followed me, in the regeneration when the Son of Man will sit on his glorious throne, you also shall sit upon twelve thrones, judging the twelve tribes of Israel. And everyone who has left houses or brothers or sisters or father or mother or children or farms for my name's sake, shall receive many

---

11 Matthew 5:2-12

times as much, and shall inherit eternal life. But many who are first will be last; and the last, first. (Matthew 19:28-30)

Even the most basic command of Christianity, to love others, is enhanced with the motivation of repayment at the resurrection of the righteous.

But when you give a reception, invite the poor, the crippled, the lame, the blind, and you will be blessed, since they do not have the means to repay you; for you will be repaid at the resurrection of the righteous. (Luke 14:10-14)

Humility itself is enjoined as the basis for reward,

But when you are invited, go and recline at the last place, so that when the one who has invited you comes, he may say to you, "Friend, move up higher"; then you will have honor in the sight of all who are at the table with you. For everyone who exalts himself shall be humbled, and he who humbles himself shall be exalted. (Luke 14:10-11)

The motivation for humility is that we will be exalted in the future and that we will have greater honor now! Even forgiveness, a decidedly personal benefit, is conditioned on our forgiving others, *"For if you forgive men for their transgressions, your heavenly Father will also forgive you"* (Matthew 6:14). Why not forgive others with no notion of personal forgiveness? Shouldn't we forgive because it is the right thing to do and not because of some benefit that accrues to ourselves? Shouldn't we secretly strive for completely disinterested reasons?

According to Jesus, the answer is, "No." Rather, we are to practice our piety in secret so that our *"Father who sees what is done in secret will reward you"* (Matthew 6:4). Critics argue that if there was ever a system of ethics grounded on mercenary considerations and dominated by the motive of recompense, it is the system that is found in the Gospels. Whatever one might urge against those who obey with "selfish" hopes of reward can, they say, be urged equally against the Gospel writers.

The problem cannot be ignored. The main thrust of Jesus's teaching is certainly that of asking people to forget themselves and focus their aspirations on God alone and on the needs of others, not on some personal benefit. This difficulty cannot be resolved unless we first acknowledge that the manner in which Jesus presents reward is completely different from our common understanding of the term and from that of His critics. We will address this problem in more detail below.

But what, we must ask, do the Scriptures say?

As discussed in the previous chapter in this book on assurance, all of the Greek words for reward—*misthos* (1 Corinthians 3:14), *antapodidōmi* (Luke 14:14), *misthapodosia* (Hebrews 10:35), *stephanos* (1 Corinthians 9:25), *brabeion* (Philippians 3:14), *antapodosis* (Colossians 3:24), and *misthapodotēs* (Hebrews 11:6)—express the idea of something obtained by means of effort, remuneration for work done, wages, or payment.

How are rewards and merit related? Even though it is clear from the New Testament that rewards are in a sense "earned" or merited, in the final analysis they are the result of grace, not our work. This is true for four reasons.

First, God was not obligated to give any reward in return for any amount of work. The fact that he chose to obligate himself in this way is an act of unmerited favor, pure grace. In view of man's depravity and the imperfection in any work one might do, God would be perfectly just never to give any reward at all. The offer to grant a reward for work was entirely his choice. The works do not obligate him. *Rather, he has obligated himself to reward the works.*

The psalmist makes this clear, saying,

> *Once God has spoken; Twice I have heard this: That power belongs to God; and lovingkindness is thine, O Lord, for thou dost recompense a man according to his work.* (Psalm 62:11–12)

Why does God reward our works? He does so, because in his "lovingkindness" (Hebrew *chesed*), he has obligated himself to do so. His *chesed,* or love and mercy, is the basis of this obligation.[12]

---

12 See R. Laird Harris, *"chesed,"* in TWOT, 306 ff. Harris demonstrates that *chesed* is granted freely, without obligation, and is related to mercy and grace.

However, some recoil at the idea that we can place God under any obligation.[13]

While we would agree that no work of ours could place any obligation on God, God himself could agree to accept an obligation to remunerate works. That he enters into obligatory relationships with his creatures is taught in many passages; they are called covenants and promises. Our good works deserve nothing from his hand, but in his grace he has chosen to grant rewards to those works, all out of proportion to their value.

We are in full agreement with Charles Hodge when he says,

> Protestants . . . teach that God does reward his people for their works. Having graciously promised for Christ's sake to overlook the imperfection of their best services, they have the assurance founded on that promise that he who gives to a disciple even a cup of cold water in the name of a disciple, shall in no wise lose his reward.[14]

Second, the rewards God grants are so astonishingly out of proportion to any work we could ever do that we can only conclude

---

13 "A. A. Hodge and Charles Hodge, commenting on the Westminster Confession, put it this way, "God's infinite superiority to us, his absolute proprietorship in us as our Maker, and sovereignty over us as our moral Governor, necessarily exclude the possibility of our actions deserving any reward at his hand. **No action of ours can profit God or lay him under obligation to us.** All that is possible to us is already a debt we owe him as our Creator and Preserver. When we have done our utmost we are only unprofitable servants. Much less, then, can any possible obedience at one moment atone for any disobedience in another moment. (4) As already proved under chapter 13, on Sanctification, our works, which could merit nothing even if perfect, are in this life, because of remaining imperfections, most imperfect. They therefore, the best of them, need to be atoned for by the blood, and presented through the mediation of Christ therefore they can find acceptance with the Father. Archibald Alexander Hodge and Charles Hodge, *The Confession of Faith: With Questions for Theological Students and Bible Classes* (Simpsonville, SC: Christian Classics Foundation, 1992).

14 Charles Hodge, *Systematic Theology*, 3 vols. (Grand Rapids: Wm. B. Eerdmans Publishing Co., 1977), 3:244.

they are the result of grace. It might be best to call them "overgenerous wages." If we do enough work to obtain a day's wage, and yet he gives us a year's worth of remuneration, that is grace. While it is true we would not receive anything if we did not do that day's labor, the amount of remuneration so far outstrips the effort such that we can only exclaim, "Praise God for his matchless grace." This is one of the teachings of the parable of the vineyard workers. Those who worked only one hour got the same as those who worked all day. God can, if he chooses, give overgenerous wages.

Third, whatever works we do would never have been done at all unless God had called us to salvation, motivated us to do them, and then, by his strengthening help, enabled us to do them.

Fourth, the main point of the parable of the laborers in the vineyard seems to be, "Do not be among the first who became last" (see discussion below). We must avoid the attitude of work for pay. We must approach our service for Christ not with an attitude that he owes us something because we have made a particular sacrifice, but rather with the attitude that we want to be faithful to him and he will do what is right. We are to take encouragement from the fact that he remembers "every cup of water" and that if he chooses to honor our service, that act is only overgenerous wages. That, Jesus says, is what the kingdom of heaven is like.

The Bible Teaches That We Should Pursue Disinterested Benevolence

Because of the strong emphasis on rewards in the New Testament, Christianity has often been accused by philosophers as being self-seeking. For example, philosopher John Hospers argues that when believers justify being moral on the basis of a doctrine of eternal rewards and punishments, this is "simply an appeal to self-interest. . . . [N]othing," he says, "could be a clearer appeal to naked and unbridled power than this."[15]

---

15 John Hospers, "Why Be Moral," in *Reading in Ethical Theory*, ed. John Hospers and Wilfrid Sellars (Eglewood Cliffs, NJ: Prentice Hall, 1970), 739. Cited by J. P. Moreland, "Ethical Egoism and Biblical Self-Interest," *WTJ* 59, no. 2 (Fall 1997): 255.

We seem to have two conflicting modes of thought: "self-centeredness" and "God-centeredness." Did not Paul make it clear that "love seeks not its own" (1 Corinthians 13:5)? How then can seeking for rewards be consistent with biblical love? If it is argued, "Virtue is its own reward," this still does not justify exhorting disciples to pursue virtue because it brings personal benefit. Are the commands of the Gospels to be obeyed because of the personal benefit such obedience might bring? Is not this thinly veiled self-centeredness, rather than love or virtue?

This view of ethics is sometimes called "disinterested benevolence."[16] This is the atheistic ethic in which good is done only for the sake of the good, with no consideration of reward for the doing of it.[17] It is atheistic because atheists do not believe in an afterlife, eternal judgment, or any final accountability for one's life. Therefore, the only appeal they have for love is altruism.

By forgetting the possibility of reward, a man supposedly honors the ethical standard in its purity. The motivation for obedience is to be found only in the command itself. Only in this manner, maintains the atheist, can the selfishness of man be crushed and a pure altruism found. This motivation is "purely moral." The reason this is the "only" way this can be done is because there is no other; there is no final accountability. As history has shown, this ethic has been catastrophically unsuccessful in prompting human betterment. Witness, for example, the 85-year experiment in the Soviet Union.

There are many objections to this viewpoint. First, it is completely contrary to what we know about human nature based on empirical observation for thousands of years. There is no such thing as pure altruism. Man's depravity means that even in the best of men, a person's altruism always contains an element of improper motive. No one performs good acts entirely or even primarily out of perfect love for others or for God. There are always other motivations lurking in

---

16 "Fackler, M.; Hopkins, Samuel," in *Who's Who in Chkristian History*, ed. J. D. Douglas; Phyllip W. Comfort (Wheaton, IL: Tyndale House, 1992), 327.

17 For a response to this atheistic ethic, see G. C. Berkouwer, *Faith and Justification* (Grand Rapids: Wm. B. Eerdmans Publishing Co., 1954), 117.

the background—the preference of one's own self-interest or of some other object less than God. Thus, even the good is tainted.

Second, the ethic of disinterested benevolence would impose on us an ethical motivation that is not only contrary to our nature but is also impossible to fulfill. For example, the "purely moral" would demand that childless couples adopt babies solely for the babies' sakes. Such an approach is naïve and far removed from the realities of life. It would be ridiculous to demand that a man who marries a woman because he loves her must do it only for the good of the woman he loves with no personal motive to have his own needs met. Of course, to marry for the single purpose of having one's own needs met would be sin, but everyone marries with a mixture of motives, and they can be good and proper motives. In fact, it was God who said it was not good for man to be alone. So, it is "good" to marry in order to have our "alone" needs met.[18]

Third, to pursue altruism, lack of self-interest, or self-sacrifice can be as calculated and ego-centered as a naked pursuit of reward. When one sets out to be selfless, he is immediately focused on some standard by which he can measure whether he is being truly altruistic, some code that will define the altruistic life. Thus, his mind is turned away from God and toward the code. This leads to endless self-examination and introspection, the error of legalism.

The history of the church is littered with the wrecks of such vain pursuits. From the self-flagellation of those seeking penance, to the scrupulous rules of behavior laid down by the monks involving poor diet, sackcloth for clothing, and hours of meditation every day, sincere

---

18 Along these lines, Moreland says, "Genuine altruism requires that an altruistic act have, as its sole, or at least main intent, the benefit of the other. An act whose sole or ultimate intent is self-interest but which, nevertheless, does result in the benefit of others is not genuine altruism. If you found out that someone 'loved' you or acted 'altruistically' toward you solely or ultimately with the intent of benefiting himself, then you would not count that as genuine love or altruism even if the act happened to benefit you in some way. Thus, 'egoistic altruism' is a contradiction in terms. Ethical egoism is consistent with pseudo-altruism but not with genuine altruism" (Moreland, "Ethical Egoism and Biblical Self-Interest," 263.

believers have vainly attempted a life void of self-interest, all the while paradoxically focusing on themselves.

Fourth, J. P. Moreland explains, "We need to distinguish between self-benefit as a by-product of an act vs. self-interest as the sole intent of an act. Scriptural passages that use self-interest may simply be pointing out that if you intentionally do the right thing, then a good by-product of this will be rewards of various kinds."[19] In other words, just because self-benefit serves as "a" motive for something, it does not follow that it is the reason that justifies the action in the first place. "The Bible may be citing self-interest as a motive for action and not as the reason for what makes the act our duty."[20] It may be that Scripture cites rewards not as the fundamental reason for an action, but as a prudent or wise reason for action, and not the moral basis or only reason for it.

I will have more to say about this objection to the biblical view of rewards in a section below where I will propose that the quest for reward is not selfish because, "Rewards are the Completion of a Life Well-lived."

The Parable of the Laborers in the Vineyard

Any discussion of the Free Grace doctrine of rewards must consider Jesus's parable of the laborers in the vineyard (Matthew 20:1-16). Scholars like Craig Bloomberg often appeal to this parable to prove that there are no degrees of glory and that in heaven all will be equally blessed. Strangely, Dr. Grudem makes no mention of this central passage on rewards.

At the outset, we must reject the unfortunate notion presented by Jeremias, Blomberg, and others that "in the parable of Jesus [as Jeremias says], the laborers who were engaged last show nothing to warrant a claim to a full day's wages. . . . [I]n this apparently trivial detail," Jeremias continues, "lies the difference between two worlds: the world of merit, and the world of grace; the law contrasted with

---

19 Ibid., 265.

20 Ibid., 266.

the gospel."[21] I disagree. The workers who were hired last certainly did "warrant a full day's wages." Why? The point of the parable is that they worked with proper motives and those who were hired first did not.

At any rate, this parable is not about the "gospel." It is about being "hired" and being first or last in the kingdom, that is, it is about status in the kingdom. While it is true that any reward can only ultimately be attributed to the generosity of the Master, rewards do involve merit, as established above. Those who were hired last actually did receive more. For one hour of work, they got a full day's wages! But rewards are only obtained by those who worked for them with the correct motives. Once this is granted, Jeremias's argument flounders. That degrees of reward are an important aspect of this parable is evident by the closing phrase, *"the last will be first and the first last"* (Matthew 20:16). Earlier in Matthew, Jesus spoke of the same concept, referring to those who would be "least" in contrast to those who would be "great" in the kingdom (Matthew 5:19). The difference, he said, was related to doing (Matthew 6:1; 7:21, 26) and to a manifestation of the inner qualities of character described in the Sermon on the Mount (5:20-28).

How does Blomberg explain the terms "last" and "first"? He says it does not refer to status, "[b]ut it may also be a vivid equivalent to the more prosaic truth that all numerical positions are interchangeable."[22] What "truth" is this? Why are all numerical positions interchangeable? Apparently, Blomberg has been "uncomfortable" with the rewards doctrine. He says, "In the twenty years of my adult Christian life I have grown progressively more uncomfortable with any formulation that differentiates among believers as regards our eternal rewards."[23] He then cites the conversation with a student mentioned at the beginning of this chapter who was psychologically harmed by the doctrine of rewards.

He also believes that since there is no "symmetry" between works and grace in regard to salvation, there can be no "symmetry" between works and grace in regard to rewards. By "symmetry," Blomberg means

---

21 Joachim Jeremias, *The Parables of Jesus*, 6th ed. (London: SCM, 1963), 139.

22 Blomberg, "Degrees of Reward in the Kingdom of Heaven?," 161.

23 Ibid., 157.

that there can be no correlation between grace and works; that is, God does not reward salvation because of works, therefore he does not reward Christian works with reward. All agree that that is true in regard to salvation. While Free Grace interpreters admit there is no legal contractual obligation between God and man in regard to rewards (the central point of the parable), there is a correlation. This is evident because, as mentioned above, all seven of the words for reward refer to payment for work done.[24]

Curiously, Blomberg admits, "There does seem to be Scriptural support for the doctrine of degrees of punishment in hell." But he denies that there could be similar gradation of reward in heaven. He argues that this could be so in heaven because, "The differences among Christians that seem to loom so large in this life could figure significantly in God's eternal reckoning. The differences in elevation between Mount Everest and the Mariana Trench seem negligible when the earth is viewed from Mars."[25] It is difficult to see why these differences, which seem significant enough for God to ordain differences in hell, would not

---

24 For example Jesus says, *"For you will be repaid at the resurrection of the righteous"* (Luke 14:14). The word for "repay" is *antapodidōmi* and means "to pay something back to someone as the result of an incurred obligation." See Louw-Nida, 1:574. See Colossians 3:24. In Romans 4:4, Paul explicitly says that a "wage" is an obligation which is owed to the worker, *"Now to the one who works, his wage [Gr. misthos] is not reckoned as a favor, but as what is due [Gr. opheilēma]"* (Rom. 4:4). An *opheilēma* ("what is due") is a "debt" or "obligation." Louw-Nida, 1:670. All these Greek words for reward (*misthos* [Matth. 10:41], *antapodidōmi* [Luke 14:14], *misthapodosia* [Heb. 10:35], *stephanos* [1 Cor. 9:25], *brabeion* [Phil. 3:4; 1 Cor. 9:25], *antapodosis* [Col. 3:24], *misthapodotēs* [Heb. 6:1, "one who pays wages," EDNT, 2:432]) express the idea of something obtained by means of effort, remuneration for work done, wages, or payment. They are singularly inappropriate terms to describe a "condition" or "cause" for final entrance into heaven which comes apart from payment, wages, work done, or remuneration but is obtained *"without cost"* (Rev. 21:6; 22:17). It is therefore lexically doubtful to say, as some Reformed thinkers do, that while believers are judged according to their works, their works have no "merits, but in that they are the effects of faith." See William G. T. Shedd, *Dogmatic Theology*, Classic reprint ed. (Minneapolis: Klock & Klock, 1979), 802.

25 Blomberg, "Degrees of Reward in the Kingdom of Heaven?." 162.

also be sufficient enough for him to acknowledge these differences in heaven.

Matthew's account of the rich young ruler (Matthew 19:16-30) is followed by the parable of the laborers in the vineyard (Matthew 20:1-16), the classic treatment of the subject of rewards in the New Testament.

To understand this parable, it is important that the conclusions reached regarding the encounter with the rich young ruler be kept in mind.[26] There, we learn that the rich young ruler was a believer who came to Jesus seeking counsel on how he could obtain an inheritance in the kingdom. He wanted to know what he must "do." He was seeking a legal arrangement in which so much work would result in so much reward. Jesus obliged him with a reminder to keep the Ten Commandments. When the man claimed he had done this (Matthew 19:20), Jesus put his finger on the fact that the man really had not. Jesus told him to sell all he had and give it to the poor and then come and follow him as his disciple. This would involve giving up all the earthly status that his culture ascribed to the rich and in which he himself trusted for a full and meaningful life. After the young ruler walked away feeling sorrowful, Peter said, *"Lord we have done all that this man refused to do, what will we have?"* Instead of rebuking him, the Lord gloriously affirmed his theology by saying,

> *Truly I say to you, that you who have followed me, in the regeneration when the Son of Man will sit on his glorious throne, you also shall sit upon twelve thrones, judging the twelve tribes of Israel. And everyone who has left houses or brothers or sisters or father or mother or children or farms for **my name's sake**, shall receive many times as much, and shall inherit eternal life. **But many who are first will be last; and the last, first.** (Matthew 19:28-30)*

Luke and Mark clarify that Matthew's "many times as much" is to be expected "at this time" or "now in the present age." What is more, there is great reward in the age to come (Luke 18:29-30; Mark 10:28-30).

---

26 See discussion elsewhere in Chapter 13, The Rich Young Ruler.

The opening word "for" in Matthew 20:1 alerts us to the fact that what follows in the parable of the vineyard workers is an elaboration in some way on the discussion of rewards that closed the preceding pericope in the account of the rich young ruler[27] (Matthew 19:27-30). The lynchpin of interpretation is the logion, "the last shall be first and the first, last," which both introduces and concludes the parable (cf. Matthew 19:30; 20:16), though, in reverse order.

This parable is probably the most variously interpreted of all of Christ's parables. Any credible interpretation must satisfactorily answer three questions. First, how is this parable in harmony with the saying about first and last that introduces and concludes it (Matthew 19:30; 20:16)?

The problem is that if all receive the same reward, a denarius, how is one last and another first? The parable is obviously intended to illustrate this principle of first and last in some way. The question is how it does this.

Second, there is a moral difficulty. How can it be fair that the laborers who labored for only an hour received the same reward as those who labored faithfully in the hot sun all day? If this principle were applied to industry today, the results would be catastrophic! The owner seems to be overly generous on the one hand and grossly unfair on the other. Many have known capricious employers who unfairly reward some more than others. Can God be unfair like this?

Third, what is the parable's main point and application to us today?

Several different approaches have been taken. For some, the key to the parable is the fact that a denarius was given to all the workers, no matter how long they worked. This, they say, shows that there are no differences of reward in the kingdom of God; all are equal.[28] Yet, however attractive this seems, it is flatly contradicted by the saying that introduces and concludes the parable. If all were rewarded equally, there would be no reversal; all would have the same rank in the kingdom.

---

27 We learn that he is a ruler in Luke 18:18.

28 Blomberg, "Degrees of Reward in the Kingdom of Heaven?," 159-72.

Others have taken the approach that God does not regard the length of time in which men are engaged in his service; rather, he considers fidelity and strenuous exertion. However, while that is no doubt true, it is purely gratuitous to assume that the laborers who were hired first did not work as hard as those who were hired last. In fact, they claim they labored hard to the point of exhaustion[29] and under the hot sun (v. 12).

Another approach is to assume that the point is no matter when a person is called into the Lord's work (as a child, a young person, or an adult), he can receive the same reward as those who have worked diligently all their lives. Some were called to Christian service as teenagers, the present writer as a college student, and C. I. Scofield at age 36. However, while this may be true and is certainly a valid application of the parable, is this the main point?

We begin by assuming that the parable is closely connected with issues raised in the encounter with the rich young ruler and also the repetitive statements about the first and the last that bracket the parable. The opening word "for" points, in the immediate context, to the concluding summary of this encounter: *"But many who are first will be last; and the last, first"* (Matthew 19:30). The rich young ruler may be "first" in this world, but he will be "last" in the kingdom *because he shunned the call to discipleship.* Peter and the other disciples, however, although last in this world, will be first in the kingdom. It seems that this refutes the common interpretation that the parable of the laborers in the vineyard was intended to correct Peter's supposedly selfish question, "What shall we have?" His question is not selfish at all. It is perfectly appropriate and is a question Jesus himself encouraged, based on this extensive teaching on rewards.

The introductory "for" does not point to that question; it points to the teaching about first and last in verse 30, which in turn points to the entire encounter with the rich young ruler. The Lord never rebukes Peter for asking this question. This parable is not a comment on Peter's

---

29 The text reads, "have borne the burden" (v. 12). Literally, this might be translated, "we bore up under very difficult circumstances, working to the point of exhaustion" (Gr. τοῖς βαστάσασι τὸ βάρος).

selfishness but on the whole notion of the great reversal and further clarification on how rewards are dispensed.

The parable describes a common scene in Palestine, the grape harvest. Often at harvest time extra workers were needed.

> *For the kingdom of heaven is like a landowner who went out early in the morning to hire laborers for his vineyard.* **When he had agreed with the laborers for a denarius** *for the day, he sent them into his vineyard.* (Matthew 20:1-2)

A denarius was the normal wage for a day's work paid to harvesters. These laborers entered into the work on a different ground than those who followed. Like the rich young ruler who wanted to know what he must do to inherit eternal life, these laborers likewise hammered out an agreement with the owner of the land. Jesus points out that position in the kingdom cannot be formally arranged as in a legal labor contract, that is, so much work results in so much compensation. Other issues are involved, such as the inward motivations and the attitudes of the workers. This wrong spirit eventually erupts into various other problems as noted in verses 11-12.

Apparently, however, as the day wore on and the hot sun ripened the fruit, it became evident to the owner of the vineyard that the harvest could not be completed without additional help. So he went into the marketplace to hire more workers at nine o'clock, noon, and three in the afternoon. The marketplace in a Palestinian village is similar to today's oriental bazaar.

> *And he went out about the third hour and saw others standing idle in the marketplace; and to those he said, "You also go into the vineyard, and* **whatever is right** *I will give you." And so they went. Again he went out about the sixth and the ninth hour, and did the same thing.* (Matthew 20:3-5)

These workers in the parable entered the work under a different arrangement with the landowner than the workers in verses 1-2. They trusted the landowner to do *"whatever is right."* Morris notes, "There is no specific offer of a job, nor is there any indication of haggling over terms or even of coming to an acceptable agreement (as in the case of the first workers)."[30] This draws us into the story, making us wonder what is right. This detail is surely important to the interpretation of the parable as their approach differs from those who were hired first and who had an agreement of so much work for so much wages.

As the day closed with the work incomplete and the fruit in danger of spoiling, the owner returns to the marketplace at the eleventh hour (five o'clock) to hire more workers. He finds a number of potential hires *standing around.*

> *And about the eleventh hour he went out and found others standing around; and he said to them, "Why have you been standing here idle all day long?" They said to him, "Because no one hired us." He said to them, "You go into the vineyard too." (Matthew 20:5-7)*

Apparently, they were not lazy, as some have suggested. The problem was that no one had hired them.

According to the Law, the workers were to be paid in the evening (Leviticus 19:13; Deuteronomy 24:15), and so when evening came (about the twelfth hour or six o'clock), the landowner ordered his foreman to summon the workers to pay them their due.

> *"Call the laborers and pay them their wages, beginning with the last group to the first." When those hired about the eleventh hour came, each one received a denarius. (Matthew 20:8-9)*

However, surprisingly, he pays those whom he hired at five o'clock (the eleventh hour) first.

Normally, those hired first would be paid first. Those who worked for only one hour must have been surprised at getting a full day's wage. They had made no bargain with their employer and had been content to trust him to do what was right. The parable speaks of the compassion of the landowner.

No doubt this suggested to those who were hired first that since they had worked twelve hours and those hired last had worked only

---

30 Leon Morris, *The Gospel According to Matthew*, The Pillar New Testament Commentary (Grand Rapids: Wm. B. Eerdmans Publishing Co., 1992), 500.

one, they would receive twelve denarii instead of the agreed upon one denarius.

> *When those hired first came, they thought that they would receive more; but each of them also received a denarius.* (Matthew 20:10)

But to their chagrin, they received what those who had worked one hour received—one denarius!

"How unjust," they thought; and they began to grumble.

> *When they received it, they grumbled at the landowner, saying, "These last men have worked only one hour, and you have made them equal to us who have borne the burden and the scorching heat of the day."* (Matthew 20:11-12)

Their gripe seems legitimate. They had labored to the point of exhaustion for twelve hours while the scorching heat of the burning east wind had blistered them all day (Isaiah 49:10; Ezekiel 19:12; Hosea 13:15; James 1:11). Yet, they received no more than those who worked for one hour in the cool evening breezes. The reader must ask himself, "Am I like these grumbling workers? If so, how?"

If rewards were a matter of strict legal recompense for each amount of work done, we would expect the landowner to say, "You are correct. I should pay you more." However, he says:

> *Friend, I am doing you no wrong; did you not agree with me for a denarius? Take what is yours and go, but I wish to give to this last man the same as to you. Is it not lawful for me to do what I wish with what is my own? Or is your eye envious because I am generous?* (Matthew 20:13-15)

"Look," he says, "I kept my bargain with you, the agreement *you* wanted, and I have a perfect right as the owner of the vineyard to be generous to others."

Therefore, there is not a precise correlation between work and reward as in a labor contract. The idea of *legal* merit is excluded (i.e., so much work obtains a contractually agreed amount of reward); only mercy is emphasized. Moreover, the point of the parable is to demonstrate that it is *God's sovereign prerogative to do as he pleases with each of us.*

He says to those hired first, "Take what is yours and *go*" (Gr. *hupagō*). We may detect here (as the accompanying rebuke regarding envy suggests) that "depart" is a better translation. The expression sometimes is a bit stronger than just "go."[31]

We are now getting close to the central issue in the parable, the incorrect attitudes toward reward that characterized these envious workers. The parable highlights three such attitudes: (1) a commercial approach to rewards, (2) their grumbling about the right of the owner to be over-generous, and (3) envy ("*Is your eye envious because I am generous?*"). They were infected with commercialism, grumbling, and envy!

To work for rewards with a sense of competition or with a desire to have higher status than others (envy) in the coming kingdom (as Blomberg incorrectly understands to be a natural consequence of the Free Grace view) is ruled out. The kingdom of heaven is not like modern industry. Taking the lowest status and becoming the servant of all is what counts before the divine Landowner, as taught in the discussion that follows the parable (Matthew 20:25-28). Only those who do not envy others for their blessings will receive overgenerous wages. Only those who work, fully confident that the Lord will always do "what is right" (who do not have a commercial attitude), and who do not worry about the amount of reward they will receive (who do not grumble), will receive any reward.

In their approach to service for the landowner, those hired first apparently wanted a guarantee, an agreement worked out in advance, so much work resulting in so much payment (v. 2). However, the other laborers agreed to trust the landlord to pay them "whatever is right" (v. 4). These are diametrically opposite approaches to working for Christ and have led to dramatically different modes of service for Christ in the history of the church.[32]

---

31 This word is used, for example, of commanding demons to "depart" (Matthew 8:32).

32 This legalistic-commercial approach was eventually perverted into the practice of indulgences. A certain amount of money would result in a specific reduction in purgatory sentence.

The attitude of the first-hired laborers may remind us of the approach of the rich young ruler who also wanted to know what he must do to obtain an inheritance in the kingdom. Did a contractual, commercial approach to rewards lurk in the mind of the rich young ruler? It had developed in the minds of the apostles. Recall how they jostled about who would be the "greatest." To Peter's question, however, the Lord immediately gives an affirming answer with no implication of impropriety on Peter's part. The parable of the laborers in the vineyard addresses the wrong attitude of the rich young ruler and the relationship between reward and work done. This teaches that the relationship is not one of contract, but of overgenerous wages—grace.

Jesus acknowledges that Peter and the other disciples have, in fact, done what is right and will obtain one-hundred-fold returns. A return of this magnitude is definitely a blue-chip investment, which is overly generous compared to the work done. Yet, since the rich young ruler wanted a contractual relationship, Jesus offered him one, *"You know the commandments,"* just as the landowner does in the parable of the laborers. The apostles, on the other hand, apparently never approached the Lord with such a contract but had simply followed him out of love and, like the other laborers in the vineyard, simply trusted the Lord to do "whatever is right" (v. 4).

In the denouement, each receives a denarius. Too much attention has been focused on the denarius. The denarius is probably a mere artifact of the story to bring out the salient lessons. The denarius is not the final reward. If anything, it would parallel the reward given in the present age promised in response to Peter's question. The man hired last did in fact receive twelve times more than those hired first, for he worked only one hour. Rather, *the final reward is being either first or last.* That is the punch line of the parable.

So, the last shall be first, and the first last. (Matthew 20:16)

Who are the last and who are the first? The *"last who will be first"* refers to those who, like the apostles, have given up everything and adopted poverty to follow Christ. They are the "unworthy." Paul would later call them the "foolish" and among the "not many mighty" and the "not many wise" (1 Corinthians 1:26) and the "weak" and the "base things of the world" (1 Corinthians 1:27). The *"first who will be last,"* then, would be those who, like the rich young ruler, had greater opportunity and capacity but were unwilling to give up the status of the rich. Evidently, those hired first were similarly proud and envious. That spirit of envy had governed their labor and was revealed only at the end of the day.

In this statement, the reward of those hired first is clear; they will be last in the kingdom. It seems that they forfeited their reward, as this sobering statement declares. In fact, they are commanded to "depart" (*"Take what is yours and go"*). They are being politely dismissed. Why? Because they had the wrong motives. They served only in order to obtain reward, not because of love for the job or the landowner. Also, they were full of envy. That is, they compared themselves with other laborers and were jealous of their honors. They were filled with an unloving and proud spirit. The other laborers, however, had served, trusting that the landowner would do what was right (Matthew 20:4). And he did. In this life, they received a greater return (three-fold or twelve-fold) over those who had labored first, and they were also given higher status in the kingdom, first instead of last. I believe that Dr. Blomberg has completely missed the central point of the parable when he says, *"From the last group of workers comes the principle that many seemingly less deserving people will be treated generously, due to the sovereign free choice of God."*[33] Those hired last were *not* less deserving. Why? They worked with the right motives: love for the Master and trust that he will do "what is right." These laborers illustrate that whatever decisions believers make now will be justly remunerated at the last day, but these laborers were not concerned about a precise correlation between their work and their wages.

The "reward" for the unworthy servants was not the denarius; it was being commanded to depart and to assume the lowest status in the kingdom (see 2 Corinthians 5:10, the "bad" reward). It was evident from their actions that they had labored with an eye toward wanting to achieve more honors than the other laborers and with an attitude that suggested that being rewarded was more important than the work itself.

---

33 Blomberg, "Degrees of Reward in the Kingdom of Heaven?," 160.

In the Lord's work, it is wrong to serve for rewards on a contractual basis with the anticipation that so much work yields so much reward. Rather, we work because we love the King and trust him to be fair and righteous. When we do, we will be astonished at his generosity, even if we started late in the day. There is nothing here about grace trumping justice. The King is both gracious and just. Rewards are not strictly tied to the amount of work done. The King will take every circumstance into consideration. But most of all we learn that he is generous. Just as he promised a one thousand percent return to the disciples, he granted the highest honor to the laborers who were hired last.

The Free Grace Doctrine of Rewards

According to Craig Blomberg, "I do not believe there is a single NT text that, when correctly interpreted, supports the notion that believers will be distinguished one from another for all eternity based on their works as Christians."[34] We believe that few in the history of the church would agree with this statement. In the discussion to follow, we will explain six of the most important aspects of the biblical doctrine of rewards.

Rewards, Good and Bad, Introduce Final Accountability into the Christian Life

A serious lacuna in Dr. Grudem's book on Free Grace theology is the omission of the biblical emphasis on rewards. No serious discussion of Free Grace theology can omit detailed consideration of the many passages in which the New Testament stresses this central biblical doctrine. For example, he never refers to key passages (such as 1 Corinthians 3:8, 15; 9:17-18; Colossians 3:24; 2 Corinthians 5:10; Romans 14:10; 1 John 2:28; 2 John 8; 1 Peter 1:17; Hebrews 11:26; Revelation 11:18; 22:12). Surprisingly, he omits the numerous statements from Christ about this central doctrine (Matthew 5:12, 46; 6:1-6; 6:16, 18; 9:41; 10:41-42; Luke 6:23, 35; 19:26). These omissions are extremely important in Free Grace interpretations of many

---

34 Ibid.

passages. A failure to interact with these texts weakens his analysis of Free Grace thinking.

Craig Blomberg says, "The greatest danger of the doctrine of degrees of reward in heaven is that it has misled many people into thinking that the very nominal professions that they or their friends have at one time made will be sufficient to save them, even if they fail to receive as high a status in heaven as they might have."[35]

Grudem agrees making a similar astonishing claim, with no proof, that Free Grace teachers would "not hesitate to say, that based upon an earlier profession of faith" that this person is saved.[36] However, had he seriously interacted with Free Grace views on rewards and final accountability, his worries about Free Grace teaching would have been assuaged. Grudem incorrectly represents Free Grace teaching as saying the saving faith is only intellectual assent. For Free Grace writers, a saving profession of faith involves more than that. It includes an inner persuasion of the truth of the Gospel and a reliant trust in the person of Christ for salvation.

The Free Grace understanding of rewards affects the interpretation of many passages and introduces accountability for our lives which Bloomberg's and Grudem's approach can never equal. Both of these scholars require (based on 2 Corinthians 13:5) that a believer must continually examine himself throughout life to discern whether or not he is truly saved.[37] This approach is virtually impossible for the majority of Christians to accept or to live by, and, therefore, they simply ignore it. This partially explains much of the apathetic Christianity in Reformed circles, which Grudem incorrectly assigns to the encroachment of Free Grace theology.

I am aware that Dr. Grudem and Dr. Blomberg will reply that, by exhorting their congregations to examine themselves to see if they are really saved, they have in fact introduced accountability. The fear

---

35 Ibid., 172.

36 Wayne A. Grudem, *"Free Grace" Theology: 5 Ways It Diminishes the Gospel* (Wheaton: Crossway, 2016), 93.

37 Ibid., 80-81.

that one is not really saved and is going to hell is supposedly a strong motivator to do good works.

Apart from the fact that this approach is noticeably absent from the Scriptures,[38] it does not work anyway. When confronted with such preaching, the average Christian does not reason, "My works are not good enough. Therefore, I may not be saved, and I must make a new beginning." Rather, he assures himself, "I *know* I am saved. Therefore, my works *must* be good enough!" He intuitively senses the very thing that Dr. Grudem knows full well. It is impossible to define a certain level of works that are adequate to calm the claims of conscience and establish that one is saved. Therefore, such preaching is simply ignored, as it should be. Thus assured, he continues in his lethargy.

More importantly, from a Free Grace perspective is the fact this this constant self-examination which Grudem and Blomberg require, in order to verify one's stoteriological status, amounts to dangling the possibility of hell over a believer's head all his life. Paradoxically, their system of Christian living is what has produced much of the legalism, guilt, shame and harsh view of God that concerns them. Notice how Blomberg impales himself on his own petard when he says, "one of the main reasons for trying to live as good a Christian life as possible is to make sure that we do in fact persevere, so that we do not lose out on eternal life altogether."[39] Granted, according to the Free Grace view of eternal security, in eternity future the differences between Moses, Paul, and the rest of us will not be occasions of eternal regret, and we will know joy unspeakable. However, for the unfaithful believer, the future Judgment Seat of Christ will be a time of profound temporary regret. The negative incentives of loss of reward and missing the Master's "Well done!" will be deeply felt. The vast body of evangelical believers sitting under the Reformed system have concluded, based on the fact they have believed and possess Grudem's "some" measure of change,[40] that they are born again. Simultaneously, they are taught (correctly) that if they are born again, they cannot lose salvation. Furthermore, they

---

38 We will comment on Grudem's misunderstanding of 1 Corinthians 13:6 later.

39 Blomberg, *Journal of the Evangelical Theological Society* 35, no. 2 (1992): 170.

40 Grudem, *"Free Grace" Theology*: 92.

are instructed that the warnings, such as those in Hebrews 6, apply not to them but only to merely professing Christians. Having trusted in glimmerings of works in their lives, these Christians conclude they are saved and that they cannot lose salvation and that it will make no significant difference at the second coming anyway. The warnings do not apply to them.

For Dr. Grudem and Dr. Blomberg, heaven is similar to a common political belief that the important thing is equality of outcomes not equality of opportunity. All are equally happy; there is no negative consequence or profound grief ("wailing and gnashing of teeth") for a failed life. Without a possible negative consequence, there is no serious motivation or final accountability, and Dr. Grudem's only negative consequence is to threaten final damnation by holding fear of hell over the believer's head all his life.

A strong emphasis on rewards, however, provides a higher and more ennobling challenge to live one's life with the end in view. The believer can live with full knowledge that he is eternally secure in God's love and grace and that he has a Great High Priest, who is sympathetic and not harsh and judgmental when we fail. He can anticipate reigning with Christ, greater opportunities to serve him, greater intimacy, and deserved honor ("Well done, faithful servant."). These motivations greatly outweigh Reformed theology's lifelong threats of final damnation.[41]

Rewards Are the Completion of a Life Well-Lived

Let us return for a moment to the difficulty some feel that the pursuit of rewards is selfish. We must not be defensive when nonbelievers and some Christian writers, citing Immanuel Kant and the Stoics, falsely assume they are on a higher moral ground, rebuking Free Grace interpreters for their mercenary motives. While it is true that rewards could be pursued for selfish motives, this is not the way the New Testament presents them. There are different kinds of rewards. Unlike

---

41 For an excellent discussion of the relationship of rewards to significance see Ken Quick, "Living for the Kingdom" (DMin diss., Dallas Theological Seminary, 1989).

biblical rewards, some kinds of rewards bear no connection with the things one does to obtain them. These are selfish. For example, as C. S. Lewis points out, "Money is not the natural reward of love; that is why we call a man a mercenary if he marries a woman for the sake of her money."[42] On the other hand, marriage is the proper reward granted to someone who loves a potential mate.

In a similar way, the general who fights for victory in order to obtain a higher rank is a mercenary. However, if he fights for victory because it is the proper reward for battle, he is not being selfish. We can see that biblical rewards are not added onto the activities of a faithful life but are, in fact, the consummation or completion of a life well lived. Victory is the reward for battle, and love and intimacy (not being "alone") are the rewards for marriage. So being honored by Christ and seeking that honor is no more mercenary than seeking love and intimacy or victory in battle. Rewards are the intrinsic outcomes and desired goals of the Christian life.

A reward is like the feeling one has when he completes a task after long effort (in this case a lifetime) and learns he has done well. Many have invested their lives in various projects, some requiring years to achieve and then experience the immense satisfaction and reward of achievement. Is that selfish? In the sphere of eternal life, Christians live well, aspiring to finish the "project" of a life well lived, and they are motivated by that distant goal. As the apostle put it,

> For I am already being poured out as a drink offering, and the time of my departure has come. I have fought the good fight, I have finished the course, I have kept the faith; in the future there is laid up for me the crown of righteousness, which the Lord, the righteous Judge, will award to me on that day; and not only to me, but also to all who have loved his appearing.[43] (2 Timothy 4:6-8)

---

42 C. S. Lewis, *The Weight of Glory* (New York: Simon and Shuster, 1975), 26.

43 To "love his appearing" could refer to his incarnation or the second coming. However, since the thrust of the context is clearly eschatological, the latter is preferable. See Philip H. Towner, *The Letters to Timothy and Titus*, New International Commentary on the New Testament (Grand Rapids: Wm. B. Eerdmans Publishing Co., 2006), 617.

Was Paul "selfish" because he lived to "fight the good fight" and yet will receive a "crown of righteousness" as a result of it? His life purpose was to fight a good fight, finish his course, and keep the faith. When the end came, he could look back with an immense sense of satisfaction and say, "By the grace of God I have done it!" A crown of righteousness,[44] an affirmation that he had invested his life well, was at the center of his daily motivation.

When the Christian practices faithfulness and experiences the sense of divine approval and inner satisfaction for having served his King, the motivation derived from that experience creates an even stronger desire to experience it fully in the life to come. He more frequently begins to view each act as a foretaste of that great future. As the fleeting moments of this experience multiply, the desire for the reward to experience "Well done" increases until it becomes a life-consuming passion. Even if the "purely moral" see this as selfish, the one before whom we will render an account clearly does not. When he exhorted us to show hospitality to those who cannot pay, he did not appeal to duty as the motive. Rather, he said, "*Although they cannot repay you, you will be repaid at the resurrection of the righteous*" (Luke 14:14). The notion that this approach to life is mercenary is a ridiculous absurdity!

Rewards Provide Opportunities for Greater Service (2 Timothy 2:12; Revelation 2:26)

Part of our difficulty is the way we view these rewards. In their most general sense they refer to the joy of participating with Christ in God's eternal purposes, the reward-inheritance (Colossians 3:14). This eternal purpose is a good and wonderful purpose: to extend the glory and blessing of God to all creation. Whatever it involves, those who know Christ as their King must strive to have a share in this. It is not a striving so much for personal benefit but persevering in good works so that we can achieve the goal of serving him as one of his co-heirs in

---

44 This is not a crown "which is" righteousness, that is, the justification of Christ, but a "righteous crown" in contrast to the unrighteous crown he was receiving from Nero. One day, the righteous Judge, the only one who matters, will say that Paul invested his life well and award him a "righteous crown."

the future reign of the servant kings.[45] Whatever our role in that great future is, it will be magnificent. Because we love him, we want to earn the right to rule with him and minister with him. So, it is our love for him and the joy set before us that motivates. The desire for future reward, so that we may serve Christ more fully in the extension of his glory throughout the created order, far exceeds and replaces altruism as a motivation. As Paul put it, *"If we endure, we will also reign with him"* (2 Timothy 2:12).

Rewards Provide Encouragement in Trials (Hebrews 10:32-36; Matthew 5:10-12)

The most characteristic context that mentions reward as a motivation is one reminding us that one day there will be a righting of all wrongs; one-day God will let us know that he remembered every cup of water; one day our sufferings now will be gloriously reversed.

> *But remember the former days, when, after being enlightened, you endured a great conflict of sufferings, partly, by being made a public spectacle through reproaches and tribulations, and partly by becoming sharers with those who were so treated. For you showed sympathy to the prisoners, and accepted joyfully the seizure of your property,* **knowing that you have for yourselves a better possession and an abiding one.** *Therefore, do not throw away your confidence, which has* **a great reward.** *For you have need of endurance, so that when you have done the will of God,* **you may receive what was promised.** *(Hebrews 10:32–36)*

> *Blessed are those who have been* **persecuted for the sake of righteousness, for theirs is the kingdom of heaven.** *Blessed are you when men cast insults at you, and persecute you, and say all kinds of evil against you falsely, on account of me. Rejoice, and be glad, for* **your reward in heaven is great,** *for so they persecuted the prophets who were before you. (Matthew 5:10–12).*

---

45 Norman L. Geisler, *Systematic Theology*, 4 vols. (Minneapolis: Bethany House, 2002), 4:310.

It is not selfish to endure for reward because we know that the universe is moral, that one day our secret choices will be remembered and honored. Jesus himself had this motivation.

*[A]nd while being reviled, he did not revile in return; while suffering, he uttered no threats, **but kept entrusting himself to him who judges righteously.**"* (1 Peter 2:23)

Rewards Are Promised Only to Those Who Love for Christ's Sake

*And Jesus said to them, "Truly I say to you, that you who have followed me, in the regeneration when the Son of Man will sit on his glorious throne, you also shall sit upon twelve thrones, judging the twelve tribes of Israel. And everyone who has left houses or brothers or sisters or father or mother or children or farms for **my name's sake**, will receive many times as much, and will inherit eternal life. But many who are first will be last; and the last, first.* (Matthew 19:28-30)

Elsewhere, Jesus says that we should become disciples *"for the sake of the kingdom of God"* (Luke 18:29-30) and *"for the gospel's sake"* (Mark 10:29).

Jesus promised reward **only** to those who had already promised to follow him with a motive other than the reward alone! For example, in the classic passage on rewards quoted above, Jesus makes it clear that the motive for the path of discipleship is first of all, "for my sake" (Matthew 19:29) and for the sake of the kingdom of God (Luke 18:29) or for "the gospel's sake" (Mark 10:29). In each case the prior motive is central. To seek reward only for the purpose of obtaining personal benefit in the next life would be to forfeit the very blessedness that was sought. In fact, the reward may also come to those who have no consciousness that they had done good at all. *"Lord, when did we see you hungry, and feed you, or thirsty, and give you drink?"* (Matthew 25:37).

Rewards Provide Us with Tokens of Worship and Gratefulness

In Revelation 4-5 the apostle John was transported to the heavenly court and stood before the throne of God. From this throne came flashes of lightning and peals of thunder. Before the throne was a sea of glass, clear as crystal. This signaled that the sea (that is, the nations) was calm and not chaotic; all was under the sovereign control of the King.

John records five hymns in response. The first two are addressed to God, the next two to the Lamb, and the last to both. As we move from hymn to hymn, the choirs become larger and larger and build to a climax where every creature sings to God and the Lamb.

The second hymn marks the praise of the twenty-four elders and the four living creatures.

> **Whenever** *the living creatures give glory, honor and thanks to him who sits on the throne and who lives forever and ever, the twenty-four elders fall down before him who sits on the throne, and worship him who lives forever and ever. They lay their crowns before the throne.* (Revelation 4:9-10)

While Bloomberg limits the casting of crowns to a single event,[46] John says this will occur whenever (Gr. *hotan*, "whenever"[47]) the elders worship throughout eternity.

Notice their posture—they fall down in submission to his majestic authority. They praise him for his worthiness. He is worthy to receive such adulation because he has created everything that exists and by his will he allows all to continue to exist (see Job 38:4-7). His power and authority are absolute; his majesty, beyond comprehension.

That being so, what do the elders do? They fall before him and repeatedly cast their crowns at the foot of the throne. These crowns

---

46 He says, "their very surrender of their crowns would prove my point: Whatever differences believers may experience on judgment day are not perpetuated throughout eternity." Blomberg, "Degrees of Reward in the Kingdom of Heaven?," 165.

47 *BDAG*, 731, "Usually of (regularly) repeated action *whenever, as often as, every time that.*"

represent honor they have received from Christ. Yet now, in the face of his overwhelming glory, they relinquish all honor to him. As Allen P. Ross says, "No one can acclaim God to be worthy of all glory, honor, and power and yet cling to one's bit of honor and power, no matter how well deserved it may be."[48]

These crowns are not to be worn throughout eternity, thus drawing attention to ourselves. Instead, they provide us with tokens of worship, symbols of relinquishment of all personal honor, which we can lay at his feet in gratitude, submission, and reverence.

Summary

The *biblical* doctrine of eternal rewards is a magnificent incitement to a faithful life. In our opinion, the church would benefit significantly in its task of motivating believers to fuller commitment if this great vision of serving with him in the fulfillment of human destiny were more frequently held before our gaze.

There is no "spiritual commercialism" or selfishness involved in the pursuit of honor, opportunities for ministry, and the desire for maximum intimacy with Christ. These are noble and inspiring goals, fully approved by Christ and his apostles. They focus ultimately on him, not ourselves.

To summarize, believers are to strive for reward (1) with a more fundamental heart motive that what we do is for Christ's sake and in response to Christ's love (2 Corinthians 5:14); (2) with a realization that, once we have done all we can do, we still have only done our duty (Luke 17:10); (3) with a heart's desire to "please the one who enlisted us as soldiers" (2 Timothy 2:4); (4) with a prior motive of serving him for Christ's sake (Matthew 19:28-30); (5) with an understanding that there is no strict contractual correspondence between a certain amount of work resulting in a certain amount of reward, for whatever we get is overgenerous wages (Matthew 20:1-16); and (6) most importantly, with the realization that rewards enable us to obtain tokens of worship

---

48 Allen P. Ross, *Recalling the Hope of Glory* (Grand Rapids: Kregel Publications, 2006), 483.

and gratitude that, like the twenty-four elders, we too can repeatedly lay at his feet (Revelation 4:10).

At the Judgment Seat of Christ, we will be summoned by the "upward call" to the victor's platform (Philippians 3:14) to hear the words, "Well done." The believers who hear those words are Christ's faithful partners (Hebrews 3:14, Gr. metochoi),[49] his servant kings, who will one day serve with him in the fulfillment of human destiny. As they rise to meet him, they will participate in the "upward call" to a better kind of resurrection.

---

49 For extensive development of the concept of "partners (Gr. metochoi) of Christ" see Dillow, Final Destiny: 141 ff.

Chapter 12

Degrees of Glory

Joseph Dillow, Th.D.

The Fulfillment of Human Destiny

For it was fitting for Him, for whom are all things, and through whom are all things, in bringing many sons to glory, to perfect the author of their salvation through sufferings. (Hebrews 2:10, NASB95)

The "glory" to which the many sons will be brought is evidently subjection of the world to come (Hebrews 2:5), the messianic salvation.

And you are those who have stood by Me in My trials; and just as My Father has granted Me a kingdom, I grant you that you may eat and drink at My table in My kingdom, and you will sit on thrones judging the twelve tribes of Israel. (Luke 22:28-30, NASB)

Authority in the kingdom and the honor of sitting at the table at the Final Gathering and enjoying the royal Messianic Banquet are plainly promised as superior rewards for superior devotion. His way is to be our way.

God purposes to equip us for rulership in the great future by preparing through suffering a race of servant kings. As an incentive to persevere in faithfulness, the Lord promises "Treasures in Heaven" for those who do. The broad term for these Treasures is the "Inheritance."

> But lay up for yourselves **treasures in heaven**, where neither moth nor rust destroy, and where thieves do not break in or steal" (Matthew 6:19–20, cf. Mark 10:21; Luke 12:33; NASB).

The various aspects of these future treasures may be summarized as (a) enhanced intimacy with God, (b) honor and praise from Christ, and (c) expanded opportunities to serve Him and minister throughout all eternity. These may be diagramed as follows.

Treasures in Heaven

Praise
Crown of Righteousness
Crown of Glory
Name in Book of Life
Imperishable Wreath
Abundant Entrance
A Special Resurrection

Reigning with Christ
Vassal Kingships
Priestly Ministry
Ownership of New Jerusalem

Honor   Service

Intimacy

Wedding Banquet
Messianic Banquet
Crown of Life
Inheriting Eternal Life
Eating from Tree of Life

Greater Intimacy with Christ

In the discussion below, we will explore in more detail each of the treasures that compose intimacy, honor, and service. We begin with what is the most important treasure, enhanced intimacy with Christ.

The New Testament uses four metaphors to describe this eschatological blessing: participation in the wedding banquet, eating from "the tree of life," receiving the "crown of life," and inheriting eternal life.

Participation in the Eschatological Banquets

There are two mentioned in the Scripture. First Jesus and his church will celebrate their marriage, the Wedding Feast of the Lamb which occurs in the New Jerusalem during the tribulation (Matthew 22:8-10; 25:1-13; Revelation 19:7). Then after Jesus descends to earth with his Church, the Messianic Banquet will inaugurate the millennial kingdom. At that banquet all the great ones of Israel's history will fellowship with all the saved in celebration (Luke 13:29-30).[1] The intimacy with Christ enjoyed by those admitted to these feasts is wonderful to anticipate, and it gives faithful believers high motivation to persevere in the midst of trials.

Eating from the Tree of Life

One expression used to symbolize this enhanced intimacy with Christ is the promise that the overcomers will "eat from the tree of life" (Revelation 2:7, 14). Eating a meal is a common Semitic metaphor for close fellowship. Free Grace interpreters understand this promise as a promise of enhanced intimacy with the King for believers who remain faithful to him.

"What is this 'tree of life'?" Numerous Scriptures relate it to character qualities and behavior, not regeneration.[2] Since partaking of the tree of

---

1   During this time, Christ will reward them for lives well-lived. This time of fellowship speaks of special intimacy with Christ that is illustrated by the wise virgins who prepared for and watched for his return (Matthew 25:1-13) and the believers who are dressed in the righteous acts of the saints (Matthew 22:11; Revelation 19:8).

2   The phrase "the tree of life" is found first in Genesis 3:22, 24. All of its other uses in the Old Testament are confined to the book of Proverbs. There the fruit of the morally upright (Proverbs 11:30), a desire fulfilled (Proverbs 13:12), a gentle tongue (Proverbs 15:4), and wisdom (Proverbs 3:18) are all called a "tree of life." This usage suggests a quality of life—rich fellowship with God—rather than the notion of regeneration. It "symbolizes the enrichment

life in 22:14 is based upon doing good works, and shared only by those who have washed their robes, that is, confessed their sins,[3] it should be understood as conditional in Revelation 2:7 as well.[4]

The tree of life will yield fruit monthly throughout all eternity (Revelation 22:2). It seems possible, therefore, to understand participation in the tree of life and eating of this monthly fruit as metaphors for

---

of life in various ways." It speaks not of obtaining life, but fully experiencing it. According to 22:12 it is a reward (Gr. *misthos*) and not a gift to all. It is not freely given. This fits well with the context of Revelation. Regenerate life comes to all "without cost" (Revelation 22:17), but "the tree of life" is presented as a conditionally earned and merited reward going to those who have not only received eternal life without cost but who also, at great cost to themselves, have overcome and persevered to the final hour.

3	While the NASB translation of Revelation 22:14 reads, "*Blessed are those who wash their robes,*" the Byzantine Majority text reads, "*Blessed are those who keep My commandments*" (NKJV). This suggests that some early editors understood washing robes to mean keeping commandments and not regeneration. Obedience to his commands, then, is necessary in order to obtain his promised reward. Obviously, eternal salvation cannot be in view because a few verses later John makes it clear that regeneration and eternal life are available freely and "without cost" (Revelation 22:17).

4	Grant Osborne, a Reformed writer, believes that "the one unifying theme is the necessity of remaining true to the Lord in order to participate in the resurrection to eternal life." He begins well, saying that the overcomer's victory is "achieved through perseverance." To eat from the tree of life requires "faithfulness and a determination that we will place living for him alone above all earthly things." He adds, "To be an overcomer in the eschatological war demands a day-by-day walk with God and dependence on his strength." With these statements one would assume that the victory is a reward to works and could not be salvation or heaven when one dies because entrance into heaven is ours by faith alone. However, we are soon disappointed to learn that this is not Osborne's meaning. We are told that the "tree of life" is the cross of Christ. He says this even after admitting that this tree in the Old Testament refers to temporal life giving qualities of wisdom (Proverbs 3:18; 11:30; 13:12; 15:40) and refers to refreshment which comes from rich fellowship with God (Ezekiel 47:12; cf. Revelation 22:2). Grant Osborne, *Revelation*, Baker Exegetical Commentary on the New Testament (Grand Rapids: Baker Academic, 2002), 789.

the regular experience of fellowshipping with God. It is inconceivable that a Christian, in whom eternal life dwells, must continually eat from a tree to obtain final entrance into heaven or maintain his presence there. Therefore, eating of the tree of life cannot refer to regeneration.[5] Donald Barnhouse is correct: "Eating of the tree of life is a reward that shall be given to the overcomer in addition to his salvation."[6]

The Crown of Life

Be faithful until death, and I will give you **the crown of life.**
(Revelation 2:10)

The crown the believer obtains is the victor's crown (Gr. *stephanos*),[7] a crown given for victory in the games, achievement in war, and places of honor at the feasts.[8] "In the New Testament it is plain that the

---

5   It is impossible that the tree of life refers to final entrance into heaven. Why? Because we are told in Revelation 2:5 that the condition for obtaining the right to eat of this tree is based upon "doing," that is, on works. Final salvation comes to us by faith alone apart from works. In Revelation 22:19, Jesus says that if anyone takes away from the words of the prophecy, "*God will take away his portion (Gr. meros) from the tree of life and from the city.*" As Marty Cauley has observed, "Obviously one cannot lose something one does not have. . . . Genuine believers are in danger of losing their right to this tree; unbelievers have no right to this tree to lose."

6   Donald Grey Barnhouse, *God's last Word: Revelation: an Expository Commentary,* (Grand Rapids: Zondervan Publishing House, 1971), 43-44. For a similar view see Richard R. Benedict, "The Use of Nikaō in the Letters to the Seven Churches of Revelation" (Th.M. thesis, Dallas Theological Seminary, 1966), 11.

7   It was woven of oak, ivy, spruce, myrtle, or olive. Jesus's crown, though made of thorns, depicted ultimate victory (Matthew 27:29). Five crowns are mentioned in the New Testament. See Ken Quick, "Living for the Kingdom" (DMin diss., Dallas Theological Seminary, 1989), 223-39. Also Eric Sauer, *In the Arena of Faith: A Call to a Consecrated Life* (Grand Rapids: Wm. B. Eerdmans Publishing Co., 1956), 59-67.

8   William E. Rafferty, "Crown," in *NISBE (1988),* 1:831.

stephanos whereof St. Paul speaks is always the conqueror's and not the king's."[9] This crown is not like the royal crown. It is a crown that is given on the basis of merit.[10]

What is the crown of life? It is not given as a result of regeneration, because regenerate life comes by means of faith alone apart from works and is not given for faithfulness under persecution. Since the crown of life is a reward given for an accomplishment after initial faith, it is probable that "life" refers to a higher quality of life in the kingdom. It would be the same as that aspect of eternal life that can be earned,[11] the special richness of eternal life merited by faithful service on the field of battle. This is the victor's crown, awarded to the one who finishes well and as a result obtains an abundant entrance into the kingdom, of which Peter spoke (2 Peter 1:11). This crown is a token of honor.[12]

---

9   Richard Chenevix Trench, *Synonyms of the New Testament*, reprint ed. (Grand Rapids: Wm. B. Eerdmans Publishing Co., 1953), 78.

10 Wayne A. Grudem, *Systematic Theology: An Introduction to Biblical Doctrine* (Leicester, England; Grand Rapids, MI: Inter-Varsity Press; Zondervan Pub. House, 2004), 813.

11 See discussion in Joseph C. Dillow, *Final Destiny: The Future Reign of the Servant Kings*, 3rd revised ed. (Monument, CO: Paniym Group, Inc., 2016; reprint, 2016), Chapter 17.

12 For some Christians the purpose of God includes severe testing, even martyrdom. This high honor will be duly compensated with a special distinction, namely, receiving the crown of life. Throughout the centuries many Christians have been called on to give their lives for Christ. This honorable heritage was pioneered by Christ and his apostles. James was beheaded in Jerusalem in ad 44. Philip was cruelly scourged and afterward was crucified. Matthew was claimed by the sword in Parthea in ad 60. Mark was dragged through the streets of Alexandria by his feet and then burned to death the following day. Luke was hanged on an olive tree in Greece. James the Less was thrown from a pinnacle of the temple in Jerusalem and beaten to death down below. Matthias was stoned and beheaded. Andrew was crucified on a cross where he hung for three days and constantly told people around him of the love of Jesus Christ. Peter was scourged and crucified upside down. He chose this posture himself because he did not think he was worthy to suffer in the same manner as his Lord. Thomas was thrust through with a spear in India.

John's readers are also reminded that even if they lose their physical lives, they will never lose eternal life. He reminds them, *"You will never be hurt by the second death* (Revelation 2:11)."[13] Dr. Grudem correctly understands this phrase to mean "condemned to eternal punishment."[14] It likely refers to the lake of fire (Revelation 20:14). However, Reformed writer Thomas Schreiner says, "The call to conquer is necessary in order to escape eternal judgment in the lake of fire."[15] We disagree. This is not a warning to those who do **not overcome**; it is a figure of speech encouraging those who do. God would not threaten true believers with a judgment He knows would never happen to them. Nor would he tell them (or non believers) that in order to secure final entrance into heaven, they must work and be successful.[16] What then does John mean?

When John says they will never be hurt by the second death, he is using a figure of speech called litotes.[17] Litotes is an "understatement in

---

Jude was crucified in ad 72. Bartholomew was beaten to death with clubs. John was condemned to a cauldron of boiling oil, though he escaped death and later died in exile on the island of Patmos. Barnabas was stoned to death by Jews in Salonica. Paul was beheaded in Rome by Nero. John Foxe, *Foxe's Christian Martyrs of the World* (Chicago: Moody Press, n.d.), 24-25.

13 The word "never" is very emphatic in Greek, a double negative (*ou mē*, "definitely not"). This expression is common in categorical and emphatic denials. J. P. Louw and Eugene Albert Nida, *Greek-English Lexicon of the New Testament: Based on Semantic Domains*, 2 ed., 2 vols. (New York: United Bible Societies, 1996), vol. 1, 664..

14 Wayne A. Grudem, *Systematic Theology: An Introduction to Biblical Doctrine* (Grand Rapids, MI: Inter-Varsity Press, 2004), 1119.

15 Thomas R. Schreiner, *Run to Win the Prize: Perseverance in the New Testament* (Wheaton, IL: Crossway Books, 2010), 39.

16 Though Schreiner strenuously denies he teaches a works salvation, we believe that he does. See extensive discussion of the warning passages in Dillow, *Final Destiny*: Chapters 33-38.

17 Martyn Lloyd-Jones, *Romans Chapter 8:17-39: The Final Perseverance of the Saints* (Grand Rapids: Zondervan Publishing House, 1976), 314 ff. Litotes is a figure of speech in which a positive statement is made by negating its opposite.

which an affirmative is expressed by the negative of the contrary."[18] For example, when Luke says of the Ephesian elders that "they were not a little comforted" (Acts 20:22), he means they were greatly comforted by Paul's parting words.[19] When we say, "Michael Jordan is not a bad basketball player," we mean he is an outstanding basketball player. So to say one will not be hurt by the second death is actually a way of expressing the positive idea that even if a person suffers physical death, *he will experience a rich eternity with God.* He is assured of an eternity with Christ. This is a great encouragement. Even though they can hurt the body, they can never take away eternal life with Christ.[20]

---

18 *Merriam-Webster's Collegiate Dictionary*, (Springfield, MA: Miriam-Webster, Inc., 2003), s.v. "litotes". For full discussion of the figure of speech litotes, see E. W. Bullinger, *Figures of Speech Used in the Bible: Explained and Illustrated*, reprint ed. (Grand Rapids: Baker Book House, 1968), 155 ff.

19 *BDAG*, 642. Or, when standing before Felix the governor, Paul says that he was from Tarsus, which is "no obscure city." He means it is a very important city.

20 There is a problem, however, with taking this promise as litotes. If it is true that one who overcomes is not hurt by the second death, then what happens if one does not overcome? Would it not follow that he *would be* hurt by the second death, that is, damned? If this is truly litotes, then the answer is, "No." If we say, "Michael Jordan is not a bad basketball player," we mean he is a very good basketball player. However, the reverse does not follow, "If you are not Michael Jordan, you are not a good basketball player." A litotes cannot be read in reverse. Ed Ediger correctly observes, "Jesus does not say that a failure to 'overcome' will result in 'the second death.' Possible implications, particularly opposite ones, are not necessarily intended by the speaker. Negative implications are not always true." Edwin Aaron Ediger, *Faith in Jesus: What Does it Mean to Believe in Him?* (Bloomington, IN: Westbow Press: A Division of Thomas Nelson, 2012), 393. For another example of the impossibility of reversing a litotes, note that Jesus used litotes when he said, "*The one who comes to me I will certainly not cast out*" (John 6:37). His meaning is something like, "I will embrace him fully." But one cannot reverse the statement and say, "The one who does not come to me, I will certainly cast out." The one who does not come to Christ cannot be cast out from a relationship with Christ because he never came into a relationship with Christ from which he could be cast out! As Marty Cauley says, "An object has to be in a container before it can be cast out of the container." It is a litotes.

Free Grace interpreters understand that not being hurt by the second death is a litotes for eternal security and a special intimacy with God in the future kingdom.[21]

Inheriting Eternal Life

A final aspect of intimacy with Christ is called, inheriting eternal life.[22] One day as Jesus journeyed south along a dusty Palestinian road, an enthusiastic young man ran to him and said,

> Good Teacher, what shall I do to inherit eternal life? (Mark 10:17, NASB)

We have discussed this encounter in considerable detail elsewhere and will not repeat it here.[23] It is enough here to say that Jesus did not think the rich young ruler was asking how to get to heaven. We know that by how Jesus answers it. He says, "You know the commandments," and then he told him to sell all he had, give it to the poor, and "follow me." If Jesus thought the young man was asking about personal salvation, he would have responded as he did to the unsaved Nicodemus, "For God so loved the world, that He gave His only begotten Son, that whoever believes in Him should not perish, but have eternal life" (John 3:16, NASB).

This young man was not an unbeliever. He was a believer. Jesus said to him, "If you want to be complete (Gr. telios)" (Matthew 19:21). The word telios means "mature." He does not want to know how to be saved; he wants to know what the next step is. Jesus did not understand this question to be about soteriology; it was about discipleship. His desire was that he might not just have eternal life in the sense of personal salvation, but that he might also have it in the sense of a full experience of it. He wanted to inherit it, that is, possess it fully; he wanted special intimacy with Christ.

---

21 For a good discussion of litotes and its significance in the overcome passages in Revelation see Marty Cauley, *The Outer Darkness*, 2 vols. (Sylva, NC: Misthological Press, 1231 Monteith Branch Road, 2012), 481-95.

22 See discussion in Dillow, *Final Destiny*: chapter 17.

23 Ibid., Chapter 22.

Eternal Honor

The well-known management consultant, Stephen Covey, identified seven habits of successful people. The second habit is "Begin with the end in mind."[24] He illustrates this way. Imagine yourself driving to the funeral of a loved one. As you get out of the car and enter the funeral parlor, you see numerous flowers, friends, and relatives. Gentle music is playing in the background. The sense of sorrow and grief permeates the air, and there are many tears. As you walk down the aisle to the front of the church to look into the casket, you gasp with surprise. When you look into the casket, you see yourself. All these people are here to honor you! This is your funeral, three years from today. These gathered friends and relatives are here to express their love and appreciation.

Still stunned by what you see, you take your seat and wait for the service to begin. Glancing at the program, you note there are to be four speakers. The first is to be from your family, both immediate and extended, representing children, brothers, and grandchildren, nephews, nieces, aunts, uncles, cousins, and grandparents. They have come from all over the country to be present at this event. The second speaker is your best friend. He is someone who can give a sense of who you are as a person. The third speaker is someone from your office. This person will, of course, have perspective on what kind of boss you were and what kind of employee you were. Finally, an elder from your church will be called on to share a few personal comments.

Now think about this scene! What would you like these speakers to say about you and your life? What kind of husband, father, employee, Christian would you like their words to reflect? What contributions and achievements would you like these people to remember? Look

---

24 Stephen R. Covey, *The Seven Habits of Highly Effective People* (New York: Schuster, 1989), 96. He has written a book which is the result of years of research in the success literature of the past two centuries. In addition, his insights have been gleaned from his twenty years of experience worldwide as a management consultant to numerous corporations. He is a recognized expert on principles of personal and organizational leadership development. His experience and studies have led him to the discovery that there are common denominators among all highly effective people, what he calls "seven habits."

carefully at the people around you. What difference does it make to them that you lived or died? What impact have you had in their lives?

Now, Covey counsels, take a few moments and jot down the thoughts that come to your mind, the answers to these questions. If you thought deeply about this scene, you discovered something about yourself that you may not have known before. You discovered some of your deep, fundamental values. To "begin with the end in mind" is to begin today with the image, picture, and paradigm of the end of your life as the frame of reference or the criterion by which everything else in your life is examined. By doing this, each part of your life can be examined in the context of the whole according to what you have concluded is most important to you. By keeping the end in mind, you can clearly evaluate whether on any given day you have violated your deepest values. You can determine whether that day, that week, that month has or has not contributed toward the vision you have of life as a whole.

The second aspect of these treasures in heaven is the honor we will receive from Christ if we have faithfully tried to live out his way of life. There are eight aspects to this eternal honor which we will discuss in this chapter: praise, the crown of glory, the crown of righteousness, a new name, a name recorded in the book of life, an imperishable wreath, an abundant entrance through the gates, and a special resurrection. First we consider praise from Christ.

Praise

It is self-evident that our motivation to accomplish a given task is directly related to how significant we feel the task is. When Paul said, "Whatever you do, work at it with all your heart, as working for the Lord, not for men, since you know that you will receive an inheritance from the Lord as a reward" (Colossians 3:23-24), he was appealing to this same motivational force. This verse reveals a central aspect of what makes us feel something is significant: a task will be viewed as significant if the people who matter to us value it as so. In this case, since it is God who determines the ultimate significance of the work, it will be perceived as highly important: "Always give yourselves fully to the work of the Lord, because you know that your labor in the Lord is not in vain" (1 Corinthians 15:58).

But one more thing is needed for us to feel that our work is truly significant. There must be recognition and affirmation by someone else. Someone other than ourselves, someone who has expertise and authority to affirm that a particular task is valuable must give his affirmation. This recognition could be given with a plaque, a word of praise, a compliment, a promotion, or a dinner in the person's honor. "But in some way one must receive the proof from the people who matter that he has done well."[25] The illustration of the imaginary funeral above illustrates the emotional impact of such praise. However, once we are gone, we will not hear it from those on earth, but we may hear it from the only one who matters.

What is evident in the interpersonal relationships in this life can now be applied to our eternal relationship with God. He is the ultimate one who will evaluate our work, and who, after we are gone, will pronounce the desired words, "Well done." And he is the one who matters more than anyone. Our eternal security gives us freedom to pursue our significance. We do not have to worry about eternal separation from our Father, that is, loss of salvation. But even though we cannot lose our justification, the warnings in the Bible tell us we can forfeit the inheritance, we can lose our eternal significance. The biblical promises that our lives can matter motivate us to make sacrifices, to take risks, to work hard, knowing that our work is not in vain in the Lord. God values whatever we do for him. The warnings that we can lose rewards should inspire the fear of the Lord in our hearts and cause us to labor to avoid that terrible consequence.

The other side of significance is final accountability. It is true that our lives can matter; they can make a difference. It is true that through service to him we can attach eternal value to the life we have lived; however, some of us will pursue this goal more diligently than others. Some Christians, to their great shame and eternal loss, will not pursue this worthy goal at all. The differences will become evident when we stand before him at the Judgment Seat of Christ.

Hearing the King's "Well done" is a powerful motivation. Who would not want to hear these words?

---

25 Ibid., 13-14.

His master said to him, "Well done, good and faithful slave; you were faithful with a few things, I will put you in charge of many things, enter into the joy of your master." (Matthew 25:21, NASB)

It may be helpful to crystalize this issue by asking yourself this question, "If God was going to personally introduce you to a person, what would you want him to say?

Crown of Glory

Christ will bestow special recognition on those who have labored faithfully to care for and disciple other Christians. It is significant that the crown of glory and the crown of righteousness (2 Timothy 4:8) have been designated as awards for those who have given their lives to evangelism and discipleship: *"Be shepherds of God's flock. . . . And when the Chief Shepherd appears, you will receive the crown of glory that will never fade away"* (1 Peter 5:1-4).

Crown of Righteousness

Paul's second epistle to Timothy exhorts him to evangelize. This epistle contains Paul's last words. He was beheaded by Nero shortly thereafter. Sensing that the end was near, he penned these moving phrases,

> *For I am already being poured out like a drink offering, and the time has come for my departure. I have fought the good fight, I have finished the race, I have kept the faith. Now there is in store for me the crown of righteousness which the Lord, the righteous Judge, will award to me on that day—and not only to me, but also to all who have longed for his appearing. (2 Timothy 4:6-8)*

For those Christians who long for Christ's return, who live their lives in view of this event, there will be special honor. The crown seems to be a reward for living a righteous life. It is "like a soldier's medal for valor in the face of battle. The medal does not contain valor, but it does declare that its possessor is valorous."[26] It is a crown of approval.

---

26 Quick, "Living for the Kingdom," 227.

Righteousness in this passage should be understood as "upright behavior."[27] It is a crown of vindication, a crown which says "Paul, you have lived well." As he wrote, Paul stood before an unrighteous judge receiving an unrighteous reward. But one day, he will stand before the only Judge that matters and that Judge will grant to him a righteous crown, a crown of vindication saying, "Paul, you were right, Rome was wrong! Thank you for serving me."

A New Name

*To him who overcomes, to him I will give some of the hidden manna, and I will give him a **white stone**, and a **new name** written on the stone which no one knows but he who receives it.* (Revelation 2:17)

What are the "white stone" and the "new name?"

The white stone has been interpreted in various ways. Mounce's suggestion fits the context well. He says, "In the context of a messianic feast (the 'hidden manna') it seems best to take the white stone as a *tessera* [a small tile] that served as a token for admission to the banquet."[28] These white stones served as admission tickets to the athletic games and to banquets.[29] So to have one's name written on it identified the holder of the ticket.[30]

---

27 *BDAG*, 248.

28 Robert H. Mounce, *The Book of Revelation*, The New International Commentary on the New Testament (Grand Rapids: Wm. B. Eerdmans Publishing Co., 1997), 83.

29 Osborne says, "It was common for members of a guild or victors at the games to use stones as a ticket for admission to feasts, and also for free food or entrance to the games." Osborne, *Revelation*: 149.

30 It is unlikely that the name written on the "ticket" was God's or Christ's. Their names were not "hidden." Another possibility is suggested by Eric Sauer who relates this to a custom of the Greek athletic games. Sauer, *In the Arena of Faith: A Call to a Consecrated Life*: 64-65. This is also mentioned by Grant Osborne. A victor's prize at the games often included objects of value and gifts of gold. According to Plutarch, winners at the Isthmian games were given one hundred drachmas and at the Olympics, five hundred. The winner received a

The believer possessing this white stone with a name on it received from the heavenly judge is recognized as a victor in the battle and has a "ticket" to the Wedding Feast of the Lamb (Matthew 22:1-14; 25:1-13; Revelation 19:7-9) and the Messianic Banquet on earth (Isaiah 25:6; Matthew 8:10-13; Mark 14:25; Luke 13:22-30; 14:16-24; 22:29-30).[31]

Even though despised on earth, he will be honored in heaven. The sentence of rejection received from earthly judges (like Nero) will be reversed. Those hated and expelled here will be honored with heavenly riches and eternal glory.

What is this "new name"? The giving of a "new name" was a Jewish custom of assigning a name at a point in life which characterizes the person.[32] In the early church James was called "camel knees" because of the calluses on his knees from so much kneeling while he was praying. Our Lord called Simon by a new name, Peter, which means "rock," signifying his future as the rock of stability in the church. Joseph, a Levite of Cyprian birth, was called "Barnabas," which means "son of encouragement." James and John were known as the "sons of thunder" and Saul of Tarsus preferred to be known as "Paul" ("little"), remembering that he was the least of the apostles and the greatest of sinners.

But perhaps the greatest illustration of the gift of the new name was the name given to a carpenter's son who grew up in a military camp town, Nazareth. Because he was obedient, even to the death of a cross, he was given a new name, "THE LORD JESUS CHRIST."[33] Just as his new name was earned by faithful obedience, so it is with the many sons he is leading to glory.[34]

---

certificate of victory with a small tablet of white stone in which the name of the victor was inscribed by an expert carver.

31 For discussion of these two banquets and their differences see Dillow, *Final Destiny*: chapter 51.

32 See Judges 6:31-32, where Gideon was renamed Jerub-Baal, which means "Let Baal contend with him" because he took a stand against Baal and cut down his altars.

33 Philippians 2:9.

34 Hebrews 2:10.

Christ will give to each overcomer a new name, a name of honor. Yet this name is known to no one but Christ and the one to whom he gives it. Each believer has his own particular life message, his own particular history of struggle and demonstration of God's life in his. God is a God of the individual as well as of the church. The secrecy of the name implies a special relationship between Christ and each overcomer. It will be a name which in some way signifies an outstanding characteristic of that person's life. This of course challenges every believer to consider the question, "What will my name be?" And more importantly, "What would I like my name to be?"

Name Recorded in the Book of Life (Revelation 3:5)

The overcomer is promised that his *name* will not be blotted out of the book of life.[35] This means either (1) that his eternal reputation is secure no matter what they do to his body under persecution (Revelation 3:2, name = reputation, ESV), or (2) it is another example of litotes, emphatically reminding them of their eternal security even if they are physically killed:

> He who overcomes will thus be clothed in white garments; and I will not erase his name from the book of life, and I will confess his name before My Father and before His angels (Revelation 3:5).

This act of persevering is to be equated with being clothed in white garments. The "white robes are the righteousness of the saints, not the [imputed] righteousness of God."[36] To have one's name confessed before the Father is to have his service and worth praised.

An Abundant Entrance "Through the Gates"

Another aspect of praise that Christ will heap on the believer who has persevered faithfully to the end is an entrance "through the gates," into

---

35 See Dillow, *Final Destiny*: 673.

36 G. Campbell Morgan, *A First Century Message to Twentieth Century Christians* (New York: Revell, 1902), 149.

the New Jerusalem. There will be twelve of these gates (Revelation 21:12).

> *Blessed are those who wash their robes, so that they may have the right to the tree of life, and may enter by the gates into the city.* (Revelation 22:14)

Some have argued that since only those who "wash their robes" can enter the city, and since entering the city will be a blessing conferred on all Christians, therefore all Christians are those who have washed their robes and are overcomers (22:14). However, John may be placing emphasis not on entering the city, but on entering *"by the gates"* into the city. Those victorious in battle gathered at the gates of a city to celebrate (Judges 5:11). This entrance was reserved for those who took the narrow way and the narrow gate, the path of discipleship (Matthew 7:13-14). John describes them elsewhere, as memorials to the twelve tribes of Israel (21:12, 14).

This is the Arch of Titus near the Forum in Rome. It was constructed after his victory over Jerusalem in AD 70. Engravings on it show Roman soldiers bringing back treasures from the temple in Jerusalem. Similarly, those Christians who remain faithful to their King will enter the city in victory and will be likewise honored.

Gates of ancient cities were for defense or honor or both. To be known "in the gates" was to sit among the "elders of the land" and have a position of high honor and authority (Proverbs 31:23). Since defense is not a function of these "gates" into the heavenly city, they are to be regarded as places of honor and authority. We are reminded of the Roman victory arches which sat astride the main thoroughfares entering into Rome. There were many entryways into Rome, but Caesar entered by the gates, by the victory arch. Through these gates, according to John, *"the honor and glory of the nations"* will enter (Revelation 21:14, 27). As Lange has suggested, to enter by the gates means to enter "as conquerors in triumphal procession."[37]

The expression "enter by the gates" is a functional equivalent for "enter with special honor." Some will enter the New Jerusalem with special honor, and some will not. This privilege goes to those who "wash their robes." This refers to confession of sin in the life of the believer and removal of all that is impure, such as sorcery, immorality, murder, idolatry, and lying (Revelation 22:15).[38]

---

37 John Peter Lange, "The Revelation of John," in *A Commentary on the Holy Scriptures*, ed. John Peter Lange, et al. (Bellingham, WA: Logos Bible Software, 2008), 12:446.

38 The need to "wash" one's robes can be paralleled with the Lord's instruction concerning the need to wash the feet, that is, daily confession of sin (John 13:10). Perhaps the only thing that can properly be alleged against this interpretation is that those who partake of the tree of life are contrasted in the next verse with nonbelievers who are outside the city (Revelation 22:15). One could legitimately argue that the opposite of a non-Christian is any Christian, not just overcomers. However, that would depend on the intent of the contrast. Is it not evident that the intent of the contrast here is moral righteousness versus unrighteousness? When making contrasts, it is appropriate to point to the extremes and not items located on a continuum between the extremes. It would therefore be quite natural to contrast the nonbeliever with the victorious overcomer and not with, for example, the lukewarm Christians of Laodicea whom God will spew out of his mouth (Revelation 3:16). Carnal Christians would simply not supply the suitable contrast John has in mind.

A Special Resurrection

A final indication of the special honors the faithful will receive is a special class of resurrection.

> *That I may know Him and the power of His resurrection and the fellowship of His sufferings, being conformed to His death; in order that I may attain to the resurrection from the dead* (Philippians 3:10–11, NASB).

We note that Paul says there is something uncertain about his future. He was not sure he will attain to the "resurrection from the dead." How can this be? The resurrection (Gr. *anastasis*) is assured to all believers. However, in this passage Paul uses an unusual word for resurrection, *ekanastasis*. The preposition *"ek"* *"out of"* intensifies the noun; it is an "out-resurrection," a "full resurrection," a fuller experience of resurrection life.[39] This is the prize/reward of the games that is awarded by the judge. It is his reward for faithful service. This is the same as the "better resurrection" of Hebrews 11 and the abundant entrance of 2 Peter 1:11. Paul equates it with the prize in Philippians

---

39 Danker distinguishes this word, *exanastasis*, from the normal word, *anastasis*, by saying, "The compound in contrast to the simple ἀνάστασις that precedes connotes a coming to fullness of life." *BDAG*, 345. Michael agrees, "But as the two forms occur in such close propinquity it is probable that there is some significance in the change of word." See John Hugh Michael, *The Epistle of Paul to the Philippians*, The Moffatt New Testament commentary (Garden City, NY: Doubleday, Doran & Company, Inc., 1929), 154. Cited by S. Lewis Johnson, "The Out-Resurrection from the Dead," *BibSac* 110, no. 438 (April-June1953): 142. George Peters also stresses the "ek", saying, "'*If by any means . . . 'I might attain unto the resurrection of the dead*,'" certainly does not give the force of the original, and it places Paul in the attitude of striving for something which is inevitable. But taking the emendation demanded by the preposition *ek*, and given by numerous critics and commentators (and admitted by some of our opponents, as Prof. Stuart), we have a reading which vindicates Paul's effort to obtain a prize, viz., *a distinguishing eclectic resurrection*. See George N. H. Peters, *The Theocratic Kingdom of Our Lord Jesus, the Christ, as Covenanted in the Old Testament and Presented in the New Testament*, reprint ed. (Grand Rapids: Kregel Publications, 1972), 298.

3:14 (Gr. *brabeion*), an award in the athletic games, which suggests that this resurrection is a prize, a special honor.

These honors greatly exceed in motivational impact any impulse toward godliness provided in the Reformed system. Instead of threatening the lukewarm Christian with the lake of fire, these biblical honors provide a more ennobling and enticing motivation for living life.

Opportunities for Service

The third aspect of the inheritance is our opportunity to serve him throughout all eternity. One day, as the Scriptures everywhere affirm, the struggle of fallen man will finally come to an end. This consummation will not be achieved by social engineering or by the successful implementation of any human ideology. Rather, it will be accomplished by a supernatural intervention of God in history, the Second Coming of Christ. Finally, history will achieve a worthy outcome—the kingdom of God. Page after page of Scripture speaks of this glorious future and the possibility that those who are Christ's servants now can be granted enhanced opportunities for ministry in the future reign of Christ's servant kings.

Reigning with Christ

> Peter answered him, "We have left everything to follow you! What then will there be for us?" Jesus said to them, "I tell you the truth, at the renewal of all things, when the Son of Man sits on his glorious throne, you who have followed me will also sit on twelve thrones, judging the twelve tribes of Israel." (Matthew 19:27-28)

> You are those who have stood by me in my trials. And I confer on you a kingdom [Gr. basileia, a "kingship], just as my Father conferred on me, so that you may eat and drink at my table in my kingdom and sit on thrones, judging the twelve tribes of Israel. (Luke 22:28-30, NKJV)

The overcomer is one who does his will to the end, either by physical death (Revelation 12:11; 2:10) or until the rapture or second coming.

As a reward, he is given a kingship within the kingdom of heaven, "*To him who overcomes and does My will to the end, I will give authority over the nations.*" (Revelation 2:26-29) Faithful believers will sit with Christ on his throne![40]

The faithful sheep who minister to the poor will receive special recognition. Jesus says to them, "Come, you who are blessed of My Father, inherit the kingdom prepared for you from the foundation of the world" (Matthew 25:34, NASB). This "kingdom" is the kingdom specifically prepared for the faithful sheep. It is not Christ's kingdom; it is a subordinate "territory ruled by a king," a kingship within the kingdom of heaven.[41] Jesus referred to them in the parable of the Minas, promising faithful servants five cities and ten cites (Luke 19:17-19).[42]

---

40 Based upon Revelation 20:4-6, some have argued that all believers will sit on his throne; therefore, all believers are overcomers. The argument is circular. We know from Revelation 2:26 that an overcomer is defined as "*he who keeps my works until the end, and I will reward him with authority over the nations.*" Therefore, those who sit upon the throne with Christ are those believers, and only those believers, who keep his works to the end. We have proven elsewhere that according to the Scriptures, not all true believers keep his works until the end (see preceding chapter). Some do and some do not.

41 *BDAG*, 169, option 2.

42 For extensive documentation of this fact, see Dillow, *Final Destiny*: Chapters 4-7. Dr. Grudem believes there is only one final judgment. This judgment, the judgment on the nations, and the Judgment Seat of Christ (2 Cor 5:10) and the Great White Throne Judgment all occur at the same time. He bases this on his belief that there is no mention of entrance into Christ's earthly kingdom in this passage and the sheep are invited to "inherit the kingdom," which he says refers to entrance into the eternal state. Free Grace adherents do not accept this view. There are two different inheritances in the Bible. There is a birth-inheritance which comes to all believers by faith alone and for no other reason (Galatians 4:7). But there is another inheritance which is a reward granted to works (Colossians 3:24), the reward-inheritance. These two kinds of inheritance can be easily seen in the Old Testament and the New. Because the inheritance in Matthew 25:34 is based upon works, this is obviously the reward-inheritance. In this same verse Jesus says, "Inherit the kingdom prepared for you from the foundation of the world." "Kingdom" in this verse refers to vassal kingships within the millennial kingdom. It is likely

Priestly Ministry

While the Jews were in exile under Persian rule in 520 BC, God raised up the prophet Zechariah. Through him some of the most amazing prophesies of Scripture were communicated to the nation. These prophesies announced the coming of the "Branch," the Messiah who will one day restore the Davidic theocracy (Zechariah 3:7-8). The high priest at that time, Joshua, was challenged to be faithful in his duties and was given this wonderful promise to motivate him.

> *Thus, says the Lord of hosts, "If you will walk in My ways and if you will perform My service, then you will also govern My house and also have charge of My courts, and I will grant you free access among these who are standing here"* (Zechariah 3:7).

His reward in the future kingdom will be threefold. First, he will "govern my house." That is, he will be in charge of the worship carried out in the millennial temple of which Ezekiel spoke (Ezekiel 40-47). Second, he will have responsibility to "guard my courts." That is, he will protect the temple precincts from any negative influences that might seek to come in. And third, he will have "free access among those who are standing there." In other words, during the millennial reign Joshua will have special access to and intimacy with God. We do not know who will serve with Joshua to help him fulfill these responsibilities. The fact is that others will be involved, and they too would have to meet the requirement to "walk in his ways," if they are to serve with him.

Jesus called those who serve in this manner "pillars" in God's temple. They will have special responsibilities in the millennial temple. Jesus says to the church at Philadelphia,

> *I am coming soon. Hold on to what you have, so that no one will take your crown. He who overcomes, I will make a pillar in the temple of my God. Never again will he leave it. I will write on him*

---

that the references to cities and kingships recalls Jesus's promise to the faithful of five cities and ten cities (Luke 19:17,19).

*the name of my God and the name of the city of my God, the new
Jerusalem, which is coming down out of heaven from my God; and
I will also write on him my new name. He who has an ear, let him
hear what the Spirit says to the churches.* (Revelation 3:11-13)[43]

The idea that having one's name written on a "pillar" signifies some
kind of honor is well established. Wilkinson notes that "it is reasonable
to believe that 'pillar in the temple' of Revelation 3:12 is intended to be
understood symbolically in the context of the coronation allusions of
this specific section."[44] The specific meaning is uncertain. Perhaps the
suggestion by Mounce is correct in that it refers to the custom that the
ruling priest would set up a pillar in the Roman temples with his name
on it.[45]

Ownership of the New Jerusalem

The overcomer is promised meritorious ownership over the New
Jerusalem, and that God will be proud to be known as his God.

---

43 The indications in the immediate context suggest that final entrance into
   heaven is not in view at all. Instead, something in addition to heaven, reward,
   is the subject. Indeed, is that not what John says, *"Hold on to what you have,
   so that no one will take your crown"* (v. 11)? If the "crown" is salvation, then
   contrary to Reformed thinking, either salvation can be lost if the person does
   not "hold fast," or the person was never saved to begin with and his failure to
   overcome proves it. Mounce does not comment on this difficulty. Rosscup
   objects to the Free Grace view that the overcomer is a saved person, saying,
   "Revelation 3:11 more probably refers to an unsaved persecutor who can 'take'
   the crown from a person who has only a professed relationship with Christ
   and his church." James E. Rosscup, "The Overcomers of the Apocalypse," *Grace
   Theological Journal* 3(Fall 1982): 272. We prefer Kistemaker's suggestion which
   fits the context well. He says, "This means that the saints are honored within
   that heavenly temple, which in fact is nothing less than the very presence of
   God." Simon J. Kistemaker, "The Temple In The Apocalypse," *JETS* 43, no. 3
   (September 2000): 444.

44 Richard H. Wilkinson, "The ΣΤΥΛΟΣ of Revelation 3:12 and Ancient
   Coronation Rites," *JBL* 107, no. 3 (September 1988): 500.

45 Mounce, *The Book of Revelation*: 104.

He who overcomes will inherit all this, and I will be his God and he will be my son. (Revelation 21:7)

This inheritance is conferred on the condition of persevering in good works. It is not an inheritance granted at birth (the birth-inheritance, regeneration) to all believers by faith apart from works. It is only granted to those believers who overcome, that is, persevere in a life of good works to the final hour. It is the reward-inheritance mentioned by Paul (Colossians 3:24). In every reference to the overcomer in Revelation, he is one who is a victor in battle.[46] The central theme of the entire book is to exhort the saints to persevere and to be victorious. If all saints persevere and are victorious, the exhortations and promises of rewards are pointless. An exhortation to do something everyone does anyway to obtain a reward that all will receive anyway is absurd.

Rewards are an Encouragement to Persevere in Time of Trial

In passage after passage, the New Testament writers invest human suffering with high dignity. It is through suffering with Christ that we are trained and equipped to join the great company of the *Metochoi*. Consider:

Therefore, among God's churches we boast about your perseverance and faith in all the persecutions and trials you are enduring. All this is evidence that God's judgment is right, and as a result you will be counted worthy of the kingdom of God, for which you are suffering. (2 Thessalonians 1:4-5)

An eternal honor is being achieved for those who persevere in suffering:

For our light and momentary troubles are achieving for us an eternal glory that far outweighs them all. (2 Corinthians 4:17)

In order for us to experience great joy at the appearing of Christ, we must rejoice (i.e., respond in faith) to the sufferings we experience now:

---

46 See also Revelation 12:11; 13:7; 15:2; 17:14.

Dear friends, do not be surprised at the painful trial you are suffering, as though something strange were happening to you. But rejoice that you participate in the sufferings of Christ, so that you may be overjoyed when his glory is revealed. (1 Peter 4:12-13)

Rewards Are Only One of the Biblical Motivations

During a Bible study on rewards with a group of missionaries, I once asked, "For some, these concepts are highly motivational. For others they are only a minor motivation, or none at all. Why?" For many of them, rewards were only a minor motivation and for some, something they never think about. Many said that the central motivation is God's love for us and our love for him. Some of the reaction to the Protestant doctrine of rewards may be blamed on the way in which the doctrine is sometimes presented by its adherents. It is a mistake to extract the reward motivation found in the Bible from other equally important or even more important motivations the biblical authors present. The chart below illustrates the context in which the doctrine of rewards should be placed.

Rewards are one of seven major motivations for following Christ's way of life.

God's Love for us. There is no question that the central motivation for following Christ is God's love for us. Because this is so important, let us consider this amazing fact in some detail. Millions of Christians in the United States wonder why they are not experiencing the fullness of resurrection life promised in the New Testament. John Maisel answers,

> *No doubt many factors are at work. But if I had to boil it down to one main issue, it would be this: You cannot experience the fullness of Christ's life unless and until you are gripped by the depth of Christ's love—His love for you. Not just knowing about His love. Not just talking about it. But personally **experiencing** His love for you.*[47]

Yes, rewards are an important and much neglected spiritual motivation, but God's love for us and our love for him are the most important. Paul states this in his prayer for us,

> *So that Christ may dwell in your hearts through faith; and that you, being rooted and grounded in love, may be able to comprehend with all the saints what is the breadth and length and height and depth, and to know the love of Christ which surpasses knowledge, that you may be filled up to all the fullness of God.* (Ephesians 3:17–19)

The heart of this prayer is not that we would love God, which is important, but that we would know God's love for us. This love "surpasses knowledge." That tells us that more than intellectual acknowledgment is meant. As Maisel explains, "To know Christ in the sense Paul is describing it means to be affected by that love at the core of who we are. We give in to it, we respond to it, we feel it thrilling our hearts, we trust it, we rest in it."[48]

---

47 John Maisel, *Radical Trust: The Two Most Important Things Jesus Wants You to Know* (Dallas: East-West Ministries International, 2012), 9-10. John's book is the most significant book on the spiritual life that I have ever read. You can order a copy from East-West Ministries at info@eastwest.org.

48 Ibid., 10.

We love because He first loved us. (1 John 4:19)

We know love by this, that He laid down His life for us; and we ought to lay down our lives for the brethren. (1 John 3:16)

Greater love has no one than this, that one lay down his life for his friends. (John 15:13)

Our Love for God. All would agree that a second motivation for following Christ is our love for him and our gratitude for what he has done for us.

For this is the love of God, that we keep His commandments; and His commandments are not burdensome. (1 John 5:3)[49]

If you love Me, you will keep My commandments. (John 14:15)

The Apostle Paul explains his central motivation this way: *For the love of Christ compels us, because we judge thus: that if One died for all, then all died* (2 Corinthians 5:14).

The word "compel" (Gr. *sunechō*) is quite strong. In this context it means "to provide an impulse, urge on, impel."[50]

For His Name's Sake. Third, Jesus says we should be motivated "for my name's sake" (Matthew 19:29). In other words, we serve for His sake and not for our own benefit. While that does not exclude the thought of our own recompense, it decidedly places it in perspective!

Because of His Forgiveness. Fourth, from the incident with the woman who had led an immoral life and received forgiveness, gratitude for forgiveness is a central motivation.

---

49 We understand the phrase "of God" to be an objective genitive meaning "love for God."

50 *BDAG*, 971. Luke 8:37, "gripped by" fear; 12:57, "distressed" until it is accomplished; Paul says he is "hard pressed" between alternatives, Philippians 1:27, etc.

Therefore I say to you, her sins, which are many, are forgiven, for she loved much. But to whom little is forgiven, the same loves little. (Luke 7:47, NKJV)

Because We Want to Please Him. Many believers are motivated by a desire to please Christ, and rewards are not a central part of their thinking. This is biblical to the core.

Therefore also we have as our ambition, whether at home or absent, ***to be pleasing to Him.*** (2 Corinthians 5:9)

No soldier in active service entangles himself in the affairs of everyday life, ***so that he may please the one who enlisted him as a soldier.*** (2 Timothy 2:4)[51]

For the Sake of the Gospel. Paul also says we should be motivated simply "for the sake of the gospel" (1 Corinthians 9:23).

Summary

The *biblical* doctrine of eternal rewards is a magnificent incitement to a faithful life. In our opinion, the church would benefit significantly in its task of motivating believers to fuller commitment if this great vision of serving with him in the fulfillment of human destiny were more frequently held before our gaze.

There is no "spiritual commercialism" or selfishness involved in the pursuit of honor, opportunities for ministry, and the desire for maximum intimacy with Christ. These are noble and inspiring goals, fully approved by Christ and his apostles. They focus ultimately on him, not ourselves.

To summarize, believers are to strive for reward (1) with a more fundamental heart motive that what we do is for Christ's sake and in response to Christ's love (2 Corinthians 5:14); (2) with a realization that once we have done all we can do, we still have only done our duty (Luke 17:10); (3) with a heart's desire to "please the One who enlisted

---

51 See also Colossians 1:10; 1 Thessalonians 4:1; 1 John 3:22 and Hebrews 13:21.

us as soldiers" (2 Timothy 2:4); (4) with a prior motive of serving him for Christ's sake (Matthew 19:28-30); (5) with an understanding that there is no strict contractual correspondence between a certain amount of work resulting in a certain amount of reward, for whatever we get is overgenerous wages (Matthew 20:1-16), and (6) most importantly, with the realization that rewards enable us to obtain tokens of worship and gratitude that, like the twenty-four elders, we too can repeatedly lay at His feet (Revelation 4:10).

At the Judgment Seat of Christ, we will be summoned by the "upward call" to the victor's platform (Philippians 3:14) to hear the words, "Well done." The believers who hear those words are Christ's servant kings, who will one day serve with him in the fulfillment of human destiny. As they rise to meet him, they will participate in the "upward call" to a better kind of resurrection (Philippians 3:14).

PART II

Biblical Texts

Introduction

Fred Chay, Ph.D.

We have attempted in Part one to examine some of the theological and historical issues involved in this most important and perennial theological topic. This has included explaining and clarifying some fundamental theological terms as well as some foundational theological topics.

Accuracy and precision are essential to construct a consistent, congruent, cogent, comprehensive and complete theology. It is the same for exegesis. Equally true is the need for theology to come forth from exegesis. Many have said that both Free Grace and Reformed theology are consistent within their systems. The question is: Are the exegetical results independent of the theological system or has bias slipped into the exegetical process?

All theologies and books of theology constructed by Evangelicals demands a high view of Scripture.[1] We are people of the book for

---

1 There appears to be an all too familiar fracturing on the issue of inerrancy. See *Five Views of Inerrancy,* Zondervan, 2013, for a description of differing views of inerrancy held by "evangelicals" today. I believe most of the Reformed theologians in this present soteriological debate and all the Free

"we believe that what Scripture says God says."[2] Hence the question is: What did God say? The answer is found using proper exegetical procedures built upon hermeneutical principles in conjunction with the leadership of the Holy Spirit by the ministry of illumination.

Free Grace theology has a history of exegetical works of analysis but only a few theological works of synthesis. This trend has been changing.[3] The charge has been made by Reformed scholars that many of the interpretations are idiosyncratic, strained, novel and artificial.[4] Although space will not permit a comprehensive dialogue, it seems prudent in Part 2 of this book to engage some of the biblical texts that are crucial for both sides of the debate.

Grace theologians hold to full inerrancy similar to the Chicago Statement on Biblical Inerrancy.

2   B.B.Warfield , *Inspiration and Authority of the Bible* (Philadelphia, Pa., The Presbyterian and Reformed Publishing Company, 1948); 299.

3   See Elliott Johnson, *A Dispensational Biblical Theology* (Allen, Tex.: Bold Grace Ministries, 2016); David Anderson, *Free Grace Soteriology*, 2nd ed. (Conroe, Tex.: Grace Theology Press, 2012); Joseph Dillow, *Final Destiny* (Monument, Col.: Grace Theology Press, 2013); David Allen and Steve Lemke, eds., *Whosoever Will*, (Nashville, Tenn.: B&H Publishing, 2010); C. Gordon Olsen, *Beyond Calvinism and Arminianism* (Lynchburg, Va.: Global Gospel Publishers, 2002); David Allen, ed., *Anyone Can Be Saved: A Defense of "Traditional" Southern Baptist Soteriology* (Eugene, Ore.: Wipf & Stock, 2016).

4   Grudem, *"Free Grace" Theology: 5 Ways it Diminishes the Gospel*, 119 and D.A. Carson, *Exegetical Fallacies*, Baker, Academic, 1984, 137.

Chapter 13

The Rich Young Ruler – Luke 18:18-30

Joseph Dillow, Th.D.

F ew passages of Scripture have exercised the ingenuity of interpreters as much as those in which Jesus interacts in one case with a lawyer (Luke 10:25-29), and in the second, with a rich young ruler (Luke 18:18-30; Matthew 19:16-30; Mark 10:17-26). Both want to know, "*What shall I do to inherit eternal life?*" The latter's question is rephrased by Matthew, "*Teacher, what good thing shall I do that I may obtain eternal life?*"

In each instance Jesus's response to these questions involves something he must *do*, apparently implying that inheriting eternal life is achieved by works. If inheriting or obtaining eternal life always refers to going to heaven when one dies, as many other interpreters believe, this seems to put Jesus in contradiction with himself in the Gospel of John where he stressed that obtaining eternal life comes through faith and no other conditions are mentioned. And it also appears to throw Jesus into conflict with the rest of the New Testament.

Interpreters from all theological backgrounds have struggled with this difficulty. One writer posits that the rich young ruler was not asking about how to obtain salvation, but rather wanted to know how he could be assured of salvation.[1] Some simply ignore the problem and leave the reader perplexed about the requirements to obey the Ten Commandments as a condition for obtaining eternal life.[2] Others suggest that because he was seeking heaven on the basis of works, Jesus speaks to him from his viewpoint and tells him what he must do if he wants to pursue that approach. Thus Jesus is not endorsing his theology but is using the man's theology to show him his shallow understanding of the commandments. Obtaining heaven by works requires perfect obedience to the Ten Commandments.[3] According to another interpreter, Jesus intended his words to show the young man that he lacked "the one all-comprehensive requirement of the law—the *absolute subjection of the heart to God,* and this vitiated all his other obediences."[4] How this can be an explanation of the way to heaven as expressed in the rest of the New Testament, which is by faith and not by works, is never clarified! Another writer simply asserts, "Faith is assumed; judgment is on the basis of performance."[5]

Another commentator says that the purpose of Jesus's citation of the commandments was to show the young ruler that money was keeping him from making a saving commitment to Christ.[6] Another writer avows that what Jesus teaches here is that the only way to enter the kingdom (i.e., go to heaven when you die) is via the route of

---

1   Louis Barbieri, "Matthew," in *BKC: New Testament,* ed. John Walvord and Roy B. Zuck (Colorado Springs: Cook, 1996), 64.

2   John L. McKenzie, "Matthew," in *The Jerome Biblical Commentary,* ed. Raymond E. Brown, Joseph A. Fitzmyer, and Roland E. Murphy (Englewood Cliffs, NJ: Prentice-Hall, 1996), 2:96.

3   William Hendriksen and Simon Kistemaker, *Exposition of the Gospel According to Matthew* (Grand Rapids: Baker Book House, 2001), 725.

4   David Brown, "Matthew," in *Commentary Critical and Explanatory on the Whole Bible,* ed. Robert Jamieson, A. R. Fausset, and David Brown (Oak Harbor, WA: Logos Research Systems, 1997).

5   Douglas R. A. Hare, *Matthew,* Interpretation: A Bible Commentary for Teaching and Preaching (Louisville: John Knox Press, 1993), 228.

6   Craig L. Blomberg, *Matthew,* New American Commentary (Nashville: Broadman and Holman Publishers, 2001), 229.

discipleship. Like many others, this writer fails to explain theologically how this can be correlated with salvation by grace through faith, although curiously, he denies that Jesus is here teaching that salvation can be gained by simple obedience to the commandments.[7]

Within Reformed circles, a new paradigm called Federal Vision or the Auburn Avenue Theology has emerged. This might be called "neonomism," the new legalism. In this view, the rich young ruler is seeking salvation by works, and that is what Jesus offers him. Salvation is a process of becoming eligible for final justification by means of non-meritorious works produced in the believer by God.[8]

A recent scholar similarly leaves us perplexed by asserting that Jesus is calling upon the young man to become a genuine (in contrast to spurious) disciple and that all Christians are genuine disciples. Thus we are again left wondering how this call to obedience can be related to the free offer of the gospel.[9]

Another scholarly work maintains that Jesus's intent was "to force the ruler to trust God and humbly rely upon him."[10] Another commentator suggests that the intent of Jesus's words is not to teach salvation by works, which is impossible, but to test the sincerity of the young man's desire for eternal life (entrance into heaven when he dies).[11]

A common Free Grace view understands the young man to be asking about heavenly reward. However, before he can obtain reward, he must first be directed to trust the Good Teacher for initial salvation.

---

7   Donald A. Hagner, *Matthew 14-28*, Word Biblical Commentary (Dallas: Word Books, 2002), 558.

8   For example, Alan P. Stanley, *Did Jesus Teach Salvation by Works? The Role of Works in Salvation in the Synoptic Gospels* (Eugene, OR: Pickwick Publishers, 2006). See also Paul A. Rainbow, *The Way of Salvation: The Role of Christian Obedience in Justification* (Waynesboro, GA: Paternoster, 2005), 155-74.

9   Craig S. Keener, *A Commentary on the Gospel of Matthew* (Grand Rapids: Wm. B. Eerdmans Publishing Co., 1999), 476.

10 Darrell L. Bock, *Luke 9:51-24:53*, Baker Exegetical Commentary on the New Testament (Grand Rapids: Baker Book House, 1996), 1482.

11 Norval Geldenhuys, *The Gospel of Luke*, New International Commentary on the New Testament (Grand Rapids: Wm. B. Eerdmans Publishing Co., 1977), 459.

For this to occur, the young ruler's self-righteous façade must be penetrated. Jesus does this by showing him that he emphatically has not kept all the commandments.[12]

Obviously, there is no consensus on the meaning of Jesus's words. According to the traditional interpretation, a young man approached Jesus sincerely wanting to know how to go to heaven, and Jesus never tells him. Instead, Jesus leaves him with the impression that to obtain eternal life he must obey God; therefore, entrance into heaven would be predicated on works. In view of the fact that many of the interpretations leave us theologically unsatisfied, or contradict each other, perhaps it is time to consider a new approach.

Contextual Setting

The encounter with this young man (Luke 18:18-34; Matthew 19:16-30) occurs within the broader context of Jesus's final journey to Jerusalem (Luke 9:51-19:48). A theme that occurs on several occasions during this section of Luke is the subject of humility as the route to significance.

The answer in the verses immediately preceding the encounter with the rich young ruler is the story of being like a little child as a condition of kingdom entrance. Like a child, one must assume lower status.[13] The key characteristic of a small child is not his faith, but his insignificance. The teaching here is that "status in the kingdom is often inversely proportional to status in the world."[14] A little child is the lowest rung on the social ladder. Keener notes that to "become as children, refers to assuming a child's low status rather than a characteristic like humility."[15] Hagner agrees, "The child's humility is his lack of status,

12 Zane C. Hodges, *Absolutely Free! A Biblical Reply to Lordship Salvation* (Dallas: Redención Viva, 1989), 187.

13 For fuller discussion of the story of Christ and the little children, see Joseph C. Dillow, *Final Destiny: The Future Reign of the Servant Kings*, 3rd revised ed. (Monument, CO: Paniym Group, Inc., 2016; reprint, 2016), 275 ff..

14 Keener, *A Commentary on the Gospel of Matthew*: 447.

15 Ibid.

not his actions or feelings of humbleness."[16] Our Lord teaches "the kingdom of heaven *belongs* to such as these" (Matthew 19:14; Luke 18:16). In Luke's expanded version, he seems to equate ownership of the kingdom with "receiving the kingdom," and both refer to obtaining high status there and do not relate to soteriological entrance.

> *And they were bringing even their babies to him so that he would touch them, but when the disciples saw it, they began rebuking them. But Jesus called for them, saying, "Permit the children to come to me, and do not hinder them, for the kingdom of God belongs to such as these. Truly I say to you, whoever does not receive the kingdom of God like a child will not enter it at all."* (Luke 18:15-17; cf. Matthew 19:13-15)

The issue is ownership of the kingdom ("belongs to"). Receiving the kingdom in Luke 19:15 = receiving royal authority there—it does not refer to receiving salvation. I suggest that "kingdom" means "royal authority."

> *When he returned, **after receiving the kingdom**, he ordered that these slaves, to whom he had given the money, be called to him so that he might know what business they had done.* (Luke 19:15)

In Luke 18:17, Jesus says that if one does not receive the kingdom by taking the lowest status, he will not "enter" it. The words "at all" are not in the Greek text. The text should be read, **"Whoever does not receive royal authority by taking the lowest status now will not enter into royal authority in the coming kingdom."** "Entering the kingdom" does not refer to going to heaven when one dies; rather, it means to enter into the experience of ruling there, or to enter into greatness (Matthew 5:19-20). It is the successful conclusion of a life-well-lived.[17]

---

16 Hagner, *Matthew 14-28*: 518.

17 For more detailed discussion of this point of view, see Chapter 14.

And immediately following this blessing on the children,

A ruler questioned him, saying, "Good Teacher, what shall I do to inherit eternal life?" (Luke 18:18; see also Matthew 19:16)

In Matthew's version we read,

And someone came to him and said, "Teacher, what good thing shall I do that I may obtain eternal life?" (Matthew 19:16)

Apparently, inheriting eternal life and obtaining eternal life are the same thing.

The teaching that only the humble can obtain ownership (ruling authority) of the kingdom fits the broader context precisely, where we have been told twice that he who humbles himself will be exalted. High honor in the kingdom comes to those who adopt the lowest status now. As Jesus put it in Matthew's account, *"Whoever wishes to become great among you shall be your servant, and whoever wishes to be first among you shall be your slave"* (Matthew 20:26-27).[18]

The encounter with the rich young ruler has a chiastic structure.

A	Receive the kingdom as a child (Matthew 19:14)
B	**The Rich Young Ruler (Matthew 19:16-29)**
A'	The first will be last, and the last first (Matthew 19:30)

Lines A and A' bracket the encounter, setting it in a context of the requirement for humility if one is to "own" or "receive the kingdom," that is, receive royal authority there. We shall see that the rich young ruler's question regarding inheriting eternal life is contextually linked

---

18 Matthew and Mark's reports of this encounter begin and end with the question of ranking in the kingdom. Luke omits the logion regarding "first and last," but the idea may be present in the promise of leaving all and receiving the reward of many times as much in the age to come (Luke 18:30).

with this *inclusio* and relates not to soteriology, but to the requirements for status.

Regarding line B in the above structure, there are three requirements for inheriting eternal life, that is, becoming "complete" (Matthew 19:20) and obtaining treasure in heaven (v. 21). They are: (1) keep the commandments (Matthew 19:17); (2) sell all that you have and give to the poor (Matthew 19:21); and (3) come, follow me (Matthew 19:21). These do not look like conditions for obtaining personal salvation which comes to us by faith alone and without cost!

Matthew begins and ends the discussion with the theme of status. He concludes with the statement, *"But many who are first will be last; and the last, first"* (Matthew 19:30), and Luke begins it with the same phrase (Luke 18:14). Some writers, starting off on this false evangelistic premise, fall into serious theological difficulties regarding works as necessary for salvation, difficulties from which they often labor without success to extract themselves.[19]

The structure of the passage tells us something else. The phrases "enter into life" and "if you wish to be complete" (Gr. *teleios*) appear to be parallel to each other. Entering into life and becoming "complete" may be related ideas. *Teleios* is a common word for spiritual maturity of a full disciple. BDAG defines it as "being fully developed in a moral sense," (p. 996). Like its cognate, *telos*, it implies a goal. The sense of "accomplishment of a task" is found in many places. Passages in the Septuagint illustrate this meaning. For example, Nehemiah refers to the fact that after the wall had been built, *"the work had been accomplished"* (Gr. *teleioō*, Nehemiah 6:16; cf. 2 Chronicles 8:16). We will discuss this point in more detail below.

Jesus apparently understands this young man to be asking about how to finish what he has begun. We will argue below that he wants to know

---

19 For example, Stanley says that works are a demonstration of salvation. "Jesus expected that anyone who will enter into life at the end of the age will have demonstrated a practical outworking of righteousness." Alan P. Stanley, "The Rich Young Ruler and Salvation," *BibSac* 649, no. 163 (January - March 2006): 58. There is nothing in the text that even hints at this. Works such as selling all that one has are not manifestations of salvation, they are conditions for obtaining it. This difficulty will be explained below.

how he can bring his initial belief to a successful conclusion. He wants to live with the end in view. He wants to know how he can *accomplish that goal*. He is asking a very significant question. This understanding is confirmed by Jesus's statement that if one does become "complete," his reward will be "treasure in heaven" (Matthew 19:21), something that is in addition to initial salvation.

Definition of Key Terms

The crux for understanding the story of the rich young ruler revolves around the meaning of some key phrases. In Matthew's account, the rich young ruler asks, "*What shall I do to obtain eternal life*" (Matthew 19:16)? Both Mark's and Luke's accounts vary the query asking, "*What shall I do to inherit eternal life?*" (Mark 10:17; Luke 18:18); and the lawyer in another encounter in Luke asks the same question (Luke 10:25). Turning to his disciples, Jesus commented about the rich young ruler, "*How hard it is for a rich man to enter the kingdom of God*" (Luke 18:25). By this phrase, the disciples understand that Jesus was explaining how difficult it is for a rich man to be "saved" (Luke 18:26). To the lawyer, Jesus simply says, "*Do this and you will live*" (Luke 10:28). In Mark's and Matthew's versions, Jesus responds to the rich young ruler by saying, "*Go, sell whatsoever thou hast, and give to the poor, and you will have treasure in heaven. Then come, follow me*" (Matthew 19:21; Mark 10:21). Matthew alone adds the phrase that by selling all, the rich young ruler can become "complete" (Matthew 19:21), and in Luke, Jesus says, "*One thing you lack*" (Luke 18:22).

The immediate impression is that the phrases "obtain eternal life," "inherit eternal life," be "saved," "be perfect," "enter the kingdom of God," "have treasure in heaven," and "you will live" are either equivalent or closely related concepts. The traditional interpretation correctly assumes this, but in my view, it is incorrect in assuming that all these terms mean "go to heaven when you die."[20] When these terms are all

---

20 Contra Robert L. Thomas, "The Rich Young Man in Matthew," *GTJ* 3, no. 2 (1982): 258. Also, even though I disagree with Thomas Schreiner's interpretation of Mark 10:17-26, he is correct when he says, "Notice that the terms 'eternal life' (v. 17), 'kingdom of God' (vv. 24–25), and 'saved' (v. 26) are

understood in a soteriological sense, the method Jesus prescribes for obtaining eternal life ("do this," "keep the commandments," "sell that which you have," "love the Lord your God with all your heart, soul, and mind," etc.) creates an interpretive problem. Does Jesus teach in these passages that entrance into heaven is based on something a person must do in contradiction to what he has said elsewhere that salvation is by faith alone (John 3:16)?[21]

A number of evangelical writers in the Reformed camp candidly admit that salvation is by faith plus works.[22] Like the Roman Catholics,

---

all synonyms in this text. There is no evidence whatsoever for distinguishing between them. Indeed, in this passage 'treasure in heaven' is also a term for eternal life (v. 21)." Thomas R. Schreiner, "Perseverance and Assurance: A Survey and a Proposal," *SBJT* 2(1998): 46.

21 "Reading Matthew 19:16–30, one might suppose that salvation is according to works: one must obey the Torah and Jesus Christ. But Matthew 20:1–15 disallows this simplistic interpretation. For it clearly teaches, albeit in a picture, that there is no necessary proportion between human work and divine reward." W. D. Davies and Dale C. Allison, *A Critical and Exegetical Commentary on the Gospel According to Saint Matthew* (Edinburgh: T. & T. Clark, 1988), 76.

22 For example, Stanley, *Did Jesus Teach Salvation by Works*: 166-293. See also Rainbow, *Way of Salvation*: 155-74. Stanley says, "It is evident that one's conduct evidently plays a role in determining one's eternal destiny," (p. 187), and "we cannot deny that Jesus demanded obedience to enter into eschatological life," 196. Stanley does not mean just that works are only an evidence of regeneration. He believes that they are an inferior cause of eternal life and that eternal life is a consequence of works (p. 198). He quotes Calvin with approval, John Calvin, *Institutes of the Christian Religion*, trans. Henry Beveridge, reprint ed. (Grand Rapids: Wm. B. Eerdmans Publishing Co., 1964), 3.14.21. From Luke 13:25-30, he derives the condition for salvation that one must "strain every nerve." He believes that salvation is "via endurance," and that endurance is a "condition" of salvation. Stanley is clear that texts speaking of endurance "say nothing about endurance being a demonstration . . . of salvation. Jesus does not say 'The one who endures to the end will demonstrate he is saved,'" Stanley, *Did Jesus Teach Salvation by Works*: 248. Stanley confusedly does not feel that "condition" carries the baggage of "gaining merit or favor." Yet that "baggage" is what Jesus referred to when he spoke about the last being first and the first being last in his summary of the encounter (Matthew 19:30).

however, they mean works of the Christian, not the works of the nonbeliever. Some who espouse this view understand these works of the nonbeliever as "works of law,"[23] and they do not avail for salvation. However, the works produced by the Holy Spirit in response to faith, they say, are non-meritorious and are a "condition" for entering the kingdom of heaven.[24] In this view salvation is a lifelong process, a pilgrimage,[25] not an event, and justification occurs in two stages. Stage one is in response to faith and involves the "initial" justification. But stage two is in response to and is conditioned on good works and occurs at the Judgment Seat of Christ, which they equate with the Great White Throne Judgment.[26] The account of the rich young ruler is a central passage to which their theology appeals.[27] What do these phrases mean?

The young man's question and Jesus's answer have spawned volumes of ink, raising a number of interesting questions. Who was this young man? Was he a believer in Christ or a nonbelieving inquirer? What does he mean by getting "eternal life"? Is he asking how to go to heaven when he dies? Opinions differ and the discussion to follow will not settle the issue, but hopefully it will point the way toward a plausible solution to the many questions this encounter raises.

Before we can answer the question, "What does Jesus mean by 'life'?" We must first ask, "Who was this young man?" If he was a believer, then we know that he already had "life" in the sense of regeneration, and this would immediately change our understanding of his real question.

Who Was This Young Man?

Was this young man a believer? We do not know for sure, but there are indications that he may have been. We are told seven things about him.

---

23 Rainbow, *Way of Salvation*: 194.

24 Stanley, *Did Jesus Teach Salvation by Works*: 197-98.

25 "My point here is simply that Jesus understands salvation to be a pilgrimage." Ibid., 142.

26 Rainbow, *Way of Salvation*: 155-74.

27 Stanley, *Did Jesus Teach Salvation by Works*: 188-219.

Luke says he was a ruler, probably meaning that he was an influential wealthy man or civic leader who was known for his piety.[28] This is impressive. Not many rulers were drawn to Christ, but this young man was; and unlike Nicodemus, he was willing to come in the light of day, indicating courage. "Despite his high social standing he made no attempt to conceal his need and his admiration for Jesus."[29] Also, he was young,[30] extremely wealthy,[31] and owned much property.[32] His approach to Jesus was respectful and enthusiastic. He likely heard the Lord Jesus speak several times and wondered if he would answer his heart-searching question. We can reasonably assume that he believed Jesus to be the Messiah, just as many among the crowds did (John 7:31; 8:31). Seeing Jesus from afar, he came running to see him, and illustrating submission and respect, he knelt at Jesus's feet.[33] He illustrates spiritual discernment and acknowledges Jesus as Lord by calling him "Good Master," which may be an indication that he believed Christ was the Messiah. He evidences a spiritual vitality and interest by asking, "*What must I do to inherit eternal life?*" He not only believes in God and sees Jesus as one sent from God, but he is morally upright. "*All these things,*" he says, "*I have kept from my youth.*" Jesus never challenges this claim. Furthermore, he came with a spirit of obedience saying, "*What good thing must I do,*" and with the spirit of a disciple desiring to be taught a matter of great importance he called Jesus "*Rabbi,*" a respectful title.[34] It should also be noted that Jesus "*loved him.*"[35] Apparently, then, the man was not insincere, as some

---

28 Suggested by Bock, *Luke 9:51-24:53*: 1476.

29 J. Sidlow Baxter, *Mark These Men: Practical Studies in Striking Aspects of Certain Bible Characters* (Grand Rapids: Zondervan Publishing House, 1960), 112.

30 Matthew 19:20

31 Luke 18:23

32 Matthew 19:22

33 Mark 10:17

34 Luke 18:18

35 Mark 10:21

have suggested. Here is a man who believes in God and Christ; he has both the character and the works that, according to Reformed writers, give evidence that his faith is real. Because he meets the required tests for genuine faith, they should grant that he is probably a saved man.

Of significance is the fact that in Luke's account, after the ruler says, "*All these things I have kept from my youth*," Jesus replies, "*One thing you lack*" (Luke 18:22). Think of it—only "one thing"! Most of us could think of many things we lack. Baxter asks, "Could there be any finer commendation of this young man's character than for Jesus to say, 'One thing you lack?'"[36] If inheriting eternal life means "get saved" and this young man lacks only one thing, surely, he who came to die for our sins would say (as he did to Nicodemus), "*Whoever believes in him will never perish*." But he does not say that because believing is not what he lacked nor was his question about how to obtain eternal salvation. Instead, Jesus gives this young man another work to do: "*Sell all that you possess, and distribute it to the poor, and you shall have treasure in heaven; and come, follow me*." It is difficult to imagine that the Savior who "loved him" would leave this man hanging on the precipice of damnation with no hope, and tell him an untruth that by obeying commandments he can earn heaven. Therefore William Brown's assertion that "it is clear that the young man did not possess eternal life" is incorrect.[37]

To explain why Jesus did not state that the way of salvation is by faith alone, Brown appeals to the other passages in the Gospel of Matthew where kingdom entrance is conditioned on works (e.g., Matthew 5:20; 7:21) and asserts (without proof) that "faith is implicit in the reception of Jesus's word and the appropriation of salvation."[38] His problem is that he equates the "appropriation of salvation" (justification) which is by faith alone with inheriting the kingdom and entering life, which, on the authority of the Lord Jesus in this passage, is obtained by faith plus

---

36 Baxter, *Mark These Men: Practical Studies in Striking Aspects of Certain Bible Characters*: 115.

37 William E. Brown, "The New Testament Concept of the Believer's Inheritance" (ThD diss., Dallas Theological Seminary, 1984), 69.

38 Ibid., 76.

works. The issue for the rich young ruler is sanctification and treasure (reward), not soteriology, as the following discussion will show.

Entering into Life

The first phrase requiring precise definition is "enter into life." What kind of life is in view, a full life now or final entrance into heaven?

> And someone came to him and said, "Teacher, what good thing shall I do that I may **obtain eternal life**?" And he said to him, "Why are you asking me about what is good? There is only One who is good; but if you wish **to enter into life**, keep the commandments." (Matthew 19:16, 17)

The young man's question is variously reported as "*What good thing shall I do that I may obtain eternal life?*"[39] or, in Mark and Luke's versions, "*What shall I do to inherit eternal life?*"[40] In response to his question, Jesus replies, "*If you wish to enter into life, keep the commandments.*"[41] Apparently "inheriting," "obtaining," and "entering" life refer to the same thing and relate to entering the kingdom as well.

The Hypothetical "Hidden Premise" View

Leon Morris assures his readers that by "life" Jesus "clearly meant life in the age to come, life in the final kingdom that God would set up."[42] However, this is not clear at all. It results in Jesus teaching that entrance into heaven is obtained by means of works, a view that developed later in the Patristic writings. As will be demonstrated below, "life" does not mean heaven when one dies, but refers to a rich experience of life now *leading to* treasure (reward) *in* heaven.

---

39 Matthew 19:16

40 Mark 10:17; Luke 18:17

41 Matthew 19:16

42 Leon Morris, *The Gospel According to Matthew*, The Pillar New Testament Commentary (Grand Rapids: Wm. B. Eerdmans Publishing Co., 1992), 489.

The traditional view of the meaning of obtaining life is that it refers to final entrance into heaven. In agreement with Morris, Bock writes,

> *The ruler is asking, "How can I be sure I'll be saved in the final resurrection?" This is a basic soteriological question not referring to reward for service but to the eternal life that comes from being God's child. This is clear from the context: 18:17 discusses entry into the kingdom and 18:28–30 makes the point that basic spiritual benefits come in this life and the next.*[43]

As we shall see, the context does not make this "clear" at all but in fact decisively argues against this viewpoint!

Those, like Bock, who understand that the rich young ruler asks how he can be sure he will enter heaven when he dies run into difficulty because entering heaven would then be conditioned on keeping commandments and selling all one's possessions. Bock then adds, "*If* one is going to earn eternal life then acts of righteousness are required."[44] Bock uses the word "if," but he has the burden of proof to establish this. Having stated that to "inherit eternal life" refers to personal salvation, Bock, in order to maintain his biblical commitment to faith alone as the only condition for personal salvation, feels he needs to introduce a word, "if," which is a hidden premise. However, this is not even hinted at in the text. This "hidden premise," that works would save *if* one could do them perfectly, is obviously added as an ad hoc explanation to solve the difficulty. Bock suggests that Jesus is not saying works are a condition for inheriting eternal life. Instead, he believes this is only a misunderstanding by the rich young ruler.

Hendriksen and Kistemaker say, "If any human being would actually fulfill this law of love to perfection, he would indeed obtain everlasting life."[45] Since no one can perfectly fulfill the law, they argue that Jesus is pointing out to the lawyer that no one can be saved using

---

43 Bock, *Luke 9:51-24:53*: 1476.

44 Ibid., 1478. (italics added).

45 Hendriksen and Kistemaker, *Exposition of the Gospel According to Matthew*: 592.

a legal approach. However, there is not even a hint in the passage that this is hypothetical. Inheriting everlasting life is clearly conditioned on works. Both of these writers end up contradicting the plain meaning of the text because they begin with the false premise that to "inherit eternal life" means "go to heaven when one dies." It is unclear how Jesus could have said it more plainly; *inheriting eternal life is indeed based on works*!

Wakefield, vigorously objects to this "hypothetical view," noting that it involves Christ making a false promise. "And worse yet, that precise combination, the fact that God offers a promise which he most certainly knows can never be actualized, makes the promise seem not just false, but deceptive, the perpetration of a divine fraud."[46] Raisanen agrees. When he explains Paul's use of the same phrase in Romans 10:5, he writes that Paul "gets involved in the cynicism that God explicitly provides men with a law 'unto life' while knowing from the start that this instrument will not work."[47] Surely, there is a better way of handling this difficulty than contradicting the plain reading of the text![48]

One can agree with Catholic interpreters that there is no evidence in the context to support the Reformed interpretation that this is a hypothetical description of what one must do to be saved if one wants to be saved by works.[49] The issue for this young man is not faith, rather

---

46 Andrew H. Wakefield, *Where to Live: The Hermeneutical Significance of Paul's Citations from Scripture in Galatians 3:1-14* (Atlanta: Society of Biblical Literature, 2003), 81.

47 H. Raisanen, *Paul and the Law* (Philadelphia: Fortress Press, 1986), 265. Cited by Stephen Westerholm, *Israel's Law and the Church's Faith* (Grand Rapids: Wm. B. Eerdmans Publishing Co., 1988), 101.

48 For thorough discussion of the hypothetical view, see Dillow, *Final Destiny*: Chapter 13, "Excursus on the Hypothetical View."

49 The Catholic apologist, Robert Sungenis, is quite right when he says, "In effect, they [Protestant interpreters like John MacArthur] say that Jesus is giving a misleading answer to the rich young man in an effort to show him that the Law cannot save him." Robert A. Sugenis, *Not by Faith Alone: The Biblical Evidence for the Catholic Doctrine of Justification* (Goleta, CA: Queenship Publishing, 1997), 179.

"in the clearest language possible, Jesus teaches that the central issue is whether he has combined his faith with works of love sufficiently to gain eternal life."[50] In fact, this man claims he has obeyed the Law for the most part, and Jesus does not challenge his claim. To the contrary, when Jesus hears him say, "*All this I have done since my youth*," Jesus "*felt a love for him*" (Mark 10:20-21) and told him, "*There is only one thing you lack*" (Luke 18:22).

The Faith-Plus-Works View

The Neonomian wing of contemporary Reformed thought agrees with Bock that "inherit eternal life" means "be saved from eternal damnation." For example, Alan Stanley argues that the ruler's question is about how he might obtain soteriological entrance into final salvation.[51] Because Jesus said, "Keep the commandments," Stanley concludes that final entrance into heaven is conditioned upon works.[52]

---

50 Ibid., 181.

51 Stanley, *Did Jesus Teach Salvation by Works*: 194-99. Stanley believes Jesus demands obedience to enter into eschatological life, that is, the glorified state (p. 196). Earlier, he defined eternal life, not only as the glorified state, but as a pilgrimage beginning with entrance and ending with perfection (ibid, 143.). Eternal life, he says, is something to be enjoyed and experienced now (ibid, 142.). A rich life now seems to be the focus in the encounter with the rich young ruler.

52 In his book, *Did Jesus Teach Salvation by Works*, Stanley is very explicit about this. He believes salvation is a "way of life rather than a one-time conversion experience" (ibid., 167.), merging justification and sanctification, as did the Council of Trent. This way of life involves discipleship (ibid., 164.). He says that when a person is initially justified, he may not yet be eligible to enter the kingdom on the last day (he feels this is soteriological entrance). But, "somewhere along the way converted sinners evidently become righteous and therefore eligible to enter the kingdom" (ibid., 175.). He is clear that salvation is "via endurance" (ibid., 248) and that endurance is not a demonstration of salvation but is a condition (ibid., 248.). Confusedly, he appears to contradict himself and says that "endurance does not cause salvation but is a demonstration of it" (ibid., 252.). He argues that this contradiction is resolved because there is an "inseparable relationship" between faith and endurance (ibid., 253.). Apparently, it is ok for works to be a condition of salvation so long as they do not cause it! Not only are works and endurance conditions of final

He argues that the rich young ruler is asking about the final stage of salvation which, in Stanley's view, is obtained by the post-conversion non-meritorious works of the regenerate man.[53]

If the above discussion is correct, both the hypothetical (Bock) and Neonomian (Stanley) solutions fail. They fail because they are both committed to the idea that "inherit eternal life" means "obtain final entrance into heaven." It does not. As the following context makes clear, inheriting eternal life and finding treasure/reward in heaven are obtained by means of becoming "complete" in one's commitment to discipleship, by saving one's soul.

Entering into a Rich Life Now

Is there another alternative? This writer finds the Free Grace viewpoint quite compelling. If this young man was indeed regenerate, what does he mean when he says that he wants to "obtain" (Gr. echō) or "inherit" eternal life? A regenerate man already has it. And why, in answer to his request, does Jesus tell him to obey the Law, sell all that he has, and follow him?

The phrase "inherit eternal life" occurs four times in the New Testament.[54] In each case, some kind of work or character quality is necessary if one is to inherit it. Therefore, it is doubtful that this has anything to do with personal salvation, which is by faith alone.[55] In

---

salvation, according to Stanley, but how we treat others is also a condition. We must not have anger (ibid., 261-67); we must love our enemies (ibid., 267-73) and forgive others, or we will be condemned to "eternal damnation" (ibid., 288). He thinks he acquits himself of heresy by asserting that these works are impossible apart from divine enablement (ibid., 208) and that "condition" does not imply merit or favor (ibid.). But in the New Testament, it makes no difference who enables works, salvation is by faith alone apart from works (Ephesians 2:8-9). The key word is "alone." To drop this word, as some do, is to ignore the distinction between two entirely different kinds of religion.

53 For full discussion of this Neonomian view of salvation, see Dillow, *Final Destiny*: chapters 36-37.

54 Matthew 19:29; Mark 10:17; Luke 10:25; 18:18

55 The related term "life" occurs 16 times in the Synoptics (Matthew 7:14; 18:8, 9; 19:16, 17, 29; 25:46; Mark 9:43, 45; 10:17, 30; Luke 10:25; 12:15; 16:25; 18:18,

the parable of the narrow way, entering life (Matthew 7:14) refers to entering into a kingdom way of living resulting in an abundant life now and greatness in the kingdom.[56]

Because a person who has placed his faith in Jesus Christ already has eternal life in the sense of regeneration, perhaps the common translation of *echō*, ("to have," or "to obtain") is not what the rich young ruler has in mind. This Greek word is used in some contexts in the sense of "to take hold of something" or "of holding fast to matters of transcendent importance."[57] For example, Paul says one of the requirements for deacons is that they should be *"holding [echō] the mystery of the faith with a clear conscience"* (1 Timothy 3:9). Timothy is instructed by Paul to *"retain [echō] the standard of sound words which you have heard from me"* (2 Timothy 1:13). Then, to the Philippians he writes, *"holding fast [epechō] the word of life, so that in the day of Christ I will have reason to glory because I did not run in vain nor toil in vain"* (Philippians 2:16). The saved *good soil* in the parable of the sower "hold[s] fast" to the word of God. Like the *good soil*, the rich young ruler wants to *"bear fruit with perseverance"* (Luke 8:15). In each instance, the idea is to hold onto a faith already in existence. This is similar to Paul's injunction, *"Fight the good fight of faith; take hold [Gr. epilambanō] of the eternal life to which you were called, and you made the good confession in the presence of many witnesses"* (1 Timothy 6:12).

This view of "have" (Gr. *echō*) explains why in Matthew's gospel the question is "What must I do to *have* eternal life?" whereas in Luke's gospel it is *"What must I do to inherit eternal life?"* Apparently "having" and "inheriting" are closely related. To "have" in English is to suggest a more passive acceptance, but to "take hold of" suggests an

---

30). In some places, the term "life" is found outside of the expression "inherit eternal life" and the discussion with the rich young ruler (see Matthew 7:14; 18:8, 9; 25:46; Mark 9:43, 45; Luke 16:25). Some writers quote these passages without comment as if they prove that "life" means regeneration or "heaven when you die" (e. g. Brown, "The New Testament Concept of the Believer's Inheritance," 67.), but it is questionable that any of these references refer to heaven or regeneration.

56 See Chapter 14 for fuller discussion of this interpretation.

57 *BDAG*, 420.

active choice. Similarly, "to inherit" something according to the New Testament involves the active choices of good works in order to obtain the inheritance as a reward (Colossians 3:24). We suggest, therefore, that Jesus is telling the rich young ruler that he must take hold of eternal life now if he wants to inherit it in the future by means of good works.

The rich young ruler wants to be one who "has eternal life abiding in him" (1 John 3:15). He wants a strong grip on it. In the discussion to follow, Jesus explains that the way the rich young ruler can "hold fast" is to obey the Law, give to the poor, and follow Christ as a disciple. This is the way he can "*have* eternal life."

If Jesus viewed the rich young ruler as an unsaved man, he would certainly have told him that "*whoever believes in him may have eternal life*," and "*[f]or God so loved the world, that he gave his only begotten Son, that whoever believes in him shall not perish, but have eternal life*" (John 3:15-16). One can "have" eternal life without cost by believing in Christ (Revelation 21:6). In these verses, "to have eternal life" comes by faith alone and for no other reason. Yet in his answer to the ruler's questions about how he can have eternal life, Jesus tells him he must obey the Law, deny himself, and follow Christ as a loyal disciple. The simplest explanation of this disparity is that having eternal life is viewed from different perspectives: either (a) initial salvation, or (b) a fuller experience of life by which one matures and becomes complete in his faith (e.g. John 17:3).

Earlier in Luke's gospel, a lawyer asked the same question, "*Teacher, what shall I do to inherit eternal life?*" (Luke 10:25). However, the usual understanding of this passage is that because the lawyer (scribe) was one of Christ's opponents, he must have been an unsaved man. This is sometimes based on Luke's comment that the lawyer was attempting to test Jesus publicly and was also trying to "justify himself" (Luke 10:29).[58] Bock understands the lawyer's question to be about "getting saved."[59]

As he did with the rich young ruler, Jesus directs him to the Law and not to faith in the Son, saying, "*What is written in the Law? How*

58 Hendriksen and Kistemaker, *Exposition of the Gospel According to Matthew*: 591.

59 Bock, *Luke 9:51-24:53*: 1023.

does it read to you?" (Luke 10:26). When the lawyer answers by saying one must love the Lord with all one's heart, soul, strength, and mind, and love his neighbor as himself, Jesus commends him saying, *"You have answered correctly; 'Do this and you will live'"* or, more clearly translated, *"Keep on doing this and you will live"*[60] (Matthew 19:17; Luke 10:28).[61]

However, it is likely that in this text Jesus does not mean "become regenerate" (or "obtain soteriological entrance into heaven," or "engage in a process of salvation leading to final justification"). Jesus is alluding to Leviticus 18:4-5:

> *You are to perform my judgments and keep my statutes, to live in accord with them; I am the Lord your God. So you shall keep my statutes and my judgments, by which a man **may live** if he does them; I am the Lord.* (Leviticus 18:4-5)

Just like the response to the lawyer (Luke 10:25-29), Moses says that obedience to the commandments of God will result in "life." When Moses said, "Do this and **you will live**," was he promising heaven when one dies on the basis of obedience to the Law? No! All interpreters agree that Moses was promising a rich life now in response to faithful adherence to the covenant. The "life" in view refers to a rich quality of life, not regeneration.[62] According to Smick, "The verb *chāyâ* 'to live' involves the ability to have life somewhere on the scale between the fullest enjoyment of all the powers of one's being, with health and prosperity on the one hand and descent into trouble, sickness, and death

---

60 Bock says that the present imperative ποίει (*poiei*, "do") speaks of an abiding love and action. Ibid., 1026.

61 Through Ezekiel, Yahweh proclaimed the same truth, "I gave them my statutes and informed them of my ordinances, by which, if a man observes them, he will live" (Ezekiel 20:11).

62 See Deuteronomy 4:1, 40; 5:29, 33. See also Hebrews 12:9-11 where submission to the Father, or as Jesus puts it, "follow me," results in life abundant. See also Preston M. Sprinkle, "The Use of Genesis 42:18 [Not Leviticus 18:5] in Luke 10:28: Joseph and the Good Samaritan," *Bulletin for Biblical Research* 17, no. 2 (2007).

on the other."[63] Kaiser argues that, in Leviticus 18:5, Moses tells them how to maintain fellowship with God and how to find a rich life now. He says, "The law has never served any purpose for justification; but it has an enormous contribution to make in the area of sanctification and living life to the fullest as God had intended his people to live [in the Old Testament, not today]."[64] Similarly, the Mishnah counsels, "Lots of the Law, lots of life,"[65] referring to the fact that study and application of the Torah leads to a rich life now under the covenant.

But are works of love toward one's God or one's neighbor the conditions for obtaining final entrance into heaven? Of course not! However, there is no problem for *sola fide* when one grants that "eternal life" is both personal salvation via faith alone and also a richer experience of that life that comes by faith plus works. In fact, most Reformed writers acknowledge this duality.[66] That being so, it is much simpler to say that this particular lawyer was a saved man who wants to know how to experience a rich life now and greater status in the coming kingdom.[67]

---

63 Elmer B. Smick, "*chāyā*," in TWOT, 279.

64 Walter Kaiser, "The Law as Guidance for the Promotion of Holiness," in *Five Views on Law and Gospel*, ed. Wayne G. Strickland (Grand Rapids: Zondervan Publishing House, 1996), 397.

65 m. Abot 2.7.

66 E.g., William Hendriksen, *Exposition of the Gospel According to Luke* (Grand Rapids: Baker Book House, 1978). These Reformed writers say, "'Everlasting life,' how beautiful the term, and how superlatively precious the essence indicated by it! It refers to the kind of life that is not only endless in duration but also priceless in quality. It embraces such treasures as 'the love of God shed abroad in our hearts' (Romans 5:5), 'the peace of God that surpasses all understanding' (Philippians 4:7), 'joy inexpressible and full of glory' (1 Peter 1:8), and 'fellowship with God the Father and with his Son' (John 17:3)." Ibid., 591.

67 To argue that this lawyer was unsaved because he wanted to publicly test Jesus and also wanted to justify himself requires us to believe that "true" believers would never want to test the Lord or be self-justifying. This is obviously not true. Furthermore, even though many of these lawyers were usually opponents of Jesus (Luke 11:45-52), some were genuinely saved or at least

According to some, the reason this young man was being excluded from heaven is that he refused to part with his wealth.[68] Surely this explanation cannot be taken seriously. The reason one is excluded from heaven is clearly stated elsewhere to be refusal to believe on the Son (John 3:18). This young man apparently did believe (he calls Jesus "Good Master," falls at his feet, and Jesus "loved him"), and there is no evidence that he did not believe in Christ.

We conclude that if we are to understand the intent of the young man's question by *how Jesus answers it*, it appears that by the phrase, "inherit eternal life," Jesus understands him to be asking about how to live life to the fullest and obtain treasure in heaven (i.e., "inherit eternal life"), not "How can I become regenerate?" or "How can I be sure I will go to heaven?"[69] Furthermore, by his answer, Jesus affirms

---

open to his message (Matthew 8:19, 21; 13:11, 52; Acts 23:9; Titus 3:12). G. H. Twelftree says, "Also, when the scribes are depicted negatively they are always associated with another group, especially with the Pharisees." See G. H. Twelftree, "Scribes," in *Dictionary of Jesus and the Gospels*, ed. Joel B. Green, Scot McKnight, and I. Howard Marshall (Downers Grove, IL: InterVarsity Press, 1992), 734. This lawyer was obviously devout, and gave Jesus the correct answer. Jesus told him he was not "far from the kingdom of God" (Mark 12:34), and that if he did just one thing, as the Scriptures demanded, he would live abundantly.

68 Stanley, *Did Jesus Teach Salvation by Works*: 199.

69 Contra Stanley (ibid., 216) who quotes rabbinical writings, rather than quoting the Old Testament, to prove his thesis that to "enter life" means to go to heaven! However, none of the Rabbinical writings he quotes even uses the phrase "enter life." Instead, they refer to entering life "in the world to come," a decidedly different concept than the Old Testament references to which Jesus refers. However, apart from the fact that these are questionable sources for understanding the gospel references, the Synoptic Gospels never refer to "life in the world to come;" instead they refer to entering into life now, abundant life by being a disciple of Christ. Neither do the pseudepigrapha or the Mishnah ever use the phrase "enter into life." Similarity does not equal equality! Equating "enter life" and "enter life in the world to come" is an excellent illustration of Samuel Sandmel's definition of parallelomania: "Two passages [enter into the world to come" in Pirke Aboth and "enter into life" in the Gospels] may sound the same in splendid isolation from their context, but when seen in context, reflect difference rather than similarity." Samuel Sandmel, "Parallelomania,"

the common Jewish belief that an inheritance is a reward for work done and is not a gift *obtained by faith alone*. This squares precisely with the way the words "inherit" and "inheritance" are used throughout the Scriptures (e.g., Colossians 3:24). It is also what Jesus teaches directly in the concluding summary of the passage (Matthew 19:29; Mark 10:30, and in Matthew 25:34-35).

We suggest, then, that N. T. Wright is absolutely correct when he says that the young man's question about inheriting eternal life has nothing to do with the modern question: "What must I do to go to heaven when I die?"[70] Instead, according to Wright, the ruler wants to know "what must I do to have a share [inheritance] in the age to come."

JBL 81, no. 1 (1962): 3. It is common in the commentaries to find references in the Talmud (400-600 years after the time of Christ) to prove this thesis. For example, b. Berakot 28b mentions "life in the future world" and b. Sotal 7b teaches that one can inherit "in the world to come" (see Hebrews 2:5). These late references prove nothing about the meaning of "eternal life" in AD 30. In fact, one can find in the pseudepigrapha a distinction between rich life in this world and life in the world to come. For example, Pirke Aboth (Sayings of the Fathers) 6:7 says, "Great is Torah, for it gives to them that practice it **life in this world** and **in the world to come**; as it is said: 'For they are life to them that find them, and health to all their flesh." And "fairer is **one hour of repentance and good works in this world** than all the life of the world to come; and fairer is one hour of calmness of spirit in the world to come than all the life of this world." Entering into life and entering into life in the world to come are not necessarily the same thing. Frankly, these references are probably irrelevant, but so are those quoted to substantiate the point that entering life means the same as entering life in the world to come in rabbinic literature and then applying this to the incident of the rich young ruler. One can prove almost anything he wants by citing Talmudic sources dated 600 years after the time of Christ. The Mishnah would be a better source, but even here the Judaism of post–AD 70 was completely reconstructed at Jabneh. This discontinuity should caution us against the rush to all things rabbinic! The life in this world is a rich life now, and life in the world to come is soteriological entrance into the kingdom. See James H. Charlesworth, ed. *The Old Testament Pseudepigrapha*, 1st ed. (Garden City, NY: Doubleday, 1983), 2:711.

70 N. T. Wright, *Jesus and the Victory of God* (Minneapolis: Fortress Press, 1996), 301. By sharing in the age to come, Wright means membership in the sense of having a possession there.

If You Want to Be Perfect

The second key phrase which has a significant bearing on one's understanding of Christ's encounter with the young ruler is his response, "*if you wish to be complete,*" or "*if you want to be perfect*" (Matthew 19:21 NIV).

According to Matthew, the rich young ruler asked, "*What must I do to obtain eternal life?*" In his reply, Jesus understood him to be asking how to become "*perfect* [Gr. *teleios*]" (Matthew 19:21). Apparently, Jesus understands the young man's question differently from the way in which modern interpreters understand it. Jesus understands him to be asking about how he can be complete, not how to enter heaven when he dies.

We must then ask, "What does it mean to be perfect?" The Greek *teleios* does not necessarily imply absolute perfection, that is, the kind of perfection needed to enter heaven when one dies, the perfect righteousness of Christ. More often it refers "to being mature, *full-grown, mature, adult.*"[71] In secular Greek, it could refer to perfection in the various stages of learning, that is, beginner, advanced, and mature.[72] The NASB nicely captures the sense by translating, "If you wish to be complete." In the New Testament it refers to one who is mature in his walk with God, not absolutely perfect in it.

The immediate impression one receives from the account of the young man's running, kneeling, and calling Jesus "Good Rabbi," is of an enthusiastic, and perhaps, immature youth[73] who has believed on Christ and now wants to know what the next step is. Jesus explains to him how he can be complete, undivided, or fully mature, and, if he is, then he can obtain (or inherit) eternal life. He tells him what is necessary to "follow him," not to become a Christian but to become a

---

71 *BDAG*, 995, option 2. See Ephesians 4:13; Hebrews 5:14; 2 Corinthians 2:6

72 Gerhard Delling, "*teleios,*" in TDNT, 8:67.

73 *Neaniskos* refers to a young man beyond the age of puberty, but normally before marriage, (Louw-Nida, 1:107). Paul often used the term in the sense of maturity. He desired to present every man "complete" (or mature) in Christ (Colossians 1:28). He contrasts *teleios* (mature) with its opposite *nēpios* (child) in Ephesians 4:13-14. Matthew tells us that this ruler was a "young man."

follower, that is, a fully committed disciple. By his answer, this seems to be how Jesus understands the young man's question. If that is so, the encounter is not about how to obtain personal salvation but how to be a complete, fully committed disciple. Why not understand the question the way Jesus did?

If becoming perfect is a condition for obtaining eternal life after this life, or entering the kingdom, or being "saved," then the requirement of selling everything and giving to the poor is perplexing. Beginning with this false assumption, most interpreters have concluded that "obviously he could not have meant that by literally and outwardly obeying this injunction, the young man would obtain a claim upon the kingdom of heaven."[74] Why is this "obvious"? The most "obvious" interpretation is that this is precisely what Jesus meant! However, "obtaining a claim upon the kingdom of heaven" does not mean "enter into personal salvation." Rather, it refers to greatness in heaven in one's status and reward.

The passage presents the concept of two categories of Christians, those who are "complete" and those who are not. The rich young ruler wants to know how he can be among the former. Unfortunately, he views the price as too high.[75]

That perfection here is to be understood as a higher level of discipleship is suggested by two factors. First, the parallel with obtaining eternal life and entering into life, as argued above, suggests that an enhanced quality of life is sought, not initial (or final) justification. Second, if one becomes complete, his reward is "treasure in heaven,"[76] which is in addition to initial salvation. It refers to the believer's reward there. It is not "heaven," it is a treasure **in** heaven. Treasure in heaven is the same as our inheritance and to obtain it is the same as to

---

74 John Peter Lange, "The Gospel of Matthew," in *Commentary on the Holy Scriptures, Critial, Doctrinal, and Hommelitical,* ed. John Peter Lange (Grand Rapids: Zondervan Publishing House, 1960), 345.

75 This is similar to some lukewarm Christians (Revelation 3:15-16) throughout history who are carnal (1 Corinthians 3:3) and are "least" **in** the kingdom of heaven (Matthew 5:19).

76 Luke 22:18

"inherit eternal life" as a reward (Matthew 19:21; Mark 10:21; 25:34-35; Colossians 3:24).

Entering the Kingdom of Heaven

It is certainly true that inheriting eternal life is synonymous in this dialog with entering into the kingdom of God, as William Brown says.[77] But entering into the kingdom of God, as discussed elsewhere, does not mean entering the future millennial kingdom in a soteriological sense. Rather, it refers to entering into a kingdom way of living now leading to future greatness, sharing in the authority to rule in that kingdom by means of living out the Sermon on the Mount now.[78] There is no place in Matthew's Gospel where the "entry sayings" unambiguously refer to initial salvation.[79] It is often simply assumed.[80]

It is also argued that the metaphor of a camel going through the eye of a needle must refer to the impossibility of entering into initial salvation. Since becoming a believer in the first place is impossible unless God works a miracle in one's heart, entrance into the kingdom of heaven must, according to this interpretation, refer to regeneration. This presses the metaphor too far. The fact that it is impossible does not mean that getting into the kingdom is totally a work of God. It means that getting in is impossible without God's help. Furthermore,

---

77 Brown, "The New Testament Concept of the Believer's Inheritance," 68.

78 See the chapter 14 in this book entitled "I Never Knew You. Also, Dillow, *Final Destiny*: 274 ff.

79 In Matthew's Gospel, there are 8 "entry sayings," including the two references to "entering into life" (Matthew 5:20; 7:13, 21; 18:3 [in verses 3 and 9, it is equated with entering into life]; 19:17, 23, 24; 23:13).

80 Matthew 7:21, of course, makes it clear that only those who do the will of the Father, that is, live out the Sermon on the Mount, will enter the kingdom of heaven in that day. However, "enter the kingdom" in Matthew 5:19-20 refers to entering into greatness in the kingdom by living out the Sermon on the Mount. The assumption is made that these false prophets must be non-Christians because they "practice lawlessness." Yet, earlier Jesus says that some who practice lawlessness are "in" the kingdom though they will be "least" there (Matthew 5:19).

the saying about the camel through the eye of the needle is hyperbole; it *is a joke*. The surrounding crowds would have burst out laughing. Therefore, this is not a statement on which to build a doctrine of salvation. We might say today, "For it is easier for Congress to balance the budget than for a lukewarm Christian to become a fully committed disciple." While it seems humanly impossible for Congress to balance the budget, we would all agree that with divine assistance, this could happen! It is far more likely that Matthew has in view Jesus's teaching in which he said, "*Apart from me you can do nothing*" (John 15:5). The impossibility in view is not that of becoming a Christian by faith, but of persevering as a disciple and entering into greatness in the kingdom without Christ's help.

Who Then Can Be Saved?

Hearing that it is difficult for rich men to "enter the kingdom of God" (Matthew 19:23), the astonished disciples ask, "*Who then can be saved?*" (Matthew 19:25). While it is correct to say, "The Twelve give unmistakable evidence that they understand entering the kingdom and salvation to be one and the same thing,"[81] one must ask, "Salvation from what?" It is doubtful that Matthew ever uses this word for salvation meaning eternal separation from God or of a process leading to heaven. Rather, in his Gospel salvation refers to deliverance from some danger,[82] from disease (i.e., being healed),[83] from persecution,[84] or from physical death.[85]

---

81 Stanley, *Did Jesus Teach Salvation by Works*: 210.

82 Matthew 8:25; 14:30

83 Matthew 9:22

84 Matthew 10:22; 24:13

85 Matthew 16:25; 24:22; 27:40, 42. There is one possible exception, "And she will bear a Son; and you shall call his name Jesus, for it is he who will save his people from their sins" (Matthew 1:21). However, even here it probably does not refer to salvation from damnation, but, as many have argued, the salvation in view is a national salvation, a return from the exilic judgment, restoration of the nation, a salvation from the consequences of their national sins. See Craig S. Keener, *The IVP Background Commentary* (Downers Grove, IL:

The closest parallel to the salvation to which the astonished disciples allude (Matthew 19:25) is Matthew 16:24-26 where Jesus told them that being saved is related to finding "life," or saving one's soul. As we have shown elsewhere in chapter 6 above, to save one's soul means to find a rich life now by self-denial, taking up one's cross, and following Christ, so that the believer is favorably recompensed at the Judgment Seat of Christ.[86]

The rich young fool (Luke 12:19-23) stored up his goods so that his *psychē* ("life") could rest and be joyous.[87] The paradox is that he must give up that selfish desire and approach to a rich life now if he desires future-kingdom status. Instead, he must lose his life if he wants to be "saved." To "save the soul" in this sense is to secure for it eternal pleasures by living a life of sacrifice now. We are apparently, according to Jesus, developing an inner character that will be preserved (saved) into eternity. There is a connection between our life of sacrifice and our capability to enjoy and experience eternal fellowship with God.

Keeping this in mind clarifies the disciple's question to Jesus in Matthew 19:25, "*Who then can be saved?*" It may refer to an eschatological salvation,[88] but if it does, it would not refer to entrance into heaven, but salvation in the sense of a reward for a life well lived. The condition for saving one's soul in Matthew 16:24 and the condition for becoming complete, finding treasure in heaven, and getting hold on eternal life, etc. are the same, self-denial. Also, both involve something one must "do." This fact should lead us to understand "save" in the sense of fulfilling one's destiny, not getting into heaven or escaping hell. This is a work passage; faith alone for salvation is never mentioned. In any case, the proximity of Matthew 16:24ff. and the use of "save" in Matthew argue against understanding "being saved" as deliverance

---

InterVarsity Press, 1993), 48. While this conclusion is not shared by all, even if it should be applied to individual salvation, it is certainly not Matthew's general usage (e.g., Hagner, *Matthew 14-28*: 19.).

86 Dillow, *Final Destiny*: chapter 15.

87 For other passages where a similar thought is expressed, see Matthew 6:25; 12:18; 26:38; Mark 12:34; Hebrews 10:38.

88 Hagner, *Matthew 14-28*: 561.

from post-mortem condemnation to the lake of fire. The disciples are asking about how to find a rich life now and a high position in the age to come.

This interpretation fits very well with *"Behold, we have left everything and followed you; what then will there be for us?"* (Matthew 19:27). He is not asking, "How do we obtain heaven?" Rather, he wants to know what reward they will receive for following him. Jesus responds with an affirming answer, an answer that has nothing to do with salvation from eternal separation from God but everything to do with the subject under discussion in the preceding context, namely, rewards. He tells them they will sit on twelve thrones judging the twelve tribes of Israel, that they will benefit in this life, and that in eternity they will inherit eternal life (obtain a reward, Matthew 19:28-29). In fact, in regard to their ranking within the kingdom, they will be first, in contrast to the rich young ruler, who will be last.

Treasure in Heaven

That the subject of the rich young ruler's question and the Lord's response is rewards to the believer and not final deliverance from eternal separation from God is further established by the fact that what is promised as a result of obeying the commandments is not heaven, but "treasure in heaven" (Matthew 19:21; Mark 10:21).

Some have understood this to mean the treasure "which is" heaven.[89] This is argued from the near context where "eternal life," "saved," and "enter the kingdom" are understood to refer to final salvation. However, this argument is circular. Rather than allow the earned reward, "treasure in heaven," to define the meaning of "inherit eternal life," they argue that "inherit eternal life" must define "treasure in heaven".[90] Elsewhere the treasure to be received is granted to those who obey his call to leave everything (Luke 18:29–30). It is a treasure

---

89 Alfred Plummer, *A Critical and Exegetical Commentary on the Gospel according to St. Luke*, 5th. ed. (Edinburgh: T. & T. Clark, 1922), 424.

90 According to Luke's understanding of rewards, it is more likely that the treasure is something in addition to heaven. See Luke 6:35; 12:33-34 (see also Matthew 6:19-20); 14:14; 16:10–11; 19:11–27.

that Jesus commands believers (not nonbelievers) to lay up "in" heaven (Matthew 6:20-21; see 1 Timothy 6:19; James 5:3). This fact of Lukan usage should have pointed the commentators toward interpreting phrases like "enter the kingdom," and "saved" in terms of "treasure" rather than regeneration or final entrance into heaven.[91]

The notion that "treasure in heaven consists of deeds of love now"[92] must be rejected. How then is it possible that "no thief comes near and no moth destroys" them (Luke 12:33). The treasures are manifestly laid up in heaven as a result of deeds of charity done now.[93] Jesus understands the man to be asking about earned reward in heaven, not initial entrance into eternal life.

Come Follow Me

Jesus's final command to the rich young ruler after he had sold all he had and given the cash to the poor was: "Come, follow me" (Matthew 19:21). We therefore disagree with Stanley when he says that Jesus is not placing an additional demand of discipleship beyond the faith requirement for salvation; that is precisely what Jesus is doing. Entering into discipleship is not synonymous with eternal life in the sense of "heaven when one dies."[94] Rather, discipleship is the condition

---

91 Curiously, Bock fails to do this. He grants that "treasure" is a reward in addition to salvation and that it parallels the terms "eternal life," "enter the kingdom," and "saved," but he does not take the obvious step of defining these parallel terms as something in addition to initial justification. He connects this treasure with rewards at the Judgment Seat of Christ, not final salvation. Darrell L. Bock, *Luke 1-9:50*, Baker Exegetical Commentary on the New Testament (Grand Rapids: Baker Book House, 1996), 481.

92 Stanley, *Did Jesus Teach Salvation by Works*: 143. Stanley then appeals to Matthew 13:44 where the kingdom of heaven is likened to a treasure in a field. However, the kingdom is compared to a treasure, and therefore a treasure in the kingdom cannot be the kingdom itself.

93 In Judaism, "the interest on this may accrue to man in this life in the form of happy results, the capital will be kept in heaven to the Day of Judgment, and then it will be paid back." Friedrick Hauk, "*thesauras*," in TDNT, 3:137.

94 Contra Stanley, *Did Jesus Teach Salvation by Works*: 144.

for entering eternal life in the sense of an enhanced experience of life, a rich life with God.

Summary

The rich young ruler was a regenerate man who had been impressed with the message of free grace in Christ and had believed on him for eternal life. He now wants to know, "What is next?" He wants to have as high a place in heaven and as rich an experience of life as possible, and so he needs to know the terms. Consistent with the broader context, the issue under discussion is taking a lower status now if one wants to be exalted (receive authority) in the kingdom. Some will receive five cities; some will receive ten.

Jesus issues a stirring call to discipleship, "Sell everything and follow me," and you will have rewards in heaven. He makes the concluding point that the issue for this young man was not initial entrance but status in the kingdom. *"But many who are first will be last; and the last, first"* (Matthew 19:30). The question for this young ruler was how to be "complete," that is, how to finish what he started.

Chapter 14

I Never Knew You – Matthew 7

Joseph Dillow, Th.D.

Several years ago, the following incident was broadcast on a Christian radio station. Apparently, the guest, a medical doctor, had made the "trip," that is, he ascended to the third heaven and returned. He reported that when he arrived, he was particularly moved by one particular revelation. He explained, "The human brain has twelve cranial nerves, and each of them is involved in specific functions of the brain. One nerve, the twelfth, is responsible for our sense of smell."

"When I was in the third heaven," he resumed, "I learned the purpose of God's twelfth cranial nerve. It enables him to smell the sweet savor sacrifices specified in the book of Leviticus."

John MacArthur reported an account of another "prophet" who, while meditating by a lakeside, suddenly saw a picture of Jesus materialize in the water. He immediately photographed it, and in a brochure announced that, for $19.95, he would send the picture to anyone who asked.

Another well-known "prophet" saw a vision of a 500-foot-tall Jesus who gave him a revelation that unless he received one million dollars in contributions to his ministry by December 31, 1987, he would die. Bumper stickers proliferated saying, "Send [name] to heaven in 87, don't give him a dime." The evangelist did receive the one million dollars on time!

On a television program last night, I watched a TV evangelist offer "miracle water" which he would send in a small plastic bag. It was guaranteed to result in a miracle in your life. All you had to do was to provide your email and your address. On a different channel, another evangelist told his viewers he believed that, if they gave $1,000 in seed money to his ministry, all of their children and grandchildren would come to the Lord.

Dr. Jones and these other would-be prophets may be believers in Christ. Perhaps they did have some unusual spiritual experiences which were very real to them, and, no doubt, some may be very sincere and honest. However, when they, in collusion with the modern TV media, promulgate this kind of silliness, they denigrate biblical Christianity and make a mockery out of the Christian faith in the minds of millions of nonbelievers.

As we will see in this chapter, these kinds of "prophets" were common in New Testament times as well.

The False Prophets from Outside the Church

Toward the end of the Sermon on the Mount, Jesus issues a warning to his disciples that they must enter through a narrow gate onto the narrow way (Matthew 7:13-14) and that only those who "do the will of the Father" will enter the kingdom of heaven (Matthew 7:21-23).

However, there is a danger. The text says that there are two kinds of prophets who can threaten the disciples' intention to pursue the narrow way: false prophets from without (vv. 15-20) and deluded miracle workers from within (vv. 21-23). When this happens, the kingdom program "suffers violence" (Matthew 11:12), and many who have already entered the kingdom in a soteriological sense are hindered from entering into discipleship.

That Jesus intends us to understand that he had two different groups in mind is suggested by a structural feature which Matthew employs. The false prophets of 7:15-20 are set off from what follows by an *inclusio*: *"you will know them by their fruits"* (v. 16), and, again *"you will know them by their fruits"* (v. 20). This feature distinguishes the false prophets from the group to follow in verses 21-23.[1] The false prophets of verses 15-20 are described as *"coming to you,"* which probably means they come from outside the church.[2]

That these false prophets appear in sheep's clothing suggests that they outwardly appear to be Christian, but they are not. The fact that they are described as wolves in sheep's clothing tells at least two things: (1) they act like sheep, that is, they have good works; (2) they are really imposters, that is, wolves. These wolves are evidently unsaved heretics who come into the community of disciples from without.

---

1   Betz and Collins note, "One should keep the two sections as separate and not treat them as one." Hans Dieter Betz and Adela Yarbro Collins, *The Sermon on the Mount: A Commentary on the Sermon on the Mount, Including the Sermon on the Plain (Matthew 5:3-7:27 and Luke 6:20-49)*, Hermeneia (Minneapolis: Fortress Press, 1995), 539. James E. Davison, citing Betz, agrees, "There are two questions that we must face here. First, is it in fact correct to identify the false prophets in v. 15 with the evildoers in v. 23? Do the pericopes in vv. 15–20 and vv. 21–23 really speak of the same group of people?" Hill and Betz have recently argued strongly that the two do not, and I am inclined to agree with them. . . . Further, the saying in verse 20, 'You will know them by their fruits,' repeats v. 16 and serves to summarize the comparison of the false prophets to bad trees (verses 16–19). The following verses (21–23), which discuss the charismatics, are only loosely joined to the preceding group. The point of association is not the identity of the groups themselves, but the element that is common to both of them: the production of bad fruits." James E. Davison, "Anomia and the Question of an Antinomian Polemic in Matthew," *JBL* 104, no. 4 (Dec. 1985): 628. Hagner also has pointed out that this is a chiastic structure, further demarcating the false prophets of verses 15-20 from the charismatics of verses 21-23. See Donald A. Hagner, *Matthew 14-28*, Word Biblical Commentary (Dallas: Word Books, 2002), 182; "Westminster Confession of Faith," in *The Creeds of Christendo*, ed. Philip Schaff (Grand Rapids, MI: Baker Book House).

2   That this group is distinguished from the first is held by several commentators. Alan P. Stanley, *Did Jesus Teach Salvation by Works? The Role of Works in Salvation in the Synoptic Gospels* (Eugene, OR: Pickwick Publishers, 2006), 176; David Hill, "False Prophets and Charismatics: Structure and Interpretation in Matthew 7:15-23," *Biblia* 57(1976): 327-48.

The way one discerns a false prophet is by examining his fruit. Otherwise, detection is difficult. But what is this "fruit?" While Dr. Grudem and many Reformed interpreters understand this fruit to be behavior,[3] elsewhere Matthew connects the fruit with their words, that is, their teaching. Indeed, their behavior was like that of sheep, it appeared good; so, the more reliable way to discern whether they were false was by what they taught. Later Jesus said that "the tree is known by its fruit" (Matthew 12:33), referring to their words. To discern a prophet's true inner nature, one must attend to his words. He explains, *"For the mouth speaks out of that which fills the heart . . . for by your words you will be justified, and by your words you will be condemned"* (Matthew 12:34, 37). The test of "fruit" is applied to those who claim to be prophets in Matthew 7:16.

Free Grace interpreters can agree with Dr. Grudem's suggestion that the presence or absence of fruit is the necessary evidence of their saved status.[4] We disagree, with his definition of fruit. Behavior is not the most important criteria, instead, it is what they teach. This criterion has a long history. Isaiah said, *"To the teaching and to the testimony! If they will not speak according to this word, it is because they have no dawn"* (Isaiah 8:20; see also Deuteronomy 18:21-23, ESV).[5]

The Charismatic Prophets from Inside the Church

Starting in verse 21 the scene changes. Now Jesus discusses those who are inside the Christian community who have confessed Jesus as Lord. However, the fact that they are not admitted to the kingdom of heaven and that Jesus calls them "evildoers," saying "I never knew you," and demands that they depart from him, has understandably led Dr.

---

3   Wayne A. Grudem, *"Free Grace" Theology: 5 Ways It Diminishes the Gospel* (Wheaton: Crossway, 2016), 89.

4   Wayne A. Grudem, *Systematic Theology: An Introduction to Biblical Doctrine* (Grand Rapids, MI: Inter-Varsity Press, 2004), 640, 705, 96, etc.; Grudem, *"Free Grace" Theology*: 89.

5   R. T. France, *The Gospel of Matthew*, New International Critical Commentary (Grand Rapids: Wm. B. Eerdmans Publishing Co., 2007), 291.

Grudem and many others to understand that they had only professed faith in Christ but, in fact, were not justified.[6]

Jesus solemnly warns them in Matthew 7:21-23:

> Not everyone who says to me, "Lord, Lord," **will enter the kingdom of heaven**, but he **who does the will of my Father** who is in heaven will enter. Many will say to me on that day, "Lord, Lord, did we not prophesy in your name, and in your name cast out demons, and in your name perform many miracles?" And then I will declare to them, "I never knew you; depart from me, you who practice lawlessness."

There are three questions about our Lord's teaching in the passage which must be considered.

- What is the "will of the Father"?
- What does it mean to "enter the kingdom"?
- What is the status of the prophets: saved or unsaved?

The Will of the Father

> Not everyone who says to me, "Lord, Lord," will **enter the kingdom** of heaven, but he who does the **will of my Father** who is in heaven will enter." (Matthew 7:21)

But what does it mean to "do the will of the Father?" Some plausibly believe this refers to believing on Christ for salvation (John 6:39-40).[7]

---

6   Grudem, *Systematic Theology*: 795. Craig L. Blomberg, *Matthew*, New American Commentary (Nashville: Broadman and Holman Publishers, 2001), p 132 A typical statement of this view is that a genuinely saved person is one who "does the will of my Father." The Greek present tense supposedly means that he is continually living in obedience to the will of God as the normal course of his life. He may fail at times, but his general course of consistency is to obey the will of the Father.

7   See Hal M. Haller, "Matthew," in *The Grace New Testament Commentary*, ed. Robert N. Wilkin (Denton, TX: Grace Evangelical Society, 2010), 36. Often,

However, it seems more likely that in the context of the Sermon on the Mount, this refers to ethical behavior consistent with the Sermon,[8] that is, the kingdom way of living. Jesus refers to what he has been talking about in the preceding two chapters, the ethical lifestyle of a disciple. The main intent of the Sermon on the Mount is to define for Christ's disciples what the will of the Father is and to challenge them to live

---

John 6:39-40 is cited to prove that the "will of my Father" is to believe on Christ. "*For this is the will of My Father, that everyone who beholds the Son and believes in him will have eternal life, and I myself will raise him up on the last day* (John 6:40). It is certainly God's will that everyone who believes on Christ will have eternal life. But is this the "will of the Father" of Matthew 7:21? It does not always mean that, even in the Gospel of John. Robert N. Wilkin, "Is Justification by Faith Alone," *JOGES* 9, no. 2 (Autumn 1996): 9. See also, René A. López, "The Pauline Vice List and Inheriting the Kingdom" (PhD diss., Dallas Theological Seminary, 2010), 132. John W. Robbins, "Justification and Judgment," *JOGES* 15, no. 1 (Spring 2002): 68. Robbins says, "Their defense should be the imputed righteousness of Christ, not their works. Many will be sent to hell because they will not mention that they are sinners saved only by the righteousness of the Man Christ Jesus." Similarly, Wilkin argues, "Jesus's point here is that no one can expect kingdom entrance on the basis of his or her works, or deeds. Far from contradicting justification by faith alone, he is proving it." Davison, "Anomia and the Question of an Antinomian Polemic in Matthew," 9.

8   Those who cite John 6:39-40 as proof that the will of God in Matthew 7:21 refers to faith in Christ ignore the fact that they could have selected John 5:30 where Jesus defines the "will of God" as good works done in obedience. He says, "*I can do nothing on my own initiative. As I hear, I judge; and my judgment is just, because I do not seek my own will, but the will of him who sent me*" (John 5:30). What about John 4:34 where Jesus says, "*My food is to do the will of him who sent me and accomplish his work*"? The will of God in that passage is not belief on Christ for salvation, it is good works done in obedience! Consider John 7:17 where Jesus says, "*If anyone is willing to do his will, he will know of the teaching, whether it is of God or whether I speak from myself.*" Doing "his will," in this context, refers to obedience to Christ's teaching. For full discussion of the view that entering the kingdom refers to entering into a kingdom way of life leading to greatness in this passage, see Joseph C. Dillow, *Final Destiny: The Future Reign of the Servant Kings*, 3rd revised ed. (Monument, CO: Paniym Group, Inc., 2016; reprint, 2016), Chaptesr 18-20.

it.[9] Therefore, this context is determinative in defining the meaning of "the will of God," instead of one reference in John.

What Does It Mean to "Enter the Kingdom?"

There are 21 so-called "entry sayings" in the New Testament.[10]

The condition for entering the kingdom—entering into life, seeking life, and seeking the kingdom—in most cases is good works. For example, the conditions for entering the kingdom are:

- Developing greater ethical righteousness than that of the scribes and Pharisees (Matthew 5:20).

- Entering through the narrow gate and proceeding on the narrow way, the way of discipleship and kingdom way of life (Matthew 7:13-14).

- Doing the will of the Father (Matthew 7:21).

- Being converted from wanting to be the greatest to adopting the lowest status, that of a child (Matthew 18:3-4; Mark 10:15; Luke 18:17).

- Selling all you have and giving it to the poor (Matthew 19:23-24; Luke 18:25-25).

- Radical discipleship signified by the metaphor of plucking out one eye (Mark 9:47).

- Being born again (John 3:3).

- Going through many tribulations (Acts 14:22).

---

9 Therefore, Nolland is surely correct in stating that the "surpassing righteousness" of Matthew 5:20 is equivalent of "doing the will of the Father" in 7:21. John Nolland, *The Gospel of Matthew: A Commentary on the Greek Text* (Grand Rapids: Wm. B. Eerdmans Publishing Co., 2005), 339.

10 The term "entry sayings" refers to these phrases: (1) "enter the kingdom of heaven" (Matthew 5:20; 7:21; 18:3; 19:23, 24; 23:13; Mark 9:47; 10:15, 25; Luke 18:17, 24, 25; John 3:5; Acts 14:22); (2) "entering into life" (Matthew 18:8, 9; 19:17; Mark 9:43); (3) "seeking life" (Luke 17:33; Romans 2:7); and (4) "seeking the kingdom" (Matthew 6:33; 13:45; Luke 12:31). These seem to be parallel and explain each other.

Apart from the single instance where Jesus says that entering the kingdom is based on faith (John 3:16) and one must be born again to enter (John 3:23), all the rest say that the condition for entrance is some good work or character quality.

Dr. Grudem plausibly believes that the prophets of Matthew 7:21-23 are professing Christians who are unsaved. He notes that Jesus does not say, "I knew you at one time but I no longer know you," nor "I knew you at one time but you strayed away from me," but rather, "I *never* knew you." They never were genuine believers.[11]

However, if they are non-Christians, then it would appear that Christ is teaching these unsaved people that salvation is based on performing the good works listed above, a view embraced by some commentators.[12] Would Christ mislead his hearers by telling them that they can work their way to heaven?

Of course, I am aware of the Reformed answer to this problem. Like Dr. Grudem, they insist that like the rest of the passages cited above, Matthew 7:71-23 is not giving conditions of entrance but are describing the characteristics of all who will enter; most importantly, that they continue in the faith to the end of life. For example, Don Carson explains,

> It is true, of course, that no man enters the kingdom because of his obedience; but it is equally true that no man enters the kingdom who is not obedient. It is true that men are saved by God's grace through faith in Christ; but it is equally true that God's grace in a man's life inevitably results in obedience. Any other view of grace cheapens grace, and turns it into something unrecognizable.[13]

---

11 Grudem, *Systematic Theology*: 795.

12 Some interpreters argue that Matthew here is in disagreement with the conclusion that salvation is by "faith alone." E.g., Luz and Koester, *Matthew 1-7: A Commentary*: 379 and n50.

13 D. A. Carson, *Jesus' Sermon on the Mount and His Confrontation with the World* (Grand Rapids: Baker Book House, 1987), 139.

Really?! What about Solomon, Saul, and a myriad other biblical examples of true believers who did not obey and persisted in their disobedience to the end of life?[14] And of course, what about the persons in Matthew 5:19? These were "in" the kingdom, that is, "saved," in Carson's terms, and yet they lived lives of lawlessness.

To come to this conclusion in Matthew 7:21-23, Dr. Grudem and Dr. Carson must import their theological system into the text with no evident contextual justification. In other words, like other Reformed scholars, they believe that is the intended meaning because their system requires it. How do they know this?

Their system is partially based on their specific misunderstanding of Matthew 24:23, "those who continue to the end will be saved," and "faith without works is dead" (James 2:14). As argued elsewhere in this book,[15] those passages have nothing to do with the Reformed insistence that works must be present to the end of life to verify the presence of genuine saving faith. But even if this was true, it is irrelevant to the entry sayings because there is no hint of this theology in any of them. The sayings are clear; works ARE necessary to enter the kingdom of heaven! They are not just an evidence of salvation; they are the condition of final entrance.

Furthermore, we have already shown that the Bible contains many examples of saved people who have not done good works to the end of life and yet will go to heaven when they die (e.g. Solomon). Therefore, entering the kingdom and going to heaven *cannot* be the same thing as is often assumed!

If these calls to enter the kingdom refer to entering into personal salvation, as Dr. Grudem believes, why is there no mention in any of these passages (except John 3:3) of the cross, Christ's death for sin, or the way of salvation by faith alone. Instead, according to Jesus, the condition for entering the kingdom is not faith alone and "without cost" (Revelation 21:6), but by good works, and it will cost one everything.

In my opinion, Dr. Grudem goes astray in his misunderstanding of the phrase "enter the kingdom." In all these works passages it does not

---

14 For extensive proof of this see chapter 10 in this book regarding Illustrations of the Carnal Christian.

15 See chapter 6.

(could not!) refer to entrance into heaven. Instead it refers to entrance onto the path of discipleship, the narrow gate and the narrow way, leading to greatness in the kingdom, as the immediately preceding context requires (Matthew 5:19-20; 7:13-14). The kingdom is not just the sphere of personal salvation; it is also a way of life described in the Sermon on the Mount.

Let us consider a few of these sayings by way of illustration of this point.

Disobedient to the least of the commandments. In Matthew 5:19-20 we read, that those who are disobedient to the least of the commandments and who teach others to do the same (like the charismatic prophets in Matthew 7:22), will be least **in** the kingdom, that is saved people. Then the Lord says, "but whoever keeps and teaches *them,* he shall be called great in the kingdom of heaven." Clearly, the issue is *status* in the kingdom and not being saved. Of course, this question was frequently on the disciples' minds.[16]

Well then, how does one become great? Jesus answers,

> *For I say to you that unless your righteousness surpasses that of the scribes and Pharisees, you will not enter the kingdom of heaven.* (Matthew 5:20, NASB95)

We know that this answer is directed at his saved disciples (Matthew 5:1-2), because Jesus emphasizes that application by saying, "For I say to **you.**" The way one becomes "great" in the kingdom is by pursuing the surpassing righteousness.

The problem, of course, is that if "enter the kingdom" refers to the sphere of salvation, and if the "will of the Father" is ethical behavior,[17]

---

16 Matthew 18:1; 23:11; Mark 9:34; Luke 9:46; 22:24-26.

17 The phrase *"will of the Father"* is used four times in Matthew (Matt. 7:21; 12:50; 18:14; 21:31) and three times in the Gospel of John (John 4:34; 5:30; 6:40). The concept of God's will is variously expressed as "your will" (Matt. 6:10; 26:42; Luke 22:42); "the will of him" (John 4:34), "his Master's will" (Luke 12:47), "his will" (John 7:17; 9:31); thus, it is found in many places in the Gospels. In no instance does it refer to belief for salvation but in each instance, it speaks of doing works of obedience. In fact, in the Lord's prayer,

Jesus would appear to be teaching salvation by works.[18] What then does it mean to "enter the kingdom"?

If entering the kingdom means entrance into personal salvation, two difficulties emerge with these two verses. First, this would mean the salvation is secured by pursuing ethical behavior (surpassing righteousness). But secondly, it places vv. 19 and 20 in contradiction to each other.

Whoever then annuls one of the least of these commandments, and teaches others to do the same, shall be called least in the kingdom of heaven; but whoever keeps and teaches them, he shall be called great in the kingdom of heaven. (Matthew 5:19, NASB95)

So, in v. 20 Jesus says that one must possess a greater righteousness (ethical standard) in order to enter the kingdom, but in v. 19 he says that those who do not have that standard are, nevertheless in the kingdom, that is, saved! This difficulty is easily removed if one is willing to abandon the idea that entering the kingdom always means entrance into salvation, the millennium or the eternal state (depending on one's eschatology). I propose that entering the kingdom in the entry sayings does not mean enter into personal salvation; instead, it means to enter through the narrow gate and proceed along the narrow way (Matthew 7:13-14), the path of discipleship, and by doing the "will of the Father" (7:21), which will lead to high status (greatness) in the kingdom.

The way one enters heaven is by faith alone apart from works (Titus 3:5; Romans 4:1-4) and without cost (Revelation 20:6), but the way one

---

Jesus instructs his followers to pray, *"your will be done,"* that is, your standards of personal righteousness be fully implemented and displayed on the earth. Surely this defines the "will of the Father" in Matthew 7:21.

18 Luz, knowing that the "will" is ethical obedience to the Sermon on the Mount, frankly admits that "doing the will of my Father is a condition of salvation." And because in his view kingdom entrance (final salvation) is based in part at least on human effort, there can "be no certainty that one will enter the kingdom of heaven. Luz and Koester, *Matthew 1-7: A Commentary*: 319. He asserts that Matthew "does polemicize sharply against the thesis that entering the kingdom of heaven is 'simply a matter of faith rather than along with faith also a matter of "doing."' Ibid., 379.

enters the kingdom of heaven is by achieving a higher level of ethical righteousness than the Scribes and Pharisees. Enter the kingdom in this passage is the answer to the question, "How can I be great in the kingdom." The answer to this question is that one must possess a "surpassing righteousness" and enter the path of discipleship, the kingdom way of living to become great.

While some have argued that this "surpassing righteousness" is the imputed righteousness of Christ, it is unlikely that Jesus is bringing Pauline theology into the context with no prior explanation. In this view, the Sermon is designed to convince men who are seeking salvation by works that they are wretched and cannot possibly live up to the perfect righteousness necessary to obtain salvation by works. In Dwight Pentecost's words, "The Lord seeks to convict the multitude of their need of Messiah by setting forth the true interpretation of what constitutes righteousness. In Matthew 5:21-7:6 the Lord's ministry is one of conviction."[19] However, the intended addressees of the Sermon are not the crowds, it is the Lord's disciples (Matthew 5:1-2). "He spoke to **them,** saying . . . "

The problem with this approach is that "righteousness" in Matthew always refers to "ethical righteousness" and not to imputed righteousness. Matthew 5:20 begins with, "For I tell you." In customary rabbinic fashion, which Jesus followed throughout the Gospels, this phrase is a title for what follows, the antitheses in verses 22-44.[20] The surpassing righteousness is defined by these antitheses. It far exceeds the righteousness of the scribes and Pharisees in six particulars: murder (5:21-25), adultery (5:27-30), divorce (5:31-32), oaths (5:33-37), retaliation (5:38-42), and loving one's enemies (5:43-48). This surpassing righteousness, in each case, goes far beyond outward acts and penetrates to **inner attitudes** and motivations.[21]

---

19 J. Dwight Pentecost, "The Purpose of the Sermon on the Mount: Part 3," *BibSac* 115, no. 460 (October-December 1958): 314.

20 Luz and Koester, *Matthew 1-7: A Commentary*: 221.

21 Reformed writer Edmund Neufeld is correct in saying "the five antitheses that complete Matthew 5, and the sections on almsgiving, prayer, and fasting give our reader more information about Jesus' kind of righteousness." Edmund K. Neufeld, "The Gospel in the Gospels: Answering the Question 'What must I

If this conclusion is correct and if "enter the kingdom" means go to heaven when you die, then Jesus is teaching salvation by works as some have concluded.[22] This creates a difficulty for Reformed exegesis.

For example, because Hagner admits that those called on to enter the kingdom are regenerate saints, he has a theological problem on his hands. He says, "The verse is addressed, it must be remembered, to those who are the recipients of the kingdom."[23] If that is true, then how can those who are already "recipients of the kingdom," that is, are saved, be called on to enter it? Haven't saved people already entered it? In response he says, "To belong to the kingdom means to follow Jesus's teaching. Hence, the kingdom and the righteousness of the kingdom go together; they cannot be separated."[24]

But, in Matthew 5:19 Jesus says they *can* be separated. The one who disobeys even the least of the commandments and teaches others to do the same "will be least *in* the kingdom." That is, to use Hagner's

---

do to be saved?' From the Synoptics," *JETS* 51, no. 2 (June 2008): 273. Davies and Allison agree, "The meaning of 'righteousness' in 5:20 is determined by the paragraphs that follow. 'Righteousness' is therefore Christian character and conduct in accordance with the demands of Jesus—right intention, right word, right deed. Hence 'righteousness' does not refer, even implicitly, to God's gift. The Pauline [forensic, eschatological] connotation is absent." W. D. Davies and Dale C. Allison, *A Critical and Exegetical Commentary on the Gospel According to Saint Matthew* (Edinburgh: T. & T. Clark, 1988), 499.

22 If "entering the kingdom" means "go to heaven when you die" and the surpassing righteousness is ethical behavior, Jesus would be contradicting himself, because elsewhere he said entrance into heaven is based on faith (e.g., John 3:16). Betz and Collins assert that Jesus does, in fact, teach salvation by works. They say, "Ethical demands should shape this way of life; but the purpose of such demands is primarily eschatological in that their *goal is to qualify the disciple for entering into the kingdom of the heavens.*" Betz and Collins, *The Sermon on the Mount: A Commentary on the Sermon on the Mount, Including the Sermon on the Plain (Matthew 5:3-7:27 and Luke 6:20-49)*: 189. Kümmel links Jesus to the Rabbis, "according to which a man must fulfill certain conditions to partake of the eschatological glory," W. G. Kümmel, *Promise and Fulfillment* (London: SCM Press, 1957), 53.

23 Hagner, *Matthew 14-28*: 109.

24 Ibid.

term, he will be a "recipient of the kingdom." The righteousness of the kingdom and belonging to the kingdom can be separated.[25]

Who is greatest in the Kingdom? The view that entering the kingdom refers to entering into a kingdom way of living leading to greatness in the kingdom is confirmed by the similar passage in Matthew 18 which opens with the statement, "*At that time the disciples came to Jesus and said, 'Who then is greatest in the kingdom of heaven?'*" (Matthew 18:1). Once again, the subject matter is "greatness" in the kingdom; once again, the passage is addressed to the regenerate Twelve, and once again, Jesus speaks of entrance.

This tells us clearly that this context, like Matthew 7:21, is not speaking about salvation, it is about status, ranking within the kingdom as mentioned in Matthew 5:19.

Jesus answers,

> *And he said: "I tell you the truth, unless you change [Gr. strephō, "inward change," BDAG, 948] and become like little children, **you will never enter the kingdom of heaven**. (Matthew 8:3)*

> *Whoever then humbles [Gr. tapeinoō] himself as this child, he is **the greatest in the kingdom of heaven**." (v. 4, NIV)*

France explains, this passage is "about accepting for oneself a position in the social scale which is like that of children, that is as the lowest in the hierarchy of authority and decision-making, those subject to and dependent on adults."[26]

---

25 Hagner weakly asserts that those who are "least" have kept the Law "for the most part"! Betz and Collins disagree. "His violation consists of the setting aside of the commandments altogether, either in their entirety or by selection. He is presented as a teacher who not only sets aside the commandments but also teaches the people to do the same. In sum, he is an apostate teaching apostasy" Betz and Collins, *The Sermon on the Mount: A Commentary on the Sermon on the Mount, Including the Sermon on the Plain (Matthew 5:3-7:27 and Luke 6:20-49)*: 185.

26 France, *The Gospel of Matthew*: 676-77.

The phrase "humbles (Gr. *tapeinoō*, 'to lose status') himself,"[27] or "take the lowly position" is the means of entrance into the kingdom in verse 4, and not by faith alone without cost. If the disciples' question about being "great" was prompted by a desire to exercise authority over others, they have started at the wrong end. Their "grown-up" sense of social position puts them out of sympathy with God's value-scale.[28]

Verse 4 begins with "whoever then" or "whoever therefore," linking it closely with the preceding. It appears that Craig Blomberg is correct when he says, "So the criterion for greatness is precisely the criterion for entrance."[29] To paraphrase our understanding of Jesus's words, we might say, "Unless you are willing to take a lower status and become a servant of all, you will not enter the kingdom way of living and obtain greatness in the kingdom." This is, of course, a common theme in Jesus's teaching.

> But Jesus called them to Himself and said, 'You know that the rulers of the Gentiles lord it over them, and their great men exercise authority over them. It is not this way among you, but **whoever wishes to become great among** you shall be your servant, and whoever wishes to be first among you shall be your slave; just as the Son of Man did not come to be served, but to serve, and to give His life a ransom for many.' (Matthew 20:25–28. NASB95)[30]

The condition for receiving high status in the kingdom is to become a servant. The condition for entrance into salvation is faith alone apart from works without cost. Therefore, entering the kingdom in Luke 18:3 does not refer to entering personal salvation; it refers to entrance into greatness in the kingdom as the parallelism suggests. As Luomanen

---

27 *BDAG*, 990.

28 France, *The Gospel of Matthew*: 676-77.

29 Craig L. Blomberg, "Degrees of Reward in the Kingdom of Heaven?," *JETS* 35, no. 2 (1992): 166. One can assume, however, that Blomberg believes all "true" believers will be great because he does not believe there are any distinctions or degrees of glory.

30 See also Mark 9:35; 10:42; Luke 22:25.

says, "it is interesting to note how Matthew answers the question about greatness *in* the kingdom of heaven by introducing the requirements of *entrance*."[31]

In order to become a servant of all, one must change his life, be "converted." This need for life change is addressed to those who are already saved, the disciples (Matthew18:1). What is in view here is the conversion of the converted, the salvation of those who are already saved. As some have noted, "the Christian life is a life of conversion."[32] To convert, that is, change one's life, in this context means to turn from not being a child to being a child, to turn from wanting to be the greatest to wanting to be the least, the servant of all.

During their time on earth, these prophets often said, "Lord, Lord." However, even though they addressed him as, "Lord," Jesus said only those who do the "will of the Father will enter the kingdom" (Matthew 7:21). Based upon our analysis above, we proposed that to enter the kingdom means to enter the kingdom way of living, which will lead to high status in the kingdom on "that day" (7:22). "That day" in this interpretation is the Judgement Seat of Christ (2 Corinthians 5:10).

We propose that the phrase "enter the kingdom" in Matthew 5:20 and 7:21 is not entrance into the sphere of personal salvation, it is, instead, entrance into the promised outcome of a life of a fully committed *kingdom way of living* which involved a greater righteousness (character and behavior), that is, doing the will of the Father. Matthew 5:20 and 7:13 refer to the beginning commitment of such a life, and 7:21 refers to the final outcome of this process on "that day," greatness. The process of doing the will of the Father and the outcome of this process, greatness, must be viewed as a whole. They are always connected.

This view of kingdom entrance coheres well with the theme of the Sermon on the Mount. It is not about soteriology, it is about the kingdom way of life. It is not a call to salvation, it is a call to discipleship. In the words of R. T. France, the Sermon is a Discourse on

---

31 Petri Luomanen, *Entering the Kingdom of Heaven: A Study on the Structure of Matthew's View of Salvation* (Tübingen: Mohr Siebeck, 1998), 240.

32 George W. Peters, "The Meaning of Conversion," *BibSac* 120, no. 479 (July - September 1963): 237.

Discipleship[33] addressed to those who are already saved, his disciples (Matthew 5:1-2). As a result of the fact that the disobedient Christian prophets had never entered the kingdom way of life while on earth, on "that day" (the future day of judgment) the Lord will say to them "I never knew you."

The charismatic prophets are saved people. It is likely that these charismatic prophets are saved people. Unlike non-believers, they were able to cast out demons and perform miracles, which Christ does not deny. Although Luther would certainly not accept the interpretation followed in this chapter, he asks the pertinent question, "What goes on here, that those who do miracles, and do them in the name of Christ, should still be numbered among the false Christians and among the evil and damned people?"[34] Good question!

How could they be doing this by the power of Satan? Unregenerate exorcists cannot cast out demons (Acts 19:14-16); these exorcists did. Christ himself says, *"If Satan casts out Satan, he is divided against himself; how then will his kingdom stand?"* (Matthew 12:25-26, 28). Elsewhere in the New Testament, attempted exorcisms by the unregenerate are catastrophic failures, but the exorcists addressing Jesus were successful.

Acts 19:13-16 refers to unbelieving Jewish exorcists using the name of Jesus ("by Jesus whom Paul preaches") who were decidedly unsuccessful. The evil spirit responded to their commands by saying, *"I recognize Jesus, and I know about Paul, but who are you?"* (Acts 19:15). Then the evil spirit caused the demon-possessed victim to jump on these evil sons of Sceva and drive them away naked and wounded!

An early Christian writing, the *Didache*, warned about these lawless Christian prophets.[35] This early teaching manual calls them

---

33 France, *The Gospel of Matthew*: 153.

34 Martin Luther, *Luther's Works*, ed. J. J. Pelikan, H. C. Oswald, and H. T. Lehmann (Philadelphia: Fortress Press, 1968), 21:270.

35 "But let everyone that cometh in the name of the Lord be received; and then when ye have tested him ye shall know him, for ye shall have understanding on the right hand and on the left. If the comer is a traveler, assist him, so far as ye are able; but he shall not stay with you more than two or three days, if it be necessary. But if he wishes to settle with you, being a craftsman, let him

the *christianos*, which is the common word for "a Christlike person," that is, a saved person (see Acts 26:28; 1 Peter 4:16). Even though they are genuine believers, these false Christian prophets are described as those "trafficking upon Christ" [Gr. *christemporos*, "one who carries on a cheap trade in (the teachings of) Christ, a *Christmonger*"].[36]

That this was a problem in the early church is clear from Paul's disclaimer to the Thessalonians, *"For we never came with flattering speech, as you know, nor with a **pretext for greed**—God is witness—nor did we seek glory from men* (1 Thessalonians 2:3-7).

Similarly, Paul exhorts Titus that those of the circumcision *"must be silenced because they are upsetting whole families, teaching things they should not teach for the sake of **sordid gain**"* (Titus 1:11).

We suggest that those to whom Jesus spoke in Matthew 7:21-23 were true believers who were "in" the kingdom but led lawless lives (Matthew 5:19; 7:23). They spoke from impurity, deceit, and with flattering speech as a pretext for greed, "sordid gain." Simon the magician may be another example.[37]

But how is it possible that Christ would allow true supernatural power from God to be used for purposes that might give credence

---

work for and eat his bread. **But if he has no craft, according to your wisdom provide how he shall live as a Christian among you, but not in idleness. If he will not do this, he is trafficking upon Christ. Beware of such men."** "Didache," in *The Apostolic Fathers: Greek Texts and English Translations of their Writings*, ed. Joseph Barber Lightfoot, J. R. Harmer, and Michael W. Holmes (Grand Rapids: Baker Book House, 1992), (10:1-12:4), 233-34.

36 BDAG, 1090.

37 Like Simon the magician in Samaria who believed, was baptized, and who followed Philip (and was therefore regenerate), these superficial, charismatic believers of Matthew 7:21-23 may have seen a profit to be made and used their gifts for selfish purposes. Concerned for fame and fortune, Simon wanted to purchase the miracle-working power of the Holy Spirit with silver (Acts 8:18-24). He seemed to fall away after a lifestyle of doing spectacular things. That Simon was in fact a regenerate saint is argued by Fred Chay and John P. Correia, *The Faith That Saves: The Nature of Faith in the New Testament* (Haysville, NC: Schoettle Publishing Co., 2008), 54-58. See discussion below pp. 518 ff.

to those who misuse it?[38] One only must turn to 1 Corinthians 12-14 where some of the spiritual gifts were being expressed in ways that caused unbelievers to think that the church was loaded with madmen (1 Corinthians 14:23), bringing discredit on the name of Christ. They were people who "build themselves up in the eyes of others" (edify themselves; 1 Corinthians 14:2; cf. 4:7-10; 13:4-5). Paul has just said that "love does not parade itself" and is not "puffed up" (cf. 1 Corinthians 13:4-5), but they were doing both.[39]

In response, Dr Grudem argues, with no proof or scriptural basis, that, "Apparently all these [miracles and exorcisms] can be produced in the natural man or woman's own strength, or even with the help of the evil one."[40] However, they cannot be the work of the evil one because that runs afoul of Christ's statement that a house divided against itself cannot stand (Matthew 12:25-26). So Grudem is left with the ad hoc explanation that miracles and demon exorcisms can be performed by an unbeliever in his own strength!

They are pleading that on the basis of their ministry in Christ's name and all the miracles they had performed, that they had entered the kingdom way of life during their time on earth and they are therefore entitled to entrance into higher status in the kingdom of heaven in "that day." For them, doing the will of the Father was their ministry of miracles, exorcisms, and prophecy. For Jesus, it was obedience to the Sermon on the Mount.

What had happened to them? Why had they fallen into such lawless living? They may have begun well, performing miracles, casting out demons, and advancing the cause of the kingdom. Apparently, they never had pure motives. At the point of their first miracle or exorcism or soon after, pride captured them and Jesus never approved of their

---

38 A current manifestation of the broad way is the "prosperity gospel," which promises a life of wealth, health, and ease to true disciples. They have led countless believers into a false system of Christian living that has harmed the faith of many. It is these types of prophets that Jesus warns against.

39 Consider Samson whom the Lord blessed (Judges 13:24) and who was carnal all his life (Judges 14:20; 16:1, 13), and yet he worked miracles by God's power (Judges 14:6, 19; 15:14; 16:28).

40 Grudem, *Systematic Theology*: 706.

ministry. But for some reason they soon fell into carnality. The text gives no explanation, but perhaps Paul's experience with the "thorn in the flesh" suggests a possible answer. Paul prayed three times that this thorn would be removed, but it was not. Why?

> *And because of the surpassing greatness of the revelations, for this reason, **to keep me from exalting myself,** there was given me a thorn in the flesh, a messenger of Satan to buffet me—to keep me from exalting myself!* (2 Corinthians 12:7)

Paul's prayer was denied because of the danger of spiritual pride![41] Billheimer is correct when he says,

> *Ego exaltation is probably the most dangerous and deadly of sins. It caused the downfall of Lucifer, with all its attending tragedies. It made the original earth a chaos, drowned in stygian darkness. It upset the balance of an entire planet. For any created being to make itself or any other thing but God the center of his world is catastrophic and self-destructive.*[42]

We may be close to the explanation for their fall into lawlessness when we suggest that these believing leaders became enamored with their spiritual experiences. Surely, "I am the man," they thought. The miracles they performed served to exalt themselves. Being granted the privilege of prophesying in Christ's name, casting out demons, and performing miracles is heady stuff. If such things endangered the apostle, it could certainly endanger these believing prophets within the community. Pride leads to lawless living.

---

41 Satan's heart was filled with pride, and this was the reason for his fall (Ezekiel 28:18). Paul recognized the same danger in appointing a youth to a position of authority (1 Timothy 3:6), and he also recognized that this danger could come on himself because of the "surpassing greatness of revelations" he had been privileged to receive.

42 Paul E. Billheimer, *Destined for the Throne*, rev. ed. (Minneapolis: Bethany House, 1975), 97.

Ministering the gospel of Christ from base motives is discussed elsewhere in Scripture. While in prison, Paul notes that some preach Christ out of selfish ambition motives (Philippians 1:15–17). In 2 Corinthians 2:17, he refers to a group who plagued the Corinthian church, peddling the word of God for profit [Gr. *kapēleuō*]. The word *kapēleuō* refers to a "huckster" who is motivated by financial remuneration for his preaching (2 Corinthians 11:20).[43] This problem was rampant with the traveling philosophers, and Paul says it was happening among Christian prophets as well.

Anyone who has watched the late-night TV evangelists can immediately see that we have the same problem today: greedy, deceitful teachers, trafficking in Christ to sordid gain. While the clear majority of these teachers are honorable men with valid ministries, some can only be described as "hucksters" by deceitfully bilking many out of their savings in order to finance their indulgent lifestyles.

Because Jesus says they are those who "practice lawlessness," this raises the question, "Can those who were workers of iniquity be found in heaven?" An immediate illustration of the fact that lawless men can be saved men is Matthew 5:19. Jesus has already declared, *"Whoever then annuls one of the least of these commandments, and teaches others to do the same, shall be called least in the kingdom of heaven."* Therefore, when he says, *"Depart from me, you who practice lawlessness"* (Matthew 7:23), we should not automatically assume that those who are addressed are unregenerate. Those described in 5:19 are clearly those who practice lawlessness, and yet they are "**in**" the kingdom, that is, saved people.

We therefore agree with David Aune when he says, "They do not appear to have been Gnostics, Zealots, or Pharisees, but rather

---

43 *BDAG*, 508. Originally, this word referred to the 'retailer' who sells on the market wares which he has bought from the ἔμπορος ('wholesaler'), and it means 'to engage in retail trade.' Both words carry with them the suggestion of trickery and avarice." It came to mean "to sell, to hawk deceitfully, at illegitimate profit." Windish, *kapēleuō*, in TDNT, 3:603. These hucksters were "suspected of corrupting by putting the best fruit on top of the basket." WPNT, s.v. "2 Cor. 2:17."

Christians whom Matthew regarded as a dangerous threat to the order and integrity of the Christian communities[44] (emphasis added).

Entering by the narrow gate and narrow way. Another passage which speaks of entering the kingdom, although using a metaphor, also leads us to the conclusion that entering the kingdom refers to entering into the kingdom way of life which leads to honor.

> *Enter through the narrow gate; for the gate is wide and the way is broad that leads to destruction [Gr apoleia], and there are many who enter through it. For the gate is small and the way is narrow that leads to life, and there are few who find it.* (Matthew 7:13–14, NASB95)

Jesus speaks of two gates and two ways. There is no need to assume that the "way" in the Sermon on the Mount is the same as "I am the way . . ." (John 14:6). The sermon is about living life, not gaining it, discipleship and not entrance into heaven. The "way" is a way of life, the kingdom way of life.

The Christian who pursues this narrow way will find life. This life refers to a rich life now and an enhanced experience of life in heaven. The phrase echoes Moses's exhortation to the Hebrews in the wilderness,

> *you shall keep My statutes and My judgments, by which a man may* **live** *if he does them; I am the Lord.* (Leviticus 18:5, NASB95)

Following the way of Torah in the Old Testament led to a rich life in the land, not heaven when one died. Similarly, following the way of the Sermon on the Mount, the way of kingdom living, leads to a rich life now and an enhanced experience of life in the future kingdom.

---

44 David Edward Aune, *Prophecy in Early Christianity and the Ancient Mediterranean World* (Grand Rapids: Wm. B. Eerdmans Publishing Co., 1983), p. 223. Contra Davies and Allison who label them "counterfeit Christians." Davies and Allison, *A Critical and Exegetical Commentary on the Gospel According to Saint Matthew*: 1:704.

"In the NT *hodós* ["way"] primarily refers to the way *of life*, the *manner of life* demanded by God (Acts 14:16; Romans 3:16f.; James 1:8; 5:20; 2 Peter 2:15, 21, etc),"[45] a meaning usually found in Matthew.[46] This is parallel to "entering the kingdom" in Matthew 5:20: *"For I say to you that unless your righteousness surpasses that of the scribes and Pharisees, you will not enter the kingdom of heaven."* Possession of an inward ethical and spiritual righteousness is necessary for entrance into the narrow way—the kingdom way of life that leads to "life" and honor. The parallelism between entering the kingdom in 5:20 and entering onto "a way" in 7:13 suggests that, like "way," the aspect of the kingdom in view in the Sermon on the Mount is a way of life, a way of life which leads to an abundant entrance into the future millennium.

The broad way, the way of ease and lukewarm commitment, leads to destruction (Gr. *apoleia*). There is no need to assume that *apoleia* refers to final damnation. The word *apōleia* is used 18 times in the New Testament. It is used eleven times of damnation,[47] four times of temporal ruin and possibly physical death,[48] twice of ruin or physical waste,[49] and once in Matthew 7:13. Therefore while the sense of damnation might be possible, Matthew only uses the word one other time, and there he uses it in the sense of waste or the "needless squandering of a resource"[50] (Matthew 26:8; cf. Mark 14:4). Its variation in meaning elsewhere should give us pause in automatically assuming it means damnation in Matthew 7:13.

---

45 Martin Völkel, "*hodos*," in EDNT, 2:491.

46 See Matthew 3:3; 5:20; 7:13-14, 24-27; 21:32; 22:16 where the way is a way of living, not "Jesus is the way" to personal salvation. (It is possible, however, that 22:16 refers to the way of salvation.)

47 John 17:12; Romans 9:22; Philippians 1:28; 3:19; 2 Thessalonians 2:3; 2 Peter 2:1, 3; 3:16 (twice); Revelation 17:8, 11.

48 Acts 8:20; 1 Timothy 6:9; Hebrews 10:39; 2 Peter 3:7.

49 Matthew 26:8; Mark 14:4.

50 James Swanson, *A Dictionary of Biblical Languages: Greek New Testament*, 2nd ed. (Seattle: Logos Research Systems, 2001), s.v. GGK724.

Perhaps the verbal form "to perish" (Gr. *apollumi*), which is found ninety times in the New Testament and often in Matthew, will give us more to work with than the one reference to the noun, *apōleia*. The verb, *apollumi* does mean "suffer damnation" in a number of places outside of Matthew, and it has only one clear instance of that meaning in the Gospels.[51] What is of interest here is that the verb is used nineteen times in seventeen verses in the Gospel of Matthew, and Matthew never uses it in the sense of damnation. It is used seven times of physical death.[52] For example, Peter was afraid of "perishing" by drowning (Matthew 8:25); Herod wanted to "destroy" Jesus (Matthew 2:13); the Pharisees likewise wanted to "destroy him" (Matthew 12:14). In one place it means "to ruin," where Jesus says that putting new wine into old wineskins "ruins" them (Matthew 9:17).[53]

The verb is commonly used of a temporal perishing or psychological and spiritual ruin of believers: "*Do not destroy* [Gr. *apollumi*] *with your food him for whom Christ died*" (Romans 14:15); "*For through your knowledge he who is weak is ruined* [Gr. *apollumi*], *the brother for whose sake Christ died*" (1 Corinthians 8:11).

Thus, it is clear that true believers can be "destroyed" in a spiritual/psychological sense. Paul speaks elsewhere of this possibility when he says, "*Remind them of these things, and solemnly charge them in the presence of God not to wrangle about words, which is useless, and leads to the ruin of the hearers*" (2 Timothy 2:14). In this passage, he uses the word *katastrophē* instead of *apōleia*. It refers in this instance to "a state of being intellectually upset to a ruinous degree."[54]

---

51 E.g., John 10:28.

52 Matthew 2:13; 8:25; 12:14; 21:41 – he will "destroy those wretches" probably a reference to the judgment in time of AD 70 on the nation and not final damnation; Matthew 22:7; 26:52; 27:20.

53 See also Matthew 10:6; 18:13-14, "to go astray;" 12:14; 15:24; 22:7; 26:52; 27:20, etc.

54 *BDAG*, 528. For a more complete discussion of "life" and "destruction," see the excursus on "destruction" at the end of this chapter, see Dillow, *Final Destiny*.

Unless Matthew 7:13-14 is an exception, there is no place in the Bible where the ways of life and death together are associated with heaven and eternal separation from God. In every case, when life or death are together, they refer to either physical or psychological/spiritual conditions in this life. Eternal destiny is never in view.[55]

In our examination of Matthew 5:19-20; 7:21-23; and 7:13-14, we can see a pattern which further establishes our interpretation of "enter in the kingdom."

---

55 Jesus told his disciples that finding true life is as difficult as getting a camel through the eye of the needle (Matthew 19:24). Apart from abiding in him, this cannot be obtained. When Paul said to the Thessalonians, "*[F]or now we really live, if you stand firm in the Lord*" (1 Thessalonians 3:8), he did not mean that if they continued to stand firm in the Lord then Paul and his companions would go to heaven when they die! Rather, he means that they would find true satisfaction knowing that their labors had not been in vain (v. 4). In the midst of their afflictions, it was a great encouragement to know that all their suffering was worth it. Their beloved disciples were doing well. This was "life" indeed. As Gene L. Green puts it, "For him and his companions the good news about this church was like a resurrection." Gene L. Green, *The Letters to the Thessalonians*, The Pillar New Testament Commentary (Grand Rapids: Wm. B. Eerdmans Publishing Co., 2002), 170. F. F. Bruce says, "The news of your unwavering faith and love is the very breath of life to us." F. F. Bruce, *The Epistles to the Colossians, to Philemon, and to the Ephesians* (Grand Rapids: Wm. B. Eerdmans Publishing Co., 1984), 67. Jesus also spoke of "life" in two senses elsewhere, "*I have come that they may have life, and have it to the full*" (John 10:10). Faithful endurance and proper response to persecution or trial may lead to a rich life. 1 Peter 3:9; Mark 9:45; and Matthew 18:18 teach that one can find true life now only if he is willing to do whatever is necessary to follow Christ. Note 2 Corinthians 4:6-11 where persecution, properly responded to, results in the "life of Jesus" being manifested in the apostles (see also 2 Corinthians 1:6). "*All discipline for the moment seems not to be joyful, but sorrowful; yet to those who have been trained by it, afterwards it yields the peaceful fruit of righteousness*" (Hebrews 12:11). "*Consider it all joy, my brethren, when you encounter various trials, knowing that the testing of your faith produces endurance. And let endurance have its perfect result, that you may be perfect and complete, lacking in nothing*" (James 1:2-4).

Scripture	Challenge	Condition	Reward
Matthew 5:19-20	Enter the kingdom	Pursue greater righteousness	High status in the kingdom
Matthew 7:21-23	Enter the kingdom	Do the "will of the Father"	Entrance into high status
Matthew 7:13-14	Enter the kingdom	Enter the way of discipleship	Life

Each passage involves a call to enter the kingdom. Each passage teaches that the path of discipleship, not faith alone without cost, is the pathway to get there. And each passage describes the outcome of kingdom entrance in various ways.

"Depart from Me"

> And then I will declare to them, "I never knew you; depart from me, you who practice lawlessness." (Matthew 7:23)

In Matthew 7:23, this terrible announcement is commonly understood by Matthew's commentators to mean exclusion from heaven and that Jesus is dooming them to eternal destruction.[56] These people, according to Hagner, "have shown by their conduct that they have not been chosen by Jesus,"[57] that is, they are not of the elect. Carson agrees, saying that the "essential characteristic of the true believer" is obedience. "True believers," he says, "will perform the will of their Father."[58] Based upon the Gospel of John, however, one would normally think that the "*essential characteristic*" of the "true believer" is faith in Christ. But, Carson assumes that obedience is the essential

56 William Hendriksen and Simon Kistemaker, *Exposition of the Gospel According to Matthew* (Grand Rapids: Baker Book House, 2001), 377.

57 Donald. A Hagner, *Matthew 1-13*, Word Biblical Commentary (Dallas: Word, 2002), 188.

58 Carson, *Jesus' Sermon on the Mount and His Confrontation with the World*: 139.

characteristic because of his belief that the Reformed doctrine of perseverance is true.

Carson's views fly directly in the face of what Jesus said earlier. As mentioned above, in Matthew 5:19 Jesus speaks of saved people who are "in" the kingdom, and yet they clearly practice lawlessness. These people were "in" the kingdom, that is, saved (in Carson's terms), and yet they lived lives of lawlessness.

Davison is correct when he says, "Matthew's real target in the passages we have examined is the problem, common to every age of the Church—and to the Old Testament community of faith—of laxity in the moral life of believers."[59] They are carnal Christians, and when they stand at the Judgment Seat of Christ, they will hear the terrible words, *"Depart from me, you who practice lawlessness"* (v. 23). They will be in the kingdom (in a soteriological sense), but they will not be *at the table*. As a result, at the Judgment Seat of Christ, they will weep and gnash their teeth in profound regret for their wasted lives and be "saved, yet so as through fire" (1 Corinthians 3:15).

While many assume that separation from Christ refers to eternal damnation, there is no indication in this passage that this separation ("depart from me") is permanent and therefore refers to damnation. In fact, some relate this to the Talmudic ban formula, the *nezipha* and the *niddui*, which do not refer to an experience of *a permanent separation, but only to a temporary separation.*[60] In a similar way, these

---

59 Davison, "Anomia and the Question of an Antinomian Polemic in Matthew," 634. Disregarding the teaching of eternal security, Davison, of course, concludes that they will be damned.

60 For full discussion of these bans see Alfred Edersheim, *The Life and Times of Jesus the Messiah*, New American Edition ed., 2 vols. (Grand Rapids: Wm. B. Eerdmans Publishing Co., 1962). 2:183. We might add here the suggestion of Jeremias and others who note that the phrases "I do not know you" and "depart from me" may refer to a teacher's order (*neziphah*), forbidding the student access to the rabbi for seven days and means something like, "I will have nothing to do with you." See Joachim Jeremias, *The Parables of Jesus*, 6th ed. (London: SCM, 1963). p.132. Jeremias is apparently referring to Marcus Jastrow, *A Dictionary of the Targumi, the Talmud Babli and Yerushalmi, and the Midreashic Literature* (New York: Judaica, 1985). The Aramaic word . . . means a "rebuke" and a "lower degree of excommunication." John

false teachers coming from inside the church (Matthew 7:21-23) are not assigned to eternal separation from God, but to receive severe rebuke and exclusion from reigning with Christ in the fulfillment of human destiny and the celebratory Marriage Banquet (the wedding supper of the Lamb), which occurs in the New Jerusalem prior to the second coming (Revelation 19:7-9; Matthew 22:1-14).[61]

"I Never Knew You"

But it might fairly be asked, "If those in this second group in Matthew 7:21-23 are truly born again, why does Jesus say to them, "*I never knew you, depart from me you who practice lawlessness*" (Matt. 7:23)?

Dr. Grudem correctly notes, "He does not say, 'I knew you at one time but I no longer know you,' nor 'I knew you at one time but you strayed away from me,' but rather, 'I *never* knew you.'" However, his conclusion that "[t]hey never were genuine believers,"[62] does not necessarily follow. It depends upon what "know" means. Jesus obviously

---

Nolland also suggests that the phrase is "reminiscent of a Jewish ban formula." John Nolland, *Luke 9:21-18:34*, Word Biblical Commentary (Dallas: Word, 2002), 734. Klyne Snodgrass, in his massive work on the parables, believes that the phrase "'I do not know you' in v. 12 may reflect a ban formula in which a disciple is forbidden access to a teacher." Klyne Snodgrass, *Stories with Intent: A Comprehensive Guide to the Parables of Jesus* (Grand Rapids: Wm. B. Eerdmans Publishing Co., 2008), 510. It is also possible that the allusion here is to the Jewish custom of being put out of the congregation, a fate that fell on any Jew who confessed Jesus as messiah (John 9:22). However, all these parallels to Jewish literature are uncertain, because they are based mainly on references from the Talmud in AD 400 to 600. It is debatable how much of this material reflects first-century Palestinian Judaism.

61 They will enter the "realm," but they will not enter the "reign." They will weep profoundly because of their exclusion from the final destiny of man in history. Elsewhere (Matthew 22:13), this experience of exclusion is called "outer darkness" (a reference to exclusion from the light and celebration inside the banquet hall, not hell). Their separation will not be permanent, but they will forfeit reward. For full discussion, of the duration of remorse see Dillow, *Final Destiny*: 322, 716 ff.

62 Grudem, *Systematic Theology*, 795.

knew them in some sense, and he knew all about their ministry. What then does this mean?

The Greek word in verse 23 ("*I never knew you*") is the common word for "to know" (Gr. *ginōskō*) found in the New Testament (222 times). It is usually more personal than the other word for know, *oida*, and communicates a "personal relationship between the one who knows and the one known."[63] However, it has a broad range of meanings. It can mean to know,[64] to learn, to be acquainted with, to have sexual intercourse with, to perceive, to recognize, to confirm, to be aware of, or even to understand (2 Corinthians 1:13).[65] The psalmist said, "The Lord knows [LXX *ginōskō*] the way of the righteous" (Psalm 1:6); that is, "The Lord *approves the manner of life* of the righteous."[66] Translations vary: he "watches over it" (NIV, NRSV, NLT) or "approves" or "guards the way of the godly" (NET); "takes care of" (NCV); "protects" (CEV); "guided and protected" (GNT). The word is also commonly used to mean "to give recognition to."[67] In secular Greek, it can even mean

---

63 E. D. Schmitz, "*ginōskō*" in NIDNTT, 2:398. However, it is not necessary to assume, as is often done, that the nature of this relationship is limited to personal salvation. It is clear that there is "knowing" and then there is "knowing." There are degrees. For example, Paul said, "*If anyone supposes that he knows (Gr. ginōskō) anything, he has not yet known as he ought to know (Gr. ginōskō)*" (1 Corinthians 8:2). One can "know" but not really "know," that is, not know as he "ought to know." To know God can also refer to fellowship or, possibly, to understand him more fully. An obvious illustration of the latter is Jesus's comment to Philip. "*Jesus said to him, 'Have I been so long with you, and yet you have not come to know me, Philip? He who has seen me has seen the Father; how can you say, "Show us the Father"?'*" (John 14:9). Here the word "know" means "to recognize who I am." Philip *did* know Christ in the sense of "being saved," but he did *not* yet fully understand who Christ really was.

64 For the various categories and related verses, see *BDAG*, 199-200.

65 Rudolf Bultmann, "*ginōskō*," in TDNT, 1:703.

66 Adam Clarke suggests "approveth the way." Adam Clarke, *Adam Clarke's Commentary*, Logos Library System electronic ed. (Albany, OR: Ages Software, 1999). See Psalm 37:18. Many understand the word in Psalm 1:6 to mean "watches over" or "protects." However, the connection to "way of life" more naturally suggests approval rather than guarding or protecting.

67 Ibid., 2:399.

"to verify."[68] This meaning is found in the New Testament, where sometimes it can shade into the sense of "to confirm."[69]

When Paul said, "*That which I do, I do not understand*" (Romans 7:15, Gr. *ou ginōskō*, lit. "I do not know"), he certainly does not mean "I do not know" or "I do not understand," as many translations render it. If there is anyone who knows and understands thoroughly what he does, it is the apostle Paul. Rather, the meaning is "I do not approve," or as the KJV has it, "I allow not."[70] Paul does not approve of what he does.

In 1 Corinthians 16:18 Paul urges, "Give recognition to [i.e., "*know* such men," or "esteem highly," or "approve," Gr. *epiginōskō*] such men," that is, to colleagues who have shown their devoted service. The translations vary: "deserve notice" (GNT); "be proud that you have such people among you" (*The Message*); "deserve recognition" (TNIV); "are worthy of honor" (NIV); "give recognition" (NIV, NRSV). It may mean "notice with approval" (see Ruth 2:10, 19). If this is the meaning of "know" in Matthew 7:23, then Jesus might be saying something like, "I never approved of your ministry," or "I never considered your work worthy of honor."[71] The Lord will not "give weight to" or "approve" the claims of the carnal prophets in Matthew 7:23 that they were doing kingdom works in his name. In these instances, *ginōskō* takes a meaning similar to the one usage of the other main word for "to know," *oida*, which can mean, "esteem highly" or "appreciate" (1 Thessalonians 5:12-13).

---

68 Bultmann, "*ginōskō*," 1:691.

69 Ibid., 1:703. See also Mark 6:38; 13:28-29; Luke 1:18; 1 Corinthians 4:19; 2 Corinthians 13:6.

70 Zodhiates, G1097. Leon Morris says, "The verb translated *understand* may point to Paul's perplexity as to why he does evil though he earnestly wants to do good. Or the word may be used in the sense 'acknowledge' or 'approve' (cf. 'the LORD knows the way of the righteous,' Psalm 1:6, RSV)." Leon Morris, *The Epistle to the Romans*, Pillar New Testament Commentary (Grand Rapids: Wm. B. Eerdmans Publishing Co., 1988), 291.

71 1 Corinthians 4:19, NIDNTT, 2:399. According to Barrett, Paul was "*unrecognized and yet recognized*," (i.e., disapproved, yet approved, *ginōskō*) (2 Corinthians 6:9). C. K. Barrett, *A Commentary on the Second Epistle to the Corinthians* (New York: Harper & Row, 1973), 189.

One lexicon suggests that, in Matthew 7:23, "know" should be understood in the sense of "recognition of a claim."[72] That could mean, of course, that Jesus does not recognize their claim to be true believers.[73] However, the context is talking about their claim to be doing ministry in his name (miracles, exorcisms, and prophecies), not their claim to be regenerate. The meaning, in that case, might possibly be something like, "I never recognized your claim to be doing ministry in my name," or "I never approved of your ministry." This is the meaning used only two verses earlier when Jesus says in regard to the unregenerate false prophets "*You will know them* [Gr. *ginōskō*, i.e., recognize their claim to be true prophets] *by their fruits*" (7:20). Jesus never knew the carnal prophets in v. 23 in the sense that he never recognized their fruit, that is, what their teaching and ministry produced.

He is using the word "know," not in the sense of an intimate saving relationship, but of recognizing the validity of one's lifestyle or one's ministry. Jesus uses the word *epiginōskō* in this sense in Matthew 17:12 when he says that the scribes did not "recognize" (Gr. *epiginōskō*) John the Baptist, that is, they did not acknowledge his ministry as that of the promised Elijah, and so they treated him with contempt. They did not "approve" of him in the sense that they never recognized his ministry as authorized by God.[74]

---

72 ALGNT 99.

73 As Davies and Allison suggest, Davies and Allison, *A Critical and Exegetical Commentary on the Gospel According to Saint Matthew*: 1:717.

74 If our proposals that such language is addressed to a justified saint seem extreme, one only has to turn to the epistle to the Hebrews to see even stronger language addressed to believers. The writer of the epistle says that "*They are crucifying once again the Son of God to their own harm and holding him up to contempt*" (Hebrews 6:6 ESV). Crucifying again the Son of God! Holding him up to contempt! No wonder these regenerate saints harm themselves. Apart from any temporal consequences, they will be severely "harmed" when the Lord Jesus says to them at the Judgment Seat of Christ, "*I never knew you, depart from me, you who practice lawlessness*" (Matthew 7:23). For proof that those addressed in the epistle to the Hebrews are regenerate saints, see Dillow, *Final Destiny*: chapter 41 and especially pp. 630 ff.

The above discussion establishes the fact that to be known by God does not necessarily mean to be unconditionally elected to salvation from eternity past, as some assume.[75]

The issue at the Judgment Seat of Christ is ethics, not enthusiasm; character, not charismata; a way of life, not signs and wonders.[76] When Jesus rejects their ministry, they will draw back in shame when they see the Lord Jesus in judgment (1 John 2:28), be saved as through fire (1 Corinthians 3:15), and lose their reward (2 John 8; Luke 19:26). There will be "weeping and gnashing of teeth," (Matthew 22:13), that is, profound regret for a wasted life.

Does This Contradict Grace?

But it may be asked, "Is this not a violation of grace?" Did not Jesus die for all our sins?[77] How can he then rebuke so severely those for whom he died and actually tell them to depart? Does this not put the average Christian under a burden of doubt and fear that he might face such a rebuke at the Judgment Seat of Christ instead of experiencing joy and reward?

No! It must be remembered that these severe warnings **do not apply to all Christians**. We are explicitly told that they apply **only** to

---

75 For a refutation of the unconditional election view, see Lawrence M. Vance, *The Other Side of Calvinism*, rev. ed. (Pensecola, FL: Vance Publications, 1991, 1999), 382-97.

76 Most modern-day "charismatics" would, of course, fully agree with this and do emphasize a kingdom way of life. There are extreme fringes among "evangelicals" as well. The passage in Matthew 7 (see also Luke 6:26) may allude to Micah 2:11, where false prophets within Israel offered a "prosperity gospel." These prophets "walk with the wind," not the Holy Spirit, says Micah. Their message is prosperity and wealth, "wine and beer," and not the strong moral demands of a true prophet. "The substance of the false teaching is the promise of material prosperity and blessings of the most sensuous character." J. M. P. Smith, W. H. Ward, and J. A. Bewer, *A Critical and Exegetical Commentary on Micah, Zephaniah, Nahum, Obadiah and Joel* (New York: Scribner's Sons, 1911), 63.

77 For discussion of the possibility of a negative judgment coming on true Christians see Dillow, *Final Destiny*: chapter 59.

those who "**practice** lawlessness," that is, lawlessness is their habitual manner of life.

No Christian who is sincerely trying to follow Christ, or, to express it in biblical terminology, "fears the Lord," no matter how imperfectly, need fret about these warnings. They do not apply to him. For that believer, there is only anticipation of joy and reward.

> *He has not dealt with us according to our sins, Nor rewarded us according to our iniquities. For as high as the heavens are above the earth, So great is his lovingkindness toward those who fear him. As far as the east is from the west, so far has he removed our transgressions from us. Just as a father has compassion on his children, so the Lord has compassion on those who fear him. For he himself knows our frame; he is mindful that we are but dust.* (Psalm 103:10–14)

Jesus "knows our frame," and he is "mindful that we are dust." That is, he understands our weakness and failure and does not condemn us but loves and accepts us.

> *Therefore, since we have a great high priest who has passed through the heavens, Jesus the Son of God, let us hold fast our confession. For we do not have a high priest who cannot sympathize with our weaknesses, but one who has been tempted in all things as we are, yet without sin. Therefore let us draw near with confidence to the throne of grace, so that we may receive mercy and find grace to help in time of need.* (Hebrews 4:14–16)

Conclusion

Christ's statement that only those who do the "will of the Father" will enter the kingdom has raised questions for interpreters of all theological persuasions. Because the context of the Sermon on the Mount has been about discipleship, most interpreters have understood the "will of the Father" to refer to personal righteousness as reflected in the preceding chapters of the Sermon. This, of course, leads to a problem. If obedience to the precepts of the Sermon is a condition of "entering the kingdom," and if the kingdom is narrowly understood as the sphere of personal salvation, as Dr. Grudem believes, that suggests that works are a condition of salvation. To resolve this difficulty, Reformed writers conclude that doing the will of the Father is not a condition of entrance, but is a characteristic of all who will enter. In their theology, all "true" believers will persevere in good works to the end of life. However, as we have demonstrated in an earlier chapter in this book, that viewpoint cannot be sustained from Scripture in view of the numerous examples in the biblical text mentioning true believers who did not persevere, such as Solomon and Saul.

Based upon usage in Matthew and the meaning of "kingdom of heaven" elsewhere in the New Testament, it is not necessary to import Reformed theology into the text. We agree with Barclay Newman that "[i]t is very important that *enter the kingdom of heaven not be understood or translated as 'go to heaven.'*"[78] He suggests an alternative that to enter the kingdom means to "be one of those over whom God rules." In other words, it refers to one who enters the kingdom way of living, obedience to God as defined in the sermon. This is quite plausible and removes much of the difficulty of a works salvation. I believe the phrase refers to entering into fully committed discipleship which leads to greatness and honor (Matthew 5:20), that is, the abundant entrance about which Peter spoke (2 Peter 1:11). This is what the charismatics wanted and what they believed their miracles and demon exorcisms should have obtained for them.

Interpreters of Matthew should not insist that "enter the kingdom" must always refer to final entrance into heaven or the millennium. R.T. France correctly notes, "To enter the kingdom of heaven does not mean to go to a place called heaven (though the eternal life of heaven will be its expected outcome (see on 18:8–9), but to come under God's rule, to become one of those who recognize his kingship and live by its standards, to be God's true people."[79]

---

78 Barclay Moon Newman and Philip C. Stine, *A Translator's Handbook on the Gospel of Matthew* (New York: United Bible Societies, 1992), 128.

79 France, *The Gospel of Matthew*: 190. Of course, for France, all who have "truly" believed will come under God's rule.

We can agree with Wayne Grudem that the "will of the Father" is obedience to the moral law of God;[80] specifically, in context, the exhortations in the sermon on discipleship. However, the charismatic prophets were not seeking salvation in Matthew 7:21; they were seeking "greatness," and that is probably the motive they had in doing all these wonderful works. It is very unlikely that those addressing Jesus as "Lord, Lord," are unsaved. Non-Christians are not able to cast out demons and perform miracles in Christ's name.

Because this entrance is based upon good works, Jesus is clearly not speaking of soteriology. To "enter the kingdom" refers to seeking surpassing righteousness and pursuing the journey along the narrow way, the path of discipleship. What Jesus has in mind here is not mere physical entrance into the kingdom but the abundant entrance the charismatic prophets thought they deserved (2 Peter 1:10-11), an entrance into greatness there (Matthew 5:19-20).[81]

The Free Grace solution suggested above understands "kingdom" as that aspect of the kingdom which refers to living life, and not entering it. To enter the kingdom is parallel to entering the narrow way, the way of life described in the sermon. The narrow way is not the way of salvation. That "way" is very broad. Many believers chose that way of life. Jesus spoke of this in Matthew 16:24-26. The path of discipleship described in the sermon, however, is very narrow.

While Dr. Grudem's conclusion that the phrases "depart from me" and "I never knew you" can refer to the rejection of false professors of faith and their assignment to damnation, that is not necessarily true.

---

80 Grudem, *Systematic Theology*: 214.

81 Those who are already saved are called on to enter into full discipleship by *"doing the will of the Father"* (Matthew 7:21), by living out the Sermon on the Mount, and by having a *"righteousness* [that] *surpasses that of the scribes and Pharisees"* (5:20). The outcome of personal salvation is regeneration and justification; the outcome of "doing the will of the Father" is "greatness" (5:19). The former refers to personal salvation, and the latter refers to application of the Sermon on the Mount, which leads to fullness of life and reward, a common theme in the Sermon (Matthew 5:12, 46; 6:1-6, 16, 18; 10:41-42; 16:24-26). These believers in 7:21-23 may be "in" the kingdom, that is, saved people, but they will be "least" there.

When Jesus says, "I do not know you," it is unlikely that he is referring to "knowing" in a saving sense. Instead, just as the Pharisees did not "know" John the Baptist in the sense that they did not acknowledge and approve of his ministry as that of the coming Elijah, neither did Jesus approve of the ministry of these false prophets. They bragged about their exorcisms and miracles instead of the more mundane requirement of obedience to the sermon. They preferred enthusiasm over ethics.

In conclusion, we suggest this understanding of the phrase "enter the kingdom":

> To enter the kingdom means to make a commitment to pursue the surpassing righteousness which will result in hearing the King say, "Well done!" at the Judgment Seat of Christ. This outcome and the initial commitment to pursue the kingdom way of life are an interconnected whole that cannot be separated. When the phrase refers to the end of the process, "that day," (Matthew 7:21) it refers to an abundant entrance into the kingdom—high honor. When no eschatological reference is found in the contexts, the other entry sayings refer to the initial commitment to enter the kingdom by the narrow gate and proceed to the narrow way of discipleship, that is, enter the kingdom way of life.

Chapter 15

Who Are the Branches? – John 15:1-2

Joseph Dillow, Th.D.

The Last Supper has been completed, and Jesus and his disciples have crossed the Kidron Valley, east of Jerusalem, and are proceeding up the slopes of the Mount of Olives. As they pass by the many grapevines lining their path that have been lifted up and tied to the supporting trellises in the vineyards, Jesus says, "I am the true vine, and my Father is the vine dresser."

The disciples have just received some frightening news. Their Master is going to be killed, and they will be left alone! In John 15–17, Jesus compassionately addresses these fears. Just as these vines have been lifted up, he wants to lift them up spiritually and psychologically and to prepare them for the difficulties ahead. His counsel in John 15 is to "abide in the vine," and if they do, they will experience enablement, fruit bearing, and answers to prayer; and they will be his "friends."

There has been much difference of opinion about the meaning of this passage. Some of the difficulty is related to the fact that the analogy emerges from an agrarian economy that is not familiar to those of us in the industrialized West. Consequently, cultural and historical data will help us know about some of the key terms and concepts in that culture.

15:1   I am the true vine, and my Father is the vinedresser.

15:2   Every branch in me that does not bear fruit, he takes away, and every branch that bears fruit, he prunes it, that it may bear more fruit. (John 15:1-2)

To correctly understand these two verses, five questions must first be answered that have significant bearing on the interpretations suggested on the following pages. (1) To whom is Jesus speaking? Is Jesus speaking about nonbelievers or believers? (2) What is the meaning of "takes away"? (3) What is a branch "in me"? (4) What is the application to the apostles? (5) What does "abide in me" mean?

To Whom Is Jesus Speaking?

Is Jesus describing those who have merely professed faith in Christ, or is he thinking of his regenerate disciples? Most expositors agree that the branches that bear fruit and are pruned represent true Christians. However, some,[1] like Dr. Grudem, believe that the branch "in me" that does not bear fruit is not a true Christian.[2]

The Meaning of "in Me"

The normal understanding of this passage creates difficulties for Grudem's Reformed view of the passage, because it shows that a truly saved person, that is, one who is "in Christ," might not bear fruit. The traditional interpretation of this phrase is stated by Bishop Westcott, "Even the unfruitful branches are true branches. They are

---

1   Charles R. Smith, "The Unfruitful Branches in John 15," *Grace Journal* 9, no. 2 (Spring 1968): 10. See also Bishop Ryle. "It cannot be shown that a branch in Me must mean a believer in Me. It means nothing more than a 'professing member of My Church, a man joined to the company of My people, but not joined to Me." J. C. Ryle, *Expository Thoughts on the Gospels* (Grand Rapids: Zondervan Publishing House, n.d.), 4:334.

2   Wayne A. Grudem, *"Free Grace" Theology: 5 Ways It Diminishes the Gospel* (Wheaton: Crossway, 2016), 123.

also 'in Christ.'"[3] To avoid this difficulty, Grudem brings his Reformed thinking into the passage and says that "in me" must not refer to a saving relationship, because in their system, all true believers bear fruit,[4] and the person in this verse did not bear fruit. The best evidence against this view is that there is absolutely no evidence for it.

Furthermore, if I understand him correctly, it seems that Dr. Grudem contradicts himself. On one hand he believes that the "in me" relationship is a *professing* relationship,[5] but on the other hand he agrees with the Free Grace view that it is a saving, united, and harmonious relationship.[6] He says, "When we stray from fellowship with Christ because of sin in our lives, we diminish the degree to which we are abiding in Christ."[7] He explains that the "in me" relationship is the "in Christ relationship."[8] To abide "in me" is to abide in fellowship.[9]

---

3   B.F. Westcott, *The Gospel According to St. John* (Grand Rpids: William B. Eerdmans Publishing Company, 1881), 217.

4   Grudem, *"Free Grace" Theology*: 121.

5   He parallels it with Matthew 7:21 where those who say "Lord, Lord," have only professed to believe (in his view) in the person of Christ but who have not done the "will of the Father" and are therefore not saved. Also he relates the "in me" relationship to the second soil in Jesus's parable that represents those who "received the word with joy," but fell away and were, in his interpretation, only professing Christians. Wayne A. Grudem, *Systematic Theology: An Introduction to Biblical Doctrine* (Grand Rapids, MI: Inter-Varsity Press, 2004), 796.

6   Ibid., 844. Grudem says, "This abiding in Christ will include not only day-by-day trust in him in various situations, but also certainly regular fellowship with him in prayer and worship." Grudem, *Systematic Theology*, 805, 44. But this is precisely the Free Grace view. See Joseph C. Dillow, *Final Destiny: The Future Reign of the Servant Kings*, 3rd revised ed. (Monument, CO: Paniym Group, Inc., 2016; reprint, 2016), 601, ff. Because Grudem believes that to be "in Christ" is to be saved, a professing Christian cannot abide in Christ.

7   Grudem, *Systematic Theology*: 505.

8   Ibid., 845.

9   Wayne A. Grudem, *Systematic Theology: An Introduction to Biblical Doctrine* (Leicester, England; Grand Rapids, MI: Inter-Varsity Press; Zondervan Pub. House, 2004), 505.

I suspect that he needs to make this switch because a professing Christian cannot abide in Christ. So, in v. 4 he switches and says, "in me" refers to a true profession of Christ. This seems more like eisegesis than exegesis. Then in 15:6 he switches again to "in me" being a non-believer because his system will not allow that a believer can be cast off and burned. Why not? Because, he believes, all "true" believers will persevere in good works to the end of life.

The phrase "in me"[10] is used sixteen times in John's Gospel.[11] A review of the sixteen usages in John shows that when he used this phrase, the Lord referred to a true Christian maintaining a life of fellowship, a unity of purpose rather than an organic connection.[12]

---

10 Gr. *en emoi*, first person, singular, dative, personal pronoun (*egō*).

11 John 6:56; 10:38; 14:10 (2x), 11, 20, 30; 15:2, 4 (2x), 5, 6, 7; 16:33; 17:21, 23

12 For example, in John 10:38, "in me" speaks of the fellowship between Christ and the Father. Consider also John 14:30 where the Lord insists that the ruler of this world has nothing "in me"; that is, he has no relationship or part with Jesus, no communion of purpose. In 14:20 the Lord says that in "that day" they will know that he is in them and they are in him. The sense seems to be that, when they see him in resurrection, they will know again the fellowship they have with him now. "That day" could refer either to the coming of the Holy Spirit at Pentecost or to the appearances of the resurrected Christ to his disciples. The preceding verse seems to connect it with the resurrection appearances. This is confirmed by John 16:16 where he also speaks of the fact that in a little while they will no longer behold him and then in a little while they will see him, a reference to his appearance in resurrection. The meaning then is that when they see Christ in resurrection, they will understand fully some things they do not understand fully now. What they will understand is that Christ was "in the Father" and that they are in Christ and he is in them. The objective knowledge of the resurrected Christ will bring about this clear perception. At this time they will see clearly that Christ has been operating in complete unity of purpose with the Father and that they are in complete unity of purpose with him. Apparently, they will know something they do not know now. They are already regenerate, but there is something they either do not know at all or only know imperfectly. What brings about the change? The text does not say, but later John states that before the disciples did not understand that he had to rise from the dead (John 20:9). Apparently seeing Christ in his resurrected state brought a flood of understanding concerning the Old Testament predictions and Christ's unity of purpose and obedience to the

While it is certain that true believers do have an organic connection with Christ, that is not what "in me" means. If this is correct, it is not possible to take it as "the sphere of profession."[13] A person "in me" is, as many interpreters have concluded,[14] always a true Christian in association or in union with Christ.[15] Alfred Edersheim, in agreement with Free Grace interpreters, notes that "merely outward profession of Christ could scarcely be described as 'a branch in' Him.'"[16]

To be "in me" is simply to be in fellowship with Christ, living obediently and with a common purpose. Therefore, it is possible for a true Christian not to be "in me" in the Johannine sense. In Grudem's

---

Father, and this solidified their commitment to him. The resurrection forever removed doubts regarding who he was and resulted in a change that lasted the rest of their lives. They committed themselves fully to follow him forever. That commitment, brought about by their seeing Christ in his resurrected state on "that day," resulted in their total unity of purpose and obedience to him. That is when they knew the experience of unity and fellowship, "you in me and I in you," with their resurrected Lord.

13 Contra D. A. Carson, *The Gospel According to John* (Downers Grove, IL: InterVarsity, 1991), 515. The Lord is not teaching that the ruler of this world has no part of his essence (who would have thought that?), but that they are not like-minded. We learn that "in me there is peace (John 16:33). Only believers who are abiding in fellowship can experience this. Elsewhere Christ specifically connects the "in me" experience with similar purposes in life (John 17:21-23).

14 We agree with Beasley-Murray's conclusion. "To 'remain' in Jesus . . . connotes continuing to live in association or union with him," George R. Beasley-Murray, *The Gospel According to John*, Word Biblical Commentary (Dallas, TX: Word Incorporated, 2002), 36:272.

15 It should be noted that this is different from Paul's usage of the concept of "in Christ." While Paul did use the phrase "in Christ" (not "in me") in this way, he often used it in a forensic (legal) sense referring to the believer's position in Christ or to his organic membership in his body (e.g., 1 Corinthians 12:13). But John never does this. For him, to be "in him" is to be in communion with him and not organically connected in union with him.

16 Alfred Edersheim, *The Life and Times of Jesus the Messiah*, New American Edition ed., 2 vols. (Grand Rapids: Wm. B. Eerdmans Publishing Co., 1962), 520.

view, the phrase "in me" in v. 2 refers only to a professing relationship with Christ. But, we ask, "How could it be that an unsaved professing Christian can 'abide in Christ,' and bear fruit?!" On the other hand, if a person "in me" is a true Christian, then Grudem's interpretation of vv. 2 and 6 that a person not abiding is cast into hell[17] conflicts with his doctrine of eternal security. This leads us to a discussion of one of John's favorite terms, "abide" (Gr. *menō*).

The Meaning of "Abide"

According to Webster, the English word "abide" means (1) to wait for; (2) to endure without yielding, to withstand, to bear patiently, to tolerate; (3) to remain stable or in a fixed state, to continue in a place.[18] Thus, it is similar in meaning to the Greek word *menō*.

The lexicons are unanimous in saying that the verb *menō* means "to remain."[19] It is used often in John, and in **every** instance, it means to remain, to stay, to continue, or to endure.[20] Christ commands his disciples to remain in him. What does it mean to "remain"? Grudem admits that this refers to "fellowship" but never explains how a professing ("in me") Christian (who is not truly a Christian) can have

---

17 Grudem, *"Free Grace" Theology*: 123.

18 Webster's Ninth New College Dictionary (Springfield, MA: Merriam-Webster, Inc. 1987), p. 44.

19 For example, Friedrich Hauck says it means "to stay in a place." Figuratively, it means "to remain in a sphere," "to stand against opposition, to endure, to hold fast" (Friedrich Hauck, "*menō*," in TDNT, 4:574-88). The word is used of the permanence of God in contrast to human mutability. God's counsel "endures" (Romans 9:11), his Word endures (1 Peter 1:23, 25), the New Covenant endures (2 Corinthians 3:11), and faith, hope, and love endure (1 Corinthians 13:13). Paul uses *menō* of the perseverance of believers in the faith (1 Timothy 2:15; 2 Timothy 2:13, 15). If we endure, we will reign with him. If we are faithless, he "remains" faithful. Karlfried Munzer says it is used metaphorically to mean to hold fast, or remain steadfast, that is, in a teaching (2 Timothy 3:14; 2 John 9), in fellowship with (John 14:10), to pass the test when one's works are judged (1 Corinthians 3:14). See Colin Brown, "remain," in NIDNTT, 3:224.

20 For example, John 1:32, 38, 39; 2:12.

fellowship with Christ. He says, "This abiding in Christ will include not only day-by-day trust in him in various situations, but also certainly regular fellowship with him in prayer and worship." However, he adds that to verify that this experience is fellowship with Christ, a person must have a "continuing relationship with Christ."[21] That is, he must persevere in abiding until he dies. If he does not, this means he was never born again to begin with. But if so, how could he have ever abided in Christ as both the text and Grudem say he did?

Chafer correctly notes that "the idea of abiding in Christ as a branch in a vine could serve as an illustration of either union [organic connection, salvation] or communion [fellowship] with Him."[22] Jesus himself clarifies which of these two options is correct when he says,

> If you keep my commandments, you will abide in my love; just as I have kept my Father's commandments, and abide in his love. (John 15:10)

Jesus abides in his Father's love by keeping his commandments. "It is certain that Christ was not attempting to preserve union [i.e., organic connection] with the Father . . . by obedience."[23] Just like those he came to save, he kept in communion (fellowship) with his Father by keeping his commandments.

What is the Meaning of "Takes Away"?

If the above discussion is correct, we have established that to be "in me" means to be walking in fellowship with Christ and does not refer to merely professing a relationship with Christ. The way one "remains" is by obedience and faithfulness. However, an interpretive problem arises when Jesus says,

---

21 Grudem, *Systematic Theology*: 804.

22 Lewis Sperry Chafer, *Systematic Theology*, 8 vols. (Dallas: Dallas Sminary Press, 1948), 3:298.

23 Ibid., 3:299.

*Every branch in me that does not bear fruit, he **takes away** [Gr. airō]; and every branch that bears fruit, he prunes it so that it may bear more fruit.* (John 15:2)

What does he mean when he says he "takes away" the unfruitful branch? This consequence has been understood in four different ways.[24] However, in the discussion to follow, we will only discuss two, Dr. Grudem's Reformed view and the Free Grace view.

Grudem's View: They Are Separated from Superficial Connection with Christ

Although in some places Grudem says that those "in me" are true Christians, he changes his opinion when he deals with John 15:2, 6 and asserts that "in me" is only a label for a professing Christian. He argues that "takes away" refers to the permanent separation of professing Christians from a superficial connection with Christ.

Why? There are two reasons. In Grudem's system, all true believers must produce fruit to the end of life. Since the believer in v. 2 did not bear fruit, his system requires that that person cannot not be a true Christian. Secondly, since the same person in v. 6 is removed and burned, and this, in his interpretation, refers to damnation, he could not be a true Christian because that would contradict the doctrine of eternal security.[25]

---

24 For discussion of this, see John A Tucker, "The Inevitability of Fruit Bearing - Part I," *The Journal of Dispensational Theology* 15, no. 44 (April 2011): 63.

25 Similarly, Darrel Bock argues the same way, realizing that a branch "in me" seems to suggest that a true believer is involved in v. 6. He says the meaning of the image must change in v. 6 and refer to "attachment" and not a saving connection. The only evidence he gives for this change is the requirement of his theology. He says those who hear his voice, follow him (John 10). Therefore, since the non-abiders do not follow, they must be merely professing Christians. Of course, it is true that true believers follow and do good works but they do not always persevere in good works to the end of life as the chapter on the carnal Christian has shown. He also argues that the text must be read from its conclusion back. Since the conclusion is that they face burning, that is, hell (his view of 15:6), then those "thrown away" must be non-believers.

If "in me" means to be in fellowship with Christ, as Grudem sometimes admits,[26] then, as pointed out above, the branch connected with the vine must be a true, not merely a professing, Christian. If the phrase "he takes away" refers only to professing Christians, then the only application to the disciples would be to warn his discouraged and fearful disciples that they may not really be born again and would go to hell, unless they can prove they are true Christians. This is hardly a likely interpretation in this atmosphere of encouragement and tenderness needed on their last night together![27]

It would seem obvious that it is possible for a Christian through disobedience to remove himself from Christ's influence and enablement. That seems to be the danger the Lord is warning about in this very passage. But that in no way implies that the one being warned is not a Christian. In fact, since he is commanded to remain in that sphere of influence and enablement, we may safely assume he was in it already and hence was regenerate.

Free Grace View: They Are Lifted Up and Encouraged

We must consider the context in which these words were spoken. Jesus is addressing the believing disciples and preparing them for their work after his departure. It is a time when they need encouragement. Would

---

Why? Because his doctrine of eternal security requires this. He overlooks the fact that there are two fires in eternity: the lake of fire and the fire at the Judgment Seat of Christ (1 Corinthians 3:15). If he could admit that a carnal Christian is a reality, his difficulties with the passage would evaporate. See Darrel L. Bock, *Jesus According to Scripture* (Grand Rapids: Baker, 2002), 507.

26 Grudem, *Systematic Theology*: 804, 44. J. Carl Laney, "Abiding Is Believing: The Analogy of the Vine in John 15:1-6," *BibSac* 146, no. 582 (January-March 1989): 64.

27 Therefore, some suggest that the analogy of the vine and the branches is intended to give the disciples instruction *concerning those to whom they would minister* and who did not bear fruit. Laney, "Abiding Is Believing: The Analogy of the Vine in John 15:1-6." Yet the text itself gives every evidence that in its entirety it was addressed *to the disciples* to tell *them* how they could bear fruit in their lives John 15:8.

Jesus spend time warning them that, unless they bear fruit, they will prove not be true Christians and be cast into the lake of fire, as Grudem maintains?[28] Does Jesus doubt that the eleven are saved? The disciples were to be the leaders of the early church. Yet now they are about to lose their leader whom they love, and their world will be turned upside down. Their need is encouragement and lifting up, not warnings of hell. This metaphor, consistent with the whole context, is about fruit bearing, not salvation.

The Immature Branch

First, let us consider the meaning of the phrase, "does not bear fruit" (ESV, NASB). The process of growing grapes often takes five years before they are harvested. During that time, the vinedresser does many things to bring them from infancy to maturity.

Like most Reformed interpreters, Dr. Grudem understands the Greek phrase, *mē pheron karpon*, to be translated "does not bear (Gr. *pheron*) fruit," implying it never did and never will. Since in his system, all true believers bear fruit to "some"[29] degree until the end of life, this means that the "branch in me" is only a professing Christian and is not born again.

Many of the translations translate, *"does not bear fruit"* (ESV, NKJV, NAB, NET, etc.), or *"bears no fruit"* (NIV, NRSV). However, the word *"pheron"* (bear) is a present participle. While these translations are accurate, they are not the only manner which one could translate a present participle. To render it "does not" is more absolute than the present participle requires. That translation might infer that this branch never has and never will bear fruit; that it is the *characteristic* of this branch. This rendering would fit better with the Reformed doctrine of holiness to the end of life. However, at the risk of being arrogant, I humbly suggest that these translations are doubtful in this context. A better translation would be "is not bearing" fruit." In other words, "it is not *presently* bearing fruit. It does

---

28 Grudem, *Systematic Theology*: 795.

29 Ibid., 788.

not say that it never did or never will, as Grudem's understanding requires.[30]

In fact, the immature vine does not bear fruit for the first three years.[31] That fact could imply that Jesus's point is that the *immature* branch does not bear fruit. Tucker correctly notes that "non-fruit bearing branches are allowed to remain so they can mature over the growing season into a fruiting branch in the future. Such branches are appropriately *encouraged* by the vinedresser and *not removed* by the vinedresser."[32] As Pink says, "It is not a branch that never bore fruit . . . but of one who is *no longer* bearing fruit."[33] Or, better, it *is not presently* bearing fruit.

There are many examples in the New Testament of the Greek word "*mē*" (not) preceding an anarthrous present participle (as it does in John 15:2, *mē pheron*), which do not imply that the person never did and never will perform the action of the main verb. When Jesus says, "The man who has two tunics is to share with him who has none [μὴ ἔχοντι]; and he who has food is to do likewise" (Luke 3:11), are we to understand that this man never had a tunic or that he is one "having none" at the time of the encounter? Many other passages could be cited.[34] Therefore, it is perfectly acceptable to translate the passage as

---

30 "The *present* participle is used for *contemporaneous* time," Daniel Wallace, *Greek Grammar Beyond the Basics* (Grand Rapids: Zondervan Publishing House, 1996), 614. The action denoted by the present participle is contemporaneous to the action of the main verb, *airō*. The branch is not bearing fruit at the time the vinedresser lifts it up. The grammar cannot be pressed to say anything beyond this. Whether the branch once bore fruit or never bore fruit must be determined by context and perhaps background information regarding 1st century viticultural practices.

31 William Barclay, *The Gospel of John*, 2 vols., The Daily Study Bible Series (Philadelphia: Westminster, 1955), 202.

32 John A Tucker, "The Inevitability of Fruit Growing: Part 2," *The Journal of Dispensational Theology* 15, no. 45 (August 11): 51-52.

33 Authur W. Pink, *Exposition of the Gospel of John*, 3 vols. (Grand Rapids: Zondervan Publishing House, 1945), 2:399.

34 When Jesus says that "every tree therefore that does not bear good fruit [μὴ ποιοῦν]" (Luke 3:9), are we to understand that he refers to trees that never

"every branch in me not bearing fruit." This translation more accurately reflects the actual growth pattern of grapevines. In fact, in this context where Jesus is speaking to his saved disciples, *"not bearing fruit"* is preferable.[35] Grapevines do not bear fruit when they are first planted; they are immature.

"Takes Away"

What, then, does Jesus mean when he says that the Vinedresser "takes away" a branch that does not bear fruit? The Greek word *airō* used in verse 2 and translated "takes away" is used twenty-six times in the Gospel of John. The lexicons often translate *airō* as "to lift from the ground," or "to lift up,"[36] or "to raise to a higher place or position, to lift up, take up, pickup,"[37] not necessarily "to take away."[38] For example, Jesus said to the paralytic, *"take up [airō] your bed and walk"* (John 5:8), and then the man *"took up [airō] his bed and walked"* (5:9). The Pharisees *"picked up"* [*airō*] stones to throw at Christ (John 8:59). Free Grace interpreters believe that the Vinedresser "lifts up" the branch that is not currently bearing fruit so it can bear fruit. This

---

bore fruit and never will? No. He refers to trees "not bearing fruit" at the present time. When Paul says, "and those who weep, as though they did not weep [μὴ κλαίοντες]," does he mean "as those who never wept and never will" (1 Corinthians 1:30)? When Paul says, "But he who stands firm in his heart, being under no constraint [μὴ ἔχων ἀνάγκην]," are we to understand that his person has never had restraint and never will? Or is Paul saying, "having no restraint" at the present time? When Paul says, "as under the Law though not being myself under the Law [μὴ ὢν αὐτὸς ὑπὸ νόμον], are we to understand that Paul was never under the law? When Jesus fed the four thousand, Mark says, "they had nothing to eat [μὴ ἐχόντων]" Mark 8:1. Does this mean they never had anything to eat and never will? No. We can translate "there was a large crowd *having at the present time nothing* to eat."

35 Some translations do translate this way. See the *Darby* and *Young's Literal Interpretation* Bibles.

36 Joachim Jeremias, "*airō*" in TDNT, 1:185.

37 *BDAG*, 28.

38 John 1:29; 2:16.

may refer to the new branches that are immature and are planted in the spring.

However, Dr. Grudem says he could not find references in the Bible dictionaries to lifting up the vines.[39]

Actually, there are a considerable number of references. In fact, Grudem even admits this. In one of the sources Grudem quotes, Pliny says that the vines are, "supported by poles or trellises (see 1 Kings 4:25; Micah 4:4; Zechariah 3:10)."[40] *The Interpreter's Dictionary of the Bible* says the vines were "propped up with forked sticks."[41] For example, Harrison says, "when the fruit-bearing branches developed they were raised above the ground on supports."[42] Grudem does admit that there is evidence that grapevines "were sometimes supported on wooden posts."[43] We ask, "How did they get up on those posts?" Obviously, they were "lifted up." This admission weakens Grudem's argument.

Apparently, Grudem is not aware of a good amount of evidence for this viticultural practice. Pliny refers to "the vine that is propped and requires a single cross-piece, and the vine that requires a trellis of four compartments."[44] Evidently, this practice was quite common in Palestine.[45] Spooner says, "grapevines are climbing plants that do

---

39 Grudem, *"Free Grace" Theology*: 122-23.

40 R. K. Harrison, "Vine," in *NISBE*, 4:986.

41 J. F. Ross, "Vine" in George Arthur Buttrick, *The Interpreter's Dictionary of the Bible*, 4 vols. (New York,: Abingdon Press, 1962), 785.

42 R. K. Harrison and F. N. Hepper, "Vine, Vineyard," in *The New Bible Dictionary*, ed. D. R. W. Wood and I. H. Marshall (Downers Grove, IL: InterVarsity Press, 1996), 1225.

43 Grudem, *"Free Grace" Theology*: 122-23.

44 Pliny, "The Culture of the Vine and the Various Shrubs which Support It," in *The Natural History* (Medford, MA: Taylor and Francis, 1855), 17:35, p. 3499.

45 It is curious that Alan Stanley would say, "The problem with this interpretation is that is relies more on historical background than on the context of the passage." However, historical background is part of the "context of the passage." Furthermore, the entire context of the passage shows that *airō* means "lift up." The need was encouragement for the disciples, not damnation if they fail!

not have their own natural support."[46] They climb upward by "twining [coil] their stems around a support."[47] The word for "lift up" used in vinedresser circles is "climbing." Annually, the vinedresser "trains" the vine so that it will climb. This refers to an annual process where the vinedresser guides the vine in the vertical direction so that as it grows, it wraps itself around the pole and, eventually, after a five-year period, arrives at the Trellis (crossbar) at the top.[48] The purpose of the annual training is so the vine will produce more buds from which the grapes come.[49] In other words, the vinedresser does this in order to encourage the vine to bear fruit. This self-climbing of the vine is a natural process by which the vine is "lifted up."

In agreement with the Free Grace view, R. K. Harrison argues that the word translated "takes away" (Gr. *airō*) is best rendered "lifts up" in John 15:2, as it is five times in John's gospel.[50] In addition to the natural tendency of the vines to climb, that is, lift themselves up after being "trained" to the poles, he says that it was a common practice for the vinedresser to lift with meticulous care vine branches that had fallen and to allow them to heal.[51] When the branches matured enough to be able to bear fruit, "they were raised above the ground on supports (Ezekiel 17:6),"[52] and "the end of the vinestock is raised by means of a cleft stick a foot or more above the surface."[53] This view of *airō* is held

---

This is what much of the Upper Room Discourse is about. Alan P. Stanley, *Did Jesus Teach Salvation by Works? The Role of Works in Salvation in the Synoptic Gospels* (Eugene, OR: Pickwick Publishers, 2006), 256.

46 Alden Spooner, *American Grape Vines and Making of Wine* (Brooklyn: A. Spooner & Co. Printers, 1846), 30.

47 https://en.wikipedia.org/wiki/Vine_training

48 Ibid.

49 Spooner, *American Grape Vines and Making of Wine*: 30.

50 John 5:8, 9, 11; 12; 8:59

51 Harrison, "Vine," 4:986.

52 Harrison and Hepper, "Vine, Vineyard," 1225.

53 E. W. G. Masterman, "Vine," in *ISBE*, ed. James Orr (Albany, OR: Ages Software, 1999).

by a number of interpreters.[54] The writer has observed this practice himself in the vineyards behind his former home in Austria.

To climb the poles under their own power and be guided (trained) by the vinedresser are all references in Pliny to lifting up to bear fruit. Thus, contra Grudem, there is a considerable amount of evidence in any book on the viticulture of grapevines stating that the vinedresser lifted up the vines *so that these vines could produce fruit*. Every statement that the vine "climbs" refers to how God lifts up the vine.[55]

Why is the Vine Lifted Up?

What then, according to Dr. Grudem, is the purpose the Vinedresser has in mind when he "removes" the vine? In his response to the Free Grace view that the correct translation of *airō* is "lifts up," he says, "Yes, but there is no evidence that the Vinedresser did this *so that these vines could produce fruit*." The text only says that the *pruned branches bear fruit*. Of course, one could respond saying, "There is no source I can find that vinedressers did not lift up the vines for the purpose of helping them produce fruit." Therefore, his argument from silence proves nothing. But more importantly, there are sources which say they are lifted up to bear fruit by naturally climbing the poles.

Pliny says that the newly planted, immature, vines grow near the ground at first. But by the fifth year they must "be *trained* to the cross-

---

54 Pink, *Exposition of the Gospel of John*. M.S. Mills, *The Life of Christ: A Study Guide to the Gospel Record* (Dallas, TX: 3E Ministries, 1999), s.v. John 15:1-8. Paul Enns, *The Moody Handbook of Theology* (Chicago: Moody Press, 1989), 352. Tucker, "The Inevitability of Fruit Bearing - Part I." William McDonald and Arthur L. Farstad, *Believer's Bible Commentary* (Nashville: Thomas Nelson, 1995), 1549. Tom Constable, *Tom Constable's Expository Notes on the Bible* (Garland, TX: Galaxie Software, 2003), s.v. John 15:2. Gary W. Derickson, "Viticulture and John 15:1-6," *BibSac* 153, no. 609 (January-March 1996). J. Dwight Pentecost, *The Words and Works of Jesus Christ* (Grand Rapids: Zondervan, 1981), 441. Chafer, *Systematic Theology*: 3:299. Gary W. Derickson and Earl D. Radmacher, *The Disciplemaker: What matters Most to Jesus* (Salem, OR: Charis Press, 2001), 161.

55 Pliny, "The Culture of the Vine and the Various Shrubs which Support It." See 17:35, p. 3514; 17:36, p. 3517.

piece"[56] and climb the poles around which they are twined or they will not bear fruit. The vines climb by their own power, guided (trained) by the vinedresser and climb higher so they can be "ripened continuously by the sun." He adds, "this is best of all for the wine."[57] To "ripen continuously" is to bear fruit. He specifically says, "When the trellis is employed [i.e., when the vine has been "trained" to go upward], wine is produced in greater quantities,"[58] that is, the vine bears more fruit. All the texts I have consulted on the viticulture of vines mention that they must be trained vertically, that is, guided to climb upward to the trellis.[59]

Grudem quotes Pliny saying, "If a vine is making poor growth, make a bonfire of its shoots and plow in the ashes therefrom."[60] From this, referring to the Free Grace interpretation of John 15:6, he concludes that this is "opposite of what Free Grace supporters argue." It is not "opposite" at all. It is exactly what Free Grace supporters believe. Some branches never respond to the Vinedresser's encouragement and are burned as trash, that is, they experience a negative assessment of their wasted, unfruitful lives at the Judgment Seat of Christ (1 Corinthians 3:15; 1 John 2:28; 2 John 8; Luke 19:26). There is no evidence in John 15:6 that this refers to damnation. That is mere assertion.

How the Vines are Lifted

Being "lifted up" and "bearing more fruit" are the end of a process. They do not happen in an instant either in vineyards or in the lives of believers. In regard to vines, God has built this tendency of the vine to wrap around the posts and climb upward. "The common grape vine is

---

56 Ibid., 17:35, p. 3504.

57 Ibid., 17:35, p. 3499.

58 Ibid., 3499.

59 Spooner notes that the vines "must be trained vertically in a serpentine form between the bearing branches on the trellis." Spooner, *American Grape Vines and Making of Wine*: 30. Apparently this "training" goes on for at least five years, and during all five years the vinedresser trains the branches. In the fifth year, not yet having reached the trellis, they "may be trained vertically." Ibid., 36-38.

60 Grudem, *"Free Grace" Theology*: 123.

a hardy . . . climber."[61] "Pliny states that the vines in Italy would climb to the very top and even out-top the highest poplars."[62] In other words, God "lifts up" the vine by a providential process (second causes) and not by a direct miracle. How does he do this? In his amazing creative design, he programmed into the genetic code, resident in the DNA, information that says to the vine's cells, "climb." In other words, the vine is genetically programmed to climb. Of course, the disciples know nothing of DNA and genes, but they see vines climbing of their own accord all the time.

What is the Application to the Disciples?

The fact that the grape vine is a climbing vine and only needs to be "trained" or guided to be lifted up on the poles is a wonderful picture of the Christian life. Believers need guidance from other Christians, Scripture and the Holy Spirit (i.e., "training") if they are to be lifted and bear fruit. Then the Holy Spirit (not DNA programming) enables them to rise. The act of lifting is for the purpose of bearing fruit. New or discouraged believers, like the disciples, need encouragement, not, as Grudem suggests, a warning that they might go to hell. To be lifted up is to be encouraged to press on in the Christian life.

The Hebrew word for "encourage" is *ḥāzaq*, and it is used many times with God as the subject. It means to "make strong" or to "strengthen."[63] The Lord "strengthened" Sampson (Judges 3:12), and he *ḥāzaq* the hands of Nehemiah. Paul said, "[M]ay the God of hope fill you with all joy and peace in believing" (Romans 15:13). The Psalmist says, "In the day of trouble . . . he will *lift me up* on a rock and now my head will be *lifted up*" (Psalm 27:5-6). "*The Lord is near to the brokenhearted, And saves those who are crushed in spirit*" (Psalm 34:17–18). "*The Lord lifts up* the meek; but brings sinners down to the ground (Psalm 146:6,

---

61 Cited by George Johnson, George Johnson, *The Grape Vine: Its Culture, Uses, and History*, vol. 1, The Gardner's Monthly Volume (Winchester, London: R. Baldwin, Paternoster Row 1847), 28.

62 J. Allen Fisk, *Culture and Treatment of the Grape Vine* (Boston: Dutton and Wentworth, 1848), 10.

63 TWOT, 276

LXX). Scripture indicates that the Christian strengthened by God will grow more and more like Christ. He will manifest the fruit of the Spirit (Galatians 5:22-23). However, like the vine, the believer goes through a training process (Hebrews 5:14; 12:11).

God uses three means to "lift up" and encourage immature or discouraged believers.[64]

First, just as God used the vinedresser to assist the vine in climbing the poles, he uses other people to encourage the downfallen or immature. "[H]ow delightful is a timely word" (Proverbs 15:23). Paul sent Tychicus to encourage the hearts of the Colossians (Colossians 4:8). Christians are to "encourage one another" (1 Thessalonians 5:11).[65]

Secondly, God also uses Scripture to encourage us (Romans 15:4). When discouraged by false accusers, the Psalmist says, "*Even though princes sit and talk against me, Thy servant meditates on thy statutes*" (Psalm 119:23). When facing terrible discouragement, he says, "*My soul weeps because of grief; Strengthen me according to thy word.*" (Psalm 119:28).

There is a third way the heavenly Vinedresser encourages us. He sends the Holy Spirit to dwell in our hearts. Jesus said, "*And I will ask the Father, and he will give you another helper (Gr. paraklētos), that he may be with you forever*" (John 14:16). The word *paraklētos* means "one who appears in another's behalf, a mediator, intercessor, helper."[66] The verbal form for *paraklētos* is *parakaleō*, which means "to call to one's side, encourage,"[67] or "to instill someone with courage or cheer, comfort, encourage, cheer up."[68] In the metaphor with the vine and the

---

64 Of course, it is doubtful that the metaphor in John 15 intends all the applications. However, it seems to be that the broader context of Scripture can be discussed here.

65 Moses is told to encourage (Heb. ⊠āzaq) Joshua (Deuteronomy 1:38). "The craftsman encourages (Heb. ⊠āzaq) the smelter" (Isa. 41:7). The one who smooths metal says to the one who solders, "It is good" (Isaiah 41:7). We are to "encourage one another day after day (Hebrews 3:13).

66 *BDAG*, 766

67 *BDAG*, 764.

68 *BDAG*, 765.

branches, the believers are enabled by the ministry of the Holy Spirit (not DNA programming) to climb upward. The earthly vine cannot do otherwise if it has been trained. However, in the application to the disciples, they must abide in the vine if they are to secure the help of the Holy Spirit and be lifted up to bear fruit. If they refuse to do this, it is at that time the warning about loss at the Judgment Seat of Christ in John 15:6 applies.

There are four categories of Christians in these verses

Category of Christian	Level of Fruit Bearing	Action of the Vinedresser	Result
New and immature believer (v.2)	No fruit	The Lord lifts him up, encourages him	Bears fruit
Mature believer (v.2)	Bears fruit	Vinedresser prunes the believer so he can bear more fruit	Bears more fruit
Abiding believer (v.5)	Much fruit		Bears much fruit
Carnal believer (v.6)	No fruit	He dries up and is cast into the fire	He suffers loss of rewards at the Judgment Seat of Christ

This verse is a divine promise that every unfruitful Christian who is not bearing fruit and *yet is walking in fellowship,* that is, is "in me," will be lifted up, that is, receive divine encouragement.

The Lord encourages the meek, and he normally does this by a process, not by a miracle. This understanding of John 15:2 fits extremely well with the whole context of Christ's last night with those whom he loved. This was a time when the disciples needed encouragement, not a time of threatening them with damnation if they do not prove to be true believers as Grudem maintains! He wants them to know that in the coming weeks, after his crucifixion and departure, the Vinedresser will tenderly care for them and lift them into the light on the trellises where they can bear fruit, even if they lay fruitless on the ground like grape vines.

Summary

The analogy of the vine and the branches is a metaphor for some kind of relationship to Christ. There are three possibilities: (1) the relationship with Christ attained by professing Christians; (2) the relationship with Christ attained by any Christian; (3) the relationship with Christ attained only by mature or growing Christians. Grudem favors the first or second (depending on how he needs the passage to fit in his theological system); and Free Grace, the third. As argued above, the Reformed view misinterprets the sense of "in me." That phrase refers not to organic union but to fellowship. Not all Christians walk in fellowship with Christ at all times and some finish life walking as mere men, saltless. The analogy signifies not an organic connection, but a dynamic fellowship. A branch "in me" is not portraying an analogy of a branch organically connected to him as a literal branch is organically connected to a vine. Instead, a branch "in me" is portraying a branch receiving strength and encouragement from Christ and living in fellowship with him (as a literal branch derives sustenance from a literal vine). This is proven by the fact that "in me" means "in fellowship with me." The analogy is used to illustrate the "in me" relationship.

John 15 tells us that when a believer is in fellowship with Christ but is not bearing fruit because of immaturity or struggles with his faith, our Lord lovingly lifts him up so that he can bear fruit. The believer who is in fellowship with Christ and who is bearing fruit is pruned so that he can bear more fruit. The analogy of the vine and the branches signifies fellowship with Christ, not organic connection with him. There is nothing here to suggest that all believers will always bear fruit. Only believers who remain in fellowship, abide in him, will bear fruit.

Chapter 16

The Vine That is Cast Out – John 15:6

Joseph Dillow, Th.D.

If anyone does not abide in me, he is cast out [Gr. ballō exō] as a branch and dries up; and they gather them, and cast [Gr. ballō] them into the fire, and they are burned. (John 15:6)

This passage is a problem for Reformed interpreters because it teaches that people who forsake a relationship with Christ might be "cast into the fire and burned." In this case, they would be forsaking the "in me" relationship because, as demonstrated earlier,[1] that is the relationship only a true believer can have with Christ. Dr. Grudem believes that this burning is a metaphor for final damnation.[2] However, there is no evidence for this. There are two fires in eternity: the lake of fire (Revelation 20:15) and the fire which symbolizes judgment on the believer's works at the Judgment Seat of Christ (1 Corinthians 3:15). John 15:6 likely refers to the latter.

---

1   See chapter 15.

2   Wayne A. Grudem, *"Free Grace" Theology: 5 Ways It Diminishes the Gospel* (Wheaton: Crossway, 2016), 123.

In this verse, Jesus states what happens to a Christian who does not "abide in me." In verse 2, Jesus spoke about the believer who is "in me," that is, the believer who is in fellowship with Christ. Now, in verse 6, he states what happens to a believer who does not "remain in me," that is, who does not *remain* in fellowship with Christ.[3] He is "cast out" (Gr. *ballō exō*). That is, he is cast out of fellowship, not out of a false profession of faith (the Reformed view held by Grudem) or out of salvation (the Arminian view). This destiny is decidedly different from that of the believer who is "in me" and is not yet bearing fruit (v. 2). That believer is lifted and encouraged.

Both Grudem and Alan Stanley argue that verses 2 and 6 are saying the same thing; verse 2 says the Lord "takes away" the fruitless branch, and verse 6 says the fruitless branch is "thrown away." Stanley says, "For the one who does not remain (v. 6) is clearly the one who does not produce fruit (vv. 4, 5). And the one who does not produce fruit is the one who is also cut off."[4] However, this assumes that *airō* must mean "remove." We believe it means "lift up."[5] If so, these verses describe two different categories of believers: those who are immature or discouraged and need to be lifted up (encouraged, v. 2) and those who persist in carnality and have their life work burned up at the Judgment Seat of Christ (v. 6).

Furthermore, the branch in verse 2 is specifically called a branch "in me," that is, a branch in fellowship with Christ. The branch in verse 6 is specifically said to be a branch that does "not abide in me," that

---

3   We established this meaning in chapter 15.

4   Alan P. Stanley, *Did Jesus Teach Salvation by Works? The Role of Works in Salvation in the Synoptic Gospels* (Eugene, OR: Pickwick Publishers, 2006), 256.

5   See chapter 15 on the Vine and the Branches where we established that the correct translation of *airō* is "lift up" and not "remove. Note the first two entries in *BDAG* for *airō* (1) "to raise to a higher place of position, lift up, take up, pick up; (2) "to lift up and move from one place to another" (*BDAG*, 28). The context determines the meaning. As demonstrated in the earlier section of this book, the viticultural practices in 1st century Palestine supports the view that these branches are lifted up from the ground in order to create better conditions for bearing fruit.

is, is not in fellowship with Christ. Verses 2 and 6 are referring to two different branches and two different outcomes.

Verse 6 states that a branch that does not abide is "cast out" (Gr. *ballō exō*, not *airō*, "lifted up"). This suggests that the heavenly Vinedresser first encourages the branches and lifts them in the sense of loving care to enable them to bear fruit in v. 2. If, after this encouragement, they do not remain in fellowship with him and bear fruit, they are then cast out. Therefore, verses 2 and 6 do not have to be referring to the same outcome. Verse 2 refers to encouragement, and verse 6 refers to the outcome for a wasted life.

The Lord is saying that, if a Christian does not remain in fellowship with him, he will be thrown away (Gr. *ballō exō*, "cast out"). In John 6:37, Jesus promises that *"the one who comes to me I will certainly not cast out [Gr. ekballō]."* Some Reformed writers understand this to be a promise that once salvation is gained, it can never be lost.[6] Yet this person in John 15:6 is cast out. Since a person who is saved can never be cast out (i.e., lose his salvation), John 15:6 must, they say, refer to a non-believer. This assumes two things: (1) the person in John 15:2 and 6 are unbelievers and (2) their destiny after being cast out is the Lake of Fire. Free Grace scholars do not believe either of those assumptions is valid.

The metaphor from viticultural practice (to be "thrown away as a branch") refers to being a useless Christian, not an unbeliever. Pliny the Elder says, "The vine throws out a great number of shoots. In the first place, however, none of them are ever used for planting, except those which are useless, and would have been cut away as mere brushwood."[7] One pushes the analogy too far to assert that the verse means "to be cast away from a saving relationship with Christ" (Arminian view), or from "a professing relationship with Christ" (common Reformed view). We need go no further than Jesus's instruction to his believing

---

6 Curtis I. Crenshaw, *Lordship Salvation: The Only Kind There Is - An Evaluation of Joseph Dillow's The Reign of the Servant Kings and Other Antinomian Arguments* (Memphis: Footstool Publications, 1995), 157.

7 Pliny, "The Culture of the Vine and the Various Shrubs which Support It," in *The Natural History* (Medford, MA: Taylor and Francis, 1855), 17:35, p. 3497.

disciples in the Sermon on the Mount in order to understand this phrase.

You are the salt of the earth; but if the salt has become tasteless, how can it be made salty again? It is no longer good for anything, except to be thrown out [Gr. ballō exō] and trampled under foot by men. (Matthew 5:13)[8]

A branch in the Vine that does not produce fruit has become, in some ways, similar to salt that has become saltless. It is no longer good for anything.[9]

Paul tells us that there are two kinds of Christians, one who is for honor and is useful to the Master and one who is for dishonor and is not.

Now in a large house there are not only gold and silver vessels, but also vessels of wood and of earthenware, and some to honor and some to dishonor. Therefore, if a man cleanses himself from these things, he will be a vessel for honor, sanctified, useful to the Master, prepared for every good work." (2 Timothy 2:20–21)

What is the ultimate fate of the believer who does not remain in fellowship? We know from other Scriptures that he faces divine discipline in time, possibly physical death, and loss of rewards at the Judgment Seat of Christ. This was the view propounded by Lewis Sperry Chafer and fits the context well.[10]

John 15:6 concludes,

They gather them, and cast [Gr. ballō] them into the fire, and they are burned. (NASB)

---

8 Cf. Mark 9:50; Luke 14:34.

9 For a fuller discussion of what it means for a believer to become "saltless," see chapter 10.

10 Lewis Sperry Chafer, *Systematic Theology* (Dallas: Dallas Seminary Press, 1947), 7:4.

We do not know for sure who "they" are. No doubt it is unimportant to the analogy but is merely a fact of viticulture and not to be pressed into service for anything in the metaphor. These hypocrites are "cast out"; that is, they dry up and are useless.

To what does the fire in John 15:6 refer? Dr. Grudem says it is the fire of damnation. He then addresses the viewpoint of one Free Grace writer who argues that the purpose of the fire in John 15:6 is for purification. Grudem says that there is "no example in Scripture of plant material or wood being purified by fire."[11] However, there is likewise no example in Scripture of vegetation or wood used as a metaphor for damnation either, unless John 15:6 is an example. In fact, "fire" in the Old Testament never has the sense of the lake of fire.[12] His argument proves nothing.

Another use of fire symbolism in the Bible is for the judgment on God's people in time (e.g., Isaiah 26:11).[13] It may or may not have either a remedial purpose or an expression of God's judgment on his people in time. In fact, in the only reference in the Old Testament to a vine being cut and burned, it refers to a temporal judgment on the people of God for their disobedience (Psalm 80:16). The outcome of

---

11 Grudem, *"Free Grace" Theology: 5 Ways It Diminishes the Gospel*: 124.

12 In the Old Testament, it always refers to a temporal judgment. The Gospels sometimes use "fire" of temporal judgment (Matt. 3:10, 12; Luke 17:29). Charles C. Bing, "Does Fire in Hebrews Refer to Hell?," *BibSac* 167, no. 667 (July-September 2010): 150. Alan Stanley argues that "the fire imagery in John 15:6 suggests eternal rather than temporal judgment." Stanley, *Did Jesus Teach Salvation by Works*: 257. To establish this thesis he cites a few passages in the Old Testament such as Ezekiel 15:4-6, which does not even refer to eternal judgment. It refers to judgment in time. He then jumps to the Synoptics and cites Matthew 3:8-12, which has nothing to do with eternal damnation but is a warning addressed to the nation regarding a coming national catastrophe in AD 70 if they do not come to national repentance and stop distorting the law. See my discussion on this in Joseph C. Dillow, *Final Destiny: The Future Reign of the Servant Kings*, 3rd revised ed. (Monument, CO: Paniym Group, Inc., 2016; reprint, 2016), 879-81.

13 For example, it is used this way in Amos 1:4, 7, 10, 12, 14; 2:2, 5. See also Isaiah 9:10; Jeremiah 21:12-14; 22:6-7; 48:45; Ezekiel 15:1-8; Hosea 8:14; Nahum 1:6; Zephaniah 1:18.

their failure to remain in fellowship, therefore, may be divine judgment in time.

It is also quite possible that John was thinking of something like Paul's comment in 1 Corinthians 3:9. We are on familiar ground here. Paul spoke of being "saved through fire" (1 Corinthians 3:15), and Jesus said that the unfaithful branches would be cast into the fire and burned (John 15:6). In his Sermon on the Mount, Jesus said that believers who do not enter the narrow gate and follow the narrow way will face "destruction," that is, spiritual and psychological ruin in time and at the Judgment Seat of Christ (Matthew 7:12-13).[14] The anonymous writer of the homily to the Hebrews informs us that when the believer's life produces thorns and thistles, this produce "ends up being burned" (Hebrews 6:8). The apostle John warns his readers that they might face "shame" at the return of Christ (1 John 2:28), loss of reward (2 John 8; cf. Colossians 2:18), and what they have will be taken from them (Luke 19:26).

The bearing of fruit may be similar to Paul's metaphor of buildings. In both cases, the quality of work and what the believer produces are things that will be submitted to fire at the Judgment Seat of Christ (1 Corinthians 3:15).[15] Paul says that the believer is the building and that the building is built up with various kinds of building materials and that the fire is applied to the building. The apostle obviously sees an intimate connection between the believer and his work. To apply the fire of judgment to the believer is the same as applying it to his work. Indeed, the believer's works are probably a metonymy for the believer himself.[16]

---

14 For full discussion see Dillow, *Final Destiny*: Chapter 21.

15 It seems like mere quibbling to say that in 1 Corinthians 3:15 the fire is applied to believer's works and in John 15:6 it is applied to the believer himself and, therefore, that John 15:6 and 1 Corinthians 3:15 could not refer to the same event (J. Carl Laney, "Abiding Is Believing: The Analogy of the Vine in John 15:1-6," *BibSac* 146, no. 582 (January-March 1989): 61.

16 A metonymy is a figure of speech consisting of the use of the name of one thing for that of another of which it is an attribute or with which it is associated.

The issue in John 15 is sanctification, not regeneration, fruit bearing, not justification; and friendship with Christ, not proof of salvation. In his summary, Jesus says,

> *You are my friends,*[17] *if you do what I command you. No longer do I call you slaves, for the slave does not know what his master is doing; but I have called you friends, for all things that I have heard from My Father I have made known to you.* (John 15:14–15)

---

17 Carson opines, "This obedience is not what *makes* them friends; it is what *characterizes* his friends." D. A. Carson, *The Gospel According to John* (Downers Grove, IL: InterVarsity, 1991), 522. It is certainly true that obedience characterizes friends of Christ. However, not all believers are characterized as friends; it depends on whether they are obedient to his commands. Obedience *does* make them friends. How could Christ have made it plainer?

Chapter 17

Justified by the Law, Known by Your Works – Romans 2

Fred Chay, Ph.D.

Introduction

One of the more difficult passages in the discussion of the nature of faith, the means of assurance, and the condition of salvation is Romans 2:1–13.

Therefore you are without excuse, every man of you who passes judgment, for in that you judge another, you condemn yourself; for you who judge practice the same things. And we know that the judgment of God rightly falls upon those who practice such things. And do you suppose this, O man, when you pass judgment upon those who practice such things and do the same yourself, that you will escape the judgment of God? Or do you think lightly of the riches of His kindness and forbearance and patience, not knowing that the kindness of God leads you to repentance? But because of your stubbornness and unrepentant heart you are storing up wrath for yourself in the day of wrath and revelation of the righteous judgment of God, *who will render*

*to every man according to his deeds: to those who by perseverance
in doing good seek for glory and honor and immortality, eternal
life;* but to those who are selfishly ambitious and do not obey the
truth, but obey unrighteousness, wrath and indignation. There
will be tribulation and distress for every soul of man who does
evil, of the Jew first and also of the Greek, but glory and honor
and peace to every man who does good, to the Jew first and also
to the Greek. For there is no partiality with God. For all who have
sinned without the Law will also perish without the Law; and all
who have sinned under the Law will be judged by the Law; *for
not the hearers of the Law are just before God, but the doers of the
Law will be justified.* (Romans 2:1-13 NASB), (emphasis added)

Paul states what seems to be a contradiction with his own words
later in Romans 3–4 and 11:6. In those passages, Paul asserts that
justification is not by works, but only and always by faith alone in
Christ alone and that eternal life is a gift given freely to a person not
based on persevering in good works (Galatians 2:16; Ephesians 2:8-9).
The exegetical options and expositional explanations are plentiful and
fully articulated by Dane Ortlund.[1]

The argument outlined by Paul is in the context of the divine
comment on the condemnation of man and the wrath of God. He
has linked immorality with idolatry and revealed that man is in
open rebellion as he tries to suppress the truth of God that has been
clearly revealed in both creation and conscience and as he exchanges
worship of the Creator for a creature (1:18-32). Paul now takes the
courtroom floor as a prosecuting attorney to describe different types
of people (pagans, moralists, and Jews) and the fact that they are guilty
as charged and therefore condemned.[2] Paul will use a Greco-Roman
literary device called a diatribe to communicate his stinging rebuke. In
this form it includes rhetorical questions and the use of an imaginary

---

1   Dane C. Ortlund, "Justified by Faith, Judged According to Works: Another
Look at a Pauline Paradox", *Journal of the Evangelical Theological Society*, 52/2
(June 2009) 323–39.

2   As Dr. Larry Moyer reminds us, "You've got to get people lost before you get
them saved."

opponent. A verse-by-verse examination of this passage reveals Paul's argument. In outline form it is as follows:

I.   God's Judgment Is According to Reality (2:1-5)

   A.   Man's Judgment Is Self-Condemnatory (2:1)

   B.   God's Judgment Is According to Truth (2:2)

   C.   God's Judgment May Not Be Immediate, but It Is Sure (2:3-5)

Man's judgment is self-condemnatory (2:1). When we judge others, we admit there is a judgment of right and wrong. "Therefore you are without excuse, every man of you who passes judgment, for in that you judge another, you condemn yourself; for you who judge practice the same things. And we know that the judgment of God rightly falls upon those who practice such things" (Romans 2:1). We who judge others are guilty by the same judgment due to our actions.

God's judgment is according to truth (2:2). "And we know that the judgment of God rightly falls upon those who practice such things" (Romans 2:2). We exchanged the truth for a lie (1:23, 25) and the Creator for the creation. Therefore, God gave us over to degradation, depravity, and death (1:24, 26, 28).

God's judgment may not be immediate (2:3-5). Verses 3-4 tell us that God's judgment may not be immediate. "And do you suppose this, O man, when you pass judgment upon those who practice such things and do the same yourself, that you will escape the judgment of God? Or do you think lightly of the riches of His kindness and forbearance and patience, not knowing that the kindness of God leads you to repentance?" (Romans 2:3-4). The fact of no immediate judgment does not preclude future judgment (2:3) and actually provides opportunity for repentance (v. 4). God's goodness and forbearance delay his coming wrath on sin.

Paul is speaking here to unrepentant moralists. This is not simply a discussion about eternal life through repentance. Paul is describing the general attitude of the moralist against God and his blindness to his own sin. It is significant that there is no mention of repentance in Romans 3:21-4:25, the chapter on justification. Repentance is mentioned only here. It is also significant that repentance is never found in the Gospel of John concerning eternal life. Notice how the grace of God is exhibited. God is kind, tolerant, and patient, even in our rebellion. A loving father to a prodigal son! This loving heart is revealed throughout the Scriptures: "Not wishing that any perish" (2 Peter 3:9); "God who desires all men to be saved and come to the knowledge of the truth" (1 Timothy 2:4).

God's judgment is sure (2:5). Eventually, God's tolerance and patience will run out (Romans 1:18). His justice must be accomplished "But because of your stubbornness and unrepentant heart you are storing up wrath for yourself in the day of wrath and revelation of the righteous judgment of God . . . " (v. 5). Wrath can come on any day, and it will come ultimately on the day of wrath, also referred to in Scripture as the day of the Lord and as the Tribulation.[3] It is the eschatological day–the Great Tribulation (Matthew 24-25; 1 Thessalonians 5:10). At that time the judgment of God will be fully displayed on mankind.[4]

Paul is looking down the corridor of time to the future day when the power of God's wrath will be unleashed as never before. Paul in effect is considering the building of wrath upon wrath in a collective way concerning all of "moral" man's sins and what they will amount to in that day when God will judge. Man's sins are piling up, accumulating.[5]

The next section of Paul's argument reveals the nature of the judgment. The argument in outline form continues as follows:

II. God's Judgment Is According to Works (2:6-10)

A. The Statement of the Principle (2:6)

B. The Application of the Principle (2:7-10)

Verse 6 contains a statement of the principle: "<u>who will render to every man according to his deeds</u>." The principle of judgment based on works runs throughout the Old and New Testaments. Paul utilizes

---

3   Peter is thinking of this topic as well in 2 Peter 3:15.

4   This wrath (*orgē* in Greek) is not hell (Revelation 4-19; see also Romans 13:4). *Orgē* is temporal.

5   See Luke 11:45-51; also 1 Thess. 2:16 ("storing up wrath to the uttermost").

the basic principle found in Psalm 62:12 and Proverbs 24:12.[6] The judgment of works is true for Christian and non-Christian. However, it is imperative to keep the nature of the judgments distinct.

For the believer, judgment will occur at the Bema Seat of Christ.[7] At this judgment, the works of the believer will be judged.[8] The unbeliever will be judged at the Great White Throne where their works are evaluated (Revelation 20:11)! These two judgments are separated by a period of 1,000 years called the Millennium (Revelation 20). Reformed theology often collapses the two judgments and makes them one.

Verses 7-10 contain the application of the principle.

to those who by perseverance in doing good seek for glory and honor and immortality, eternal life; but to those who are selfishly ambitious and do not obey the truth, but obey unrighteousness, wrath and indignation. There will be tribulation and distress for every soul of man who does evil, of the Jew first and also of the Greek, but glory and honor and peace to every man who does good, to the Jew first and also to the Greek.

We must remember that Paul is getting ready to speak about eternal life (v. 7).

In any communication, it is imperative that terms be defined lest communication be muddled. We often assume we are defining terms in the same way, but often it is only later that we realize we are speaking across or engaged in cross talk because we actually are not measuring meaning with continuity due to confusion of terminology. This is

---

6   See also Ecclesiastes 12:14; Jeremiah 17:10; Hosea 12:2; Matthew 7:21; 1 Corinthians 3-4; 6:9; 9:24-27; 2 Corinthians 5:10; Philippians 3:14; Romans 14:10; Ephesians 6:8; Colossians 3:24; 2 Timothy 4:14; 1 Peter 1:17; 1 John 2:28; 2 John 8; Revelation 2:23; 22:12.

7   See John 5:24; 1 Corinthians 3-4; 9:24-27; 2 Corinthians 5:9-10; Romans 14:10; 1 Peter 1:17.

8   See Romans 2:6. Ἀποδίδωμι ("pay back") was used in papyri for the paying of a debt (MM, 61) (see Romans 12:17; 13:7; 1 Thessalonians 5:15; 2 Timothy 4:14). Ἀποδίδωμι is also used in the Septuagint in Psalm 17:21; 93:23; Isaiah 65:6-7; 2 Chronicles 6:23; and Job 33:26.

even more important in theology. Precision must be the hallmark of all theological dialogue, especially for those who hold to a high view of Scripture as being inspired and inerrant and reflecting the very revelation of the mind of God.

In considering the theological term "eternal life", it is essential, although we all think we know what we mean by it, that we take care to be clear what it actually means. "Eternal life" may be more flexible and not as technical of a term as we assume. The term "eternal life" is used 41 times in the Greek New Testament. The phrase consists of "eternal" (αἰώνιος) and "life" (ζωή).

In defining "eternal life," it is important to understand that the term has both quantitative and qualitative aspects. The term can be used to describe <u>quantity of time</u>, that is linear time. As such, it is seen to be possessed in the present, but the emphasis is on the future. It is also understood to be something that is given or is gifted. The term can also be used to refer to a <u>qualitative aspect</u>—a present quality of life. As such it involves the present, and it involves our works and reward for such merit. Louw and Nida understand that the term can possess both aspects and elements of unending duration—quantity as well as qualitative aspects.[9] Perhaps this is the meaning of John 10:10 where Jesus declared that he "came to give life and life more abundantly" (John 17:3).[10]

These aspects of quantity and quality are delineated in multiple passages of Scripture. The quantitative aspect of eternal life can be seen in John 3:16-17, arguably the most recognizable passage on eternal life. After discussing with Nicodemus the necessity of being born again for "seeing the kingdom of God" (3:3) and "entering the kingdom of God" (3:5), Jesus makes his famous proclamation: "For God so loved the world that he gave his only begotten Son, that whoever believes in him *shall not perish*, but have eternal life. For God did not send the Son into the world to judge the world, but that the world might *be saved* through him" (3:16-17; emphasis added). Here the emphasis is on passing out of death (the just penalty of sin) and into life (salvation

---

9 See *Louw & Nida, Greek-English Lexicon of the New Testament based on Semantic Domains*, Vol. 1 p. 642. United Bible Society New York, 1989.

10 See also *BDAG* on ζωή 2b.a and b with αἰώνιος.

from death and entry into the kingdom) (cf. John 5:24 where eternal life is connected with passing out of death and into life).

This quantitative aspect of eternal life can also be seen in John 4:14 where Jesus speaks with the Samaritan woman at the well. Taking opportunity from the location by a well, Jesus uses water as a symbol of that which gives life. "[B]ut whoever drinks of the water that I will give him shall never thirst; but the water that I will give him will become in him a well of water springing up to eternal life" (4:14). That duration of life is in view is supported by the phrase "never thirst;" the effect of the water will never end. In these passages where eternal life denotes quantity of life (duration), it is given freely to those who "believe" or receive what is given.

In other passages of Scripture, eternal life denotes a quality of life that is described by such metaphors as an inheritance that is not forfeited, a reward that is earned, a harvest that is reaped, and a treasure that is stored up, metaphors that imply some level of cost for the believer. In Matthew 19:29, Jesus tells his disciples, "And everyone who has left houses or brothers or sisters or father or mother or children or farms for my name's sake, will receive many times as much, and *will* <u>inherit eternal life</u>." The future aspect λήψεται ("will receive") is reinforced by the future inheritance aspect κληρονομήσει ("will inherit"). Notice that the inheritance is given to those who perform the good work of sacrificing for Jesus's name's sake.

In John 12:24-26, Jesus says, "Truly, truly, I say to you, unless a grain of wheat falls into the earth and dies, it remains alone; but if it dies, it bears much fruit. He who loves his life loses it, and he who hates his life in this world will keep it to *life eternal*. If anyone serves Me, he must follow Me; and where I am, there My servant will be also; if anyone serves Me, the Father will honor him" (emphasis added).

Jesus is going to die in rendering his service for mankind and obeying his Father. Jesus's disciples come to him saying that there are some Greeks who wish to meet with him (12:20-22). Jesus tells his disciples that he has other plans and informs them of some important theological truth (12:23). This message is similar to the theological truth in the texts found in Luke 9:24, Mark 8:35, and Matthew 10 and 16. In light of the Matthew 16 passage and Peter's role in the instruction, it is probable that this is the same truth that Peter has in mind in 1 Peter

1:9, i.e. the "saving of the soul".[11] The conditions in John 12 seem quite distinct from the faith alone that is required to appropriate the free gift of eternal life seen in John 1:12, 2:22, 3:15-16, 4:14, 5:24, 6:40 and other passages that include faith alone in Christ alone. John 12 includes not loving the joys of this life and, in reality, hating the pleasures that this life can bring. The result is to be honored by the Father for such a life of sacrifice. Hence, the concept of eternal life here may have a qualitative aspect that is being considered.

The Apostle Paul wrote to the churches in Galatia, "The one who is taught the word is to share all good things with the one who teaches him. Do not be deceived, God is not mocked; for whatever a man sows, this he will also reap. For the one who sows to his own flesh will from the flesh reap corruption, but the one who sows to the Spirit will from the Spirit reap *eternal life*. Let us not lose heart in doing good, for in due time we will reap if we do not grow weary. So then, while we have opportunity, let us do good to all people, and especially to those who are of the household of the faith" (Galatians 6:6-10; emphasis added).

Paul is instructing believers to sow so that they may reap. The result of reaping is the reception of eternal life, and reaping is the result of works on the part of the believer. Thus, to say that the eternal life in this verse refers to eternity in heaven (the quantitative sense) would be to affirm salvation (specifically, justification) by works. Also, if the quantitative sense of eternal life were in view here, the loss of eternal life would be the loss of heaven (which is an Arminian view of the passage). Since that is not theologically possible based on the exegesis of other passages,[12] then it seems that Paul is guiding the church to do good work so they can reap eternal life in the qualitative sense, both now and later (cf. Galatians 6:4 "reason for boasting" and John 10:10 "life and abundant life"). There is no mention that believers need to do good to prove they are saved in the first place (the salvation of the

---

11 See, *Textual and Theological Exposition of the Logion: The Salvation of the Soul*, Fred Chay, Ph.D. dissertation Trinity Theological Seminary 2003. Also see, "The Cost of Discipleship: Losing One's Life for Jesus' Sake", *Journal of The Evangelical Theological Society*, 56/1. (2013), 43-61

12 Some texts that affirm the impossibility of losing eternal life (i.e. heaven) are John 6:39; 10:28-29; Rom. 8:31-39; 2 Tim. 2:11-13; and 1 Pet. 1:3-5.

audience is assumed by Paul) or that if they do not they will fail the future and final vindication at the Great White Throne.

In 1 Timothy, Paul exhorts his young protégé to "[f]ight the good fight of faith; take hold of the *eternal life* to which you were called, and you made the good confession in the presence of many witnesses" (1 Timothy 6:12). Timothy is a pastor and a believer.

Hence, it is hard to see how he could be instructing Timothy to become a believer and gain eternal life (the quantitative sense). Rather, Paul is exhorting him to live his life now in such a way that he will have great reward later. That this is Paul's meaning is confirmed by what he says to Timothy a few statements later, exhorting him to instruct the rich people in his church not to be conceited but to be "rich in good works," because by doing so they will be "storing up for themselves the treasure of a good foundation for the future" and will be able to "take hold of that which is life indeed" (1 Timothy 6:17-19; cf. 2 Timothy 4:7-8). Eternal life in the qualitative sense is in view in this passage.

These passages confirm that eternal life can be understood as a gift one receives freely (the quantitative sense) or as a reward to be earned with a cost (the qualitative sense). The exhortation of John 3:16 is not the same as Luke 14:25-35.

We now come to the essential problem of the Romans 2 passage because it raises a quintessential question: Is justification by faith alone or by works or by a faith that works or by both faith and works? The answer to this question has been the focus of much theological discussion.

In verses 7-8, Paul begins his general application of the principle that God's judgment is based on deeds. It should be noted that the explanation of this passage must be tied to verse 13 and an understanding of what Paul means when he writes, "doers of the Law will be justified before God."

Returning to our outline, we can see how verses 7-8 fit into Paul's argument.

II. God's Judgment Is According to Works (2:6-10)

    A. The Statement of the Principle (2:6)

    B. The Application of the Principle (2:7-10)

1. General Application (2:7-8)

    a. Eternal life to those who do good (2:7, cf. 2:13 "doers of the Law will be justified")

    b. Wrath to those who do unrighteousness (2:8)

Here, we have four major interpretations to consider.

1. Salvation by Works View

In his commentary on Romans, Thomas Schreiner observes that "many scholars contend that Paul describes Christians whose obedience to the law is a means by which they will be saved in the eschatological day (e.g., Mundle 1934; Flückiger 1952; K. Barth 1956b: 304; Souček 1956; König 1976; Cranfield 1975: 152–62; Fitzmyer 1993c: 297)."[13] The context of 2:13 does seem to suggest that the issue is justification by works of the law.[14]

Furthermore, many would look at Jesus's encounter with a lawyer in Luke 10:25-28 as supporting this view. The lawyer asks Jesus, "Teacher, what shall I do to inherit eternal life?" Jesus asks the lawyer what the Law says. When the lawyer recounts the two greatest commandments (love God and love neighbor), Jesus affirms his response and references Leviticus 18:5, "Do this and you will live." (But this passage should be examined in light of the above discussion of the two senses of "eternal life." Is the lawyer asking how to get into the kingdom of God, or is he asking how he can secure an inheritance in the kingdom, i.e. eternal life in a qualitative sense?)

Some simply merge faith and works (i.e. obedience) as being synonymous in that faith alone is the same as works alone. Ernst Käsemann writes, "Here 'by works alone' in fact coincides with 'by faith alone' (Althaus). The misunderstanding of 'partly by faith and partly by works' is ruled out. It is not that faith has to be succeeded

---

13 Thomas R. Schreiner, *Romans* (vol. 6; Baker Exegetical Commentary on the New Testament; Grand Rapids, MI: Baker Books, 1998), 114.

14 See Alan Stanley, *Did Jesus Teach Salvation by Works?* Pickwick Publications, Eugene, Oregon, 2006, 58,324. Originally from, "The Evangelical Theological Society Monograph Series", Volume 4.

by moral conduct which alone will be judged at the last (e.g. Kuhl)."[15]
Kent Yinger gives a succinct description of such interpreters as
"those who take ['works'] here as simply another way of saying 'faith.'
That is, 'patiently doing good' is not a human work, but is actually
Christian belief, so that it is 'according to faith' they are judged (and
vindicated)."[16]

The difficulty with this view is that Paul tells us in Galatians 2:16
and Ephesians 2:8-9 that no amount of law keeping can save/justify
a person from the penalty of sin. Indeed, in the continuation of
Paul's argument in Romans, he will go on to provide a catena of Old
Testament passages which confirm that there is none who does good
(3:12), and thus there is none righteous, not even one (3:10). At the
end of chapter 3, Paul draws his major conclusion: justification is a gift
of God found only in Christ (3:24), specifically by faith in Christ and
apart from works of the Law (3:28). He then points us to the examples
of Abraham, whose belief was credited to him as righteousness (4:3),
and David, who spoke of the blessed man that God credited with
righteousness apart from works (4:6-8).

2. Assurance by Works View

Another way of interpreting what Paul is saying here in Romans
2 is put forth by those who hold that works serve as evidence of true,
saving faith and provide assurance of salvation to the believer. The line
of reasoning runs something like this: We are saved by faith alone but
the faith that saves is never alone. Works do not save us, but they give
evidence that we are saved. If you are regenerated, then you will act like

---

15 Ernst Käsemann, *Commentary on Romans* (ed. Geoffrey W. Bromiley Grand
Rapids, Mich.: William B. Eerdmans, 1980), 58.

16 Kent L. Yinger, *Paul, Judaism, and Judgment According to Deeds*, (Cambridge,
UK: Cambridge University Press, 1999), p. 147. See also, James D.G. Dunn,
Romans 1-8, (Dallas, TX: Word Books, 1988), p. 85. A new work also seems
to articulate this view as the author seeks to blend both Roman Catholic and
Reformed protestant views together and define faith as active, enduring and
continual allegiance to Jesus. See Matthew Bates, *Salvation by Allegiance
Alone: Rethinking Faith Works, and the Gospel of King Jesus*, (Grand Rapids
MI, Baker Academic Press, 2017).

it. If you do not, then you are not saved. Works are necessary for eternal life, but not the grounds of eternal life. Regeneration necessarily results in good works. This is often explained as works being a manifestation of salvation not the merit of salvation.[17]

Bradley Green, in his work *Covenant and Commandment: Works, Obedience, and Faithfulness in the Christian Life* addresses Romans 2 and critiques the hypothetical view of the passage, which will be taken up below. Green writes, "Christians, even if they have already been justified by faith apart from works (in the past), will ultimately be justified (in the future) because they are 'doers of the law'. As attractive (tempting?) as it might be to consider Romans 2:13 as hypothetical, that simply will not do."[18]

Schreiner seems to equivocate on the value of the hypothetical view as he states:

> Paul elsewhere teaches that works are necessary to enter the kingdom of God (cf. 1 Corinthians 6:9–11; 2 Corinthians 5:10; Galatians 5:21). Since Paul asserts that works are necessary for salvation and also that, one cannot be justified by works of the law, it is probable that he did not see these two themes as contradictory. Paul's insistence elsewhere that works are necessary to enter the kingdom suggests that the similar theme here cannot be dismissed as hypothetical. The promise of eternal life for those who do good works in Romans 2:7, 10, in any case, seems straightforward enough.[19]

---

17 Ibid., 161.

18 Bradley G. Green, *Covenant and Commandment: Works, Obedience, and Faithfulness in the Christian Life*, (Downers Grove, Ill.: InterVarsity Press, 2014), 107. In a personal correspondence with Dr. Green, he made it clear that we are saved by faith alone but that faith must have works to prove it is the right kind of faith that actually saves. One's faith will be validated and vindicated at the final judgment based on Romans 2:6.

19 Thomas R. Schreiner, *Romans* (vol. 6; Baker Exegetical Commentary on the New Testament; Grand Rapids, MI: Baker Books, 1998), 115.

Schreiner defends the thesis that Paul believed "works are necessary for justification" and asserts that Romans 2:13 says "those who keep the law will be justified." [20]

Another advocate of this view and an author who has articulated that salvation can only be validated and vindicated at the great white throne judgment is Paul Rainbow, professor of New Testament at North American Baptist Seminary. He declares, "Since deeds express faith and are the index of faith's genuineness, deeds will be the criterion." [21]

Robert Mounce's discussion of Romans 2:5-6 explains that,

> Here we have a basic principle of divine judgment. God will "give to each person according to what that person has done" (cf. Psalm 62:12; Proverbs 24:12; Matthew 16:27). But you say, I thought Paul taught clearly that a person is saved by faith. That is true. A bit later he affirmed that a person "is justified by faith apart from observing the law" (Romans 3:18). But in the immediate context Paul was not teaching how we are made right with God but how God judges the reality of our faith. Faith is not an abstract quality that can be validated by some spiritual test unrelated to life. God judges faith by the difference it makes in how a person actually lives. A. M. Hunter is right in saying that "a man's destiny on Judgment Day will depend not on whether he has known God's will but on whether he has done it." That is why Jesus taught that those who respond to the needs of the hungry, the thirsty, the stranger, the sick, and the prisoner will be rewarded with eternal life; but those who fail in these down-

---

20 Thomas R. Schreiner, "Did Paul Believe in Justification by Works?", *Bulletin for Biblical Research* 3 (1993): 131, 152.

21 Paul A. Rainbow, *The Way of Salvation: The Role of Christian Obedience in Justification*, (Waynesboro, GA: Paternoster, 2005), 194. I had the pleasure of having dinner with Dr. Rainbow at the Evangelical Theological Society national convention banquet and dialoguing over his conclusions. I told him he sounded very neo-Catholic, which quite surprised him.

to-earth tasks will "go away to eternal punishment" (Matthew 25:31–46).[22]

With a lack of clarity, Stuhlmacher writes, "In the final judgment, one's works, as a visible expression of the nature of a person, are evaluated. What is pleasing before God is rewarded; what is evil or was neglected will be punished" (Romans, 46).[23]

Matthew Black says there is no necessary contradiction between this teaching of Paul and his doctrine of justification sola fide. "The Pauline doctrine deals with the conditions of entering on the Christian life—that life rooted and grounded on faith alone. But in the life that follows, 'works,' as the spontaneous expression of the life of faith . . . are no less an integral part of the life which will one day be judged by God—only they are no longer simply the result of conformity to an external code."[24]

Noting that Protestantism has always found serious difficulty with the idea of eschatological retribution according to works, Käsemann comments that "Roman Catholics have seized on it, not without malicious joy, as support for their dogmatics."[25]

John Calvin informs us that this is not that difficult a passage. He explains:

But there is not so much difficulty in this verse, as it is commonly thought. For the Lord, by visiting the wickedness of the reprobate with just vengeance, will recompense them with what they have deserved: and as he sanctifies those whom he has previously resolved to glorify, he will also crown their good works, but not on account of any merit: nor can this be proved from this verse; for though it declares what reward good works are to have,

---

22 Robert H. Mounce, *Romans* (vol. 27; The New American Commentary; Nashville: Broadman & Holman Publishers, 1995), 90–91.

23 Peter Stuhlmacher, *Paul's Letter to the Romans: A Commentary* (trans. Scott J. Hafemann; Louisville, Kent.: Westminster/John Knox Press, 1994), 46f.f.

24 Matthew Black, *Romans*, (Grand Rapids, Mich.: Eerdmans, 1989), 47.

25 Käsemann, *Romans*, 57.

it does yet by no means show what they are worth, or what price is due to them. And it is an absurd inference, to deduce merit from reward.[26]

C. K. Barrett contends: "The reward of eternal life, then, is promised to those who do not regard their good works as an end in themselves, but see them as marks not of human achievement but of hope in God." (Barrett, *Romans*, 46–47).[27]

Dr. Ben Witherington III, from a more Arminian perspective, recognizes the tension:

Just as there is a tension or balance in Paul's theology between divine sovereignty and viable human choice, so there is also a tension between salvation by grace through faith and judgment of works. It is a mistake to affirm one side of the conundrum at the expense of the other, since Paul affirms both. Perhaps the real problem is that we cannot always see or understand, especially this far removed from the context of Paul's thinking, how such apparent antinomies go together."[28]

One of the major contributors and modern voices in defense of this view is John Piper, who asks in a sermon on Romans 2,

Or should these verses be taken at face value, so that they mean that the path to heaven is really the path of obedience, and judgment really will accord with works?

Would it be a contradiction with the gospel of free and sovereign grace if that gospel were powerful enough that all who truly

26 John Calvin and John Owen, *Commentary on the Epistle of Paul the Apostle to the Romans* (Bellingham, WA: Logos Bible Software, 2010), 89–90.

27 C.K. Barrett, *A Commentary on the Epistle to the Romans* (New York: Harper & Row, 1957), 46-47.

28 Ben Witherington III and Darlene Hyatt, *Paul's Letter to the Romans: A Socio-Rhetorical Commentary* (Grand Rapids, MI: Wm. B. Eerdmans Publishing Co., 2004), 81.

believed it were radically changed by it and came to heaven on the path of persevering obedience? If that were true—and I think it is true—then the works that count would be the works of faith, and at the judgment they would be the evidence of saving faith in Christ. And our salvation would accord with them, but not be based on them.[29]

In the next week's sermon on the same passage, Piper answers the question, "What does verse 7 mean?" After mentioning the hypothetical view (see below), Piper goes on to suggest another explanation:

The other answer would say, it means that God does indeed give eternal life to those who persevere in obedience not because this obedience is perfect or because it is the basis or the merit of eternal life, but because saving faith always changes our lives in the power of the Holy Spirit so that true believers persevere in doing good. In other words, a changed life of obedience to God's truth (verse 8) is not the basis of eternal life, but the evidence of authentic faith, which unites us to Christ who is the basis of eternal life.

Now, I think this second way of viewing these verses is correct. This is why verse 6 says, "[God] will render to every person according to his deeds," not "on the basis of" his deeds, or "because of the merit of his deeds." Eternal life is always based on Jesus Christ and through our faith. But since faith, by the Holy Spirit, always sanctifies or changes us into the image of Christ (one degree at a time, 2 Corinthians 3:18), there will be deeds that "accord with" this saving faith. So while eternal life will be awarded only to believers, it will be awarded "according to"—there will be an accord with—their deeds. There will be a way of

29 John Piper, "The Final Divide: Eternal Life or Eternal Wrath, Part 1," n.p. [cited 25 February, 2015]. Online: http://www.desiringgod.org/messages/the-final-divide-eternal-life-or-eternal-wrath-part-1.

life that God can put on display to demonstrate to the world that this person's faith was real.[30]

John Piper again puts it this way:

Now, in none of these texts does it say that eternal life is earned by or merited by or based on good deeds. They simply say, in effect, that the final verdict of eternal life will accord with good deeds. They go together. And the reason they go together is not that works has replaced faith or that merit has replaced grace, but because the gospel of justification by faith is the power of God unto salvation. It is not a weak thing. The gospel does not come into a life and leave it under the dominion of sin. It comes in the power of the Holy Spirit. And where it is believed, trusted and cherished, it produces what Paul calls "the obedience of faith" (Romans 1:5; 16:26). And eternal life always accords with that."[31]

However, the question that must be posed to this view is always: How much, which ones, and how long? How much change in the believer must be present to prove that salvation has genuinely occurred, and how much sin disproves it? Which good works must be present, and which sins cannot be present? How long must the believer persist in these good works to demonstrate genuine, saving faith, and how long can a professor of faith continue in sin before we say his profession of faith is spurious? The answer that is often given is: Perfection is not

---

30 John Piper, "The Final Divide: Eternal Life or Eternal Wrath, Part 2," n.p. [cited 6 December, 2015]. Online: http://www.desiringgod.org/messages/the-final-divide-eternal-life-or-eternal-wrath-part-2. Piper would tie this theology to his view that "faith working through love" (Galatians 5:6) is the only kind of faith, and if there are no deeds of love then there was no saving faith (*The Future of Justification: A Response to N.T. Wright*, [Wheaton, Ill.: Crossway, 2007], 109-110, 114. He also declares, "Faith, which becomes effective through love, avails justification. The clause, 'which becomes effective through love,' is an adjectival modifier of faith. It tells what kind of faith avails justification." Ibid., 206.

31 Piper, "Final Divide: Part 2," n.p. Also, see Piper, *The Future of Justification*, 120-127.

required, but regular, habitual, and continual sin is no longer possible." Piper puts it this way: "A changed life—not a perfect life—always comes as the fruit of being united to Christ. So, a transformed life is a necessary condition of eternal life, but does not earn or merit eternal life."[32]

How much of a transformed life is he talking about? Where are the lists of infractions and the frequency tables that let us know when we are over the line or, in fact, never got into the game? And if God can keep me from sinning too much, why can he not keep me perfect and free from sinning at all?

Notice the pastoral implications of this view in terms of assurance of salvation. Again Dr. Piper states:

> There is a clue in verses 4b-5 [of Romans 2] that Paul, in these verses, does not have perfect obedience in mind as the path to eternal life. ". . . not knowing that the kindness of God leads you to repentance? But because of your stubbornness and unrepentant heart you are storing up wrath for yourself in the day of wrath . . . " Notice the importance of repentance.

> It's because they have unrepentant hearts that they are storing up wrath in the judgment. So if they had repentant hearts, they would not store up wrath at the judgment day. This is a pointer to the fact that Paul is not thinking in an all-or-nothing way about righteousness here. He is thinking that God is kind and merciful and willing to forgive people for their sins if they will repent and turn to him for mercy. He doesn't stress yet what the basis of that mercy is in Christ's death, but he does show that "perseverance in doing good" probably includes a repentant heart that depends on mercy for forgiveness for failures. That's the path to eternal life.[33]

---

32 John Piper, "The Final Divide: Eternal Life or Eternal Wrath, Part 3," n.p. [cited 22 December, 2017]. Online: http://www.desiringgod.org/messages/the-final-divide-eternal-life-or-eternal-wrath-part-3.

33 Piper, "The Final Divide: Part 2," n.p.

In another sermon on Romans 2, Piper makes the following argument:

> Jesus himself was even stronger in stressing that you cannot finally pass muster at the judgment day if your life has not been changed in keeping with his commandments. . . .
>
> Here is the crucial clue: on judgment day we will be judged according to our deeds, including the acts of our tongue, because deeds are the infallible sign of what fills the heart. "From the fullness of the heart the mouth speaks." You can judge a tree by its fruit and you can judge a heart by its deed. The issue is not really, Are we saved by faith in Christ or by good deeds? The issue is, On the judgment day how will God make manifest that his judgment is just? And the answer is, He will certify to the world that we have saving faith by calling our deeds to attest to its reality.[34]

But Piper's discussion of the judgment does not account for believers who will stand before the *bema* seat of Christ with no deeds worthy of reward. According to the apostle Paul in 1 Corinthians 3:10-15, there will be believers who built upon the foundation of Christ in their lives with wood, hay, and straw, which represent a life devoid of good deeds. Paul says that their works will be burned up in the judgment, yet these believers will be saved, although as through fire. These believers are saved by faith and have had Christ laid as a foundation in their lives, but they failed to build on the foundation with good deeds. They will suffer loss, but the loss is not eternal life; rather, it is the loss of reward for good deeds. There is no place for such believers in Piper's understanding of the judgment.

Finally, Michael Bird states in accordance with Romans 2:6 that, "Nonetheless, justification according to works is entirely biblical. . . . Thus justification is on the basis of faith, while judgment is congruent

---

34 John Piper, "Final Judgment: Eternal Live vs. Wrath and Fury," n.p. [cited 25 February, 2015]. Online: http://www.desiringgod.org/messages/final-judgment.

with the life of obedience. . . . Second, we must highlight that good works really are good and are necessary for salvation."[35]

This view has a long history of acceptance in dealing with a difficult passage that seeks to understand and explain Pauline theology. It seeks to remain true to its Reformed basis of justification by faith alone but must add that the faith that saves is never alone and must be evidenced by good works, so that final vindication and validation of salvation can be assigned at the great White Throne to all those who are truly saved. The impact on a person's assurance of salvation is self-evident. The difficulty of the connection between faith and assurance was felt within the Reformation of the 16th century, was carried over to colonial America by the Puritans in the 17th century, and continues in the Neo-Puritan movement of the 21st century.[36]

3.   The Hypothetical View

According to the hypothetical view of Romans 2, man could theoretically earn eternal life by continuing to do good, but, in reality, no one ever has or ever will be able to do this. Paul clarifies this point in the very next chapter, where he quotes the Old Testament teaching that "there is none righteous, not even one" and "there is none who does good, not even one" (Romans 3:10 & 12; cf. Romans 3:19; Galatians 3:8-12). Jesus even used this logic with the rich young ruler, who asked him, "What good thing shall I do that I may obtain eternal life?" Jesus initially responds by telling him to keep the commandments. "Which ones?" the young man asks, to which Jesus responds by

---

35 James K. Beilby and Paul R. Eddy, *Justification: Five Views*, (Downers Grove, Ill.: IVP Academic, 2011), 155.

36 See R.T. Kendall, *Calving and English Calvinism to 1649*, (Oxford: Oxford University Press, 1979); M.C. Bell, "Saving Faith and Assurance of Salvation in the Teaching of John Calvin and Scottish Theology," (PhD diss., University of Aberdeen, 1982); Robert Letham, "Saving Faith and Assurance in Reformed Theology: Zwingli to the Synod of Dort," (PhD diss., University of Aberdeen, 1979); and Randall C. Zachman, *The Assurance of Faith: Conscience in the Theology of Martin Luther and John Calvin*, (Louisville, KY: Westminster John Knox Press, 2005).

quoting the commandments pertaining to our relationships with other men (essentially commandments 5 through 10). When the rich young ruler asserts that he has kept all these commandments from his youth, Jesus drives home the point that he has not kept the first four commandments, his duties to God. The young man's wealth is his idol. He has not kept the commandments after all. As Jesus demonstrates, this is an excellent pre-evangelism device: use the Law to show it is God's standard of righteousness, then show that no one ever has or ever could meet that standard. In this way, the Law points us to the only one who is righteous, namely Christ, whose righteousness we can have by faith in him (cf. Romans 3:28; 4:1-8; Philippians 3:9; Galatians 3:24; 1 Timothy 1:8-11).

Schreiner acknowledges the acceptability of this view:

> Probably the dominant interpretation is that these verses are hypothetical. Eternal life would be given if one did good works and kept the law perfectly, but no one does the requisite good works, and thus all deserve judgment. The advantage of this interpretation is that it retains the focus of this section of Romans: judgment on all who sinned. It also neatly harmonizes with 3:19-20. No one can ever be justified by the works of the law since no one practices what the law commands.[37]

Even John Stott, a committed Lordship salvation proponent, understands Romans 2 as hypothetical. He says, "This is a theoretical

---

37 Schreiner, *Romans*, 114. Schreiner provides the following footnote to his comments: "See, e.g., Calvin 1960: 56; Kuss 1957–78: 64–68; Leenhardt 1961: 78; Kuhr 1964; Mattern 1966: 130–33; van Dülmen 1968: 76–82; Synofzik 1977: 80–83; Bassler 1982: 141–45; Moo 1991: 139–41; Thielman 1989: 94–96; Thielman 1994a: 172–74; Aletti 1988; Lincoln 1995: 141–42. Melanchthon (1992: 87–88) resolves the conflict by appealing to the law/gospel contrast, and argues that verse 13 (pp. 88–89) demands perfect obedience for justification." Also, see Zane Clark Hodges for this view in *Romans: Deliverance from Wrath*, (Corinth, TX: Grace Evangelical Society, 2013), 63ff (Hodges used to hold to the reward view as described in the next section below).

or hypothetical statement, of course, since no human being has ever fully obeyed the law (cf. 3:20)."[38]

We need to hear these words as an actual principle, not as factual reality. This has to do with what is called the illocutionary force of a statement. Locution refers to what is actually said. Illocution has to do with what is meant. The atmosphere of the statement must be sensed. When we fail to notice the atmosphere, we misunderstand the statement. For example, someone may say, "Well, you're a fine person!" The person hearing it may miss the sarcasm and understand it as straightforward praise. Or similarly, someone may ask, "Are you hungry?" What they really mean is, "Let's go get something to eat." Paul's locution may point to the principle that a person who does good could earn eternal life, but this does not mean there is anyone who actually does good. With this even Calvin agrees.[39]

4. The Reward View

Paul may be building on the idea that for the believer there is the opportunity to gain reward for faithfulness. This would fit the idea of 1:16-17 ("the righteousness of God is revealed from faith to faith"). Hence, the use of "eternal life" needs to be seen in the qualitative sense with regard to future rewards. This use of "eternal life" is not without precedent in the New Testament (cf. Mark 10:29-30, Galatians 6:8).

The basic idea here is that eternal life must first be granted as a gift through faith. Then it can be built upon and result in reward, if one lives his life for that which is worthy of reward. This understanding of the judgment of the believer's works is known as *bema* theology. According to this doctrine, there will be a judgment of believers before the *bema* of Christ (cf. Romans 14:10-12; 1 Corinthians 3:10-15; 2 Corinthians 5:10). This judgment is separate from the Great White Throne judgment, which determines who enters heaven and who is cast into the lake of fire (Revelation 20:11-15). Most who hold to this view believe these two judgments will be separated by the 1,000 year

---

38 John R.W. Stott, *Romans: God's Good News for the World*, (Downers Grove, Ill.: InterVarsity Press, 1994), 86.

39 John Calvin, *The Institutes of the Christian Religion* 3.17.13.

millennial reign of Christ. The purpose of Christ's *bema* seat judgment is to dispense rewards to believers who lived faithfully for Christ after having been gifted eternal life by faith apart from works.[40]

In the natural world you need to be physically born before you can grow and enjoy all the potential of life. So also in the spiritual life, you need to be born again and then grow as a believer. As Jesus put it in John 10:10, "I came that they might have life (quantitative sense on the basis of grace through faith) and have it abundantly (qualitative sense on the basis of faithfulness, perseverance, and good deeds)."

Joseph Dillow provides a superb articulation of this view in his magisterial work, *Final Destiny*:

> The Christian who perseveres in doing good works can obtain the reward of eternal life, that is, an enriched experience of that life given to him freely at justification through faith alone. It is true that no unjustified man can obtain rewards in heaven by works, but the regenerate saint can. The unjustified can never earn honor, glory, and peace, but the justified can if he shows *"persistence in doing good"* (Romans 2:7).

> The Reformed doctrine of perseverance in holiness has often based its scriptural appeal on many of the passages discussed in the preceding chapters. "The perseverance of the saints," they say, "reminds us very forcefully that only those who preserve to the end are truly saints." Romans 2 is often used to support their view. We suggest, however, that the aspect of eternal life in that chapter is not final entrance into heaven as the Experimentalist maintains. Instead, it refers to that enriched experience of life gained by faithful perseverance in doing good and which finally results in hearing the Master say, "Well done!"[41]

---

40 There are those in the Free Grace movement that hold that the bema seat will include negative consequences for works done in the body. See: *The Rod: Will God Spare It?* J.D. Faust (Schoettle Publishing N.C. 2002)

41 Joseph C. Dillow, *Final Destiny: The Future Reign of the Servant Kings*, (Monument, CO: Paniym Group, 2012), 227 (but see the entire section from 221-227).

There are over 15 views of Romans 2:6-10. The four summarized in this chapter give us enough problems. The important fact is that the traditional Reformed view of assurance based on works is an exegetical option but only one of fifteen options. As we seek to merge Romans 2:5-7 with 2:13, which says, "the doers of the law will be justified," it seems that the options are:

1. Salvation by works? (Contra Romans 3:20; 11:6; Galatians 2:16; Ephesians 2:8-9)

2. Assurance by works? (Contra John 3:16; 5:24)

3. A Hypothetical Case? ("If you could, you would; but you can't, so you won't—so don't talk about it!" Romans 3)

4. Reward based upon works? (Both an Old Testament and New Testament truth that fits with Romans 14:10)

It seems that when it comes to the interpretation of Romans 2, dogmatism is not warranted. The diversity of opinions among those in the Reformed camp is evidenced by those who validate option 1 in certain formulations, option 2 universally and option 3 to a very large degree. The diversity among those in the Free Grace camp finds supporters in favor of options 3 and 4.[42] It is to be noted that

---

42 In the interest of completeness, my entire outline of Romans 2:1-16 is provided here:
I.   God's Judgment Is According to Reality (2:1-5)
    A. Man's Judgment Is Self-Condemnatory (2:1)
    B. God's Judgment Is According to Truth (2:2)
    C. God's Judgment May Not Be Immediate, but It Is Sure (2:3-5)
II. God's Judgment Is According to Works (2:6-10)
    A. The Statement of the Principle (2:6)
    B. The Application of the Principle (2:7-10)
        1. General Application (2:7-8)
            a. Eternal life to those who do good (2:7)
            b. Wrath to those who do unrighteousness (2:8)
        2. Specific Application (2:9-10)
            a. Wrath to those who do evil (2:9)
            b. Glory to those who do good (2:10)

in Dr. Grudem's book critiquing Free Grace theology he does not mention Romans 2 at all. In fact, his massive *Systematic Theology: An Introduction to Biblical Doctrine*, never mentions Romans 2:1-13. Therfore, it is difficult to state his view.

As to the charge that the Free Grace interpretations are novel, highly unusual, unprecedented, and unlikely interpretations of Scripture, this appears to be unwarranted concerning Romans 2.[43]

C.   Confirmation of the Principle (2:11-16)
    1.   The Principle of No Partiality (2:11)
    2.   The Practice of No Partiality (2:12-16)
       a.   The Law is not the issue (2:12)
       b.   The Law is both inward and outward, and the impartial judge will take both into consideration (2:13-16)

43 See Wayne Grudem, *"Free Grace" Theology: 5 Ways It Diminishes the Gospel* (Wheaton, Ill.: Crossway, 2016) for these and other pejorative descriptors.

Chapter 18

The Do-It-Yourself Kit – Romans 7-8

David R. Anderson, Ph.D.

How would you like to have a Do-It-Yourself kit for the Christian life? I once saw a cartoon that reminded me very much of Romans 7. It showed a man standing at the counter of a Do-It-Yourself shop. Apparently, he had bought a Do-It-Yourself TV kit, but his attempt blew up on him. As he stood before the counter with a broken picture tube in one hand, another tube sticking out of his ear, and a bent-up TV antenna under his arm, he asked the clerk, "Do you have an 'Undo-It-Yourself' kit?" This is essentially what Paul will be asking by the end of Romans 7.

Recall that Paul introduced this entire section by identifying his readers as "those who know the law" (7:1). The Law once appealed to Paul like a Do-It-Yourself kit for righteousness, and he now shares the results of that kind of thinking with those in Christ who might be tempted to revert to the Law to bear righteous fruit (6:19, 22). The kit came packaged with "ten simple steps to spiritual maturity." But when Paul tried to follow the instructions, he couldn't get the formula to work. Everything blew up on him. When the smoke cleared, Paul was looking for an Undo-It-Yourself kit: "[W]ho will deliver me from this body of death?" (7:24).

The problem is there are no Do-It-Yourself kits for the Christian life. The Law *appears* to be such a kit, but our Sin Nature in Adam only exploits the Law to deceive us into thinking we can or must do it ourselves. This is the false appeal of our inadequate flesh, but the self-reliant pursuit of the Law only leads to "death." The sense of "death" in Romans 5–8 is captured by the progression: *defeat, disillusionment,* and *despair.* Just as when we revert to *Sin* through the flesh in 6:15-23, death is also the daily ration meted out by the Sin Nature when we try in our own ability to submit to *the Law* as our "commander." The harder *I* try, the harder *I* fall.

Romans 7:7-12 dealt with the inevitable failure of our self-sufficient attempts to fulfill righteousness. Our problem there was falling prey to the illusive appeal of our own *performance* to make us feel good about ourselves. This is one of the four great lies whispered in our ears by the devil to keep us defeated. This lie is that we must meet a certain standard of performance in order not only to feel good about ourselves but also to be loved by God. Now in Romans 7:13-17, which I call "The Arena of Despair," we bump up against the second great lie. It is that we must have the approval of people, or a certain group of people, in order to feel good about ourselves. In the first lie, other people are not necessarily involved. But in the second lie we are tempted to allow other people to evaluate our performance, our person, our personalities, and our appearance. With this lie comes all the power of peer pressure.

In 7:13-25, Paul answers a second anticipated objection by at least some of his readers, that the Law must be evil if it only makes us even more sinful and miserable. If true, one solution might be to avoid God's Word altogether, since it reveals the Law to us; ignorance is bliss. "God forbid," Paul replies. That is like claiming that since so many marriages wind up in divorce and unhappiness, people should not get married. "Absurd," Paul would say, "there's nothing wrong with marriage; there's something wrong with *us.*" In order to show *why* the Law is good (7:12), Paul provides a sequential three-step argument in 7:13-25. Each step follows the same cycle of a *statement,* followed by *logical support,* and concluding with a *summary.* Our overall outline looks like this:

ROMANS

In the first cycle, "Arena of Despair" (7:13-17), the statement appears in v. 13, the logical support in vv. 14-16, and the summary in v. 17.

A. ARENA of Despair   7:13-17

1. The *Statement*   13

Has then what is good become death to me? Certainly not! But sin, that it might appear sin, was producing death in me through what is good, so that sin through the commandment might become exceedingly sinful.

Is the law the cause of death? No, says Paul, the cause of death is our Sin Nature. But law plays a key role in making us fully aware that the death we experience is in fact due to the Sin Nature. The same law Satan uses to *provoke* sin, God uses to our *advantage*: that we might recognize our sin, be held fully accountable for it, and see our death as the just consequence for it.[1] Again, by "death" Paul is not referring to spiritual death or necessarily even to physical death, although that may be a final consequence of the struggle in Romans 7. Rather, "death" refers to the agony of defeat—disillusionment and despair—that robs us of anything we might call life and keeps us from bearing righteous fruit (see 6:19-22). Indeed, the person in this arena sometimes wishes he *were* literally dead.

Paul identifies the culprit that leads to such death. The Sin Nature uses the Law or the Word of God—which is *good*—to bring defeat and despair, but ultimately even *this* is meant by God for good. It may seem counterintuitive, but let's explore how it works.

Before conversion, we are naturally prone to self-reliance (we are "in the flesh," 7:5). At the moment of conversion we are happy and positive about our new life in Christ and look to the Word for growth in our spiritual life. But with life's inevitable challenges and adversity, we are distracted from our purpose in Christ: to bear righteous fruit to holiness (6:19, 22). So we reach for our "mountain climbing equipment" (our "flesh" = *natural ability* in Adam) and set out to climb the "Mt. Everest" of our dreams. And "those of us who know the law" (7:1) may approach the Bible as a Do-It-Yourself kit to be more like Jesus, have a happy home, be a success, or gain financial freedom. But

---

1   Paul counters the imagined objector's negative insinuation by explaining the *positive* role played by the law ("the commandment") in exposing sin as he had demonstrated in 7:7-11. His logic in these verses is rooted in his prior explanation of the *purpose* of the Law in 2:14-16 and 5:13-14, 20-21. The key is to recognize that the two purpose clauses in 7:13 parallel Paul's logic about the role of the law in 5:13 and 5:20a. The purpose clause "that it might *appear* sin" is better translated "that it might *be exposed* as sin." The premise that sin is *not* at first evident recalls Paul's claim that *sin is not imputed when there is no law* (5:13). This was a problem, for without law there was no way to warrant death as a just condemnation or sentence for sin. The second purpose clause "so that sin through the commandment might become exceedingly sinful" can be read "*more abundantly* sinful" and seems to echo 5:20a, "[T]he law entered that the offense might abound." Since the latter clause resolves the problem raised in 5:13, Paul's parallel conclusion in 7:13 is now clear. The law is *good* (7:12) because it makes us aware of our own sin and holds us *fully accountable* for that sin, so that death can be *fully seen* as the just consequence of that sin.

before we get half way up we find ourselves slipping and falling. Time after time we get up, only to fall again; it becomes such a struggle, we finally lose hope and give up, defeated. "What's the use?" "I have no impact in my world." "I can't be a holy, submissive wife." "I can't control my anger or my tongue." Eventually, we fall into total disillusionment and despair. Our vision and passion are dead, and so is our spiritual life.

This is the "death" Paul describes. We can't blame it on the Bible; we can't say, as many of us do, that it just "doesn't work." So *how can this utter failure be seen as "good" (7:12)?*

2. The *Support*   14-16

¹⁴For we know that the law is spiritual, but I am carnal, sold under sin. ¹⁵For what I am doing, I do not understand. For what I will to do, that I do not practice; but what I hate, that I do. ¹⁶If, then, I do what I will not to do, I agree with the law that it is good.

The key to Paul's explanation for the dilemma of law-induced "slavery to sin" is the Greek word *sarkinos*, translated here as *carnal*. This is simply the adjective form ("fleshly") of the noun *sarx*, translated "flesh" in Romans 7:5, 18, and 25. As we discovered in our discussion of Romans 7:1-6, "the flesh" in Romans 7 is Paul's label for our bent toward self-sufficiency inherited from Adam. So one who is "fleshly" tries to behave *autonomously* and thus (for "those who know the law," 7:1) to keep the law by *self-effort*. When Paul says, "the law is spiritual," he is saying that the goal of righteous behavior that is *reflected* by law *goes beyond* "the letter" (7:6).² Unlike the law, self-reliance is *not* "spiritual," and herein is our hope in disillusionment and despair: *the law can drive us to the Spirit to fulfill the law's "righteous requirement,"* as Paul first suggested in 7:6 and will conclude in 8:4.

The problem emerges when we use the law's standard (the Word of God) to *dictate our performance* in earning God's favor for righteous

---

2 This is precisely Jesus' point in the Sermon on the Mount about *the righteousness of God*. If we are to be *perfect* ("spiritual") like our Father in heaven (Matt 5:48), our righteousness must *transcend* the "letter" (5:21-47).

behavior, whether in this life or the next. This is like trying to ride a ten-speed bike in tenth gear up a steep hill. We will not get very far. We soon run out of strength. Our chances greatly improve when we use the principle of "gear-ratio" ("abundance of grace," 5:17b) to get us up the hill, as Paul will elaborate in Romans 8. Does that mean we are free of obligation? One housewife asked, "Does what you're teaching on the law mean I don't have to do it? Guess what. I don't feel like doing my housework today." If we don't feel like doing things that seem burdensome, does grace mean we don't have to? The answer is yes and no. No, we do not *have* to do these things to "buy" God's continued favor. But yes, God *does* ask us to be his "agent" in specific circumstances *out of love* to display his righteousness and bring life (6:22-23). The key to avoiding the mere "letter" of the law is to realize when *God* is asking, and that our "obligation" is to his Spirit's lead and not to our flesh (8:12-14).

The problem in Romans 7:7-25 is that the Spirit (7:6) is *nowhere in sight*. The entire struggle going on here is to bring Paul, or any self-reliant believer, to the point that he realizes he cannot fulfill what God asks of him out of his own power. Even though the believer is no longer "in Adam" via his new position "in Christ," he can still revert to living a self-reliant life through the flesh. God wants us to come to the point where we realize we can't pedal up that hill in tenth gear. He is waiting for our strength to run out so he can fill us with his—it is God who gives us the basic desire and power to do them (Philippians 2:13). "And whatever you do, do it heartily, as to the Lord and not to men" (Colossians 3:23); we may actually find the joy of the Lord bubbling forth as we work for *him*, not for our earthly boss or parents or husband or wife, but for the Lord.

So we see that there are some things mentioned in the Bible that are a total delight. We will put them into one circle, the Circle of Delight. Other things may be drudgery to us. We will put them into a second circle: the Circle of Drudgery. Obviously, these things that are drudgery are not things that I desire to do in and of themselves. However, the secret to doing these things without putting ourselves under the law principle is to broaden our perspective in order to realize that God has asked us to do these things, and he has given us the basic desire and power to do them (Philippians 2:13).

Therefore, both the Circle of Delight and the Circle of Drudgery fit into a larger Circle of Desire to do his will, whatever that may be. So, if he asks me to clean commodes, or dig ditches or any of many other distasteful tasks, I can do them heartily with a song on my lips because he asked me to, and I desire to please him. "Whatsoever you do, do heartily as unto the Lord, not unto men" (Colossians 3:23). And as we do this we may actually find the joy of the Lord bubbling forth. He can transfer tasks out of the Circle of Drudgery right into the Circle of Delight as I do them for him, not for my boss on earth or my parents or my husband or my wife.

The result of this kind of life—empowered by the desire to fulfill God's righteous goals in us—will be a life of discipline with integrity, nothing less than conforming our Condition (behavior *that reflects his righteousness*) to our Position (*in Christ*), whether it is fun or not. But this is not the same as what we usually think of as self-discipline. Before I believed in Jesus and for some time after that, I equated discipline with *willpower*—a Do-It-Yourself system doomed to the failure of Romans 7:7-25. Remember, *he* gives us the power to do his good pleasure, his will (Philippians 2:13). As Charles Trumbull said, "The effortless life is not the will-less life. We must exercise our will to submit to His. Not my will but thine be done."[3] The key here is to be *aware* of what his will *is*, as we are led by the Spirit (Romans 8:14). We maintain our integrity as his people when the power source is the Holy Spirit, not "fleshly" self-effort.

Thus, Paul's contrasting assertion in v. 14, "The law is spiritual, but I am carnal, sold under sin," is reminiscent of Galatians 3:3, "Having begun in the Spirit, are you now being made perfect *by the flesh?*" A "fleshly" person cannot fulfill a "spiritual" law, for such a person is "sold under sin." The verb "sold" recalls the slave trade, and its perfect tense implies a state of being—as long as this person insists on self-reliance he continues in a *state* of *slavery to sin* and cannot possibly fulfill a spiritual law (Romans 7:15). Thus, Paul agrees from his own experience (7:16) that the Law *is* good and "he is sold under sin" (7:13-14).

---

3 Charles G. Trumbull, *Victory in Christ* (Fort Washington, PA: Christian Literature Crusade, 1972), 51.

In verse 15, we stand in the middle of the Arena of Despair. Paul finds that as he does his best to live the Christian life on his own, he is completely stymied. In self-reliance he is a *slave* to his Sin Nature (v. 14), kept from doing what he wants to do: "I just can't figure myself out. I really *want* to do what is right, but I keep doing what is wrong. What gives?" This is the man who desperately wants to stop lying, but as soon as he opens his mouth, out pops another lie. It is the wife who desperately seeks some peace and love in her home, yet before her husband has been home five minutes she opens her mouth and starts in on him again. It is all who want to break addictive behaviors but succumb again before the day is over. It is the cry of despair saying, "Sometimes I just hate myself," a groan which booms out of the arena of Romans 7:15. It is proof positive that this is a defeated Christian sold to the Sin Nature as its slave.

So, how does Paul know that the Law is spiritual (7:14a)? Because when he really wants to do what God asks of him (7:15), he finds that in his fleshly self-reliance (7:14b) he does things he really does not want to do (7:16a) and thus agrees that the Law has spiritually convicted him, so it must be good (7:16b, compare 7:12, "holy, just, good"): it exposes our inadequacy (7:17).

3. The *Summary*   17

But now, it is no longer I who do it, but sin that dwells in me.

Paul summarizes the whole situation by saying in v. 17, "It must be the Sin Nature dwelling in me that causes me to do these things I hate." His main point in v. 13—realizing that it was *not* the Law that caused his death-like state of despair—is now completed with the discovery that the *culprit* is his *Sin Nature* and the *arena* ("in me") is *his flesh* (see 7:18). In v. 17 he has thus come full circle around the Arena of Despair: Statement (13b), Support (14-16), and Summary (17).

As depressing as this Arena of Death can be, there is some encouragement to be found in light of this "spiritual schizophrenia." The "I" here is the one who has died with Christ (7:4), but when we choose to operate in our flesh ("me"), the Sin Nature within us brings us down. As we grow in Christ, we become more aware of the heinous depth of depravity that takes refuge in our flesh. We are shocked by our thoughts: "How can we be Christian and still feel such anger, bitterness, lust, envy?" This is when we can take hope in knowing that these sinful dispositions or actions arise not from our New Identity but from the Sin Nature that dwells "in us," in our *unredeemed flesh* (7:14, 18). That's why they are called "works of the flesh" (Galatians 5:19).

Most first person references in the New Testament outside of Romans 7 are to our New Identity in Christ. Once we believe in Jesus as our Savior, we are new creatures in Christ (2 Corinthians 5:17). We are no longer children of wrath; we are children of the King of kings. With Christ, the Father, and the Spirit living inside of us we are no longer the Old Man (all that we were before Christ). We are held to account for our sinful deeds and attitudes, but they do not express who we really are in Christ. We can admit that our Sin Nature will not disappear this side of eternity, yet we can still resist the devil's appeal to our flesh—we simply acknowledge the source (our Sin Nature acting through our flesh) and denounce it: "That evil thought came from the wicked factory within me, but I don't have to obey it, and I flatly deny it is an expression of who I really am in Christ."

The Arena of Despair is a place of disillusionment for the believer who submits to the law principle where the Sin Nature uses law as a whip to *keep us enslaved* and *defeat* us, rather than bring the life Christ came to offer: *freedom* from slavery to Sin. Where is this arena? It is internal. It is that place of struggle where I choose to do good but find myself doing evil. It is Romans 7:15. We imagine ourselves to be spiritual schizophrenics, split personalities. We cannot figure ourselves out. We are confused when we see how easily Satan deceives us by using something *good* (the Law, 7:12) to enslave us again, just as when we were "in the flesh" (7:5). So why do we believe the lie? Fortunately, Romans 7 is not the "end of the story." In Romans 8, God offers a way out of our pain that does not hurt us or others, especially those we love. But this reassurance in turn raises a nagging question. If the Sin Nature causes so much defeat, disillusionment, and despair for the Christian, yet God still loves us and wants us to have an abundant life, why didn't he just eradicate our Sin Nature when we died with Christ? Why does he allow Sin to drag us like gory gladiators into the Arena of Despair day after day to battle against it until Christ returns?

We find the answer in the stated purpose of the book of Romans, the heart of the gospel (1:16-17). The primary goal of our salvation in Christ is that we display the righteousness of God by faith as our Condition conforms to our New Identity in him. If there were no Sin Nature, we would not need Christ's power within us to reveal the righteousness of God in our behavior. We could "pedal up the steep hill in tenth gear" out of self-effort, thus obviating the need to depend on God to deliver us. Since all pride and sin is rooted in the demand for independence—"God, I don't need you. I can do it myself" (Genesis 3:5)—God left the Sin Nature in us and let us use our Do-It-Yourself kit to show us *the gross inadequacy of self-reliance* and our need to depend on God by abiding in Christ and walking by the Spirit (Romans 8:1-13). We cannot really understand our need for Romans 8 until we have experienced the failure of Romans 7—out of death issues life, out of despair comes dependence. God waits until we have *exhausted our own strength* so that he can work in us and we can *share his glory* as sons (8:14-39).

As C. I. Scofield says, the Arena of Despair (Romans 7) is the stepping-stone to Romans 8.

Not everyone, by any means, has had the experience of the seventh of Romans, that agony of conflict, of desire to do what we cannot do, of longing to do the right we find we cannot do. It is a great blessing when one gets into the seventh of Romans and begins to realize the awful conflict of its struggle and defeat; because *the first step* to get out of the seventh chapter and into the victory of the eighth, *is to get into the seventh.* Of all the needy classes of people, the neediest of this earth are not those who are having a heart-breaking, agonizing struggle for victory, but those who are having no struggle at all, and no victory, and who do not know it, and who are satisfied and jogging along in a pitiable existence of ignorance of almost all the possessions that belong to them in Christ.[4]

---

4 C. I. Scofield, quoted by Miles J. Stanford, *The Complete Green Letters* (Grand Rapids, MI: Zondervan, 1983), 56-57 (emphasis added).

It is better to have tried a Do-It-Yourself Kit in the Christian life than never to have tried at all. We can be assured when we enter the Arena of Despair in Romans 7 that our defeats are but stepping-stones to the full deliverance of Romans 8. When our Do-It-Yourself Kit has finally blown up on us, we can come humbly to God and ask for his "Undo-It-Yourself Kit."

THE RAT

Romans 7:18-25

Every day we wake up we are faced with a struggle against our Sinful Nature, which we shall call the rat inside us. And often the inner pain caused by our own losing struggles with the Rat leaves us looking for someone else to blame for our troubles: our parents, our company, our church, maybe even our God. After all, he is the One who made this mess of a person. We may finally decide everything is hopeless: "We cannot change. There is no way out. We are just victims of circumstances beyond our control." As previously mentioned, behind the law-keeping mindset of Romans 7 there are four lies that our Sin Nature (the Rat) uses to trap us in a life of disillusionment and despair. These lies are listed by RAPHA ministries:[5]

1. **Performance.** I must perform up to a certain standard in order to feel good about myself.

2. **Approval.** Certain people must approve of me in order for me to feel good about myself.

3. **Blame.** Someone or something outside myself is the cause of my failures and rejections.

4. **Shame.** There is something wrong with me that cannot be repaired. I am what I am. I was born this way. I cannot change.

---

5 Robert S. McGee, *The Search for Significance* (Houston, TX: Rapha Printing, 1990), 43-116.

All four lies feed the choice of *self-reliance* to meet righteous expectations and culminate in the despair expressed by the end of Romans 7. Like Paul, a lot of believers find themselves in utter despair. Recall the three cycles of *Despair under the Law* in Romans 7:13-25, each comprised of a Statement, Support for the Statement, and a Summary. Here we cover the last two cycles:

3. Despair under the Law	**7:13-25**
a. *Arena* of Despair	13-17
b. *Agent* of Despair	18-20
c. *Admission* of Despair	21-25

There is a way out, but first we have to understand how we get stuck in this "death spiral." Paul identifies the critical relationship between the Sin Nature and our flesh in Adam.

B. AGENT of Despair   7:18-20

1. The *Statement*   7:18a

For I know that in me (that is, in my flesh) nothing good dwells.

Paul's reason for *failure in pursuing law* ("I am 'fleshly,'" 7:14) parallels his prior explanation for our *failure in pursuing sin* ("because of the weakness of your flesh," 6:19). Again, the "flesh" here is *not* identical to our Sin Nature, which Paul designates in near context (7:17, 20) with the term *hē hamartia* ("the" sin); "flesh" is the Greek word *sarx*, and it designates *all that we carry from Adam* (body, soul, spirit) that remains unredeemed.[6]

---

6   Paul later identifies this "vehicle" for the Sin Nature as *the flesh* (6:19; 7:5, 14, 18, 25c; 8:3a). But Adam "is a type of Him who was to come" (5:14c), in that Christ was *also* sent "in the likeness of sinful flesh" (8:3); and since Christ was "without sin" (Heb 4:15) he could offer *another* type of inheritance: in *him* we are no longer condemned to sin and death but *released* to righteousness and life (Rom 5:15-21).

This does *not* mean that an unbeliever can do *nothing* good. In declaring all our righteous deeds are like filthy rags, Isaiah concedes (64:6) that we do righteous deeds in our fallen state. Paul's point is that if we could do nothing while we were **in Adam** to bear the fruit of God's righteousness *in the flesh* (7:5), then we can do nothing *by that same flesh* now that we are **in Christ** to produce righteous deeds that bear fruit to *holiness* (= *sanctification; visibly set apart to God, 5:12-21; 6:19-22*). Remember, we *carry our flesh from Adam forward* into our new life in Christ, and it will tarnish that "visibility" *whenever we trust it* to produce righteous deeds in our lives—*this* is what Paul will refer to as *kata sarka* ("according to the flesh") in 8:1-13. Even the greatest works of man by his own efforts are still tainted by sin. Such is our fallen condition in the flesh.

2. The *Support*   7:18b-19

For to will is present with me, but how to perform what is good I do not find. ¹⁹*For the good that I will to do, I do not do; but the evil I will not to do, that I practice.*

The word "for" tells us that Paul is explaining his claim in v. 18a. As new Creations in Christ we want to do the right thing, but as limited humans we simply do not have the inner power to pull it off consistently—this will require the power of the Spirit who dwells in me (8:1-4). My New Nature is prone to worship, but my Sin Nature is prone to wander. This flies in the face of humanism, which claims that man has the power within himself to solve his own problems. We are not saying man cannot send someone to the moon without God's enablement. The "will" in question is the ability to perform—and thus reveal—the righteousness of God (1:17; 3:21; 5:17, 21; 6:18-20); and this amounts to Sanctification. All our human efforts do nothing to "deliver" us in our spiritual condition. We may achieve moral victory through our own efforts in one area, but then comes spiritual defeat in another and we really do not surpass the mere *letter* of the law (7:6) to display *the righteousness of God.*[7]

---

7   On the parallel between 7:6 and Matt 5 in this regard, see note 2 of the previous section, "The Do-It-Yourself Kit."

Paul is now ready to make the concluding observation that a "rat" lives inside of him—that is, **Sin** working through his flesh—which drives him to do the evil he does not want to do.

3. The *Summary*   **7:20**

Now if I do what I will not to do, it is no longer I who do it, but sin that dwells in me.

Paul returns to the Sin Nature (*tē hamartia,* "the" sin) as the Agent of Despair. Let us recall how Paul is using "I" and "me" in 7:13-25 (see again our discussion of 7:14, above). "I" is one in Christ who has free will yet opts to fulfill the righteous requirement of the Law *in his own ability* ("me" = "the flesh," 7:18a). He realizes that the Sin Nature (the "Rat") takes over *as soon as the flesh is engaged* to fulfill the law's righteous requirement. This surfaced in a discussion I had with a Christian brother on a separate issue when he said, "Well, don't you trust me?" I replied, "Trusting *you* is not the issue. I don't trust your Sin Nature . . . and I don't trust mine either. It's not that we can't work together but we need to admit that evil dwells in each of us—that is, in our flesh" (7:18a). It's the same old Rat.

Thus, it is not that we are *too weak* in our self-reliance to overcome temptation. We are *not weak enough*, and this awareness drives Paul to his own Admission of Despair, so that he will finally capitulate to *grace* by the Spirit rather than *law* by the flesh (7:6, *realized* in Romans 8).

C. ADMISSION of Despair   **7:21-25**

1. The *Statement*   **7:21**

I find then a law, that evil is present within me, the one who wills to do good.

Paul uses the word "law" in Romans in a number of ways: The Law of Moses (2:11-13; 3:19); the Law of conscience (2:14-15); the Law Principle (dominion by law) (3:21; 6:15; 7:1-6); the Law of Faith (3:27); the Law of God (6:15; 7:1, 4-16, 22, 25); the Law of Sin (7:23, 25; 8:2);

the Law of my Mind (7:23); and the Law of the Spirit of life (8:2). So, what is this *new* law that Paul has discovered about the operation of evil within us? It is "another law" (7:23) that he will finally identify in 7:25b—a law that is closely linked to the Law of Sin. Here Paul is taking the approach of a moral scientist in order to identify this "new" law. In fact, the word for "find" at the beginning of the verse is the Greek word from which we get the exclamation, "Eureka!" As a moral scientist, Paul has just made a new discovery, meaning he has observed something new regarding his failure to do righteousness according to God's standard (7:15-20).

Paul had a moral Observation (7:15-17)—the things I do not want to do I am doing, and the things I do want to do I am not doing. That observation led to a Hypothesis (7:18-20)—there must be something evil (Sin Nature) within me leading me to do these things I do not want to do. From the Hypothesis, the scientist tests his observation and guess in a controlled environment to see if it can be repeated. If the Hypothesis can be repeated over and over without exception, the scientist postulates a Theory. If the Theory can be verified without exception, we have a Law. And that is what Paul does in 7:21. Something within him is allowing the Sin Nature to have its way with him against his will. No exceptions. It is there in every single one of us.

The support for Paul's statement?

2. The *Support*   7:22-25a

²²For I delight in the law of God according to the inward man. ²³But I see another law in my members, warring against the law of my mind, and bringing me into captivity to the law of sin which is in my members. ²⁴O wretched man that I am! Who will deliver me from this body of death? ²⁵I thank God—through Jesus Christ our Lord!

Again, the word "for" tells us that Paul is *substantiating* his statement that evil is present within him. And "I" is still the Christian who has determined to fulfill the righteous requirement of the Law in his own inability (the *flesh*). Note Paul's prolific wordplay on the notion of "law":

- **Law of God**—this is God's *standard of righteousness*
- **Law of My Mind**—conscience-mediated *awareness of*, and *agreement with*, the standard of righteousness defined by "the Law of God" (see 2:15)
- **Law of Sin**—the Sin Nature (*tē hamartia*) *leads to "death"* when "activated" in my body ("members" refers to the *body*, 6:12-14) by awareness of the Law of God (7:7-12)
- **"Another" Law in My Members**—a "flaw" inherited from Adam that opposes the Law of my Mind and *enslaves me to the Law of Sin*; it is the **Law of the Flesh** (7:24, 25b), and only the **Law of the Spirit of Life** can *release us from this slavery* (8:2).

The present participles "warring" and "bringing" describe the ongoing pull of the Law of the Flesh in his members that enslaves him to his Sin Nature when incited by the Law of God, the perfect standard of righteousness. It is like the force of gravity acting on a book sitting on a desk. I might not be *aware* of this force until I pick up the book. When I attempt on my own to "hold up the book"—to live according to that perfect standard—the law of gravity wears me out with its continuous force until the book falls; that is, this "law in my members" (the Sin Nature working through the flesh) keeps on working until I exhaust my strength and stop trying. Some have more natural strength than others, but in time *everyone* will "put the book down."

The Law of the Mind seems to work from the *inside out*, while Sin gains its beachhead in the flesh ("in my members") from the *outside* through the law. This does not mean that the "body of death" is itself evil; God created it, and it was good. But the human body can be used as an accomplice to the Sin Nature to bring us defeat and despair. The body "houses" our flesh, which is in turn exploited by Sin to defeat the "inward man" that is trying to meet God's righteous requirement. Paul describes this state as "wretched." Some believe that this could not possibly describe Paul as a believer, so it must depict his pre-conversion state. But without going into all the exegetical details, it describes the life of an "incarcerated" believer trying to live the Christian life through his own power—by the flesh. To quote James D. G. Dunn:

In a word, it is not the cry of the non-Christian for the freedom of the Christian; rather it is the cry of the *Christian* for the full freedom of Christ. . . . If we have understood Paul aright, and if Romans 7, 14-25 is a transcript of Christian experience, then we must not hide or ignore this. Proclamation of a gospel which promises only pardon, peace and power will result in converts who sooner or later become disillusioned or deceitful about their Christian experience.[8]

In alluding to "this body of death," Paul intended to be very graphic: It was sometimes Roman practice to chain a murder victim's body to his murderer as punishment. Paul likens his wretchedness to just this kind of sentence: chained to a rotting body! Paul's best efforts to fulfill God's righteous standard were doomed instead to serve the Sin Nature with the "dead body" that houses his flesh. Paul then realizes the only solution is to *leave law's dominion* and return to the realm of *grace* (6:14; 7:1), and this is what he finally realizes he has done in Christ: thank God, the Lord Jesus Christ has delivered him from this dreadful incarceration (7:25a)!

When we enter the realm of grace, we display the intent of Romans 5:17—*those who receive abundance of grace and of the gift of righteousness will reign in life*—which in turn anticipates the *freedom* and *full deliverance* of Romans 8.

3. The *Summary*   7:25b

So then, with the mind I myself serve the law of God, but with the flesh the law of sin.

Here Paul recapitulates the entire argument of 7:13-25. Recall that the "Law of the Mind" is our conscience-mediated agreement with the Law of God—his *righteous requirement* (1:32; 2:14-15, 26). Paul now confirms in the example of his own life that the "law in my members" opposing the Law of my Mind (7:23) is in fact the **Law of the Flesh**.

---

8 "Romans 7, 14-25 in the Theology of Paul," *Theologische Zeitschrift* 5 (September/October, 1975): 268, 272.

In my Adamic self-reliance, I am caught in a tug of war between the Law of the Mind and the Law of the Flesh by which Sin enters. Once hosted by the flesh, Sin—like a parasite—*enslaves* me, and that is the Law of Sin.

This leads to a sense of resignation that Robert McGee calls the Shame Game, namely "the wrong belief that there is something wrong with us that can never be repaired."[9] Behind this lie there is another: "I must always be what I have been and live with whatever self-worth I have. I am what I am. I cannot change. I am hopeless." It is actually "the Rat"—the Sin Nature—that cannot be repaired. We cannot escape it. The shame in this case is a "deep feeling of guilt, sadness, and hopelessness that we experience when we become convinced that past failures, bad habits or poor appearance have made a permanent scar on our self-worth."

But Paul knew the way out of the Shame Game. It is not through some inner power, but a power that penetrates from without. Only the supernatural power of the risen Lord Jesus Christ can deliver us (Romans 5:10). God took Paul's past and buried it; he took his present and ignored it; he took his appearance and utilized it. Christ gave him a *new man* to put on, a *new goal* to live for, and a *new hope* to die for, and it drove him to share the means of achieving this deliverance in Romans 8. The contrast with Romans 7 could not be more striking.

We may be in a prison of darkness and despair caused by past failures, persistent habits, or rejection by others. And the Rat will take these negative experiences in our lives to spin his lies. Romans 7 helps us to acknowledge Satan's strategy and focus on God's truth. When you know the truth, it will set you free. The keys of God's truth can open the prison doors of darkness and despair. Yet freedom for freedom's sake is not our ultimate goal; we are freed from the power of sin to "reign in righteousness to eternal life" (5:21) and thereby reveal the righteousness of God to all Creation (1:17). We are set free when we forsake our self-reliant flesh and follow the Spirit (7:5-6). And that is just where Paul is headed.

---

9 McGee, *Search for Significance*, 101.

WAR AND PEACE
Romans 8:1-4

Paul introduced us to spiritual warfare in Romans 6 by depicting our Sin Nature and God as opposing generals. Paul's appeal to those in Christ was to use their "members" as weapons of warfare in the King's army and thereby be delivered from the tyrannical rule of the Sin Nature to *freedom* (ironically) as "slaves of righteousness" (6:16-20). Such freedom was contingent on living not under the dominion of *law* but under *grace* (6:14-15), so we were warned about how readily the Sin Nature uses the law to gain a beachhead in the flesh and drag us back into the Arena of Despair: a slavery to Sin that brings defeat, disillusionment, and despair (Romans 7). Paul now aims to show *how* we are to live under grace and enjoy full deliverance from slavery to Sin to bear the fruit of righteousness, the incentive for which is a quality of life unknown by the world, something the Bible calls "eternal life" (6:21-23).

Thus, we leave the agony of defeat (Romans 7) and come with joyful anticipation to the thrill of victory in Romans 8, what some have called the "Red Rose of Romans," the Fulfillment of the Vision. Godet called it "that incomparable chapter."[10] Newell wrote: "The believer is like the storm-tossed mariner who has come to his home harbor and casts anchor when he comes into the light of Romans 8."[11] Here Paul virtually *trumpets* full deliverance to life and peace, and the key to this deliverance is the power of the Holy Spirit. Conspicuous by his scarcity in Romans 7 (a single introductory allusion in 7:6), the Spirit in effect *pervades* Romans 8 (19 times).

The Spirit can deliver us *from* Sin and "Death" (defeat, disillusionment, despair) to an abundant life (8:1-17) and he can deliver us *through* Suffering to a glorious inheritance (8:18-39). The entire chapter is therefore integrated by the **life** and **hope** that **the Spirit**

---

10 Frederick Godet, *Epistle to the Romans*, (New York: Funk & Wagnalls, 1883), 287.

11 William R. Newell, *Romans: Verse by Verse* (Grand Rapids, MI: Kregel, 1994), 287.

supplies us as children of God, so that we might live a righteous life *now* and rule with Christ over *the world to come* as "sons indeed." In the first major section Paul explains how the Spirit *displaces* the Law of Sin and Death (8:1-11), so that we may be fully released from the tyranny of Sin and Death to live out our calling as mature "sons of God" (8:12-17).

ROMANS 5–8

I. SIN	(1:1–3:20)
II. SALVATION	(3:21–4:25)
III. SANCTIFICATION	(5–8)
A. Freedom from Wrath	(5)
B. Freedom from Sin	(6)
C. Freedom from Law	(7)
D. Freedom from Despair	(8)
1. Victory over Sin	(8:1-17)
a. Delivered from the Law of Sin and Death	(8:1-11)
1) Principle of Deliverance	1-4
2) Process of Deliverance	5–8
3) Prospect of Deliverance	9-11
b. Delivered from a Life of Sin and Death	(8:12-17)
2. Victory over Suffering	(8:18-39)

I. PRINCIPLE of Deliverance   **8:1-4**

Here we look at the first four verses, which introduce us to the Principle of Deliverance from the Law of Sin and Death (7:23a, 25b; 8:2). Following the "carnage" of Romans 7, Paul wants to shift his readers' thinking from **death** *through the flesh* (introduced in 7:5) to **life** *through the Spirit* (introduced in 7:6), beginning with his victorious *proclamation*.

A. PROCLAMATION of Deliverance 8:1-4

1. The *Text*

Most translations rely on a Greek text that reads something like: *There is therefore now no condemnation to those who are in Christ Jesus.* Preachers typically use this verse as a guilt reducer, reminding us of our position "in Christ": we have been completely forgiven of all our sins, past, present, and future (= justification). So when we still drag around a wheelbarrow full of guilt, we need to recall that there is no longer any condemnation; we should stop beating ourselves up. It preaches well. However, 98% of existing Greek manuscripts conclude the verse with a qualifying clause:

> *There is therefore now no condemnation to those who are in Christ Jesus,* **who do not walk according to the flesh, but according to the Spirit.**

This reading suggests that absence of condemnation depends on walking according to the Spirit rather than the flesh. Which text is right? Some would settle this discrepancy based on *external evidence*—that is, the *most numerous* manuscripts (98%), or the *oldest* (2%), or both. That debate is beyond the scope of this book, but even if we accept the oldest manuscripts as more reliable, and the qualifying clause above is not present in 8:1, the truth of 8:1 is tightly argued all the way through v. 4 and therefore depends on the same condition as in 8:4, that we *walk* according to the Spirit, and not the flesh.

This is another factor that helps us decide which manuscript tradition is preferable, and it is called *internal evidence*. The internal evidence also includes the intended meaning of the word translated "condemnation," a word we have already encountered in Romans 5:16 and 18. So does it mean condemnation to hell or something different from that?

2. The *Technicality*

The most reputable dictionary available on the Greek New Testament (BDAG) points out a critical difference between two words[12] that play a key role in our understanding of 8:1 in light of 5:16 and 18:

> *Krima* = the **courtroom verdict**—a statement of one's legal standing or Position as a result of *judgment* (see 5:16a). The verb form for this courtroom verdict is *katakrinō* (Rom. 8:34). Note the contrast with *katakrima*. The switch from –*krinō* to –*krima* (just a letter change) takes it from the courtroom to the outworking of the sentence; from our Position to our Condition. This observation cannot be overemphasized.

> *Katakrima* = the **sentence** handed down for a "guilty" verdict— the **Condition** that *results* from the *verdict* ("incarceration under a death sentence," see 5:16a, 18a). To quote BDAG directly: "not 'condemnation', but the punishment following sentence, *punishment, doom*."[13]

The relationship between *krima* and *katakrima* in 5:16 establishes the meaning of *katakrima* in 8:1, where its use is parallel to 5:16, 18. The word *krima* denotes Adam's "guilty" verdict (5:16a). To be consistent, if Paul had wanted to denote a sense of *judicial* condemnation (the verdict) in 8:1, he would have used the word *krima*. So Paul is not alluding to the *judicial* condemnation we escaped when Christ took on our sins, was found guilty, and died on our behalf. In what sense, then,

---

12 Walter Bauer, *A Greek-English Lexicon of the New Testament and Other Early Christian Literature*, rev. and ed. by Frederick William Danker (Chicago: University of Chicago Press, 2000), 518, 567 [hereafter *BDAG*].

13 Arndt, W., Gingrich, F. W., Danker, F. W., & Bauer, W. (1979). A Greek-English lexicon of the New Testament and other early Christian literature: a translation and adaption of the fourth revised and augmented edition of Walter Bauer's Griechisch-deutsches Worterbuch zu den Schrift en des Neuen Testaments und der ubrigen urchristlichen Literatur (p. 412). Chicago: University of Chicago Press.

do we escape condemnation if not by Christ's *judicial* condemnation on our behalf?

It is not a statement of Position, but of Condition. We left our Position back in Romans 6. Truly, our Position in Christ is the basis for an abundant life (Romans 6:23). But the *basis* is not the *building*; the foundation is not the superstructure. So in Romans 7, Paul was addressing our miserable Condition as we serve the Sin Nature through a misdirected focus on law keeping. If a Christian pursues life by reverting to the "flesh" in his present experience (6:19; 7:5, 14, 18, 25), the tyranny of his Sin Nature working *through* the flesh will incur *katakrima* "penal servitude" (MM, 327-28) to his Sin Nature, which results in doom (BDAG) and gloom (7:24) in his Condition on earth, for the wrath of God is poured out impartially against *all* sin (1:18). Our freedom in Position has already been won by Christ's *death*, but the man of 7:24 is still in a wretched, enslaved Condition because of the Law of the Flesh (7:25b).

So as we enter Romans 8, Paul anticipates his release from this slavery and praises Jesus Christ (7:25a), the One who delivers us from this Condition by his *life* (4:25b; 5:9-10). Clearly, Paul is still dealing with our Condition, and the Spirit provides the key to releasing the Christian from his ongoing "penal servitude" according to the flesh. So just as Paul uses "walk" to advance from Position to Condition in Ephesians 4:1, he also uses "walk" in Romans 8:1-4. And—just as in 6:19; 7:5, 14, 18, 25—"the flesh" should be seen to refer to our continuing human inadequacy or "inability" inherited from Adam and carried forward in this present life (5:12, 19).

Consider Bob, a seminary graduate and evangelist, in fact, a very successful evangelist. But his giftedness and success seduced him away from his family like a wanton mistress. In time, his wife left him; he lost his ministry and found himself bankrupt. In his wretchedness, he said, "Where is this God I have been preaching? I trust the cross for my salvation, but I don't see that I am any different than before I became a Christian. I sense no power from the Holy Spirit. I've been a jerk all my life. It would be better for everyone if I just died." That despair is voiced by a man who read Romans 8:1 too narrowly as an affirmation of *justification*. He believed and preached the message of justification (the substitutionary *death* of Christ) but he desperately needed to hear and believe the message of *sanctification* (the substitutionary *life* of Christ).

This substitutionary life of Christ offers real hope that the wretchedness of Romans 7:24, the self-condemnation, can end. But how? This leads us to the *Precept* of Deliverance.

B. PRECEPT of Deliverance   8:2

For the law of the Spirit of life in Christ Jesus has made me free from the law of sin and death.

The verse begins with "for" to explain *why* "there is now no condemnation to those who do not walk according to the flesh but according to the Spirit" in 8:1. We have already seen the Law of Sin and Death at work in Romans 7, but there is a higher law, the Law of the Spirit of Life, which "trumps" the Law of Sin and Death to free the wretched man of 7:24 from his enslaved Condition. The verb "has made . . . free" (*ēleutherōsen*) is in the aorist tense which may refer to the past, but not necessarily. One use of this tense is called the gnomic aorist,[14] which (as we noted in 5:12) speaks of a general principle or rule or law of life: "makes . . . free." Hence, some grammarians also think the aorist in Romans 3:23 should not be translated, "For all *have sinned* . . . ," but rather as *gnomic*, "For all *sin* . . . " One can argue that a newborn child has not sinned, even though he *has* inherited a Sin Nature. It would therefore be expressing a general principle: "all [of mature conscience] *sin*" (compare 2:14-15; 3:20; 5:13-14; 20a).

In commenting on Romans 8:2, Cranfield believes this is an *ingressive* aorist (an action which begins at a point in time and continues as an ongoing process):

First of all it must be said that this "has set free" refers to the *beginning* of an action, not to its completion. . . . The completion of our liberation from the power of sin and of death is not until our death and resurrection. . . . Paul is affirming that the Roman

---

14 Daniel B. Wallace, *Greek Grammar Beyond the Basics* (Grand Rapids: Zondervan, 1996), 562.

Christians are people, the bonds of whose enslavement to sin, to the tyranny of self, God's Spirit has *begun* to loosen. . . . The liberation of which Paul speaks *is setting free* to resist sin's reign over one's life.[15]

An *ingressive* aorist in this context, then, would signify that once I opt to walk according to the Spirit, the law of the Spirit of life *begins to set me free* and is in the process of setting me free from the law of sin and death. If *ēleutherōsen* is translated as a *gnomic* aorist, the verse would read, "For the law of the Spirit of life . . . *sets me free* from the law of sin and death" as a general principle. In any case, this is not much different from Cranfield's ingressive sense.

Borrowing from our prior analogy of the law of gravity for the Law of Sin and Death (see our discussion of 7:22-25a), suppose I lift a rather heavy book lying on a table to see how long I can hold it up. Since the moment I pick it up the law of gravity begins working to oppose my efforts to hold it up, I will sooner or later have to put the book down, no matter how strong I am. There is no hope of continuing to hold up the book in my own strength. However, in the world of physics, there is a "higher" law to help me. It is the law of *displacement*. This is what causes a helium balloon to rise. Depending on the weight of the book and the size of the balloon, if I tie a helium balloon to the book, it might help me hold up the book. The heavier the book, the more helium balloons are needed, but we can safely conclude that enough balloons tied to the book will enable me to hold up the book as long as I wish, or even carry the book away.

In our Christian lives, the "heavy book" is God's perfect standard of righteousness. I may see the book and decide it would be a wonderful way to live, but when I pick it up, the Law of Sin and Death begins to oppose my efforts and works to make me put it down (Romans 7). Not until I depend on a higher *power* (Jesus Christ, 7:25a) can the higher *Law* of the Spirit of Life in Christ Jesus displace the Law of Sin and Death.

---

15 C. E. B. Cranfield, "Paul's Teaching on Sanctification," *Reformed Review* 48 (Spring, 1995): 220-21, emphasis added.

Someone might well object, "I have asked my Savior to deliver me from my sinful life-style, but it has not worked." But consider this: while tying only one balloon to the book may not hold or lift up the book, it is a *law*. If I *keep* tying balloons to the book, sooner or later the book will go up. The law of displacement begins to work with the very first balloon. So, I come to Jesus the first time and pray, "Lord, I simply *cannot* love brother Bob in my own strength the way you want me to. Please live in me. Love him through me." Balloon number one. The more consistently we pray a prayer like that, the more we focus on Jesus, and the more "balloons" we tie to the book. It is only a matter of time until the book goes up, and I find myself loving brother Bob through Christ who strengthens me.

Some of our sins are sins of *commission*, meaning things we know we are doing wrong and wish to stop. Others are sins of *omission*, meaning things we know we are to do and should start doing. Either way, when we go forward in our own strength (the "energy" of our flesh), the law of sin and death begins to pull us down. So exactly how do we engage this "displacement" of one law by the other? Whenever we look to the substitutionary life of Christ, the law of the Spirit of life enables us to quit our old, bad habits and begin new, good ones.

C. PLAN of Deliverance   8:3

> *For what the law could not do in that it was weak through the flesh, God did by sending His own Son in the likeness of sinful flesh, on account of sin: He condemned sin in the flesh, . . .*

1. The Flesh = Our Frail Humanity Inherited from Adam

Charles Darwin's theory of evolution had an impact on far more than biology. Social Darwinism bought into the idea that man is getting better and better in a *moral* and *social* sense. Hence, the notion of postmillennialism became popular: man is getting so good he can bring in a kingdom of righteousness for a thousand years, after which Christ will come. Science can solve the ills of society. Eugenics (eliminating undesired genes and promoting desired genes) was an easy sell. But one notorious proponent of eugenics and Social Darwinism proved that mankind is far from getting better. Hitler used the best science of his day to play God with the human race and commit the greatest atrocities imaginable against mankind. The "weakness" remained because it resides in our *flesh* inherited from Adam (Romans 6:19a). Every aspect of our being has been affected by the Fall: our minds, darkened; our emotions, degraded; our wills, degenerate; our bodies, decaying. While humanism puts its faith in the powers of man, its end result will always be disillusionment. No, those who look to men to solve mankind's problems will be sorely disappointed.

When one of my daughters was about four years old, she was so in love with Christopher Reeves (the Hollywood actor that played Superman) that she would climb up on my lap and try to give me a spit curl like Christopher Reeves so I could look more like Superman. One day as she was curling away, I said, "You know, Laura, I really am Superman." Her eyes got wide. *Really?* "Sure. You want to fly?" Of course she did. So I put her on my back and walked out into the street. "OK. Are you ready?" *Ready.* So I started to run down the street, slowly picking up speed (very slowly). She began kicking me like a horse. *Come on, Superman,* she cried, *let's fly.* I finally ran out of steam and stopped. *What's wrong?* "I forgot my cape." *Let's go get it.* "Can't. I think mom has it in the laundry. We'll have to try again when it's washed and pressed." I never got off the ground, of course, that day or any day.

Have we come to the place where we realize we are not Superman? The vision of Christ-likeness is asking us to fly; unfortunately, we cannot fly on our own. We cannot fulfill the law, God's perfect standard of righteousness, in our own strength, the flesh. But there is a Super Man living within us who has supernatural power; *He can* fly. So how does he do this within us? It is the effect of "displacement."

2. God's Plan = The Substitutionary Life of Christ

God sent his Son to do what we cannot. Christ took on human flesh to become our *substitute in death*—God "condemned sin" in Christ's flesh—and released us to *life* (5:18, compare Hebrews 2:14-18). But once we identify with him in death, he also wants to be our *substitute in life* (Romans 6:4-5). Our deliverance in Christ is not so much a *changed* life as an *exchanged* life; it is *trusting*, not *trying*. We trusted his substitutionary *atonement;* why not trust his substitutionary *enthronement?* He *lives* in us; why not let him *replace* us at the controls so *we become the righteousness of God in him* (Galatians 2:20; 2 Corinthians 5:21)? Paul's meticulous choice of words now makes this explicit.

D. PURPOSE of Deliverance   8:4

> ... *that the righteous requirement of the law might be fulfilled in us who do not walk according to the flesh but according to the Spirit.*

1. "Righteous Requirement" = Standard of Righteous Behavior (*dikaiōma*)

The word for righteousness in Romans (*dikaiosunē*) represents an umbrella concept or "genus" that is further specified by a variety of "species"—it encompasses both righteousness *credited* to us in the courtroom of heaven (Romans 4:3, our New Position) and Christlike righteous *behavior* on earth (Romans 6:13, 16, our Intended Condition). Paul uses *dikaiōma* ("righteous requirement of the law") as the "species" of *dikaiosunē* that strictly denotes *righteous behavior*, not "justification."[16] Paul had used the same word *dikaiōma* (1:32) to explicitly link this *desired righteous behavior* (5:16b) to *Christ's righteous work* on our behalf (5:18b). Thus, God's free gift of grace (5:16b, 17b—Christ's *atonement* on the cross and *life in us* in the resurrection, 4:25) is meant to result in *righteous behavior*

---

16 As developed in our exposition of Romans 5:16 (in our book *Portraits of Righteousness*), translating *dikaiōma* as "justification" does not adequately convey Paul's intent to designate righteous *behavior*—not just *judicial status*— as the ultimate goal of Christ's work on our behalf (5:18). Paul's choice of *dikaiōma* in 8:4 to describe this righteous behavior in light of our inability in Adam reflects our need to *receive* the *abundance* of the free gift of grace in Christ (5:17b) in order to fulfill the *intended goal* of our "absolution-and-release" (*dikaiōsin*) with a view to life (*zōēs*) (5:18b; see note 12, Chapter 4, "Humanity, We Have a Problem" in *Portraits of Righteousness*). This goal is *God's righteousness revealed through us to the world by faith* (1:17; 5:17b, 21b; 6:19-22).

(5:16b) *fulfilled* (*plerōthē*) *in us* as the *righteous requirement of the law* (8:4).[17]

However, this "righteous requirement" is fulfilled in us only by *walking* "according to the Spirit" and not by the self-reliant "flesh." So what does it mean for us to "walk according to the Spirit"?

2. "Walk" = Conduct of Life (see Ephesians 4:1, 17; 5:2, 8, 15; Colossians 3:7; 4:5)

Those in Christ who are free from condemnation (doom and gloom in their Condition) (8:1) are better described by "walking" than by "working." But in *walking* by the Spirit, they will also be *working* for God's kingdom. We need to distinguish "walking by the Spirit" from other ministries of the Spirit that are often claimed as the means to full deliverance and freedom in Christ.[18] Some say we must be *baptized* by the Holy Spirit for power.[19] They usually believe in two baptisms of the Holy Spirit: one which puts us into the Body of Christ, and another by which we are baptized for power. Yet, there is only "one baptism" (Eph. 4:5) and given the context of the Body of Christ (Eph. 4:11-16), this

---

17 The mention here of *fulfillment* of the Law marks a crucial turn in Paul's argument that the purpose of the "gospel of God" (1:1, 16-17) is to *set us apart to reveal the righteousness of God*. This righteousness is consummated when we *fulfill* the Law, which is "holy, and just, and good" (7:12) and *spiritual* (7:14). Two other New Testament passages elucidate how this goal is fulfilled *not* under *law* but under *grace* (6:14-15). In the Sermon on the Mount, Christ declares that all the Law is to be fulfilled *in him*, so that to be "great" in the Kingdom of God one must embody *his* righteousness, and exceed even the greatest *self-sufficient* righteousness—it is the *perfect* righteousness of God (Matthew 5:17-20; 48). This is modeled for us by Abraham, our father in *faith*, whose imputed righteousness did not fulfill the Law until he *obeyed* God and his faith was *perfected* (James 2:21-23); thus, like Abraham we *enact* God's imputed righteousness not by *law* but by *grace*—Christ's resurrection life in us—received through *faith* (Romans 4:13-25; 5:17b).

18 See "Digging Deeper: The Basis for the Abundant Life in Romans 6:23," Chapter 7, "Freedom through Slavery" in *Portraits of Righteousness*.

19 Stanley M. Horton, "The Pentecostal Perspective," in *Five Views on Sanctification* (Grand Rapids, MI: Zondervan, 1987), 129-30.

"baptism" cannot be referring to water. It is the *singular* baptism of/by the Holy Spirit.

Others affirm that the *filling* of the Holy Spirit is what gives us power to bear fruit. If so, it is not even mentioned in the two greatest fruit-bearing chapters in the New Testament: Galatians 5 and Romans 8. In the two instances where the Greek verb *plēroō* is used (Ephesians 5:18ff and Acts 13:52), it refers to group worship. And in all the instances where the verb *pimplēmi* is used (John the Baptist, Zacharias, Elizabeth, the Upper Room, Peter, and Paul), the filling did not depend on first dealing with sin. The filling came on the person only for a short period, was for a special witness, and came with unequivocal physical effects.

By contrast, in Galatians 5 and Romans 8 we find the verbs "walk" and "lead"; from our perspective we *walk* with or by the Spirit; from his perspective he *leads* us. The following chart contrasts the differences among these three ministries of the Holy Spirit.

BAPTISM	LEADING	FILLING
1 COR. 12; ROM. 6	ROM. 8; GAL. 5	LUKE 1; ACTS 2, 4, 9
Indwelling	Enabling	Intoxicating
Permanent	Progressive	Periodic
"Fact"	"Faith"	"Feeling"

We can see that *baptism* by the Holy Spirit is a permanent indwelling—he seals us until the day of redemption (Ephesians 4:30). But the Holy Spirit's *leading* (8:14) is a progressive enabling that prevails over the lusts of the flesh to bear righteous fruit to holiness (Romans 6:19). In other words, as we grow in Christ, we log more and more time walking by the Spirit. This requires that we exercise faith, for there are times the Holy Spirit will lead us into a desert with adversity, just as he did with Jesus (Luke 4:1). *Filling* seems to come at the Holy Spirit's sovereign discretion for special ministry and is not expected to last hours or days on end until we knowingly sin. The person filled knew something special was happening; he could feel it, but it was never described as the key to full deliverance and freedom in the Christian life. Conjuring up formulas by which we can co-opt the Spirit into filling us smacks of manipulating God, or what might be called "magic."

So what is the Purpose of our Deliverance? It is that Christ's righteous work (*dikaiōma*) might be fulfilled (*plerōthē*) in us (8:4); in short, it is *Christ-likeness* (8:29). And how will we know we are fulfilling that purpose by walking by the Spirit? While the Scriptures give accounts of those who spoke in tongues and those who went around witnessing, the only reliable evidence of one who is walking by the Spirit is that they demonstrate the fruit of the Spirit as opposed to the works of the flesh (Galatians 5). One who is full of anger, envy, and lust is walking by the flesh; one characterized by love, joy, and peace is walking by the Spirit (see also Ephesians 4:22–5:11). We need to recognize that we are in a *war*.

Those who are trying hard yet suffering defeat in this battle against Sin need desperately to *rest* in their foundational Position and learn the Law of the Spirit of life (Romans 8:2): to *let* the Holy Spirit lead them through the darkness and deserts by faith. Through him they can bear his fruit in the midst of any storm. There will still be pain in this life, sometimes very excruciating pain. But Jesus knew something about pain. Though he was acquainted with grief, he knew how to walk by the Spirit and he endured the cross on our behalf for the joy set before him. Likewise, the Spirit will be there to sustain us and imbue our lives with "eternal-life quality" (6:22-23), even when we are led down paths of great pain (8:23-27).

So, for those of us who are on the front lines and know it, be of good cheer. By one free gift that *leads to righteous behavior* (*eis dikaiōma*, Romans 5:16), the "appointed" Son has already won the victory (1:2-4). Now this "firstborn of many brethren" (8:29) wants to lead *many sons to glory* (8:18-19; compare Hebrews 2:10), as Christ's *righteous work is fulfilled* (*dikaiōma plerōthē*) in those who walk by his Spirit (Romans 8:4). Tragically, some of God's soldiers do not even know they are in a war, and they are in the greatest peril. They could go through their entire Christian lives, not realizing that their enemies (the world, the flesh, the devil) are blocking God's intent to reveal his righteousness in them (1:17). What a waste.

Chapter 19

Examine Yourself to See If You Are in the Faith – 2 Corinthians 13:5-6

Fred Chay, Ph.D.

In any theology of assurance, the perennial passage that is claimed by all theological systems is 2 Corinthians 13:5-6. Everyone thinks they understand its theological truth, but oftentimes with quite different theological conclusions with resulting divergent theological and pastoral consequences. In 2 Corinthians 13:5, Paul writes:

Examine yourselves as to whether you are in the faith. Test yourselves. Do you not know yourselves, that Jesus Christ is in you? - unless indeed you are disqualified. (NASB)

Based on the apostle Paul's declaration, Dr. Grudem writes:

This verse poses a challenge for Free Grace advocates because they do not think it appropriate to tell regular churchgoers who profess to be Christians that they should "examine themselves" to find out if they are really born again or not. That comes too close to saying that good works are a necessary result of saving faith, which is contrary to Free Grace teaching.[1]

Dr. Grudem's theology of assurance uses this verse specifically: "The New Testament authors do not hesitate to warn their readers that *some who are among them might not be saved*. I expect this is an unpopular teaching in many circles today, but I cannot see the New Testament as teaching anything else." In the beginning of this section of his book, Dr. Grudem emphasizes that: "New Testament epistles frequently warn churchgoers that some of them might not be saved. The remedy for this situation, according to the New Testament, would be to ask churchgoers (and those who claim to be Christians but don't go to church) to examine their lives to see if there has been a genuine change as a result of being born again."[2]

Clearly, Dr. Grudem understands this apostolic warning as a demand for these "saints" to examine their lifestyle to determine if they are regenerated and born again.[3] The assumption is that they are not, given their behavior.[4]

---

1   Grudem, "*Free Grace*" *Theology*, 131. In fact, this is exactly what Paul Rainbow says regarding the necessity of works given that they are the "grounds" of justification. *The Way of Salvation: The Role of Christian Obedience in Justification* (Milton Keynes, UK: Paternoster Press, 2005), 83, 193-194, 208-10.

2   Grudem, "*Free Grace*" *Theology*, 79. However, he does admit, "It is important to realize that this judgment of believers will be a judgment to evaluate and bestow various degrees of reward (see below), but the fact that they will face such judgment should never cause believers to fear that they will be eternally condemned. Jesus says "He who hears my word and believes him who sent me has eternal life: *he does not come into judgment,* but has passed from death to life" (John 5:24). Wayne Grudem, *Systematic Theology: An Introduction to Biblical Doctrine* (Grand Rapids: Zondervan Publishing House, 1994), 1143.

3   See 2 Corinthians 1:19. Paul calls these people "saints" or "holy ones" twice in 1 Corinthians 1:1-2. Two NT translations tip their hand as to their theological commitment by stating: "Test yourselves to discover whether you are true believers. Put your own selves under examination." (Weymouth NT) "Examine yourselves to see if your faith is genuine. Test yourselves. Surely you know that Jesus Christ is among you; if not, you have failed the test of genuine faith" (NLT).

4   This is both the Arminian and Reformed view. The difference is that Arminians understand that these are Christians who lose or forfeit their once possessed

Free Grace Positions

There are three views that Free Grace theology has contributed to understanding this verse and the resulting theology.[5] However,

---

eternal life, and the Reformed view holds that these "Christians" never truly were saved. For the Arminian perspective, see Chris VanLandingham, *Judgment & Justification in Early Judaism and the Apostle Paul*, (Peabody, MA: Henrickson Publishers, Inc., 2006), 203-204; Robert Shank, *Life in the Son: A Study of the Doctrine of Perseverance* (Springfield, MO: Westcott Publishers,1960), 37, 95, 201, 288. See also I. Howard Marshall, *New Testament Theology: Many Witnesses, One Gospel* (Downers Grove, IL: InterVarsity Press, 2014), 289 and *Kept by the Power of God: A Study of Perseverance and Falling Away* (Downers Grove, IL: InterVarsity Press, 2004), 289 and *Kept By the Power of God* (Minneapolis: Bethany Fellowship, 1969), 122. Concerning 2 Corinthians 13:5, both Shank and Marshall are less than forthcoming in their theology within the text. If you read closely, their view that Christians can lose their salvation comes forth, but it is not extremely transparent. It sounds similar, but not exactly, like the traditional Reformed view. Stephen Travis is more precise and articulate of the view that salvation once gained can be lost based on 2 Corinthians 13:5. See *Christ and the Judgment of God: The Limits of Divine Retribution in New Testament Thought* (Colorado Springs: Hendrickson Publishers, 2008), 157-158. For a clear Reformed perspective see C. K. Barrett, *Second Epistle to the Corinthians: A Commentary*, Harper's New Testament Commentaries (New York: Harper Publishing, 1973), 33; Joel Beeke, *Assurance of Faith: Calvin, English Puritanism, and the Dutch Second Reformation*, American University Studies (New York: Peter Lang, 1991), 51, 148-149; Frank Thielman, *Theology of the New Testament: A Canonical and Synthetic Approach* (Grand Rapids: Zondervan, 2005), 694: and G. K. Beale, *A New Testament Biblical Theology; The Unfolding of the Old Testament in the New* (Grand Rapids: Baker Academic, 2011) 510, 534, 536, 864; Thomas Schreiner, *New Testament Theology: Magnifying God in Christ* (Grand Rapids: Baker Academic, 2008), 583, 587; Michael Bird, *Evangelical Theology: A Biblical and Systematic Introduction* (Grand Rapids: Zondervan Publishing House, 2013), 605. *The Race Set Before Us: A Biblical Theology of Perseverance & Assurance* by Thomas Schriener and Ardel Caneday, (Downers Grove, IL: InterVarsity Press, 2001), 181 provides a good survey of options as well as their unique perspective of the topic. A good historical and theological perspective is found in *The Assurance of Faith: Conscience in the Theology of Martin Luther and John Calvin* by Randall Zachman (Minneapolis: Fortress Press, 1993), 198.

5   It is somewhat gratifying to note that Dr. Dan Wallace in his endorsement on the back cover of Dr. Grudem's work offers both a commendation and

we must observe the context that Paul writes within. We must be reminded that Paul goes to great lengths to affirm the Corinthians' eternal justification as opposed to questioning it.[6] We must also notice that Paul does not tell them to examine their works. Certainly, after two books of apostolic reflection and rebuke, their works are definitely an issue: both what they did and what they did not do, not to mention their motives.[7] But that is not what they are to view. Paul also does not tell them to examine their faith. What Paul does ask is for them to examine if they are "in the faith." Perhaps this phrase is a reference to orthodoxy as in Titus 1:13 and Jude 3.[8]

The First View: The Content of the Faith Delivered to the Saints

The first view perceives that the issue is the content of the faith once for all delivered to the saints, rather than a subjective appropriation of the saving message. If so, then Paul is responding to the Corinthians' challenge to whether Paul's theology is in the bounds of what they saw as the new orthodoxy since the new generation of apostles (10:2,12,18;

---

condemnation as he says, "The soteriology of this movement (Free Grace) is thoroughly consistent and deeply flawed". It is expected, given that Free Grace theology came from exegetical study and not based on a theological system, that consistency would be its virtue. This does not mean that an error, if consistently replicated, is still anything but an error given its origin.

6   2 Corinthians 1:2,1:21-22, 3:2-3, 6:14, 8:9 and 1 Corinthians 1:2, 6:11, 12:13.

7   The judgment of their works was very much a concern to Paul for this church. But the judgment was at the bema seat (1 Corinthians 3, 4, 9:24-27; 2 Corinthians 5:9-19) where believers will be evaluated, not at the Great White Throne (Revelation 20:11-12). In personal conversation, Dr. Grudem explained that he holds to a form of judgment for the believer at the bema (see Grudem, "Free Grace" Theology, 143-44) while he states that all the judgments are actually one judgment: "The view taken in this book is that these three passages (Matthew 25:31-46, 2 Corinthians 5:10, Revelation 20:11-15) all speak of the same final judgment, not of three separate judgments." See Grudem, Systematic Theology, 1141.

8   Dr. Frank Thielman would also include Titus 1:1; 1 Timothy 3:9, 4:1. Theology of the New Testament: A Canonical and Synthetic Approach (Grand Rapids: Zondervan Publishing House, 2005), 694.

11:5; 12:11) has brought another message. Paul, as their apostle, is warning them to check whether their new "beliefs," acquired from the false apostles, are within the body of Christian teaching that their true apostle taught them (11:5; 12:12).

The phrase "in the faith" supports this interpretation. This phrase is also found in 1 Corinthians 16:13, where Paul exhorts the Corinthians to "stand firm" and 2 Corinthians 13:5 where Paul asks the Corinthians to "test yourselves." Both of these "in the faith" statements come at the end of each of these respective books.

A Second View: The Reflective Principle

Perhaps Paul is using a touch of irony and the reflective principle much as he uses the concept of being an imitator or mimic as a guide for this wayward church.[9] This view is articulated by Dr. Charles Bing:

> Paul is writing to the believers in the Corinthian church. They have many problems, some of which seem to be the result of false apostles undermining Paul's ministry. To exalt themselves, the false apostles are claiming that Paul is a false apostle (10:2). One of Paul's purposes for writing is to defend and humbly reassert his apostleship (5:12-13; 10:1-11:33; 12:11-33). The Corinthian Christians are confused and want "proof" (from dokimén, passing a test, being approved) that Christ is speaking through Paul (13:3). Paul tells them his power is from Christ, as they will see when he visits (13:1-4, 6).
>
> The false teachers seek to "disqualify" (from adokimos, not passing a test, unqualified, disapproved) Paul as one who does not pass the test of an authentic apostle. But when Paul arrives, the Corinthians will see that he is not disapproved by God. The Corinthians themselves are his credentials of authenticity (3:1-3). Christ is in him because Christ is in them! Because they are surely saved, the Corinthians should know that Paul is not disqualified (13:6).

---

9   See 1 Corinthians 4:16 and 11:1 for the mimic or imitator role of Paul to his audience.

Thus Paul proves his authenticity by pointing the Corinthians to their own salvation experience. In the original language, "yourselves" is emphatic in the sentence throwing them back to verse 3 where Paul says, "since you seek proof of Christ speaking in me . . . " They should not examine Paul for Christ's presence, but themselves! Of course Christ is speaking through Paul, because Paul preached Christ to them and they were saved (1 Corinthians 15:1-2; 2 Corinthians 1:19), so Paul must be authentic. His argument here is the same as in 10:7 - "If you are Christ's, then we are Christ's." Only if they fail the test, would he.

One key to interpreting this passage is to note Paul's use of rhetoric and irony. In 2 Corinthians Paul uses highly emotional rhetorical language for emphasis (note especially the irony in chapters 10-12). The way the question is asked in verse 5, "Do you not know yourselves that Jesus Christ is in you?" expects a positive answer—"Of course you know that Christ is in you!" The wording of the original language in the phrase after that, "unless indeed you are disqualified," uses irony to mean the opposite—obviously they know they are not disqualified from eternal salvation. Verse 6 then follows with more irony—the readers were questioning Paul, but after looking at their own salvation they should know he has passed the test of authenticity too."[10]

---

10 Charles C. Bing, *Grace, Salvation, & Discipleship*, (Grace Theology Press, 2015) 168, and Grace Notes. This seems to also be the view of Chrysostom. Epistle of Paul to the Corinthians 29.4 found in Gerald Bray and Thomas Oden, eds., *Ancient Christian Commentary on Scripture*, vol. VII, *New Testament 1-2 Corinthians* (Downers Grove, IL: InterVarsity Press, 1999). See also Murray J. Harris, *The Second Epistle to the Corinthians*: A Commentary on the Greek Text (NIGTC) (Grand Rapids: Wm. B. Eerdmans Publishing Co., 2005), 921. Harris also cites P.E. Hughes, *Paul's Second Epistle to the Corinthians* (NICNT) (Grand Rapids: Wm. B. Eerdmans Publishing Co., 1962). But see also Paul Barnett, *The Second Epistle to the Corinthians* (NICNT) (Grand Rapids: Wm. B. Eerdmans Publishing Co., 1997), 607.

The Corinthians wanted "proof" (δοκιμὴν, v. 3) of Paul's authority in Christ—the same One who had worked and was working so mightily in them. So, in verses 5–7 Paul uses terms related to δοκιμὴν to turn their scrutiny back on themselves. In verse 5a, he tells them to "examine" themselves, using the related verb δοκιμάζετε, and in verse 5b he introduces the idea that they might "fail the test" (ἀδόκιμοί ἐστε; lit. "be unapproved"). Again at the end of verse 6 he uses ἀδόκιμοί: ἡμεῖς οὐκ ἐσμὲν ἀδόκιμοι ("we ourselves do not fail the test").[11] Then in verse 7, Paul uses both δόκιμοι and ἀδόκιμοι, "approved" and "unapproved." The Corinthians want proof that Paul is the man he had seemed to be when they first knew him. So, he gives them proof, but not the kind they expect.[12]

Ironically, Paul's best arguments for and proof of his apostolic authority are the Corinthian believers who have been transformed by his ministry—the same ones who are now doubting him. Paul introduces this line of reasoning earlier in 2 Corinthians when he writes, "Are we beginning to commend ourselves again? Or do we need, as some, letters of commendation to you or from you? You are our letter, written in our hearts, known and read by all men; being manifested that you are a letter of Christ, cared for by us, written not with ink, but with the Spirit of the living God." (2 Corinthians 3:1–3) And again, "You are looking at things as they are outwardly. If anyone is confident in himself that he is Christ's, let him consider this again within himself, that just as he is Christ's, so also are we" (2 Corinthians 10:7).

The logic of Paul's argument is compelling: If the Corinthians want proof of whether Paul's ministry is from Christ, they must look at themselves, not him, because Paul had ministered the gospel to them (Acts 18:1–11; 1 Corinthians 2:1–5). They are the fruit of his ministry, and they would know him by the reality of their own salvation. "The

---

11 It is of no little significance that Paul includes himself in the same group as the Corinthians ("we ourselves). He is not speaking as a believer to a group of unbelievers, but to fellow Christians.

12 This is a summary of the argument from Perry C. Brown, "What Is the Meaning of 'Examine Yourselves' in 2 Corinthians 13:5?", *Bibliotheca Sacra* 154 (1997): 178.

proof they seek of Christ speaking in him [Paul] (v. 3) they will find in their own saving relationship to Christ."[13]

Perry Brown captures this interpretive option as he states:

To summarize, might the Corinthians have found themselves disqualified if they examined themselves too closely? Not at all! Paul knew they were Christians, and the Corinthians knew it too. Why then did Paul make such probing remarks? He made them because of the absurdity of questioning his motives and authority in the first place. The Corinthians were Christians; there can be no doubt about it from the way Paul structured his remarks. His ministry had introduced them to Christ; there is no doubt about that either. So when the Corinthians looked at themselves and realized they were who they were because of God's power and authority working in Paul, then the apostle could close his argument by saying, "But I trust that you will realize that we ourselves [ἡμεῖς, emphatic in Greek] do not fail the test" (v. 6). If the Corinthians considered themselves to be "in Christ" (and they did), it was pure foolishness to scrutinize the authority of the man who had introduced them to Christ! The Corinthian believers needed only to look in the mirror to find proof that Christ was working in Paul.[14]

---

13 Ibid., 181.

14 Perry C. Brown, "What Is the Meaning of 'Examine Yourselves' in 2 Corinthians 13:5?", *Bibliotheca Sacra* 154 (1997): 187. This is also the view of Murry Harris. "Rather than demanding proof (*dokimē*) that Christ was speaking through Paul (v.3), the Corinthians ought to be examining and testing (*dokimazō*) their own selves. The repeated *heautous* ("yourselves") is in each case emphatic by position. Paul continues like this: "Don't you know yourselves [*heautous*] sufficiently well to recognize that Christ Jesus lives within each of you [cf. Rom 8:9] and that therefore you are in the faith?" Although for the sake of emphasis he adds "unless, of course, you fail the test [*adokimoi*]," he does not believe the Corinthians are counterfeit and knows that no Corinthian is likely to form such a conclusion about himself. As v.6 implies, the Corinthians' belief in the genuineness of their faith carried with it the proof of the genuineness of Paul's apostleship and gospel, for he had become their father in Christ Jesus through the gospel (1 Cor 4:15). They

A Third View: Sanctification and the Bema Seat

The understanding of the purpose of the book that Paul is writing is essential if we are to understand why he wrote each section of the book.[15] As David Lowery states:

> What concerned Paul preeminently was the presence of false teachers claiming to be apostles, who had entered the church. They promoted their own ideas and at the same time sought to discredit both the person and message of the apostle. Second Corinthians was written to defend the authenticity of both his apostleship and his message.[16]

In regards to the specific theological topic under consideration, again Lowery clarifies:

> Paul's question is usually construed with regard to positional justification: were they Christians or not? But it more likely concerned practical sanctification: did they *demonstrate* that they were in the faith (cf. 1 Corinthians 16:13) and that

---

themselves as men and women in Christ formed the verification of his credentials (cf. 3:2, 3). Only if they doubted their own salvation should they doubt Paul's claim to be a true "apostles of Christ Jesus" (1:1). If they did not fail the test, neither did he (v. 6). Frank E. Gaebelein and J. D. Douglas, ed., *Romans – Galatians*, vol. 10, *The Expositor's Bible Commentary* with The New International Version of The Holy Bible, in 12 volumes (Grand Rapids, Mich.: Regency Reference Library, Zondervan Publishing House, 1976), 403 – 404.

15 The seminal work of E.D. Hirsch, Jr., *Validity in Interpretation* (New Haven: Yale University Press, 1967) first opened the doors for the evangelical world regarding the importance of not only authorial intent but also the concept of heuristic genre and intrinsic genre that enable the interpreter the ability to "zero in" on the exact meaning of a text as the relationship of the whole and parts are subjected to examination. This becomes the Hermeneutical Circle and Hermeneutical Spiral.

16 David Lowery, "2 Corinthians," in *The Bible Knowledge Commentary*, ed. John F. Walvoord and Roy B. Zuck (Wheaton: Victor Books, 1983), 552. Dr. Lowery is Professor of New Testament Studies at Dallas Theological Seminary and received his Ph.D. from University of Aberdeen.

Christ was in them by their obeying His will? To stand the test was to do what was right. To fail was to be disobedient and therefore subject to God's discipline. The words *fail(ed) the test* (2 Corinthians 13:5–6) and *failed* (v. 7) render the Greek word *adokimoi* ("disapproved"; cf. *adokimos* in 1 Corinthians 9:27).[17]

Paul has been placed in competition by the Corinthians with other men who are seen, and who desire to be seen, as associated with the original apostles. But Paul makes it clear that he himself is not inferior to the most eminent apostles (11:5; 12:11) —the Twelve. Both Paul and the upstarts are claiming association and therefore legitimacy. But Paul is able to back up his claim with the signs of a true apostle and the power of God that worked in him.[18] These men are being looked to by the Corinthians, who thought that Paul was the old guard and not demonstrating the power or manifesting Christ in his life up to their standards.[19] This is confirmed by the emphasis on the term and theme of weakness.[20] The Corinthians are viewing Paul as weak and no longer the "go to" man and so looking for the next generation of leaders. But Paul is concerned that this will result in needing to assert himself in judgment based on his apostolic authority when he visits these believers.[21] His concern is that they are acting in the flesh,

---

17 David Lowery, "2 Corinthians," in *The Bible Knowledge Commentary*, 584-585.

18 2 Corinthians 12:12. Also, Paul was aware of the power the Lord had given him for building up the Church but that same power could be used for destroying (2 Corinthians 10:8).

19 A typical problem for the Corinthians. (See chapters 1-2 for their cultic personality behavior.) This issue is expressed by Paul. (See 2 Corinthians 10:2 "some who say…;" 10:10 "For they say…;" 10:12 "those who commend themselves…;" 10:22-23 "Are they… so am I.")

20 "ἀσθενείας.» See 2 Corinthians 11:30; 12:9 (twice), 10 (twice); 13:4,9.

21 Paul's concern is that he might have to come to discipline his people with severity and tear them down. See 2 Corinthians 10:8; 13:2,10. This would be in addition to the judgment at the *bema* seat. Paul hopes they will listen to his words of exhortation now and be spared the rebuke by the Lord later

given the list of vices they continue to practice, and his fear is that he will be displeased with them and need to discipline them (12:20-21, 13:10!). This is one angry apostle speaking to the church and his fellow believers who refuse to repent of their impurity, immorality and sensuality. There is nothing new about this behavioral issue for these people. But the overall context of both 1 and 2 Corinthians is clear that the sins of these people will have a consequence at the *bema* seat and possibly in the near future on earth (1 Corinthians 11:30 & 2 Corinthians 13:10).

One can imagine that the following words and the illocutionary element is one of sobriety and sternness motivated by love from their father in the faith.

> This is the third time I am coming to you. Every fact is to be confirmed by the testimony of two or three witnesses. I have previously said when present the second time, and though now absent I say in advance to those who have sinned in the past and to all the rest as well, that if I come again, I will not spare *anyone*, since you are seeking for proof of the Christ who speaks in me, and who is not weak toward you, but mighty in you. For indeed He was crucified because of weakness, yet He lives because of the power of God. For we also are weak in Him, yet we shall live with Him because of the power of God *directed* toward you.

> Test yourselves *to see* if you are in the faith; examine yourselves! Or do you not recognize this about yourselves, that Jesus Christ is in you—unless indeed you fail the test? But I trust that you will realize that we ourselves do not fail the test. Now we pray to God that you do no wrong; not that we ourselves may appear approved, but that you may do what is right, even though we should appear unapproved. (2 Corinthians 13:1-7)

(1 Corinthians 3-4, 9:24-27; 2 Corinthians 5:9-10). See also Rom. 14:10; Ecc. 12:13-14.

Paul declares that when he comes, after the double warning[22] he will not spare anyone (13:1-2). They are seeking for "the proof of the Christ that works in me and is mighty in you. . . ." Paul is saying, do not worry about my credentials or the proof that Christ is using me or that Christ is in me empowering my ministry since I am weak (13:3) toward you in ministry. Instead, just as Christ came in weakness (13:4) and I am weak (13:4) do not worry yourselves about that. Instead test yourselves to see if Christ is operational in you! Examine your own life to see if you see the power of Christ in you. It seems obvious that Paul did not see much godliness in their lives at this time or over the past two letters. But his warning is in regards to the Bema, which he has reminded them about in both letters.

Paul has corrected their behavior throughout both of the Corinthian correspondences. He has declared that he wishes to come to build them up but he may come in authority and not spare them and may need to tear them down (12:20-21, 13:2, 10!). Notice he does not share the gospel with them. He does challenge them to understand there is a day of judgment (2 Corinthians 5:9-10; 1 Corinthians 3:11-12, 4:3-5, 1 Corinthians 9:24-27) and a time that the Lord will determine if a man is approved (*dokimos*) or unapproved (*adokimos*). Paul realizes that the Corinthians might find themselves unapproved. But he already said this by declaring to them that some will have all their works burned up (1 Corinthians 3:14) and that some of them were killed for their sin at the Lord's table (1 Corinthians 11:28-30). In fact, they need to "examine" (*dokimazo*) themselves concerning this. Paul is certain the he was approved at least at that moment. In 1 Corinthians 9:24-27 he uses the same term to tell the Corinthians that he beat his body and brought it under control and into subjection lest he be disapproved or disqualified (*adokimos*) at the *bema*. Paul does not conclude in 13:10 with an altar call for them to become a Christian or become saints. They already are (1 Corinthians 1:2). He demands that they act like it (12:20-21) or he will come with severity and tear them down (13:2, 10).

---

22 Perhaps a reference to "the witness of two or three" from the OT law. See Deut. 19:15, 17:6.

The issue is not that Christians are to regularly examine their lifestyle to see if they are behaving good enough and not to question their salvation. It is to question their behavior regarding sanctification and realize the severity of the consequences both now (sickness and death—1 Corinthians 11:28-30) and in the future (2 Corinthians 5:9-10) at the *bema* if they fail to obey the Lord.[23]

The conclusion to the Corinthian correspondence coming right after such a severe rebuke (13:10) contains the tender words of a spiritual father combining an affirmation of their family relationship with both the apostle Paul, themselves and their brothers in the body of Christ capped off with a Trinitarian declaration of blessing (13:11-13). Far from doubting their family inclusion, Paul declares their lineage in the body of Christ.

The Reformed view of this passage is certainly an option but it is only one of many options as to how to interpret the passage. In fact, when theological bias is left at the door, other views seem much more likely. In fact, based on exegetical details one of the best options is a Free Grace view.

---

23 See Galatians 6 for the vice and virtue lists that Paul exhorts his fellow Christians to consider in terms of walking in the flesh or walking in the Spirit. The choice is not hypothetical. It is a real moral choice that each believer must make daily.

Chapter 20

Faith Working Through Love
Galatians 5:6

Fred Chay, Ph.D.

One of the most interesting passages in the Pauline corpus utilized to provide a functional description of faith and its relationship to works is Galatians 5:6:

> [3] And I testify again to every man who receives circumcision, that he is under obligation to keep the whole Law. [4] You have been severed from Christ, you who are seeking to be justified by law; you have fallen from grace. [5] For we through the Spirit, by faith, are waiting for the hope of righteousness. [6] For in Christ Jesus neither circumcision nor uncircumcision means anything, but *faith working through love*. [emphasis added]

One can see the inherent danger of creating a theology that includes a direct role of works, as in Roman Catholicism. The Roman Catholic Church argues for the role of love (a shorthand for works) as being that which ignites faith, forms faith, and accompanies faith to play a direct role in justification.[1] The Reformation's response defended the indirect role of love/works in justification.[2]

Many from the Reformed tradition understand that the only type of justifying faith is a faith that endures, and their understanding, argued from Galatians 5:6, is that justifying faith is "faith working through love."[3] Wayne Grudem asserts the importance of this passage when he quotes John Calvin saying, "I wish the reader to understand that as often as we mention faith alone in this question, we are not thinking of a dead faith, which worketh not by love, but holding faith to be the only cause of justification (Galatians 5:6, Romans 3:22)."[4] One of the most able proponents of this view is John Piper. In his book, *Future Grace*, almost every page of which he attributes to the teaching he gained while under Daniel Fuller's[5] tutelage, he cites Galatians 5:6 fifteen times, more than any other biblical passage in his book. He states:

> My aim is to understand and explain how it is that justifying faith works through love (Galatians 5:6). My argument is that the reason justifying faith is never alone, is that it is the nature of faith to sanctify. There is something about the essence of justifying faith which makes it a morally transforming agency. Or, to put it more precisely, there is something about the faith through which pardoning grace justifies, that makes it a

1 Douglas J. Moo, *Galatians*, Baker Exegetical Commentary on the New Testament (Grand Rapids MI: Baker Press, 2013) 330.

2 Moo reminds us that it was Augustine, from which Calvin derived all of his "five points," that used Galatians 5:6 to bridge the gap between Paul and James regarding the role of faith and works. Moo, *Galatians*, 330. See also J.B. Lightfoot, *Saint Paul's Epistle to the Galatians* (Andover: Warren F. Draper, 1881) cited in Moo, *Galatians*, 331.

3 See D. A. Carson, Peter T. O'Brien, and Mark A. Seifrid, *Justification and Variegated Nomism* (Grand Rapids, MI: Baker Academic, 2001), 2:269.

4 Wayne Grudem, *"Free Grace" Theology: 5 Ways It Diminishes the Gospel* (Wheaton, IL: Crossway, 2016), 29.

5 See Daniel Fuller, *The Unity of the Bible* (Grand Rapids, MI: Zondervan, 1992).

suitable and efficient means through which empowering grace always sanctifies. My point in this book is that the faith, which is the occasion of justification, is the same faith through which sanctifying power comes to the justified sinner. There are three assumptions here. The first assumption is that justifying faith is persevering faith. Perseverance in faith is, in one sense, the condition of justification; that is, the promise of acceptance is made only to a persevering sort of faith, and the proper evidence of it being that sort is its actual perseverance.[6]

Piper elaborates his theological perspective and its implications as he states the necessary results of saving faith:

These are just some of the conditions that the New Testament says we must meet in order to be saved in the fullest and final sense. We must believe in Jesus and receive him and turn from our sin and obey him and humble ourselves like little children and love him more than we love our family, our possessions, or our own life. This is what it means to be converted to Christ. This alone is the way of life everlasting.[7]

Piper's exegesis of Galatians 5 is presented in his book, *The Future of Justification*,[8] in a separate appendix that reveals the priority of this text to his theology. The book provides an excellent critique (done with a superbly irenic spirit) of N.T. Wright's version of the New Perspective on Paul, a topic that has drawn many critiques and evaluations. Piper's is the most recent in a long line of presentations since the 1977 entry of E.P. Sanders's seminal study concerning what he deemed "covenantal nomism" (which was called the "New Perspective on Paul" by James D.G. Dunn).

---

6 See John Piper, *Future Grace* (Sisters, OR: Multnomah, 1995), 26. Douglas Moo appears to agree, indicating that "it is by living this way that people can have a sure hope of righteousness." Moo, *Galatians*, 331.

7 John Piper, *Desiring God* (Sisters, OR: Multnomah, 1986), 69-70.

8 John Piper, *The Future of Justification* (Wheaton, IL: Crossway Books, 2007).

Piper's interpretation of Galatians 5:6 is a combination of possible grammatical nuance and theological assumptions concerning the lexical meaning of "faith." The verse receives such emphasis from Piper because, in his view, much of the divide between Protestantism and Catholicism came from the interpretation of what the phrase "faith working through love" means.[9] He goes to great lengths to discuss the inference of the middle voice of the participle "working" to refute the Catholic idea that love is a "form" of faith due to a reflexive concept of the middle voice.[10] He finds a close parallel in grammar with James 5:16 and then, after establishing the grammatical parallel, comes to his theological conclusion:

> A literal rendering of James 5:16 would be: "The prayer of a righteous man, becoming effective, avails much." This corresponds in Galatians 5:6 to "The faith becoming effective through love avails [justification]." The only point I want to make is that prayer is not rain. That is, when James says that Elijah prayed and it "became effective" in drought and rain, he was not saying that prayer "expressed itself" in drought and rain. He was saying that prayer had the effect of producing drought and rain. That is analogous to how faith relates to love.

---

9   Piper, *The Future of Justification*, 204. This view seems closer, but not exactly similar in terms of resultant theology, to Paul Rainbow, *The Way of Salvation: The Role of Christian Obedience in Justification* (Eugene, OR: Wipf & Stock, 2012); Chris VanLandingham, *Judgment and Justification in Early Judaism and the Apostle Paul* (Peabody, Mass.: Hendrickson Publishers, 2006). Alan Stanley, *Did Jesus Teach Salvation by Works?* (Eugene, Ore.: Pickwick Publishing, 2006).

10 In English, verbs can be either active or passive, but in Greek there are three voices: active, middle, and passive. The function of the middle voice is often difficult to define because of the many nuances it encompasses. Daniel Wallace lists seven different ways the Greek middle voice can be interpreted (*Greek Grammar Beyond the Basics: An Exegetical Syntax of the New Testament* [Grand Rapids, MI: Zondervan, 1996], 414-430). Generally speaking, the middle voice draws special attention to the subject that is performing the action of the verb. Wallace cites A.T. Robertson's definition: "[T]he subject is acting in relation to himself somehow" (Wallace, *Greek Grammar*, 415).

I conclude therefore that the use of ἐνεργουμένη in the middle voice does not have the nuance implication of extending itself, with the implication that the love in which this self-extension happens is part of what faith is. That cannot be shown from the words as they are used.

Moreover, the grammar of the verse suggests that Paul is saying that justifying faith is the kind of faith that produces love. The anarthrous participle (ἐνεργουμένη) following an anarthrous noun (πίστις) is naturally construed as having an attributive relationship. That is, the natural way to read it is: "faith, which through love becomes effective." "The attributive participle stands both with and without the article and is equivalent to a relative clause" (Piper citing Moulton p. vol. 3:152).

Therefore, even though it is possible that ἐνεργουμένη is adverbial ("faith, by means of becoming effective through love, avails justification"), this is not obvious. In fact, the effect of this unnecessary translation is to make love "the instrument of the instrument" of justification (justification is by faith love). This translation is then used as an argument that justification is not by faith alone apart from works of love, but rather that justification is by faith by means of works of love. This, I think is the opposite of what Paul teaches in Romans 3:28; 4:4-6; 5:1; 10:3-4; Philippians 3:8-9; Galatians 2:16; 3:8, 24.[11]

Piper recognizes the importance of this passage. He states:

In one sense, the Reformation hinges on how love and faith are related in Galatians 5:6. Luther summed up the battleground this way in reference to Galatians 5:6: "This place the schoolmen do wrest unto their own opinion, whereby they teach that we are justified by charity or works. For they say that faith, even though it be infused from above . . . justifieth not, except it be formed by charity." In other words, what Luther was willing to fight over was whether ἐνεργουμένη was attributive, defining the kind of faith

---

11 Piper, *The Future of Justification*, 204-205.

that justifies (his own view), or was doubly *adverbial, explaining how faith justifies* by *means* of extending itself through love. And (2) δι' ἀγάπης has an adverbial force in that it implies that the essentially justifying instrument is faith formed by love—that is, faith in the form of love.

I would argue that we stay closer to the mind of Paul by giving δι' ἀγάπης ἐνεργουμένη a simple attributive meaning. "Faith, which becomes effective through love, avails justification." The clause "which becomes effective through love" is an adjectival modifier of faith. It tells what kind of faith avails justification. Therefore, love as an expression of faith is not the instrument of justification—it does not unite us to Christ who is our perfection. Only faith does. But this faith is the kind of faith that inevitably gives rise to love.[12] (emphasis original)

This interpretation with its theological implications of the nature of faith is consistent with his book *Future Grace* concerning the historical creeds.[13] This view clarifies that justification is by faith alone but the faith the saves is never alone; it must be loving in action to be justifying.[14]

---

12 Ibid., 205-6.

13 See especially pages 21-25.

14 As Calvin stated, "It is not our doctrine that the faith which justifies is alone. We maintain that it is always joined with good works. But we contend that faith avails by itself justification." John Calvin, *Calvin's Commentaries: The Epistles of Paul the Apostle to the Galatians, Ephesians, Philippians, and Colossians,* trans. T. H. L. Parker, eds. David W. Torrance and Thomas F. Torrance (Grand Rapids, MI: William B. Eerdmans, 1965), 96. This view has an interesting consequence for the doctrine of assurance. I know I am saved because I love, which proves I have the type of faith that saves. Hence, works are essential for proof of salvation, and no works means no salvation. Therefore, we cannot be saved without works. Works are the means that we know we are saved. The logical circular reasoning is hard to escape. Again, as Moo states, "Faith and love must be distinguished: but with the same clause Paul emphasizes that the two, while separate, are inseparable." *Galatians,* 331. And in conclusion, "[I]t is by living this way that people can have a sure hope of righteousness." Ibid., 331.

However, there are some questions that must be addressed before this interpretation is accepted. First, there are some who would see the use of ἐνεργουμένη as a verb in the passive voice and not the middle voice,[15] although the middle is preferred by many commentators.[16] In the present tense, there is no distinction in the form of the verb between the middle and the passive, making determination of form a subjective matter of interpretation, not simply translation. We must tread carefully when making such a large assertion over a point for which there is no objective evidence![17]

Second, the language used in some of Piper's evidence must not be missed. He states, "Moreover the grammar of the verse *suggests* that Paul is saying that justifying faith is the kind of faith that produces love" [emphasis added].[18] Piper realizes that the grammar itself "suggests" and is not a clear or dogmatic aid to the interpretation. His conclusion

---

15 Ben Witherington III, *Grace in Galatia* (Grand Rapids, MI: Eerdmans, 1998), 370.

16 F.F. Bruce, *Galatians*, The New International Greek Testament Commentary (Grand Rapids, MI: Eerdmans, 1982), 232; Ernest De Witt Burton, *A Critical and Exegetical Commentary on the Epistle to the Galatians*, The International Critical Commentary [on the Holy Scriptures of the Old and New Testaments] vol. 35 (Edinburgh: T&T Clark, 1921, 1950), 281.

17 Although Bruce (following Lightfoot) says a good case can be made for the middle in every use of this term in the New Testament (See F.F. Bruce, *Commentary on the Galatians, New International Greek Testament Commentary*, [Grand Rapids, MI: Eerdmans Publishing 1982] 232), this is challenged by Fung with support from J.A. Robinson and G.S. Duncan who favor the passive. Ronald K. Fung, *The Epistle to the Galatians*, The New International Commentary on the New Testament (Grand Rapids, MI: Eerdmans, 1988), 228. As professor Jeff Phillips say from a personal conversation, "If the middle voice is accepted as in Piper's view (and many others), love becomes the product of faith and a necessary product if the faith is genuine, justifying faith. If the participle is passive, love is not the product of faith but the means by which faith is energized or becomes effective. In other words, there is faith and there is love; love does not proceed from faith but acts upon faith (as an instrumental means to energize it)." This has been championed by the Roman church for years.

18 Piper, *The Future of Justification*, 205.

is that the participle is functioning in an attributive manner and not adverbially in the clause. It is interesting that most of the grammars, except for the one he cites,[19] do not comment on this verse concerning the use of the participle.[20] In fact Burton believes that it is actually adverbial.

Finally, there is a lexical predisposition that assumes that faith has a more active nature than it actually does.[21] In order to explain the need for an attributive rather than an adverbial force, Piper appears to follow Luther's as well as Calvin's formula that we are "saved by faith alone, but the faith that saves is never alone." Thus, the construction must be talking about justification, and since faith always expresses itself in love, that must be what Galatians 5:6 is referring to. Piper explains the nature of faith in Galatians as he states:

---

19 J.H Moulton, *A Grammar of the Greek New Testament*, vol. 3 (Edinburgh; T & T Clark, 1963), 3:152. However, the difficulty concerning the syntax of participles is noted by Wallace. "It is often said that mastery of the syntax of participles is mastery of Greek syntax. Why are participles so difficult to grasp? The reason is threefold: (1) usage–the participle can be used as a noun, adjective, adverb, or verb (and in any mood!); (2) word order–the participle is often thrown to the end of the sentence or elsewhere to an equally inconvenient location; and (3) locating the main verb–sometimes it is verses away; sometimes it is only implied; and sometimes it is not even implied! In short the participle is difficult to master because it is so versatile. But this very versatility makes it capable of a rich variety of nuances, as well as a rich variety of abuses." *Greek Grammar*, 613.

20 See Wallace, *Greek Grammar*; C.F.D. Moule, *An Idiom Book of New Testament Greek* (Cambridge, Eng.: University Press, 1959); A.T. Robertson, *Grammar of the Greek New Testament in Light of Historical Research* (New York, NY: George H. Doran Company, 1919); Max Zerwick, *Biblical Greek Illustrated by Examples* (Rome: Pontificii Instituti Biblici, 1963); and H.E. Dana and Julius R. Mantey, *A Manual Grammar of the Greek New Testament* (Toronto: Macmillan, 1957).

21 See the earlier chapter by David Anderson on the lexicography of "Faith". Also see Fred Chay and John Correia, *The Faith That Saves: The Nature of Faith in the New Testament* (Eugene, OR: Wipf & Stock publishers, 2008) and the insightful Reformed theologian Gordon H. Clark regarding the meaning of faith: *Faith and Saving Faith* (Jefferson, MD: The Trinity Foundation, 1983).

Now with that understanding of faith and works let's ask why genuine faith inevitably produces love, according to Gal. 5:6. Paul isn't saying that we are justified by two things: faith and works of love. He is saying we are justified by one thing, faith, and this faith is of such a nature that it produces love like a good tree produces good fruit. Being a loving person is absolutely essential to being saved, because the faith which saves by its very essence works through love. Therefore, it is tremendously important that we see how saving faith produces love.[22]

There is no qualitative or quantitative scale given for this "absolutely essential" loving aspect that a person must have in order to be saved. This understanding seems similar to Luther who states:

Faith must of course be sincere. It must be a faith that performs good works through love. If faith lacks love it is not true faith. Thus, the Apostle bars the way of hypocrites to the kingdom of Christ on all sides. He declares on the one hand, "In Christ Jesus circumcision availeth nothing," i.e., works avail nothing, but faith alone, and that without any merit whatever, avails before God. On the other hand, the Apostle declares that without fruits faith serves no purpose. To think, "If faith justifies without works, let us work nothing," is to despise the grace of God. Idle faith is not justifying faith. In this terse manner Paul presents the whole life of a Christian. Inwardly it consists in faith towards God, outwardly in love towards our fellow-men.[23]

Analysis

We share with Piper a desire to distance ourselves from a Catholic understanding of justification that requires works as a means. With this

22 John Piper, "Saving Faith Produces Love" (sermon, June 5, 1983), *Desiring God,* http://www.desiringgod.org/messages/saving-faith-produces-love.

23 Martin Luther, *Commentary on the Epistle to the Galatians* (1535), trans. Theodore Graebner (Grand Rapids, MI: Zondervan Publishing House, 1949), 194-216.

common desire, there is another approach to Galatians 5 that might give a more contextually balanced understanding of the passage while at the same time allowing that the grammar of the participle may well be adverbial in nature without resulting in the Catholic interpretation.

Context

In exegesis, as in theology, there needs to be a coherent, consistent, and comprehensive understanding of the text. This has been aptly articulated by E.D. Hirsh.[24] In his approach, he calls for understanding the genre of a passage, which entails consideration of all of the parts to govern the whole. Hence, not only has Hirsh demanded that we seek for the author's intent but also that intent can only be validated as each part of the text produces a whole that can be demonstrated by the parts. Perhaps another name for this is seeking contextual comprehension that is consistent and cohesive. This means that context is king.

In the passage at hand, it is critical that the context be understood. First, in the general and greater context, Paul is speaking to Christians about moving forward in their Christian life (i.e. sanctification).

- Paul is addressing believers in the churches of Galatia, reminding them that they were justified by faith and not by works of the law (2:16). In fact, he is perplexed that, having begun by the Spirit, they wish to continue by the law and the flesh (1:6; 3:2-3).

- Paul argues that the law is of no value to believers since their lives are to be lived in the life of Christ (2:20-21).

- The Spirit is in their hearts (4:6), and they have come to know God or to be known by him (4:9). How could they wish to go back to the law (4:9b-10)?

- The issue has to do with the fact that there are some who are trying to move the believers away from their freedom and back into the system of Mosaic Law and its entanglements

---

24 E.D. Hirsch Jr., *Validity in Interpretation* (New Haven, CT: Yale University Press, 1967), 78, 88, 111.

that could not nor cannot justify anyone; nor can it aid in sanctification (4:17; 5:7, 12).[25]

The specific context of 5:6 reveals that the audience is people who have already been set free and yet who are being tempted to go back to the law (5:1). In fact, the specific aspect of the law being addressed is circumcision; if the Galatians would be persuaded to submit to circumcision, they would also be required to keep the entire law (5:2-3).

It is apparent that there are some among them that are preaching such a gospel and that Paul's desire is that those opponents would mutilate themselves (utilizing a play on words and theme) (5:12). However, the believers have already been known by God and received the true gospel. They were called forth for freedom (5:1, 13), but now are in danger of consuming one another (5:15). The issue is not that they are not justified but that they need to continue in sanctification that is by the Spirit and not by the law.[26]

The key to discerning Paul's intent in 5:6b is understanding the nature of the issue at hand. Paul's concern is that the believers who had received Christ and had been justified were seeking to be sanctified by works of the law. If they were to go back to that system as if they needed what the law could provide, it would be of no benefit to them. In fact, it would be a detriment to them in that the law cannot provide for them, nor produce in them, what Paul desires or what God demands. If they go back to the law, they are "severed" from Christ since they seek to be justified by the law. They have been cut off from Christ and "fallen" from grace (5:4).

The Arminian camp would see this as a clear proof that Christians can lose their justification.[27] The Calvinistic camp sees this as clear

---

25 This is perhaps similar to the issue seen in Acts 15:5, where the argument was not over the requirements of justification but rather over the prerequisites of sanctification among non-Jewish converts. This idea was suggested to me by Zane Hodges in a personal conversation 1980.

26 That the topic is sanctification in some sense in 5:6 is understood by Fung, *Galatians*, 229, note 47.

27 See I. Howard Marshall, *Kept by the Power of God* (Paternoster Digital; 2005), 110 and Robert Shank, *Life in the Son* (Springfield, MO: Westcott Publishers,

proof that they never had truly received justification. But the people in question had received the gospel from Paul and were willing to at least go blind for him (4:12-16). In fact, Paul declares of his readers that "we through the Spirit by faith are waiting for the hope of righteousness" (5:5). Paul sees himself with his audience in that they are justified and righteous and wait for the future manifestation of hope that such a righteousness will provide, namely, ultimate vindication and glorification of the believer in the presence of Christ.[28]

In 5:6, Paul clarifies the inability of the law and specifically of circumcision. The law, in regard to justification, can accomplish nothing. It is unable. It is ἰσχύω. It does not have the power to save or to sanctify.[29] Paul specifically ties this to the fact that "in Christ" the law is powerless. The audience and the topic have to do with Christians who have been justified. They are already "in Christ." This phrase (or an equivalent) is used no less than 11 times by Paul in Galatians,[30] and seems a shorthand way of addressing the community of the justified. In 3:12, Paul calls the Galatians "brothers," and in 3:15, he asks them where their sense of blessing has gone. This fits well with Paul's admonitions in the beginning of chapter 3 that they began their walk according to the Spirit by faith, but now were reverting to legalism for their standing with Christ and in the church. This was Paul's major concern with Peter in chapter 2.

1960), 176, 313.

28 It is understood in Free Grace circles and by some Reformed theologians, based upon the New Testament, that salvation is a past act (justification), a present activity (sanctification), and a future hope (glorification). See Earl D. Radmacher, *Salvation*, (Nashville: Thomas Nelson Publishing, 2000), 6. The fact is that we have been saved from the penalty of sin; we can be saved from the power of sin; and in the future we will be saved from the presence of sin. On this theological axiom the likes of Lewis Sperry Chafer and the Gospel Coalition can agree.

29 In the Old Testament, perhaps the dual function of the Law was to reveal God and regulate his people. Its function was not to justify or save them in an eternal manner.

30 1:6, 22; 2:4, 17, 20; 3:14, 22, 26, 28; 5:6, 10

The law will not function as an aid now that they have already come to Christ. This was clearly explained by Paul in 3:23-25 where he expounded that the law was a tutor or a guide until Christ came. These people had received Christ, and so the law was not only of no benefit for justification, it was also not to be used for sanctification. They had already begun by faith in Christ in the Spirit (5:1). They were also instructed to walk by the Spirit (5:22-25). There was no need to go forward by law and the flesh. Paul knew they were running well but were in danger of being hindered from this truth (5:7,18). Therefore, in 5:6 the faith in question is manifested by love.

Grammar

It may be, as Burton comments, that the participle is adverbial.[31] In fact, Piper admits that this is a grammatical possibility.[32] As Wallace[33] notes, if the participle were preceded by the article we would know that it is functioning adjectivally; even if it is anarthrous, though, it may still be functioning as an attributive adjective. Wallace[34] notes that the "fourth attributive position" (i.e. no articles on either the noun or the adjective, as is the case in our passage) can be used in an attributive sense, but that is only determined by context.

If the participle is indeed adverbial, our contextual analysis above does not indicate that the Catholic view of this verse is correct. Instead, if Paul is discussing sanctification rather than justification, the apparent tension in justification by grace through faith literally vanishes.[35] The

---

31 See Burton, *Galatians*, 281.

32 Piper, *The Future of Justification*, 205. The reason that he does not accept that possibility is his strong insistence that the passage is addressing justification rather than sanctification, which is addressed in the above contextual analysis.

33 Wallace, *Greek Grammar*, 617.

34 Ibid., 310-11.

35 J. Phillips comments on the significance of the sanctification contextual clues, "Continuing with the idea of the passive and accepting Piper's contention that the context is about justification (rather than sanctification), justification does not happen by faith alone but by faith energized by love. Thus, we now have the situation where justification is by faith plus something else, namely

adverbial sense may indeed be accepted because Paul is saying that the manner or means of faith is manifested by acts of love as opposed to the law. Justification is by faith, not by works of the law. Sanctification, likewise, is "by means of faith which is energized by love" (accepting a passive voice). The verse can still be interpreted as, "Circumcision or uncircumcision means nothing [for our walk with Christ], but rather faith, becoming effective by means of love, [means everything for our walk with Christ]."[36]

However, it seems likely that Piper is correct that indeed the participle ἐνεργουμένη is acting adjectivally. In fact, it would appear rather that the entire phrase δι' ἀγάπης ἐνεργουμένη is modifying πίστις. The fact that Paul adds the modifier δι' ἀγάπης ἐνεργουμένη to πίστις tells us that, indeed, he is being very careful in his discussion. In no other instance of πίστις in Galatians does Paul qualify it in any way beyond addressing its object (i.e. "faith *in Christ*");[37] the addendum of δι' ἀγάπης ἐνεργουμένη to πίστις in this case should lead us to cautious and careful evaluation. Even if we accept Piper's analysis, though, the

---

love. But if Paul's concern in the passage is sanctification, then love is indeed necessary, not for justification, but for sanctification. This correlates well with James 2, where faith without works is dead, or ineffective, for service in the body (James is not concerned with justification from the penalty of sin but faith working itself out through love for the brethren). The justification of James 2:24 is justification before men who can only see our works, not our hearts. Indeed, this was the very issue that Jesus was addressing when he said, 'By this all men will know that you are my disciples, if you have love for one another' (John 13:35). Thus, faith alone justifies apart from any works, including works of love. But faith is useless for serving one another in the body, useless for witnessing to the world, and useless for our sanctification unless it is energized by means of love." From personal conversation. Also see Joseph Dillow's comments on James 2:14-26 in this book.

36 The quotation marks are our adaptation of Piper's interpretation of the adverbial sense (205), substituting "sanctification" for "justification."

37 Likewise in Romans Paul never qualifies faith. The sole exception to this is in Romans 3:28, when Paul clarifies that the faith he is discussing is "apart from works of the Law." Paul seldom qualifies the noun πίστις in his writings. Some see Romans 1:5 and 16:26 as obedience qualifying faith. It may simply be in apposition: Obedience to the gospel is faith.

attributive relationship does not prove that justifying faith shows itself in love. Rather, if contextually Paul is discussing sanctification, then his main point is that faith is energized or "becomes effective"[38] for sanctification by means of love.

In fact, the ensuing context reveals that the issue *is* sanctification, which is accomplished by the power of the Spirit as seen through love. Paul argues strongly that our walk with Christ is not by means of the flesh as motivated by law. The famous section concerning the "fruit of the Spirit" is contrasted with the works of the flesh and the manipulation of the law.

This context sheds light on the issue of 5:6. The contrast is love versus law in the life of the Christian. Paul describes the obvious conditionality and caution that walking in the Spirit was not an automatic result of the Christian life.[39] In fact, he is concerned that if they do not maintain

---

38 Piper's interpretation of the middle voice (204)

39 "As Paul says, 'If we live by the Spirit, let us also walk by the Spirit.' The use of the subjunctive in the apodosis implies the conditionality of walking by the Spirit. Paul is exhorting (hortatory subjunctive) the Galatians to walk by the Spirit if they live by the Spirit. The implication is that some can live by the Spirit (i.e. be justified) but fail to walk by the Spirit (i.e. be sanctified). This statement brings Paul back to the beginning of his main argument in the letter (3:3, 'Having begun by the Spirit, are you now being perfected by the flesh?'). The Galatians are in danger (a real danger, not hypothetical), after having been justified by faith (3:2), of losing their freedom in Christ and becoming slaves again to the elemental things of the world (4:3; 5:1). One can see in Galatians (the earliest of Paul's writings we possess, coming at least 15 years prior to Romans), the seeds of his later epistle to the Romans where these ideas are expanded upon. In Romans 1-4, Paul makes the case that all are condemned under sin and that the Law cannot justify us, only faith in Christ apart from the Law. Romans 5 transitions from the issue of justification to sanctification and is followed by chapter 6 where Paul exhorts Christians not to submit to the slavery of sin any longer. In chapter 7, he explores the futility of trying to be sanctified by the Law; just as the Law cannot justify, it also cannot sanctify. The power for sanctification is found in chapter 8, namely walking according to the Spirit, as it is here in Galatians 5" (From a personal conversation with J. Phillips). This fit well with David Anderson's understanding of Romans articulated in this book earlier. Also see Zane C. Hodges, *Romans: Deliverance from Wrath*, (Corinth, Texas, Grace Evangelical Society, 2013).

their walk of faith, which is energized by love, they will harm each other (5:15). At the end of the chapter (an unfortunate and illogical breaking point), Paul issues a last challenge against becoming boastful, challenging one another or envying one another (5:26). In the following chapter (6:1), Paul mentions the fact that some will fail to walk in the Spirit and actually walk in the flesh, be caught in trespass and sin, and be in need of restoration since they have fallen. Paul as a pastor is painfully aware that just because a caution is issued, the conditionality is not merely hypothetical but actually possible.[40] Paul knew that there would be believers in Galatia who would continue to backslide into legalism, and he admonished them to restore each other gently.

Conclusion

Faith is only known before men by deeds and actions, either by law or love demonstrated in linear time. Faith before God is known to God intuitively and instantaneously with simultaneity of all knowledge of all things.[41] Paul instructs the Christians at Galatia, having come to Christ by faith and not by law (2:16), that they are to grow in their faith by love and not deeds of the law (2:20; 5:6, 16). Faith is indeed manifested before men by means of love. But that does not mean that the nature of faith itself inevitably results in works or in deeds of love. As Bornkamm has warned,

> We must guard against the misunderstanding current especially in Catholic theology (though Protestantism is far from exempt) that only faith made perfect in love leads to justification. This represents a serious distortion of the relationship between faith, love, and justification. In speaking of justification Paul never talks of faith *and* love but *only* of faith as receiving. Love is not therefore an additional prerequisite for receiving salvation, nor

---

40 Peter ended his last letter with both an appeal to faithfulness and a recognition of the danger of retrogression. (2 Peter 3:17-18).

41 This is grounded in the attributes of God's infinity and simplicity which operate perfectly given his magnificent multidimensionality.

is it properly an essential trait of faith; on the contrary, faith animates the love in which it works.[42]

The contextual clues, as well as the grammatical analysis, leads to the conclusion that Paul was not attempting in this passage to delimit the kind of faith that is effective for justification. Rather, he seeks to help the Galatians see that their standing with Christ began with faith, and in Galatians 5:6, he teaches that their sanctification continues by faith energized or "made effective" through love.

---

42 See Günther Bornkamm, *Paul* (Minneapolis: Fortress, 1971) cited in Fung, *Galatians*, 230.

Chapter 21

The Nature of Death – Ephesians 2:1

David R. Anderson, Ph.D.

And you were dead in the trespasses and sins (ESV)

And you *he made alive,* who were dead in trespasses and sins (NKJ)

Καὶ ὑμᾶς ὄντας νεκροὺς τοῖς παραπτώμασιν καὶ ταῖς ἁμαρτίαις ὑμῶν

The first observation we need to make is that the words *"he made alive"* in the NKJ are in italics, which means there are no Greek words in the original text behind these words. Some might even suggest that the translators are betraying their theology by sticking these words in the text, meaning, many theologians think we must be regenerated (born again) before we can believe. Much of that approach comes from their understanding of the word "dead."

I listened to a debate between James White and Dave Hunt on Calvinism.[1] During the first twenty-two minutes of the debate White made reference to this verse at least four times. What he was trying to establish as the foundation for his Calvinistic point of view is that

---

1 http://www.youtube.com/watch?v=q61K6ZITck4, accessed October 9, 2014.

spiritually speaking every man or woman is a spiritual corpse before regeneration—dead. Once the word corpse is on the table, the logic flows from there.

Can a corpse eat? No. Can a corpse talk? No. Can a corpse breathe? No. Can a corpse think? No. Can a corpse **believe**? No. This is a primary recruiting tool used by Five-Point Calvinists. If a man or woman is a spiritual corpse, and if a corpse is completely incapable of eating, speaking, breathing, thinking, or believing, then one is completely incapable of believing before regeneration.

Sounds quite logical, and it is. But the problems are twofold: first of all is the misuse of the word "dead," and second is the fact that we already concede that on his own a person cannot believe. Let's look at the misuse of the word "dead."

White is using "dead" here in the sense of "inactive" like a dead church or youth group. This completely overlooks the word "in." We are in a book about **Position** (Ephesians 1-3) and **Condition** (Ephesians 4-6).[2] Chapter one begins with all the spiritual blessings we have "in Christ" in heavenly places. But chapter two begins with our **Position before** we were baptized by the Holy Spirit into Christ. We were dead in sin. This kind of death is not talking about a spiritual corpse but rather a spiritual separation. Our human spirits were separated from God. Physical death is a separation—the material part of man from the immaterial. Spiritual death is also separation—the spirit of man from God. Physical life comes when God breathes the breath of the spirit of life into the material part of man. And spiritual life (post-Pentecost) comes when the Holy Spirit unites with our human spirit. Life is union; death is separation.

It is easy to show that the human spirit of an unbeliever is quite active and functional even though it is separated from God. In Genesis 41:8 we are told that Pharaoh's spirit was troubled within him. In 1 Kings 21:5 we are told that Ahab's spirit was sullen. In 1 Chronicles 5:26 it says God stirred up the spirit of Tiglath-Pileser. In 2 Chronicles 36:22 God stirred up the spirit of Cyrus the Persian to free the Jews. In Daniel 2 it says Nebuchadnezzar's spirit was troubled and anxious and

2   See Dave R. Anderson, *Condition and Position: A Commentary on Ephesians,* (Grace Theology Press, 2017).

in 5:20 it was hardened with pride. Surely we would argue that none of these mentioned was a believer. But their spirits were not corpses. They were quite active. They were separated from God, but they were capable of a number of activities.

Zechariah 12:1 says the Lord forms the spirit of man within him. To what purpose? To be a corpse? No the spirit of the unbeliever has many functions, as we have seen. I would even argue that our conscience is a function of our human spirit, and this is precisely where the Holy Spirit convicts the unbelievers of sin, righteousness, and judgment.

In 1 Corinthians 2:11 we read, "For what man knows the things of a man except the spirit of the man which is in him?" The context calls for a non-Christian in this verse, but the spirit within him knows the man. If this man's spirit is dead like a corpse and cannot breathe, eat, think, or believe, how is it that this spirit in the unbeliever can "know" the things of the man?

In Luke 16:19ff Jesus tells the story of the rich man and Lazarus. The rich man dies. His body is buried. His spirit goes to hell. While in hell, the spirit of the rich man can see, feel, talk, and think. Does this sound like a spiritual corpse to you? Not exactly. The only possible response to this is to say the spirit of the unbeliever is a corpse while his body is alive on earth, but then is regenerated when sent to hell so it can function as observed. Wait a minute. You've got a regenerated spirit in hell? Not likely.

To conclude, "dead in trespasses and sins" is a statement of spiritual separation (death) from God, the spiritual state of an unbeliever. It does not mean dead like an inactive volcano. It means separated from God, but alive and kicking.

Chapter 22

The Conditional Nature of Unconditional Assurance Colossians 1:22-23

Joseph Dillow, Th.D.

This passage has a long history of various interpretive options.[1] It is commonly cited by Reformed writers in support of the view that assurance of salvation can only be obtained if one continues in the faith. For example, F. F. Bruce says, "If the gospel teaches the final perseverance of the saints, it teaches at the same time that the saints are those who finally persevere—in Christ. Continuance is the test of reality."[2] Grudem also believes that this passage proves that continuing

---

1   For a summary of the five major views see the discussion by , Charles C. Bing, "The Warning in Colossians 1:21-23," *Bibliotheca Sacra* 164, no. 653 (January - March 2007): 85-87.

2   F. F. Bruce, *The Epistles to the Colossians, to Philemon, and to the Ephesians* (Grand Rapids: Wm. B. Eerdmans Publishing Co., 1984), 79. Similarly, Willard Aldrich says, "If we do not continue in the faith, we have not been saved." Willard M Aldrich, "Perseverance," *BibSac* 115, no. 457 (1958): 17.

in the faith is the necessary evidence that one has been reconciled, that is, saved.[3]

Both Arminian and Reformed expositors appeal to this passage in support of their positions:

> *Yet he has now reconciled you in his fleshly body through death, in order to present you before him holy and blameless and beyond reproach--if indeed you continue in the faith firmly established and steadfast, and not moved away from the hope of the gospel that you have heard.* (Colossians 1:22-23)

Arminians find support here for their teaching that salvation can be lost if the Christian fails to continue in the faith.[4] Some Reformed scholars argue that the Greek conditional clause here suggests certainty in the outcome. In other words, Paul could be saying, "If you continue in the faith, *and you will*, then you will be presented holy and blameless."[5] To be presented "holy" in this view is to be presented clothed in the perfect righteousness of Christ.

Only those who continue in the faith, they say, will be presented as justified, that is, legally "blameless," having been clothed with the blameless righteousness of Christ. Therefore, in their view, justification and continuance in the faith are always linked.

In Greek, this is technically a first-class condition, that is, the condition is assumed to be true. This is said to indicate that reality of one's faith is that one will continue in the faith. O'Brien, for example, asserts, "The Greek construction εἴ γε, translated 'provided that,' does not express doubt."[6] Or, to say it differently, "You will be presented holy and

---

3   Wayne A. Grudem, *"Free Grace" Theology: 5 Ways It Diminishes the Gospel* (Wheaton: Crossway, 2016), 89. Wayne A. Grudem, *Systematic Theology: An Introduction to Biblical Doctrine* (Grand Rapids, MI: Inter-Varsity Press, 2004), 792.

4   For example, B. F. Westcott, *Colossians: A Letter to Asia*, reprint ed. (Minneapolis: Klock & Clock, 1914), 75.

5   D. A. Carson, "Reflections on Christian Assurance," *WTJ* 54(Spring 1992): 17.

6   Peter T. O'Brien, *Colossians, Philemon*, vol. 44, Word Biblical Commentary (Dallas: Word Inc., 1998), 69.

blameless because (or 'since') you will continue in the faith." Therefore, their argument is that only those who persevere are truly Christians.[7]

This interpretation not only assumes that "holy and blameless" refers to absolute holiness and blamelessness (i.e., justification), which is doubtful (see below), but it is also an overreach in the use of the Greek conditional clause. It is incorrect to say that a first-class condition guarantees that the conditional clause is certain. Rather, as Wallace states: "The first-class condition indicates *the assumption of truth for the sake of argument. The normal idea, then, is if—and let us assume that this is true for the sake of argument—then*."[8] It does *not* always mean "since" as is sometimes assumed.[9] But more importantly, the conditional clause in Colossians 1:23 does not begin with "if" (Gr. *ei*), but with "if indeed" (Gr. *ei ge*). That clause (*ei ge*) does *not* always assume a condition that is assumed to be true. Had Paul wanted to signal a higher degree of certainty, perhaps he would have used *ei*. Even so, it would only assume certainty for the sake of argument and not reality.[10]

Douglas Moo is very explicit in his comment on this passage that final salvation "depends on" perseverance to the end. Moo says,

*He wants to confront the Colossians with the reality that their eventual salvation **depends on their remaining faithful** to Christ and to the true gospel. Only by continuing in their faith can they hope to find a favorable verdict from God on the day of judgment.*[11]

---

7   William Hendriksen and Simon Kistemaker, *Exposition of Colossians and Philemon* (Grand Rapids: Baker Book House, 1964), 83-84.

8   Daniel Wallace, *Greek Grammar Beyond the Basics* (Grand Rapids: Zondervan Publishing House, 1996), 690.

9   Ibid.

10 Pak points out that *"ei ge"* does not really convey the condition which is assumed to be true (cf. Galatians 3:4). Joseph K. Pak, "A Study of Selected Passages on Distinguishing Marks of Genuine and False Believers" (PhD diss., Dallas Theological Seminary, 2001), 271.

11 Douglas J. Moo, *Colossians and Philemon*, The Pillar New Testament Commentary (Grand Rapids: Wm. B. Eerdmans Publishing Co., 2008), 144.

Since this kind of statement would normally be understood as dangerously close to a works salvation, qualifications must be added. Moo explains that this is only the human responsibility side of the equation. On the one hand, Moo says that God will work "to preserve his people so that they will be vindicated in the judgment; but, at the same time, God's people are responsible to persevere in their faith if they expect to see that vindication."[12]

This seems to place the final arrival in heaven, in part, in the hands of the persevering believer and a salvation is, in part, based upon works. Reformed theologians respond that their opponents do not understand the mysterious connectedness between divine sovereignty and human responsibility. But we do. We simply do not agree with their understanding of that connectedness. This retreat to the unexplainable and to "mystery" leaves the average Christian wondering, "How does this work?"

Apparently, no explanation is necessary. As Reformed writer Lorraine Boettner put it, the Calvinist is "under no obligation to explain all the mysteries connected with these doctrines."[13] However, such a response is simply a fig leaf for a system of theology that makes no rational sense.

Does Perseverance in Faith Prove Salvation?

Grudem cites this passage to prove that all Christians will be presented holy and blameless, and therefore only perseverance in the faith to the end can prove that one is really saved.[14] He believes that Free Grace interpretations cannot hold up under scholarly review.[15]

---

12 Ibid.

13 Loraine Boettner, *The Reformed Doctrine of Predestination* (Pittsburg: Presbyterian and Reformed Publishing Co., 1932), 124.

14 Grudem, *"Free Grace" Theology*: 89.

15 If anyone disagrees with his interpretation, Grudem accuses their point of view of being idiosyncratic, Ibid. 119. It is surprising to him that Free Grace Interpretations "are done by seminary graduates who have the ability to use technical tools such as concordances and reference books for New Testament Greek giving their arguments the appearance of scholarly argument." Imagine

Reformed scholar Joseph Pak also argues for this perspective in two ways. He says that (1) the conditional clause is "most likely" to be connected with the main verb, "be reconciled" (v. 22), and (2) the parallel passage in Ephesians 5:26-27 includes the believers' glorification (Gr. *endochos*) with the nouns "holy, blameless and beyond reproach."

Regarding (1) above, does the conditional clause "if we continue in the faith" refer to "*in order to present you . . . holy and blameless*," or to "*be reconciled*"? If it is connected with "be reconciled," the meaning is:

He has now reconciled you . . . if indeed you continue in the faith.

Therefore, Grudem would be correct, and we would have a test of salvation. The proof of reconciliation is grounded on the believers continuing in the faith.

Free Grace theologians, however, connect the conditional clause with "holy and blameless." Therefore, we read that Christ will:

Present you before him holy and blameless and beyond reproach—
if indeed you continue in the faith.

Which is correct? Joseph Pak thinks that it "is highly improbable that a conditional clause would not modify the main verb 'be reconciled.'"[16] He continues, "A reasonable explanation is that Paul is presenting present continuation in the faith as a test of past reconciliation."[17] Thus he says, "If you continue in the faith, then you have

---

that! How could anyone trained in scholarly work disagree with Grudem and his fellow Reformed colleagues! He falsely claims that Free Grace interpretations "cannot stand up after careful scrutiny by evangelical scholars outside the Free Grace movement." Ibid., 138. As we will demonstrate in a later chapter in this book, that claim is not only arrogant and condescending, it is patently ridiculous. For one response, see also, Joseph C. Dillow, *Final Destiny: The Future Reign of the Servant Kings*, 3rd revised ed. (Monument, CO: Paniym Group, Inc., 2016; reprint, 2016), 1072-78.

16 Pak, "A Study of Selected Passages," 274.

17 Ibid., 277.

been reconciled."[18] The difference is significant for the interpretation of the passage. If we are reconciled and presented before him glorified only if we persevere in faith, that is one thing. However, if we are to be presented before him holy and blameless and beyond reproach, only if we persevere in faithfulness, that is another. Free Grace writers believe that all Christians will be presented before him and be finally saved, but only some will be presented holy, blameless, and beyond reproach. The latter are Christ's *Metochoi*,[19] his Servant Kings who will share in kingdom rule with Christ in the fulfillment of human destiny.

Pak gives no support for his assertion that the conditional clause should be linked to the main verb, "reconciled," instead of the near antecedent infinitive, "in order to present you." In fact, there are many instances of a main verb, followed by an infinitive, followed by a conditional clause in which the conditional clause is connected with the infinitive and not with the main verb.[20]

Douglas Moo (*contra* Pak) says, "The if clause is probably to be attached to the word 'present' in v. 22: 'God has reconciled you with the purpose of presenting you as holy before him—but you will, in fact, only be presented as holy before him if you continue . . . .'"[21] Similarly, Murray Harris observes that the phrase refers to "the future divine 'presentation' (but not the reconciliation)."[22]

Christ Presents the Believer Holy and Blameless

Regarding Pak's second point (2), one must ask whether the purpose clause ("in order to present you . . . blameless," etc.) refers only to the

---

18 Ibid., 278.

19 Hebrews 3:14, "partners," NASB: Gr *metochos*.

20 For example, Matthew 24:24; Mark 13:22; Acts 20:16; 1 Corinthians 16:7.

21 Moo, *Colossians and Philemon*: 144.

22 Murray J. Harris, *Exegetical Guide to the Greek New Testament: Colossians and Philemon* (Grand Rapids: Wm. B. Eerdmans Publishing Co., 1991), 60. Pokorny agrees, "The condition refers only to the final clause in 1:22b." Ptr. Pokorny, *Colossians* (Peabody, MA: Hendriksen Publishers, 1991), 92.

sanctification of believers without regard to their final stage, i.e. the glorification, or if it includes it, as Bruce and Grudem do.[23] To support his interpretation that final glorification is included, Pak appeals to Ephesians 5:25-27.

He argues that "there is no compelling reason to conclude that Paul is excluding final glorification as the purpose of Christ's reconciliation of believers in v. 22."[24] That may be true, but more importantly, there is no compelling reason to believe that the phrase includes it. He says, "It is more probable that future glorification is also in view."[25] Why is it "more probable"? Pak substantiates this in two ways. First, he argues from Ephesians 5:26-27.

*So that he might sanctify her, having **cleansed her by the washing of water** with the word, that he might present to himself the church in all her glory, having no spot or wrinkle or any such thing; but that she would be holy and blameless.* (Ephesians 5:26–27)

Pak says that the phrase "the church in all her glory" refers to the believer's perfected, resurrected bodies. But does the context suggest that?

The members of the church have been regenerated ("having cleansed her by the washing of water") and Christ's purpose is that he might (aorist subjunctive) also "sanctify her." The purpose of this sanctification is that he "might" (aorist subjunctive), present to himself a church holy and blameless, etc. The subjunctives indicate uncertainty. Sanctification is a process involving both God and man. While it is certainly true that God's intention is that all believers be sanctified, it is obviously true that this does not always occur, because sanctification is not "all of God;" man's response is required. Pak admits this when he says, "Although sanctification invariably follows justification, it is

---

23 Bruce, *The Epistles to the Colossians, to Philemon, and to the Ephesians*: 79. Grudem equates the believer's perfect glorification at the resurrection with being "holy, blameless, and beyond reproach" Grudem, *Systematic Theology*: 1202.

24 Pak, "A Study of Selected Passages," 275.

25 Ibid., 276.

difficult to describe the lives of certain believers [Corinthians] as holy, blameless, and irreproachable."[26]

He adds,

> "Since this happened while the lives of at least some of them [referring to the Corinthians] were still characterized by carnality (division in the church, immorality, idolatry, etc.), it would be difficult to say that in their lives, God's purpose of making them holy, blameless, and irreproachable has been accomplished."[27]

This glaring admission, buried in a footnote, negates his interpretation of Colossians 1:22-23, which seeks to prove that the regenerate always has a life of works and always perseveres in faith to the final hour.

Obviously, recognizing this problem, he explains,

> It is also reasonable to view even these Corinthian believers reflected at least **some difference** in their lives from the lives of unbelievers in the city because when a member within [the] Corinthian church committed a serious sin in a defiant manner, not as an act of ignorance (1 Corinthians 5:1-15), Paul seems to have considered such a person as unsaved. [28]

So, like Grudem's requirement of merely "some" change,[29] only "some difference" is all that is necessary. But Paul does not say the Corinthians are unsaved. He says they walk as "mere men" (1 Corinthians 3:3). Also, the descriptions of their vices leave one perplexed about the "some difference" Pak and Grudem would see between the Corinthians and the surrounding culture. According to Pak, on the one hand "sanctification invariably follows justification" but on the other hand it does not. Apparently, all that is necessary for the believer to validate

---

26 Ibid., 274, n. 78.

27 Ibid., 274, n. 78.

28 Ibid., 274, n. 78.

29 Grudem, *"Free Grace" Theology*: 92.

that he has been reconciled is that there is "some difference" between his life and that of nonbelievers.

Pak argues that because the word "glorious" is linked to being presented "holy and blameless" (Ephesians 5:27), the believer's glorification in a resurrection body is included.[30] However, he confuses a theological idea, the glorification of the believer in a resurrection body, with the Greek word "glorious" (Gr. *endochos*). This Greek word has no theological connection to the concept of the believer's final transformation at the resurrection, which Pak wants to draw from it.

Instead, it speaks of the relative glory and honor resulting from a well-lived life. As Charles Bing expresses it, "In this view the *quality* of that presentation, not the fact of it, is conditioned. All believers will be presented before the Lord, but only those who persevere faithfully and hold firmly to their hope will be presented without reproach."[31]

To suggest that the goal of Christ's reconciliation is to provide his church with glorified bodies removes the moral import of this context. To counter this problem, many interpreters want it both ways, that is, growth in sanctification in this life issuing in glorious perfection at the resurrection.[32] His goal is to present the church brilliant in purity, mature, and composed of a people who have honored him with their lives. The word "glorious" (Gr. *endochos*) never refers to absolute perfection in the New Testament.[33] Final glorification in Colossians 1:22-23 and Ephesians 5:25-27 is not included in the word for glory. Rather, the glory of a life lived faithfully to the end, pure, and unashamed is in view.

---

30 Pak, "A Study of Selected Passages," 276.

31 Bing, "The Warning in Colossians 1:21-23," 85.

32 For example, F. F Bruce suggests, "the holiness which is progressively wrought in his life by the Spirit of God here and now is to issue in perfection of glory on the day of Christ's Parousia." Bruce, *The Epistles to the Colossians, to Philemon, and to the Ephesians*: 187.

33 *Endochos* is used four times in the New Testament, once of the "glorious" garments of John the Baptist (Luke 7:25), once of being without "honor" (1 Corinthians 4:10), once in regard to the "wonderful" deeds of Christ (Luke 13:17), and here in Ephesians 5:27 of a "glorious" church.

A more significant issue involves something Pak overlooks. In the marriage parallel there is no sense in which sanctification of the wife by the husband includes the notion of perfection. The whole context speaks of the husband's sacrificial love for his wife as being a relative purifying influence, not an absolute perfecting influence on his wife. Sanctification is a setting apart in order to effect moral purity.[34] Calvin correctly relates this passage not to final glorification (or including it) but to Christ's "inward work through which 'the fruits of that hidden purity become afterwards evident in outward works.'"[35]

This passage teaches that just as Christ's sacrificial love for his church is intended to promote practical holiness and righteous acts (sanctification), so the husband's sacrificial love for his wife is intended to do the same. It would be a fiction to maintain that a husband's sacrificial love would result in perfect sanctification or include it. It is also fiction to assume that Christ's sacrifice results in absolute perfection in this life, and the context of Ephesians 5:26-27 is not about the resurrection body but about the moral growth in grace of the church. These verses parallel Colossians 1:28 where Paul says that his goal is to "present every man *complete* in Christ." Similarly, the goal of Christ is to "present to himself the church in all her glory." This is referred to in Revelation 19:8 as the "righteous acts of the saints." These acts will not be perfect, but they are commendable. Furthermore, just as the wife's growth in purity and blamelessness is also dependent on her responses (and not just her husband's love), so is the church's. The blamelessness in Ephesians 5:26-27 comes as a result of moral choices and is not the automatic purity of the resurrection body.[36]

---

34 Andrew T. Lincoln, *Ephesians* (Dallas: Word Books, 1990), 375.

35 John Calvin, *Ephesians*, electronic ed., Calvin's Commentaries (Albany, OR: Ages Software, 1998), s.v. "Ep:5:27".

36 The idea that marriage partners by their godly behavior can effect change in one another is found in other places (1 Peter 3:1-2). Indeed, Christ, by his example (1 Peter 2:21), has led many a wayward lamb back into the fold (1 Peter 2:25).

Holy, Blameless, and without Blemish

Probably, the major reason for understanding this passage with reference to salvation is that the words "holy," "blameless," and "without reproach" are taken absolutely as Grudem does.

The focus here in Colossians 1:22-23 is on being presented holy, blameless, and beyond reproach. But does this refer to an absolute or a relative blamelessness? These are people who were "formerly alienated" from God and who are now reconciled (Colossians 1:21-22). They are regenerate people who must "continue in the faith." Nonbelievers do not have faith in which to continue.

At issue here is not arrival in heaven but whether believers will arrive there "holy, blameless, and beyond reproach."[37] This is the goal toward which Paul labors (Colossians 1:28). This is a goal of sanctification, not salvation.

But what do the terms "holy," "blameless," and "irreproachable" mean in Colossians 1:22-23? Some agree with Grudem and understand this to mean perfectly holy, blameless, and irreproachable.[38] However, elsewhere in the New Testament, the terms are used to describe imperfectly holy and imperfectly blameless Christians. Elders of the church, for example, are to be "beyond reproach" (Titus 1:6; 1 Timothy 3:10). When the 144,000 stands before the throne, they are declared blameless, not because of their justification but because of their growth in progressive sanctification. There was no deceit in their mouth (Revelation 14:5). And believers are exhorted in 1 Corinthians 7:34 to be holy in both body and spirit. This obviously refers to an imperfect experiential relative holiness, not absolute justification.

---

37 Lohse suggests that "the words 'before him' in Colossians do not primarily refer to the future day of the Lord. Rather, they express that the Christians' present lives are lived in God's presence." Eduard Lohse, *Colossians and Philemon A Commentary on the Epistles to the Colossians and to Philemon*, Hermeneia (Philadelphia: Fortress Press, 1971), 65. We would partially agree. However, this presentation is certainly eschatological, but we agree that what is presented is the present quality of life of the believer.

38 Hendriksen and Kistemaker, *Exposition of Colossians and Philemon*: 84. Robert G. Bratcher and Eugene Nida, *A Handbook on Paul's Letter to the Colossians and to Philemon* (New York: UBS Handbook Series, 1993), 32.

Also, Paul clearly relates these words when combined together to refer to a relative and not an absolute blamelessness.[39]

> Do all things without grumbling or disputing; so that you will prove yourselves to be **blameless** and **innocent**, children of God **above reproach** in the midst of a crooked and perverse generation, among whom you appear as lights in the world. (Philippians 2:14–15)

Paul's goal for them is not that they will attain sinless perfection (he knows that is not possible) but that they will be mature and experientially blameless, innocent, and above reproach in comparison to the rotten world in which they live.

Peter echoes a similar thought:

> Therefore, beloved, since you look for these things, be diligent to be found by him in peace, spotless and blameless. (2 Peter 3:14)

Becoming "spotless and blameless" does not come about through obtaining a glorified body, but by means of being "diligent" (Gr. *spoudazō*, "take pains, make every effort").[40]

The notion of being "blameless" in the sense of being experientially righteous is grounded in the Old Testament. "Blameless" never means perfectly blameless in the Bible. Beginning with Job we are told,

> There was a man in the land of Uz whose name was Job; and that man was blameless, upright, fearing God and turning away from evil. (Job 1:1)[41]

---

39 This is not to deny that Paul uses the term "holy" (Gr. *hagios*) in the sense of absolute perfection in some contexts. We have been sanctified in an absolute way through the blood of Christ.

40 *BDAG*, 939.

41 The Hebrew *tām* is translated *amemptos* in the LXX in this verse and variously translated elsewhere in the NASB as "guiltless" (Job 9:21), "blameless" (Psalm 37:37), "integrity" (Job 8:20). In no case is absolute perfection implied.

The psalmist declares,

How blessed are those whose way is blameless, who walk in the law of the Lord. (Psalm 119:1; cf. Deuteronomy 18:3)

The Hebrew word for "blameless" (Heb. *tāmîm* in Psalm 119:1 [LXX Psalm 118:1]) was translated into Greek in the LXX as *amōmos*, the same word Paul uses in Ephesians 5:27 and Colossians 1:22. When the psalmist refers to a man who is blessed because his ways are blameless, he refers to the man's lifestyle: he does nothing wrong (v. 3), he observes God's statutes, and he seeks him with all his heart (v. 2).

Similarly, David pleads for vindication saying,

Vindicate me, O Lord, for I have led a blameless [tōm] life; I have trusted in the Lord without wavering. (Psalm 26:1)

Elsewhere he says,

He whose walk is blameless [tāmîm] will minister to me. (Psalm 101:6)

Tāmîm is an adjective (also used as a substantive) that means "honest or devout" when applied to people. It refers to "purity, innocence, blamelessness, [one who] walked in *integrity*."[42] Abraham was told that if he personally was to experience the blessings of the unconditional Abrahamic covenant, he must be "blameless." Waltke defines this as "wholeness of relationship and integrity rather than no sin."[43] This is not the absolute blamelessness of justification, but the experiential and relative blamelessness of one who is mature and walks in God's ways.

---

42 James Swanson, *Dictionary of Biblical Languages: Hebrew Old Testament*, 2nd ed. (Seattle: Logos Research Systems, 2001), #9448, s.v. "tom".

43 Bruce K. Waltke, *Genesis: A Commentary* (Grand Rapids: Zondervan Publishing House, 2001), 259.

In Pauline thought, to be "blameless" is to be relatively pure and mature. Explaining his reason for admonishing and teaching men, he says,

> *that we may present every man complete [Gr. **teleios**] in Christ. And for this purpose also I labor.* (Colossians 1:28-29)

While some interpreters understand "complete" to mean perfect glorification in a resurrection body,[44] most interpreters of the New Testament understand Paul's use of *teleios* to refer to maturity. This is the completeness to which James referred when he said we must endure trials joyfully so that we will be "perfect and complete, lacking in nothing" (James 1:4). This is the "mature man" to which Paul refers elsewhere when he says:

> *Until we all attain to the unity of the faith, and of the knowledge of the Son of God, to a **mature** [Gr. teleios] man, to the measure of the stature which belongs to the fullness of Christ. As a result, we are **no longer to be children**, tossed here and there by waves, and carried about by every wind of doctrine, . . . but speaking the truth in love, we are **to grow up in all aspects** unto him.* (Ephesians 4:13-15)

In other words, while his goal is to produce "mature" (Gr. *teleios*) Christians, he certainly knows that this will not always happen. But he presses on to promote the growth of his converts so that they will be relatively holy, relatively blameless, and relatively beyond reproach when they stand before the King at the Judgment Seat of Christ. These terms do not refer to the believer's future glorification. They refer to his present sanctification.

In conclusion, it is better to understand Colossians 1:22-23 not as a proof that those who are truly reconciled will necessarily continue in a life of holiness to the final hour. Rather, it is a passage that teaches that believers will be presented mature and relatively blameless and

---

44 Kenneth M. Gardonski, "The Imago Dei Revisited," *Journal of Ministry and Theology* 11, no. 2 (2007): 36.

beyond reproach only if they remain steadfast, unmovable, and firmly established in their faith. The goal is not to present them as saved people, but to present them as faithful Christians. Some will be faithful, and some will not, but all who are genuinely born again will arrive in heaven when they die regardless of their faithfulness in this life.

Chapter 23

Make Your Calling and Election Sure
2 Peter 1:10-11

Joseph Dillow, Th.D.

A central verse of the Reformed view of assurance is 2 Peter 1:10-11.

> *Therefore, my brothers, be all the more eager to make your calling and election sure. For if you do these things, you will never fall, and you will receive a rich welcome into the eternal kingdom of our Lord and Savior Jesus Christ.*

Wayne Grudem, like most who accept Reformed soteriology, views this as a passage in which Peter challenges us to be sure we are saved.[1] As we shall see, Free Grace advocates have a different interpretation.

---

1 Wayne A. Grudem, *"Free Grace" Theology: 5 Ways It Diminishes the Gospel* (Wheaton: Crossway, 2016), 86.

What does it mean to "make your calling and election sure?" Arminians see it as an exhortation to guarantee that we do not fall fatally and lose our salvation.[2] Grudem believes that this passage applies to the conscience. In other words, by the doing of good works, by the adding of the various qualities of the preceding context to faith (1:3-7), we prove to our conscience (and others) that we really are saved people. As the troubled conscience reflects on the presence of these qualities in life, it is supposedly quieted and assured.[3] Salvation, Reformed writers say, is sure from the viewpoint of the counsels of God, but from the human side it is "insecure unless established by holiness of life."[4] We must "produce a guarantee of [our] calling and election"[5] or "make [our] calling and election secure."[6] Others, such as Calvin, do not connect this with conscience but simply with the need for some external evidence as proof that we are saved.[7]

Grudem understands "fall" as falling away from a profession of faith, and being "sure" as a subjective confidence in the heart that one is saved.[8] He says,

> If they fall away from their profession of faith in Christ and life of obedience to him, they may not really be saved—in fact, the evidence that they are giving is that they are not saved and they never really were saved.[9]

---

2   For example, R. C. H. Lenski, *The Interpretation of the Epistles of St. Peter, St. John, and St. Jude* (Minneapolis: Augsburg Publishing Co., 1966), 277.

3   Wayne A. Grudem, *Systematic Theology: An Introduction to Biblical Doctrine* (Grand Rapids, MI: Inter-Varsity Press, 2004), 591.

4   Henry Alford, "2 Peter," in *The Greek Testament* (Chicago: Moody Press, 1966), 4:394.

5   R. J. Strachan, "The Second General Epistle of Peter," in *The Expositor's Greek Testament*, ed. W. Robertson Nicoll (New York: George H. Doran), 5:128.

6   For example, Alford, "2 Peter," 4:394.

7   John Calvin, *2 Peter*, electronic ed., Calvin's Commentaries (Albany, OR: Ages Software, 1998), s.v. "2 Peter 1:10".

8   Grudem, *Systematic Theology*, 805.

9   Ibid.

However, once a person has verified to his conscience that his status with God is "sure," that is, he is of the elect, he will never stumble. If he is truly regenerate, he must be growing in Christ, and a maturing Christian will not stumble. Grudem says there must be a long-term pattern of growth.[10] Edward Blum agrees, "[A] Christian by growing in grace becomes assured of having been called and elected by God."[11]

However, we believe that Grudem's interpretation of Peter's words is unlikely for several reasons. For one thing, it suffers from the fact that the immediate context defines the "sureness" as a *bulwark against falling, and not a subjective confidence to the heart* that one is saved. Peter says that the way we make one's calling and election sure is by "doing these things." This evidently refers to 1:3-7 where he exhorts believers to add various virtues to their Christian lives. The apostle is concerned, not with their assurance, but with their perseverance and their fruitfulness. He says:

> *For this very reason, make every effort to add to your faith goodness; and to goodness, knowledge; and to knowledge self-control; and to self-control, perseverance; and to perseverance, godliness; and to godliness, brotherly kindness; and to brotherly kindness, love.* (2 Peter 1:5-7)

He wants his readers, having begun well, to finish well. He explains why:

> *For if you possess these qualities in increasing measure, they will keep you from being ineffective and unproductive in your knowledge of our Lord Jesus Christ.* (2 Peter 1:8)

Being effective and productive in our knowledge of Christ will result in our calling and election being "sure," morally impregnable against falling into sin. Elsewhere, Peter expressed a similar thought:

> *But resist him, firm in your faith, knowing that the same experiences of suffering are being accomplished by your brethren who are in the*

---

10 Ibid.

11 Edward Blum, "2 Peter," in *The Expositor's Bible Commentary*, ed. Frank E. Gaebelein (Grand Rapids: Zondervan Publishing House, 1976), 270.

*world. And after you have suffered for a little while, the God of all grace, who called you to his eternal glory in Christ, will himself **perfect, confirm, strengthen and establish you.*** (1 Peter 5:9-10 NASB)

Rather than calling into question the salvation of those who may lack these qualities, as Grudem does, Peter does just the opposite. He affirms they are saved.

*But if anyone does not have them, he is nearsighted and blind, and has **forgotten that he has been cleansed from his past sins.*** (2 Peter 1:9)

The absence of these qualities does not necessarily cast doubt on one's justification. But it does indicate that a believer has forgotten the motivating benefits of the grace of God.

The result of doing these things is that we will not stumble and fall. This immediately suggests that sureness in this context is a sureness that prevents stumbling and not a sensation of assurance or proof of salvation. This fits well with his concern that some of his believing readers have become "entangled," that is, stumbled, even after having escaped the defilements of the present world (2 Peter 2:20). So, in 1:10, we see his warning about stumbling, in 2:20, his concern about them becoming "entangled," and in 3:17, his concern that they might "fall."

Peter's exhortation follows an Old Testament pattern. *"Those who love Thy law have great peace, And nothing causes them to stumble"* (Psalm 119:165). To love God's law is a statement of Peter's exhortation that believers should be "doing these things." As a result, they will not stumble.

Furthermore, the general thrust of the book, as summed up at the end in 2 Peter 3:17, is concerned with perseverance, not assurance. The Greek word for "sure," *bebaios,* never has a subjective sense (that is subjective confirmation to the conscience) in biblical or extra-biblical Greek. *Bebaios* is often a technical term for a legally guaranteed security,[12] but that is probably not the sense here. In classical Greek, *bebaios* and

---

12 James Moulton and George Milligan, The Vocabulary of the Greek Testament (Grand Rapids: W.M.B. Eerdmans Publishing, 1930), 107,108.

related words[13] meant "fit to tread upon" or a "firm foundation." A few verses later Peter refers to the prophetic word which is "more sure" (*bebaios*) than the subjective experience Peter enjoyed after witnessing the transfiguration of the Lord on the mountain (1:19).

This is the meaning of the verbal form in Colossians 2:7 where Paul exhorts his readers to be rooted and built up in him and "strengthened [Gr. *bebaioō*] in the faith." "It is good," says the writer of the epistle to the Hebrews, "for the heart to be strengthened [*bebaioō*] by grace" (Hebrews 13:9). It is important to notice that in two passages Peter himself seems to explain what he means by "make sure."

We are to make our calling and election "sure" as a protection so that we will never stumble, that is, fail morally or spiritually, in our Christian lives (1:10). The word "stumble" (Gr. *ptaiō*) is never used of damnation; it refers instead to personal failure in the Christian life. It means "to lose one's footing." As James put it, "for we all stumble [*ptaiō*] in many ways" (James 3:2). The thought of stumbling is central to Peter's epistle and is brought out again at the end: "*You therefore, beloved, knowing this beforehand,* be on your guard *lest, being carried away by the error of unprincipled men, you* **fall from your own steadfastness**" (2 Peter 3:17). "Fall from your own steadfastness" is manifestly the same as "to stumble" in 1:10.

To "make [our] calling and election sure" means to guarantee, by adding to our faith the character qualities in 2 Peter 1:5-7, that our calling and election will achieve their intended aim. What is that?

But as he who **called** *you is holy, you also* **be holy in all your conduct.** (1 Peter 1:15 NKJV)

But when you do good and suffer for it, if you take it patiently, this is commendable before God. For **to this you were called.** (1 Peter 2:20-21 NKJV)

Not returning evil for evil or reviling for reviling, but on the contrary blessing, knowing that **you were called to this,** *that you may inherit a blessing.* (1 Peter 3:9 NKJV)

---

13 *Bebaioō,* "to establish," and *bebaiōsis,* "confirmation."

The aim of our calling and election is holiness in this life, perseverance in suffering, and inheriting a blessing in the life to come. It does not refer to our calling to salvation, as Grudem believes.[14] "Calling and election" in 2 Peter 1:10 are united under the same article. This sometimes signifies that the nouns in such a structure may have some close relationship to one another.[15] Calling and election are very practical and experiential concepts in the New Testament. We often talk of *election* rather than *election to be holy*. We speak of an efficacious call rather than a call to suffer and persevere. In other words, we discuss the initial event, calling and election, separately from the intended effect, a holy, obedient life."[16] First-century readers would have seen the terms as signifying the totality of their Christian experience. To them it is probable that the two words taken together are a merism representing the totality of their Christian lives and the intended aim of calling and election.[17]

His reference to an "abundant entrance" suggests something beyond mere entrance. By making our calling and election "sure" we are not only protected against falling and entanglements now, but also we will obtain an abundant entrance into the future kingdom (1:11).

The expression "calling and election" is used one other time by our Lord in Matthew 22:14.[18] In that passage this phrase referred to

---

14 Grudem, *Systematic Theology*: 805.

15 This is not Granville Sharp's rule, which only applies to personal nouns.

16 The concepts of calling and election are so profound and problematic that they fully justify such a treatment. But readers of the New Testament would not do this. They saw the ideas of initial event and intended result as all part of the same term, "calling and election."

17 This phrase has merismic tendencies in that it seems to be looking at the Christian life as a totality by using the words that signify the beginning and the end of the process. For further explanation of merism, see A. M. Honeyman, "Merismus in Biblical Literature," *JBL* 71(1952): 11-18.

18 The NKJV (Majority text) includes a reference at the end of the parable of the vineyard workers (Matthew 20:16). However, I am in agreement with the critical text and view it as inauthentic. For extensive discussion of the parable from a Free Grace viewpoint, see Joseph C. Dillow, *Final Destiny: The Future*

those who had been called (invited) and chosen (selected) to attend the Wedding Banquet of the Lamb, which will transpire in the New Jerusalem during the tribulation. Those chosen to attend were clothed with the appropriate wedding clothes (v. 11), the "righteous acts of the saints" (Revelation 19:8). The believers in 2 Peter 1 were those who had added to their faith various works and character qualities. It is likely that Peter had his Lord's teaching in view and, like him, spoke of those called to a holy life and were chosen for an abundant entrance into the kingdom. That abundant entrance was Peter's way of describing the reward of participation in the Wedding Banquet. We can diagram the parallelism this way:

Scripture	Called to Righteousness	Condition	Chosen for Reward
2 Peter 2:10-11	"calling and election" (v. 10)	Make your Christian life firm by adding the qualities of vv. 5-7	"the entrance into the eternal kingdom of our Lord and Savior Jesus Christ will be **abundantly supplied to you**" (v.11)
Matthew 22:14	"invitation [called] to the wedding feast" (v. 9)	Dress yourself with the righteous acts of the saints (vv. 11-12)	"gathered together [chosen/elected]" "the hall was **filled** with wedding guests" (v. 10)

Reign of the Servant Kings, 3rd revised ed. (Monument, CO: Paniym Group, Inc., 2016; reprint, 2016), Chapter 49, esp. p. 781. For an alternative Free Grace approach see the article by Gregory P. Sapaugh, "A Call to the Wedding Celebration: An Exposition of Matthew 22:1-14," *JOTGES* 5, no. 1 (Spring 1992).

The Reformed theologians say that to make our calling and election sure is to discover if we are elected by looking at our works. But Peter is saying something different. To make our calling and election sure is to add virtues to our faith so that we (1) build a firm foundation, impregnable against falling into sin, and (2) obtain a rich welcome when we enter the kingdom (1:11, "abundantly supplied").

Chapter 24

Fellowship with the Father – 1 John

David R. Anderson, Ph.D.

1 John 2:3-4

Now by this we know that we know him, if we keep his commandments. He who says, "I know him," and does not keep his commandments, is a liar, and the truth is not in him.

It is hard to come up with a passage leaned on more than this one by Reformed theologians that want to buttress their marriage of justification with sanctification. Here, according to them, is how to tell if you are elect. In fact, some of them find eleven tests in 1 John to help measure one's elect status.[1] But none of these tests speaks louder to the issue of whether or not someone is headed for heaven than this one. The argument is pretty simple: here is how we can know that we know Jesus, if we keep his commandments. Furthermore, anyone that claims to know Jesus and does not keep his commandments is simply a liar. Pretty straightforward, isn't it?

---

1 John MacArthur, *Saved Without a Doubt* (Colorado Springs, CO: Victor Books, 1992), 67-91.

Except that it isn't. Without addressing the context of these verses for the moment, let's look more closely at them in the original language. Don't worry if you don't read Greek. I want to show you something you can pick up on just by looking at the Greek:

Καὶ ἐν τούτῳ *γινώσκομεν* ὅτι *ἐγνώκαμεν* αὐτόν, ἐὰν τὰς ἐντολὰς αὐτοῦ τηρῶμεν. ὁ λέγων ὅτι *ἔγνωκα* αὐτὸν καὶ τὰς ἐντολὰς αὐτοῦ μὴ τηρῶν, ψεύστης ἐστὶν καὶ ἐν τούτῳ ἡ ἀλήθεια οὐκ ἔστιν·

Can you look at the three verbs italicized above and see that the last two begin with *ἔγνωκα*? So, although they are from the same word (*ginōskō*) as the first verb, they are both in a different tense than the first verb: they are in the perfect tense, while the first verb is in the present tense. As far as I know, all evangelicals believe Scripture is inspired by God. That means if he changed tenses, there was a reason for it. If we miss this deliberate shift on John's part, we miss his intent for the verse. Others have pointed out that the root word for "know" (*ginōskō*) speaks of "experiential" knowledge as opposed to intuitive knowledge. Greek grammarians call it a "stative" verb because it describes a state of being as opposed to a verb of action. In other words, to "know" or to "believe" speak of inner truths but not outward actions.

K.L. McKay, a Greek grammarian, has written an excellent article dealing with the perfect tense of stative verbs in which he demonstrates that putting a stative verb into the perfect tense has the effect of intensifying the basic meaning of the verb.[2] It is a deeper state of the meaning of the verb. Constantine Campbell describes the effect as the verb being "sharpened" beyond its normal usage.[3] In this case, the verb

---

2   K. L. McKay, "On the Perfect and other Aspects in New testament Greek," *Novum testamentum* XXIII, 4 (1981), 297. See also Constantine Campbell, *Basics of Verbal Aspect in Biblical Greek* (Grand Rapids, Mich.: Zondervan, 2008), 110.

3   Ibid. Campbell gives some examples of this sharpening effect on other New Testament verbs. For example, the verb φοβοῦμαι (*phoboumai*) in the present means "I am afraid," but the sense of the perfect (πεφόβημαι, *pephobēmai*) would be "I am terrified."

means "to know" in the sense of an experience. So, putting it into the perfect tense means "to know intensely," "to experience deeply," or "to know fully."

None of the commentators who take the "tests of life"[4] view of 1 John have observed the significant change in tenses here in 2:3. Some of the translations have noticed this change, such as the NASB, which says, "And by this we *know* that we *have come to know* Him, if we keep His commandments." But this does not solve the problem, nor does this translation reflect the perfect tense of the *stative* verb. This point cannot be stressed enough, since 2:3 is referenced more than any other "test of life" in 1 John by those who believe this letter was written to tell believers how to know if they are true Christians or not.

The perfect tense in the Greek language has the basic meaning of "completed action in the past with present results." But, according to its use in context, a typical verb can put its emphasis on the completed action in the past *or* on the present results. When the translator thinks the emphasis is on the completed action in the past, he will translate it with the English word "have" to emphasize the completed action: "have heard," "have written," "have finished," "have been sanctified." But when the translator thinks the emphasis is on the present results of the completed action in the past, he translates the verb like an English present tense: "It is finished" (*tetelestai*—Christ's statement on the cross). But within a stative verb, McKay's point is that it should normally or "mostly"[5] be translated with the emphasis on the present results. In other words, "have come to know" does not recognize the significance

---

4   Reformed theologians see 1 John as containing various "tests of life" for the Christian to discern whether he is truly saved. They take 5:13 as the purpose statement of the entire letter. See, for example, John MacArthur, *1-3 John* (Chicago: Moody Publishers, 2007), 9; 202-203. On the other hand, Free Grace interpreters see 5:13 as an expression only of the purpose of the immediately preceding section (5:1-12; John uses the clause "These things I have written…" or similar statements several times throughout the epistle—1:4; 2:1; 2:26; 5:13). The purpose of the entire epistle, according to the Free Grace view, is at the beginning of the letter, where John expresses his concern that believers enjoy fellowship with the Father as he does (1:3-4). Thus, if 1 John contains tests of anything, they are tests of fellowship, not tests of life.

5   McKay, "On the Perfect," 297.

of a stative verb in the perfect tense. A more accurate reflection of the emphasis on the intensified state of experiential knowledge here would be, "And by this we *know* that we *know* him *intensely.*" And what is intense knowledge if not deep, intimate knowledge? Once again, the emphasis here is on *fellowship*, not on whether a relationship exists or not. Grudem seems completely unaware of McKay's work on the perfect tense of stative verbs, or he chooses to ignore it because it does not fit with his theology. It is not a test of whether a person is born again; it is a test of whether a person is having close fellowship with God.[6]

And, after all, doesn't a test of *fellowship* fit better with the argument of a book, the proclaimed purpose of which is that we might "have fellowship" with the Father and his Son Jesus Christ (1:3)? When it comes to fellowship, there is room for relativity. In other words, when it comes to intimacy with Christ, there is close, closer, and closest. The more consistently a believer keeps his commandments, the closer he is to the Savior (John 14:21). But when it comes to having a saving relationship with the Savior, there is no room for relativity at all. He is either one's Savior, or he is not. As the analogy goes, one cannot be a little bit pregnant. Hence, since no one keeps his commandments absolutely, how could anyone ever know he or she has a saving relationship with Christ? How good would someone have to be? How many commandments would a person have to keep? How consistently would he have to keep his commandments?

1 John 3:6

No one who lives in him *keeps on* sinning. No one who *continues to* sin has either seen him or known him. (NIV)

This is another verse in 1 John commonly used by Reformed theologians as a test of one's election. According to Reformed theology, there is no such thing as a carnal Christian (1 Corinthians 3:1-3);

---

6 Grudem does deal with this passage in his book *"Free Grace" Theology: 5 Ways It Diminishes the Gospel* (Wheaton, Ill.: Crossway, 2016), 81, note 3; 91; 95. However, he does not discuss the verb tenses and how they bear upon exegesis of the passage.

therefore, an elect person cannot continue in sin. Just what "continuing in sin" means is hard to pin down. How long is "continuing"? We don't know. Could I have one sin habit but not two? What if I have a relatively innocuous sin habit on the scale of evil, like maybe overeating or smoking? Does that qualify for "continuing in sin"? These are embarrassing questions to all but the most self-righteous of the Reformed because most people that name the name of Christ have some sort of peccadillo that they drag around. Are they all excluded from the pearly gates?

Reformed people like Wayne Grudem love 1 John 3:6 because, depending on how you translate the verse, it can be good ground to support their point that an elect person cannot continue in sin.[7] Many well-known preachers say this verse means if a person who claims to be a Christian "sins," he simply professes Christ but does not possess Christ. That statement has a nice ring to it, but it is a problem for anyone who has read 1 John from the beginning.

Back in 1 John 1:8, we were warned that the Christian who claims he has no sin in his life is self-deceived. Of course, those that say the person in 3:6 is not a Christian also say the person in 1:8 is not a born-again believer. But the subject of 1:8 is "we," a "we" which includes the apostles (when "we" is traced from 1:1 through to 1:8). To say the "we" in 1:8 does not refer to believers does all sorts of violence to the text. You might as well say the apostles were not born-again believers. But if these are believers in 1:8, then it appears we have a contradiction between 1:8 and 3:6.[8] We must explain this apparent contradiction somehow.

Those who say 3:6 is not referring to born-again believers must do something with the fact that all humans still fall short of the absolute holiness of God. In other words, they are still sinful. This includes Christians and non-Christians, possessors and professors, the elect and the non-elect. Therefore, they argue that 3:6 could not mean absolute sinlessness. But absolute sinlessness seems to be the meaning that arises from a basic translation from the Greek into English. So

---

7   See ibid., 81, note 3.

8   See Dave R. Anderson, *Maximum Joy*, (Grace Theology Press, 2013), 53.

when we cannot explain the text from the apparent meaning in the English translation, we like to retreat to Greek grammar. No problem. Sometimes that is very helpful (such as in 2:3-5). But we need to be sure our Greek grammar is correct.

Those who want to get the born-again person out of 3:6 tell us that *hamartanō*, the Greek verb used in the original text, is in the present tense. So far, so good. But this is where some get off track. They want to tell us that the basic meaning of the present tense in the Greek language is *continuous* action. In other words, a true believer does not *continue* to sin. Anyone who claims to be a Christian but *continues* to sin has neither seen nor known him, that is, he is simply not a genuine believer.

You can see this interpretation without going to a commentary by just looking at the NIV above. The NIV translates 3:6 as such: "No one who lives in him keeps on sinning. No one who continues to sin has either seen him or known him." Here they not only change the word "abides" from the original *menō* to "lives" (which would be a completely different word in the Greek), but they reveal their interpretation of the present tense as *continuous* action when they translate the verb *hamartanei* as "keeps on sinning." They translate it this way in the first half of 3:6 and, in the second half, as "continues to sin" (the same root verb).[9]

Unfortunately, there is nothing inherent in the Greek present tense that tells us this is *continuous* action. For example, Jesus refers to his single act of coming to the earth at his incarnation in the present tense in John 6:33 when he says, "For the bread of God is he who comes down

---

9 In the second half of the verse, *hamartanō* is in the form of a substantival present participle. Imposing the idea of continuous action on a substantival present participle is even more tenuous than it is for the verb in the first half of the verse. Dan Wallace points out that while verbal aspect of a substantival participle is not entirely diminished, the "aspect of the *present* [emphasis original] participle can be diminished if the particular context requires it." He points out that in Mark 6:14, John *ho baptizōn* ("the baptizer"; substantival present participle) cannot mean that John continuously baptizes, "for otherwise John would be baptizing without a head" since he is dead at this point in the narrative. *Greek Grammar Beyond the Basics* (Grand Rapids, Mich.: Zondervan, 1996), 620 (see also note 19 on the same page).

from heaven and gives life to the world." Is there anyone that would like to tell us that the present tense here means *continuous* action, that is, that Jesus is continually coming down from heaven? I don't think so. The present tense *can* mean continuous action, but that is only one of its ten different uses, and it is a fairly rare usage.[10] There need to be other indicators in the context of the verb before we conclude that the meaning is *continuous* action. So, I hope you see the problem. What is our suggested solution?

Once again, we think the passage, and the book as a whole, is about our *fellowship* with God, not our *relationship* with God. Why might an informed interpreter think the issue in this verse is fellowship instead of relationship? The first clue is the word *abides*. This word should be a clue that John's subject is fellowship instead of relationship. In John 15:5–11, Jesus tells branches that are "in the vine" to "abide in the vine." If they are in the vine, they are "in Christ," to use Paul's words. But now they are told to "abide in Christ," which makes no sense to those that believe in eternal security unless "abide" is taking us away from relationship truth into fellowship truth. So, when we see "abide" in 1 John, we should begin with the working assumption that he is giving us some more truth about fellowship, unless there is strong evidence to the contrary.

Our second clue is John's choice of the *perfect* tense for the verbs *seen* and *known*. Just as in 2:3-5, especially for verbs describing a state of being (*to know*) as opposed to verbs of action (e.g., *to hit*), the perfect tense expresses an intensified state. In other words, "to know" in the perfect tense becomes "to know intensively" or "intimately." "To see" in the perfect tense becomes "to see very closely." These are verbs of *close fellowship* with the Savior. A Christian in close fellowship with Jesus wants sin out of his life. The Christian who can dismiss the sin in his life as no big deal has never caught a close vision of the Savior and does not know him very intimately. It is *a contradiction* to claim close fellowship with the Savior and to sin without remorse, confession, or repentance.

---

10 Wallace discusses the several options for interpreting verbs in the present tense, of which continuous action (which he calls the "Customary [Habitual or General] Present") is only one, in his *Greek Grammar*, 514-539.

But how can we reconcile this claim in 1 John 3:6 that Christians in fellowship (abiding) do not sin when 1 John 1:8 says they do? Well, as we have already discussed, one approach is to say that the present tense of the verb "to sin" means "to continually sin." However, as mentioned, that meaning is not inherent in the present tense. To mean continual action, the text will usually employ other words along with the present tense to make that meaning obvious, such as: 1) *diapantos*—"continually" (Luke 24:53; Hebrews 9:6; 13:15) or 2) *eis to dienekes*—"continually" (Hebrews 7:3; 10:1).

J. P. Louw demonstrates convincingly that the present tense in 1 John has no such meaning.[11] It is, in fact, "a zero tense of factual actuality." We will look at this again when we get to 3:9, which would be a direct contradiction to 1:8, if the *continual* meaning of the present tense is imported into both verses. Thus, the NIV demonstrates questionable scholarship on this point when it imports the "continual" translation here. That is an interpretative choice made by the translators, but the choice comes from a theological point of view they have imported into the text, not from a careful study of Greek grammar.

And who of you really wants to take the verbs in verse six as continual action? Have any of you wrestled with an ongoing problem with a particular sin? Better asked, who of us has not? The only people that can raise their hands are the hypocrites or the self-deceived, which are precisely the errors of the Christians in 1:6 (hypocrisy) and 1:8 (self-deception). Going down that road can lead into deep darkness. This leads us to 1 John 3:9.

1 John 3:9

No one who is born of God will *continue* to sin, because God's seed remains in them; they cannot *go on* sinning, because they have been born of God.

Like verse six, this verse appears to say that a genuine, born-again Christian does not sin and cannot sin. But that contradicts 1:8, which

---

11 J. P. Louw, "Verbal Aspect in the First Letter of John," *Neotestamentica* 9 (1975): 99-101.

says Christians do sin, and the truth is not in them if they deny this. Suggested solutions are as follows:

1) The people in 1:8 are not genuine, born-again Christians. But, then, as we have asked before, who are the "we" of 1:1-7? It includes the apostles. Surely they are genuine, born-again Christians.

2) The present tense of 3:9 means a genuine, born-again Christian does not and is not able to *continually* sin. As in verse six, this is the approach of the NIV: "No one who is born of God will *continue* to sin, because God's seed remains in him; he cannot *go on sinning*, because he has been born of God" (emphasis mine). But, as we saw in 3:6, the present tense in 1 John does not mean continual action. Try sticking the "continuous action" present tense in 1:8—"If we say that we do not continually have sin, we deceive ourselves, and the truth is not in us." If the present tense means continuous action in 3:9, consistency argues for continuous action in 1:8. But that makes 3:9 a direct contradiction to or inconsistent with 1:8. Consistency cannot breed inconsistency. The law of non-contradiction prevails.

3) Perhaps the best answer lies in understanding the meaning and significance of "*his seed*." This is a reference to God's nature. His divine nature is passed down through his divine seed. The new birth places his seed in us. Just as my physical seed cannot produce something outside its genetic code, so God's seed cannot produce something contrary to his nature, that is, sin. God's nature cannot produce sin. God's nature in us (his seed) cannot produce sin.

This passage may be best understood as a parallel to Paul's statements in Romans 7:14-25. The evil which I do is done by me, but not really; it is done by my sin(ful) nature. So, the divine good that I do is not done by me; it is done by my divine nature. Both of these natures dwell in the child of God simultaneously. However, even though the sin(ful) nature from our "B.C. days" stays with us after we are born again (as does our physical body, our personality, our core intelligence, et cetera), the addition of God's divine nature with the indwelling Holy Spirit changes our identity forever. We are radically, fundamentally different from the Old Man (all we were before we met Christ or were born-again). We now have the mind of Christ (1 Corinthians 2:16). "For I delight in the law of God according to the inward man" (Romans 7:22). When I obey the lusts of the flesh, my new inner man

(the divine nature) is disgusted and repulsed. I can only cry out with
Paul ("Oh, wretched man that I am!") when I choose to follow the lead
of my sinful side. This inner disgust was not present in my Old Man.
Conviction from the Holy Spirit, yes; disgust and anguish such as Paul
was reeling from in Romans 7:24, no. The new creature in Christ (2
Corinthians 5:17) knows that when the believer knowingly sins, he is
not acting in accordance with this fundamental change that has taken
place within him when he was born again. He longs with the mind of
Christ to act in harmony with his new identity. In fact, that is the only
way he can manifest or make visible who really is a child of the King.
And that's what the first half of verse ten tells us.

1 John 5:1a

**Everyone who believes that Jesus is the Christ has been born
of God. (ESV)**

Whoever believes that Jesus is the Christ is born of God. (NKJ)

Amazingly, some Reformed scholars are now resorting to 1 John
5:1 in support of their belief that *regeneration precedes faith* in the
ordo salutis. In a recent paper presented to the Evangelical Theological
Society, John Piper, who is not a New Testament Greek scholar, is
cited as saying that 1 John 5:1 is the clearest text in the New Testament
supporting the position that regeneration precedes faith.[12] The
suggestion might not need to be addressed if it were not for the noted
Reformed scholars cited in support: Stott, Ware, Frame, Murray, et al.

The argument rides under cover of a misinterpretation of Greek
grammar, especially the meaning of the Greek **perfect tense**. Mounce,
Wallace, Zerwick, and Moulton (all accomplished Greek grammarians)
explain the basic force of the perfect tense as *completed action in the
past with present results.* While the Greek verb "born" in 1 John 5:1 is

---

12 John Piper, *Finally Alive* (Scotland: Christian Focus, 2009), 118, quoted in
   Matthew Barrett, "Does Regeneration Precede Faith in 1 John?" (paper
   presented at the 62nd Annual Meeting of the Evangelical Theological Society
   in Atlanta, GA, November 2010). Barrett has since published a book
   containing the same quote. *Salvation by Grace: The Case for Effectual Calling
   and Regeneration* (Phillipsburg, New Jersey: P&R Publishing, 2013), 158.

in the *perfect* tense, the verb "believes" is a *present* participle. These Reformed scholars argue that since the action of the main verb ("born") is completed in the *past*, while the subject of the sentence is *pas* (Πᾶς) followed by a *present* participle ("who is believing"), the action of the main verb ("born/regenerated") must precede the "result" of believing. But the paper goes further to propose that since regeneration *precedes* faith, it therefore *causes* faith, and/or *results in* faith, and Five-Point Calvinism follows on its heels.

Granted, just as in English grammar, it is easy to get lost in Greek grammar. But the proposal needs to be examined further in order to expose that the entire argument is based on a simple error in Greek grammar. And before delving further, it should be noted that whereas some Reformed scholars employ the perfect tense of "is born" in 1 John 5:1 to support their understanding that regeneration precedes faith, *none* of the grammarians cited does so—they know better. So, what does 1 John 5:1 actually say?

> **Whoever believes** that Jesus is the Christ **is born** of God, and whoever loves him who begot also loves him who is begotten of him.

> Πᾶς ὁ πιστεύων ὅτι Ἰησοῦς ἐστιν ὁ χριστός, ἐκ τοῦ θεοῦ γεγέννηται, καὶ πᾶς ὁ ἀγαπῶν τὸν γεννήσαντα ἀγαπᾷ [καὶ] τὸν γεγεννημένον ἐξ αὐτοῦ.

The subject of the sentence, "whoever," is followed by a present participle in the original Greek. Since the Greek participle (ὁ πιστεύων) has what looks like an "o" in front of it, it is an "articular" participle which functions as an *adjective* and not as an *adverb* connected to the verb. The ESV reflects this by translating "Everyone who believes." Only if the participle were *not* preceded by the article could it then be connected to the main verb, "is born," and in some way describe or qualify the state, "born of God."[13] Thus, as an *adjectival* participle

---

13 There are eight ways an adverbial participle can describe the action of an independent verb: *temporal, manner, means, cause, condition, concession, purpose,* and *result* (Wallace, 612). Take Ephesians 5:18-21, for example: The

describing the *subject* of the sentence (Πᾶς), it does not in any way specify the *results* of the main verb or what the main verb *causes*.

Grammarians also speak of the particular verbal "aspect" the author wants to emphasize by using the perfect tense, whether **completed action in the past** (*has been born*, an extensive perfect) or **present results** (*is born*, an intensive perfect). We see this latter aspect emphasized in translations of Jesus's cry on the cross: *tetelestai*, a verb in the perfect tense. Most translators aptly put the emphasis here on the **present results** of the crucifixion by translating this in the *present—it is finished*, although they *could* have put the emphasis on the **completed action in the past**—*it has been finished*. Likewise, the NKJV translators of 1 John 5:1 emphasize the **present results** of the Greek perfect tense verb in John's use by rendering it in the English *present* tense: *is* born. The ESV translators put the emphasis on the completed action in the past: "has been born."

Finally, 1 John 5:1 is not specifically discussing the *original* faith of the current believer. A person who was born again in the past can be currently believing and demonstrating that faith by loving God and others that are born of God. But they can also be currently *dis*believing, and *not* loving God or others. John is concerned about *abiding* in faith. His point is that everyone that believes, at whatever stage of their faith journey (see 2:12-14), is still born of God and shows their pedigree (compare 3:9) by *abiding* in the love of God and others born of God. Since John is emphasizing a **general principle**, the participles "whoever believes" and "whoever loves" both exemplify a **gnomic** use of the present tense as they parallel "also loves" (present tense) in the last clause.

---

readers are told to "be filled" (main, finite verb). This main verb is followed by five participles (speaking, singing, making, thanking, and submitting). None of the participles has an article (the little "o") preceding it, so they may be (and indeed are in this case) adverbial participles describing the action of the main verb in some way. Of the eight options, the two that make the most sense are *means* or *results*: 1) Be filled *by means of* speaking, singing, making, . . . ; 2) Be filled, *with these results:* speaking, singing, making, ... So the participles are most likely telling the Ephesians *how* to be filled (means) or the *results* of being filled (result). But since they are all adverbial participles they are directly modifying the main verb, *be filled*.

Throughout his paper Barrett confuses the grammar in claiming that regeneration actually *causes* faith. If this is what the verse says, it would support Reformed theology. But *cause* and *result* can only be predicated of an *adverbial* participle in relationship to the main verb. Unfortunately for his argument, the participles he cites are *all* adjectival. Consequently, the verse says nothing at all about believing as a *result* of, or *caused* by, the new birth (regeneration). To suggest that the new birth *causes* or *results in* believing is like saying **everyone running** (present participle) in a race **has been pinned** (perfect verb) with a race number and then claiming that being pinned with a number *caused* them to run the race. Or, "My barber, who eats bacon and eggs for breakfast, completed his first marathon last week," and then concluding that completing the marathon caused my barber to eat bacon and eggs. No connection. The entire paper is built on a simple mistake in Greek grammar. And it is not a debatable one.[14]

---

14 For an additional critique of the Reformed use of 1 John 5:1 as a proof text for their *ordo salutis*, see Brian J. Abasciano, "Does Regeneration Precede Faith: The Use of 1 John 5:1 as a Proof Text," *The Evangelical Quarterly* 84, no. 5 (October 2012), 307-322.

Conclusion

Final Thoughts . . . A Final Plea

Fred Chay, Ph.D.

I
t has been said, "We need to be spiritual enough to desire the truth, astute enough to grasp the truth, and brave enough to proclaim the truth."[1]

All sides of this theological discussion desire to know the truth. However, as theologian Helmut Thielicke proposed, "Do we not have to accept the fact that under the shadow of forgiveness different decisions are possible and different loyalties and liberties may exist?" To ask the question is to answer it. Different decisions and different loyalties have been the hallmark of the church with its diverse theological articulations and declarations. The challenge is how to handle those differences.

For Martin Luther, the idea of challenging the Roman Catholic Church seemed inconceivable until it wasn't. So today, challenging the prevailing dogmatic articulation may also seem inconceivable, but we must. As a form of Roman Catholic theology was accepted for 1,000

---

1   Attributed to Dr. Bill Jackson

years before Luther fully challenged and partially corrected the theology of that day, so it appears today that, as the apostle Paul declared, "it is necessary that there must be divisions among you in order that those who are approved may be made manifest" (1 Corinthians 11:19).

This is not the first time, nor will it be the final time, but it has become an essential time that the doctrine of grace and what has been called Free Grace theology must be clarified. We have presented a historical and theo-bibliographic timeline to demonstrate that the Free Grace theological perspective is not new or novel. We have attempted to clarify theological terminology, such as the biblical concepts and constructs of faith and repentance and their relation and role in soteriology. We have also endeavored to clarify theological doctrines, such as the assurance of salvation, the perseverance of the saints, and rewards for faithfulness.

It is our hope that the purity and simplicity of the free gift of eternal life, given by God's grace alone, received by man's faith alone in our only savior Christ alone, and the birthright and confidence of assurance of that eternal life are always based upon what Jesus did by dying for us and not on what we do by living for him.

It was the practice of Johann Sebastian Bach to begin every musical composition by scripting "*JJ*" at the top of the manuscript. The initials stand for *Jesu, juva* "Jesus, help me." At the completion of the future masterpiece, he wrote *SDG* at the bottom. *Soli Deo Gloria*, "To God alone be the glory." May that be our prayer.

Scripture Index

New Testament

Contributors

David R. Anderson, Ph.D.

Dr. Anderson and his wife, Betty, have pastored in the Houston area for thirty years and have helped to plant eight churches. Dr. Anderson served as the Senior Pastor at Faith Bible Church in The Woodlands, Texas, for eighteen years. During that time, he also served as an Adjunct Professor for Dallas Theological Seminary, teaching in three different departments (Greek New Testament, Bible Exposition, and Theology). He has been an Adjunct Professor for Jordan Evangelical Theological Seminary and taught graduate courses in several other foreign countries.

Dr. Anderson was the founder and president of the Greater Houston Bible Church Association, which is a cooperative effort of churches in the association to reach Greater Houston with the gospel. Dr. Anderson is also one of the founders of the Free Grace Alliance. He is also the founder and president of Grace School of Theology, a Houston-based seminary with teaching locations throughout the state of Texas and online. In addition to his presidential responsibilities, Dr. Anderson teaches at Grace in the areas of theology and biblical languages. He is the author of *Maximum Joy*, an exposition of First John, and *Free Grace Soteriology*.

Fred Chay, Ph.D.

Dr. Chay has been in the ministry for more than 40 years. He has pastored churches in Arizona, California, and Texas and also served as the Western Director of the Christian Medical Association. He was a professor of Theological Studies at Phoenix Seminary and was the Director of the D.Min. program for over twenty years. He is the founder and president of Grace Line, a ministry devoted to motivating Christians toward maturity in their faith. He is currently Dean of Doctoral Studies and Professor of Theological Studies at Grace School of Theology.

He is also Managing Editor of Grace Theology Press. He is the author of *The Faith That Saves-The Nature of Faith in the New Testament*, *The Glorious Grace of God*, *Medical Ethics*, and *Suffering Successfully*.

Joseph Dillow, Th.D.

Jody (Joseph) Dillow came to Christ while majoring in Electrical Engineering at Oregon State University in 1963. Upon graduation from the University of Oregon in Science, he went to Dallas Theological Seminary, where he majored in New Testament Greek and received his Th.D in 1978 in Systematic Theology. While there, he directed the Campus Crusade work at SMU and later at Cornell University in Ithaca, New York. In 1977 he served briefly as a visiting professor in systematic theology at Trinity Evangelical Divinity School in Deerfield, IL. In 1978, God led Jody and his wife, Linda, to Vienna, Austria, where they were used of God to found and direct the ministry which is now known as BEE World (Biblical Education by Extension World). For 14 years they ministered behind the Iron Curtain, and then they moved to Hong Kong in 1992 to launch BEE in China, South Korea, and Vietnam. BEE's mission is to provide extension biblical training in closed countries to those who might not otherwise have access to it. In 1995, they returned to the United States, where they are carrying on the same ministry today. For information about BEE World, visit beeworld.org.

Dr. Dillow is the author of several books including *The Reign of the Servant Kings: A Study of Eternal Security and the Final Destiny of Man*, *Final Destiny: The Future Reign of the Servant Kings*, *The Pre-*

Flood Vapor Canopy, Speaking in Tongues, Solomon on Sex, and with his wife Linda and Dr. Pete and Lorraine Pintus – *Intimacy Ignited.* The Dillows live in Colorado Springs, Colorado. They have five grown children and ten grandchildren.

J. Paul Tanner, Th.M., Ph.D.

Dr. J. Paul Tanner is the Middle East director for BEE World, traveling frequently to various Middle Eastern countries to teach courses for Arab believers in Christ. He holds a Th.M. from Dallas Seminary in Hebrew and Old Testament, and a PhD from The University of Texas at Austin in Hebrew Literature and Culture. Over the course of his career, he has taught at five seminaries around the world. For five years, he and his wife lived in Amman, Jordan. During this time, he was professor of Hebrew and Old Testament studies at the Jordan Evangelical Theological Seminary, and served as the academic dean of the school. Prior to coming to the Middle East, he and his family lived in Singapore for eight years. During part of this time, he was a lecturer in Hebrew and Old Testament at Singapore Bible College.

Dr. Tanner has had several articles published in evangelical journals, including *Bibliotheca Sacra,* the *Journal of the Evangelical Theological Society,* and *Trinity Journal.* He is the author of *Worshiping God in the Psalms* and *Daniel: Man of Faith, Integrity and Insight* (courses written for BEE World), and has written a commentary on the epistle to the Hebrews for *The Grace New Testament Commentary.* He is also the author of the forthcoming commentary on the book of Daniel for the Evangelical Exegetical Commentary series.

Ken Wilson, M.D., D. Phil.

Dr. Wilson graduated as a medical doctor from the University of Texas system, followed by an Orthopedic Residency and Hand Fellowship. He then taught as a full-time academic professor at Oregon's medical school for many years. While maintaining his hand surgery practice, Dr. Wilson decided to pursue theology. He graduated magna cum laude from Faith Lutheran Seminary with a M.Div. degree, then magna cum laude from Golden Gate Baptist Theological Seminary with a

Th.M. degree. Dr. Wilson attended The University of Oxford in the United Kingdom where he received his doctorate in theology, D. Phil., with the thesis, "*Augustine's Conversion from Traditional Free Choice to 'Non-free Free Will': A Comprehensive Methodology.*" His Oxford D. Phil. thesis is published by Mohr Siebeck (2017).

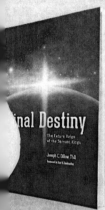

CPSIA information can be obtained
at www.ICGtesting.com
Printed in the USA
FFOW02n0631071017
40764FF

9 780998 138541